Death of a Generation

Death of a Generation

Generation

How the Assassinations of
Diem and JFK
Prolonged the Vietnam War

HOWARD JONES

OXFORD
UNIVERSITY PRESS
2003

OXFORD
UNIVERSITY PRESS

Oxford   New York
Auckland   Bangkok   Buenos Aires   Cape Town   Chennai
Dar es Salaam   Delhi   Hong Kong   Istanbul   Karachi   Kolkata
Kuala Lumpur   Madrid   Melbourne   Mexico City   Mumbai   Nairobi
São Paulo   Shanghai   Taipei   Tokyo   Toronto

Copyright © 2003 by Howard Jones

Published by Oxford University Press, Inc.
198 Madison Avenue, New York, New York 10016

www.oup.com

Oxford is a registered trademark of Oxford University Press

Library of Congress Cataloging-in-Publication Data

Jones, Howard, 1940–
Death of a generation : how the assassinations of Diem
and JFK prolonged the Vietnam War / Howard Jones.
p. cm.
Includes bibliographical references (p.   ) and index.
ISBN 0-19-505286-2
1. Vietnamese Conflict, 1961–1975.
2. Kennedy, John F. (John Fitzgerald), 1917–1963—Assassination.
3. Ngo, Dinh Diem, 1901–1963—Assassination. I. Title.

DS557.7 .J67   2002   959.704'3—dc21   2002014475

1 3 5 7 9 8 6 4 2
Printed in the United States of America
on acid-free paper

For those who died in Vietnam

CONTENTS

Acknowledgments   ix
List of Abbreviations   xi

Introduction: Toward a Tragedy   1

1
Counterinsurgency in South Vietnam: Averting a Quagmire   13

2
Democracy at Bay: Diem as Mandarin   29

3
Counteraction to Counterinsurgency: The Military Solution   49

4
Waging a Secret War   70

5
Subterfuge in the Delta   93

6
The Strange Seduction of Vietnam   114

7
A Decent Veil of Hypocrisy   143

8

De-Americanizing the Secret War   170

9

From Escalation to Disengagement   200

10

End of the Tunnel? A Comprehensive Plan for South Vietnam   221

11

Mandate from Heaven? The Buddhist Crisis
and the Demise of De-escalation   247

12

The Fire This Time   268

13

The Road to a Coup   297

14

At the Brink of a Coup—Again   322

15

Toward a Partial Withdrawal   348

16

President Kennedy's Decision to Withdraw   377

17

Fall of the House of Ngo   407

Conclusion: The Tragedy of JFK   443

Notes   457
Bibliography   537
Index   547

ACKNOWLEDGMENTS

O VER THE PAST DECADE and a half, I have incurred many debts in writing this book, none of which I can adequately repay. Several people gave generously of their time, making this work much better than it would have been without their assistance.

I especially appreciate those who read all or parts of the manuscript or who offered helpful suggestions in extended conversations. Colleagues at the University of Alabama proved to be friends and interested scholars more than co-workers. David Beito volunteered to read the work because of his interest in Kennedy and provided encouragement at times I needed it the most. Ron Robel, who has forgotten more Asian history than I could ever hope to know, read a section on the Buddhist revolt that saved me from error. Tony Freyer shared his deep knowledge of history, helping me to bring focus to my ideas. Forrest McDonald, who is the only other person besides me to read all my writings, once again made incisive proposals that found their way into the manuscript. James K. Galbraith, professor in the Lyndon B. Johnson School of Public Affairs at the University of Texas, not only read the manuscript and offered useful recommendations, but he facilitated my interview with his dad and then shared documents, his own writings, and a deep personal devotion to the topic that was an inspiration. Paul Hendrickson, long-time feature writer for the *Washington Post* and author of a highly acclaimed work on Robert McNamara, provided perceptive comments that reflected his extensive familiarity with the period. Ken Hughes, a Non-Resident Fellow with the University of Virginia's Miller Center of Public Affairs' Presidential Recordings Project, asked to read the manuscript, furnishing a careful examination derived from his intimate knowledge of Kennedy materials. Don Rakestraw of Georgia Southern University, a friend and co-author with me on other subjects, similarly asked to read the work, providing insightful recommendations. Last but not least, my long-time friend and candid critic, Pete Maslowski of the University of Nebraska, brought his expertise to the work, forcing me to sharpen my arguments by strongly disagreeing with them.

For sharing their firsthand knowledge with me, I owe the deepest gratitude to Daniel Ellsberg, John Kenneth Galbraith, Roger Hilsman, Jack Langguth, Robert McNamara, Walt Rostow, and Dean Rusk.

For help in securing documents and other materials, I thank Tim Dixon for gathering references and showing continued interest in the project; George Eliades, whose transcriptions of pivotal Kennedy tapes were essential; Jennie Kiesling for securing a copy of an elusive article; Jon White for making copies of documents; Samuel C. Wilson for his collection of news articles; Francis J. Gavin of the Lyndon B. Johnson School of Public Affairs, who put me in touch with key people; Matt Fulgham and John Taylor of the National Archives in College Park, Maryland;

Jim Cedrone, Kara Drake, and Suzanne K. Forbes of the John F. Kennedy Library; Eric Voelz and Cheryl A. Moe of the National Personnel Records Center in St. Louis, Missouri; Nancy E. Mirshah of the Gerald R. Ford Library; and the library staff at the University of Alabama. Michael Parrish of the Lyndon B. Johnson Library was helpful in so many ways that I could not possibly list them all.

For assistance in gathering photos for the book, I thank James B. Hill and Jen Mohan of the John F. Kennedy Library; E. Philip Scott of the Lyndon B. Johnson Library; Sylvia Baldwin, administrative assistant to John Kenneth Galbraith; and the Audio-Visual staff at the University of Alabama.

For financial and research assistance, I thank the Earhart Foundation, whose help (again) combined with a sabbatical leave to relieve me of teaching responsibilities for a year of research and writing; the Lyndon Baines Johnson Foundation of the Lyndon B. Johnson Library for a Moody Grant-in-Aid of Research; and at the University of Alabama, Provost Nancy Barrett, James Yarbrough and David Klemmack of the Dean's Office of the College of Arts and Sciences, and President Andrew Sorensen, who has fostered a research atmosphere on the campus.

Oxford University Press again demonstrated that a big publishing house can still maintain a remarkable degree of warmth, understanding, and personal support. Sheldon Meyer saw value in my proposal years ago and arranged a contract. Joellyn Ausanka oversaw the production process with her kind and interested manner. Thomas LeBien read the early chapters and offered penetrating comments. Susan Ferber showed unending patience in waiting for the manuscript and then used her superb editorial skills to shape my writing into something that I hope proves readable and persuasive.

Finally, I dedicate this book to the central people in my life: Mary Ann, my spouse, confidante, and closest friend, who has enriched my life beyond measure and who has lived through the Kennedy experience as emotionally as I have; my daughters Debbie and Shari, who have been wonderfully supportive while enduring my time away in research and writing; my son, Howie, who I hope would have liked the book; my mother and father, who made it possible for me to study history and who now live next door and have been waiting for "the Kennedy book" for more years than I care to admit; and my grandchildren, Timothy, Ashley, Lauren, Tyler, and Katelyn, who I hope will come to appreciate our nation's heritage as much as I have.

Northport, Alabama   Howard Jones
Fall 2002

ABBREVIATIONS

AP	Associated Press
ARVN	Army of the Republic of Vietnam
CIA	Central Intelligence Agency
CINCPAC	Commander-in-Chief, Pacific
CIP	Counterinsurgency Plan
COSVN	Central Office for South Vietnam
DMZ	demilitarized zone
DRV	Democratic Republic of Vietnam (Hanoi)
FLAG	Foreign Liaison Assistance Group
FRUS	U.S. Department of State, *Foreign Relations of the United States*, various dates
ICC	International Control Commission
JFKL	John F. Kennedy Library
LBJL	Lyndon B. Johnson Library
MAAG	Military Assistance and Advisory Group
MACV	Military Assistance Command, Vietnam
NATO	North Atlantic Treaty Organization
NLF	National Liberation Front
NSAM	National Security Action Memorandum
NSC	National Security Council
NSF	National Security File
PAVN	People's Army of Vietnam
PLAF	People's Liberation Armed Forces
POF	President's Office File
SDC	Self-Defense Corps
SEATO	Southeast Asia Treaty Organization
USIA	United States Information Agency
USIS	U.S. Information Service
USOM	U.S. Operations Mission
USVR	U.S. Department of Defense, *United States-Vietnam Relations, 1945–1967* [The Pentagon Papers], 12 vols. Washington, D.C.: Government Printing Office, 1971.
VOA	Voice of America

Death of a Generation

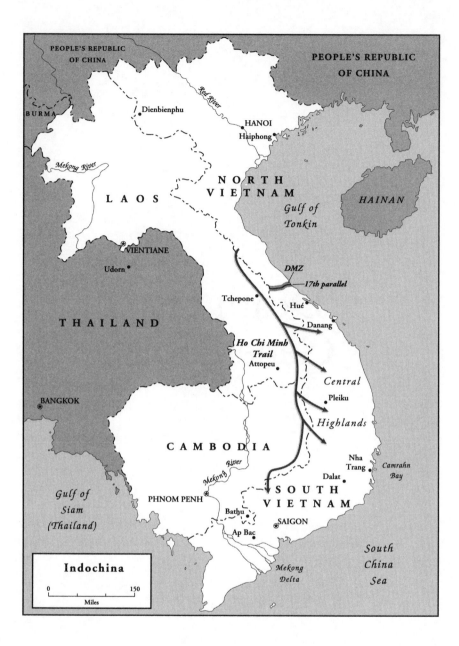

PEOPLE'S REPUBLIC
OF CHINA

PEOPLE'S REPUBLIC
OF CHINA

BURMA

Dienbienphu

Red River

HANOI

Haiphong

Mekong River

NORTH
VIETNAM

Gulf of
Tonkin

HAINAN

L A O S

VIENTIANE

Udorn

DMZ

17th parallel

Tchepone

Hué

T H A I L A N D

Danang

Ho Chi Minh
Trail

Attopeu

Central

BANGKOK

Pleiku

Highlands

C A M B O D I A

River

Mekong

Nha
Trang

Camrahn
Bay

Dalat

Gulf of
Siam
(Thailand)

PHNOM PENH

Bathu

SOUTH
VIETNAM

Ap Bac

SAIGON

South
China
Sea

Mekong
Delta

Indochina

0   150

Miles

INTRODUCTION
Toward a Tragedy

THRONGS OF PEOPLE had gathered along the streets of downtown Dallas during their lunch hour, attempting to catch the first glimpse of the presidential motorcade as it rolled toward them that warm afternoon of November 22, 1963. The youthful, handsome president rode in an open limousine, waving at the crowds on both sides. President John F. Kennedy had come to Texas to begin his race for a second term in the White House, as well as to heal a split in the state's Democratic party between conservative Governor John Connally, seated in the same automobile, and liberal Senator Ralph Yarborough, who was riding a few cars back with Vice President Lyndon Johnson. At 12:30 P.M. Central Standard Time gunshots rang out, mortally wounding the president and seriously injuring Connally. Half an hour later Kennedy died, never regaining consciousness after taking one bullet through the neck and another in the head.

"If President John F. Kennedy had lived, he would not have sent combat troops to Vietnam and America's longest war would never have occurred," say Kennedy apologists. The assassination, they insist, had killed more than the president; it was responsible for the death of a generation—of more than 58,000 Americans, along with untold numbers of Vietnamese on both sides of the seventeenth parallel.

When I first began this study, I was dubious about these assertions, but as my research progressed, many of my doubts disappeared. President Kennedy staunchly resisted the relentless pressure for combat troops, but, critically important, he never called for a total withdrawal. Instead, by the spring of 1962 he sought to roll back the nation's military involvement to the less provocative advisory level he had inherited when taking office more than a year earlier.

What strikes anyone reading the veritable mountain of documents relating to Vietnam is that the only high official in the Kennedy administration who consistently opposed the commitment of U.S. combat forces was the president. Numerous staff studies and White House discussions of South Vietnam's troubles from 1961 to 1963 demonstrate his acute understanding of the issues. Admittedly, he and his advisers initially faced more pressing matters in Cuba, Laos, and the Congo. But a large number of documents show the administration's belief that the problems in Vietnam fit into the global context of Cold War. This is not surprising in light of Kennedy's public declaration while senator in 1956—that Vietnam was "the cornerstone of the Free World in Southeast Asia."[1]

Kennedy joined other presidents of the turbulent post–World War II era in becoming a hostage of the Cold War. U.S.–Soviet rivalries all over the world transformed the most remote areas into hot spots deemed vital to American interests and therefore worthy of a military investment. Traditional rules of engagement no longer applied as the United States after 1945 entered a global contest that meshed ideological with economic and military warfare. The critical standard for judging any regime in the Cold War era was its opposition to communism; hence, one Washington administration after another embraced unsavory foreign leaders as long as they were anti-Communist. Kennedy, like Harry S Truman and Dwight D. Eisenhower before him, believed that containment strategy could thwart the destructive impact of a domino theory, which held that the collapse of a country to communism could similarly bring down its neighbors like falling dominoes. The result was that successive presidential administrations propped up governments such as that of Ngo Dinh Diem in South Vietnam. The White House thus hoped to stop the spread of communism, whether it came from the Soviet Union, the People's Republic of China, their presumed proxy of North Vietnam, or the Vietcong, whose forces were carrying the bulk of the war in the late 1950s and early 1960s.

By the time Kennedy became president, Washington's policymakers had defined the low-intensity conflict in Vietnam as a key battleground in the Cold War. From their point of view, South Vietnam's government was under siege from an insurgency engineered by North Vietnam in collaboration with its Communist friends in Moscow and Beijing. Although the United States had not signed the Geneva Accords of 1954 ending the Indochinese war, the Eisenhower administration filled the power vacuum left by the French defeat and sought to build a nation in southern Vietnam that would provide a democratic model for others to emulate. Hanoi's involvement in the insurgency of the late 1950s, according to Washington, was a violation of the Geneva terms, because its infiltration of men and supplies into the south constituted interference in South Vietnam's domestic affairs and an infringement of its sovereignty as a nation.

The Hanoi government sharply disagreed with the U.S. interpretation, insisting that the Geneva settlement had called for a *temporary* military demarcation of Vietnam at the seventeenth parallel, followed by national elections in 1956 to reunify the country. The United States had illegally implanted Diem as premier in 1954 and proceeded to block the elections. The struggle in Vietnam was, in their view, a civil war in which the Vietnamese in the north were helping fellow Vietnamese in the south to throw out Diem and his imperialist U.S. sponsor. The charge of infiltration was unfounded, and the United States must withdraw from Vietnam and allow the Vietnamese to resolve their domestic problems.[2]

The U.S. argument rested on shaky legal and historical ground that would dog the nation throughout its long stay in Vietnam. Not only did competing nations reject the U.S. view, but so did many of its closest allies. The Kennedy White House found great difficulty in trying to explain away the specific Geneva terms that stipulated the provisional nature of the settlement. It faced enormous problems in attempting to justify its actions in Vietnam on the basis of Hanoi's alleged violations of the Geneva agreements that no American had signed. It amassed countless pieces of evidence demonstrating North Vietnamese assistance to the south, only to find that the documentation carried little weight among those nations that believed it an internal conflict and thought the United States paranoid in its fear of communism. Finally, it failed to realize that the perceived Soviet–Chinese Communist threat was not monolithic and that Hanoi and Beijing had a long history of deep enmity. Indeed, evidence suggests that the Chinese, along with the Americans, opposed the national elections that would have reunified and strengthened their long-time regional antagonist. The Kennedy administration, however, continued the course laid out by its predecessor, insisting that America's role as freedom's guardian warranted its intervention in South Vietnam. This argument remained specious, offering a weak response to Hanoi's consistent demand for a U.S. withdrawal from Vietnam that would enable its people to settle their own differences.

The Kennedy administration termed Hanoi's assistance to the south "infiltration" and tried to resolve that problem in a simple and direct fashion. Both civilian and military advisers advocated a military solution as the quickest remedy to the Communist insurgency in South Vietnam that the north, they insisted, had sponsored by steadily expanding its infiltration of Vietcong cadres and matériel into the south. Once the White House had categorized the conflict as externally driven, its arguments for a deepening U.S. military involvement became eminently logical. An American troop presence would raise South Vietnamese morale while sending a message to allies, neutrals, and the Communist world that the U.S. commitment to Diem was sincere. Deployment of combat forces would demonstrate U.S. credibility and stave off direct intervention by either Moscow or Beijing. The discipline, training, and professionalism exemplified by Americans in uniform would furnish a model for the Army of the Republic of Vietnam (ARVN) while bolstering Diem's beleaguered regime in Saigon. U.S. soldiers could patrol the long and treacherous frontiers of South Vietnam, halting infiltration and freeing the ARVN to take the offensive against the Vietcong.

Yet President Kennedy preferred an expanded advisory role. Why?

He had long regarded the war as South Vietnam's alone to win or lose. As a young congressman, Kennedy had visited Vietnam and become a close friend to Edmund Gullion, the minister and political affairs officer in the U.S. embassy in Saigon. Kennedy had enthusiastically supported Diem's becoming premier in 1954, only to modify his thinking after Gullion insisted that Diem as a Catholic did not represent his people and could not win the war. Such a stand, argues former White House adviser Roger Hilsman, guided the president's policy throughout his abbreviated term in office. Diem's poor performance as premier confirmed this early assessment. Kennedy's position, however, drew little support from determined advisers who argued that only American combat troops could salvage the besieged country. Instead of taking over the war, Kennedy made every effort short of direct U.S. combat involvement to turn the verdict in Saigon's favor. He listened to opposing arguments and refused to make hasty decisions. He emphasized the need for civic action programs that would build a popular base for the Saigon government and thereby facilitate the unity so vital to winning the war. "Postpone for further study" became the bywords of his administration, particularly regarding the question of combat troops. Although the president used this approach in part to avoid the appearance of weakness, he also recognized that an outright "no" to troop use would result in a bitter fight within his administration.[3]

Kennedy's strategy was risky, for it encouraged the hard-liners to believe that the door remained open for a military solution. Before the pressure became insurmountable, Kennedy hoped that American advisers and training personnel would improve the ARVN's fighting performance to the extent that it could bring the insurgency under control and Americans could resume their low-profile advisory role. The key question, of course, was what he would do if the ARVN failed to improve and he faced the choice of either accepting defeat or committing combat forces. Kennedy realized, however, that the United States confronted problems all over the world and opposed sending American boys to fight a war in the jungles and rice paddies of Asia that had the makings of a quagmire. Had not General Douglas MacArthur warned the president against Asian land wars?

Like many of his advisers, President Kennedy narrowly depicted the central threat as guerilla warfare and became an avid proponent of counterinsurgency shortly after entering the White House in January 1961. Political and military actions to squelch a revolt against a civil government—these were the tactics of cunning and adventure. Such a multifaceted and colorful program offered enormous appeal to the young executive because it called for social, political, and economic correctives as well as those of a military nature. But the Vietcong waged a more broadly conceived strategy of revolutionary warfare (people's war) with the objective of building a new social order, not merely changing the state or government. In the early 1960s the insurgents were in the initial stage of their struggle—guerrilla tactics based on terror and violence. Then would follow a transitional period in which they would pursue a mixture of guerrilla and conventional measures before moving into the final phase: a general uprising fueled by full-scale military operations of both regular and irregular forces. Communist warfare was thus appropriate to the jungle environment and hence capable of combatting the most sophisticated forms of Western technology. The president, however, focused on the guerrilla struggle as a match of wits and welcomed the challenge.[4]

U.S. Air Force general and former CIA operative Edward Lansdale provided the most convincing argument for this strategy. Dapper, daring, and never at a loss for words, he had engaged in psychological warfare (psywar) during the 1950s to protect the Diem regime from perceived North Vietnamese aggression. He recommended a broadly based counterinsurgency program that, by sheer coincidence, paralleled the arguments advocated by the U.S. Country Team in South Vietnam. Both Lansdale and the American advisers in Saigon emphasized the civil as well as the military dimensions of that approach, assigning priority to the personal security of the South Vietnamese people in an effort to attract the popular support essential to suppressing an insurgency. The U.S. role was to train the South Vietnamese army, Civil Guard, and Self-Defense Corps in counterinsurgency techniques so that they could restore domestic stability. The United States would then terminate its special military assistance resulting from the recent emergency and scale back its involvement to the advisory level authorized by the Geneva Accords of 1954.

The Kennedy administration only initially accepted Eisenhower's insistence that the Communists in Laos posed the central threat to freedom in Southeast Asia; by April 1961 it regarded the Vietcong insurgency in South Vietnam as a vital arm of the Communist menace spreading throughout the region. The Communist insurgency led by the Pathet Lao in neighboring Laos seemed inseparable from Vietnam's growing instability because of the administration's belief that the North Vietnamese worked through the National Liberation Front (NLF) in providing the Vietcong with manpower and material goods through Laos below the seventeenth parallel. Farther south, Cambodia likewise served as a veritable thoroughfare for infiltration into South Vietnam. About 700 miles of the Laotian–Cambodian frontier lay open to the insurgents, much of it pockmarked by natural hideouts containing munitions, foodstuffs, and infirmaries. Estimates varied, but the White House calculated that by 1961, North Vietnam was filtering in 2,000 men per year down what became known as the "Ho Chi Minh Trail" and that the Vietcong in South Vietnam already numbered 12,000.[5] Furthermore, to the east lay the coastal area, a major source of infiltration by sea that stretched 1,000 miles from the seventeenth parallel to the country's southern tip at the Camau Peninsula. Any effort to seal off Laos and Cambodia from South Vietnam was futile. Most successful insurgencies have a privileged sanctuary as well as a depot for facilitating the inflow of manpower and supplies from outside the country. Counting North Vietnam, the Vietcong had three.

The problems in South Vietnam proved enormously complex and yet, President Kennedy hoped, susceptible to a resolution without direct U.S. military involvement. At forty-three the youngest person ever elected to the presidency, he impressed many observers as highly intelligent, witty, and graceful in style. Eager to make his mark on history, the Harvard graduate in political science readily accepted the growing global challenges of the office. His highly publicized "New Frontier" in domestic and foreign policy committed the United States to containing communism and protecting human rights. But at the same time he recalled his fighting experiences in World War II and, combined with Gullion's negative assessment of Diem, refused to regard military force as the first option. Kennedy became convinced that the solution to South Vietnam's problems depended on closing the Laotian border (along with those of Cambodia and North Vietnam); creating a neutralist government in the Laotian capital of Vientiane that included no Communists; introducing social, economic, and political reforms to the Saigon government that made it more responsive to the people and more effective against the Vietcong; and establishing an anti-Communist policy toward Southeast Asia built on the cooperation of members of the Southeast Asia Treaty Organization (SEATO). Victory in South Vietnam rested on safeguarding its frontiers and developing a counterinsurgency program that guaranteed internal security.

The Kennedy administration's Vietnam policy developed under the lead of Secretary of Defense Robert McNamara, whose hard-core managerial tactics transformed the U.S. involvement into a cold and business-like proposition. The former Ford Motor Company executive virtually computerized the U.S. effort, attracting the support of the military by his tireless emphasis on the role of statistics in defining success and failure. Secretary of State Dean Rusk, a Georgia-born farm boy turned Rhodes scholar and specialist on the Far East during the Truman administration, had delegated Vietnam to McNamara, thinking the move would win the Pentagon's support by giving it a greater sense of participation. W. Averell Harriman, veteran diplomat and senior adviser to the new administration, thought this decision a mistake, because it made Vietnam into a military matter. "From the very beginning," he asserted, "we didn't take fully into account the kind of political developments, the kind of economic developments and social developments which were necessary, which would have been more possible in the early days." Rusk, Harriman continued, "thought that things were going to be difficult and it would be easier to divest himself of that responsibility." The secretary of state focused on Berlin, Cuba, and the need for collective security in preventing war. His preoccupation with Europe and Latin America left McNamara to oversee the Vietnam problem, which he, as head of the defense department, sought to resolve by reducing the measure of effectiveness to sheer numbers. When a White House adviser questioned the possibility of saving Vietnam, the defense secretary bolted upright and stormed back: "Where is your data? Give me something I can put in the computer. Don't give me your poetry."[6]

Like numerous others in Washington, McNamara knew little about South Vietnam and simply categorized it as one of many weak countries in need of U.S. help against communism. This naïve assumption was not entirely his fault. The nationwide hysteria of the 1950s known as McCarthyism had hounded many East Asian experts out of the state department, often resulting in unsophisticated, one-dimensional analyses of regional issues. But, as Hilsman recently noted, the East Asian specialists who remained in the state department warned the defense secretary against a deepening involvement—advice he did not heed. Rather than attribute Vietnam's instability to its domestic social, political, and economic problems, McNamara blamed Communist China for masterminding a campaign aimed at gaining regional control.[7]

Laos and Cuba, however, were more crisis-ridden than Vietnam in early 1961 and therefore headed the new administration's list of foreign policy concerns. Neutralization of Laos appeared to be the only way to save it from communism. No one disputed the Eisenhower administration's claim that Laos was unsuitable for making a stand against the Communists: The landlocked country sat in a strife-torn region and lacked the political and economic potential to become a bastion of the Free World. Its people were anti-Communist but had shown little inclination to fight their adversary. Cuba, barely ninety miles off the U.S. shore, posed a more immediate problem. Guerrilla chieftain Fidel Castro had seized power in 1959 and, growing more belligerent by the day, appeared ready to embrace communism. The bearded young lawyer had left the impression that he had allied with the recklessly aggressive Soviet premier, Nikita Khrushchev, to spread the Communist gospel throughout Latin America.[8]

By the spring of 1961, the Kennedy administration considered South Vietnam the most feasible place to achieve a major victory in the Cold War. Strategic access to coastal waters, the West's concessions in Laos, the Bay of Pigs humiliation in Cuba, and the confrontations with the Soviet Union over Berlin—all had combined to elevate South Vietnam to global importance.

The White House attempted to deal with Southeast Asia by implementing a multifaceted policy based on the principles of flexibility and restraint. Two weeks before Kennedy's inauguration, Walt Rostow, an economics professor at the Massachusetts Institute of Technology who became one of the president's most influential foreign policy advisers, warned Rusk that the Eisenhower administration's reliance on nuclear threats did not constitute a suitable remedy to the Communist guerrilla challenge in Indochina. Communism preyed on underdeveloped countries by infiltration, subversion, and guerrilla warfare. To counter this "disease," Rostow advocated a multilayered response that focused on developing a greater mobility for fighting limited battles and an economic program designed to deter Communist insurgencies through nation-building programs. Such a broad approach called for both military and civil measures to provide the vast number of peasants in Laos and Vietnam with "a stake in the system, a sense of identification with it, and a commitment to its survival." Such a flexible and restrained approach could fulfill the promise highlighted in President Kennedy's inaugural address to help "those people in the huts and villages of half the globe struggling to break the bonds of mass misery." Only in this fashion could the United States avoid direct combat involvement.[9]

But the optimism of this inaugural moment eventually faded. By the time of the president's assassination, he had come close to finalizing a process for withdrawing most of America's soldiers in accordance with the "Comprehensive Plan for South Vietnam." Indeed, the first thousand troops would begin their scheduled pull-out in early December.[10] To be sure, Kennedy's initial approach to South Vietnam had led to the assignment of nearly 17,000 U.S. troops, but none had the authority to engage in combat unless under attack. Their official purpose remained advisory, supportive, and symbolic, even though their very presence drew more than a few of them into combat, whether as military advisers, logistics specialists, airplane pilots, or simply ground personnel. The White House tried to conceal this secret war in Vietnam in an effort to avert domestic unrest and to maintain limitations on the real war between the Communists and the Free World. If the ARVN pushed back the Vietcong, and if Kennedy won reelection in 1964, he intended to continue the phased withdrawal program aimed at having the great bulk of U.S. soldiers home in 1965. Those remaining behind would total 1,500, all advisers and considerably closer in number to the strictures of the Geneva Accords.

But as the situation in South Vietnam dramatically worsened during the fall of 1961, President Kennedy became convinced that, at least for a time, he must emphasize the military correctives contained in counterinsurgency doctrine. The president tried to maintain the thin line between support duties and direct combat with the Vietcong. Yet that line blurred as uniformed Americans in South Vietnam grew in number and were put at risk on a daily basis. How could a U.S. military commander restrain his men under attack? Could not self-defense graduate into an offensive that Americanized the war? By the spring of 1962, the president sought to pare back the U.S. military involvement to the level of early 1961. This withdrawal effort stalled in the wake of the Buddhist uprising of May 1963 and ultimately came to a halt in the aftermath of Kennedy's own death some six months later.

Much of the failure in Vietnam was attributable to President Diem and his family. A Catholic in an overwhelmingly Buddhist country, Diem found it difficult to refute charges of religious persecution. Cold, aloof, and nepotistic, he never revealed any propensity for democracy and preferred to keep power in the hands of himself and his family. Indeed, he was so averse to carrying on a dialogue that, to avoid having to use the toilet, the U.S. embassy had instructed its officials not to drink any liquids for three hours before calling on the premier. Diem's belief in "personalism" reflected his elitist, mandarin background and his profound distrust of people outside the Ngo family—including Americans. Had not his family remained loyal in late 1960, when disgruntled military officials launched their narrowly abortive coup attempt? Was it not certain (at least to him) that the U.S. embassy and the CIA had accepted if not promoted his demise? Consequently, Diem (who was not married) sought advice almost exclusively from his equally distant and seemingly emotionless brother, Ngo Dinh Nhu, who held no executive position in the government, and his sister-in-law, Madame Nhu, who had become Diem's "First Lady." A vivacious and acid-tongued critic of U.S. reform efforts in South Vietnam (caricatured by news correspondents as the "Dragon Lady" after the comic book character), Madame Nhu was a former Buddhist who had converted to Catholicism and preferred a closed society based on puritanical moral standards that she alone defined. "Not only sunlight," she pointedly observed, "but many bad things fly in."[11] By the time Kennedy became president, Diem had survived numerous palace crises since entering office in 1954, when the United States underwrote his regime with large-scale military and economic assistance shortly after France's defeat at the legendary battle of Dienbienphu.

In a tragically misguided move, the Kennedy administration in 1963 promoted the generals' coup against Diem, thinking that a change of government would improve the war effort and thereby facilitate the U.S. withdrawal from Vietnam. When the ARVN generals staged their coup in early November, they did so with full knowledge of American approval, albeit without direct collaboration and participation. The White House nonetheless bore heavy responsibility. The president had become an accomplice in the coup by signaling the conspirators that Diem would receive no U.S. assistance. Earlier overtures by the generals to the United States through the CIA had brought no such assurance, making them pause the previous August. But stories had spread that Nhu had privately contacted North Vietnam about ending the war without consulting outside powers. What would be the generals' fate, given their known dissatisfaction with the Saigon regime? Diem's crude handling of the Buddhist crisis finally combined with the ARVN's bumbling war effort, the Kennedy administration's open criticisms of the Saigon regime, and the persistent rumors of Nhu's secret negotiations with Hanoi to drive the generals into a coup that culminated in the deaths of both Diem and Nhu.

Wild celebrations engulfed the generals in Saigon as a grateful populace praised them for sweeping out the hated Ngo family. Domestic stability had seemingly returned to South Vietnam. The efficiency with which the generals dispatched the regime left the popular perception that they would easily defeat the Vietcong. But this euphoria lasted only momentarily. The generals' decision to kill Diem and Nhu opened a visceral division among them and led to bitter turmoil in Saigon. Then, in three weeks, President Kennedy himself lay dead—and with him the Comprehensive Plan for South Vietnam.

President Kennedy's close associates have confirmed his intention to reduce the American involvement in Vietnam. John Kenneth Galbraith, the U.S. ambassador to India and long-time friend and confidant of the president, stated that Kennedy had decided to disengage America's special military forces from Vietnam. Hilsman and McNamara agreed, magnifying even more the tragedy of Kennedy's assassination.[12]

Particularly striking was Galbraith's assertion that, to promote a withdrawal, President Kennedy had planned to replace Rusk with McNamara as secretary of state after the presidential election of 1964. Galbraith is convinced that Kennedy intended to "Vietnamize" the war after his expected reelection—to reduce the U.S. commitment to the advisory level it occupied when he first took office. The president's greatest obstacle was the military. He had been burned by Pentagon officials (and the CIA) during the Bay of Pigs fiasco and hesitated to trust them afterward. By late 1962, the president searched for a way to maintain control over the military while phasing out the nation's special military aid to Vietnam. One means for doing so, according to Galbraith, was to change the leadership in the state department. Kennedy had come to regard Rusk "as a committed cold warrior and given, as in Vietnam, to a military solution or, more precisely, non-solution." Indeed, Rusk's perspective on Communist aggression derived from the West's experiences at Munich in 1938. "When one views the sad events of the 1930's in Europe," he wrote in his memoirs, "I think that the United States and Western democracies, with our pacifism, isolationism, and indifference to aggression, were guilty of 'tempting thieves.'" The president's only hesitation about the McNamara shift was that without him heading the defense department, the military might take charge of the war. Kennedy, Galbraith declared, considered McNamara the only person capable of standing up to the Joint Chiefs of Staff and the Pentagon.[13]

Galbraith's claim has merit. Hilsman likewise insists that Kennedy "was clearly going to pull out" and that he intended to normalize relations with South Vietnam. One means for doing this, Hilsman declared, was to remove Rusk. Although Rostow had left the White House in late 1961, he was aware of a withdrawal plan sometime afterward. McNamara had indeed become convinced by the fall of 1963 that the United States should withdraw its thousands of "advisers." Indeed, according to Galbraith, the great unspoken truth within the administration's innermost circle was that the United States could not win the war and should recall all special assistance put in place since January 1961. When asked about Galbraith's claim that the president had decided to change secretaries of state, the former defense secretary responded that the president had not asked him to make the switch but that "Robert Kennedy did."[14]

Galbraith's assertion places McNamara even more under the shadow of Vietnam. Although the defense secretary called for withdrawal in 1963, he expressed no such idea when President Johnson escalated the war later that year. McNamara explained to me that the Vietcong's activities had heated up and that only military action could resolve the dire situation. Hilsman insists, however, that McNamara was "inconsistent" and "mixed up" and never intended to pull out.[15] In December 1963, Johnson did what his predecessor had so skillfully avoided: He adhered more closely to the views of the Joint Chiefs of Staff regarding Vietnam. While vice president, Johnson had not been privy to the secret White House proceedings relating to the coup and, when learning of the Kennedy administration's clandestine involvement, strongly denounced that decision. As president, Johnson wanted to get the nettlesome war out of the way so that he could implement his domestic reform program.

For good reason, historians are reluctant to speculate on what might have happened in Vietnam had President Kennedy lived. Then why examine this issue? Kennedy died in Dallas, cynics declare, rendering it meaningless to debate whether he might have adopted an alternative policy in Vietnam that could have averted the deaths of millions.

It is not speculation, however, to examine President Kennedy's policies toward Vietnam in an effort to discern whether or not a pattern of withdrawal was in the making. As the pivotal figure in this drama, he argued that only the South Vietnamese could win (or lose) the war. Repeatedly he defined success as reducing the Vietcong insurgency to a level that the Saigon government could police on its own.

The materials undergirding this study demonstrate that President Kennedy intended to reverse the nation's special military commitment to the South Vietnamese made in early 1961.[16] After receiving continued mixed reports on the war's progress, he turned toward a phased military reduction that would begin in late 1963 and, after his presumed reelection in autumn 1964, succeed by the end of 1965 in returning America's military status to its 1961 advisory level. His appointment of Henry Cabot Lodge as ambassador to South Vietnam in the fall of 1963 was a telling event. A leading Republican, Lodge and his party would share the political blame in the event of failure in Vietnam. Indeed, Lodge became a strong proponent of the coup, communicating directly with the president and making that business bipartisan in nature. Doubting South Vietnam's capacity to win the war and staunchly opposed to U.S. combat troops, President Kennedy sought to halt the move toward Americanizing the war in a process that President Richard M. Nixon would make known as "Vietnamization."

Not everyone will accept the findings of this study. The story that emerges in these pages is unsettling and difficult to refute. The president at first joined others in the incongruous strategy of withdrawal through escalation but soon realized that military disengagement offered the only feasible avenue out of the morass. The president then promoted the coup in a miscalculated effort to advance a withdrawal that, for political reasons, would take place during his second term in office.

President Kennedy was not solely to blame for these events. U.S. intervention in Vietnam in the years preceding his presidency had thrust the United States into South Vietnam's domestic and foreign affairs. Emmet John Hughes, former political adviser and speechwriter for President Eisenhower, noted that the United States as an interventionist nation could not "save the very freedom of another nation *without* becoming critically involved in its whole conduct and destiny." There was no way to separate involvement in foreign and domestic matters. "The point is that to be fastidiously aloof from the internal political life of an ally *is* to 'interfere.' It is the interference of acquiescence." So deep was the American involvement that it could not have escaped blame for a coup, regardless of what it did or did not do.[17]

Still, the president does not belong on the high road that befitted the idealistic image of Camelot. Kennedy encouraged a coup that ran out of control and led to Diem's death rather than his expected exile. Some contemporaries suspected the president's involvement in the coup, but they did not push the issue because of his own assassination so soon afterward. Had Kennedy lived to win reelection, there is no reason to believe that he would have changed his views about wanting to get out of a war that had become a lost cause. Is it fair to criticize him for postponing a withdrawal on political grounds? Was he justified in asserting that a withdrawal before the election would ensure a Republican victory based on the charge that the Democrats had lost Vietnam as they had lost China? In T. S. Eliot's dramatic play, *Murder in the Cathedral*, the English Archbishop of Canterbury, Thomas Becket, declared, "The last temptation is the greatest treason; To do the right deed for the wrong reason."[18] But what do the motives matter if the outcome might have spared a generation?

1

COUNTERINSURGENCY
IN SOUTH VIETNAM
Averting a Quagmire

For the first time, . . . [I have] a sense of the danger and
urgency of the problem in Vietnam.

President John F. Kennedy, January 30, 1961

OR ALMOST TWO WEEKS in early January 1961, U.S. Air Force Brigadier General Edward Lansdale secretly conducted a firsthand inspection of South Vietnam at the request of the outgoing secretary
of defense. The former CIA operative presented his findings in a twelve-
page report to Washington that, within a week of John F. Kennedy's inauguration as president, had wound its way through the CIA, to Eisenhower's
secretary of defense, to McNamara, and, finally, to Rostow. "It was an ominous draft," Rostow muttered before heading for the Oval Office.

"Mr. President," Rostow declared, "I think you ought to read this."

"Look," groused Kennedy. "I've only got a half-hour today. I've got an
appointment afterwards. Do I have to read it all? Can you summarize it?"

"No, sir. I think you must read it."

Taking the memorandum, the president quickly read through it, absorbing its most important ideas. He looked up and somberly declared,
"Walt, this is going to be the worst one yet." A moment of silence followed
before Kennedy spoke again. "I'll tell you something. Eisenhower never
mentioned the word Vietnam to me." Silence again. The president asked
for reading material on guerrilla warfare. "Get to work on this, Walt."[1]

I

THE TIMING was right for Lansdale's report. Barely two months earlier in
November 1960, a military coup had failed only at the last minute to oust
Diem, but its close brush with success highlighted the popular dissatisfac-
tion with the Saigon regime. The following December, Communist leaders

in Hanoi had promoted the establishment of the National Liberation Front as an umbrella organization that welcomed Diem's opponents, both Communist and non-Communist. Then, in early January 1961, Khrushchev delivered a fiery speech aimed at the Chinese Communists but interpreted by Kennedy as a challenge to the United States. The Soviet Union, declared the premier, wholeheartedly supported "wars of liberation" by "colonial peoples against their oppressors." McGeorge Bundy, the new national security adviser, informed Rusk, McNamara, and CIA Director Allen Dulles that the president's "concern for Vietnam is a result of his keen interest in General Lansdale's recent report and his awareness of the high importance of this country." Rostow agreed. "I am sure that, to the end, Kennedy regarded Vietnam as the worst of his problems. It was so far advanced by the time we got to it."[2]

The background of North Vietnam's interest in the south is clear. In the summer of 1954, just after the Vietminh's victory over France at Dienbienphu, the Communist Lao Dong (or Vietnamese Workers' party) gathered at the Sixth Party Plenum in Hanoi, where President Ho Chi Minh called for reunifying the country through nationwide elections. That objective in mind, the party established the Fatherland Front to, as General Vo Nguyen Giap put it, "rally all the forces that are susceptible of being rallied." But, Giap charged, Diem as prime minister under Emperor Bao Dai arbitrarily postponed the Geneva-mandated elections of 1956 and engineered his own sham election as president of the newly created Republic of Vietnam. Once in that position, he launched a brutal assault on the Fatherland Front and other dissidents that by 1956 had reduced the Communist party's membership in the south by 90 percent. The following year, the Communists began a terrorist campaign in the south that, Giap insisted, had no direct assistance from the north. As one party member put it, they "tried to kill any [government] official who enjoyed the people's sympathy and left the bad officials unharmed in order to wage propaganda and sow hatred against the government." In January 1959, Communist party leader Le Duan returned to Hanoi after completing a secret inspection of South Vietnam and presented his report to the Politburo of the Central Committee. Diem's harsh policies, Le Duan asserted, had endangered fellow Vietnamese in the south and deepened their hatred of the Saigon regime. With U.S. assistance, Diem had denied sustenance to the Vietcong by creating a series of fortified communities called "agrovilles," and his government's police force had arrested thousands, many of whom it later tortured and executed. This period was, according to a spokesman for the Democratic Republic of Vietnam in Hanoi, the revolution's "darkest hour."[3]

Diem had, however, failed to meet the peasants' needs and therefore offered new hope for the Communist party as the Fifteenth Plenum convened in Hanoi in January of 1959. Some of the delegates were southern cadres who appealed for help against Diem; others had left the south following the Geneva Conference of 1954 and now wanted to return home and protect their comrades. Le Duan urged the Central Committee to build up insurgent forces and promote the revolution in the south. But party leaders split over the question, some favoring immediate assistance and others warning that military escalation in the south would drain sparse materials from the north while it was trying to build a socialist community at home. Still another group feared that an armed conflict would alienate the Soviets and the Chinese by provoking U.S. intervention. Ho Chi Minh warned his colleagues to act cautiously, waiting for the right moment to make a strike for final victory.[4]

The result was a compromise that revealed a tactical division in the plenum over timing and *not*, it is important to note, between north and south. The party approved a revolutionary struggle aimed at liberating the south from "the imperialists and the feudalists," completing the "national democratic revolution," and reunifying Vietnam by using "the strength of the masses, with political strength as the main factor, in combination with military strength to a greater or lesser degree depending on the situation." At this point the party preferred negotiations over fighting. The Central Committee proposed Resolution 15, which would authorize a mixed political and military struggle aimed at national reunification but approved an emphasis on military means if this broadly based tactic failed. Ho and Giap had not ruled out force, but it was not yet time, Ho insisted, to abandon the political approach.[5]

The implications of this party division are enormously significant. If the main drive for escalating the struggle in the south came from southerners, then the revolution was primarily indigenous in that Diem's actions had aroused resistance from within. Hanoi was therefore reluctant to act, preferring observer status over active participation. But if party leaders in the north largely determined the stepped-up activity in the south, then Hanoi bore chief responsibility for the revolution.[6]

The truth appears to be that the war was national and not regional, a revolutionary war directed by Hanoi but whose combatants on both sides came from all Vietnam. The Communist Lao Dong had masterminded the revolution, but Diem's brutal tactics had spurred the movement by overturning what the Communists thought they had achieved during their war against France and at Geneva—a united Vietnam, free of foreign rule. In waging this people's war, the Lao Dong party had two central objectives whose priority shifted back and forth throughout the period: establishing socialism in the north and liberating the south as the first step toward national reunification. The north imposed order onto a widely disparate group in the south that opposed Diem. Indeed, the insurgents doubtless would have ousted Diem if he had not had U.S. assistance. The revolution in the south could not make significant advances without northern direction and organization. It also could not succeed without assistance from the cadres sent south in the period following the Fifteenth Plenum who were, to further confuse the matter, primarily native southerners. The troubles in South Vietnam stemmed from north *and* south.[7]

After the plenum's adjournment, Ho Chi Minh traveled to Beijing and Moscow, seeking support for the party's new stand. No one knows the specific content of his discussions with Chinese and Soviet leaders, but after his return to Hanoi, the Central Committee in May 1959 opened the way to a greater military orientation in policy by approving Resolution 15. That same month, the party's leaders ordered the establishment of a secret military communication line to provide goods for the revolution in the south. The first infiltration down what became known as the "Ho Chi Minh Trail" began in June of that same year and reached the south in late August. Aided by this new supply line, the south initiated a revolutionary war that Le Duan defined as a protracted political struggle intended to buy time for building the military base for victory. The party's Politburo declared that "the time has come to push the armed struggle against the enemy." By mid-summer of 1959, the party notified cadres in the Central Highlands that it had given "the green light for switching from [a] political struggle alone to [a] political struggle combined with [an] armed struggle."[8]

Hanoi had made this decision in part to save lives and thin resources but also to comply with the wishes of both the Soviet Union and China to avoid a widened war. Khrushchev sought peaceful coexistence with the West and preferred an observer status regarding Vietnamese events as long as they remained internal in scope. But the Lao Dong's decision to move toward an armed struggle aimed at national reunification caused concern in the Kremlin that the Chinese might seize the opportunity to expand their influence in Southeast Asia. Mao Zedong would not hinder Vietnamese objectives, but he wanted to concentrate on China's domestic problems following the Korean War and did not want another confrontation with the United States. He had told Ho in the summer of 1958 that the time was not yet right for revolution in the south and that the first priority must be to complete the socialist changes in the north. Now, however, Mao praised the Vietnamese quest for national liberation. This objective in mind, he approved military assistance and heightened propaganda, all the while calculating that the United States might overextend its commitment to Diem and facilitate China's strategic interests in the region.[9]

Hanoi thus acted on its own, albeit cautiously because it too feared a direct U.S. military intervention. Le Duan restrained his militant approach to advocate throughout the remainder of 1959 the development of "regroupees," those young Vietnamese from the south who had come north after the Geneva Conference for insurgency training and who now returned to the south as cadres to lead a revolution that depended on the participation of men, women, and children. Nearly 90,000 refugees had moved north in 1954, many of them attending the Xuan Mai Training School outside Hanoi. North Vietnam infiltrated these regroupees into the south in groups of forty to fifty, first by truck into the mountains of lower Laos and then by foot through jungle paths that wound west of the demilitarized zone through Laos and Cambodia. Once in South Vietnam, the cadres assumed leadership positions within the party.[10]

The Communist party, according to one member in March 1960, had become locked in a "tug-of-war" with Diem and the Americans and was not yet able to overthrow the Saigon government. The ultimate objective was "an armed general uprising" aimed at seizing control of the south. But for the time being, the party remained an auxiliary to a political program that called for "peace, re-unification, independence and democracy." This restrained approach would change, however, because of "the policy of cruel terrorism of the Americans and DIEM." Victory would come through arming "village self-defence units" to facilitate the political struggle.[11]

In September 1960, the Third National Congress of the Lao Dong party in Hanoi declared that the purpose of the "Vietnamese revolution" was to push the "socialist revolution in North Viet-Nam while at the same time stepping up the National People's Democratic Revolution in South Viet-Nam." Before 576 delegates, Ho Chi Minh exalted the principles of socialism and proclaimed that they must work toward reunifying the nation by peaceful methods. Le Duan insisted that the people must lead the revolution. It would be "a long and arduous struggle, not simple but complex, combining many forms of struggle" and necessitating the flexible use of legal *and* illegal means. At no time did he speak of direct military involvement from the north. The party settled on a five-year plan to bring socialism to the north, but when it elected Le Duan as first secretary and thus second only to Ho Chi Minh, it was clear that national reunification would become the prime objective of the 1960s. Furthermore, three South Vietnamese were now in the Politburo: Le Duan, Pham Hung, and a leading military figure, Nguyen Chi Thanh, who as General of the Army held a rank equivalent to Giap's. The Politburo also included Le Duc Tho, who was not a native southerner but had been Le Duan's deputy during the war against the French. The party's focus would soon be on the south.[12]

With the revolution in the south as the chief objective of the Communist party, its leaders discussed the establishment of a new united front of workers and peasants in the south that would seek Diem's fall without provoking direct U.S. intervention. The organization must recruit those people unhappy with the Saigon regime and operate under the party's direction. The southern front would say nothing of communism and would follow the pattern of the Vietminh Front by consisting of a central committee and a series of cells extending down to the village level.[13]

On December 20, 1960, the National Front for the Liberation of South Vietnam, or National Liberation Front, came into existence at a secret meeting of about sixty people in a group of small buildings in South Vietnam close to the Cambodian border. As one of its participants proudly declared years afterward, "each individual in the hall was aware that he was participating in a historic event." The NLF's chief objective was to win independence and freedom for the "Fatherland" against the "U.S. imperialists" who had sided with "Diem and his clique" in terrorizing the people and blocking democracy. The NLF had a number of goals, not made public until mid-January of 1962, but chief among them was the overthrow of Diem.[14]

The generals' foiled coup attempt of November 1960 had convinced the Politburo in Hanoi in mid-January 1961 to take advantage of the south's growing instability and intensify the political and military activities. The party secretly reestablished the Central Office for South Vietnam (COSVN) in the south, which had operated under the direction of the Central Committee during the war against France and had been dissolved after the Geneva Conference of 1954. That same month of January 1961, the Lao Dong party approved the NLF's political program and emphasized that Vietnamese Communists and non-Communists shared the same objectives. "Nothing," Ho Chi Minh repeatedly emphasized, "[was] more precious than independence and liberty." Central to this effort was the use of terror and violence in the broad sense of assassinations, kidnappings, sabotage, and any other measure designed to undermine the credibility of the Diem government. South Vietnam had become an "American colony," charged Communist party leaders. Diem's forces under U.S. directives had "taken out the bowels, cut off the heads, stripped off the flesh, eaten the livers, and drunk the blood of our compatriots, including old ladies, pregnant women and babies in the cradle." They had resorted to guillotines and torture in making the south into a "huge prison" that was ripe for revolution.[15]

This was the war in Vietnam that President Kennedy encountered on entering the Executive Office in January 1961.

II

THE PRESIDENT'S OPPORTUNITY for meeting this Communist threat came from Lansdale, who, in his early fifties and now Deputy Assistant to the Secretary of Defense for Special Operations, had become a legend in his own time. A hardened veteran of the Office of Strategic Services in World War II, he had engaged in psychological warfare while working as a CIA agent in the Philippines during the early 1950s campaign against the Huk insurgency. He soon became CIA station chief in Saigon, where he helped to preserve the Diem regime against its enemies during the latter part of that decade by engaging in premium CIA tactics that included a sophisticated propaganda campaign against Hanoi and bribing would-be coup leaders with all-expenses-paid vacations in the Philippines. Once again, at the start of the Kennedy administration, Lansdale's expertise came into play. As the only Pentagon official with counterinsurgency experience in Asia, he appealed to a venturesome president who read James Bond spy novels, fancied himself a dashing young prince from King Arthur's roundtable of wise statesmen and brave warriors, and considered guerrilla warfare a fascinating battle of wits rather than a mindless use of brawn.[16]

Kennedy's move toward a deeper and more active intervention in Vietnam also grew out of the dynamics of the new administration. The confidence and hope that characterized the post-Eisenhower White House encouraged innovation and bravado. The president's resident historian, Arthur M. Schlesinger, Jr., was a Pulitzer Prize–winning author from Harvard who years afterward recalled the euphoria in Washington. "The future everywhere . . . seemed bright with hope. . . . The capital city, somnolent in the Eisenhower years, had come suddenly alive. The air had been stale and oppressive; now fresh winds were blowing. There was the excitement which comes from an injection of new men and new ideas, the release of energy which occurs when men with ideas have a chance to put them into practice. . . . We thought for a moment that the world was plastic and the future unlimited." Another contemporary in Washington, Seymour Deitchman from the defense department, remembered the same atmosphere. The dawning of the Kennedy era was "one of change, of ferment, of self-confidence—of 'knowing' what had to be done and of unquestioning 'can do.'" Kennedy regarded Khrushchev's early January speech as a gauntlet thrown down at the feet of U.S. leaders. Had not the new executive sent copies to his advisers? Had he not sought comments after reading the speech aloud to his advisers gathered in the Oval Office, to his cabinet members, and to his guests at dinners? The only way to confront this menace, Deitchman declared, lay in rebuilding the South Vietnamese military and the government. "That challenge may appear shadowy and full of braggadocio from the vantage point of the bitter experience of all parties in the late sixties. But who can deny that it was uttered seriously, and was meant to succeed, if it could, ten years earlier?"[17]

President Kennedy's attraction to insurgency warfare had become evident before his election, when he became an ardent admirer of a 1958 novel entitled *The Ugly American*. Written by political scientist Eugene Burdick and U.S. Navy Captain William Lederer, the book became a bestseller in the midst of the 1960 presidential campaign. The story featured fictitious U.S. Army Colonel Edwin Barnum Hillandale, who stood almost alone in winning popular support in the imaginary country of Sarkhan (Vietnam) in Southeast Asia. Whereas most Americans on the scene had alienated the native populace by their crude and arrogant behavior, Hillandale won a huge following by his simple homespun manner—particularly by playing "ragtime" songs on his harmonica in the villages. Most U.S. emissaries in that turbulent region of the world, however, failed to influence the political direction of the new countries. The young Senator Kennedy was so taken by the book that he and five other leading Americans purchased a full-page advertisement in the *New York Times* declaring that they had given copies to every U.S. senator. Most striking, Burdick and Lederer had patterned Hillandale after Lansdale.[18]

In his report to the president, Lansdale painted a dismal picture. South Vietnam was in "critical condition." The Vietcong had made so much progress in the south that the United States "should treat it as a combat area of the cold war" in need of "emergency treatment." It required the presence of Americans who genuinely liked Asia and its people, who were willing to risk their lives for freedom, and who exuded the vigor and sincerity essential to winning popular support and instilling confidence in their government.[19]

The new administration had to redefine the U.S. role in South Vietnam. Washington should recall its ambassador in Saigon, Elbridge Durbrow, who had been in the "forest of tigers" for almost four years and did not realize how "tired" he had become or "how close he [was] to individual trees in this big woods." Indeed, the Diem regime suspected Durbrow (and correctly so, according to Lansdale) of sympathizing with (if not aiding and abetting) the coup attempt of November 1960. A new ambassador (Lansdale meant himself) should be in place before the April elections in South Vietnam, ready to counter the Vietcong. U.S. military advisers must accompany the Vietnamese army into combat areas. Members of the Military Assistance and Advisory Group (MAAG) in Saigon were "hardly in a position to be listened to when they are snug in rear areas and give advice to Vietnamese officers who have attended the same U.S. military schools and who are now in a combat in which few Americans are experienced." Lansdale saw no problem in making such a policy adjustment. All MAAG personnel, including their chief, the gruff and outspoken General Lionel McGarr, expressed strong interest in joining ARVN forces in the field.[20]

Lansdale insisted that the United States support Diem "until another strong executive can replace him legally." This task would not be easy. Diem "[felt] that Americans have attacked him almost as viciously as the Communists, and he [had] withdrawn into a shell for self-protection." His brother and closest adviser, Ngo Dinh Nhu, had fostered the premier's isolation by encouraging him to rely solely on family. If we do not like "Brother Nhu," Lansdale continued, "then let's move someone of ours in close." To edge South Vietnam toward democracy without undermining the strong leadership needed to defeat the Communists, the United States must send "a mature American" as the new ambassador. This "unusual American" must be sensitive to Vietnamese feelings and work toward the creation of a two-party political system in which the "loyal opposition" helped to develop a popular national program. Americans on the scene, Lansdale complained, had taught Diem's opponents "to be carping critics and disloyal citizens by [their] encouragement of these traits."[21]

The only areas in South Vietnam not under Communist control were those protected by loyalists using counterguerrilla methods. The insurgents' armed forces below the seventeenth parallel probably numbered close to 15,000, but more alarming, Lansdale asserted, were the thousands of Communists who were well trained in "proletarian military science" and already entrenched in the most economically productive areas of South Vietnam. The Vietcong controlled most of the country's heartland, that vast center of rice and rubber production extending from the jungle foothills of the High Plateau above Saigon all the way down to the Gulf of Siam. The Saigon government held only the urban area of Saigon–Cholon and those narrow regions protected by the Civil Guard and Self-Defense Corps. These paramilitary forces had proved fairly adept in counterguerrilla tactics and in winning the support of villagers who in turn provided information on Vietcong locations.[22]

Unlike the guerrilla wars in the Philippines and Malaya, the Communist insurgents in South Vietnam were not as vulnerable to a military strategy based on isolating and then destroying the enemy. South Vietnam's extensive borders stretched more than a thousand miles and featured a rough terrain that was virtually impossible to patrol. Vietcong cadres easily infiltrated South Vietnam from Laos and Cambodia. After the Geneva Accords of 1954 had authorized the relocation of Vietminh forces to the north, many left their families in the south. These so-called "stay-behind organizations" provided the nucleus of the Vietcong insurgency. Many former Vietminh contingents now returned to their homes and, along with those in the south recruited on a local basis, received North Vietnamese assistance passing through the jungles of Laos and Cambodia.[23]

Saigon itself was not safe from Communist infiltration. Radio Hanoi kept the city in turmoil by levying a prolonged and bitter propaganda assault on both South Vietnam's leaders and their American friends on the scene—in particular, MAAG. Diem insisted that the Communists' goal was "first the mountains, then the countryside, and then the city." In two of the Communists' greatest successes in the 1950s—Manila and Hanoi—government forces had been shocked by the Communists' establishment of secret networks throughout the cities. "I believe," Lansdale declared, "that the people in Saigon–Cholon have been the target of considerable subversive effort by the Communists and that it takes an in-place organization to carry this out."[24]

The United States must stand behind Diem, insisted Lansdale. Admittedly, he and Diem were friends, but this was not "a blind friendship": The premier had exiled or jailed some of Lansdale's Vietnamese friends. Diem wanted to delegate authority, but he had found most colleagues either too soft to make hard decisions or too proud to assume difficult tasks. He leaned too heavily on Nguyen Dinh Thuan, secretary of state for the presidency, who had acted as a "hatchet man" in ridding the government of incompetents. Vice-President Nguyen Ngoc Tho was "so soft-hearted" that he never took action against those in need of a reprimand or an outright dismissal from office.[25]

The White House must recognize Diem's untenable position and work within its parameters. Those who criticized Diem, Lansdale cryptically remarked, had failed to realize that he "is human and doesn't like the idea of people trying to kill him out of hatred"—most notably, "at 3 A.M. by bursts of heavy machine gun fire into his bedroom in an obvious try at liquidating him in his bed." For seven years, the Communists had leveled a "venomous attack" on his regime. The only way for Diem to quiet this verbal assault was to curtail freedom of speech. This he refused to do.[26]

Lansdale laid some of the blame on the U.S. embassy but not on either the CIA or MAAG. Diem believed that many Foreign Service personnel held him in such contempt that they had adopted the same critical tactics used by the Communists. Americans must drop their "holier than thou" approach to Diem. If they viewed him as "a human being who has been through a lot of hell for years—and not as an opponent to be beaten to his knees—we would start regaining our influence with him in a healthy way."[27]

Lansdale concluded that the United States should "help those who help themselves, and not have a lot of strings on that help." The South Vietnamese could win the war if the United States sought to provide security for the populace and to devise a sound course of action against the Vietcong. South Vietnamese civil and military officers, in turn, must implement these policies as well as psywar techniques. The U.S. military must oversee the program.[28]

President Kennedy encountered a strong adversary in Vietnam, against which he now thought he had an appropriate, equivalent response that rested on his administration's central principles of flexibility and restraint. Counterinsurgency measures and continued support to Diem—these two steps offered a rational and limited reaction to a Communist menace in Vietnam that allowed the White House to deal with other Cold War problems at the same time. And the great attraction of this low-key approach lay in its emphasis on the United States's helping the South Vietnamese themselves to win the war. Any decision to withdraw such special assistance could take place much more easily if the administration did not send Americans to fight the war.

III

ON SATURDAY MORNING of January 28, 1961, McNamara telephoned Lansdale at his home in Virginia and ordered him to the White House within the hour. What could be so urgent? Lansdale wondered, as he dashed out the door. When the general arrived, he was rushed to the waiting area outside the Cabinet Room, where the president was presiding over a meeting with more than twenty advisers, including Rusk, McNamara, Vice President Lyndon B. Johnson, General Lyman L. Lemnitzer (chair of the Joint Chiefs of Staff), CIA director Allen Dulles, Assistant Secretary of Defense for International Security Affairs Paul Nitze, and Assistant Secretary of State for the Far East Graham Parsons. Lansdale could not have known this, but their focus of concern was Cuba, about which Dulles had prepared a briefing on the CIA's plan developed under Eisenhower for invading the island and removing Castro from power. In the aftermath of what Lansdale sensed was an intense discussion, he was ushered into the room to sit at the long table opposite the president. Those in attendance exchanged looks of bewilderment, most of them having never seen Lansdale and puzzling over why this uniformed man was there. With the general's report in front of him, the president introduced his special guest as a recent visitor to Vietnam and praised his written analysis without revealing its contents. "For the first time," Kennedy asserted with satisfaction, "[I have] a sense of the danger and urgency of the problem in Vietnam." And then, without having consulted Rusk, Kennedy motioned to his secretary of state before asking Lansdale, "Did Dean tell you that I'd like you to go over there as the new ambassador?" Silence blanketed the room. Lansdale, just as surprised as the others, flushed and politely replied, "I'm a regular military officer over at the Pentagon and it's a great honor and thank you very much, but I don't think my place is in diplomacy."[29]

One can only imagine the astonished looks on the faces of Rusk and his colleagues as the president, clearly energized by Lansdale's findings (Did he not personify the fictional James Bond?), made this startling and unorthodox nomination. Then, before anyone could say anything, Kennedy asked Parsons to summarize another report on South Vietnam then under consideration. Parsons felt uneasy. He was familiar with Lansdale's CIA exploits and did not like them. Lansdale, Parsons later complained to Rusk, was a "lone wolf and operator" with a "flamboyant" manner who did not feel bound by higher authority and was too politically driven and monstrously outspoken. When Rusk, ever the loyal team player, seemed willing to endorse Lansdale for the Saigon post, Parsons hotly protested, warning of the threatening message sent to observers the world over in appointing a general and former CIA agent to a diplomatic post in a country under Communist siege. Although he dissuaded Rusk (who simply ignored the president's statement and allowed the idea to die quietly—he had not, after all, given a specific order), Parsons now found himself in the uncomfortable position of advocating his own study without knowing whether it agreed with Lansdale's findings that the president had so enthusiastically endorsed.[30]

As it soon became clear, Parsons's conclusions were remarkably similar to Lansdale's in highlighting the military, political, economic, and psychological aspects of a "Basic Counterinsurgency Plan for Vietnam" (CIP) recently submitted by the Country Team in Saigon. The defense department under President Eisenhower had called for a plan of action, which led to the appointment of a committee in the Saigon embassy that was composed of representatives from MAAG, the CIA, the U.S. Operations Mission (USOM), and the U.S. Information Service (USIS). The study group called for a 20,000-man increase in the South Vietnamese army, rapid counterinsurgency training under MAAG's direction of a Civil Guard raised by 32,000 to a total of 68,000, and a massive reorganization of the Saigon government in security and intelligence matters. Thus the defense and state departments had combined in placing priority on improved internal security against a Communist-led insurgency. The South Vietnamese military could take the offensive against the Vietcong and bring the war to a close in eighteen months.[31]

Since December 1959, the Country Team declared, Vietcong terrorism had sought to bring down Diem. Black propaganda, forced taxation, kidnapping and murder of village and hamlet officials, ambushes along canals and roads, and repeated armed attacks on agrovilles, land development centers, small army units, and Civil Guard and Self-Defense Corps posts—all these scare tactics had undermined popular confidence in the Saigon government's capacity to protect its constituents. The Vietcong intended to take advantage of growing disenchantment with the Diem regime in particular and the Ngo family in general. Widespread discontent focused on brothers Nhu and Ngo Dinh Can as directors of the corrupt and semicovert Can Lao party, and on Madame Nhu as a staunch advocate of governmental policies that reflected no concern for popular needs. At a time when the Diem regime desperately needed the allegiance of its people, it had alienated the military, peasants, members of the government, the Cao Dai and Hoa Hao religious sects, intellectuals and other elitists, and, to some extent, labor and urban business groups.[32]

The Diem government's central task was to restore individual security in the face of a preponderant military threat. Indeed, South Vietnam was unique in having to defend itself against Communist subversion inside the country while, according to the Country Team's findings, facing a potential conventional attack from North Vietnam. At present, the greater danger came from the insurgents. Diem had hurt the country's defense system by refusing to delegate authority to his generals for fear of another military coup attempt similar to the close call of November 1960. In truth, the ARVN was in no shape to launch an offensive against the Vietcong. Not only did its soldiers lack discipline, training, matériel, and morale, but nearly 75 percent of them were preoccupied by pacification efforts, with about half assigned to static guard and security responsibilities. The Vietcong had meanwhile sabotaged communication lines, buildings, agrovilles, and many other structures left unguarded.[33]

According to the Country Team, South Vietnam would fall to the Communists within the next few months if the United States failed to come to its defense. Saigon's leaders must take emergency measures to improve their government and win popular support. The ARVN must clear the Vietcong from its main political and military operating base—the rice-rich Mekong Delta—while the United States helped the South Vietnamese wind down the insurgency. In conclusions similar to those advocated by Lansdale, the Country Team insisted that Saigon stop the flow of North Vietnamese matériel into South Vietnam while attacking the Vietcong and building a defense against outside aggression. Only with U.S. military, economic, and advisory assistance could the South Vietnamese prevail.[34]

Top priority was a national plan intended to counter the domestic and foreign threat. Such a comprehensive strategy entailed tightened internal security, improved intelligence and communications, the creation of border and coastal patrols to stop infiltration, a major military offensive, and the installation of leaders who could build a spirit of national unity by demonstrating greater sensitivity to popular needs. Furthermore, the Saigon government should keep both the press and public informed. The army and the people must develop a "mutuality of interests."[35]

Some of the ideas contained in the Country Team's report were so similar to Lansdale's that, in a questionable piece of protocol, he interrupted to speak on its behalf. Victory depended on full South Vietnamese involvement in the proposed counterinsurgency program, he asserted. The Communists' "big year" was 1961. To defeat them, the United States must instill an aggressive spirit into the South Vietnamese by underwriting an expansion of their military forces and then encouraging them to take the offensive.[36]

Lansdale drew a sharply negative reaction when he declared that Diem no longer trusted the United States and then rejected the Country Team's claim that the central problem was military. Members of the embassy and the Foreign Service, he alleged, were "defeatist" and showed no genuine interest in South Vietnam's welfare. Diem still had confidence in MAAG and the CIA but believed that "there are Americans in the Foreign Service who are very close to those who tried to kill him" during the November 1960 coup attempt. Kennedy expressed concern over Diem's suspicions and asked Lansdale to assess Durbrow's performance.

"I'm a little hesitant," Lansdale responded, "but you're the president and you need the truth. So I'll just tell you right now, I think he's a very ill man. His judgment's impaired by his physical condition. He's a fine professional Foreign Service officer and could be used someplace, but don't keep him on in Vietnam anymore. He's sick, he's on his back a lot of the time, and you need someone very alert, whoever it is. And pull him out."

Rusk could contain himself no longer. "You're off your subject, boy," he indignantly declared in his southern drawl.

"Well, Durby's an old friend of mine," Lansdale responded, "and I like the guy. I saw a lot of him when I was in Vietnam on this brief visit. I think it's a shame that the guy's kept on there because he was quite ill, in bad shape."

Durbrow and his staff in Saigon, the secretary of state hotly insisted, did not seek Diem's overthrow. They had had an especially trying time during the past three and a half years in attempting to convince him of the necessity of reform while assuring U.S. friendship. "This was never easy," the usually staid Rusk sharply asserted, "nor was President Diem an easy person."[37]

Lansdale's remarks had set off a heated discussion that intensified when President Kennedy took his visitor's side in the remedies proposed. He first questioned the wisdom of expanding South Vietnam's armed forces when the real problem, as Lansdale argued, involved politics and morale. Diem, it appeared, had shown no interest in an antiguerrilla campaign. If the problem was a lack of motivation among South Vietnam's armed forces, how would additional troops guarantee an ARVN offensive? If the Vietcong numbered only a few thousand, why raise the South Vietnamese army from its present level of 150,000 to 170,000? In any event, the injection of new military personnel could have no impact sooner than a year or two. Parsons was visibly upset with the president's preference for Lansdale's ideas and defended the Country Team's call for more South Vietnamese troops. The ARVN had two major responsibilities, Parsons emphasized: to put down the growing insurgency and to prevent a conventional attack by North Vietnam's army of 300,000. An enlarged South Vietnamese army was critical.[38]

The president could not reject Parsons's argument out of hand, but he clearly leaned toward Lansdale's conclusions and urged prompt action based on them as well as the Country Team's call for a counterinsurgency program. Counterguerrillas must "operate in the north," Kennedy asserted. Such covert actions drew support from a number of White House advisers, including the brothers McGeorge and William Bundy, McNamara, Rostow, and the president's own brother and attorney general, Robert Kennedy. Indeed, the antiguerrilla operations in the north advocated by President Kennedy marked the first step in a covert campaign that got under way in full force in 1964 and lasted into the early 1970s as "Operation Plan 34A"

(OPLAN 34A). Rusk recommended the creation of a task force on Vietnam similar to the one already at work on Cuba. Its responsibility would be to determine the necessary measures for implementing the Counterinsurgency Plan submitted by the Country Team. Vietnam, the president observed, was one of four crises (the others were Laos, Cuba, and the Congo) in need of emergency attention. He wanted McGeorge Bundy to supervise a course of action aimed at making notable progress in South Vietnam within three months.[39] Such impatience would continually bedevil U.S. efforts against an enemy that pursued a long-term approach.

President Kennedy supported the Counterinsurgency Plan as a vital part of a greater U.S. initiative on behalf of Diem. At a National Security Council meeting on February 1, just two days after the acrimonious exchanges in the White House, he approved an expenditure of $28.4 million to expand South Vietnam's military forces by 20,000 (due in part to the slipping situation in Laos), and another $12.7 million to establish a training and supply program for the additional 32,000 members of its Civil Guard. He also directed the defense secretary to consult other agencies in determining the means for developing counterguerrilla forces. In a small act that revealed his zest for counterinsurgency warfare, the president scrawled the words "Why so little?" next to the figure of $660,000 allotted to "Psychological Operations" found in the Country Team's report.[40]

Lansdale's conclusions had combined with many features of the Country Team's lengthy study to become the essence of a counterinsurgency strategy in South Vietnam. One of the president's chief advisers, Roger Hilsman, was a graduate of West Point and a hard-nosed member of a World War II commando force known as "Merrill's Marauders." Drawing from his own guerrilla experiences in the Burmese hills, Hilsman had gone on to serve both the OSS and CIA and now strongly supported the counterinsurgency approach. Guerrilla warfare, he declared from his position as director of the state department's Bureau of Intelligence and Research, was "a new kind of aggression in which one country sponsors internal war against another." In a statement that fitted Rostow's thinking, Hilsman insisted that counterinsurgency was vital to promoting the economic development of poor countries. Kennedy meanwhile studied the writings of guerrilla theorists Mao Zedong and Che Guevara and soon instructed the army to do the same. Mao's most basic warning became the fundamental principle underlying White House efforts: Guerrilla warfare would fail "if its political objectives do not coincide with the aspirations of the people and their sympathy, cooperation and assistance cannot be gained." Indeed, Kennedy often quoted Mao's statement that "guerrillas are like fish, and the people are the water in which fish swim." The way to kill the fish was either to dam up the water or change its temperature. Thus the president emphasized *non*military tactics in defeating Communist "wars of national liberation."[41] Most noteworthy was his determination to help the South Vietnamese win a guerrilla war that was theirs alone to fight.

PRESIDENT KENNEDY had defined the most pressing problem in Vietnam as a Communist insurgency that had originated in North Vietnam and that would become increasingly dependent on cadres and matériel entering South Vietnam through Laos and Cambodia. He had avoided the term "counterrevolution," which would have classified the Vietcong as revolutionaries and hence suggested that the United States sought to put down an indigenous movement for independence. In doing so, however, he had failed to grasp the full scope of the Communists' strategy. The administration had become involved in a different kind of war, an unconventional conflict that guaranteed confusion in defining the enemy. Indeed, wrote Paul Kattenburg, former head of the Vietnam task force, "U.S. counterinsurgency did not view the guerrillas as men and women of the villages themselves." They were "clearly alien and distinct elements, who intruded suddenly and after long forced marches from secure rear bases equipped by China and Russia upon peaceful rice-growing villages which they would then terrorize mercilessly." In February 1961, a secret meeting took place in military Zone D above Saigon, where paramilitary groups in the Mekong Delta joined those forces in the Central Highlands to form the People's Liberation Armed Forces (PLAF), which became the military arm of the NLF that Diem derisively called the Vietcong or Vietnamese Communists. The Vietcong, Kattenburg argued, was not simply comprised of villagers fighting for independence or domestic reform. Its leaders were Communists who sought global conquest.[42]

The administration's broadly based Counterinsurgency Plan rested on improving the South Vietnamese military forces by enhanced U.S. military and economic aid. Related components were the neutralization of Laos, the sanctity of its border and that of Cambodia's touching South Vietnam, and the institution of economic and political reforms in Saigon. The president opposed a direct U.S. military involvement because the South Vietnamese themselves must win the war. Victory did not entail the total destruction of the Vietcong because of Vietnam's rugged jungle terrain and the insurgents' privileged sanctuaries in Laos and Cambodia. Success would come when South Vietnam sharply reduced the intensity of the conflict. A quagmire in the making it was—and one that the president sought to avert through carefully calibrated counterinsurgency tactics.

2

DEMOCRACY AT BAY
Diem as Mandarin

Everything must be brought into play to insure [*sic*] the
survival of Vietnam.

Wolf Ladejinsky, February 24, 1961

IEM'S COOPERATION was the major requirement for a successful
counterinsurgency campaign in South Vietnam. His distrust of
Americans did not bode well for a warm relationship, and his
suspicion had deepened each time Ambassador Durbrow called for democratic reforms as a prerequisite for U.S. assistance. Diem's reasoning was,
on the surface, eminently practical: A decentralized government would endanger the war effort by inviting the opposition into the decision-making
process. Such a move, he insisted, would threaten the chain of command and
permit dissidents to undermine national unity. But Diem's stand against de-
centralization ran deeper than wartime considerations. To delegate more
authority to field officers would provide the military with the means for staging
another coup attempt.

The supreme irony is that the democracy advocated by the United
States to save the Diem regime was exactly what could bring it down. Although the White House promoted the image of the premier as a proponent of democracy, the truth was that Diem remained an autocrat. The
revolution he sought was reactionary in nature: the restoration of imperial
rule along the lines of his nineteenth-century Chinese role model, Emperor Minh Mang. Diem's philosophy was Confucian in principle, emphasizing a bureaucratic order that placed him at the top as the "Son of Heaven,"
served by well-educated civilian and military figures known as mandarins,
whose authority extended down to the district and provincial levels. U.S.–
South Vietnamese relations would further deteriorate if the White House
conditioned its assistance on Diem's forsaking his mandarin principles and
granting democratic reforms. The immediate casualty would be President
Kennedy's counterinsurgency program; the long-range result could be the
end of Diem's rule.

I

AT A PRESS CONFERENCE on February 6, 1961, Diem announced a series of reforms and urged popular participation in the struggle against the Vietcong. Durbrow publicly praised the reform program while reminding Rusk that similar programs had appeared over the years without effect. Yet Diem's appearance before both foreign and domestic journalists suggested that he had embarked upon important changes. Governmental administration would improve—*if* Diem delegated authority to subordinates from the provincial level down to the villages. But his only democratic proposal was the election of youths to the village councils. Security problems, Diem explained, prevented general elections. Durbrow nevertheless concluded that Diem's program was "substantial, forward-looking and, if properly implemented, should provide [a] solid base to build on."[1]

The liberal-minded undersecretary of state, Chester Bowles, likewise emphasized the need for land reform, a just legal system, and popular participation in government. In a meeting with the Vietnamese ambassador to Washington, Tran Van Chuong, Bowles cited the successes in Thailand and Japan in reiterating the importance of providing land for the peasants. Social reforms would lay the basis for long-range peace and stability, Bowles contended. The nations of Southeast Asia must develop "a sense of common destiny" that rested on "justice and more equality." Only then would the Vietnamese people realize that their enemy was the Vietcong and not their government in Saigon.[2]

Bowles's call for land reform drew enthusiastic support from the director of the state department's Southeast Asia Affairs Division, Kenneth Young, who urged his home government to exercise more guidance without assuming South Vietnam's burden. Young had visited South Vietnam during the advent of the guerrilla crisis in early December 1959, and he had noted an impressive program that relocated thousands of people to protect them from the Vietcong. Diem had also attempted to safeguard the Pleiku area in central Vietnam by erecting clusters of population centers across the southward route of enemy infiltration that would make guerrilla movements more difficult to hide. The outcome of these ventures depended on the capacity of the Vietnamese people to make their own livelihood. What struck Young most was "the absence of American advisors on the spot or direct assistance," marking "a major demonstration of Vietnamese 'do-it ourselves.'"[3]

After a three-month stay in Southeast Asia during the summer and fall of 1960, Young offered further recommendations on improving the situation in South Vietnam as a vital step toward curbing the Communist Chinese threat to Asia. Diem's responsibility, Young insisted, was to convince the young professionals and rural people to support the government's recently announced reforms. They appeared promising: a Department of Civic Action, a National Economic Council, a Department of Rural Affairs, and a stream of village, municipal, and provincial councils. Diem's agroville program, an effort to relocate peasants in barbed-wire enclosures safe from the Vietcong, was a sound idea, but it had struggled because the government did not compensate farmers for their labor.[4]

South Vietnam, Young argued, needed a new village program based on a small military force that fought the Communists while other soldiers conducted civil work. Such a broad effort would promote urban and rural community development and thereby encourage monetary investment in the Mekong River Basin. Young advocated what he called "agrimetro" reform, which aimed at creating "compound communities" within a "village cluster." Integral to this project was a mobile village defense system dependent on a company of 120 specially trained village commandos assigned to each compound community. Guerrilla attacks on villages or hamlets in the compound community would meet resistance from all defense units in the area. To facilitate this approach, South Vietnam needed a special warfare school.[5]

President Kennedy's interest in counterinsurgency had led to several detailed studies that supported Young's findings. At a planning session in late February 1961, Rostow welcomed the task of analyzing the value of antiguerrilla warfare in resisting communism in South Vietnam. The advisory group talked about taking two items before SEATO: the institution of counterguerrilla operations and the use of local military personnel and matériel to develop the economy.[6]

Lansdale meanwhile continued his campaign for counterinsurgency by urging the South Vietnamese government and army to adopt civic action projects that promoted communal safety. The counterinsurgency program must have a social as well as military dimension. He sent the White House a speech he would give on February 24 to the Special Warfare School at Fort Bragg, North Carolina, which stressed the civic action dimension of counterinsurgency. Citing the teachings of ancient Chinese general Sun Tzu, Lansdale underscored the importance of having leaders imbued with the "moral law" in winning popular support through civic action projects. The Communists in North Vietnam acted on this principle. Two decades earlier, Mao Zedong had sought to ally China's army with the people. The Communists' success in their "guerrilla phase" depended on using Sun's first "constant factor" of moral leadership, which governed "the art of war." The future of counterinsurgency rested on ensuring security.[7]

Thus, a major element in undercutting the guerrillas (of equal importance with military measures, Lansdale argued) was the development of civic action programs that implemented Sun's moral emphasis on meeting popular needs. President Kennedy, Lansdale believed, recognized the government's moral responsibility to pursue social, political, and economic policies intended to safeguard the people and win their support. The army was inseparable from the government and must make the soldier "a *brother* of the people, as well as their protector." Civic action encompassed "basic military courtesy and discipline" as well as "formal projects." Good behavior by army patrols was essential in guerrilla territory. "A stolen chicken, a carelessly driven jeep, may well make villagers so angry that they would withhold information and let an ambush succeed."[8]

Lansdale's counterguerrilla theories offered a viable alternative to an all-out military assault on the Vietcong that the ARVN was not prepared to launch. His emphasis on civic action did not rule out military measures. But the killing of Vietcong must not spill over into the civilian sector and thereby undermine the government's war effort. Lansdale, however, failed to address one of the government's most fundamental problems in countering guerrilla warfare: how to determine which Vietnamese civilians were clandestine supporters of the Vietcong. And yet, the government's attempts to distinguish between loyalists and traitors seemed more attractive than simply killing everyone.

Robert Taber's *The War of the Flea* did not appear until 1965, but its ideas were precisely those that Lansdale sought to avert. At one point in the book, Taber argued that "there is only one means of defeating an insurgent people who will not surrender, and that is extermination. There is only one way to control a territory that harbours resistance, and that is to turn it into a desert. Where these means cannot, for whatever reason, be used, the war is lost." To a friend, Lansdale wrote that if the "only alternative is to kill every last person in the enemy ranks [then] I'm not only morally opposed to this alternative, but I'm convinced that it's humanly impossible."[9]

The move toward counterinsurgency warfare received another boost from a U.S. civilian adviser and agricultural specialist on the scene, Wolf Ladejinsky, who insisted that Diem must build political ties with his people. In a memo to the president, Rostow enclosed a letter from Ladejinsky, who, like Young and Lansdale, supported Diem. Ladejinsky had worked as a U.S. adviser in Japan's post–World War II land reform program. After leaving his governmental position, he arrived in Saigon in 1956, where he advised Diem on agrarian affairs and became a close friend. Indeed, Ladejinsky lived in a house next to the palace and had breakfast with the premier on a regular basis, often discussing how to implant the land reform program that Ladejinsky had drafted for South Vietnam. Ladejinsky insisted that Diem was not aware of the failures in the program and often circumvented the law because he thought it was for the common good. He moved in people he could trust—"refugees"—to the farm communities and distributed land to them for political and security reasons. He then told them what to grow in accordance with "the greater good." But the closeness between Diem and Ladejinsky did not last. Durbrow had asked Ladejinsky to bring up with the premier the subject of corruption in the government and other matters that went beyond land reform. Lansdale guessed that Ladejinsky probably became "very political" in his talk and alienated Diem. Rostow assured President Kennedy that Ladejinsky was "a wise old boy on Asia as a whole, as well as Vietnam."[10]

Ladejinsky warned that recent economic progress in South Vietnam might grind to a stop if the Communist attacks persisted. The Saigon regime had not been prepared to counter the subversion, and its feeble efforts at economic improvement had failed to bring political stability. Despite U.S. aid and hard work by the Vietnamese people, economic advances had stalled in the face of "political ineptitude and misdirected military preparation—above all the former."[11]

The military situation was abysmal. Americans, Ladejinsky insisted, failed to understand that the Vietminh's victory over the French had stemmed from the principles of guerrilla warfare. U.S. military efforts rested on the mistaken assumption that the fighting in Vietnam would be similar to the straightforward military offensive employed in the Napoleonic Wars. Widespread discontent within the ARVN derived from Diem's personal direction of his military forces and an inadequate intelligence system that hampered the army's capacity to counter "the widespread, mobile, well organized, well-armed and well-directed communist subversion groups." The military establishment must fight the same type of war waged by the Communists. Only in this manner could the government provide security to the peasants and retain their loyalty. "The multitude of fence-sitters in the countryside, driven into that position by communist terror, would be materially reduced, and a greater measure of internal security would be attained."[12]

The government must also move away from the exclusiveness of Diem's mandarin principles. Ladejinsky was not the only contemporary to recognize the heavy costs borne by the South Vietnamese because of their premier's mandarin thinking. Democratic Senator J. William Fulbright, chair of the Foreign Relations Committee, informed the president that Ho Chi Minh had expressed great pleasure on learning that the mandarins from the north had moved south. "Good!" Ho responded. "That is the best news I have heard in a long time. With that crowd now in the South, how can we lose?" Diem's mandarin loyalties had led him to emphasize military objectives at the expense of domestic political reforms. The absence of communication between government and people threatened to undermine the regime.[13]

Diem personified a complex mixture of good and bad. He was, Ladejinsky declared, "a man of the highest moral principles, of strong will and, above all, a man who never panics, fully confident that he is the invisible hand of the Lord in everything he does." But he also had "political blind spots" that resulted from "great caution, monumental stubbornness and equally monumental prejudices." With the war under way against the Communists, Diem preferred "the form rather than the substance of democracy." His strong belief in self-rule precluded any delegation of authority. Diem erroneously believed that the struggle against the Communists was purely military and that his government would suffer from a broadened political base. The November 1960 coup attempt, he naively insisted, lacked political motivations.[14]

Ladejinsky thought that South Vietnam could become an economic "showcase" once its people felt secure. The major threat came from the Communists of North Vietnam, who received support from the Chinese. The United States must help Saigon prepare its defenses against a certain armed assault from the north. In words strikingly similar to those of Kennedy's while a young senator, Ladejinsky declared that South Vietnam was "the heart of Southeast Asia" and the "cornerstone" of the independence of Laos, Cambodia, and Thailand. "Everything must be brought into play to insure [sic] the survival of Vietnam."[15]

This assessment bolstered President Kennedy's support for counterinsurgency. In an effort to install a counterinsurgency program over the next two years, he created a task force under the leadership of the CIA's Special Assistant for Planning and Coordination, Richard Bissell. It quickly became clear that the British success in quashing the insurrection in Malaya would provide a guideline for South Vietnam. Priority would go to military assistance. A search began for more military personnel—including British or Malayan, the state department made clear—to train the South Vietnamese in counterguerrilla warfare. The task force recommended twenty-one additional ranger companies and their eventual increase by forty. It called for infiltrating the Vietcong and improving border patrol, village transceivers, and civic action. The state department advocated a broad "Operations Plan," which stipulated a cooperative relationship with Cambodia, safe operational bases for the ARVN, the election of youths to village councils, and social programs in Vietcong-cleared areas that included the assignment of health, education, and agricultural specialists.[16]

Durbrow approved of these measures but warned again of Diem's reluctance to share power with nonfamily members. The ambassador was about to leave his post, a pivotal move because it suggested an imminent change in U.S. policy. No longer would the administration condition assistance on Diem's willingness to grant reforms. Durbrow knew this, as did Diem. Durbrow insisted that the Saigon government would not act without pressure from Washington. The entire approach depended on Diem's distributing power to people outside his family. This he refused to do.[17]

Durbrow came away with a mixed response after an hour-long attempt in early March 1961 to convince Diem to accept the Kennedy administration's Counterinsurgency Plan. General McGarr had reached an oral agreement with Thuan on a military command structure that directly connected the Chief of South Vietnam's Joint General Staff with his operational units in the field. The agreement contained other features: a centralized logistics system that reached down to the corps level; the use of psywar operations and improvements in intelligence, communications, and border and coastal patrols; and a national planning system for counterinsurgency and national security. Durbrow pushed for more: one or two members of the non-Communist opposition in Diem's cabinet; the dissolution of the secretive Can Lao party or at least its becoming open and providing a precedent for requiring the Communists and all other covert parties to do the same; and the establishment of better relations between South Vietnam and Cambodia. A broader government was possible, Diem implied, because many opposition members now realized that had the November coup attempt been successful, it would have helped the Communists. On the Can Lao party, however, he offered no assurances. Finally, Diem saw little chance of working out any arrangement with Cambodia, because its leader, Norodom Sihanouk, showed no interest in establishing good relations.[18]

Albeit with reservations, Durbrow felt encouraged by Diem's progress toward instituting reforms. The premier still hesitated to provide even modest remuneration to peasants who worked in the agrovilles but did not live there to receive their benefits. Those peasants who lived outside the agrovilles, he asserted, could turn to nearby markets, schools, hospitals, and maternity wards. On several other matters, he preferred to wait until after the April 1961 elections to avoid charges that he had approved changes merely to win votes. Diem, however, seemed confident of success, and for the first time he promised to implement the counterinsurgency measures where possible.[19]

And yet, the reality was far different from the appearance: The White House and the Saigon government had embarked on a collision course. Diem couched his reform assurances with equivocation. At no time did he promise to broaden the government, remove secrecy in politics, or end popular intimidation. Nor did he guarantee support for counterinsurgency. Diem rejected any governmental changes he deemed detrimental to his regime. He remained suspicious of Durbrow, underscoring the need to replace him with someone more sympathetic to South Vietnam's interests. The White House recognized that its Counterinsurgency Plan depended on Diem. The open democratic process advocated by the Kennedy administration, along with the Counterinsurgency Plan, remained elusive.

II

A NATIONAL INTELLIGENCE ESTIMATE in late March 1961 confirmed Diem's continued opposition to reforms. South Vietnam's problems, according to the study, stemmed from Communist guerrillas whose terrorist tactics had undermined popular confidence in the Diem regime. Admittedly, Diem had exerted stronger governmental controls while permitting some reforms. He had also intensified military actions against the Vietcong and improved the ARVN's antiguerrilla capacity. Still, he had not faced up to the social, political, and economic causes of the November 1960 coup effort and could soon confront another takeover attempt by non-Communists. The Communists, of course, intended to exploit the chaotic situation.[20]

Later that month, Thuan met with Rusk and Durbrow in the U.S. embassy in Bangkok to discuss South Vietnam's problems. Foreign correspondents, Thuan complained, had criticized his government's undemocratic features without recognizing the gravity of the Vietcong threat or his country's economic and political backwardness. Since 1959, the Vietcong had relied on terrorism. Rising numbers of trained cadres had arrived from the north as part of Hanoi's publicly announced objective of promoting Diem's collapse. Ho Chi Minh's long-time trusted general, Vo Nguyen Giap, declared that his government sought to replace Diem with a "friendly" leader who would support a reunified Vietnam in line with the Geneva Accords of 1954. This seemingly innocuous statement meant, Thuan insisted, a Communist-controlled "front" government in Saigon.[21]

South Vietnam was at war, Thuan emphasized. Each month the Vietcong killed nearly 300 ARVN troops and numerous civilians. In the decade before Diem's arrival as premier in 1954, the forerunner of the Vietcong—the Vietminh—had occupied much of the countryside. Its forces had then indoctrinated many peasants with communism and kidnapped a large number of youths from families migrating north under provisions of the Geneva Accords. Many Vietcong members were married to South Vietnamese women or were brothers or sons of people in the south. Thus, the Vietcong could easily intimidate relatives into collaboration. When Diem took office, the outgoing French controlled only the main towns and highways. During the next two years he had worked to regain the countryside and establish internal security. He had been so successful that the Vietcong resorted to terrorism.[22]

Thuan insisted that his government supported the proposed Counterinsurgency Plan but lacked the funds necessary to underwrite the effort. Only by levying new taxes, collecting old taxes, and floating a loan through local banks could the government meet the heavy expenses of 1961. Even then, the banks stipulated that half of the loan go to economic development and not exclusively to the military program. Meeting the costs of 1962 appeared to be out of the question.[23]

In response to this unsettling news from Bangkok, Rostow urged President Kennedy to exert more pressure on Diem to approve the Counterinsurgency Plan. Rostow also took on the task of convincing others in the administration to support the president's counterguerrilla strategy. Although himself a strong military advocate, Rostow assured Sorensen that "the struggle of these hard pressed areas against Communist pressure can never be wholly a military struggle." Economic development was a vital part of the battle against communism. Yet the most immediate need, Rostow told Kennedy, was "an effective counter-offensive in Viet-Nam." After Diem's certain reelection victory on April 9, the United States could approach him "directly and with vigor on the Counter-Insurgency Plan." To cultivate Diem's trust while emphasizing the necessity of both political and military remedies, the government turned to the ambassador-select to South Vietnam, Frederick Nolting, a disarming, soft-spoken Virginian. The United States must use its "unexploited counter-guerrilla assets on the Viet-Nam problem: armed helicopters; other Research and Development possibilities; our Special Forces units." Rostow wanted McNamara to activate this program. "It is somehow wrong to be developing these capabilities but not applying them in a crucial active theater. In Knute Rockne's old phrase, we are not saving them for the Junior Prom."[24]

Rostow recommended that the president use "various subterfuges" to evade the strictures contained in the Geneva Accords, especially the stipulated limitation on MAAG's size. Others involved in the Geneva agreement—most noticeably, North Vietnam in collaboration with the Communists in Laos and Cambodia—were openly violating the accords, Rostow noted. Support had grown for ignoring the terms, particularly since the United States was not a signatory nation to the 1954 agreements.[25]

In the midst of this flurry of activity, the problem again arose of whether or not to condition U.S. aid on Diem's institution of reforms. Diem, as expected, overwhelmingly won reelection in a highly suspect process that the *Pentagon Papers* termed "an essentially meaningless formality." Rostow went into action. The president must reassure Diem of continued U.S. support by sending the vice president on a good-will mission to South Vietnam, inviting Thuan to the United States, pressing Diem to broaden his government and decentralize its administration, and raising MAAG's ceiling unless there was some other way to introduce a "substantial number of Special Forces types." Diem had recently spent two hours with news columnist Joseph Alsop, complaining that the United States did not fully support his government in Saigon. Durbrow again urged the White House to warn Diem that if he did not cooperate with the United States, it would withhold funds for increasing his military forces.[26]

Both Lansdale and Rostow opposed issuing an ultimatum to Diem. Durbrow, according to Rostow's staff assistant Robert Komer, had "an obvious personality clash" with Diem and should not "lay down the law to the President." Rostow agreed with Komer and staunchly opposed Durbrow's advice to condition the force increase on Diem's implementation of the Counterinsurgency Plan. These were Durbrow's last days in Saigon, and he lacked leverage, Rostow argued. Once Nolting assumed his new post as ambassador, he should negotiate with Diem on the matter.[27]

Then, in mid-April 1961, two events further enhanced the U.S. role in South Vietnam. First, the Kennedy administration agreed to a cease-fire in Laos, followed by neutralization talks in an attempt to wind down the Communist insurgency and sanctify the border touching South Vietnam. Second, its approval of the CIA's plan to overthrow the Castro regime in Cuba had resulted in one of the greatest debacles in the history of U.S. foreign policy. Cuban military forces either killed or captured every member of the small group of Cuban exiles involved in the landing at the Bay of Pigs, and Castro publicly blasted the White House for engineering the coup attempt.

The setback in Cuba nearly traumatized the Kennedy administration, leading to a major reassessment of its foreign policy. The president's credibility plummeted, causing him to doubt the wisdom and honesty of the CIA and the Joint Chiefs of Staff and to rely instead on his brother Robert, along with Sorensen as chief counsel and a small coterie of others who had helped him get into office. "All my life I've known better than to depend on the experts," the president moaned. "How could I have been so stupid, to let them go ahead." On April 21, four days after the aborted invasion, the president bitterly noted at a breakfast meeting with Rusk and other advisers that the morning's newspapers did not include the joint chiefs in the stories attributing blame to government agencies. The Pentagon had whitewashed its culpability.[28]

Later that same day, Kennedy brought retired Army General Maxwell D. Taylor into the administration to analyze the failure at the Bay of Pigs and to make recommendations on future Cold War strategy. Taylor, a veteran of World War II and the Korean War, had served as Chief of Staff in the Eisenhower administration until pressured out after advocating a measured strategy of "flexible response" in the John Foster Dulles era of brinkmanship and massive retaliation. The United States, Taylor warned, must be prepared to deal "with anything from general atomic war to infiltrations such as threaten Laos." After retiring from the army in 1959, Taylor wrote *An Uncertain Trumpet*, which criticized Eisenhower's defense strategy and, in Kennedy's words, was "most persuasive" in "shap[ing] [his] own thinking." Taylor proved an exception to the president's negative image of generals. According to one state department observer, Taylor "talked with an elegance unexpected in a soldier, and he looked exactly as a general should: clean-cut, scholarly, handsome, and resolute."[29]

The administration was in "deep trouble," Kennedy solemnly told Taylor. Indeed, the general's homecoming in the midst of the Cuban disaster took on a funereal bearing. "I was ushered into the Oval Room," Taylor later wrote, "and there met President Kennedy, Vice-President Johnson, and McGeorge Bundy along with a few other officials who drifted in and out. I sensed an air which I had known in my military past—that of a command post that had been overrun by the enemy. There were the same glazed eyes, subdued voices, and slow speech that I remembered observing in commanders routed at the Battle of the Bulge or recovering from the shock of their first action." The new administration had "engaged in its first bloody action and was learning the sting of defeat."[30]

If the U.S. experience with Laos was not another defeat, it certainly was not a victory, and, for that reason, it combined with the Cuban fiasco to assign special importance to South Vietnam. "What happened," according to state department Asian specialist James Thomson, Jr., was that "we discovered that the Laotians were not Turks." They would not fight. "And, once we discovered that the Laotians were not Turks, it seemed advisable to pull back from confrontation in Laos." It suddenly became clear that "the place to stand one's ground . . . was Vietnam because the Vietnamese were Turks." Years afterward, William Sullivan, former Far Eastern Affairs expert in the state department, confirmed this observation. "Laos was a secondary problem . . . a poor place to get bogged down in because it was inland, had no access to the sea and no proper logistics lines . . . it was rather inchoate as a nation; . . . the [Laotians] were not fighters." In a view shared by Rusk, Sullivan asserted that Vietnam was a more appropriate site for a confrontation because it had "logistical access to the sea and therefore, we had military advantages. It was an articulated, functioning nation. Its troops were tigers and real fighters." The White House regarded Vietnam as the "main show," not a potential quagmire but a "more solid instrument for settling" the ongoing battle between the Free World and the Communists.[31]

The move toward a Laotian compromise had frightened the South Vietnamese into believing that the same outcome awaited them. President Kennedy adamantly rejected numerous proposals by the military to send troops into Laos to save the U.S.-supported regime. To adviser and historian Arthur M. Schlesinger, Jr., the president declared, "If it hadn't been for Cuba, we might be about to intervene in Laos." Waving a pile of cables from General Lemnitzer, Kennedy noted that they urged military intervention and disgustedly remarked, "I might have taken this advice seriously." He was even more emphatic in a conversation with Sorensen. "Thank God the Bay of Pigs happened when it did," the president remarked in September. "Otherwise we'd be in Laos by now—and that would be a hundred times worse." John Kenneth Galbraith, former economics professor at Harvard and Kennedy's ambassador to India, sarcastically warned his good friend in the White House that "as a military ally the entire Laos nation is clearly inferior to a battalion of conscientious objectors from World War I." The president realized that the northern border of Laos was China, which raised the chances of a bigger war. Moreover, he recognized the primacy of Cold War demands. As he told *New York Times* writer Arthur Krock, Khrushchev must not misinterpret Laos and Cuba as signals that the United States was in "a yielding mood on such matters as Berlin." Critics charged that the president possessed more profile than courage and that he was anything but the best and the brightest. The president knew that the United States must take a stand against communism somewhere, and, as he told James Reston of the *New York Times*, "Vietnam looks like the place."[32]

In the aftermath of the Cuban disaster, the administration had to re-establish U.S. credibility in the quickly intensifying Cold War. Rostow warned the president that the Cuban humiliation had severely jolted the Western alliance and urged him to tighten U.S. military and economic ties with Atlantic friends. The White House had handled the Congo problem through the United Nations and dealt with Laos through SEATO in a way that held together its European and Asian members while keeping the neutrals "more or less with us." Those same SEATO meetings, however, had fostered a greater international awareness of the problems in South Vietnam.[33]

Rostow agreed that Vietnam was "the place where—in the Attorney General's phrase—we must prove that we are not a paper tiger." The Vietcong had no international right to pursue an aggressive policy against South Vietnam. The United Nations should confront this "indirect aggression" by sanctioning military forces to block further infiltration from the north. The United States should accept the British offer to help South Vietnam and therefore "internationalize the effort to the maximum." It should emphasize to India that South Vietnam's fall to communism would have a negative impact throughout Southeast Asia. Finally, it must convince Diem that his domestic political problems stemmed not only from the Communist opposition but also from his failure to make necessary reforms. Presidential adviser McGeorge Bundy put it bluntly: "At this point we are like the Harlem Globetrotters, passing forward, behind, sidewise, and underneath. But nobody has made a basket yet."[34]

Accordingly, the administration established a secret committee called the Presidential Task Force to devise a plan for saving South Vietnam. At a cabinet meeting on April 20, President Kennedy asked McNamara to appoint the deputy secretary of defense, Roswell Gilpatric, as head of a group that included Lansdale, Rostow, Sorensen, Alexis Johnson from the state department, and Desmond Fitzgerald from the CIA. Gilpatric later explained that his appointment as chair of the new task force had reflected the president's lack of confidence in the state department because of his dissatisfaction regarding Laos. The president was also unhappy with the lack of leadership shown by the Joint Chiefs of Staff, who at one point had given him five different recommendations for what to do. McNamara informed the president that Gilpatric would have a plan of action by April 28. To monitor progress, Robert Kennedy served as the president's liaison with the committee, attending nearly every meeting and reporting directly to his brother.[35]

Lansdale's membership on the committee raised a bitter ruckus. About two weeks earlier, Rostow had suggested that the president place greater emphasis on Vietnam and appoint Lansdale as a "full time first-rate backstop man." In characteristic fashion, Lansdale responded to the news by writing a lengthy paper. He recommended that President Kennedy create a new study group on Vietnam and that he, Lansdale, hold an executive position on it. Gilpatric considered Lansdale "a very useful, knowledgeable assistant" even though he was "a soldier-of-fortune type." Professional foreign service officers did not trust him because of the independent course he had taken in the Philippines and South Vietnam. Hilsman considered him "an eight ball, an odd ball," who took "great delight in manipulating personalities. He's very much of a CIA type." Lansdale's January 1961 memo on Vietnam "might have influenced Kennedy in the beginning, but he had none after that." Gilpatric admitted that Lansdale was a "sort of solo performer, an operator who didn't go along with the usual channels and guidelines in the foreign service field." But Gilpatric did not share the state and defense departments' negative assessment. Lansdale "was in the doghouse with both of them. And I was convinced they were wrong."[36]

Before the committee had met, state department representatives expressed sharp disapproval of Lansdale's involvement. According to the *Pentagon Papers*, "State objected, successfully, to having an Ambassador report to a Task Force chaired by the Deputy Secretary of Defense, and with a second defense official (Lansdale) as executive officer." Lansdale also encountered staunch opposition from the joint chiefs, who sought to maintain control over the military program and felt threatened by his position in the defense secretary's office. The first draft had designated him "Operations Officer for the Task Force," which entailed his returning to Vietnam after the program received President Kennedy's approval and then, following discussions with U.S. and South Vietnamese officials, making recommendations on how to implement its provisions. But the state department infuriated Lansdale by feverishly working to reduce his status on the committee. On the same day that Gilpatric informed the president of Lansdale's assignment to the Task Force, the general hotly withdrew his name, leaving Gilpatric to offer the lame explanation that the defense department preferred the general's serving as Task Force representative.[37]

Lansdale's demotion reflects how political and controversial he had become. The files contain McNamara's copy of Gilpatric's memo to the president with the defense secretary's handwriting changing the statement that Lansdale "will proceed to Vietnam immediately" to "will proceed to Vietnam *when requested by the Ambassador.*" In view of the state department's opposition to Lansdale, this statement blocked his return to Vietnam. It is unclear whether McNamara made this change before or after Gilpatric's memo went to the president. The *Pentagon Papers* believe the change was in the memo when it went to the president, suggesting that Kennedy had approved McNamara's opposition to Lansdale.[38] More likely, however, McNamara altered the Lansdale reference *after* the memo went to the Oval Office. Kennedy's favor for Lansdale had not diminished. Why would he oppose sending the counterinsurgency expert to Vietnam for the purpose of making recommendations, particularly when the administration's program of counterinsurgency rested heavily on Lansdale's January 1961 report? But the president was also a political realist who recognized the danger of forcing the general onto the state and defense departments. Kennedy maintained his preference for limited military measures, again reflecting his support for Lansdale's program.

III

THE FIRST MEETING of the Presidential Task Force on April 24 so quickly degenerated into derisive personal exchanges that Gilpatric ill-advisedly turned over the chair's duties to Lansdale. "Gee, I don't know," Gilpatric declared to the general. "There's an awful lot of emotion on these meetings. I think I'm going to be too busy to go. Please take them over." Lansdale also demonstrated a lack of wisdom in agreeing to do so. "This is going to be rough on me, you know." He did not make it easy on himself by employing blunt methods. To the state department representatives at the meeting, he opened with an invitation assured of raising their ire: "I know, hearing some of your remarks, you don't like what I'm thinking." He then added: "You've got to say some things about me, so let's start the meeting. You get it out of your system. Say all the nasty things you want about me, and when you're through, let me know. Don't take too long with this, and then we'll get to work." The feud was in the open. "Have you got all the hate out of your system now? Let's go on with the meeting." But these sarcastic remarks only strengthened the venom. "Well look, we really do have some problems here we've got to get to, and if you want, I'll meet you afterwards and have lunch or something, and you can spoil my lunch by telling me what a heel I am or something. But we've got work to do." In an amazing understatement, Lansdale later observed, "They didn't like it at all."[39]

Somehow the Task Force survived the rancor and formulated a multifaceted strategy for saving South Vietnam. The United States would encourage the formation of a two-party system of non-Communist groups, send an economic team to find ways to bolster the economy, help the Diem regime become more responsive to its people, and make the South Vietnamese into a "polarizing spirit" against communism in all Southeast Asia. Militarily, the United States should emphasize the need to seal off the Cambodian border, underwrite the costs of adding 20,000 troops to South Vietnam's armed forces, and promote counterguerrilla warfare by sending 100 more MAAG personnel than the 685 allowed by the Geneva Accords (a violation advocated earlier by Rostow) as "close-up advisors" in "selected combat operations." It should also enhance internal security by instituting air surveillance by radar and halting enemy entry by water through additional assistance to Vietnam's junk force. To reassure Diem of continued U.S. support, Lansdale would accompany Vice-President Johnson on a good-will visit to South Vietnam. Gilpatric intended to present the Task Force's plan to the president by the end of the week.[40]

The mixed reaction to the report reflected the consternation felt by both sides over a greater U.S. military commitment. Clearly shaken by the Bay of Pigs debacle, Sorensen represented McGeorge Bundy and David Bell, director of the Bureau of the Budget, in warning President Kennedy to support "only the basic concept of an all-out internal security effort to save Vietnam." It seemed highly doubtful that the report's two basic premises would work—that Diem would grant reforms and that Saigon, even with U.S. assistance, could close South Vietnam's borders to infiltration. According to Sorensen, "There is no clearer example of a country that cannot be saved unless it saves itself—through increased popular support; governmental, economic and military reforms and reorganizations; and the encouragement of new political leaders." General McGarr, however, warned that the South Vietnamese must first establish a "military seal" along the Cambodian border that would stop the assaults across the frontier as well as the covert introduction of Vietcong, which would require about 30,000 troops. To assume the required training duties, MAAG must raise its troop ceiling. McGarr later informed Admiral Harry Felt, Commander-in-Chief, Pacific (CINCPAC), that President Kennedy was willing to violate the Geneva Accords to save South Vietnam and, in a statement rendered meaningless because it rested on so many contingencies as well as on McGarr's own interpretation of the president's words, also showed a "possible willingness" to send U.S. troops to Laos and South Vietnam.[41]

An April 27 meeting of the National Security Council (NSC) and others exposed the deep divisions among Washington's leaders over whether

or not to become militarily involved in Laos and, by extrapolation, in Vietnam. Indeed, state department adviser Alexis Johnson considered the meeting "the turning point on Laos," and Rostow called it "the worst White
House meeting he had ever attended in the entire Kennedy administration." On April 26, the Communist-led Pathet Lao had opened a major
offensive aimed at seizing as much territory as possible before the cease-
fire went into effect. Late that night the joint chiefs warned Felt that the
navy might have to retaliate with air assaults against North Vietnam and
perhaps even southern China. The next day, the same day that the Task
Force delivered its report on Vietnam, Admiral Arleigh Burke, Chief of
Naval Operations, warned that military intervention in Laos could lead to
war with Communist China and the use of nuclear weapons. Rusk, nevertheless, argued that the best way to avoid war in Southeast Asia was to
demonstrate a willingness "to use force." McNamara and congressional
leaders at the large meeting, both Democrat and Republican, opposed military intervention. Felt urged a limited involvement designed to protect the
Mekong Valley. It became clear that no one wanted to take over Laos.
"The issue," according to Johnson, "was simply whether you could best
protect Thailand and the rest of Southeast Asia by stopping the Communists where they were and holding the Mekong River Valley part of Laos."[42]

The president made no commitment to any position but asked questions that showed his caution about using combat troops. Did the United
States have the ability to defend the airfields in Laos? What would be the
troop position on the airfield at the capital of Vientiane and other places
along the river? What would happen if the United States withdrew? According to Alexis Johnson, Kennedy "was very, very deeply disturbed at
exposing a body of Americans to a situation in which he might have to take
very extreme measures to protect them." Johnson believed that the
president's opposition to military intervention in Asia stemmed from General MacArthur's warning that the Communist Chinese would overwhelm
U.S. ground forces. Had not MacArthur spoken from firsthand experiences in the Korean War? In the midst of this controversy, MacArthur met
with the president in New York and, in a piece of advice that Sorensen said
Kennedy "never forgot," warned against committing troops in a frontal
assault. Laos, the general insisted, was a totally unacceptable place to make
a stand, although, according to the president's notes of the meeting,
MacArthur supported "a rear-guard action in the southeast of Asia" *if* the
area sought U.S. protection. Kennedy, Johnson thought, "seized upon the
Chiefs' . . . very inept presentation of the military situation to rationalize
and justify his own instinct that he didn't want to get involved."[43]

The Task Force, however, feared that neutralization of Laos would
guarantee Communist control of its eastern mountains and thereby provide the path for an invasion of South Vietnam. It therefore recommended

that the United States support the addition of two divisions to the South Vietnamese air force. To train these men, the United States would have to provide a force of 1,600 men for each division, along with a 400-man special forces team to train the South Vietnamese in counterinsurgency warfare. The Kennedy administration would also have to inject 3,600 men over the 100 additions already approved for MAAG. Consequently, President Kennedy approved the Task Force recommendations on Vietnam in the midst of the Laotian crisis. In a speech that evening at a Democratic dinner in Chicago, the president declared, "We are prepared to meet our obligations, but we can only defend the freedom of those who are determined to be free themselves. We can assist them—we will bear more than our share of the burden, but we can only help those who are ready to bear their share of the burden themselves." The next day, CINCPAC warned of the need to send 5,000 forces to Udorn, Thailand, and to Tourane (Danang) in South Vietnam.[44]

The central issue in this growing controversy over combat troops focused on which aspect of counterinsurgency doctrine should receive priority. Even though the president preferred the nonmilitary steps, he recognized that certain military actions had to precede the safe implementation of civil reforms. But his approval of such measures did not include American soldiers in a fighting role. Many of his advisers, however, saw the opening for military expedients and argued for a quick solution: the use of Americans in combat. If the Korean War had sufficiently warned the president about the dangers of a ground war in Asia, the lesson had escaped his military leaders. According to Gilpatric, General George Decker, Chief of Staff of the Army; General Earle Wheeler, later chief of staff and then chair; and General David Shoup, Marine Corps Commandant, all considered the dispatch of amphibious forces into Vietnam as "just one more military engagement." Gilpatric recalled no "haunting feeling that this would be something which would bog us down as we were in Korea."[45]

Just before an NSC meeting on April 29, a large group of advisers met in the state department to explore the military options in Laos and to relate them to South Vietnam. The real issue in Laos, according to McNamara, was whether or not the United States could land military forces in Vientiane because of the threats from Communist Chinese air power, Pathet Lao resistance, and sabotage. Admiral Burke nonetheless supported U.S. military intervention. "If pushed we could retreat across the river, reinforce from Udorn and go back and fight." The first task was to use troops to secure the airfield. McNamara worried that the United States would need thirty-six sorties a day to cover troop movements into Laos. In a glaring understatement, McGeorge Bundy warned that "if we took this action we would be doing something which most countries would not appreciate."[46]

The call for U.S. combat involvement possessed a simplistic allure. Robert Kennedy had attended this meeting at his brother's behest and played the devil's advocate in goading the advisers into revealing their innermost thoughts. "Where would be the best place to stand and fight in Southeast Asia, where to draw the line?" Thailand and South Vietnam, McNamara responded. The central question, argued the attorney general, was whether the United States "would stand up and fight." Rusk leaned toward putting U.S. troops in Vientiane and standing ready to evacuate them by helicopter if they could not hold the airfield. With less than measured consideration, he asserted, "This would be better than sitting back and doing nothing." Burke felt confident that the United States could hold Danang, but General Curtis LeMay, Air Force Chief of Staff, went farther in assuring his colleagues that U.S. air power could stop the Pathet Lao. Shoup concurred. B-26 bombings before troop landings would make it "possible to obtain a cease-fire and get the panhandle of Laos."[47]

The meeting's aggressive tone underlined the growing sentiment within the highest levels of the Kennedy administration for using U.S. military power in Southeast Asia. Deputy Assistant Secretary of State John Steeves warned that if the problem in Laos was "unsolvable, then the problem of Viet-Nam would be unsolvable." If the United States wrote off Laos, it was "writing the first chapter in the defeat of Southeast Asia." McNamara argued that the United States had to attack Hanoi if it gave up Laos. Decker admonished his colleagues to understand that "if we go in, we should go in to win, and that means bombing Hanoi." He admitted that "there was no good place to fight in Southeast Asia but we must hold as much as we can of Viet-Nam, Cambodia and Laos." Burke agreed. "Each time you give ground, it is harder to stand next time." If the United States conceded Laos, it "would have to put U.S. forces into Viet-Nam and Thailand." Indeed, the United States "would have to throw in enough to win—perhaps the 'works.'"[48]

Faced with the prospect of defeat, the appeal of direct U.S. military intervention had gained momentum. Decker suggested that the United States move troops into Thailand and South Vietnam in an effort to foster a cease-fire in Laos. LeMay did not believe a cease-fire possible without "military action." When Burke asked what would happen if no cease-fire followed, Decker crisply replied that "we would be ready to go ahead." The United States could conduct the entire operation by air, LeMay argued. B-26s could slow the enemy while more sophisticated bombers halted the influx of supplies and bought time for the Laotian forces to improve their fighting skills. Even Bowles, who later opposed U.S. military involvement in Vietnam, insisted that "the main question to be faced was the fact that we were going to have to fight the Chinese anyway in 2, 3, 5 or 10 years and that it was just a question of where, when and how." The Chinese would not escalate their involvement, LeMay insisted. In a statement that suggested no awareness of the nearly disastrous consequences of the Chinese intervention in the Korean War, he blithely asserted that "the worst that could happen would be that the Chinese Communists would come in."[49]

U.S. military intervention, these advisers suggested, might have to be total. In view of the recent embarrassment at the Bay of Pigs, Robert Kennedy strongly warned against a partial commitment to Southeast Asia. "We would look sillier than we do now if we got troops in there and then backed down." The real issue was "whether we are ready to go the distance." If so, Rusk solemnly insisted while appealing to the wisdom of collective security, "we would want to get the United Nations mixed up in this." "The question to be faced," Steeves thought, "was whether we could afford to lose Southeast Asia." That area was the "prize." Burke declared that "only the United States could pull its own chestnuts out of the fire." McNamara gloomily observed that "the situation was worsening by the hour and that if we were going to commit ourselves, then we must do so sooner rather than later." On that dour note, Rusk adjourned the meeting.[50]

Advisers in the Kennedy administration went beyond the president's wishes, irresistibly drawn to a misleadingly simple and fast resolution to the problem. Rusk, as an ardent Cold Warrior, joined McNamara and the military figures at the meeting in advocating stern military action. Particularly striking was LeMay's call for all-out military force. The general was notoriously reckless but attracted a strong political and military following that compelled the president to pay homage to his recommendations, no matter how extreme. But, according to Gilpatric, every time Kennedy saw LeMay, "he ended up in a sort of a fit. I mean he would just be frantic at the end of a session with LeMay because, you know, LeMay couldn't listen or wouldn't take in, and he would make what Kennedy considered . . . outrageous proposals that bore no relation to the state of affairs in the 1960s." Galbraith agreed with Gilpatric's assessment. Years afterward, the then ambassador to India noted that President Kennedy once remarked about the incautious general, "Can any civilized country have people like General LeMay?"[51] From thousands of miles away in Washington, from the vantage point of policymakers who had, in most instances, never been in South Vietnam, the solution was clear: Close the infiltration routes by interdiction bombing, and authorize U.S. soldiers to end the Vietcong threat, even if it meant a direct assault on Hanoi.

President Kennedy emphasized the civil dimensions of counterinsurgency in an effort to avert a direct U.S. military involvement. One positive result of the Bay of Pigs fiasco soon came into play, however: The president had adhered to military and intelligence experts in approving the plan to overthrow Castro. They had been wrong once and could be wrong again. Hilsman insisted that the president preferred advisers as "a token to keep the military quiet" while he implemented counterinsurgency and worked to improve Diem's military forces. Kennedy did not want U.S. troops with white and black faces pursuing the Vietcong. Their actions would drive the peasants into the Communist camp. The Vietnamese must do the job themselves. Hilsman recommended using American soldiers only "to protect the people; don't chase the Vietcong." In the background would be social, political, and economic reform programs. "The sea of people in which Mao says the guerrillas swim like fish will have dried up."[52] The task would not be easy. Pressure for a military involvement came not only from military personnel but from civilian leaders as well. President Kennedy's reason and instincts persisted in pointing to counterinsurgency and continuing support to Diem.

SEVERAL IMPORTANT FEATURES of the administration's aid program to South Vietnam reflected the president's wish to avoid a deeper involvement. First and foremost, he accepted Lansdale's arguments for a counterinsurgency program and for standing by Diem. Second, Kennedy recognized the importance of convincing Diem to support counterinsurgency—even if it meant relaxing the U.S. policy of conditioning aid on his institution of reforms. Third, the president realized that a U.S. troop involvement would Americanize a war that was South Vietnam's alone to fight. Kennedy knew that he faced a certain battle with advisers who advocated U.S. combat forces. He also grasped the interrelated nature of Laos, Cambodia, and South Vietnam to stopping communism in Southeast Asia and promoting America's Cold War efforts. All these considerations demonstrate the president's opposition to U.S. combat involvement.

The realities were evident. U.S. success depended on the support of the South Vietnamese people; and without Diem's cooperation in molding a government more responsive to their needs, the chances for defeating the insurgency would decline in proportion to the sinking popularity of his rule. Either Diem would have to change his mandarin philosophy, or a coup might change the government.

3

COUNTERACTION TO COUNTERINSURGENCY
The Military Solution

If we are given the right to use nuclear weapons, we can guarantee victory.

> General Lyman Lemnitzer, chair of
> Joint Chiefs of Staff, April (?), 1961

U.S. forces should be deployed immediately to South Vietnam.

> Joint Chiefs of Staff, May 10, 1961

THE MARTIAL SENTIMENT expressed by the White House advisers at what the *Pentagon Papers* called a day of "prolonged crisis meetings" posed a major problem for President Kennedy as he attempted to limit the U.S. military involvement in South Vietnam. A few of his counselors openly sought a military solution; others by their very silence concurred. No one present—including Rusk and McNamara—argued for counterinsurgency. The military, asserted Schlesinger, did not prefer ground troops unless they numbered "at least 140,000 men equipped with tactical nuclear weapons." A dangerous pattern had begun to develop, he insisted. The Pentagon opposed limited action unless President Kennedy gave prior approval to every escalated step it thought should follow, including the nuclear bombing of Hanoi and Beijing.[1]

It soon became clear that the chair of the joint chiefs, General Lemnitzer, likewise supported an all-out military response to what the president had called "the subterranean war." The general had been in Laos at the time of the NSC meeting, but on his return to Washington he assured the NSC that "if we are given the right to use nuclear weapons, we can guarantee victory." The president sat in moody silence until someone testily declared, "Mr. President, perhaps you would have the General explain to us what he means by victory." Kennedy sighed and called the meeting to a close. Afterward he cynically remarked that since Lemnitzer "couldn't think of any further escalation, he would have to promise us victory."[2]

Despite the president's outspoken support for counterinsurgency, nearly everyone around him preferred a military solution. Counterinsurgency required patience and time, all the while seeking a partial victory at best. Once South Vietnam, with U.S. assistance and advice, had reduced the Vietcong's activities to domestic disturbances, the Diem regime would emerge victorious. But those propounding a military remedy had little faith in South Vietnam's ability to win the war by itself. More important, they had no confidence in Diem. President Kennedy continued to oppose an Americanization of the war and insisted that only the South Vietnamese could determine its verdict.

I

THE "PROGRAM OF ACTION" submitted by the state department's Task Force to the president at the NSC meeting on April 29 termed the Vietnamese situation as "critical, but not hopeless" and initially adhered to Kennedy's preference for counterinsurgency. The central thrust in the assistance effort, declared the report, must be to achieve internal security by implementing "mutually supporting actions of a military, political, economic, psychological and covert character." SEATO's military intervention was permissible should that step prove necessary. Also vital was the cooperation of Laos and Cambodia in halting Hanoi's infiltration of personnel and supplies into South Vietnam.[3]

The Task Force did not dismiss the role of nonmilitary measures. To promote joint cooperation between the nations, the vice president must use his goodwill visit to exalt Diem as "a man of great stature and as one of the strong figures in Southeast Asia on whom we are placing our reliance." The administration should seek a multilateral involvement by working with the British in training South Vietnamese personnel and extending financial assistance as a means of encouraging similar support from others in the Western alliance. The report also called for an enhanced civic action program that included the construction of roads, schools, markets, wells, and irrigation ditches, the expansion of agricultural and veterinary assistance, and the introduction of medical dispensaries and other health services. In addition to meeting the immediate needs of the rural community, the reform programs must build a healthy political and economic infrastructure based on a decentralized government and long-range economic development. The United States, concluded the Task Force, must approve a five-year assistance program to South Vietnam.[4]

The Task Force continued in the same balanced vein until it came to the necessity of reestablishing Diem's faith in U.S. motives; at that point, it joined the Country Team in taking a subtle turn toward a military remedy. Diem, according to the Task Force, remained convinced that Americans had adopted an "equivocal attitude" toward the November 1960 coup attempt, and he now ignored the need for political reforms. Diem had proven incapable of protecting his people from the Communist insurgents. Military correctives had therefore emerged as the top priority, automatically reducing the importance of the social, political, and economic recommendations contained in the Counterinsurgency Plan.[5]

The Task Force program then sharply veered from the president's stand against U.S. combat troops, either alone or as part of an allied force. "While there is still time, the inhibitions of the Geneva Accords, which have been violated with impunity by the Communists in both Laos and Viet-Nam, should be done away with." The United States must negotiate a defensive alliance with Saigon that authorized the dispatch of U.S. or SEATO troops to South Vietnam. Such a move would free the ARVN of static defense duties and permit it to take the offensive against the Vietcong. The U.S. forces, it became clear, would train the South Vietnamese, provide a border patrol to halt infiltration, and deter a Chinese Communist invasion. Furthermore, the United States would send 400 Special Forces to Nha Trang to train South Vietnamese soldiers in counterguerrilla warfare. These pivotal moves admittedly entailed risks: Neutral nations might oppose the United States's direct military involvement in South Vietnam; the Communists would gain excellent propaganda material; and Hanoi might ally with the Chinese Communists in a major military escalation that could necessitate a "significant commitment" of U.S. troops from the Pacific to the Asian mainland. The French, the report noted, had deployed 200,000 troops in a losing cause. Without exploring the implications of U.S. troop involvement, the advisers insisted that the benefits derived from a show of force outweighed the risks. The White House must consider a "formal rejection of the Geneva Accords," and the newly appointed Ambassador Nolting should meet with Diem about negotiating a defensive alliance. The Joint Chiefs of Staff and CINCPAC should meanwhile determine the number of U.S. troops required.[6]

President Kennedy recognized the dangerous ramifications of the Task Force proposals and approved only those military actions deemed integral to counterinsurgency doctrine. Sorensen agreed, but he doubted that Diem could defeat the insurgency without instituting pacification measures that won the support of his people. "We do not want Vietnam to fall," Sorensen wrote the president. "The chief purpose of insisting upon such conditions should not be [the] saving of American dollars but the saving of Vietnam."[7]

But the president, too, was willing to violate the Geneva Accords in an effort to achieve his definition of victory. In a move that Rusk termed the president's "most important decision," he approved an unpublicized increase in MAAG's advisers by 100 over the present 685 authorized at Geneva to train the 20,000-man addition to the 150,000 soldiers already in the ARVN. This move, according to the *Pentagon Papers*, marked "the first formal breach of the Geneva agreement." Kennedy also agreed to enlarge MAAG's duties to include advising and supporting the 40,000-member Self-Defense Corps. He then concurred with the recommendation to increase support for a Civil Guard expanded from 32,000 members to 68,000. To safeguard the country against outside threats, he approved an expanded border patrol, a radar surveillance system to warn of Communist overflights (no evidence existed of such aerial activity), and a greater use of the South Vietnamese junk force in closing off infiltration by water. Particularly appealing to the president was the deployment of a Special Forces Group of 400 U.S. Army personnel (the first open violation of the Geneva Accords), trained in counterinsurgency and wearing green berets to signify their elitist status. Most notably, however, he withheld approval of U.S. "conventional, non-nuclear forces," including the assignment of a marine brigade plus support troops to either Danang or Nha Trang. This proposal he assigned to further review.[8]

In a move that carried great potential for international trouble, the president approved the Task Force's call for covert actions, both in North and South Vietnam and in Laos. Counterintelligence agents gained sanction to penetrate Communist organizations throughout the Vietnams, and "American or Chinese Nationalist crews and equipment" could assist the South Vietnamese in gathering photographic intelligence. On the basis of this pilfered information, these agents should develop "networks of resistance" through sabotage and harassment operations. Under joint MAAG–CIA supervision, the First Observation Battalion already in South Vietnam could work with the CIA in recruiting South Vietnamese civilians. To stem Vietcong infiltration, teams of South Vietnamese "under light civilian cover" and trained by the CIA and the Special Forces were to engage in hit-and-run assaults on Vietnamese Communist strongholds in southeastern Laos.[9]

The White House supported still more actions that violated the Geneva Accords. Those measures aimed at North Vietnam included the use of MAAG-trained ARVN soldiers in conducting ranger raids and other low-key military operations and the deployment of South Vietnamese planes to drop leaflets encouraging popular resistance to the Communists. Those steps in the south were more striking, for they had the potential to alienate the regime if uncovered. They focused on infiltrating the Saigon government, opposition political groups, and the armed services in an effort to determine loyalty to Diem, provide warning of coup attempts, and identify potential leaders in the event of his fall from power.[10]

The military assistance program had grown dramatically in light of the heightening Vietcong threat, but, according to the Task Force, it needed to expand even more. In 1959 the allotted funds were $59 million, but in

1961 the amount reached $73.6 million, and the defense department recommended another increase to $110 million in 1962. The last figure included the Program of Action for South Vietnam, but this sum provided only the minimum amount necessary to sustain the newly enlarged force of 170,000 soldiers and a Civil Guard then numbering 32,000 before the scheduled increase to 68,000. If aid went to 200,000 armed forces (South Vietnam sought another 30,000), all 68,000 in the expanded Civil Guard, 40,000 in the Self-Defense Corps, and the 400 Special Forces added to MAAG, the Military Assistance Program for 1962 would require $140 million of funding.[11]

Lansdale angrily warned that the new military direction of the proposal would ensure South Vietnam's defeat. The Task Force, it was clear to Lansdale, had made a profound shift in emphasis: Instead of balancing the military and civil aspects of counterinsurgency, it had made military assistance the priority by urging the use of U.S. combat troops, either by themselves or in conjunction with SEATO forces. Lansdale complained that "the U.S. past performance and theory of action, which State apparently desires to continue, simply offers no sound basis for winning as desired by President Kennedy."[12]

It was easy to detect flaws in the military orientation advocated by the Task Force. Its members did not explain how to secure the cooperation of either Diem or the leaders of Laos and Cambodia. They did not explore the consequences of sending in U.S. troops. In a remarkable lack of foresight, they almost casually admitted that the presence of U.S. soldiers might provoke a military intervention by the North Vietnamese and the Chinese Communists. They then capitalized this bald understatement by blandly asserting that the United States would respond with a major military commitment. What would be the extent of a Communist troop involvement? Did the United States have the manpower and logistical means to meet the new challenge? Had not the Chinese military intervention in the Korean War graphically demonstrated the dangers of a land conflict in Asia?

The president must have pondered these questions. Singularly absent from his response to the Program for Action was approval of U.S. combat troops. His counterinsurgency strategy remained intact though leaning toward military correctives on a temporary basis. MAAG's advisory and training mandate was to increase the effectiveness of the ARVN, Self-Defense Corps, and Civil Guard. Attempts to end infiltration from North Vietnam came in the form of radar surveillance, larger border patrols, and assistance to South Vietnam's junk force. Psywar operations in both Vietnams and Laos would seek to undermine Hanoi's effectiveness while U.S. advisers explored the alternatives to Diem in the event of a coup. In the most vivid instance of Kennedy's counterinsurgency emphasis, he approved the addition of 400 Special Forces to MAAG for training the South Vietnamese in limited warfare. The remedy was to create a specially trained group of commandos whose task was to stop infiltration from the north. As for U.S. combat forces, the president again assigned this issue to further study. Every call for their use, he realized, rested on what Sorensen termed "assumptions and predictions" not subject to verification: on Laotian and Cambodian assistance in closing the borders, on Diem's reforming his army and government, and on his cultivating popular support and undercutting the Communists.[13] The president's actions supported the military dimension of counterinsurgency strategy without ignoring civic needs. His central objective remained that of facilitating South Vietnam's efforts to win the war on its own.

A second Task Force meeting a few days later demonstrated that President Kennedy's opposition to a military solution had not slowed the ardor of his advisers. In a revised version of the report, Gilpatric only momentarily returned to the principle of counterinsurgency by emphasizing the necessity of interweaving the military and nonmilitary correctives in South Vietnam. His chief interest lay in securing the U.S. soldiers needed to fulfill the military part of the program. If required, he declared, a marine brigade could be in South Vietnam in twelve hours and army reinforcements from Hawaii shortly thereafter. He expressed concern that the fourteen-nation conference on Laos scheduled to open in Geneva on May 15 might result in a Communist effort to impose a freeze on the number of military forces brought into Southeast Asia.[14]

The president's close adviser on foreign affairs, Walt Rostow, likewise focused on the military side of counterinsurgency *without* supporting the Task Force's call for combat troops. Rostow wanted the failure of the Geneva Accords to become known through its International Control Commission, established to guarantee the sanctity of South Vietnam's frontiers. Any U.S. troops sent to the troubled area must have only one function: to promote the Counterinsurgency Plan. Gilpatric argued that the injection of U.S. soldiers would free the ARVN to fulfill its offensive role in the counterinsurgency program. Rostow agreed and added three other justifications: Their presence would provide stepped-up training against the insurgency, furnish a "trip wire" warning of enemy assaults, and counter an "anticipated major ChiCom invasion." When asked by Lansdale how many troops it would take to meet counterinsurgency demands, Rostow thought that hundreds might be sufficient if inserted on a gradual basis. Such a move "was quite a different matter from putting in U.S. combat units."[15]

Rostow's call for troops of a noncombat nature amounted to a dangerous game in semantics that could lead to a full-scale military involvement. Although instructed to avoid combat, the very presence of armed men in uniform would constitute an upgraded military bearing that guaranteed trouble. Would the enemy regard the rising number of U.S. troops as part of an advisory operation or as the initial step toward Americanizing the war? Was not advising an army on how to improve its kill functions tantamount to joining the military effort? The perception of U.S. combat involvement would outweigh all disclaimers.

II

As IF GUIDED by some magnetic force, the White House discussion returned to the question of U.S. combat troops. U.S. Army General Charles Bonesteel (Secretary of the General Staff) noted that the joint chiefs had estimated the number of U.S. fighting forces needed in Laos but not in South Vietnam. He joined the CIA's William Colby in expressing doubt about whether a few hundred U.S. soldiers could close the long Laotian border. The Task Force, Bonesteel declared with a sense of relief, had finally raised the central issue in the assistance effort: How serious was the United States about preventing Communist domination of South Vietnam? Success required "very sizeable force commitments." If Americans intended to stop communism, "the commitment of U.S. combat forces would be worthwhile though a major undertaking."[16]

The push for combat troops became relentless, buttressed by the presidential advisers' lame attempts to downplay its dangerous ramifications. Gilpatric emphasized that their immediate task was to resolve the insurgency problem. Bonesteel argued that the presence of U.S. marines "would carry important symbolic value as an indication of U.S. willingness to fight." Colby noted the "important psychological advantages" gained from a troop introduction. Rostow was dubious, warning that "we must be honest in assessing the ability of U.S. military power to be effectively employed against the Viet-Cong guerrilla effort." Bonesteel retorted that his remedy was "by no means solely a military effort." And yet, the other correctives he mentioned could result only from military measures: a favorable settlement in Laos (*not* through neutralization) and secured borders between Laos and South Vietnam and along the seventeenth parallel. The U.S. success in the Greek civil war of the late 1940s, Bonesteel insisted, had demonstrated the need to safeguard a troubled country's frontiers. He failed, however, to mention the exorbitant military expenditures required to crush the Greek insurgency.[17]

Not all of the president's advisers recommended a military solution. Rostow correctly observed that the U.S. assistance program in Greece had profited from the vast number of loyalists to their government as well as from Yugoslavia's decision to close its border to the insurgents shortly after its break with the Soviet Union. George Ball, Undersecretary of State for Economic Affairs, warned that the presence of U.S. combat troops would elevate the conflict in South Vietnam into a Cold War struggle between the Free World and the Communists.[18]

Even though a battle had begun inside the Kennedy administration over the direction of the assistance program, its passage still hinged on winning Diem's support for internal reforms. At the inauguration reception in Independence Palace on April 29, Diem had taken Durbrow aside to ask whether the White House had approved the Counterinsurgency Plan. The outgoing ambassador told him no and, in a statement demonstrating his lack of awareness of the new military thrust of the Task Force, asserted that the Saigon government first had to take "certain minimum actions" that included the establishment of a central intelligence organization, the assignment of counterinsurgency operations to the military command, and the implementation of the reforms announced by Diem in early February. Diem assured Durbrow that his ministers had the Counterinsurgency Plan under study but warned that its enactment took time. In his continued effort to exact reforms as a quid pro quo for assistance, Durbrow emphasized that he could not support the planned 20,000-man increase in South Vietnam's armed forces until Diem met the above conditions.[19]

Durbrow's repeated calls for domestic reforms had worn on Diem's patience, raising questions about whether the premier would ever change. The ambassador was skeptical that Diem's ministers were studying the Counterinsurgency Plan, especially since Vice President Nguyen Ngoc Tho had told him the day before that he knew of the plan but had not seen it. Indeed, Tho expressed doubt that any minister had seen the plan. Durbrow suspected that Diem had shown it only to Thuan. When Durbrow explained its contents to Tho, the vice president seemed supportive, remarking that Diem needed to take advantage of the popular favor that had resulted from the government's ability to hold elections despite the Vietcong's obstructionist tactics. Lansdale recommended that President Kennedy craft a letter calling for cooperation and *not* insisting on Diem's "being a good boy" by accepting U.S. conditions. Such a paternalistic approach ran "exactly contrary to Asian psychology." Nolting must not climb into "the same trap as Ambassador Durbrow found himself in."[20]

Pressure for U.S. troops had likewise increased outside the Task Force proceedings. From the NSC staff, Robert Komer warned McGeorge Bundy that the use of American ground forces would reassure Diem and avert another Laos by "seal[ing] off" South Vietnam from infiltration. Admittedly, the troops' presence would violate the Geneva Accords, but so would the increase in MAAG advisers provide the Communists with the opportunity to "raise hell" at the conference on Laos. Komer suggested that Diem abrogate the accords before the conference opened. "After it starts, he will get an even bigger black eye if he does." Diem could also request membership in SEATO and ask for soldiers through that organization. The United States would then have a legal basis for sending troops.[21]

Komer thought the Pentagon so wrapped up in the traditional military approach of engaging the enemy that it was bent on sending forces "too large and unwieldy for early action." The objective of dispatching troops, Komer insisted, was *not* to fight guerrillas but to reassure Diem (and the worried Thai prime minister, Sarit Thanarat) of U.S. support in the certain aftermath of shock resulting from the imminent neutralization of Laos. Neither the Counterinsurgency Plan nor Vice President Johnson's trip could sufficiently relieve the anxious Saigon government. A neutralized Laos would permit Communist involvement in its government and open the door to a North Vietnamese invasion of the south. Only a U.S. battalion supported by naval power, Komer argued, could restore the region's confidence in the United States.[22]

This call for U.S. troops as a demonstration of credibility rather than for combat suggested little understanding of the implications of such a move. Komer insisted that their purpose was not primarily to fight but to prove a commitment to South Vietnam. And yet he did not speculate about the chances of the Vietcong's regarding them as a direct military challenge. Nor did he examine the consequences of an enemy attack on these soldiers. If they did not respond decisively, would not their restraint encourage more aggression and thus make a mockery of U.S. power and prestige? If they did respond, would an assault on an elusive, shadowy band of insurgents retreating into the jungles have a measurable, positive impact? Would not U.S. commanders request more men? Ironically, a battalion was both too large and too small. It provided an easy target for the enemy and yet it was of insufficient size to take the offensive. Indeed, the presence of a small number of U.S. soldiers would actually *invite* Vietcong attacks.

Rusk attributed the White House reluctance to deploy troops more to timing than to reasoned analysis, thereby leaving the question open to debate. The National Security Council emphasized the necessity of assuring Diem that the United States would not abandon Southeast Asia. But Rusk warned that sending combat troops at this juncture would complicate the Geneva Conference on Laos. If trouble developed in South Vietnam after the conference was under way, he hastened to add, the United States could send troops. That same day, Rusk approved a staggered increase in MAAG by 100 military personnel. No one was to discuss this increment with either the United Kingdom or the International Control Commission. In what had become a White House pattern, he declared that the question of adding U.S. combat forces would undergo further study.[23]

President Kennedy had meanwhile become concerned about an appearance of weakness and engaged in a risky show of force that aimed at saving Laos from the Communists while emphasizing to the Soviets the need for a cease-fire. That May, when the U.S. military reserves were low and he faced a Soviet ultimatum on Berlin, the Communists launched a major push from the Plaine des Jarres toward the Mekong River. Should the 10,000 marines in Okinawa land in Laos through Thailand? Congressional leaders overwhelmingly opposed such a move. Kennedy recognized the danger but readied the marines, knowing that Soviet spies would note the action and hoping that the Kremlin would want a settlement. The gamble paid off. Without attempting to hide their dispatch to Southeast Asia, the administration convinced Moscow and Hanoi that it was sending half of the marine contingent to Laos and the other half to South Vietnam. The White House then instructed veteran diplomat W. Averell Harriman to notify Khrushchev through Indian Prime Minister Nehru that the United States would not abandon Laos—even if it meant military action. Harriman emphasized that President Kennedy preferred a neutralized Laos built on the Soviets' halting their military assistance to the Pathet Lao. Khrushchev considered Laotian neutrality preferable to a Chinese brand of communism, and Ho Chi Minh knew that the injection of U.S. troops would prolong the reunification of Vietnam. The president's strategy worked. Harriman secured a UN-supervised cease-fire in Laos on May 5, 1961.[24]

The settlement in Laos had direct bearing on the Diem regime. *Time* magazine criticized the Laotian cease-fire as "a cold war defeat" for the United States that could extend to South Vietnam. What had happened to President Kennedy's highly heralded inaugural promise to "pay any price" in guaranteeing liberty? Laos would have "a Communist sympathizer" heading the government, Communists holding governmental posts, and Communist troops controlling half of the nation. The country would "quickly go behind the Iron Curtain." If the White House intended to save South Vietnam, "it must be willing to get far more deeply involved—to the point of fighting, if necessary." Kennedy slammed down the magazine. "Sons of bitches. If they want this job they can have it tomorrow."[25]

In the meantime, General Lemnitzer attended a series of meetings in Saigon that further convinced him of the wisdom of a military buildup. To the Country Team, Durbrow expressed disappointment with Diem for failing to implement the three essentials of a sound counterinsurgency plan: a single chain of command, a central intelligence network, and political and economic reforms. Lemnitzer, however, had little sympathy for this argument. Having just inspected Laos, he complained about working on a "shoe string" caused by the Geneva ceiling on military assistance, and he strongly opposed the administration's policy of stipulating conditions on military aid to South Vietnam. The first objective, according to the joint chiefs chair, must be to save the country; reforms could follow. An expanded military effort was essential.[26]

The air of emergency became more prominent after Lemnitzer's two-hour meeting with Diem. The fall of Laos, Diem warned, would open the door to massive infiltration or to an actual invasion of his country. He did not want U.S. combat troops, however. Asians should fight Asians. Chinese Nationalists offered a potential source of manpower, but only if the U.S. Air Force and the Seventh Fleet filled the resulting vacuum in Formosa caused by the reassignment of Chinese troops to South Vietnam. More than 2,000 Vietcong had entered South Vietnam since December, Diem reported. He needed help in closing the long land frontiers and coastline.[27]

Lemnitzer warned his joint chiefs' colleagues that South Vietnam threatened to take the same catastrophic path as Laos. The United States must approve the 20,000-man increase in South Vietnam's armed forces. But an argument had developed over whether the United States or South Vietnam should pay for the addition. The aid process, Lemnitzer angrily declared, had ground "to a dead halt with critical loss of time in initiating the long training period required." Did the United States wish to prevent South Vietnam from becoming another Laos and thereby avert the loss of all Southeast Asia? Did it want to protect South Vietnam's independence and maintain its close alignment with the West? Lemnitzer warned that if the administration did not stop wrangling over details, South Vietnam would join Laos and North Vietnam in going "down the drain of Communism."[28]

Lemnitzer insisted that the key to preserving U.S. prestige in the world was to take strong military action in South Vietnam. And yet, he complained, the U.S. embassy in Saigon foolishly opposed the small but necessary increases in MAAG. The Military Assistance Program aimed only at maintaining the status quo under normal conditions and thus offered little hope for success against the growing threat to South Vietnam's domestic security. The persistent quibbling over whether the United States should assume the costs of a moderate increase in South Vietnamese forces had endangered the entire effort against the Vietcong. "Each day lost," the general asserted, "can never be regained."[29]

The pressure for U.S. combat troops had become inexorable. The joint chiefs argued that their deployment could discourage a North Vietnamese or Chinese action, free South Vietnamese soldiers to engage in counterguerrilla actions, help in training South Vietnam's forces, provide a fulcrum of support for either additional U.S. soldiers or a possible SEATO military move in the region, and demonstrate the U.S. commitment to all Asia. MAAG argued that American forces would deter the Communists and raise the morale of the South Vietnamese while enhancing support for SEATO. U.S. combat support units were also necessary, including helicopter and aviation companies, air force transport groups, and air–ground control facilities. MAAG admitted that this was a "politico-military situation" but insisted that military measures were a necessary prerequisite to a political solution. "The solution is NOT entirely military." The remedy included the use of political, military, psychological, economic, and sociological methods "in a balanced, coordinated mix, tailored to the time in history and the environment of the country marked for take over." But "there is absolutely no substitute for adequate military force of the right kind in being at the required time and place."[30]

General McGarr remained confident that the president would use military force. His recent visit to Washington had convinced him that the administration was determined to halt the global decline in U.S. prestige resulting from the recent setbacks in Cuba and Laos. President Kennedy and now General Lemnitzer had repeatedly declared that South Vietnam must never fall behind the "Bamboo Curtain." The problem as they saw it, according to McGarr's reading of the two men, was primarily military in nature. The White House supported a broadened advisory and training effort by MAAG and the insertion of additional military personnel and war goods. The recommended 100-man increase was not enough. MAAG needed an immediate infusion of 156 military forces with 272 more to follow over a three-month period. More could come later.[31]

McGarr was wrong in his assessment of the president. Although both Kennedy and Lemnitzer recognized the primacy of military correctives, the president had not moved into the general's camp. Kennedy preferred civic action, but he was aware of Diem's resistance to reforms, and he had come to realize that the sense of urgency in South Vietnam required a relaxation of these stipulations for assistance. As Lemnitzer declared, reforms could follow the reestablishment of domestic order. Lemnitzer, however, regarded the solution in South Vietnam as exclusively military. McGarr listened to the two leaders and heard what he wanted to hear. In truth, the president kept the military tactic within the context of counterinsurgency strategy; the general regarded the military effort as the strategy itself.

The battle lines had been forged within the Kennedy administration over the level of military escalation needed to resolve the problem in South Vietnam. The president must have thought the matter settled when he approved the counterinsurgency program and vented every call for combat troops with recommendations for further study. But the widely based push for a military solution did not abate. Lemnitzer had once been the only member of the joint chiefs to endorse a limited commitment, but he switched his position in light of the feared loss of Laos to communism. Lemnitzer and most of the president's other advisers favored a military solution.

III

AT A MAY 5 press conference, President Kennedy announced that Vice President Johnson would soon leave on a fact-finding mission to Asia. The vice president had not wanted to go.

"Mr. President," Johnson responded to a third entreaty, "I don't want to embarrass you by getting my head blown off in Saigon."

"Don't worry, Lyndon," Kennedy assured him. "If anything happens to you, Sam Rayburn and I will give you the biggest funeral Austin, Texas, ever saw."[32]

Johnson had no choice. Four days after the press conference, the vice president, accompanied by his wife and the president's sister and brother-in-law, Jean and Stephen Smith, left Washington, arriving in Saigon at 6:40 in the evening of May 11. After settling in the guest house at Independence Palace, the party joined Ambassador Nolting for dinner at the restaurant atop the Caravelle Hotel. During his one-day stay in Saigon, Johnson met with Diem twice and delivered a speech before the National Assembly that Nolting described as the "high point" of the visit.[33]

The growing clamor in Washington for a military solution in South Vietnam had underscored the importance of the vice president's trip to Saigon. In view of the certain neutralization of Laos, his assignment was to restore Diem's confidence in the U.S. commitment to Southeast Asia in general and to South Vietnam in particular. This goal the vice president could never achieve, despite the misleading impression afforded by his warm welcome. Johnson purveyed the image of a simple, homespun Texas cowboy who could mingle comfortably with anyone on the street. "I must confess I don't know where [the] U.S. is or who is Mr. Johnson," asserted a sugarcane vendor after shaking hands with his American visitor; "but I know him now. . . . I think [the] American people must be even more democratic than he, so I am glad to be friends of [the] American people."[34]

Johnson's mood was garrulously upbeat—too much so in light of the deteriorating military situation in South Vietnam. His public comparison of Diem to Winston Churchill and George Washington did not fit with the Vietcong's successes, the feeling of insecurity and questionable loyalty among the populace, and the sullen defeatist demeanor that permeated the South Vietnamese army. His several toasts to Diem as "the Franklin D. Roosevelt of Vietnam" did not seem appropriate in that the premier's April 1961 election victory had garnered nearly 90 percent of the votes only by rigging the results. Journalist Stanley Karnow remarked that Johnson acted as if he were "endorsing county sheriffs in a Texas election campaign" when he plunged into the crowds, shaking hands and praising the Vietnamese people and their leader while anxious security agents stood nearby.[35] No evidence suggested that the South Vietnamese premier ever entertained the notion of sharing his rule with anyone other than his family. The vice president's transparently phony outpourings of flattery did not fool Diem into believing that the United States sought an ally on an equal basis.

Despite Johnson's effusive praise of Diem, there was design in his unorthodox diplomacy. His task was to assure the premier that the imminent neutralization of Laos would not likewise take place in South Vietnam. Not that the White House held high hopes for Diem. Rostow saw no alternative, even as he admitted to the possibility of a coup. If Diem fell, Rostow told the president, the United States should work with the younger members of the army. Indeed, a change in leadership might yield the military and political reforms long desired, but, Rostow hastened to add, Americans should do nothing to encourage a coup because of its unpredictable outcome. Nolting must reconcile the differences between Diem and the army by persuading him to grant his officers more field control. The central problem, Rostow insisted, lay in Diem's refusal to implement reforms. Flattery might work. "We still have to find the technique for bringing our great bargaining power to bear on leaders of client states to do things they ought to do but don't want to do."[36]

The morning after Johnson's arrival, he met with Diem for nearly three hours. The meeting began on a cordial basis, but it suddenly degenerated into disagreements over the specifics of U.S. aid before ending on a positive note. Johnson presented Diem with a gift—a set of *American Heritage* books—before turning to substantive talks based on a letter from President Kennedy to Diem. Cooperation between the nations, the vice president drawled through an embassy officer as interpreter, was the key to success against the Vietcong. Diem, however, abruptly switched the direction of the conversation to remind his visitor of long-standing requests for a 20,000-man increase in the army and more military assistance for the Civil Guard. Johnson quickly returned to the president's letter by focusing on the need for collaboration in the Counterinsurgency Program and by raising the possibility of increasing the ARVN beyond Diem's present request of 170,000 soldiers.[37]

That evening Johnson met with Diem again, this time raising the prospect of a direct U.S. military intervention. Following the evening banquet, Johnson asked whether Diem was interested in U.S. combat troops and a bilateral treaty with the United States. Only in the event of an invasion from the north, the premier responded. Either step—the injection of foreign troops or the negotiation of a bilateral treaty—would undermine his nationalist reputation and substantiate the Communists' highly trumpeted charge of his being "My-Diem," or American Diem.[38]

Although Johnson's inquiry about combat troops may seem unexpected in light of President Kennedy's opposition to such a measure, there is a plausible explanation. At first glance, it appears that the vice president had either expressed his own feelings or bowed to the wishes of the state department's Task Force and the joint chiefs. Indeed, he had come under pressure from MAAG's Chief, General McGarr, who had asked for 16,000 U.S. combat troops (he would accept 10,000 if Diem rejected the larger number), ostensibly to train South Vietnamese soldiers. And yet it would not be out of Kennedy's character to authorize his emissary to examine all options in an effort to understand the situation in both Laos and South Vietnam. At the president's May 5 press conference, the question had risen about whether he intended to send U.S. combat forces to South Vietnam. "The problem of troops," Kennedy responded, "is a matter . . . still under consideration." This circular answer left the door open for the vice president to discuss the matter with Diem.[39]

Even as Johnson prepared for his Asian visit, the movement had intensified in Washington for sending combat troops to South Vietnam. On May 10, the Joint Chiefs of Staff responded enthusiastically to Gilpatric's recommendation that the United States deploy military forces to South Vietnam. Without offering any thoughts on the size and makeup of the contingent, the joint chiefs four times in a single memo urged McNamara to approve the proposal. It would prevent South Vietnam from becoming another Laos, furnish "a visible deterrent" to North Vietnamese and Chinese Communist aggression, and, by freeing the ARVN from static defense duties, allow its "fuller commitment to counterinsurgency actions." In a recommendation not justified by any provision in the SEATO charter, the joint chiefs wanted Diem to ask the United States to "fulfill its SEATO obligation" by assigning soldiers to South Vietnam.[40]

The president remained skeptical about the use of combat troops. At an NSC meeting the next day, he reviewed the Task Force's Program of Action in South Vietnam and made a number of decisions that reaffirmed his opposition. After approving the "mutually supporting" military, political, economic, psychological, and covert actions, he again pushed aside the question of combat troops by instructing the defense department to examine the "diplomatic setting" in which such a move would take place and to conduct a thorough analysis of the size and composition of the forces required. While Vice President Johnson was making every effort to raise Diem's confidence in the United States, the administration was open to negotiations with other Asian leaders aimed at improving South Vietnam's relationship with neighboring countries. In the words of the *Pentagon Papers*, Kennedy had made no military commitments, issuing "a near-minimal response which avoided any real deepening of our stake in Vietnam."[41]

Ironically, Kennedy's nightmarish experience in Cuba had made it easier to oppose the joint chiefs' call for combat troops. No longer did he feel bound by their recommendations simply because they were the experts. Had not these same experts counseled approval of the Bay of Pigs operation? And yet he knew that the perceived failure to save Laos had strengthened the call for combat troops in South Vietnam. What made the military proposal especially difficult to counter was the circuitous route it took in both the defense and state departments. Gilpatric had strayed from broadly conceived counterinsurgency tactics by leaning heavily on military measures. He had secured the joint chiefs' approval of a heightened military involvement that rested on a questionable reading of the U.S. obligations under SEATO. No one asked how that pact's provision for consultation had become transformed into an assurance of combat troops. Rusk, too, had left the door open for a military solution when he admitted that a further decline in South Vietnam's situation might necessitate ground forces.

Without promising troops to Diem, the president intended to demonstrate his commitment to the region. Since early May, American newspapers had reported the administration's ongoing consideration of sending troops, and Diem could not have been surprised that Johnson raised the subject. Indeed, had the vice president avoided the issue, Diem would have suspected a lack of commitment by the administration. On May 20, before Johnson's return, the widely read *Saturday Evening Post* carried an article that had come at the president's private instigation. Entitled "The Report the President Wanted Published," it was the essence of Lansdale's January 1961 report on Vietnam under the byline of an American officer "whose name, for professional reasons, cannot be used." Kennedy had told McGeorge Bundy that Lansdale's account of Vietcong activities would make "an excellent article for something like *The Saturday Evening Post*," and the state and defense departments found someone to write it without identifying Lansdale.[42] The article emphasized counterinsurgency and continued support to Diem, *not* combat troops.

Kennedy had surely expected the troop question to arise in the vice presidential visit, but he felt confident that Diem would oppose the idea for exactly the reasons he gave—to avoid the appearance of being an American puppet. Diem did not *want* U.S. combat forces. Had he *ever* asked for them? Had he not balked at any sort of bilateral arrangement that might turn over the war to the Americans and destroy his image of independence? Diem's predicted response, the president realized, could undermine the argument among his White House advisers for combat forces. Risky thinking if so, but had Diem replied in the affirmative, Kennedy could have followed his familiar pattern of relegating the matter to further study.

President Kennedy's emphasis on a balanced civil and military approach seemed to have triumphed when Diem promised support for a counterinsurgency effort based on "parallel political and economic action of equal importance with military measures." Diem agreed to an increase in MAAG personnel; to MAAG's supporting and advising the Self-Defense Corps; to military assistance for all 68,000 members of the Civil Guard; to an expanded junk force aimed at halting Vietcong infiltration by water; to an immediate joint study of border control efforts and renewed talks with Cambodia over the matter; to assistance to South Vietnamese armed forces in village health, welfare, and public works programs; and to the use of foreign non-American specialists in counterguerrilla warfare who would operate under Saigon's control. Diem then gave Johnson a memorandum seeking more military assistance. They closed their meeting with an agreement to issue a joint communiqué summarizing their talks.[43]

The Johnson party flew out of Saigon early the following day of May 13, bound for Manila and a whirlwind round of stopovers in the Philippines, Taiwan, Hong Kong, Thailand, India, and Pakistan, before heading home on May 24.[44]

Soon after returning to the United States, Vice President Johnson submitted his report on the mission. In language that state department analyst Alexis Johnson thought stronger than the White House considered "wise at that time," the vice president termed the Diem regime salvageable and urged the administration to save it. The ongoing Geneva Conference on Laos, Johnson continued, seemed destined to neutralize that country, casting a pall over South Vietnam and other neighboring states by raising questions about the U.S. determination to resist communism. The region's leaders wished to remain friends of the United States, Johnson declared, but the expected outcome in Laos had made these nations "hypersensitive to the possibility of American hypocrisy toward Asia." The neutralization of Laos would cause a "deep—and long lasting—impact" of "doubt and concern" about the U.S. commitment to Southeast Asia. Diem and others conceded that the United States sought to make "the best of a bad bargain" on Laos, but they remained deeply troubled over the ramifications of a neighboring coalition government that included Communists. The approaching summit talks in Vienna between Kennedy and Khrushchev had led Asians to fear that the U.S. focus was on the West and not Asia. Leaders of Southeast Asia wanted actions to follow words. "We didn't buy time," Johnson asserted; "we were given it."[45]

The vice president insisted that the situation in South Vietnam was less critical than that reported by "journalistic sensationalism," but he also warned that these conditions could worsen. The U.S. mission in Saigon had become obsessed with security concerns. Admittedly, terrorists roamed the jungles and rice paddies, "significant numbers" of government officials had been assassinated, and Saigon was a hotbed of "anti-government, noncommunist plotting." But Johnson saw no need for panic. A coup attempt was unlikely. The real danger was a progressive loss of Diem's control over his people that stemmed from either the Vietcong's successes in forcefully recruiting the South Vietnamese or the Saigon government's failure to satisfy their social, political, and economic needs.[46]

The United States, Johnson warned, "must decide whether to support Diem—or let Vietnam fall." South Vietnam needed an additional $50 million of military and economic aid. Diem had agreed to Kennedy's proposed joint economic mission, and Johnson recommended its immediate implementation. A continued deterioration in governmental control would reduce the Diem regime to a "glittering façade" held up only by "a modern military establishment and an oriental bureaucracy both maintained for the indefinite future primarily by the United States Treasury." Under those circumstances, the Communists would triumph because of the lack of promising leaders among the non-Communist opposition. A government responsive to popular needs could not come from "men in white linen suits whose contact with the ordinary people is largely through the rolled-up windows of a Mercedes-Benz."[47]

If the United States failed to provide Diem with the necessary guidance and assistance for defeating the Vietcong, Johnson warned, it might have to send combat troops. The regime lacked the "self-dedication and self-sacrifice" needed to inspire popular confidence. Indeed, "there are disturbing suggestions that the government not only fears the Viet Cong cadres and terrorists but its own people as well." Diem's followers had squelched all resistance to the regime, but in doing so they had alienated local government officials who were not sympathetic to the Vietcong. "Ultimately, perhaps even our direct military involvement may be required to hold the situation."[48]

Johnson emphasized, however, that Diem wanted additional economic and military assistance, *not* U.S. combat troops. His people had recently emerged from colonial rule and, except in the unlikely event of a North Vietnamese attack, vehemently rejected "the return this soon of Western troops." The United States might gain South Vietnamese support if it sought contributory economic and military assistance from other countries and thereby removed the colonial stain. The vice president therefore recommended a three-year program of expanded military and economic aid. In a warning laden with bitter irony in light of his own White House experience a few years later, Johnson declared that before the United States considered sending combat troops, "we had better be sure we are prepared to become bogged down chasing irregulars and guerrillas over the rice fields and jungles of Southeast Asia while our principal enemies China and the Soviet Union stand outside the fray and husband their strength."[49]

The heightened aid commitment, Johnson admitted, would thrust the United States deeper into South Vietnam's domestic affairs. Americans involved in military assistance must nonetheless work more in the jungles and less in the cities. Those dispensing economic aid must abandon the safety of Saigon to establish closer contact with the people in the outlying areas. Only in this manner could U.S. assistance win the allegiance of the Vietnamese people and culminate in victory over the Communist insurgents. U.S. casualties would occur, but they would be fewer than would result from direct combat with the Vietcong.[50]

Americans must remain sensitive to the Diem regime's feelings even while insisting on the assistance plan. Those in the mission must quietly persuade Saigon's officials from the president down to associate with the people and deal with their grievances. "Handshakes on the streets of Vietnamese leaders and people is the concept that has got to be pursued. And shirt-sleeves must be the hallmark of Americans." If this happened, the educated groups in South Vietnam might be willing to serve the government, thereby providing new leadership should Diem fall from power.[51]

SEATO was not the answer, Johnson insisted. Neither France nor Britain supported decisive action. Besides, Asians distrusted both European nations as former colonial powers interested only in regaining their predominant positions. If the Geneva Conference failed to safeguard Laos, SEATO would no longer be meaningful. At that point, the United States must develop a new collective security approach based on allying all free nations in the Pacific and Asia and emphasizing social and economic reforms.[52]

Johnson placed South Vietnam's problems within the Cold War context by darkly warning that if the United States did not stop communism in Southeast Asia, it must surrender the Pacific and establish defenses on America's home shores. Without Southeast Asia to hold back Communist expansion, "the island outposts—Philippines, Japan, Taiwan—have no security and the vast Pacific becomes a Red Sea." South Vietnam and Thailand were "critical to the U.S." in terms of credibility and defense. The United States must either help them "or throw in the towel in the area and pull back our defenses to San Francisco and a 'Fortress America' concept."[53]

Johnson concluded with a declaration that the United States must decide whether to act now or give up the attempt to stop Communist expansion in Southeast Asia. Such a program entailed heavy expenditures in money, effort, and prestige. The White House must also consider the possibility that "at some point we may be faced with the further decision of whether we commit major United States forces to the area or cut our losses and withdraw should our other efforts fail." In ringing words, he proclaimed, "We must remain master of this decision."[54]

For the most part, congressional members approved Johnson's assertions, but, in a change of heart that shoved the Korean experience out of mind, some of the more outspoken legislators leaned toward sending in U.S. combat troops. The vice president had earlier received a note of warning from the newest addition to the Senate Foreign Relations Committee, Democrat Thomas Dodd of Connecticut, who had recently toured the Philippines, Vietnam, Thailand, Laos, and Taiwan. U.S. prestige in Asia had plummeted as a result of the Cuban affair, he concluded. Were not the Communist Chinese calling the United States a "paper tiger"? Now, in Congress, the strongly anti-Communist senator theatrically expressed his colleagues' concern that "the drama which may toll the death knell for the United States and for Western civilization is now being played out in southeast Asia." The area's people were experiencing a "crisis of confidence" in America, which necessitated a sharp increase in aid. Counterguerrilla forces

must cross the seventeenth parallel into North Vietnam "to equip and supply those patriots already in the field; to make every Communist official
fear the just retribution of an outraged human-communications center,
and [to consider each] transportation facility a target for sabotage; to provide a rallying point for the great masses of oppressed people who hate
Communism because they have known it." Indeed, the United States should
"carry the offensive to North Vietnam, and wherever else it may be necessary." First-year Republican Representative Paul Findley of Illinois denounced the vice president's opposition to military escalation. "U.S. combat
forces are the most effective deterrent to aggression, and we should publicly offer such forces to South Vietnam without delay." Such an early commitment would ward off a Communist attack.[55]

Kenneth Young, who had accompanied Johnson and would soon become ambassador to Thailand, praised the trip while reiterating the warning against combat troops. The vice president and his wife "came, saw, and
won over." Johnson had met with key people in all four capitals and brought
a human aspect to America's interests in the region while establishing a
warm personal relationship with Diem and other leaders. "Diem showed
no appetite for American combat troops mixing among the South Vietnamese people." In the absence of "large scale hostilities or infiltration,"
the White House should exercise extreme care toward this "sensitive internal issue." South Vietnam's interest in economic progress and social
justice was so much in harmony with the objectives advanced by the vice
president that Diem and his cohort took on the image of "new frontiers-
men." A taxi driver in Bangkok best summed up the impact of the visit:
"Your Vice President he good man. He talk people."[56]

Despite Young's overly optimistic tone, his assessment was important
in emphasizing the region's opposition to U.S. combat troops. Not surprisingly, the vice president received a royal welcome from Southeast Asian
allies deeply concerned about the coming neutralization of Laos. Predictably, they expressed their intention to institute social, political, and economic changes long advocated by the United States. On the surface it
appeared that the Johnson mission had restored Southeast Asia's confidence in the United States. But this feeling, even if accurate, had not translated into a desire for direct U.S. military involvement in South Vietnam.
These people sought security without incurring outside obligations detrimental to their independence. Diem and other leaders in Asia requested
more military and economic assistance—*not* U.S. fighting forces.

DIEM OPPOSED a bilateral treaty for the same reason he resisted combat
troops: Both measures invited a formal U.S. military involvement in South
Vietnamese affairs that would provide Hanoi with more propaganda to use
against his collaboration with U.S. imperialists. Indeed, a bilateral treaty
would most likely authorize U.S. troops in the event of an emergency.

Diem's lack of interest in joining SEATO provided additional insight into his opposition to a bilateral treaty: South Vietnam already reaped SEATO's benefits without incurring any cost. Diem understood that the United States was the real source of power in the regional pact and that if North Vietnam invaded the south, the United States, with or without SEATO assistance, would intervene on his behalf.

Johnson's shower of praise on Diem had hardened instead of softened his opposition to change. Why should the premier buckle under when the Americans exalted his leadership as vital to the world's freedom? Nhu assured his brother that the United States would never abandon its aid effort and insisted that they did not have to make reforms.[57] Diem wanted more assistance—but with no strings attached.

Diem's claims to independence had a hollow ring in light of America's deepening involvement in his affairs. Nolting had opposed a bilateral treaty, but he strongly supported the Kennedy administration's decision to disregard the Geneva Accords in raising the U.S. military ceiling in South Vietnam and to cite North Vietnamese infractions as the basis for doing so. Convinced of the rightness of the U.S. position, Rusk reversed previous policy and informed the British, French, and Canadians that the United States intended to dispatch 100 additional MAAG forces as the first of several increases in response to Hanoi's infiltration of the south. International law, he argued, authorized noncompliance with a treaty when one of the parties to the agreement broke its provisions. Article 24 of the Geneva Accords made clear that the armed forces of each party "shall commit no act and undertake no operation against the other party." In a transparent effort to conceal America's growing involvement in South Vietnam, Diem recommended securing acceptance by the International Control Commission of an additional 1,000 new MAAG personnel for training his army units. He then approved more U.S. military personnel for training the Civil Guard and Self-Defense Corps but stipulated that the soldiers conceal their military status by wearing civilian clothes. Nolting did not believe that the International Control Commission would condone these military increases or that the discarding of uniforms would fool anyone.[58]

Diem's concern was personal as well as professional. Could he trust the United States? Had it not abandoned Laos by supporting neutralization? To grant military power to those not under his direct control could place the sword in the hands of his enemies. He had survived several assaults on his rule. In 1955 his regime had barely succeeded in putting down a widespread sect crisis. Two years afterward, an assassin missed from five paces and then his automatic pistol jammed before he could fire again. And in 1960, disgruntled generals led a coup that narrowly failed. Would the United States be next in seeking his overthrow? As the *Pentagon Papers* later observed, an expanded U.S. military presence in South Vietnam provided a greater capacity for "American ability and temptation to encourage a coup."[59]

4

WAGING A SECRET WAR

[Counterinsurgency offered the best chance at winning] the
hearts and minds of the people.

USAF Major General Bela K. Kiraly,
Summer (?), 1961

[The presence of U.S. troops would arouse] race-hatred,
hatred of the white man in general, originally of the French,
now converted by clever Communist tactics into a hatred of
Americans.

Theodore H. White,
October 11, 1961

The initial responsibility for the effective maintenance of the
independence of South Vietnam rests with the people and
government of that country.

President John F. Kennedy,
October 11, 1961

THE COLD WAR intensified during the spring of 1961, raising South
Vietnam's importance in the Kennedy administration's delib-
erations. In early June, the president's tense two-day summit
meeting with Khrushchev in Vienna culminated in the premier's warning
that if the United States did not leave Berlin by the end of the year, the
Soviet Union would sign a separate peace with East Germany, forcing the
West to negotiate with the East Germans for continued access to West
Berlin. "If the West tries to interfere," Khrushchev assured Kennedy, "there
will be war." The president did not shrink from the challenge. "Mr. Chairman," came the sharp response, "there will be war. It is going to be a very
cold winter."[1]

Kennedy, according to James Reston of the *New York Times*, had been
"shaken and angry" by the way Khrushchev "had bullied and browbeaten"
him. In an interview in the U.S. embassy after the conference, the president expressed his feelings. "I think I know why he treated me like this. He
thinks because of the Bay of Pigs that I'm inexperienced. Probably thinks

I'm stupid. Maybe more important he thinks that I had no guts." The White House must demonstrate to the Soviets that it would defend the national interest. "I'll have to increase the defense budget. And we have to confront them. The only place we can do that is in Vietnam. We have to send more people there."[2]

South Vietnam's importance had notched upward within the heightening Cold War. That same month, the fourteen nations gathered in Geneva issued a declaration on the neutrality of Laos that would terminate its use as a "corridor to South Vietnam," and they called for the withdrawal of all foreign soldiers, except the French, under supervision of the International Control Commission and with the Geneva cochairs supervising compliance. But beneath these cosmetic changes in Laos were the realities of a CIA-sponsored "secret war" in which 9,000 Hmong tribesmen had received arms to carry out paramilitary measures intended to halt further infiltration into South Vietnam. The White House now prepared to conduct the same type of clandestine warfare in South Vietnam.[3]

I

THE PRESIDENT'S ATTEMPT to control the military aspects of his administration's counterinsurgency program in South Vietnam suffered a severe blow when an economic mission to Saigon took a military turn. As part of the agreements resulting from the Johnson visit, President Kennedy sent to Saigon a six-member "Special Financial Group," comprised primarily of government employees but headed by Eugene Staley, a private economist and head of the Stanford Research Institute, whose task was to develop an economic plan for South Vietnam. Just before the team's departure in mid-June, however, Diem requested financial support for another increase in South Vietnam's armed forces—this time from 170,000 to 270,000—and the result was a series of exchanges between the governments that monopolized the business of the Staley mission and led it to focus on military issues. In Washington, President Kennedy told South Vietnam's secretary of state, Nguyen Dinh Thuan, that Diem's requested "increase should be done quietly without publicly indicating that we did not intend to abide by the Geneva Accords."[4]

The Staley Group thus became a virtual conduit for sending military information back and forth between Saigon and Washington on whether or not to raise South Vietnam's troop level. Drawing on information provided by the U.S. military, the economic advisers strayed beyond their original mandate to furnish military advice as the basis of this "Joint Action Program." If the insurgency maintained its present intensity, the Staley Group reported, Diem should receive an additional 30,000 men to the

170,000 already in uniform. But if the insurgency intensified, Diem must have 270,000 men, with the United States providing support up to the 200,000 level. Furthermore, the economic team urged the White House to underwrite the recently approved 20,000-man increase in South Vietnam's armed forces, and it supported Diem's call for a hundred more agrovilles as integral to counterinsurgency warfare. The Staley Group agreed with the U.S. military in arguing that security was the vital prerequisite to a successful economic and social program.[5]

The question of raising South Vietnam's military force level had developed in accordance with the demands of the escalating Cold War and led Rostow to believe that the Communists were stepping up the insurgency in South Vietnam in harmony with the growing tensions in Berlin. Agreement came from Sterling Cottrell, a member of the state department's Task Force on Vietnam, who insisted that the call for a larger South Vietnamese armed force suggested the need for a firsthand inspection by General Maxwell Taylor in his capacity as the president's military representative. Rostow warned Deputy Undersecretary of State Alexis Johnson that "we were in a brief interval before great heat might be put on us in Viet Nam." It would not be surprising if the Vietnam issue "should come to a head at the time of the Berlin crisis."[6]

Rostow viewed all these problems within the global context of the Cold War and advocated a stronger initiative against what he perceived as the external source of trouble plaguing South Vietnam. Conventional forces were not sufficient to counter Khrushchev's covert tactics in Southeast Asia, Rostow warned the president. "We must be prepared to increase the risk of war on his side of the line as well as facing it on ours." U.S. protection of South Vietnam did not entail merely countering a guerrilla war below the seventeenth parallel but also putting Moscow, Beijing, Hanoi, and other world leaders "on notice that an expansion of the attack on Diem may lead to direct retaliation in Vietminh territory."[7]

Speaking before the June 1961 graduation ceremonies of the Special Warfare School at Fort Bragg, Rostow argued that guerrilla warfare posed the central threat to underdeveloped nations such as South Vietnam. In a speech read beforehand by Lansdale and given to the president, Rostow emphasized that the internal parties alone must fight a guerrilla war. Such a conflict was "an intimate affair, fought not merely with weapons but fought in the minds of the men who live in the villages and in the hills; fought by the spirit and policy of those who run the local government." Hanoi's operation against Saigon was an act of aggression, just as North Korea's attack on South Korea was in June 1950. Outsiders cannot by themselves win such a war, but they can foster conditions that determine its outcome.[8]

Rostow argued that the chief remedy to this threat was a counterinsurgency program that struck a balance between military and nonmilitary correctives. "A guerrilla war mounted from outside a transitional nation" was "a crude act of international vandalism." The Communists relied on "a systematic program of assassination" aimed at undermining personal security. Not only must the legitimate government guarantee safety through a strong military establishment, but it must also introduce civic action programs aimed at developing secure villages.[9]

As part of the counterinsurgency effort, Rostow noted a few days later, the South Vietnamese government must stop Vietcong infiltration. To Chalmers Wood, deputy director of the Vietnam Task Force, Rostow observed that the ARVN's sweeping operations presently under way in Vinh Binh province seemed effective in driving out Vietcong forces, but what would prevent their return after the troops left? Wood noted that in Malaya the British had used "framing operations" to isolate, encircle, and destroy the guerrillas. Rostow's eyes brightened as Wood suggested that such tactics begin in Saigon and move northwest to the Cambodian border and then along the border in a northeastern and southwestern direction until the Vietcong forces retreated to the frontier and had the choice of leaving the country or facing certain death. At that point, Rostow jumped to his feet and exclaimed, "This is the first time I have heard a practical suggestion as to how we should carry out our operations in Viet-Nam." The Task Force should contact Saigon about developing a plan for pushing the Vietcong out of the country.[10]

The attempt to stop outside interference in the war necessitated concerted actions in both North and South Vietnam. The White House must prepare for three levels of reaction, Rostow insisted: a major increase in the number of Americans sent to South Vietnam for training and support duties; a counterguerrilla program in the north, perhaps supported by U.S. air and naval forces and aimed at inflicting the same degree of damage there as the North Vietnamese had caused in the south; and, in the event of a military invasion from the north, a limited military action above the demilitarized zone (DMZ) that included seizure of the port of Haiphong. The purpose of presenting the aggression in South Vietnam as an international issue, Rostow told Rusk, was "to free our hands and our consciences for whatever we have to do." The threat of U.S. military action against North Vietnam would provide leverage in negotiations over Southeast Asia. "I would assume that a posture aimed more directly against North Viet-Nam is more likely to be diplomatically persuasive."[11]

Rostow's stance remained primarily consistent with that of the president's in calling for a counterinsurgency program that emphasized both military and nonmilitary remedies. Like Kennedy, Rostow recognized the immediacy of the military threat and sought to meet it with unconventional measures intended to provide the security requisite to social, political, and economic reforms. Unlike Kennedy, however, Rostow seemed more willing to challenge North Vietnam. Still, neither man advocated direct U.S. combat against the Vietcong. The military solution, as promoted by the joint chiefs and others, had not won White House support. Through continued aid and advice, the Kennedy administration sought to cultivate conditions unfavorable to the Vietcong. Only then could the South Vietnamese win a war that was theirs alone to fight.

Toward that end, the White House reversed its earlier position, perhaps because of the Staley Group's prodding, and funded the 20,000-man addition to South Vietnam's armed forces. At first the U.S. government agreed to commit only some of the resources, and even that concession rested on the stipulations that Saigon furnish the balance of the cost and mobilize without delay. But this arrangement proved unsatisfactory. South Vietnam had no financial resources, Thuan assured Nolting. The ambassador was convinced. On the basis of his strong recommendation, the White House agreed to absorb all the expense by releasing the last $4.5 million remaining in the fiscal year 1961 budget. Rusk expressed concern that unconditional approval of this expanded military aid would suggest a waning interest in Washington for economic reforms in South Vietnam. But he relented because of his greater fear that refusal to assume this cost would undermine South Vietnam's confidence in the United States.[12]

On June 14, President Kennedy met with Thuan to discuss a letter from Diem that sought U.S. compliance with the communiqué he had worked out with Vice President Johnson calling for increased American aid. Among Diem's requests was an increase in South Vietnam's armed forces from the 170,000 just approved in May to 270,000 regulars over the next three and a half years. Such a massive growth, of course, necessitated a corresponding expansion of MAAG, a move that General McGarr had already advocated. In Diem's words, the additional soldiers would "serve the dual purpose of providing an expression of the United States' determination to halt the tide of communist aggression and of preparing our forces in the minimum of time." When Kennedy inquired about the feasibility of sending guerrillas into North Vietnam, Thuan responded, "A few highly trained troops were available but . . . if Viet-Nam were to risk these men in an attempt to stir up unrest in North Viet-Nam, the United States should be prepared to make a major effort to give them the full support needed to carry out such an action to a successful conclusion."[13]

The president's approval of covert actions in North Vietnam greatly enhanced the role of the CIA. The Washington office instructed its station chief in Saigon, William Colby, to take over the program. "We pressed ahead," Colby later recalled. "Flights left Danang in the dusk headed north with Vietnamese trained and equipped to land in isolated areas, make cautious contact with their former home villages and begin building networks there. Boats went up the coast to land others on the beaches, and we started leaflet drops and radio programs designed to raise questions in North Vietnamese homes about their sons being sent to South Vietnam to fight and about the vices of Communist rule."[14]

President Kennedy had approved an escalated assistance and advisory program that did not include combat troops but whose military direction and shift northward soon unsettled many observer nations, including neutralist India and the Soviet Union. Although assured that the United States had no plans for taking over the war in South Vietnam, India had reports from Laos that U.S. officers had accompanied its local forces to the front and feared that they might do the same with the ARVN in South Vietnam. Furthermore, Rostow had recently complained to an Indian official that the Communists were systematically assassinating potential leaders of South Vietnam and hinted at strong U.S. counteractions aimed at the problem's source in Hanoi. Indeed, some press reports suggested that the White House was considering attacks on North Vietnam. Such developments, India warned, would provide the Communist Chinese with an excuse to intervene in South Vietnam and cause another Korea. The Soviet embassy in Washington joined India in voicing concern about a U.S. assault on North Vietnam.[15]

Violence in South Vietnam meanwhile continued to spread. In the mid-afternoon of July 8, two men on a motor bicycle threw a grenade that bounced off Nolting's car without exploding. The assailants escaped, and the ambassador at first urged Washington to give the incident "no special notice." After instructing his staff to exercise more care in its daily activities, Nolting assured Washington that the attack "was not part of a campaign of terror directed against Americans but was more probably an isolated incident instigated by overzealous but unskilled Viet Cong cadres." He later became convinced, however, that the act had been part of a Vietcong "scare campaign" intended to undermine U.S. influence in the country.[16]

In mid-July the South Vietnamese and American Special Financial Groups officially recommended approval of the "Joint Action Program" based on the principles of counterinsurgency. The only way to defeat this Communist threat was for the United States to support a full-scale mobilization of South Vietnam's social, economic, political, military, and psychological forces. The prime short-range objective was to restore domestic security in the south as a prerequisite to long-range nonmilitary reforms. The solution necessitated massive social and economic changes, particularly in the countryside, and all closely intertwined with the military effort.[17]

The military approach nonetheless maintained priority, as demonstrated by Taylor's recommendations to the president. The Joint Chiefs of Staff, he declared, must develop an overall plan for Southeast Asia that secured enough of the Mekong Valley and Laotian panhandle to halt infiltration while preventing a conventional assault on South Vietnam (and

Thailand) that would originate from northern Laos and North Vietnam. Air attacks along with a guerrilla offensive against these latter two areas might prove essential. The United States must also prepare for a possible naval assault on North Vietnam.[18]

Predictably, the combat issue rose again when Taylor warned the president that the above objectives might require direct U.S. military assistance. Securing the Mekong Valley and launching an air and land offensive from the Laotian panhandle demanded optimal use of South Vietnamese, Laotian, and Thai ground forces. The United States should provide logistical support only. But if these indigenous forces proved insufficient, the joint chiefs must determine the number of U.S. combat troops needed. Hopefully, these Americans would be limited to air forces, ground troops to protect U.S. air and supply depots, and Special Forces to train the South Vietnamese in counterguerrilla warfare. By implication, however, Americans might have to engage in combat.[19]

The drive for a greater U.S. military participation in the war continued on another front as well. Assistant Secretary of Defense William Bundy asked the joint chiefs to consider retaliatory measures against Hanoi that included a naval blockade and air patrols above the seventeenth parallel. In accordance with the Task Force's suggestion, Bundy asked for the joint chiefs' views on the establishment of U.S.–South Vietnamese coastal patrols from Cambodia's border to the mouth of the Mekong River. Such steps "would supplement those actions recently approved by the President" and were justifiable in light of Hanoi's aggressions. All air and naval operations against North Vietnam would be "our equivalent of the guerrilla operations which the Viet Minh are conducting in South Viet Nam."[20]

The Kennedy administration also authorized research into new psywar methods that were peculiarly suited for counterguerrilla warfare. Among the innovations introduced to the ARVN were a lightweight and highly maneuverable power glider capable of aerial reconnaissance for lengthy periods on a single tank of gasoline ("an airborne Volkswagen," according to the minutes of the meeting); a paddlewheel boat run by a steam engine burning cane alcohol and capable of moving in just three inches of water while carrying up to thirty men; an armolite rifle, which was a high-propellant, 22-caliber weapon light enough for the smaller South Vietnamese Rangers to use; dogs to facilitate South Vietnamese night patrols; a silent alarm system that any villager could activate to warn the ARVN as much as twenty-five miles away; and a defoliant capable of destroying all vegetation in border infiltration areas over a three-year period.[21]

Robert Komer from the National Security Council staff argued for a greater military escalation. He called for a massive increase in military assistance to guarantee victory before the growing crisis in Berlin became hot by the end of the year. Such strong action would demonstrate to the

Soviets and Chinese that the United States meant to hold the line against communism. To reassure America's allies in Asia, Komer recommended that the president show "moxie" by taking off "all wraps" on the counter-guerrilla war. *"We would regard this as a wartime situation in which the sky's the limit* [emphasis in original]." The United States had little to lose if the new military initiative failed. "Are we any worse off than before? Our prestige may have become a little more heavily engaged but what else?" The failure to save Laos and a probable confrontation over Berlin made it incumbent on the United States to safeguard South Vietnam.[22]

Komer's argument, like that of others before him, lacked sound reasoning. Inexplicably, he saw no danger in an unrestricted U.S. military involvement that placed the nation's prestige on the line. Even if he had not advocated direct American combat, he knew that the presence of uniformed personnel could draw enemy fire and that a return volley would erase the thin line between defensive and offensive action. Any damage to U.S. credibility could broaden the commitment and lead to the use of combat troops. Combined with the widely perceived defeat in Laos, anything less than a full-scale victory in South Vietnam would undermine U.S. prestige in the Cold War.

Taylor and Rostow nonetheless assured President Kennedy of the need for a comprehensive military plan for all Southeast Asia, and, with the support of the Southeast Asia Task Force, they insisted that it include military action against North Vietnam. Rostow's steady conversion to military priorities had become complete. The most effective way to halt infiltration through the Laotian panhandle, he agreed with Taylor, was to establish a military base below Laos. Covert action, according to the Task Force, was crucial to relieving North Vietnam's pressure on the south; if unsuccessful, the United States must quietly warn Hanoi of "direct retaliatory action." Taylor and Rostow concurred. The United States could find a "convenient political pretext" for attacking Hanoi while preparing for a Chinese Communist involvement. The Task Force bluntly declared that U.S. forces should strike Hanoi, with or without SEATO's approval.[23]

In a late July White House meeting, the president found himself in the uncomfortable position of having to resist this mounting pressure for stronger military action in both Laos and North Vietnam. Robert Johnson from the National Security Council staff supported an approach already under consideration: a combined military force of Laotian, Thai, South Vietnamese, and U.S. soldiers that would occupy southern Laos and close the border. The proposal also included an air and naval assault on Hanoi or Haiphong if Vietcong infiltration picked up dramatically. Harriman strongly opposed a U.S. troop commitment, and he did not favor Rostow's call to "bomb Hanoi." Indeed, Kennedy privately dubbed Rostow the "Air Marshal" because of his zeal for bombing. The president's probing questions, however, revealed that no one had made a detailed logistical study of such a far-reaching plan. Nor was anyone clear about the specific steps involved in any operation in southern Laos, the impact that an attack on Hanoi or Haiphong would have on North Vietnam, or the chances of the allies' holding on to any areas taken.[24]

The president emphasized the importance of securing accurate assessments before making such grave decisions. Equally optimistic estimates about Laos, he pointed out, had proved incorrect. The military proposal before him seemed impractical because Laotian airfields were run-down and the overall situation there had deteriorated so badly. The American people, numerous military leaders, and the British and French governments opposed a U.S. troop involvement. Johnson countered that the United States must develop a broad plan and attract outside support by making a public commitment that affirmed its readiness to intervene. Kennedy reminded his advisers of General Charles de Gaulle's recent warning that the French had pursued the same logic and lost the war.[25]

Kennedy's wariness had struck at the heart of military strategy. Supporters of expanded military action had no satisfactory response. They called for a sweeping plan (without specifying the practical steps necessary for success), emphasized the importance of securing help from allies (without explaining how to convert the British and French to intervention), advocated a public pledge of support to Saigon (without noting how such a threat would cause Hanoi to terminate its help to the Vietcong, particularly when the United States was assisting Saigon), and relied on two Laotian air fields for bringing in heavy equipment (without a prior examination of their conditions). The air fields turned out to be of limited utility.[26]

President Kennedy refused to approve a military expedition into Laos and chose instead to focus on South Vietnam by accepting the Staley Group's recommendations and by sending a special mission to analyze the military situation. In agreeing to a 200,000-man army, he had concurred with the joint chiefs' recommendation, though knowing that the increase would take place over a year's time and that he could raise the number at a later date. The United States would assume the bulk of the costs, although the president urged Diem to share in the expenses and to admit his non-Communist political opponents into the government. Rusk upbraided his colleagues for arguing that military intervention was cheap and easy; *any* other tactic was less expensive. The president explained his rationale for a special mission. Anyone making military recommendations should examine other instances of intervention and compile information on present needs. General Taylor would head the mission.[27]

Not surprisingly, Kennedy's reluctance to declare outright opposition to military escalation encouraged its growth. A few days after the late July meeting, Rostow and Taylor sent a memo to the president, attempting to summarize his views for purposes of clarity. They understood the reasoning behind his attempt to examine every alternative before "either positioning U.S. forces on the Southeast Asian mainland or fighting there." This "graduated pressure" on Hanoi "could take the form of air strikes against the land lines of communications and supply centers, and sea interdiction of logistical traffic along the east coast of Viet-Nam. It could also include a naval blockade in the Gulf of Tonkin to isolate the Port of Haiphong." Furthermore, the United States might take action against China if it intervened in Vietnam. Kennedy left the impression of moving toward a military solution when he sought Rostow and Taylor's advice on making the world aware of North Vietnam's aggressions in the event that the United States had to resort to direct military measures. "I agree with you that ground work has to be laid or otherwise any military action we might take against Northern Vietnam will seem like aggression on our part." Robert Johnson reiterated his call for strong measures, declaring in a memo to fellow NSC members that the time had come "to bite the bullet." Saving southern Laos and the Mekong region might require "a substantial U.S. manpower contribution." Rostow, too, had edged closer to a military reaction. But he did not want the United States to take over the war. He sought to demonstrate the U.S. commitment to Southeast Asia by raising the morale and resistance of the Communists' victims and thereby "minimizing the chance that U.S. troops will have to fight."[28]

President Kennedy had not reduced his support for counterinsurgency, but he left the impression of having done so. In approving a sizable ARVN increase and in calling for a special mission to South Vietnam, he had encouraged advocates of the military solution. As Sorensen observed, the president did not want to appear weak. Yet his refusal to make a decision during these meetings encouraged those advocating a military approach to feel that he did not oppose their position. Kennedy's indecisive response proved dangerously misleading. He still maintained that military measures were only a means toward establishing social and economic reforms.[29] His interest in a firsthand examination of the military situation did not suggest a loss of confidence in the nonmilitary aspects of counterinsurgency. But in trying to ascertain the military realities, he left the door open for military escalation.

II

IN ACTUALITY, Saigon was fairly secure, but in the countryside the growing Vietcong influence reaffirmed the need for a counterinsurgency program. A June report revealed that the Vietcong had stepped up its activities in the first half of 1961. Someone shot up a U.S. Operations Mission officer's car about ten miles outside the city. Guerrillas and terrorists had assassinated more than 500 local officials and civilians, kidnapped more than 1,000, and killed nearly 1,500 South Vietnamese military personnel. The Vietcong's regular forces numbered about 25,000; guerrillas and terrorists probably reached 17,000 in number. The North Vietnamese had become concerned about the escalated U.S. military involvement in the south, and in June, Prime Minister Pham Van Dong traveled to Beijing to seek help. The Chinese did not extend assistance at this time, but Mao expressed approval of South Vietnam's armed resistance, and Zhou Enlai emphasized the importance of "blending [the] legal and illegal struggle and combining [the] political and military approaches."[30]

"The situation gets worse almost week by week," wrote veteran journalist and author Theodore H. White to the president. Having been in China during the 1930s and 1940s, initially as an aide to Nationalist leader Chiang Kai-shek and then as a correspondent for *Time* magazine, White brought a firsthand knowledge and keen eye to Asian affairs that commanded respect. Only disaster lay in a deeper U.S. involvement in Vietnam, he warned. "The guerrillas now control almost all the southern delta—so much so that I could find no American who would drive me outside Saigon in his car even by day without military convoy." A major "political breakdown" had occurred, resulting in vast numbers of South Vietnamese who did not seem to care about the house falling down around them. "I find it discouraging to spend a night in a Saigon night-club full of young fellows of 20 and 25 dancing and jitterbugging . . . while twenty miles away their Communist contemporaries are terrorizing the countryside." White asked a number of questions that must have been disconcerting to the president. If the army tried another coup, should the United States support it? What if none occurred? "Should we incubate one?" Remaining in Vietnam much longer could force such a decision. "If we feel bound by honor not to pull or support a coup, shall we lay it on the line to Diem and intervene directly . . . or should we get the Hell out?" If the United States decided to send combat troops, did it have "the proper personnel, the proper instruments, the proper clarity of objectives to intervene successfully?"[31]

President Kennedy had little time to reflect on the issues raised by White, for the escalated Vietcong threat had led Diem to ask for a greater U.S. military commitment. On June 14, Thuan forwarded the White House a letter from Diem that sought American troops to train South Vietnamese "combat leaders and technical specialists," an ARVN enlargement from 170,000 to 270,000, and a "considerable expansion" of MAAG in "selected elements of the American Armed Forces." Diem had called for nearly double the 150,000 authorized in 1961 and more than the 100,000 prescribed in the Kennedy administration's Counterinsurgency Plan. His concern focused on recent events in Laos and uncertainty about Cambodia.[32]

President Kennedy meanwhile tried to promote the counterinsurgency approach by shifting the responsibility for covert operations from the CIA to the defense department. In large measure attributable to his disenchantment with the CIA over the Bay of Pigs debacle, he approved three National Security Action Memoranda in late June: NSAM 55, 56, and 57. NSAM 55 drastically reduced the CIA's authority over paramilitary actions by transferring that power to the Joint Chiefs of Staff. NSAM 56 authorized the defense secretary to draft the objectives of paramilitary warfare. And NSAM 57 established the guidelines for planning and implementing such strategy. The CIA would still handle covert operations that fell "within the normal capabilities of the agency"—those "wholly covert or disavowable." NSAM 57, however, tied important activities to the defense department. "Any large paramilitary operation wholly or partially covert which requires significant numbers of militarily trained personnel, [and] amounts of military equipment" will mean those that "exceed normal CIA-controlled stocks and/or military experience of a kind or level" required for such operations. Those bigger needs would become "the primary responsibility of the Department of Defense with [the] CIA in a supporting role."[33]

In early August the president approved part of the Staley Report. He raised the ARVN's size by 30,000 while deferring the balance of the requested increase. Hopefully, the war would be about over by the time the ARVN reached the 200,000 level in late 1962. The group had recommended 200,000 if the insurgency did not abate and 270,000 if it notably intensified. President Kennedy emphasized that Diem must agree to a plan for using these new forces. The issue of a U.S. troop deployment remained unsettled.[34]

South Vietnam appeared to be on the verge of adopting counterinsurgency strategy. The government had included a national counterinsurgency plan in a twenty-page field command directive for the ARVN entitled, "Concepts of Pacification Operations." It focused on psywar techniques, military measures, civic action, and civil–military cooperation. To share the successful features of the Malayan experience, Robert G. K. Thompson, Britain's former Permanent Secretary of Defense in the Malayan Federation and an expert in guerrilla warfare, would soon be in Saigon to head the civic action and civil intelligence aspects of the British Advisory Mission. A special South Vietnamese delegation was also to leave for Malaya to study the methods used by the Special Police Force that had led the successful antiguerrilla campaign.[35]

Such measures proved necessary in light of the sudden upswing in Vietcong activity during the fall of 1961. Lansdale's January warning had been correct. From September to October of 1961 the Lao Dong party in North Vietnam upgraded the Central Office for Vietnam (COSVN) and

soon afterward approved a resolution calling for greater military and political resistance against the Americans in Vietnam. NLF operations quickly
intensified.[36]

"The Vietcong," *Time* magazine reported in mid-September, "are everywhere: furtive little bands of Communist guerrillas, dressed in black
peasant pajamas or faded khakis tossing grenades into isolated villages in
the rice fields in the south." Veteran China observer Henry Luce ran the
magazine, lending credibility to the story. Born in China as the son of
Christian missionaries, Luce had witnessed the Communists' rise to power
and warned against their doctrines. "If the U.S. cannot or will not save
South Viet Nam from the Communist assault, no Asian nation can ever
again feel safe in putting its faith in the U.S.—and the fall of all Southeast
Asia would only be a matter of time."[37]

Earlier in September, Vietcong actions surged in the Second Corps
area, along the Laotian–Cambodian border, and in the Central Plateau.
Armed with submachine guns, machine guns, automatic rifles, and mortars, the Vietcong seized control of southern Laos and most of the northern border of South Vietnam and would escalate their military operations
once the rainy season had ended. The most alarming incident came at one
in the morning of September 18, when nearly a thousand Vietcong forces
wielding rifles and machetes broke through the earth and barbed-wire bar-
ricade to seize the provincial capital of Phuoc Vinh, located less than sixty
miles north of Saigon. The fifty-man Civil Guard unit put up little resistance, and the two ARVN ranger companies on patrol nearby fled into the
jungle, their leader afterward lamely explaining that he had wisely laid in
wait "to ambush the guerrillas when they withdrew."[38]

The aftermath of the Vietcong assault on Phuoc Vinh proved as shocking as the event itself. Casualties numbered nearly eighty villagers, forty-
two of them dead. In the course of holding the area for about six hours, the
Vietcong confiscated a hundred rifles and thousands of rounds of ammunition before releasing 250 accused Communists from the local jail. After
staging a "people's trial" before distraught villagers, they beheaded the
provincial chief and his assistant in the marketplace for committing "crimes
against the people."[39]

No incident prior to Phuoc Vinh so graphically revealed the Diem
regime's inability to protect its people. The Vietcong had captured its first
provincial capital and for the second time during the past eighteen months
had executed a provincial chief. Although Phuoc Vinh had been particularly vulnerable to the Vietcong because of the thick jungle cover outside
the province, the attack on an area so close to Saigon demonstrated again
that infiltration through Laos had soared to an alarming level. At stake was
not only the Mekong Delta but all of South Vietnam.[40]

The state department in Washington approved several emergency measures to counter the growing crisis. The ARVN, Civil Guard, and Self-Defense Corps would undergo accelerated training and receive night lights, more dogs, and portable communication devices to facilitate patrols. They would also get more barbed wire, upgraded small arms, mines to close trails and protect outposts, and bulldozers for clearing the thickly forested regions. South Vietnam's Air Force would soon have more Caribou and other kinds of aircraft, along with defoliants, manioc killer, and napalm for use along the Laotian and DMZ frontiers.[41]

Less than two weeks after the attack on Phuoc Vinh, Diem showed his growing alarm by reversing his stand against a bilateral treaty and calling for a mutual defense pact with the United States. His request had resulted from the deteriorating situation in Laos, the growing infiltration out of that country, and the probability that the lack of Anglo–French support would prevent the United States from taking action in accordance with the SEATO Treaty. Most important, the latest Vietcong assaults would undermine national confidence in his rule. Diem sought a public assurance from the United States that it would not let his country fall to the Communists.[42]

Diem's proposal, perhaps surprisingly, attracted little interest in Washington. A mutual treaty would help only South Vietnam without providing the United States any leverage over Diem. Such a pact would cause serious problems over the Geneva Accords, SEATO, and the constitutional provision requiring Senate approval. The state department recommended action only under the collective defense principles contained in the SEATO Treaty.[43] Given the heightened Vietcong activities and the president's opposition to direct U.S. military action in the war, the White House had no interest in a bilateral treaty that would make the United States a wartime ally of South Vietnam.

The Kennedy administration continued gathering evidence of Vietcong infiltration in its effort to persuade the United Nations to condemn Hanoi's aggressions. In mid-August the president had sent to South Vietnam William Jorden, a former *New York Times* correspondent and current member of the state department's Policy Planning Council, to document infiltration from the north. In his late September report, Jorden cited convincing evidence from Saigon that North Vietnam directed the insurgency: North Vietnamese Communist party resolutions and declarations calling for a "liberation movement" in the south; propaganda highlighting the central role of the Lao Dong party (Communist); information on the Vietcong's intelligence and infiltration routes; interrogation notes of Vietcong prisoners who had entered the south from Laos; the meal record found at a substation, which revealed the high level of manpower infiltration during a three-month period; the diaries of a substation commander citing matériel brought from the north and of a Vietcong soldier's trek through Laos and into South Vietnam; Vietcong maps printed in Hanoi and a medical chart printed in Beijing; Soviet bloc medical supplies taken from a Vietcong unit; and aerial photographs of Vietcong bases in Cambodia. The chances were slim of securing a U.N. condemnation of Hanoi, but the presence of a U.N. observer mission might curtail Communist actions. Jorden concluded that there was "external interference in the affairs of South Vietnam by the Communists and, specifically, by the North Vietnamese."[44]

A National Intelligence Estimate substantiated Jorden's findings. The CIA reported that armed Vietcong numbered about 16,000, including a jump by 4,000 in the last three months. One-fifth of the Vietcong's strength came from the north through the mountain trails of southern Laos; the great bulk of the cadres, however, came from the 90,000 Vietnamese Communist forces who had migrated to North Vietnam during the 1954–55 evacuation of Vietnamese Communist army units after the Indochina War. These experienced guerrilla fighters, most of them former Vietminh from southern and central Vietnam, had returned to their homes in the late 1950s and were now fighting in South Vietnam. Although some of the Vietcong's weapons had come from North Vietnam, no one had made a positive identification of Communist-bloc military goods. Their arms were primarily of U.S. or French origin, most of them left over from the Indochina War or captured from South Vietnamese forces. Thus the huge majority of Vietcong recruits were transplanted South Vietnamese who had trained in the north and, with Hanoi's help and organization, had easily infiltrated back into the south. According to one source in the ARVN, "trying to locate crossing points [at the] SVN/Laos border [was] like trying to tell which hole in a sieve water comes out of."[45]

It is not clear that the White House knew this in 1961, but evidence compiled for a state department report in 1968 (corroborated by Hanoi's official history) suggested that North Vietnamese regular army involvement had begun in the south by late 1961. Documentation regarding the charge against the People's Army of Vietnam (PAVN) came from interrogations of five crew members captured on a North Vietnamese sampan near Danang in 1961. One was a PAVN officer who had been in the Vietminh during the 1940s and received training in 1959 as a Vietcong liaison with South Vietnam. On his first mission south, he met with an agent at a museum in Danang and traveled with him to the north; two months later he accompanied him back to the south. When captured in 1961, the PAVN officer had become cell chief and commander of the sampan, and he had made six visits to the south. Each time he came to Danang, he transported long messages written on onion skin paper from a liaison officer in the north to a female Vietcong agent in Danang. On his last voyage south, he carried coastal maps, a Minox camera for photographing identification papers, and other useful documents. His only mission, he declared, was to pass documents between Liaison Bureau posts. The second prisoner was a PAVN Warrant Officer assigned to a Liaison Bureau, who had made more than seven trips south with the PAVN officer mentioned above. The third prisoner was a member of the Lao Dong party, who in 1957 took a six-day political course administered by the Fatherland Front. The following year he and two others—now prisoners in late 1961—operated a sampan that made more than seventeen voyages transporting materials and agents between the north and south.[46]

All these pieces of evidence highlighted the central enigma in America's involvement in Vietnam—that of defining the conflict. Was it a civil war or a war of aggression waged from the outside? Or was it a combination? From the U.S. perspective, the fighting had originated in an offensive engineered by Hanoi. South Vietnam was a sovereign nation under siege by another nation. But North Vietnam's view was markedly different and, legally speaking, on sounder ground: The provisional military demarcation line dividing Vietnam in 1954, according to the Geneva Accords, was temporary and did not create a separate nation of South Vietnam. All difficulties between north and south were domestic in nature, meaning that men and goods arriving from the north did not constitute outside infiltration but were merely internal assistance to fellow countrymen threatened by the U.S.-sponsored Diem regime. In short, it was a revolutionary war. Hanoi's purpose was that of the signatories to the Geneva Accords: to reunify Vietnam, which meant that the conflict did not involve outside interests.

Herein lay the problem facing the United States: how to convince the world that South Vietnam was a nation under siege from external, Communist-led forces. Nowhere in the Geneva agreements did the signatories denominate two sovereign governments in Vietnam. Nowhere was there reference to a country called South Vietnam. The burden of proving North Vietnamese aggression (perhaps aided or encouraged by the Soviets or Communist Chinese) rested on the United States. And even if the Kennedy administration amassed incontrovertible evidence of such infiltration, Hanoi could point to the Geneva Accords in declaring the conflict domestic in nature and of no concern to the United States. The outside aggressors, according to North Vietnam, were the imperialistic Americans seeking to reestablish a Western colony by manipulating their puppet regime in Saigon. Popular opposition to Diem had grown, Hanoi's leaders declared, justifying assistance to their southern countrymen as a critical step toward reunifying Vietnam. At a Politburo meeting in Hanoi in October 1961, Ho Chi Minh emphasized the importance of continuing guerrilla warfare as one step toward a victory that could come only "bit by bit." The United States could prove nothing significant by demonstrating Hanoi's assistance to the insurgency.[47]

III

To halt the alleged infiltration, Rostow proposed a border control plan that the Joint Chiefs of Staff roundly rejected. He called for 25,000 SEATO forces to protect the seventeenth parallel and the Laotian and Cambodian frontiers. Such a move, he argued, would raise Diem's spirits while intimidating both the Chinese and the Russians as well as the North Vietnamese. The proposal would not work, the joint chiefs insisted. It would spread SEATO forces too thinly over several hundred miles of territory, exposing them to attack or permitting the Vietcong to maneuver around them. They would also operate in the areas of weakest defense against a North Vietnamese or Communist Chinese assault. The placement of military forces along the seventeenth parallel was useless because the Vietcong seldom traversed this area. Furthermore, Hanoi might interpret the move as the first step toward an all-out attack and escalate its involvement.[48]

The joint chiefs wanted to send *American* troops into Laos. Within the broad context of protecting Southeast Asia, they argued, the military defense of Laos was premiere. The loss of the central and northern part of this country would open three-fourths of Thailand's border to Communist military assault. The loss of southern Laos would expose both Thailand and South Vietnam along with Cambodia. At least three divisions of U.S. troops plus another two divisions of support units were needed to stop the Vietcong and protect Laos. Rather than dispatching its forces throughout Southeast Asia, the United States should focus on Laos and thereby safeguard that country along with Thailand and South Vietnam. If "politically unacceptable," the joint chiefs offered a "limited interim course of action" that would help South Vietnam regain its own lands while freeing its forces to take the offensive against the Vietcong.[49]

The joint chiefs renewed their call for SEATO Plan 5, which aimed at establishing a defense perimeter along the Mekong River. The first step was to station a brigade-sized force of 12,000 men (with U.S. air and logistic support) in the Central Highlands near Pleiku, just opposite major Vietcong infiltration routes and targets. Another measure was to maintain outside Southeast Asia a central reserve of 5,000 men, including one American unit of brigade, all ready to move into the area if needed. The joint chiefs also wanted the freed-up South Vietnamese troops to intensify counterguerrilla warfare, and they sought to broaden the rules of engagement to allow the SEATO commander to take actions outside South Vietnam. This approach would prove America's "determination to stand firm against further communist advances world-wide." The United States must not become so "preoccupied with Berlin" that it ignored Southeast Asia, which was "more critical from a military viewpoint."[50]

Available forces included one U.S. Brigade Task Force Team stationed in Thailand. SEATO ground and air units would position themselves in South Vietnam to protect its border touching Laos down to Cambodia, except for that part of the seventeenth parallel held by South Vietnamese forces. One division of SEATO ground forces (about 11,000) would locate in the high plateau of Pleiku, freeing the ARVN to take the offensive elsewhere. The United States would contribute 5,000 ground troops of 9,600 total, with another 850 in the air component. The total SEATO force, including support personnel, would be 22,800, including 13,200 Americans. U.S. naval forces from the Seventh Fleet would backstop SEATO operations either by halting Vietcong sea infiltration or by providing a carrier strike potential.[51]

The joint chiefs then set out the rules of engagement. SEATO forces could take any action deemed essential to their security. They could go on the offensive only if the Vietcong endangered the borders of South Vietnam or the SEATO forces themselves. Such action included the use of SEATO air and ground contingents in Laos. If North Vietnam intervened militarily, SEATO could approve air strikes against military targets in that country. If North Vietnamese regulars intervened, the SEATO command would be enlarged from its one-division status to twelve divisions, along with seven Regimental Combat Teams and five battalions. Together, the joint chiefs confidently asserted, these SEATO forces could defeat North Vietnam. The United States would contribute two army divisions, one marine division/ wing team, and five air force tactical squadrons then deployed in Thailand and South Vietnam. U.S. forces would jump from 13,200 to 129,000, a figure that did not include those from the navy. One of these divisions must come from the continental United States, which would necessitate calling up one division plus others to maintain the nation's strategic reserve.[52]

If the Chinese Communists intervened, questions would arise about whether to attack certain targets in south China with conventional weapons or to use nuclear weapons against targets directly supporting Chinese movements in Laos. To counter such Chinese action, SEATO forces would need to grow to fifteen divisions and eight Regimental Combat Teams (278,000 men). The United States would contribute three ground divisions deployed in Thailand and South Vietnam, along with one marine division/wing team, ready for amphibious operations against North Vietnam. Two divisions and additional air forces would come from the continental United States, which entailed two more divisions along with other forces needed to keep the strategic reserve.[53]

In the event of a North Vietnamese or Chinese involvement, SEATO would defend all of Southeast Asia. Such action included air and naval attacks, air and naval interdiction of communications lines, and an all-out air and naval offensive intended to destroy the enemy's war-making capacity.[54]

The pressure for U.S. combat troops had become inexorable. From the office of International Security Affairs, William Bundy urged McNamara to pursue an "early and hard-hitting" military program headed by SEATO forces. The time "*is* really now or never" for stopping the Vietcong. The administration had a 70 percent chance of providing Diem an opportunity to win the war. "The 30% chance," Bundy continued, "is that we would wind up like the French in 1954; white men can't win this kind of fight." Alexis Johnson submitted a state department paper entitled "Concept of Intervention in Vietnam," which advocated the initial use of about 60,000 U.S. combat forces, followed by more "at the earliest stage that is politically feasible." They could fight any enemy contingents "encountered in any reasonable proximity to the border or threatening the SEATO forces," and they could engage in "hot pursuit" into both Laos and Cambodia. According to the *Pentagon Papers*, the primary objective was to inject U.S. combat troops into Vietnam, "with the nominal excuse for doing so quite secondary."[55]

Taylor did not support the joint chiefs' assessment. He informed the president that SEATO Plan 5 aimed to counter overt aggression (which did not exist) and offered no means of coping with growing infiltration out of southern Laos. Even if the plan were feasible, the problem remained of securing contributions from member nations. The so-called SEATO force would be primarily American soldiers, raising the question of whether the United States had the necessary manpower to meet its commitments to Berlin and NATO while pursuing this broadly based action in Southeast Asia. Taylor thought the present military size insufficient to meet both obligations. The administration must decide whether to mobilize more troops or to accept the limitations on the nation's military capabilities in Southeast Asia "as a permanent fact."[56]

In the midst of this growing dispute over a deepened U.S. involvement in the war, correspondent Theodore H. White again urged the president to resist the temptation to send U.S. combat troops to South Vietnam. They would receive little local assistance because Diem had failed to mobilize his people against the Communists. The presence of U.S. troops would arouse "race-hatred, hatred of the white man in general, originally of the French, now converted by clever Communist tactics into a hatred of Americans." It was not wise to make a military commitment to the malaria-ridden Mekong Valley and "so far from the main arena of action" in Berlin. "This South Viet-Nam thing is a real bastard to solve." The United States could either withdraw or allow younger military officers to "knock off Diem in a coup" and hope for the best from a military regime. U.S. troops could not succeed without a South Vietnamese government capable of inspiring its people to oppose communism to the death.[57]

At a White House meeting on the morning of October 11, President Kennedy approved a special mission to South Vietnam that was clearly military in thrust and membership. Headed by Taylor, it included Rostow, Lansdale, Cottrell, Jorden, and representatives from CINCPAC, the CIA, and the defense department. No high-ranking state department official accompanied the mission, leaving Rostow as the only member comparable to Taylor in rank but, as the headstrong general made clear, acting as his deputy. Rusk had condoned this arrangement because he too considered Vietnam as primarily a military issue whose resolution belonged to the secretary of defense. Kennedy sought to discourage speculation about the imminent introduction of U.S. combat troops by announcing the mission's purpose as an economic survey, although the truth was that he authorized it to consider establishing a U.S. military presence in that beleaguered country by increasing assistance and training of South Vietnamese soldiers and providing helicopters, light aircraft, trucks, and other means of ground transportation.[58]

President Kennedy made additional decisions that gave impetus to the ongoing secret war both in Laos and now developing rapidly in Vietnam. In the ground war, he authorized U.S. advisers to accompany South Vietnamese commandos in attacking Communist holdings at Tchepone and other key points in Laos; in the air war, he approved the use of planes in an operation code-named "Farmgate," which involved air commandos from the recently established U.S. Air Force's 4400th Combat Crew Training Squadron (known as "Jungle Jims"). Ostensibly sent to train South Vietnamese pilots, crew, and support personnel in counterinsurgency tactics, the air commandos were volunteers who had undergone extensive screening before their acceptance into a program that was combat-oriented. This elite group resulted largely from LeMay's efforts to create a Special Forces unit in the air force as a counterpart to that of the army's. Indeed, it collaborated with the army's Special Forces along the frontier. As a mirror to the sprightly attire that President Kennedy had selected for the army's Green Berets, the air commandos wore outfits of LeMay's choosing: fatigues and Australian-style bush hats with brims tilted upward. The air commandos' officially stated purpose of training pilots was a subterfuge; their leader, Colonel Benjamin King, claimed that LeMay had emphasized training the Vietnamese for combat.[59]

The Jungle Jim Squadron was easily adaptable to counterinsurgency warfare. The aged and slow-flying, propeller-driven planes were lightweight enough to land on sod runways and maneuver slowly over the jungle while engaging in reconnaissance, bombing, airlifts, and close support actions for ground troops. President Kennedy knew that they would become involved in combat. He agreed with McGeorge Bundy that the Jungle Jims' "initial purpose" was combat training, implying that their responsibilities would expand. Gilpatric's notes on that October 11 meeting stated that they would be part of MAAG's training mission and were not for combat "at the present time."[60]

The U.S. Air Force quickly joined the war. On October 12, it dispatched the first contingent of a training squadron to a rundown, former French air strip at Bien Hoa Air Base just above Saigon. In another poorly disguised effort to hide their involvement in the fighting, the U.S. pilots wore civilian clothes while Vietnamese military personnel sat at their sides, initially flying sixteen twin-engined C-47 (changed to SC-47 after modification) transports, eight T-28 fighter-bombers (armor-plated and packing two machine guns and 1,500 pounds of rockets and bombs) from the navy, and eight B-26 twin-engine attack bombers (carrying machine guns and 6,000 pounds of rockets and bombs) from Air Force Reserve units—the last renamed "Reconnaissance Bombers" (RB-26s) in a transparent attempt to circumvent the Geneva ban on sending bombers into Indochina. In early December, when the U.S. pilots arrived in Vietnam (125 commissioned officers and 235 enlisted personnel), McNamara approved U.S. participation in combat, as long as someone from the Vietnamese military was on the plane. This directive was a mere formality since the line between training and fighting was never clear. Questions from the press received the stock answer: "No USAF pilot has ever flown in tactical missions except in the role of tactical instructor."[61]

The president used various tactics to stop the rush to all-out action. In draft instructions to Taylor (which Taylor actually wrote), the general was "to evaluate what could be accomplished by the introduction of SEATO or United States forces into South Vietnam." This statement proved too strong for the president. In a revealing move, he struck it from his final instructions of October 13 and inserted more moderate wording in an attempt to restore balance to the counterinsurgency program. "While the military part of the problem is of great importance in South Vietnam, its political, social, and economic elements are equally significant, and I shall expect your appraisal and your recommendations to take full account of them."[62]

Kennedy had moved more clearly against the employment of combat forces, although he had left the door open by again assigning the matter to further study. Taylor observed that this letter summarized the attitude of the president and most of his advisers and was consistent with the policy he had approved the previous May. In that memo, Kennedy had authorized a counterinsurgency approach based on "mutually supporting actions of a military, political, economic, psychological and covert character." At that time and later, however, he considered military measures a necessary prelude to establishing the security needed to permit social, political, and economic changes. He had serious misgivings about interfering in what he termed to *New York Times* columnist Arthur Krock "civil disturbances caused by guerrillas." In a telling observation, the president declared that "it was hard to prove that this wasn't largely the situation in Vietnam." Military correctives alone were not the solution. Success came more by "nation-building rather than in numbers of enemy killed and battles won." Like Rostow, the president hoped that the South Vietnamese would fight well enough to remove any need for U.S. combat units. In a striking maneuver, Kennedy privately arranged for the *New York Times* to run a story that appeared on the front page of the October 15, 1961, edition: "High administration sources said today . . . the President remains strongly opposed to the dispatch of American combat troops to South Vietnam."[63]

The president was not alone in resisting the push for U.S. soldiers. The heart of the problem, according to a U.S. Marine major after three months of firsthand observation, was the *manner* in which the United States extended assistance and advice. MAAG's chief was isolated from military operations, undermining both the morale of his men and their respect for him. Advice went to the South Vietnamese through "awkward and large booklets and directives rendered by tedious translation." The South Vietnamese attitude was "show me, don't tell me." U.S. advice at the field level was good, but not enough advisers were in the field. Some 90 percent of South Vietnam's forces were not engaged in the fighting, with most of them garrisoned except for those holding defensive positions along the northern border. Despite these problems, MAAG showed no sense of urgency: The men worked from 8 to 12 in the morning and from 2 to 5 in the afternoon during the week, and took weekends off. The South Vietnamese, concluded the major, could win the war with suitable advisers along with air, logistical, and technical assistance. U.S. troops were not necessary.[64]

More than one U.S. military officer on the scene in South Vietnam advocated counterinsurgency as the best route to success. The war's outcome, a U.S. Air Force major general insisted, depended on a combination of social, economic, political, and military measures aimed at winning "the hearts and minds of the people." McGarr concurred that "significant military progress cannot be fully effective until this political progress is made." An integrated civic–military program of pacification must develop in the villages and hamlets. A "National Plan" must rest on the "amoeba principle" of clearing key areas and systematically expanding the sanitized regions until the entire country was safe.[65]

McGarr warned that the increased infiltration of guerrillas into South Vietnam had made the situation so perilous that the expected ARVN increments would lead to victories in battle that paradoxically resulted in a defeat in the war. The ARVN had received Ranger training "to the full extent allowed by hot war operations here." And yet, Diem and the Joint Military Staff had severely weakened the ARVN by draining off its best leaders and enlisted men to form more Ranger companies. "What we need to win is National *control and coordination* [emphasis in original] of effort, not just hardware!" The U.S. Army must not "be placed in the position of fighting a losing battle and being charged with the loss." In a prophetic conclusion, McGarr declared that until Washington's civilian leaders realized that the key to victory in South Vietnam was to seal off Laos, "the military will be blamed for a situation here which is not of its own making and for which it has not been adequately supported by our country."[66]

WITHIN THE FEVERED PITCH of the Cold War, the pressure for a military solution in South Vietnam continued to swell. Even Taylor shifted his position to reveal an inclination for direct U.S. military action. If the counterinsurgency effort failed, he warned Kennedy, the White House must "do the unpalatable." At a news conference on October 11, the president announced the Taylor mission, stressing the ongoing search for ways to preserve South Vietnam's independence. He knew that the move would leave the appearance of an imminent decision to order U.S. troops to the troubled region. In response to a reporter's question about sending Americans into combat, Kennedy fueled more speculation by declaring that in light of stepped-up Vietcong activities in South Vietnam, Taylor would provide "an educated military guess" as to the status of Diem's government and "we can come to conclusions as what is best to do." At a White House meeting two days later, the president expressed great concern over the spate of stories declaring that the United States was about to dispatch combat troops. And not only was this notion coming from the press. Lemnitzer wrote Felt that Taylor's public objective was to assess whether the present aid program needed expansion; but, the joint chiefs chair added in a chilling forecast, "you should know (and this is to be held most closely) General Taylor will also give most discreet consideration to [the] introduction of U.S. Forces if he deems such action absolutely essential."[67]

5

SUBTERFUGE IN THE DELTA

[Any U.S. soldiers sent to the Mekong Delta must arrive]
expecting to fight . . . and [be] prepared for [an] extended
commitment.

Lieutenant General Lionel McGarr, October 30, 1961

T HE INVOLVEMENT of the U.S. military in South Vietnam became
more pronounced in the fall of 1961 as the two governments
graduated from an advisory relationship to a limited partnership.
The situation in Saigon had become so threatening that the Kennedy administration encountered growing support either to send combat troops
or, a few observers whispered, to promote a coup. Infiltration from the
north steadily increased, causing more of Washington's policymakers to
advocate a direct assault on Hanoi. Rusk assured Indian officials that Hanoi
had masterminded the Vietcong's growing activities in South Vietnam.
The evidence for this charge, he insisted, came from captured documents,
confessions of prisoners, Hanoi's public support for the Vietcong, and the
growing number of Vietcong entering South Vietnam through the Laotian corridor following the cease-fire. Such increases had become clear in
the High Plateau opposite southern Laos and from battalion-sized Vietcong
assaults bolstered by PAVN regulars from North Vietnam. From 25 to 40
percent of the Vietcong now came from the north and provided leadership
for the insurgency. "Without them there would be no war in Viet Nam."[1]

Diem meanwhile continued to frustrate U.S. advisers by refusing to
delegate meaningful authority to ARVN officers in the field. There was
reason behind what appeared to be an unreasonable stand. The move, he
well knew, entailed the concession of power to those in the military who
bitterly opposed him. Diem had not forgotten the generals' coup attempt a
year earlier. Indeed, he feared his senior military commanders as much if
not more than the Vietcong, which helps to explain his sudden interest in
a foreign military force that would be under his personal control. Ironically, victory for either antagonist in the war—the ARVN or the Vietcong—
ensured his own fall from power. The growing crisis led the Taylor mission
to recommend a limited partnership that included U.S. combat troops.

I

PRESSURE HAD CONTINUED to mount for a deepened U.S. military commit-ment to South Vietnam as the Taylor mission prepared to leave Washing-ton on October 17, 1961. In a paper given to the general before his departure for Saigon, the defense department and other government agencies ex-plored a wide range of advisory and patrol assignments for U.S. combat forces—none advocating a direct engagement with the Vietcong but all necessitating a rise in numbers that would violate the Geneva Accords of 1954. If Admiral Felt condoned American soldiers only as a last resort, he nonetheless insisted that the way to shut down infiltration from Laos was to dispatch a large contingent of ground forces. Preferably, they would be from SEATO and include Americans, although he was not averse to send-ing U.S. soldiers on their own. Their responsibility for the moment, Felt told Taylor in an extensive briefing at CINCPAC headquarters in Hono-lulu, should be to perform logistic chores for engineering and helicopter units—*not* to engage in combat. Rostow, however, advocated a "limited but systematic harassment" of North Vietnam by U.S. planes authorized to cross the seventeenth parallel and engage in hit-and-run actions as well as to drop and remove landing parties assigned to destroy military targets. Communist strategy aimed at circumventing the United States's central strength in the region—the Seventh Fleet—while exploiting its "main weak-nesses": Diem and "the political limitations on the role of white men in an Asian guerrilla war." The United States must likewise focus on North Vietnam's "fundamental weakness": the "Hanoi-Haiphong complex."[2]

Diem's interest in outside assistance fed the call for an expanded U.S. military involvement that came from American advisers in both Saigon and Washington. Nolting supported a military commitment that included fighter-bomber and transport aircraft, SEATO ground forces, and U.S. combat troops, all to end infiltration across the seventeenth parallel and the Laotian and Cambodian frontiers. The heightened Vietcong threat had led Diem to reverse his opposition to a bilateral defense treaty with the United States and, reported Nolting, to seek combat forces—"though ostensibly for guard duty, not for combat unless attacked." According to Nolting, Diem feared that the Communists planned to isolate Hué from Saigon, slicing South Vietnam in half and promoting its collapse. The premier's alarm had become so intense that he would accept long-time hated Chinese Nationalist soldiers as part of his defense force.[3]

In the meantime, problems had developed between Taylor and Lansdale, the latter accompanying the mission at the president's request. When Kennedy approached him about the assignment, Lansdale thought he was to go alone and only later realized that Taylor headed the mission and did not want him as a member. "He was just getting a ride on my airplane," Taylor later remarked. He had called Lansdale to the White House, where he had a list of about eight people who would join the mission. Lansdale noticed a line drawn across the list just above his name.

"What's that line?" asked Lansdale.

"People above that get in to see presidents and everything and the others are working parties."

During the long flight to Saigon, relations between the men sharply deteriorated. Taylor had called an organizational meeting of all those on board the plane. "Everybody give me a list of things that you think you're qualified to look into." Lansdale instead submitted a long list of people he knew in Vietnam who could provide insights into its problems. Taylor termed it "a very interesting list" but told Lansdale not to see Diem or any others.

"Look, these are old friends of mine. If you'd like, why I'll do anything I can. You can hit them high, and I'll hit them low if you want. We can get some things done that way."

"You aren't on our protocol list, so you don't attend any of these calls on the President." Taylor then asked Lansdale to "please work on building a defense on the border."

"What sort of defense?"

"A system of fortifications or a wire like the Iron Curtain in Europe."

"Good God, you aren't going to do that, are you?"

"Look into it."

Lansdale was to determine the costs and manpower needed to build an electronic fence along all of South Vietnam's borders that would end Vietcong infiltration. "That's not my subject," Lansdale protested. "I'm no good at that. . . . [It's] a waste of my time." Taylor refused to budge, and Lansdale did not argue. He knew he could assign the task to MAAG and it would cost billions of dollars that Washington would not approve.

"Well," Lansdale snidely remarked, "I'm an old friend of Diem's. I can't go to Vietnam without seeing him. I'll probably see him alone." In a razor-like tone, he posed the question, "Is there anything you want me to ask him?" Taylor abruptly ended the discussion.[4]

Lansdale's premonition about meeting with Diem rang true. On deplaning in Saigon, Taylor immediately found himself surrounded by reporters while Lansdale, sidestepping the group, suddenly found himself face to face with Diem's personal secretary. "The president would like to see you immediately." "I better check with my boss on this," Lansdale replied. Seeing Taylor busy with the press, Lansdale pulled Rostow aside and informed him of the surprising development. "Diem has invited me to the palace," Lansdale explained. "I might be there for dinner. I don't know." "Go ahead," Rostow declared. In a statement that Lansdale must have relished making, he asked, "Would you please tell the boss this isn't a protocol call? I'm going to see an old friend."[5]

At Independence Palace that evening, Lansdale learned that the situation had worsened since his visit less than a year ago and that Diem had compounded his difficulties by surrendering too much authority to his brother, Ngo Dinh Nhu. That evening, while Taylor talked with the press and Lansdale was en route to his dinner engagement, Diem delivered an alarming address to the National Assembly, declaring a national emergency in light of the Vietcong threat. As the two men dined in the palace, Diem expressed concern about the Taylor mission. "What's this mission doing here?" "What are you all up to?" "What's he like? What's he want? What's he going to ask me?" "I don't know," Lansdale replied. "Why don't you wait, and they'll be in here to have a meeting with you tomorrow, and you'll find out. You can handle yourself all right on this."[6]

Then the conversation became personal as they talked as long-time friends. Diem's nephew, Nhu's son, was there—and had a new toy missile, a rocket with a launcher. Lansdale tried to explain to the young boy how it worked while squatting on the floor next to Diem as he continued to eat. "You don't point this at him," Lansdale warned. He had no idea about the strength of the spring and joked about "whether it would take his head off." Lansdale taught the boy to launch the rocket into the ceiling's ventilating fan. "We spent dinner, actually, taking parachutes and things out of the ventilating fans, and the kid and I were climbing up a ladder to get these things out. . . . This was very different from an official protocol meeting."[7]

After dinner, Nhu entered the room and sat next to Lansdale. From that point, the atmosphere became impersonal as Nhu repeatedly interrupted the conversation by answering every question Lansdale asked Diem. This was a "very strange relationship," Lansdale later remarked. Diem seemed "very hesitant in his talk," as if there was "something physical as well as a mental hazard or something." Diem "wasn't as sure of himself as he had been when I had seen him less than a year before." Lansdale had talked with Diem just after the assassination attempt of 1960, and he had shown no lack of self-assurance. "So it hadn't been an outside, physical happening like that that had caused the change." Diem was not superstitious; he was "very rational" and "pragmatic." But he had changed.[8]

Diem asked whether he should request American troops. Lansdale expressed surprise. "What do you want U.S. troops for? Are things that bad here? Have you reached that point in your affairs that you're going to need them to stay alive? Do you need them?"

"I asked you a question," Diem replied.

Lansdale countered, "I'm asking you a very legitimate question on this thing. Are you ready to admit that you have so lost control of your situation that you can't cope with it here? You'd have to do that before you ever turn around and ask for American troops in here."

"I shouldn't have asked you that, should I?"

"Answer my question," Lansdale demanded. Nhu interjected to explain that the troops would bring stability. "I asked your brother this," Lansdale sharply retorted, "and I want to know for sure."

"No, we can still handle things," Diem finally responded.

Almost in a whisper, Lansdale advised, "Stay with that then." As he later explained, "I was against U.S. troops going [into] combat [there]. I'd seen the French and figured we'd do much what they did—even with good intentions." We would be "dirty foreigners."[9]

Especially disturbing was Nhu's domineering presence. Diem, Lansdale suggested, had come so heavily under his brother's control that the locus of power had shifted out of the premier's hands. Lansdale finally tired of Nhu's repeated interruptions to questions addressed to Diem. "Can't the two of us talk together?" Lansdale impatiently asked the premier. "Your brother can be in on this, but is he running things or are you?" After a tense moment of silence, Diem explained that, out of exasperation over the continual stories of coup plots, he had authorized his brother to ferret out conspirators. The result, Lansdale later remarked, was a wave of brutal arrests that highlighted Nhu's power and made a mockery of the country's alleged move toward democracy. "It shocked me to see Nhu taking over the place. That worried me."[10]

Immediately afterward, Lansdale briefed Taylor about the meeting with Diem and Nhu, but he did not believe that the general fully comprehended the issues threatening to tear the country apart. "Very few of the military minds," Lansdale explained years later, "understood the problem they were facing or who the enemy was or how he was trying to fight, the political basis behind their military activities, the political results they were trying to achieve through their military and other psychological and economic actions." Lansdale lamented, "We went out to kill the enemy—a very different thing—and wouldn't try to understand him." Taylor feared a conventional war with North Vietnam or Communist China more than he did the insurgency and, like Rostow, leaned toward a stronger U.S. military commitment to Saigon that included possible direct action against Hanoi.[11]

Lemnitzer's analysis reinforced Taylor's feelings. The joint chiefs' chair recognized the advisability of using counterinsurgency tactics where applicable. But despite the similarities between the British experience in Malaya and the situation in South Vietnam, the differences were so striking that the latter required military action. The rebels in Malaya had been denied a safe haven in neighboring Thailand; the Vietcong enjoyed that privilege in both Laos and Cambodia. The racial features of the Chinese insurgents in Malaya had distinguished them from the native populace; the Vietcong were not discernible from South Vietnamese loyalists. Food was scarce in Malaya but plentiful in Vietnam, meaning that the Vietcong had ample supplies. The most important differences, however, lay in leadership and field performance: The British had commanded well-trained Commonwealth troops, whereas the ARVN forces suffered from inadequate training and low morale that became evident in their poor fighting record. Despite all these British advantages, it took twelve years to squelch an insurgency in Malaya that was considerably weaker than the one led by the Vietcong.[12]

The most immediate need in South Vietnam, Lemnitzer insisted, was a massive infusion of military aid. In two other successful government campaigns against terrorists—in the Philippines and in Burma—the chief remedy was a concentrated military campaign. Indeed, the Vietcong's increasingly larger units had focused their assaults on the poorly trained Civil Guard rather than the army, not only inflicting heavy losses on those units but confiscating their weapons and supplies. McGarr warned that excessive dependence on the Civil Guard for police functions would undermine the counterinsurgency effort.[13]

Taylor's inclination toward an expanded U.S. military involvement received further support during his initial talks with Diem on October 18. The premier did not heed Lansdale's advice against requesting U.S. combat troops. Diem initially called for additional South Vietnamese armed forces along with more Civil Guardsmen and Self-Defense Corps to protect the hamlets against growing infiltration from Laos. Taylor urged greater offensive action, but Diem pointed out how easily the Vietcong disappeared in the endless trails leading into and out of South Vietnam. The Vietcong's objective, Diem explained, was to launch more raids on central Vietnam in an effort to draw the ARVN from the south and expose Saigon to attack. Increased infiltration through Laos had necessitated his request for either U.S. or SEATO troops to guard the border. His people would welcome a foreign troop presence, he insisted, because they considered the Communist threat of international origin and thought a formal defense commitment from the United States the only guarantee against a withdrawal similar to that about to take place in Laos.[14]

Taylor's conference with the ARVN's field commander, General Duong Van Minh, made clear that no degree of military enlargement could by itself remedy Diem's inept rule and deep suspicion of his army. The six-foot-tall, burly general surprised Taylor by so openly criticizing Diem, particularly to a non-Vietnamese. "I had not yet acquired experience with the Vietnamese bent for running down their closest associates to the casual passer-by." "Big Minh," as the general was known, had been instrumental in the regime's late 1955 victory over the Binh Xuyen, a notorious organization of thugs who had run Saigon's brothels and police force. Minh had a warm personality and was popular with the people and with his men, but he carried an impressive yet empty title because of Diem's distrust of his military leaders. Minh moaned that the situation was "extremely grave" because of poor leadership in Saigon. The regime blatantly courted certain groups, classes, races, and even religions. It selected only those military personnel as provincial chiefs whose authority derived from Diem. Two chains of command had resulted: The provincial chief controlled the Civil Guard and Self-Defense Corps, and the generals nominally commanded those ARVN troops sent on major operations. Cooperation between the fighting groups proved impossible. Even though Diem had declared a national emergency, he had not mobilized all the nation's resources. Furthermore, Minh insisted, Diem wanted "to downgrade the military" by rejecting any delegation of authority to the ARVN's officers. Minh and his colleagues felt that "they were on a plane in a dive, and that they would soon reach a point where it would have to be levelled off or it would be too late."[15]

Diem's own ministers likewise attested to his flaws. Vice President Tho told Taylor that Diem must improve his leadership skills. The peasants supported the Communists out of fear alone and would welcome Saigon's protection. The ARVN had mistakenly prepared for modern warfare when the enemy's guerrilla tactics necessitated ranger forces capable of unconventional fighting. If the government failed to protect the countryside, its people would continue flocking into the cities, causing more economic problems and rampant unrest. Tho blamed Diem and urged a more active U.S. intervention to ensure a better use of arms and aid.[16]

Support for this bleak assessment came from Takashi Oka, a Japanese journalist educated in the United States and now the *Christian Science Monitor*'s East Asia correspondent in Saigon. In a letter to her home office that made its way into President Kennedy's files, she asserted that *Diem* was the problem and that a change in government was imminent—either under U.S. pressure or from an army coup. Diem had "lost all touch with reality" and feared a coup more than he feared the Vietcong. Despite his emergency proclamation, his brother's wife, Madame Nhu, was preoccupied with an attempt to ban nightclub dancers as immoral and put them in paramilitary formations, while Diem sat in long cabinet meetings, absurdly planning the spacing of trees in new agrovilles and land development centers. For the past six months, news correspondents had been able to extract only an unbroken monologue out of Diem that went on for hours without focusing on anything of substance. His refusal to delegate authority had resulted in administrative bottlenecks that obstructed mobilization of resources and seriously damaged the war effort. The Vietnamese did not want to go Communist, Oka insisted. Yet a "clearsighted leader" told her, "If I have to choose between dictatorships, I will choose the Communist one, because it is more efficient."[17]

These grave circumstances caused some White House advisers to ponder the wisdom of dropping Diem. As preparation for a possible change in rule, the state department asked the Saigon embassy to compile a list of persons and groups considered to be acceptable alternatives. In accordance with the Vietnamese constitution, the first choice would be Vice President Tho. Not only was he popular, but he also had the potential to bring together the country's civilian and military leaders. Tho had been a friend of Minh's since their sharing a French jail cell during the early part of the Indochina War. Another viable candidate was the Secretary of State for the Presidency, Nguyen Dinh Thuan, who likewise enjoyed good relations with the army and was once a civilian official in the defense department. A "military caretaker government" under General Minh was acceptable. Casting support for someone already in an official position would ease the transition and arouse support from influential countrymen who found more fault with Diem than the government.[18]

The state department's contingency actions were defensible because Diem's government was in deep trouble, as graphically evidenced by the Vietcong's growing terrorist activities in the areas directly above Saigon. The city was in near panic. Three scenarios seemed possible, none of which could leave Diem in power: a palace revolution, a military coup, or a Communist overthrow of the government. Chances were even for one of the first two, but highly unlikely for the third because the Communists lacked the military strength required. A palace revolution appeared to be under consideration by senior government officials, who welcomed the involvement of moderate anti-Communist figures. Under this arrangement, Diem would remain in office to handle policy issues but leave their execution to an emergency council. Only the military had the capacity to engineer a coup, with its likelihood increasing in proportion to the Vietcong's successes in the field.[19]

II

DESPITE THE STUMBLING of the war effort, the state department wanted to give Diem another chance to make changes. It took a turn toward past policy by advocating a stronger demand for reforms in exchange for continued assistance. President Kennedy should urge Diem to create an Internal Security Council that could activate the Counterinsurgency Plan. Otherwise, the United States would withdraw support. "Such a move would require preparation, secrecy, surprise, and toughness."[20]

Most observers, however, insisted that the key to victory lay in using U.S. troops to halt infiltration. That objective in mind, McGarr warned Taylor that an injection of combat forces had to be substantial in size because of the need to seal the entire border around South Vietnam. The minimum force required was two divisions along with helicopters and other reinforcements. The ARVN would help close the border by consolidating its many isolated posts into a smaller number of larger and more defend-able border bases whose security rested on interlocking patrols. When Rostow explored the possibility of sending U.N. observers to the areas, he had to admit that the border was a virtual "sieve" of countless jungle trails, making tight surveillance impossible.[21]

Another obstruction was the lingering shadow of the past. Diem had survived a number of assaults on his rule. The dilemma was peculiarly his: To reward his most talented officers with greater responsibility carried the seeds of his own destruction; failure to do so would help the Vietcong topple his regime. And this was not the only piece of history that bore heavily on Diem's calculations. His brother, Ngo Dinh Nhu, told Lansdale that the certain neutralization of Laos had stunned the South Vietnamese people. That agreement alone would signal SEATO's collapse and the U.S. abandonment of its resistance to communism. Taylor's visit had provided a huge psychological lift because it suggested impending action. But if noth-ing decisive followed, Nhu implied, the message would become clear that Diem was on his own.[22]

Nhu also argued that the Saigon government was waging the wrong kind of war. The Communists sought tactical victories by the use of terror in securing strategic positions that kept the South Vietnamese people off balance and allowed them no time to prepare a defense. The South Viet-namese likewise needed tactical victories rather than decisive encounters on the field. "We must increase the number of ambushes of the Viet Cong," Nhu insisted. Such tactical conquests required "method and a thorough follow-through which really is quite foreign to Asians." ARVN troops should have "the primary mission of liquidating the Viet Cong ambush on the line of march." The United States must train the officers to take the initiative by "drawing the tiger out of the forest."[23]

The recent Vietcong torture and assassination of Colonel Hoang Thuy Nam, chief of the South Vietnamese Liaison Mission to the International Control Commission (ICC), heightened the alarm in South Vietnam. The Vietcong had long regarded Nam as a major obstacle to its success. Vietcong agents had kidnapped him on October 1, and more than two weeks later, on October 17, authorities pulled his badly mutilated body from the Saigon River close to a bridge on the northern edge of the city. Nam's caretaker of the farm, Nguyen Van Honshow, confessed to providing information about Nam's whereabouts to the Vietcong, who had threatened Honshow and his family if he refused to help. Led by Nguyen Van Chang, a Communist and long-time acquaintance and resident of the same village as Honshow, ten Vietcong members of an organization called the "Front for the Libera-tion of the South" abducted Nam from his farm and killed him.[24]

On the same evening that Nam's body was discovered, the Diem government sent a letter to the ICC, accusing Hanoi of the murder. The next morning the commission asked Saigon for evidence of North Vietnamese complicity. Ambassador Nolting termed this request a major breakthrough since the commission had the obligation to consider all information presented, including that gathered by the Jorden mission about border infiltration. The ICC letter offered Saigon an "unprecedented opportunity" to justify military actions that came into conflict with the Geneva Accords.[25]

The Saigon government argued that Nam's assassination was part of Hanoi's plan to take over South Vietnam. The Lao Dong party (Communist) had passed a resolution in September 1960 designating Hanoi as the linchpin of a revolution intended to overthrow the Saigon government and "liberate the South." Evidence revealed close ties between Hanoi and an organization called "Forces for Liberation of the South," which followed the directives of Le Duan, general secretary of the Lao Dong party. At the Third Party Congress held in Hanoi in September 1960, Le Duan had advocated "subversion and aggression" against the Republic of Vietnam. That same month, the *Hanoi Daily* called for the "overthrow of the dictatorial and Fascist regime of the American–Diemist clique" in Saigon and its replacement with a "national democratic coalition government."[26]

Hanoi, the letter continued, had founded the Forces for Liberation of the South to make it appear that a "spontaneous popular movement" against South Vietnam was under way. In actuality, the organization was subordinate to the Lao Dong party, whose loyalty lay with the Communist leadership in Hanoi. The party's Central Committee had ordered a general offensive in the south aimed at exploiting the unsettled situation in Laos and the rest of Southeast Asia. In February 1960, Radio Hanoi took responsibility for an assault on the military post at Tay Ninh in South Vietnam by the Forces for Liberation of the South. In September 1961, Radio Hanoi called the attack on Phuoc Thanh a party victory. At the last conference of the Interparliamentary Union in Brussels, Belgium, earlier that same month, each delegate received an envelope from the North Vietnamese embassy in Moscow containing propaganda for use by the Forces for Liberation of the South.[27]

The liberation front, according to the Diem regime, was thus the military instrument of expanded Vietcong aggression against South Vietnam. Interrogations of captured Vietcong cadres showed them to be well trained and brought in by sea, across the seventeenth parallel, or through Laos and Cambodia. The total Vietcong in central Vietnam had grown from a thousand at the end of 1959 to five times that number by mid-1961. The Saigon government had secured confessions or diaries establishing many Vietcong as natives of South Vietnam who had regrouped in the north and reentered the south either through Laos or along the coast of Quang Tri Province. Documents seized at Ca Lu showed that from October 1960 to February 1961, the Vietcong had carted in weapons and munitions by sea and mountain trails through Quang Tri (in addition to those transported illegally across the frontiers of Laos and Cambodia). The growing arsenal included machine guns, submachine guns, pistols, carbines, grenades, and grenade launchers.[28]

Vietcong methods had intensified in brutality since the end of 1960. Until then, the Vietminh had sought to undermine the Diem regime by propaganda and terror. But the pace of activity had quickened along with its savagery. Millions of party pamphlets propagated lies about the Saigon government, while the Vietcong engaged in abductions, murders, and mutilations. When the Vietcong hit the capital of Phuoc Thanh province in mid-September 1961, they brazenly executed its chief, his assistant, and ten civil servants and inhabitants, including a woman and child. As recently as October 12, the International Control Commission received reports of 806 deaths and 770 kidnappings. Photographs recorded grisly sights: numerous beheadings of women and children along with government officials and teachers. The Communist party spread the saying, "*Kill the Land Robbers,*" to encourage the wanton seizure of land from Diem's supporters. "*One naily board for each square of land,*" its party members declared in laying metal or bamboo spikes in weeds or marshy areas. Vietcong recruitments also learned to block roads by building thorny bamboo barricades with grenades concealed in the branches. All these horrors, the Diem regime bitterly charged, were basic to the "Machiavellian plan of international Communism" to seize control of South Vietnam.[29]

The Saigon government's assessment of Hanoi's objectives and methods was correct, even if it overestimated North Vietnam's control over the Vietcong. The Lao Dong party in Hanoi had approved a revolutionary war in the south that called for the eventual use of armed force in overthrowing the Diem regime. A campaign of terror had ensued, driven by intimidation, kidnapping, and assassination. Communists led the recently organized National Liberation Front (NLF), but it had attracted a wide following by calling for the overthrow of the "disguised colonialist regime of the US Imperialists and the dictatorial government of NGO DINH DIEM, lackey of the US," and the establishment of "the people's democratic and coalition government." Emphasizing that the U.S.–Diem forces exploited the Vietnamese population, the NLF instructed its cadres to "respect their customs and habits" and "respect local cadres" by "never consider[ing] ourselves as their masters" and always avoiding "the likely embarrassing atmosphere between a host and his guest." Most important, the NLF's organization and direction had come from Communist party leaders in Hanoi. Although they had begun the revolution with the intention of using political tactics to promote the peaceful reunification of Vietnam, Diem's repressive policies had pushed them into a more militant strategy aimed at his forceful overthrow.[30]

The conflict had reached crisis proportions by the time Taylor entered Saigon in October 1961. To anxious South Vietnamese, his visit, combined with Diem's declaration of a national emergency and Colonel Nam's public funeral, underscored the danger. Security seemed so fragile that the government canceled the October 26 National Day celebrations, lamely explaining that it intended to devote the allotted resources to helping those thousands of South Vietnamese left homeless by a recent flood in the Mekong Valley. Particularly disturbing was the lack of confidence felt by senior government and military officials in the premier's capacity to handle the growing crisis. Nolting warned Washington that these two groups might collaborate in a coup.[31]

Taylor noted a "great cloud of doom" in Saigon. South Vietnam suffered from "a deep and pervasive crisis of confidence" resulting from a feared Communist takeover of Laos, the Vietcong's rapid growth, and the hardships resulting from a massive flood in the Mekong Delta. It was a "double crisis of confidence," according to Schlesinger years afterward: "doubt that the United States was really determined to save Southeast Asia; doubt that Diem's methods could really defeat the Viet Cong." The ARVN's military campaign had sputtered due to a lack of intelligence about enemy movements, the hazy command structure, and the static nature of its operations. The Vietcong had taken the offensive, choosing targets at will and openly harassing and intimidating the populace. Although Saigon's atmosphere was explosive, Taylor found no hard evidence of a coup in the making. But loose talk could jell into action.[32]

In these anxious surroundings, the issue of U.S. troops became the paramount topic in the Saigon discussions. Diem bounced back and forth on the issue, at first opposing them before reversing himself in a later meeting. Taylor likewise discerned a need for ground forces after talking with the regime's civilian and military advisers. The devastation in the Mekong Valley, he calculated, provided a fortuitous occasion for introducing combat forces under the appellation of flood control units. Taylor intended to justify their use for well-publicized humanitarian reasons but, in McGarr's revealing statement, "with subsequent retention if desirable." Nolting was not supportive, complaining that these so-called combat engineers would actually be "a self-contained unit" of infantrymen acting "under the rather transparent cover of flood relief." A U.S. troop presence would cause an international uproar over the violation of the Geneva Accords while "shuffling off" the ARVN's war responsibilities to "the much stronger, better equipped Americans." McGarr disagreed. The flood presented "an excellent opportunity to minimize adverse publicity" by disguising U.S. troops as humanitarian relief workers. This approach permitted a withdrawal at any time, and it meshed combat troops with those soldiers specializing in logistics, transportation, and medicine.[33]

The Taylor mission recommended increased numbers of U.S. military personnel and closer cooperation with Saigon. Top priority was an ARVN offensive that hinged on improved intelligence and provincial security, a more mobile army, and a ranger force capable of blocking infiltration from Laos. But Taylor regarded the injection of U.S. military forces as key to success. In a written summation of "personal ideas" that he entitled "Introduction of U.S. Combat Troops" and gave to the Vietnamese, he announced his intention to furnish helicopter reconnaissance of areas in need of a "flood relief task force, largely military in composition," that consisted of engineering, medical, signal, and transportation personnel, as well as combat troops to protect relief workers. "Obviously," Taylor asserted, "such a military force would also provide [a] U.S. military presence in Viet Nam and would constitute [a] military reserve in case of [a] heightened military crisis."[34]

Taylor reported Diem's concurrence with this "new phase in the war." The mood in Vietnam "was the darkest since the early days of 1954," but it was "one of frustrated energy rather than passive acceptance of inevitable defeat." Vietnamese morale would continue to dip without a "hard U.S. commitment to the ground." To show the world that the struggle had reached a "turning point," Taylor urged an appeal to the United Nations, Diem's public assurance of governmental reforms, and an exchange of letters between President Kennedy and Diem that publicly proclaimed their partnership. Diem felt confident that the introduction of U.S. soldiers in connection with flood relief would attract the support of Saigon's National Assembly.[35] He realized that the arrival of American combat units would feed Hanoi's claims to his being a puppet of U.S. imperialism, but the Vietcong posed more of a threat than did Communist propaganda. A stronger U.S. military presence would facilitate his stay in power.

The plan seemed foolproof. Although the flood relief task force would consist primarily of logistical troops, Taylor insisted that its presence would assure Diem of "our readiness to join him in a military showdown with the Viet Cong." The program's humanitarian aspect would avert charges that the United States intended to take over the war. With the troops' task specifically stated, they could pull out without a loss of honor. "Alternatively," Taylor noted in a suggestive statement found in an "Eyes Only" cable to the president, "we can phase them into other activities if we wish to remain longer." The optimum number of troops was 8,000, a force that contained enough combat units to protect relief workers along with any areas occupied by U.S. forces. Their involvement would raise the nation's morale by demonstrating heightened U.S.–South Vietnamese cooperation.

Of course they would be at risk. "Any troops coming to [Vietnam] may expect to take casualties."[36]

During Taylor's last meeting in Saigon on October 25, Diem itemized his war needs. Taylor emphasized that Americans would pilot the helicopters as American units under American commanders. Language problems had impeded Thuan's request for American instructors of the Civil Guard, but he thought either Chinese or Koreans would be acceptable for both the Civil Guard and the Self-Defense Corps. Diem preferred Chinese instructors and had learned from Jiang Jieshi (Chiang Kai-shek) that he was leery about sending troops but amenable to providing nonuniformed personnel who could, if required, engage in combat. Thuan remarked that even though the number of those forces might reach the thousands, their presence could more easily remain secret than troops in uniform. In view of the coming harvest season of November and December, Diem sought U.S. assistance in spraying deadly chemicals on rice crops in the high plateau that the Vietcong regularly confiscated. He also repeated his request for armored boat assistance in the struggle over the delta's bountiful rice supplies. Thuan urged destruction of the Vietcong base at Tchepone in Laos, because it permitted the enemy to shell South Vietnam with recently introduced artillery. Finally, Diem asked that the White House assign Lansdale to Saigon—to which some unidentified person from the state department scrawled in the margin of the report, "No. No. NO!"[37]

Admiral Felt approved sending some military items to South Vietnam even before Taylor submitted his report to the president. Helicopters, in particular, would bolster the strength of both the central government and the provinces. He had no preference over whether the pilots "should be in uniform or sheep-dipped," but he knew that Diem considered the aircraft essential to his forces' mobility. Echoing the Taylor mission's thoughts, Felt agreed that the administration should use the flood "as an immediate cover." He also recommended that army engineers and navy Seabees prepare for an extended American stay by constructing an oil pipeline from the Saigon docks to the airport and a road east from Attopeu in Laos. U.S. combat troops could protect those work crews. Finally, he called for a T-28 (Jungle Jim) armor-covered aircraft from the navy and the use of Chinese Nationalist forces, who could be naturalized as Vietnamese and sent to the delta, where they would join a substantial number of ethnic Chinese already there.[38]

One member of the Taylor mission, Sterling Cottrell, expressed alarm over its unvarnished military thrust and recommended that the United States seek reforms while furnishing military and economic assistance. In an unsettling statement, however, he expressed doubt that the Saigon government could survive even with U.S. military aid. The introduction of combat troops could serve no purpose at this time, even if their presence boosted

South Vietnamese morale. But the troops should remain ready in case the guerrilla conflict graduated into conventional war. The United States must help South Vietnam, Cottrell admitted, but only in an expanded advisory capacity. Direct involvement by either U.S. or SEATO military forces would provide the Communists with the opportunity to remind the Vietnamese of their past colonial experience with the French. That Diem had requested Lansdale as adviser provided an "ideal entree" for an escalated advisory effort.[39]

Taylor, however, insisted that a flood relief force was not a cover for introducing U.S. combat troops. He too had gotten the "impression" that observers regarded the idea as a "cover plan" for injecting U.S. soldiers. "Such is not my view." The flood had caused an emergency that Saigon had to handle with relief measures as well as with military efforts necessary to safeguard the region from Vietcong forces who had fled the swollen waters and would return after their recession. "This concept does not amount to a cover as it undertakes to conceal nothing." The flood provided a "good reason" for sending military personnel, which, in turn, would satisfy Diem's request for troops to close the borders.[40]

Taylor could not have believed his own words in denying that the flood had provided a cover for inserting U.S. troops. The U.S. chargé in Saigon, William Trueheart, bluntly termed the move a "subterfuge" for bringing in U.S. soldiers to close the borders and prevent an invasion from the north, thereby permitting South Vietnamese forces to dispense with the guerrillas. Rusk was among several policymakers in Washington who joined Felt and McGarr in noting the convenient opportunity afforded by the flood to enlarge the U.S. military program.[41]

Taylor had leaned toward the use of troops before he left Washington. Years afterward, he admitted that he had departed for Vietnam in late 1961 "knowing the President did not want a recommendation to send forces." On his arrival, he became convinced of their need. His final report, however, did not contain the arguments for troops found in the "Eyes Only" cables sent to the president, leaving the erroneous impression that the general had not made such a proposal. He had attempted to reduce the chances of combat by recommending limitations on their number, having them wear civilian clothing, and assigning only noncombat duties. Yet he realized that a single American soldier in Vietnam constituted a military commitment and that the chances were good for a military encounter. Did he not point to an imminent confrontation when the Vietcong returned to areas previously under flood waters? William Colby from the CIA station in Saigon likewise noted the conventional nature of Taylor's military ideas. Despite its innocuous label, the flood relief task force would consist of U.S. military personnel. Whether in uniform or, as Felt put it, "sheep-dipped," the presence of thousands of U.S. soldiers would trumpet a direct challenge to the Vietcong and Hanoi.[42]

III

THE ONLY EFFECTIVE RESTRAINT on the Taylor mission could be President Kennedy, who remained insistent on exhausting all other counterinsurgency measures before considering a military solution. He was willing to increase the size of the Military Assistance and Advisory Group, approve additional military support for the Civil Guard, upgrade the training of the Self-Defense Corps and Special Forces, grant more assistance to the ARVN's civic action programs, tighten border controls, and enhance psywar methods. He hoped to seal off the Laotian corridor to the Vietcong and close their sanctuary. Kennedy also realized the importance of stabilizing the Cambodian border and establishing good relations with that country. Finally, he intended to work closely with Saigon in seeking the assistance of other nations, particularly the British, in countering the guerrilla war. So touchy was the troop question, however, that the president directed Taylor to refrain from discussing his conclusions with anyone outside the mission until he returned to Washington and they agreed on policy.[43]

The Saigon government meanwhile left the illusion of making changes in accordance with Taylor's recommendations. It established a broadly based organization aimed at providing nationwide help to flood victims. Diem accepted Thuan's call for reorganizing the country's intelligence services, and government ministers discussed the creation of survey teams to examine security in the provinces. On a border force, Thuan considered Lansdale the "ideal choice" to organize and command the Americans involved. Thuan also reported the possibility of appointing a top-level executive board in the government comprised of Nhu as chair and up to four cabinet members, including Thuan himself. In defending the proposal, Thuan argued that Nhu was the only person Diem trusted and should therefore receive a specific cabinet duty closely aligned with the government official in charge of national security. Nolting agreed. "It was the only feasible way to bring about a delegation of authority by the President and have it stick."[44]

But Diem continued to oppose any surrender of power, meaning that the changes under way left only the veneer of progress. The key element was the creation of an executive board to implement his directives. Although Washington expected that group to act independently of Diem, its hope was far different from the reality. Cabinet members came from the Ngo family, and from this narrow bank of people would come Diem's appointments to the executive board. Its chair would be his brother, Ngo Dinh Nhu. Diem's unbending resistance to delegating authority ensured continued frustration in Washington and prolonged instability in Saigon.

Diem's opposition to reforms led Jorden, mission member and author of the forthcoming report on Vietcong infiltration, to explore the possibility of a coup, perhaps directed by the United States. Pressure for political and administrative changes had reached the "explosion point," he told Taylor, leaving the United States with a choice of approaches that ranged from supporting the Saigon government to "engineering a coup against the Diem regime." If change did not occur in an orderly fashion, it would "almost certainly come through forceful means carried out by an alliance of political and military elements." Jorden did not advocate U.S. promotion of a coup at this time, largely because it was "not something we do well." But the United States must prepare for a coup by identifying with the South Vietnamese people and not their rulers. Diem's refusal to delegate authority had caused a "near paralysis" in administrative work in which his family dominated governmental affairs and "Madame Nhu presides over the women of South Vietnam like an Empress." The ultimate step was "to back a coup that would remove Diem from power." But for now, the United States must support changes that reduced Diem's status to "figurehead and symbol."[45]

Jorden was not the only U.S. observer to recommend preparation for a coup: The National Security Council in Washington had just received the same advice from Frank Child, who had spent two years in South Vietnam as member of a public administration training group under contract with Michigan State University. Child argued that Diem "can only postpone defeat . . . he cannot win." Without a massive infusion of U.S. combat troops (which Child opposed), Diem could not survive past eighteen months. Child discerned the distinct possibility of a military coup and urged the White House either to break with Diem beforehand or to take the lead in his overthrow. In the November 1960 attempt, three battalions of the army's elite paratroopers had led "a sort of *coup d'etat*" that sought to force out Diem's objectionable advisers while convincing him to terminate his political control over the military establishment. The coup fell short only when its leaders accepted a negotiated settlement. "Their political naivete, their apparent lack of political aspirations or political connections left them isolated, inactive, and ineffective during the crucial hours." South Vietnam had capable alternative leaders, Child insisted, but they were powerless. "A military *coup*—or an assassin's bullet—are the only means by which this leadership will ever be exercised." The White House must "prepare for or . . . prepare such an eventuality."[46]

The United States had two major options: either promote a coup, which it preferred not to do, or enhance the American military presence, which more than a few presidential advisers were willing to do. Child's analysis drew praise from two members of the National Security Council staff, Robert Johnson and Robert Komer. Johnson added, however, that the administration would more than likely give Diem another chance. With Diem now supporting U.S. military intervention, the White House might possess the leverage to condition assistance on governmental reforms. Komer again called for military intervention, this time asserting that "over-react-ing" was "best at this point." U.S. stature in Southeast Asia could not sur-vive the loss of South Vietnam after the expected U.S. failure in Laos. Perhaps there were other options. But Komer doubted it. The question of combat troops would arise again. It was wiser to act before the war spread and required "a Korean type commitment." Komer did not want to be-come involved in what he called "another squalid, secondary theatre in Asia. But we'll end up doing so sooner or later anyway because we won't be willing to accept another defeat. If so, the real question is not whether but how soon and how much!"[47]

Taylor hoped that Diem would institute reforms once additional U.S. advisers were in place. The establishment of a "limited partnership" neces-sitated a major alteration in MAAG's role in South Vietnam. "It must be shifted from an advisory group to something nearer—but not quite—an operational headquarters in a theater of war." In its new role of "limited partner," the United States must maintain a middle position, "avoiding formalized advice on the one hand, trying to run the war, on the other." Admittedly, the first installment of U.S. forces might prove insufficient to close the frontier and end the insurgency. Indeed, "there is no limit to our possible commitment (unless we attack the source in Hanoi)."[48]

The call for military action against North Vietnam permeated the Taylor mission's report. General William Craig warned that U.S. combat forces would have no positive impact in South Vietnam unless they went into Laos to cut off infiltration. Rostow insisted that the United States must clarify its "intention to attack the source of guerrilla aggression in North Vietnam and impose on the Hanoi Government a price for partici-pating in the current war." Cottrell declared that Americans should apply "graduated punitive measures" to North Vietnam "with weapons of our choosing." Taylor insisted that his push for heightened military measures marked no change in direction, but simply "an intensification of [the] ef-fort toward the current policy." The root of the problem lay in Hanoi. Hence the call had risen for "an attack at the source." Taylor denied that he and Rostow had recommended bombing. They intended to tell the presi-dent that "the real enemy, the real trouble is in Hanoi. If we can't accom-plish our purpose down here, we're going to have to do something in North Vietnam."[49]

Although Lansdale continued to oppose U.S. fighting forces, he pre-sented two plans, both rejected by Taylor, that would send in Chinese Nationalist soldiers under the guise of workers or advisers. The first was a "human defoliation" proposal, offered as an alternative to chemical war-fare. A Chinese Nationalist firm would receive timber concessions in the Communist-controlled hardwood forests north of Saigon and then send in armed workers, who would fell the trees while protected by South Vietnamese soldiers. "They might very well have to fight to get to the trees," Lansdale shrewdly observed, "so they would clean up the Viet Cong along the way." His second proposal called for 2,000 Chinese Nationalist veterans, aged thirty-five to forty, from the army's Special Forces to enter Vietnam as Vietnamese after being "sheep-dipped" in Saigon's Chinese sector of Cholon and given Vietnamese names. They would train the villages' Self-Defense Corps in "weaponry, patrol, and intelligence reporting." Taylor was not interested in either plan. "Lansdale was an idea man, and he could turn out ideas faster than you could pick them up off the floor, but I was never impressed with their feasibility."[50]

The counterinsurgency approach still drew McGarr's support, although he joined Lemnitzer and Taylor in giving it a military predominance. If the United States failed to take decisive action, McGarr warned, the unconventional tactics now used by the Vietcong could give way to conventional warfare by North Vietnam. In his first twelve-month report as MAAG's chief, McGarr focused on the threat of overt aggression from North Vietnam. The only way to win this protracted guerrilla conflict was through "an integrated program of civic action, intelligence and psychological means, during the Preparation Phase," followed by the "Military Operational Phase," and concluding with the "Security and Reconstruction Phase."[51]

The central need, McGarr emphasized, was additional military personnel to close the border between Laos and the high plateau of South Vietnam. Increased infiltration from Laos had led to a significant Vietcong buildup in the northern and central regions of South Vietnam. The best estimate was that 17,000 "regular, numerically designated Viet Cong units" were in Vietnam—more than double that of a year before. Evidence of the ballooning infiltration came from ever-increasing Vietcong assaults along with sharply intensified political and subversive activities in the southern part of the Mekong Delta. The most important source of Vietcong strength was in the south—10,000 in number, and the best trained and equipped— all poised to strike Saigon.[52]

The insurgency's advanced status made the most immediate threat military in nature, McGarr insisted. Vital to long-range success was the coordination of governmental and military efforts through the creation of a National Plan and a Central Intelligence Organization. Government forces must adhere to the "amoeba principle" in clearing an area and slowly expanding their control over the entire nation. Military morale suffered from the widespread frustration resulting from "inadequate civil–military follow through measures" that permitted the Vietcong to return to areas after the ARVN pulled out.[53]

McGarr thought that the Taylor mission's "most significant proposal" was the call for U.S. military forces—"to be accomplished, at least initially— under a cover plan" based on the flood. "However, I am now convinced that unless deployed in sufficient strength the Viet Cong, both for military and propaganda reasons, will eventually consider U.S. troops a prime target." American soldiers sent to the Mekong Delta must arrive "expecting to fight" and "prepared for [an] extended commitment."[54]

McGarr realized that U.S. troops could not stop enemy infiltration without becoming involved in the conflict. The war's increasing tempo pointed to direct U.S. participation. Vietcong prisoners along with documents removed from their dead comrades had verified the ARVN's claim that thousands of Vietcong had recently infiltrated the south through Laos. If the war continued to escalate, Nolting concurred with McGarr, Americans might *have* to fight.[55]

Despite the heavy risks of a widened war, White House planning focused on Taylor's thinly disguised combat force. The Mekong Delta was the center of the Vietcong's strength, and that was the area hit hardest by the flood. Taylor termed the introduction of U.S. troops an "essential action," arguing that they would "conduct such combat operations as are necessary for self-defense and for the security of the area in which they are stationed." Furthermore, they would "provide an emergency reserve to back up the Armed Forces of the GVN [Government of Vietnam] in the case of a heightened military crisis." Finally, they would "act as an advance party of such additional forces as may be introduced if CINCPAC or SEATO contingency plans are invoked." Although the ARVN would fight the Vietcong, the U.S. forces would constitute a "general reserve" in fighting "large, formed guerrilla bands which have abandoned the forests for attacks on major targets." South Vietnam was "not an excessively difficult or unpleasant place to operate" and the "risks of backing into a major Asian war" were not high. North Vietnam was "extremely vulnerable to conventional bombing." Finally, "there is no case for fearing a mass onslaught of communist manpower . . . particularly if our air power is allowed a free hand against logistical targets."[56]

Taylor's proposal was seductively simple but highly dangerous, for it entailed a potential long-range military commitment. It would establish a base for later U.S. military actions aimed at building security while averting charges of intervention. It would permit continued freedom of action regarding any combat commitment while providing a face-saving way out in the event of failure. It would demonstrate the U.S. intention to stand by South Vietnam in what Taylor had earlier termed a military showdown. The well-known physical and environmental hardships associated with South Vietnam's rough terrain and weather, the threat of a Chinese Communist intervention, the questionable effectiveness of bombing expeditions—all these considerations Taylor dismissed as inconsequential. Acceptance of his proposal would force the Kennedy administration to abandon counterinsurgency measures in favor of a military escalation. Robert

Johnson offered the most incisive observation. "If we commit 6–8,000 troops and then pull them out when the going got rough we will be finished in Viet Nam and probably in all of Southeast Asia."[57]

ROBERT JOHNSON had put his finger on the central enigma in any U.S. troop commitment: How many soldiers were enough? Taylor's plan for introducing combat forces would paradoxically signal a major escalation in the nation's military involvement without providing enough men to make a difference in the war. Several members of the administration expressed concern, including Alexis Johnson and McNamara, who warned that Taylor might tie the helicopters to his flood relief plan in an effort to facilitate the movements of U.S. soldiers. Rusk appeared to favor U.S. troops but hesitated because of Diem's refusal to delegate authority to military commanders. Without that pivotal change, it was difficult to see how a "relative handful [of] American troops" could have a "decisive influence" on events. Rusk nonetheless opposed a "major additional commitment [of] American prestige to a losing horse."[58]

The implication of Rusk's statement was unmistakable: The U.S. commitment to South Vietnam could not waver, which meant that Diem must either reform his government or leave it.

6

THE STRANGE
SEDUCTION OF VIETNAM

As I knew from experience with my French friends, there was
something about Vietnam that seduced the toughest military
minds into fantasy.

George Ball, Autumn 1961

T HE PRESIDENT was deeply perplexed by Taylor's call for combat
troops. Kennedy had resisted the pressure from the joint chiefs
and other military and civilian advisers, but Taylor's abrupt change
of course threw a different light on the matter. Although the president held
a visceral distrust for military figures, he regarded Taylor as a masterful combination of intellect and common sense whose personal and professional
qualities had meshed with his sensible call for a flexible and restrained foreign policy. Taylor's record had suggested a natural opposition to committing U.S. ground forces to Asia. The Undersecretary of State for Economic
Affairs, George Ball, had hoped for better judgment from the general. "Yet,
as I knew from experience with my French friends, there was something
about Vietnam that seduced the toughest military minds into fantasy."[1]

I

THE TROOP QUESTION became more complicated when the president sought
the views of a fellow Irish-Catholic and trusted friend during their Senate
days together, Democrat Mike Mansfield of Montana. Mansfield had long
opposed European involvement in Asian affairs as dangerously entangling
and purely imperialist. In earning a master's degree in history, he wrote a
thesis that criticized the late-nineteenth-century U.S. involvement in Korea. Later awarded a Ph.D., he taught Far Eastern history at the University
of Montana, where in his classes he expressed disapproval of the French
involvement in Indochina. After his 1954 visit to Indochina, Mansfield wrote
a report that influenced the Eisenhower administration to support Diem.

In 1956, Senator Kennedy spoke before the lobbying group known as the American Friends of Vietnam, where he praised Mansfield as "a great friend of Vietnam."[2]

In a stand that could not have been surprising, Mansfield staunchly opposed a military solution in Vietnam. The most effective resistance to communism, he now argued in a statement that fitted Kennedy's predilections, came not from armed force but from broad social, political, and economic changes that fostered democracy in the villages and provinces. The United States could increase military and economic assistance, but it must not assume the central task of stopping Communist infiltration and subversion. In a statement that also was in harmony with the president's sentiments, Mansfield insisted that the responsibility for winning the war belonged to the South Vietnamese alone. A U.S. troop involvement could lead to four adverse results: (1) great fanfare followed by an embarrassing retreat; (2) an indecisive and draining conflict similar to that in Korea; (3) an all-out war with China while the Soviet Union stood on the side; (4) global war.[3]

The United States, Mansfield warned, must *not* send combat troops. Its key allies would not join a fight against "third-string communist forces" from North Vietnam. The Chinese Communists might intervene and make South Vietnam "a quicksand for us." The big question was, "Where does an involvement of this kind end even if we can bring it to a successful conclusion?" In Saigon? Hanoi? Beijing? Any level of troop involvement in Asia would drain already thin manpower resources and endanger U.S. commitments elsewhere while stirring up ugly memories of Western colonialism. A military victory in South Vietnam would require a massive commitment of American lives and treasure. If the United States lost, "we will suffer disastrous repercussions throughout all of Asia and we will indeed become the laughing stock of the world."[4]

President Kennedy had received a similarly negative analysis from Harvard economist John Kenneth Galbraith. As an undergraduate at Harvard, the young Kennedy had met the professor, and later as senator had turned to him for economic advice before asking for his help in the presidential race of 1960. Unfailingly blunt and cuttingly witty in his remarks, Galbraith had won the president's trust not only in economic and political matters but in foreign affairs as well. On the same day Taylor submitted his report, Galbraith was in Washington for a state visit of Indian Prime Minister Jawaharlal Nehru and, at the president's request, expressed his views on Vietnam. The situation, Galbraith warned, was "perilously close to the point of no return." The Taylor mission's military proposal included "all the risks of the operation in Korea of ten years ago, without the justification of a surprise attack across the boundary, without the support of the United Nations, and without a population determined to fight for independence."[5]

Galbraith insisted that the time was right to end the war in Vietnam and seek a U.N.-supervised peace. The Geneva Conference on Laos was about to close; the Communist front had weakened because of the growing rift between Moscow and Beijing; Nehru was a respected neutral who could transmit information between East and West; and the Taylor mission's suggestion of U.S. military intervention had raised Washington's bargaining power with the Soviets, Communist Chinese, and neutrals. The first prerequisite was to replace Ambassador Nolting with someone more forceful. Governor W. Averell Harriman of New York, Galbraith argued, could stand up to both Diem and the U.S. military in insisting on government reform. Recently appointed Assistant Secretary of State for Far Eastern Affairs, Harriman had served as ambassador to the Soviet Union during World War II, and he now headed the U.S. delegation in the Laotian negotiations. Second, Galbraith continued, some country not closely associated with the United States should call for a U.N. resolution confirming South Vietnam's independence, and the Saigon government should request U.N. observer teams to investigate its charges of infiltration. Third, a neutralized Laos was vital to prevent it from becoming a staging area for further Vietcong operations in South Vietnam. Since India was chair of the International Control Commission in Vietnam, the United States should ask Nehru to approach Ho Chi Minh about calling for a cease-fire. Ho must realize that Washington's objective was an independent South Vietnam not necessarily allied with the United States, and, once peace came, he must approve the establishment of commercial relations between North and South Vietnam and accept both Vietnams into the United Nations.[6]

On the surface, Galbraith had suggested an enticing way for the United States to pull out its special military forces from South Vietnam without either abandoning the country or resorting to a major military involvement. The chief U.S. failure, he later asserted, derived from "military miscalculation." During a 1961 visit to Vietnam, U.S. military leaders had briefed him an entire morning without giving sufficient attention to the negative impact of jungle conditions on military operations. Galbraith insisted that the "jungle terrain had its own implicit defenses" that undermined the United States's traditional military approach. Not only did the landscape and environment lessen the impact of superior firepower, but the Vietcong could attack American troops and the Americans could not distinguish the Vietcong from the citizens. Communism was irrelevant. On a long trip north of Saigon one Sunday, Galbraith wondered how Americans could discern a "Communist jungle from a free enterprise jungle." U.S. military officers never discussed these points, starkly exposing their failure to understand the war.[7]

Forty years later, Galbraith believes that the war was unwinnable. He admits to having been mistaken in the early 1960s by asserting that Diem was the central problem and that, by extrapolation, a change in leadership might have changed the outcome. The Vietnam war was never winnable because of the natural advantages held by the guerrillas in knowing the land and being able to fade away into the population. But Diem's poor leadership had created the illusion that *he* was the problem and that the simplest and most effective remedy was a coup. Like Mansfield, Galbraith called for a military withdrawal.[8]

Kennedy realized that such an action would hurt U.S. credibility by leaving an image of retreat. He could not adopt such a measure in a heightening Cold War that turned so heavily on posture and perception that the mere appearance of defeat had a negative impact. The approaching neutralization of Laos had already inflicted a major blow to U.S. prestige throughout the region. Kennedy, partly in reaction to Laotian events, had conveyed so many assurances to South Vietnam that a military withdrawal would constitute a humiliating surrender guaranteed to damage U.S. stature for years. Although Galbraith's argument was appealing in theory, it was impossible in practice. The White House could not order a military reduction without first being in the position to claim that South Vietnam could stand on its own.

Another problem with Galbraith's proposal became clear. He (and most contemporaries) failed to grasp the depth of North Vietnam's commitment to reunifying the country under Hanoi's control. Although the Vietcong bore the brunt of the fighting, the great mass of evidence of North Vietnamese assistance that the United States and South Vietnam had compiled should have convinced the most hardened skeptic that Hanoi would not retreat from its intention to drive all foreign peoples out of Vietnam. Nothing short of South Vietnam's destruction as a self-proclaimed nation could satisfy North Vietnam and the Vietcong. Galbraith nonetheless argued that South Vietnam should come under U.N. sanction as a sovereign nation. His recommendation had no chance without victory on the battlefield.

And, according to at least one news correspondent on the scene, that victory was unlikely, for the Communists were winning this "hot war" in the jungle. Robert Martin from *U.S. News and World Report* asserted that the ARVN's military situation had settled into "the dry rot of hopelessness," strikingly similar to that of the Chinese Nationalist Army after World War II. A young South Vietnamese officer hesitated to take the offensive. "Why should I fight? I get no support. My men have had no leave for two years. My promotions depend not on what I do but on keeping out of trouble." The army sought to avoid contact with the enemy. In central South Vietnam, alongside 165 miles of Laotian and Cambodian borders containing hundreds of mountain trails, one ARVN division of 6,500 men (3,000 fewer than the normal size) had the responsibility of protecting four provinces encompassing 17,000 square miles of territory. Its headquarters was an outpost made of bamboo sticks ten miles away but requiring three hours of difficult travel to reach because of a one-track road made of glue-like mud in rainy seasons that clung to the wheels of jeeps and trucks. Vietcong recruitments were successful not only because of intimidation but also because its cadres promised fighters a gun, monthly pay, and the right to remain in their own villages. Cash bonuses went to peasants who deserted the home guards and brought their weapons with them. One captured woman declared that she was one of many females who had received training in the north to mobilize women in the south, perform theatrical shows filled with propaganda, and "comfort" Vietcong cadres. Many rural schools had closed, village clinics lacked adequate medicine because of the danger of the Vietcong's seizing the supplies, and farmers feared attending agricultural extension programs because of Vietcong threats. Transportation had come to a virtual standstill, which meant that the cities were unable to send manufactured goods into the countryside and rice became scarce in the cities. U.S. military advisers were already in the field, armed for protection but authorized only to give technical advice. Concluded Martin: "Time is running out in Vietnam."[9]

There is no reason to believe that President Kennedy thought the situation desperate and in need of a changed policy. He concurred with Mansfield and Galbraith's opposition to U.S. combat troops, but he was not willing to risk the certain strategic and political fallout of a military withdrawal. Mansfield's warnings against direct military participation convincingly forecasted an entangling, open-ended involvement. Galbraith's plan offered the attraction of averting armed U.S. intervention, calling for South Vietnam's independence, and, by seeking to diminish North Vietnam's reliance on Communist China, easing the tense Sino–Soviet struggle for Southeast Asia. But Kennedy knew that South Vietnam could not stand on its own. He also realized that the United States could not curtail its military involvement without sustaining a heavy political cost. Neither Mansfield nor Galbraith had presented a viable solution to the fundamental issue dividing Washington and Hanoi: the U.S. objective of sanctifying an independent, non-Communist South Vietnam, and North Vietnam's demand for a reunified country in line with the Geneva Accords of 1954. This irreconcilable difference threatened to make war the ultimate solution.[10]

While the president pondered the alternatives to a troop involvement, the Taylor mission submitted its report, entitled "A Limited Partnership," directly to him on November 3, 1961. At four o'clock in the afternoon, Taylor and the mission members filed into the Oval Office to wait for the president. As the group milled around the historic room, Taylor lightheartedly remarked that he wanted to soak up every detail of his surroundings so he could answer the excited inquiries of his daughters. He then eased into the president's famous rocking chair and began swaying to and fro—at precisely the time the president walked into the room. The startled general bolted upright, bringing the chair with him since it had been a tight squeeze. Kennedy ignored Taylor's embarrassment as he, much to Lansdale's undisguised delight, hurriedly wriggled out of the chair and returned it to its original position.[11]

Taylor quickly turned the attention of the meeting to the mission's recommendation for combat troops. They would train the South Vietnamese Air Force, relieve ARVN forces at Danang in the northern sector of the country, and advise on engineering projects and the use of military equipment. Although Taylor emphasized that they would fight only if attacked, he admitted the potential for direct action. If Hanoi did not call off its guerrilla war on South Vietnam, the United States would have to decide whether or not to continue sponsoring a war that crossed international borders. Did those under attack have the "right to strike the source of aggression, after the fact of external aggression is clearly established?" The United States must "cover action in Southeast Asia up to the nuclear threshold." Taylor ensured success "if the right men are sent to do the right jobs." In private afterward, he and Rostow grimly warned the president that Diem could not last more than three months without U.S. military help.[12]

Despite Diem's request for Lansdale's return to Vietnam, the general would not do so immediately. After the Taylor team presented its report and left the room, the president asked Lansdale to remain for a few moments. "I want you to work on Cuba," Kennedy declared. The Bay of Pigs fiasco still weighed heavily on the president's mind, causing him to regard the Caribbean troubles as more pressing than those in Vietnam. Lansdale would soon attempt to mastermind the fall of Fidel Castro through a top-secret operational plan code-named "Mongoose." He would not return to Vietnam until mid-1965.[13]

The Taylor report, the president realized, left the door open for a full-scale U.S. combat engagement. Based on a section written by Rostow, the general argued in his cover letter to Kennedy that the United States must strike at the source of the Soviet Union's "wars of liberation." Taylor wished years afterward that he had taken an even stronger stand. "Had I known what the future held, the better course would have been to introduce a strong American combat force right then, and see whether that wouldn't deter the enemy when they saw that indeed the United States was ready to fight for this place if necessary." The time might come when the United States must "attack the source of guerrilla aggression in North Vietnam and impose on the Hanoi Government a price for participating in the current war which is commensurate with the damage being inflicted on its neighbors to the south."[14]

Since South Vietnam was in such dire straits, Taylor preferred a counterinsurgency strategy that tilted sharply toward military correctives. The U.S.

experiences in the Philippines and Greece suggested that the best approach to putting down a Communist insurgency was to take the offensive. Rangers and specially equipped company-size ARVN units must pursue the guerrillas into the jungles, using hunter–killer tactics aimed at putting them on the defensive. U.S. military and civilian personnel would act as advisers and collaborators (as in Laos) in pacifying areas cleared of Vietcong. U.S. helicopters would enhance the ARVN's mobility and flexibility, and defoliation projects would eliminate the Vietcong's food supplies. The United States *must* undercut the Communists' claim that the Vietcong was "the local wave of the future."[15]

The mission concluded that the United States must establish a "limited partnership and working collaboration with the Vietnamese." Such a sweeping program necessitated changing MAAG from an advisory group to "an operational headquarters in a theater of war." Only joint U.S.–South Vietnamese efforts could achieve civil–military cohesion.[16]

The next day, in Rusk's conference room on the morning of Saturday, November 4, Taylor and several of the president's advisers focused on raising the number of combat troops higher than the 8,000 called for in the proposal. Taylor reported that President Kennedy "instinctively" opposed their use, even though they would focus on flood relief and withdraw within a "matter of months." McNamara expressed the prevailing sentiment among the group in declaring 8,000 soldiers an insufficient number to save South Vietnam and that the White House might have to use all the nation's resources against North Vietnam. In a position not consistent with his recollection years afterward, Ball spoke not only in favor of a troop commitment but for expanding its number beyond that recommended by the Taylor mission. The dispatch of the "8,000-man force," he shrewdly observed, actually committed the United States to "unlimited action." If troop deployment was a fait accompli, "Why wait on going at Hanoi?" The American people would understand a total commitment but not one of a limited nature. "A larger force is preferable." Lemnitzer agreed. "We must commit the number of troops required for success." Rostow assured his colleagues that neither Hanoi nor Beijing posed a significant risk to American action. Taylor and others preferred a "Berlin-type commitment." Thus the debate did not focus on *whether* to commit U.S. fighting forces; it centered on the number necessary to complete the task. The real issues at the meeting were, as William Bundy noted, "dissatisfaction with the half-in, half-out, nature of the 'flood relief task force,' and a consensus of disbelief that once thus engaged the US could easily decide to pull the force out."[17]

The sentiment for combat troops was overwhelming. President Kennedy had expected Taylor to provide feasible alternatives to a military buildup. Instead, Taylor had joined the hard-liners even before he left for Saigon and, once there, became an ardent supporter of sending American troops. Realizing, however, that the president did not want to commit American boys to the war, the general offered a bogus alternative.

The November 4 meeting placed even greater pressure on Kennedy to intervene. Even Ball, who later opposed American combat troops, fell in line with the others. His memoirs, written in 1982, self-servingly declare that he was "appalled at the report's recommendations" and feared that with such a commitment we "would find ourselves in a protracted conflict far more serious than Korea." The Vietcong were "mean and tough," as the French came to realize in the 1950s, and a direct U.S. military involvement could provoke the Chinese to intervene as they did in Korea. No outright invasion had occurred in Vietnam, making this a "revolutionary situation" heavily tinged with anticolonial sentiment. "To my dismay, I found no sympathy for these views."[18] Even though Ball had come closer than others in recognizing the struggle as revolutionary in nature, the official record shows that he too had succumbed to the strange seduction of Vietnam. The pressure for U.S. combat involvement in the war had reached formidable dimensions that only the stiffest presidential opposition could resist.

Later that same day, the state department instructed Nolting to approach Diem about delegating governing authority in exchange for U.S. acquiescence in a "joint effort" to win the war. Washington had a new idea: the establishment of a National Emergency Council in South Vietnam (growing out of Diem's October declaration of a national emergency), headed by Tho and with Thuan as secretary. All business between Diem and the departments of government would pass through the council, with Nhu acting as liaison. Furthermore, "a mature hard-headed" American would participate in all council decisions. Nolting did not believe that Diem would make any governmental changes that divested him of power. He might agree to a council having executive authority, but only with Nhu as chair and both Tho and Thuan as members. Moreover, Diem could not permit an American "to participate in all decisions" because this idea suggested a concession of governmental control to the United States. Diem's resistance to change had narrowed the Kennedy administration's options.[19]

The greatest danger in a U.S. troop commitment lay in a matching Vietcong escalation followed by a Russian or Chinese involvement. A special intelligence analysis asserted that the United States could airlift more materials to the ARVN, deploy 8–10,000 troops as a flood relief unit, send 25–40,000 combat troops, and, with each step, threaten to bomb North Vietnam if its help to the Vietcong did not end. But it also noted that such air assaults would not stop the infiltration and that Moscow and Beijing might intervene. Despite the joint chiefs' call for sending U.S. troops, Generals MacArthur, Eisenhower, and James Van Fleet warned against doing so. Escalation ensured a wider war.[20]

II

RUMORS OF U.S. TROOPS had drawn a strongly negative reaction from Communist nations, neutrals, and even America's allies. North Vietnam, Communist China, India, France, and the United Kingdom urged the Kennedy administration to reject such a provocative measure. A North Vietnamese official announced at a late October press conference in Geneva that the Vietnam Democratic Party (Communist) had warned against the insertion of combat troops, and North Vietnam's foreign minister, Ung Van Khiem, had proclaimed to the National Assembly that "the U.S. imperialists must be held responsible for the consequences" of such a "dangerous move." Less than a week later, the Vietnam Fatherland Front asserted that if either American or SEATO troops entered the conflict, the 16 million people in North Vietnam "would resolutely stand beside their 14 million compatriots in the South." The front appealed to the Geneva cochairs and the International Control Commission to halt U.S. intervention as a violation of the Geneva Accords, which Hanoi had "consistently upheld." At the ongoing Geneva Conference on Laos, the Communist Chinese delegate warned that the introduction of U.S. troops in Vietnam would undermine any Laotian agreement. And at a luncheon in the home of Jacqueline Kennedy's mother and stepfather, Indian Prime Minister Nehru informed the president of his adamant opposition to U.S. soldiers. The White House countered that Hanoi had engineered the insurgency and that a Communist victory in South Vietnam would provide a pattern for conquest that might spread into other troubled areas throughout the world.[21]

This international opposition to U.S. combat troops failed to dissuade Rusk. He admitted that the arrival of U.S. soldiers at that touchy time might endanger the Laotian negotiations. He realized that increased commitments to Saigon would come during the ongoing Berlin crisis and might encourage Hanoi to take advantage of the U.S. preoccupation with Germany to raise the level of infiltration. "I didn't necessarily oppose sending combat troops to Vietnam," Rusk later observed; "I just wanted Kennedy to realize that this was truly a fateful decision with enormous consequences." The flood cover was not wise. "If we wanted to send troops, we ought to be straightforward about it."[22]

Rusk joined other advisers in thinking the mission's recommended number of soldiers insufficient. After all, he warned the president, the dispatch of combat forces to South Vietnam would signal "the ultimate possible extent of our military commitment in Southeast Asia." Perhaps the only way to save South Vietnam was to convince the Communist nations of Washington's "willingness to commit whatever United States combat forces may be required to accomplish this objective." In an assertion that must have startled the president, Rusk declared that the number of ground forces available was six divisions, or about 205,000 men, which, he insisted, would not endanger the administration's Berlin policy.[23]

Rusk was not the only adviser victimized by his illusions. William Bundy wrote a memorandum summarizing the range of "good" and "bad" scenarios based on U.S. intervention that, he declared in his first draft, "took the Taylor recommendations to their logical conclusion." The best scenario, Bundy asserted, rested on Diem's making all the desired changes because of the infusion of 8,000 American forces and Hanoi's calling off its offensive. "Only trouble is—it's unlikely!" Before the memo went to the president, Bundy added the words "inclined to recommend" a heightened military commitment to South Vietnam because of the "steady growth of doubt all that week" in Vietnam. Taylor's naval aide, Lieutenant Commander Worth Bagley, agreed that the major purpose for sending combat forces was to raise South Vietnam's morale and not to engage in any "positive military task other than that of self-defense." Their very presence would encourage Diem to make administrative changes long wanted by the United States. A notable increase in U.S. assistance along with the assignment of "a small American force" would signify South Vietnam's importance to America's own security "and should be just as convincing to the 'other side' whether we commit 8,000 men or 80,000 men." In a curiously naïve statement, Bagley asserted that the United States did not seek a "positive military objective," making it "difficult to see how our forces can become mired down in an inconclusive struggle."[24]

Bundy and Bagley's ideas underlined the narrow understanding that Washington's policymakers had about the ramifications of deploying U.S. combat troops. They argued that the mere presence of such forces would lift South Vietnam's morale, lead Diem to implement reforms, and convince Hanoi that its efforts were hopeless. The Americans would not engage in offensive operations, eliminating the danger of their becoming bogged down in Asian jungles or rice paddies. In the meantime, the ARVN would shield the Americans from the Vietcong. This was naïveté to the extreme. Americans in the beleaguered area would become exposed to enemy fire, ensuring a direct combat involvement. As Bagley later admitted, they would "take up the sword and try to win the war."[25]

McNamara nonetheless joined Rusk in urging the president to send a contingent larger than that called for by the Taylor mission. The defense secretary agreed with Gilpatric and the joint chiefs that the proposed 8,000-man force was not sufficient to convince "the other side (whether the shots are called from Moscow, Peiping [Beijing], or Hanoi) that we mean business." The 8,000 men should therefore constitute the "initial" installment of a number that would grow in accordance with need. McNamara assured Kennedy that if Hanoi and Beijing intervened directly (as Rusk had declared), the United States could amass 205,000 ground forces without endangering its Berlin policy. A major intervention would avert a web-like affair by showing the enemy that "we mean business," whereas a limited involvement "would be almost certain" to cause the United States "to get increasingly mired down in an inconclusive struggle." The White House must make a public commitment to preserving South Vietnam from communism and warn Hanoi that its continued help to the Vietcong meant certain "punitive retaliation" against North Vietnam. "The chances are against, probably sharply against, preventing that fall by any measures short of the introduction of U.S. forces on a substantial scale."[26]

Like the joint chiefs, the secretaries of state and defense regarded U.S. combat forces as crucial to South Vietnam's salvation. Their major concern was timing: A troop introduction prior to a Laotian settlement could cause the Communists to break the cease-fire in that country and force a decision on whether to send U.S. armed forces there as well. But if troops went into South Vietnam *after* a settlement in Laos, they might reaffirm U.S. determination throughout the region and stabilize both countries. Negotiations over South Vietnam were not possible because the Communists insisted on a neutralization settlement similar to that about to take place in Laos. This step was not "desirable or necessary, given the scale of Viet Cong action and the stronger position of the GVN [Government of Vietnam] and the greater accessibility of Viet-Nam to the United States and SEATO."[27]

Thus the president's two top advisers advocated dispatching almost twenty-eight times the number of combat troops to South Vietnam that the Taylor mission had recommended. The first contingent would locate just below the seventeenth parallel, assigned the responsibility of warding off any North Vietnamese invasion and thereby releasing ARVN forces to take the offensive. Ancillary to this central military task was the improved training and equipping of the Civil Guard and Self-Defense Corps by U.S. advisers, the use of American helicopters and light aircraft to enhance the ARVN's mobility, and the creation of a specialized border ranger force to halt infiltration from Laos. The United States would also provide airlifts, special intelligence, air–ground support, and aerial reconnaissance and photography.[28] The essential component in the expanded U.S. military commitment was combat troops.

Rusk and McNamara were like Taylor in failing to see that *one* American soldier in South Vietnam signified a full-scale commitment. All three advisers ignored reality in suggesting that 8,000 American military personnel did not constitute a large-scale intervention and that this show of force would convince the enemy to relent. What if 8,000 combat troops failed to back down Hanoi? Could 205,000 American soldiers accomplish the task? If not, what would be the next level of commitment? This shallow thinking guaranteed a steadily escalating involvement.

In a short time, Ball came to fear the snowball effect of a troop commitment, and, in a reversal of his stand just three days earlier, he privately warned Kennedy against Taylor's troop recommendations. The international lawyer and undersecretary of state for economic affairs had had first-hand experience with the French during their final days in Indochina during the mid-1950s, and he no longer believed that the White House should become militarily involved. Years afterward, he recalled McNamara making many assurances of victory that rested on computerized analyses. "Well, Bob, look," Ball interjected on one occasion, "I've heard all of that before; the kill ratios, the cost effectiveness aspects of various operations, the body counts. The French had exactly the same statistics and they lost." Now, to Kennedy, Ball issued the same warning. "To commit American forces to South Vietnam would . . . be a tragic error. Once that process started, . . . there would be no end to it. Within five years," Ball darkly predicted, "we'll have three hundred thousand men in the paddies and jungles and never find them again. That was the French experience. Vietnam is the worst possible terrain both from a physical and political point of view." To Ball's surprise, the president appeared unwilling to explore the matter. "George, you're just crazier than hell. That just isn't going to happen."[29]

At first it is difficult to explain the president's reaction to Ball's warning. Critics claim that Kennedy leaned toward troops but felt confident that he could maintain restraints on their number. Others argue that the president remained opposed to combat forces and dismissed Ball's fears out of hand. Ball later expressed uncertainty about Kennedy's response and would not venture a guess about his real feelings. But based on the president's consistent reluctance to commit troops, it is certain that he regarded a single troop commitment as the beginning of an elastic involvement. The initial installment would automatically lead to a second and a third, until the entanglement became virtually irreversible. The result would be either a full-scale war that offered no assurance of victory or a humiliating withdrawal that dealt a crippling blow to U.S. prestige.[30]

In an early November conversation with Schlesinger, Kennedy moaned about his shortsighted advisers: "They want a force of American troops. They say it's necessary in order to restore confidence and maintain morale. But it will be just like Berlin. The troops will march in; the bands will play; the crowds will cheer; and in four days everyone will have forgotten. Then we will be told we have to send in more troops. It's like taking a drink. The effect wears off, and you have to take another." Kennedy, Schlesinger later asserted, meant that Americanization of the war would not occur during his presidency and that Ball need not worry about seeing "300,000 American troops in the rice paddies of Vietnam." The president thus "disagreed with Ball's prediction *because* he agreed with Ball's analysis." The war was South Vietnam's to win or lose, Kennedy continued to believe. If it became "a white man's war," the United States would duplicate the French debacle.[31]

The president's fears were warranted: His advisers wanted to go beyond merely patrolling South Vietnam's borders to hitting Hanoi. Had not Rusk and McNamara raised the initial troop ceiling from 8,000 troops to 205,000? U.S. military forces, they asserted, should stand ready "to strike at the source of the aggression in North Viet-Nam." Rostow wanted the immediate dispatch of 5,000 U.S. (or SEATO) forces to the seventeenth parallel as replacements for the 3,500 ARVN forces already there. The U.S. soldiers could help put down the insurgency "short of engaging in detailed counter-guerrilla operations but including relevant operations in North Viet-Nam." They could also deal with an "organized Communist military intervention." No one, Rostow emphatically declared, envisioned their fighting in the paddies and jungles. "No one is proposing at this stage—although the issue may have to be faced—selective action in North Viet Nam if Communist infiltration does not stop." But the United States must "move without ambiguity—without the sickly pallor of our positions on Cuba and Laos." The Communists would "back down."[32]

Once again, the president's advisers failed him by not examining all the implications of a troop injection. They were correct in asserting that a military presence would demonstrate U.S. determination while bolstering Saigon's flagging spirits. But the other side of the issue outweighed that intangible positive impact. The move would imperil the delicate Geneva negotiations over Laos (a point admitted by Rusk and McNamara), and it would encourage an unlimited U.S. commitment, regardless of the original force size.[33] If American soldiers failed to act when circumstances demanded, Hanoi would gain a major propaganda victory. If they reacted decisively, the U.S. involvement could become complete, making the war no longer South Vietnam's to win or lose. Either outcome undercut the wisdom of sending U.S. fighting forces into Vietnam.

President Kennedy again resisted the pressure for combat troops by advocating alternative measures. In a White House meeting on November 11—the same day the memos arrived from Rusk, McNamara, and Rostow—the president asked several probing questions. Could the assistance program succeed without combat forces? How could the administration overcome the opposition of Democratic Senator Richard Russell of Georgia and others in Congress? If the administration decided against sending soldiers, what reasons should it give Diem? What changes in South Vietnam would force a reconsideration? How did the question relate to the ongoing talks on Laos? How much of the U.S. commitment to Diem was conditional on his instituting reforms? The president agreed with Rusk and McNamara in opposing the immediate dispatch of combat troops, but he rejected their call for a "categorical commitment to prevent the loss of South Vietnam." Would not such a commitment necessitate combat troops? Those advisers at the meeting concurred with Ball in warning that "a flat commitment without combat forces was the worst of both worlds." The president declared that "sending organized forces was a step so grave that it should be avoided if this was humanly possible." He would approve U.S. troops only as "a last resort"—and even then only as part of a SEATO force.[34]

The military solution thus remained an option. Washington notified Nolting that it would not send combat units in lieu of other public and diplomatic measures intended to halt infiltration. The president preferred a "partnership" with Diem. The defense department, however, continued "preparing plans for the use of U.S. combat forces in SVN under various contingencies, including stepped up infiltration as well as organized . . . (military) intervention." The administration sought to exhaust all expedients short of U.S. ground forces. In the meantime, it expected to participate in decisions on military, political, and economic matters that affected South Vietnam's security.[35]

The president had not taken an unequivocal stand against combat troops, thereby encouraging supporters of the move. Taylor later insisted that Kennedy had felt no compunction to declare a commitment to South Vietnam because he had already done so in NSAM 52 of May 11, 1961. The president, Taylor wrote, "never indicated any opposition of which I was aware to the thesis that we must be prepared to go all the way if we took this first step—one of the prime lessons of the Bay of Pigs." Rostow confirmed this interpretation by recalling that after the president had approved all parts of the Taylor report except that of sending troops, he stood up and asserted: "If this doesn't work perhaps we'll have to try Walt's Plan Six; that is, [a] direct attack on North Vietnam." As Rostow wrote, Kennedy "took the minimum steps he judged necessary to stabilize the situation, leaving its resolution for the longer future, but quite conscious that harder decisions might lie ahead."[36]

III

THE PRESIDENT'S middle-of-the-road position drew a mixed reaction. Robert Johnson spoke for several state department colleagues in declaring this a "strategic moment" for sending combat troops and proving that "we are prepared to prevent the fall of Viet Nam." Two veteran diplomats, Harriman and Bowles, opposed any military involvement in South Vietnam. Harriman warned against tying U.S. prestige to Diem's "repressive, dictatorial and unpopular regime." Bowles, as undersecretary of state, urged both Rusk and Schlesinger to accept a political solution. In supporting Diem, the

United States was "headed full blast up a dead end street." Both Harriman and Bowles favored a negotiated military withdrawal.[37]

Harriman advised the president to accept an approach similar to that followed in Laos. The grizzled veteran of the diplomatic wars had been greatly distraught at the situation in the state department when assuming his new position as Assistant Secretary of State for Far Eastern Affairs. The McCarthy witch hunt of the previous decade had devastated the state department's Asian bureau after China's conversion to communism in 1949. "A wasteland," Harriman lamented. "It's a disaster area filled with human wreckage." The United States must take advantage of the Soviet Union's interest in stabilizing Southeast Asia by concluding the negotiations over Laos in such a manner that no country could use it as a staging area against South Vietnam. The United Kingdom and the Soviet Union, as cochairs of the Geneva Accords of 1954, should then assemble the powers directly concerned about Vietnam—the United Kingdom, the Soviet Union, the United States, Communist China, France, North and South Vietnam, and India—to seek a settlement based on the following terms: an immediate cease-fire; a temporary division of Vietnam with a mutual renunciation of force and the establishment of commercial arrangements between the sectors; a strengthened or replaced International Control Commission to observe and enforce agreements; and the possibility of elections in reunifying the country. Once hostilities eased, the United States would reduce its military presence.[38]

Given the administration's Cold War mindset, the chances for negotiations over Vietnam seemed minimal. President Kennedy showed no interest, particularly while infiltration continued from the north. Rusk likewise opposed negotiations. The other side would seek U.S. concessions in exchange for stopping illicit actions that were tantamount to "highway robbery." Kennedy feared that postponing stronger measures in an effort to encourage talks with the Communists would appear to be a "major crisis of nerve." Concurrence came from Democratic Senator Stuart Symington of Missouri, former Secretary of the Air Force under President Truman and now an influential member of the Armed Services Committee and chair of the Subcommittee on the Middle East and South Asia. Symington had just returned from a visit to the embattled region. The White House, he told the president, must take direct military action. "Whether it be Saigon, or Berlin, or some other place, I do not believe this nation can afford further retreats."[39]

Kennedy recognized the need for strong measures, even appearing to ponder the use of combat troops while, in reality, slowing the momentum in that direction by requesting more information and working toward a partnership with Saigon. In other instances of firm U.S. action—Iran, Greece, Berlin, Lebanon and Jordan, Quemoy and Matsu—"we have come home free." He asked Rusk and McNamara to examine the nation's 1947 intervention in Greece. What was the U.S. commitment in men and money? "Are we prepared to send in hundreds and hundreds of men and dozens and dozens of ships?" Anything less seemed ineffective. "Or am I misinformed?" He questioned the guns used in counterguerrilla warfare. Were they too heavy for the small Vietnamese soldier? Picking up one of the long-range but heavy U.S. Army M-14 rifles then in use, Kennedy pointed it to the window of the Oval Office and keenly observed that the thickness of the jungles made close-up firing more likely and raised questions about the present rifle's utility. The shorter-range, lightweight carbine that he had used in the Pacific during World War II seemed more acceptable. "You know, I like the old carbine. You aren't going to see a guy 500 yards in the jungle."[40]

The president's tactics did not ease the pressure for combat troops. Rostow saw no danger of Chinese intervention as long as U.S. ground forces did not cross the seventeenth parallel. "Then—but only then—do I believe they would go to war with us." Just before a morning meeting of the National Security Council on November 15, McGeorge Bundy submitted a memo to the president, reporting a conversation with Rusk in which he argued that the White House should announce a "Rusk–McNamara Plan and fire all concerned if it doesn't work." The United States "*must* meet Khrushchev in Vietnam or take a terrible defeat." A White House commitment to a single division of combat troops would not escalate the conflict. "*With* this decision," Rusk insisted, "I believe the odds are almost even that the commitment will not have to be carried out." Bundy was convinced that this idea had the support of Rusk, Taylor, Rostow, and the vice president. "That is why I am troubled by your most natural desire to act on other items now, without taking the troop decision. Whatever the reason, this has now become a sort of touchstone of our will."[41]

This conflicting advice weighed heavily on the president at the National Security Council meeting as he repeated his reluctance to commit U.S. troops to South Vietnam except, perhaps, on a multilateral basis. "Korea was a case of clear aggression which was opposed by the United States and other members of the U.N. The conflict in Viet Nam is more obscure and less flagrant." In an irrefutable statement, he declared, "[I] could even make a rather strong case against intervening in an area 10,000 miles away against 16,000 guerrillas with a native army of 200,000, where millions have been spent for years with no success." The French would provide no support, to which remark Rusk noted British opposition as well. The secretary of state nonetheless thought that a firm policy in South Vietnam similar to that in Berlin might work without forcing Americans into combat. Kennedy sharply disagreed, insisting that the issues and opposing sides were clear in Berlin, whereas in South Vietnam the situation was "vague and action [was] by guerrillas, sometimes in a phantom-like fashion." The United States must avoid any action that suggested a unilateral violation of the Geneva agreements. It must "place the onus of breaking the accords on the other side and require them to defend their actions."[42]

The president nonetheless considered it imperative to appear strong wherever the Communists posed a threat. McNamara countered that direct U.S. military intervention would clarify matters in South Vietnam by aiming U.S. power at the sources of Vietcong strength, including those in North Vietnam. Hanoi was the most important area and "would be hit," Rusk declared, while admitting that an attack would "raise serious questions" because it was more of a "political target than a military one." Any military actions in North Vietnam must first disable all Vietcong airlifts into South Vietnam "to avoid the establishment of a procedure of supply similar to that which the Soviets have conducted for so long with impunity in Laos." But, the president asked, where would the United States base its operations? On aircraft carriers? Were they not vulnerable? Lemnitzer affirmed the need for carriers but added that Taiwan and the Philippines would provide the bases of action. McNamara admitted the need for a larger injection of U.S. troops, planes, and matériel than previously thought.[43]

The president still doubted the wisdom of a major military escalation. Would McNamara recommend such a move if SEATO did not exist? Yes, grimly responded the defense secretary. What would be the rationale? Lemnitzer tersely replied that a "Communist conquest would deal a severe blow to freedom and extend Communism to a great portion of the world." As with Laos, Kennedy found it difficult to justify strong actions in South Vietnam while doing nothing in Cuba. Lemnitzer snidely added that the joint chiefs felt that "even at this point the United States should go into Cuba." Overlooking this gratuitous remark, the president expressed concern about the reaction of neutral nations and the American people and Congress. Rather than make a decision at this time, Kennedy again tried to defuse the pressure by asserting that he wanted to discuss the matter first with his vice president, who had been unable to attend the meeting.[44]

Later that same day, Rusk directed Nolting to seek Diem's reaction to the administration's decision to accept everything in the Taylor report except U.S. combat troops. In exchange for the premier's agreement to a joint program along with the implementation of reforms, the United States would increase its military and economic aid. The relationship would be "much closer" than advisory in that the United States expected "to share in the decision-making process in the political, economic and military fields as they affected the security situation." In the meantime, more U.S. military personnel would assume "operational duties" aimed at helping South Vietnam win the war. Such responsibilities were "more suitable for white foreign troops than garrison duty or missions involving the seeking out of Viet Cong personnel submerged in the Viet-Nam population."[45]

And yet, the call for more stringent military action did not abate, for shortly after the president's decision, Hilsman joined Taylor and other advisers in continuing the push for combat troops. As director of the state department's Bureau of Intelligence and Research, Hilsman had overseen a recent study of guerrilla warfare that recommended correctives focusing on civic action, intelligence gathering, police work, and "constabulary-like counterguerilla forces." But South Vietnam's problems, he believed, had reached emergency proportions. The flood afforded an opportunity to combine strategic with humanitarian objectives by sending in 8,000 American forces as the "entering wedge" for more. Indeed, this proposal could provide the opportunity to implement the U.S. Army's new concept of a Foreign Liaison Assistance Group (FLAG), which entailed a three-step introduction of U.S. troops as first humanitarian or civic action teams, then Special Forces, and, finally, as regulars. The dispatch of the initial contingent "should be undertaken only as part of a more fundamental decision to follow through with a Korean-scale action if need be."[46]

The president realized that these military measures would Americanize the war and inquired into their legality. The state department's legal counselor and member of the Harvard law school faculty, Abram Chayes, doubted the U.S. case for attacking North Vietnam. The doctrine of "hot pursuit" permitted immediate retaliatory action on enemy bases located near the Laotian or North Vietnamese borders, but a direct assault on Hanoi or other strategic positions deep inside North Vietnam would go beyond the self-defense guarantees found in international law or in the U.N. Charter. The right of individual or collective self-defense contained in Article 51 of the charter came into play only after "a direct external attack upon one country by the armed forces of another." An armed attack justified an immediate counteraction that did not necessitate U.N. approval. "In cases of aggression that fall short of armed attack, however, it would not be consistent with the purposes of the United Nations for the United States as a UN member to proceed to the use of armed force to defeat acts which it considers aggressive." The U.N. member must seek a judgment from the United Nations Organization itself.[47]

The Kennedy administration remained open to sending combat troops. In a circular telegram to selected embassies, the state department indicated that even though it did not contemplate sending combat forces to South Vietnam, "nothing currently envisaged rules this out should it become necessary." Such action would involve exceeding the ceilings understood by the International Control Commission and the Geneva Accords. The emphasis must be on the violations by North Vietnam. The forthcoming

Jorden White Paper would focus on Hanoi's aggression and thereby gain support for the American position.[48]

With the issue of combat troops still very much on his mind, the president asked Galbraith to inspect the situation in Saigon en route back to his post in India. Not only did the president's invitation suggest his growing attraction to Galbraith's views, but it also demonstrated the ambassador's important place in the president's inner circle of confidants. Kennedy knew that Galbraith would recommend pulling out and leaving the problem to the Vietnamese. This command to visit Vietnam was particularly gratifying to Galbraith. After the Taylor mission's visit to the White House, its report was on the desk in the Oval Office, and Galbraith asked to see it. Rostow asserted that it was top secret and doubted that Galbraith had security clearance. Galbraith grabbed the copy, huffily declaring that his clearance was the same as Rostow's.[49]

It did not take long for Galbraith to send his reaction, which, he later declared, was "well received by the president and not by his advisers." Taylor's flood relief task force was an "exceedingly half-baked" ruse for sending troops. "Once there, they would use a shovel with one hand and deal with the guerrillas with the other." A resort to U.S. troops would be a mistake. "[S]ince there can't be enough of them to give security to the countryside[,] . . . their failure to provide security could create a worse crisis of confidence." Galbraith opposed the use of force and called military involvement a "slippery slope" that would broaden U.S. participation. Based on his experience as director of the U.S. Strategic Bombing Survey in 1945–46, he considered bombing "random cruelty" and militarily ineffective. The president must break with Diem, who had recently capitalized his troubles by becoming the center of "intense theological disputes" at home. Many observers lamented that Diem was "a great but defamed leader" whose administration had become "exceedingly bad." No major conflict could depend on logistic support backpacked by peasants over jungle trails. Indeed, he scoffed at White House concern over the insurgents. "Washington [was] currently having an intellectual orgasm on the unbeatability of guerrilla war." If guerrillas were effective in a ratio of one to fifteen or even more, "the United States would hardly be safe against the Sioux."[50]

"The only solution," Galbraith concluded, "must be to drop Diem." It was "politically naïve" to believe that he could make substantive changes at home. To win the war, he would have to assign more power to the army, and the result would be his own fall from power. Coup rumors were rampant—to the point, according to Nolting, that a mere nod from the United States could set one in motion. "It is a cliché," Galbraith continued, "that there is no alternative to Diem's regime. . . . This is an optical illusion arising from the fact that the eye is fixed on the visible figures. It is a better rule that nothing succeeds like successors." The South Vietnamese army presented a viable option that would buy time until the return of civilian rule. The U.S. cause was not hopeless—unless "we marry our course to that of a man who must spend more time protecting his own position and excluding those who threaten him than in fighting the insurgency." As matters stood, "we are now married to failure."[51]

Rostow adamantly disagreed with Galbraith's assessment. He assured the president that Galbraith had failed to grasp the international dimensions of the war. Infiltration from the north had increased the number of guerrillas from 2,000 in 1959 to the present total of 16,000 (not counting the Communist Civil Guards). On one route into South Vietnam, more than 400 a month had migrated during the first half of 1961. Nearly 70 percent of the growing enemy force were local recruits; 25 percent were South Vietnamese trained in the north and returned to the struggle; only 5 percent were North Vietnamese regulars. The infiltrators comprised well-trained "political cadres and soldiers, the hard core of the Viet Cong effort." The open frontier provided the chief means of escape from army pursuit. The Greek government of the 1940s, Rostow declared, had put down the Communist insurgency only when the Stalin–Tito rift forced a closing of the Yugoslav refuge. In Malaya and the Philippines, the established governments prevailed because the Communists had no frontier. Galbraith, Rostow hotly declared, had "grossly underestimated the military significance of the infiltration process."[52]

Rostow again dismissed the widespread concern about a U.S. troop presence leading to a full-scale war. No one, he emphasized, expected American soldiers to join "sweeps through Vietnamese territory." But they could conduct special missions if the struggle went badly and necessitated an escalated involvement. They would release ARVN forces for fighting by providing "a plateglass presence" along the seventeenth parallel and by protecting the towns in the countryside, both in the plateau and along the coast. U.S. forces could help build roads and participate in other engineering and logistic projects. Finally, they could assist the South Vietnamese if the Vietcong initiated open warfare.[53]

In a startling recommendation, Rostow told President Kennedy that the White House must consider instigating a coup if Diem failed to make changes. The administration, Rostow argued, must not permit the Vietcong to claim it legitimate to wage a guerrilla war across a border. In an appeal to the president's concern over his place in posterity, Rostow insisted that the "New Frontier will be measured in history in part on how that challenge was met." There was no way to dodge the issue. "No amount of political jiu-jitsu is going to get us off that hook." If the United States could overcome South Vietnam's political and administrative problems through a combination of "partnership and pressure, we shall get a lift of confidence which would, among other things, make it more safe to help induce a coup."[54]

About a week later, Galbraith wrote the president again, likewise suggesting the possibility of a coup, though not one inspired by the United States. From New Delhi, Galbraith warned Kennedy that South Vietnam was "a can of snakes." Although he considered himself accustomed to Oriental politics and government, "I was not quite prepared for Diem." A proposal recently made to Taylor revealed a lot about the premier. That proposal was to have a helicopter carry Diem from the palace to the airport. Transport by car necessitated a motorcycle escort for protection, and all residents along the route had to take in their laundry, close all windows, keep their heads in, and stay off the streets. Travel by helicopter "would make him seem more democratic." If Diem left Saigon even for a day, he required all cabinet members to see him off and welcome him back. He suffered from a lack of intelligence information, the need for centralized army control, the confusion resulting from the provincial governors' dual responsibility as army generals and political administrators, and the "subservient incompetence" of these political administrators. Diem saw a "greater need to protect himself from a coup than to protect the country from the Viet Cong."[55]

IV

GALBRAITH WAS WRONG in his negative assessment of the Vietcong's capabilities but correct in discerning the threat of a military coup. His error about the enemy's resiliency would not become clear for some time, but his second point concerning a coup threatened to materialize in the near future. Hilsman cited "two reliable reports" that high-ranking military leaders in Saigon were planning to overthrow Diem. Much of the generals' animosity focused on the Nhus, who had recently launched a strident newspaper campaign against the United States. In late November, General Minh strongly criticized his government when talking to the U.S. Army attaché. The general had rushed to the attaché on the same day that the anti-American newspaper barrage had started, so fearful of Nhu's agents that he had a bodyguard with him. Diem's alleged reforms in the military, Minh insisted, were "shams" designed to fool the United States. Interference by Diem and his family in military matters had spawned an alarming situation. Brigadier General Le Van Kim, a subordinate of Minh's and a long-time critic of Diem, concurred. The next day, Colonel Pham Van Dong, Deputy Commander of the Third Army Corps, confided to the attaché that he had discussed the possibility of a coup with the commander of that corps, Brigadier General Le Van Nghiem, who wanted to "wait and see how things go before we take sides." According to Minh, Diem had become a "puppet" of his brother Nhu, who, Dong interjected, intended to seize control of the government. Rostow urged the White House to investigate the likelihood of a coup if Diem failed to make changes.[56]

In the event of a coup attempt, the United States put several contingency plans in place. Above all, the administration must not become identified with a coup that failed. Relations with Diem would be at "almost dead end." It seemed probable that all the United States had to do to ensure a coup was to declare its preference for the constitutional succession of Vice President Tho. Nhu, however, had already criticized Tho and would probably seek his assassination. If a struggle for power developed, it would involve Diem, the ARVN officers, Nhu and his Can Lao agents, the Communists, and the religious sects—all of which would lead to chaos and profit the Communists. U.S. involvement should be on the side of the military officers and seek to end the takeover as quickly and cleanly as possible.[57]

The president rejected the coup route, choosing instead to approve a tightened joint effort with South Vietnam that would provide a safe middle ground between Galbraith's recommendation to drop Diem and the Taylor mission's call for combat troops. NSAM 111 accepted all the Rusk–McNamara recommendations of November 11 except the call to make a full commitment to saving South Vietnam. The United States agreed to furnish an air lift and uniformed personnel to South Vietnamese forces, more equipment and manpower for air reconnaissance and related activities, and small craft and uniformed advisers and operating personnel for coastal and inland water assignments. It accelerated training and equipping of the Civil Guard and Self-Defense Corps, and it provided the personnel and equipment needed for improving the military–political intelligence system beginning at the provincial level and moving upward. It also arranged for operational collaboration with South Vietnamese military forces, expanded economic and relief assistance, more administrators and advisers, and a joint survey of provincial conditions affecting the counterinsurgency program. In turn, the Saigon government must put the country on a war footing and welcome non-Communist participation in making decisions. About a week later, the president authorized a "selective and carefully controlled joint program of defoliant operations" ("Ranch Hand") aimed at undermining the Vietcong by killing tall weeds and thick underbrush along key infiltration routes and by denying food in areas where a resettlement plan and alternative food source were available for the peasants. NSAM 111 did not authorize U.S. combat troops.[58]

It would be easy to agree with those critics who insist that President Kennedy was a Cold Warrior who intended all along to escalate the war, even to send combat troops. NSAM 111 carried the suggestive title of "First

Phase of Viet-Nam Program," which implied the imminence of more decisive measures. Had he not mobilized U.S. military forces against the Soviets during the Berlin Wall crisis that previous August of 1961? Had he not asserted to McNamara and Rusk that only U.S. resolve in other world crises had allowed it to "come home free"? But these actions were misleading. The president wished to retain his options while trying every expedient short of U.S. fighting forces. He never wavered from his stand that only South Vietnam could win the war.[59]

The public impression remained, however, that the White House seemed inclined toward a deeper involvement in the war. Rostow called for U.S. help to the Saigon government to clear out all villages in the border area with North Vietnam that ran from the seventeenth parallel south to Cambodia and label this a "kill area" in which ARVN forces would shoot everything that moved. The war, he insisted, was not winnable without a sealed-off Laotian border. A neutral Laos under supervision of the International Control Commission might reduce infiltration. Just across the border in Laos, the Vietcong had captured the towns of Tchepone, Muong Phine, and Saravane, allowing its forces to control the Lao Bao Pass and countless elephant trails into South Vietnam. Some American experts wanted "special forces" to hit North Vietnam's key communication and transportation facilities.[60]

The president's call for closer cooperation with Diem drew flack as the Vietnamese press, secretly spurred by the Nhus, viciously attacked the United States's conditional aid plan as another instance of raw imperialism. "Vietnam Not a Guinea Pig for Capitalist Imperialism to Experiment On," proclaimed one editorial headline. Nolting thought that Diem had told the truth in declaring that his government had had nothing to do with the articles, although the premier hotly insisted that the White House call for a "quid pro quo" arrangement "played right into the hands of the Communists" by providing them with "a monopoly on nationalism." Dang Duc Khoi, a government officer who soon became its press representative, assured the U.S. embassy's Public Affairs Office that Madame Nhu had engineered the bitter press campaign. The Nhu family had had "a fit of temper" because of NBC correspondent James Robinson's critical account of an interview with Madame Nhu. She directed the Director General of Information, Tran Van Tho, to unleash an assault against the American press—without Diem's knowledge. Not until Thuan and Tuyen informed Diem did he know that she had been responsible.[61]

Tho's directives to the press went farther than Madame Nhu had envisioned. The criticisms focused on U.S. "interference" with Saigon's government and using the leverage of "conditional aid." Tho reminded the U.S. embassy of his long-standing opposition to freedom of the press and cited the recent controversy as justification. The articles in the *Thoi Bao* would inflame the populace against Americans as "capitalist–imperialists." Tho assured John Anspacher, the embassy's counselor for public affairs, that if he convinced the American press to "report correctly" about South Vietnamese affairs, the Saigon government would "persuade" the South Vietnamese press to stop the anti-American stories. Anspacher responded that his government could not regulate the American press and that U.S. officials were "walking on eggs."[62]

Nolting reported a "marathon" session with Diem and Thuan on December 1 that lasted for more than four hours and was somewhat encouraging. Diem repeated that U.S. influence in his government would hurt the war effort, and yet he expressed appreciation for President Kennedy's help and understood his reasons for attaching aid conditions. Even though the atmosphere of the meeting was friendly, Diem was "evidently smarting" from the attacks on him and his family in the American press. Nolting again denied his government's role in the press accounts, particularly those in *Time* magazine that emphasized the need for South Vietnamese "concessions" in exchange for more aid. Thuan noted that the stories raised nationalist feelings and interfered with a joint program. "I cannot overstress [the] disservice which certain press stories and obvious leaks have done, and are doing, to our cause here."[63]

Diem assured Nolting that he had already made changes intended to widen the base of his government. He planned to reactivate the National Internal Security Council and have it meet twice a week as a "war cabinet." He would soon appoint the "most active anti-communist patriots" to Provincial Councils having advisory and real powers. Eventually they would hold office by election. On the issue of military command, Diem declared that he had already delegated full authority to the Field Command to plan and carry out operations. Diem approved what McGarr had been doing for months: helping General Minh plan and take the offensive. Diem still opposed American participation in administrative decisions because of certain resentment from nationalist South Vietnamese and the opportunity this opened to Vietcong propaganda. How could he publicly declare that he needed Americans to carry out his national revolution? Americans became frustrated when matters failed to go "their way," which then aroused resentment among South Vietnamese. He and Thuan, however, agreed to invite selected Americans to take part.[64]

Nolting expressed mild encouragement regarding the recent changes. Diem insisted that before attempting to build a "superstructure" of democracy, he wanted an "infrastructure of democracy" based on education, civic responsibility, administrative capabilities, and political toleration. The prerequisite to success was personal security, which made the war a battle for the "hearts and minds" of the South Vietnamese people. Diem intended to become more accessible to the people by meeting with them and giving monthly radio talks. But he refused to broaden his government by inviting in "dissidents or fence sitters." The improved "public image" of Diem wanted by Washington, Nolting added, could come only with victory in the field. In the meantime, the few concessions agreed to by Diem along with others that might come on a gradual basis should ultimately turn the war around and lead to the Vietcong's defeat.[65]

In early December 1961 the greatly expanded U.S. aid effort, code-named "Operation Beef-Up," got under way, but not without complaints about American infringements on South Vietnam's sovereignty. Diem reacted coldly to the White House overture about helping the Saigon government make decisions. South Vietnam, the premier retorted, "did not want to be a protectorate." The state department softened its demands. The result was, according to Rusk, a partnership "so close that one party will not take decisions or actions affecting the other without full and frank prior consultation." The "Memorandum of Understanding" approved by Diem on December 4 established a "limited partnership" that rested on South Vietnam's maintaining responsibility for winning the war and on its building an "infrastructure of democracy."[66]

Rostow wanted faster action and urged the president to send Lansdale back to Saigon. "I do not believe that all the choppers and other gadgetry we can supply South Viet-Nam will buy time and render their resources effective if we do not get a first class man out there." Rostow was not alone in making this proposal. In a surprising reversal of form, the state department had also pondered the advisability of sending Lansdale to Saigon as an "explainer" of the U.S. position. Lansdale warned the president and others in a White House meeting that Diem feared a U.S. attempt to repeat the French experience of placing its people in key positions and gradually assuming complete control. Lansdale opposed a return to Vietnam for reasons he had explained in late November to General Samuel Williams. Lansdale had rejected the claim that South Vietnam could not win the war with Diem as leader. "So, one of the thoughts being ginned up is that I go over as his personal advisor and, presumably, clobber him from up close. I pointed out that this was a duty without honor and I'd be damned if I'd do that."[67]

To justify the expanded U.S. military commitment to South Vietnam, the White House on December 8 authorized the public release of William Jorden's long anticipated state department "White Paper" documenting infiltration from the north. Entitled *A Threat to Peace: North Vietnam's Efforts to Conquer South Vietnam*, it argued that under the doctrine of "collective self-defense," Saigon could request outside help. The irony is that Jorden's report sent a message to Diem that his biggest threat came from the outside, supporting his argument that domestic reforms were secondary to stopping infiltration. He became convinced that the United States regarded South Vietnam as so integral to the Free World's fight against communism that the Kennedy administration had no choice but to help his government.[68]

On December 11 the first two contingents of about thirty-three U.S. helicopters landed in Saigon, accompanied by four single-engine training planes and 400 uniformed personnel as pilots and ground crews. Although assigned to the ARVN in the field, the helicopters would remain under U.S. Army control. The following day the *New York Times* called this program "the first direct military support by the United States for South Vietnam's war against Communist guerrilla forces." The story, however, did not appear on the front page of the *Times*, even though it considered the move "the first fruits" of the Taylor mission. The three-member International Control Commission recognized the pivotal nature of the U.S. decision. Its Canadian, Indian, and Polish representatives held several emergency meetings to determine whether to terminate their functions in South Vietnam in light of the recent U.S. military buildup that had violated the Geneva Accords by raising its uniformed personnel to nearly 1,500 in number. Less than a week after Jorden's report appeared, on December 14, the White House formally announced a program of enhanced U.S. assistance to Saigon brought on by North Vietnam's violations of the 1954 agreements. The following day, the administration publicly released the letters between Kennedy and Diem that signified a formal agreement to expand the U.S. assistance program in South Vietnam.[69]

To facilitate the new partnership, the United States made the enlarged MAAG secondary to a much more broadly organized group known as the Military Assistance Command, Vietnam (MACV), and subordinate to CINCPAC in Honolulu. The U.S. military's dominant role became evident when MACV dutifully acknowledged the dual political and military thrust of the counterinsurgency program but could not hide the notable absence of the word advisory from the title (as in MAAG). Like the Greek experience of the 1940s, the senior U.S. military officer would help plan and make decisions about military operations; but if the conflict intensified, as it had in Korea, he could assume responsibility for its conduct. MAAG thus faded into the background in the face of a "military assistance command" that had a joint staff headed by the "Commander, US Military Assistance Command, Vietnam."[70]

For the new position as Commander of MACV, McNamara and Rusk approved Taylor's nomination of Lieutenant General Paul Harkins, who had been General George Patton's deputy chief of staff in North Africa and Europe during World War II. After serving as Taylor's chief of staff of the Eighth Army in Korea, Harkins became Field Force Commander for SEATO and, when Taylor assumed the superintendent's office at West Point, his commandant of cadets. Although well acquainted with South Vietnam, Harkins had no experience with insurgency warfare. Gilpatric had mild reservations. Harkins, Gilpatric later declared, "was diplomatic all right, to a fault, in a sense that I think he didn't have strong enough convictions." The president recognized these dangers but accepted McNamara and Rusk's recommendation. Over Hilsman's protests, Kennedy emphasized the impossibility of pushing past the joint chiefs a young officer with no guerrilla warfare experience over a general: "The military would crucify me." Taylor called Harkins "a natural" and led the way in promoting him to a four-star general. McNamara outlined the requirements for advisers in South Vietnam to the secretary and the army's chief of staff. He called for a greater number of officers and men capable of field duty in a semicombat role— particularly that of unconventional war in a rigorous climate. "We have got to have the first team there; I am not sure we do now." The joint chiefs considered Harkins an excellent choice for assuming what McNamara termed "the most difficult job in the U.S. Army."[71]

The new arrangement could not have pleased McGarr. Lemnitzer informed the general that the administration had approved a U.S. military assistance command and that its head as the senior U.S. military representative in South Vietnam would have the dominant voice in military matters, on both the American and the South Vietnamese side. To impress Diem with the heightened counterinsurgency effort, a four-star U.S. general would assume control and MAAG would serve under his command. Lemnitzer realized that the new command structure would be "something less than a Christmas present" for McGarr, but felt confident that he would make the adjustment.[72]

In the meantime, Nolting's claim that Diem had changed his attitude toward reform proved overly optimistic. General Minh had recently informed the premier of the use of task forces as provided in a military campaign plan worked out by CINCPAC. Diem became immediately suspicious and demanded to know why the task forces were to operate under the field command. Minh explained that they would focus on specific actions against heavy Vietcong centers and thus help corps commanders fulfill their pacification responsibilities. Diem strongly disapproved. Then on several occasions afterward, senior officers close to Nhu suspiciously asked whether Minh sought control of the task forces in an effort to carry out a coup. When Minh later presented a border control plan to Diem that was similar to that drawn up by MAAG and modified by the field command, Diem told him to "hold off" while he studied a British proposal. Minh complained that he felt like an "officer without portfolio." Armed agents, he insisted, regularly followed him, and his own guards had arrested two armed men near his house who were identified as Thuan's "private detectives."[73]

Diem's fear of a coup had prevented him from delegating authority to his military officers from the chain of command all the way down to field units. Antiguerrilla operations required tactical flexibility and great initiative in reacting to sudden dangers. This "vicious circle," Rostow argued, would break only if a coup succeeded, "but for us to encourage one would involve grave risks." Lansdale understood Diem's apprehension about a coup—especially when his field commander, Minh himself, had been "outspoken" about one. Only an enhanced U.S. military involvement in South Vietnam could stabilize the political situation and unify the country's armed forces.[74]

The U.S. military buildup came at precisely the time that the Vietcong, under Hanoi's direction and as Lansdale had warned President Kennedy, expanded its activities. By late 1961, the Vietcong had developed an operational base in the Central Highlands. The Communist party had just issued a circular declaring, "The People's Revolutionary party has only the appearance of an independent existence; actually our party is nothing but the *Lao Dong* Party of Vietnam, unified from North to South under the direction of the central executive committee of the party, the chief of which is President Ho." On December 11, North Vietnam's foreign ministry denounced the United States for accusing Hanoi of doing what the United States itself was doing. The "U.S. imperialists" had installed a military program that violated the Geneva Accords. The United States and its "puppet Ngo Dinh Diem administration" had then gathered "a pile of faked documents" that criticized Hanoi for breaking the 1954 agreements. For seven years the United States had violated Vietnam's sovereignty by importing thousands of U.S. military personnel and untold amounts of armaments.[75]

Not all was harmonious within the Communist camp. Beijing's leaders had become concerned about the Vietcong's upgraded military actions. In December 1961, senior diplomat Zhang Yan proclaimed before the National Conference on Foreign Affairs that large-unit operations were "inappropriate" in that the Communist Vietnamese had "exposed themselves too much." Guerrilla warfare should continue for perhaps another ten years to permit the Vietcong to expand its size. Marshal Ye Yianying, president of the People's Liberation Army's Military Science Academy and an acquaintance of Ho Chi Minh, led a military delegation to Hanoi late that same month to celebrate the seventeenth anniversary of the creation of the People's Army of Vietnam. While there, he urged Hanoi's leaders to be patient. The only way to destroy the Diem regime was through guerrilla warfare and not by battalion-sized military operations. China's caution was primarily attributable to its nearly devastating internal economic problems, which discouraged policies conducive to a confrontation with the United States.[76]

The Vietcong's heightened offensive had severely challenged the U.S. aid program. Part of South Vietnam's problem lay in the lack of qualified servants in the provinces. In addition, the Vietcong had killed thousands of people, including government officials and village chiefs. "And some of the best ones," according to Alexis Johnson in the state department, "were the ones that were murdered." They were the "targets," leaving the government with a small number of trained personnel. Continued U.S. support to Diem remained the only option.[77]

BY THE END of 1961, MAAG had more than doubled to 2,067 military advisers, causing great concern among Americans on the scene about the growing military orientation of an aid program now spearheaded by MACV. The U.S. chargé in Saigon, William Trueheart, thought that MACV's establishment had overemphasized the military's role in Vietnam and raised questions about the ambassador's status. The most obvious sign of this change was the provision that MACV would report directly to the joint chiefs and the secretary of defense. Lemnitzer pointed to the overarching need for broader military advice and assistance in training and security. Nolting protested and even considered resigning, but Rusk would not bend. McNamara bluntly responded that the joint chiefs had hotly declared that "no four-star general is going to be under an ambassador." Peering directly at Nolting, the defense secretary firmly and slowly asserted, "Look, on this one the Joint Chiefs have got me over a barrel. I can't do anything about it."

Shortly before noon on December 22, 1961, twenty-five-year-old Army Specialist Fourth Class James Davis of Livingston, Tennessee, became the first American killed by Communist guerrillas in Vietnam. He and nine South Vietnamese soldiers had been aboard a radio-detection truck as it lumbered west on Provincial Highway No. 10, scattering huge clouds of dust from the gravel that softly settled on the few Vietnamese peasants working in the rice paddies. Out of the eerie stillness came the explosion of a land mine under the truck's rear that threw it thirty yards into a ditch. As its ten occupants clambered back onto the road with their rifles, about twenty Vietcong arose from the watery paddies to spray the road with automatic gunfire. Davis was shot through the head, dying instantly. All ten soldiers died in the ambush, their bodies found hours later covered with flies and their weapons and electronic gear gone.[78]

Two days earlier, MAAG had received official approval to use all means at its disposal in self-defense. Nolting had reminded his home office that just as the Vietcong depended on political, economic, psychological, guerrilla, and military means, so should the counterinsurgency program maintain a multifaceted orientation. The line of restraint dramatically blurred with Davis's death. In a surprising development, McGarr appeared chastened and expressed opposition to the new military focus. Civilian policymakers, he complained to Lemnitzer two days after Christmas, were trying to settle a "very unconventional situation in a basically conventional manner." Military measures could not provide permanent solutions to a massive problem that had political, economic, psychological, *and* military dimensions. Defeating an insurgency required "long range coordinated action on all fronts."[79]

How prophetic were these words as the United States embarked upon a limited partnership with South Vietnam that pointed to an Americanized war.

7

A DECENT VEIL OF HYPOCRISY

> We have not sent combat troops in the generally understood
> sense of the word.
>
> President John F. Kennedy, February 14, 1962

THE RAPIDLY ESCALATING U.S. military involvement in South Vietnam alarmed many observers that the Kennedy administration intended to Americanize the war. As part of "Project Beefup," MACV assumed control of military matters, relegating MAAG to an ancillary position and suggesting a U.S. takeover of the war. By the end of 1962, military assistance more than doubled and the number of advisers almost tripled to more than 9,000. U.S. pilots bombed and strafed South Vietnamese villages suspected of harboring Vietcong, while helicopters provided mobility to the ARVN and, for a time, terrified the Vietcong peasants. "Roaring in over the treetops," Hilsman recalled with immense satisfaction, the helicopters "flushed [the Vietcong] from their foxholes and hiding places, and running in the open, they were easy targets."[1]

Counterinsurgency, however, remained the official U.S. strategy. The Diem regime, pushed by U.S. and British advisers, instituted the Strategic Hamlet Program, which, patterned after the now defunct agrovilles, called for the construction of thousands of interconnected and fortified encampments aimed at safeguarding villagers from the Vietcong and thereby building popular loyalty to the central government. Integrally related to this pacification effort was the use of defoliants to kill ground cover concealing enemy movements and the chemical destruction of crops to deny foodstuffs to the Vietcong. At the center of the U.S. involvement was the U.S. Army's Special Forces. Trained in counterinsurgency warfare and adorned in colorful camouflage garb, the Green Berets shared their expertise and enthusiasm with South Vietnamese soldiers, attempting to inject a strong sense of optimism that made victory seem inescapable. U.S. involvement in unconventional warfare provided a glimpse into future low-intensity conflicts, affording onlookers and participants an exciting opportunity to witness and perhaps even make history.

The Kennedy administration waged a secret war in Vietnam even as it denied the obvious. An admission to combat engagement would acknowledge violation of the Geneva Accords as well as endanger the ongoing negotiations over Laos. Most important, it would mark a breach of faith with the American people. But how to hide these clandestine actions? On January 13, 1962, the first U.S. planes participating in the secret Farmgate operation flew a mission in support of Vietnamese aircraft under attack. A pattern developed so quickly that, by the end of the month, Americans had engaged in 229 combat sorties. More than a few anxious observers feared that the United States had gone to war in Vietnam. Before an executive session of the Senate Foreign Relations Committee on January 12, Nolting admitted that a U.S. *adviser* had died but assured his inquisitors that "as of now" U.S. advisers were not in combat. Three days later, a news correspondent asked the president at a press conference, "Are American troops now in combat in Viet-Nam?" "No," he responded. The administration's repeated denials failed to ease the mounting suspicions. In mid-February, the *New York Times* chastised the White House for concealing the truth, and columnist James Reston asserted that "the United States is now involved in an undeclared war in South Vietnam."[2]

The secret war in Vietnam could not remain secret for long. Trueheart acknowledged that the enhanced military program violated the Geneva Accords. When U.S. military personnel confronted questions about the new equipment and people, the standard response was "No comment." Trueheart also admitted that the U.S. government made every attempt to hide its military involvement from the American public. "I knew about what they were doing with the equipment as they turned it over to the Vietnamese," he asserted. "I knew we were also, of course, flying the Farm Gate airplanes. There were many questions about whether in fact there was always a Vietnamese in the back seat or the front seat or whichever seat he was supposed to be in." Indeed, the Vietnamese aboard the plane became known as a "sandbag." Hilsman confirmed this assessment, calling the Vietnamese a "nominal pilot." Trueheart defended the use of defoliants around military installations, but he could not justify crop destruction, because it hurt the villagers and not the enemy. The Vietcong could always secure food. Such a practice alienated the very people that the Diem regime needed to befriend.[3]

A major impetus to exposing the U.S. military involvement came from the arrival of a different brand of news correspondent: young and sometimes inexperienced American reporters assigned to what they regarded as the backwaters of Vietnam. Hoping for professional advancement and driven by the exuberant spirit of the times, David Halberstam from the *New York Times* (who replaced Homer Bigart in August 1962), Neil Sheehan of United Press International, and Malcolm Browne of Associated Press were among those who intended to assume the role of wartime correspondents similar to their illustrious predecessors during World War II. Not only did they expect to be privy to secret plans and operations, but they also hoped to accompany U.S. and South Vietnamese soldiers into battle and, like Ernie Pyle and other giants before them, gather exclusive firsthand information and write career-making stories. The atmosphere was ripe for trouble, however, because America's military advisers bitterly rejected any criticisms of their performance and refused to divulge privileged information to the press. Cries of censorship came from the correspondents, arousing deep resentment within the Kennedy administration. Halberstam was "pink, if not red," exclaimed General Samuel Williams from MAAG.[4] An accommodation was especially difficult because the correspondents attributed the lack of progress in the war to errors in analysis and strategy, whereas the analysts and strategists insisted that their policies would succeed if the press left them alone.

The White House soon lowered a veil of secrecy over its military involvement in South Vietnam that directly affected all journalists. The Saigon regime proved especially sensitive to press criticism from well-known figures such as Bigart, who had covered the Greek Civil War of the late 1940s; François Sully from *Newsweek*; and James Robinson from NBC, the latter two of whom infuriated Diem by criticizing both him and Madame Nhu. When Nolting informed Diem that the U.S. government could not quiet the press because of the fundamental right of freedom of speech, the premier further withdrew into himself. More was at stake than Diem's personal displeasure. The fury over these newspaper accounts could undermine the U.S. assistance program in South Vietnam.

The year 1962 proved pivotal to the U.S. involvement in South Vietnam in that it opened with the promise of a success that led the Kennedy administration to consider withdrawing most of its military forces and returning to a low-key advisory program. General Harkins and other U.S. military leaders doubtless believed the positive assessments they gave to the press. President Kennedy had faith in a counterinsurgency program that, he proudly asserted, depended more on special skills than sheer firepower. Harkins predicted victory within a year, and McNamara offered the same grandiose assurances, albeit over three years. The strategic hamlets would soon be in place, crop destruction would starve the Vietcong, and the expanded U.S. military presence would energize the ARVN into launching a final offensive.

In this Alice-in-Wonderland atmosphere, private discussions began in Washington about a phased cutback in the U.S. involvement. But before the United States could begin a partial withdrawal, it had to build up South Vietnam's capacity to stand on its own. Such an objective led to the ultimate irony in the war: The only way to lower the U.S. involvement was to raise the U.S. involvement. All the while, the Kennedy administration became deeply entrenched in a secret war in Vietnam, and, to keep this reality from the American people, it arranged the facts in a manner that did not always reflect the truth.

I

AT A TOP-LEVEL MEETING in Palm Beach, Florida, on January 3, 1962, President Kennedy reiterated his opposition to a direct U.S. military involvement in the war while paradoxically taking one step closer to it. He told those present—including the Joint Chiefs of Staff, the vice president, McNamara, Taylor, Harkins, and Gilpatric—that Harkins as MACV's commander would possess more powers than those held by the chief of MAAG. As a four-star general, Harkins would control U.S. military policy, operations, and aid in South Vietnam. He could discuss both U.S. and Vietnamese military matters with Diem and his military leaders, and he answered directly to the joint chiefs and secretary of defense. The president turned to Harkins and clarified his task. "I want you to go out and help President Diem do everything he can to stop these communist inroads and build up his army. There are about eight hundred advisers there now, and if you need more let us know and we'll do everything we can to help." The U.S. advisory role now approximated that of a joint military command. Kennedy nevertheless emphasized that "the U.S. military role there was for advice, training and support of the Vietnamese Armed Forces and not combat."[5]

The Kennedy administration recognized the political wisdom in maintaining a low profile and attempted to delude the public into believing that nothing had changed. The joint chiefs chair received instructions to work with the departments involved in developing "a suitable cover story, or stories," for any U.S. action affecting public affairs or security issues.[6] The White House had justified deception to conceal its deepening military commitment to South Vietnam.

The Saigon embassy expressed great concern over the North Vietnamese and Communist Chinese reaction to the enhanced American military presence. It warned the White House that Hanoi would escalate its military response as a well-publicized defensive move, hoping to confuse world opinion and avert a direct U.S. intervention. In a penetrating admonition, the embassy asserted that "the game could become one of the patience of the contending forces, with the DRV [Democratic Republic of Vietnam, or North Vietnam] aware of the political disadvantages which would confront the US forces in a prolonged match." The White House should not attempt to relieve pressure on the south by expanding military operations in the north. Threats to use U.S. combat forces in North Vietnam would encourage Hanoi to seek Communist Chinese assistance out of fear that the United States intended to reunify Vietnam by force. The Chinese might even enter the war, as they did in Korea in 1950.[7]

The U.S. embassy was correct in its concern over a widened conflict, for Hanoi had intensified its efforts to attract Chinese help. In late January 1962, more than 1,500 people had gathered in a Beijing rally hall, where a huge NLF banner stretched over its entrance and NLF representative Huynh Van Tam received a standing ovation. The Americans, Huynh announced, had expanded their combat role in Vietnam. They had helped the Diem regime in torturing and maiming half a million people, and in killing 90,000 and injuring another 23,000 by bombs. They had participated in mopping-up operations, and they had poisoned crops in liberated areas. In the last seven years, they had worked with Diem in setting up 847 prisons holding about 300,000 inmates and 262 agrovilles that placed millions under house arrest in "another form of concentration camp." According to Liu Chang-sheng, vice president of the All-China Federation of Trade Unions, the 650 million people in China supported the effort to throw out "U.S. imperialism and the Ngo Dinh Diem clique." The United States, Liu proclaimed, sought to convert South Vietnam into a "colony and military base for aggression against southeast Asia and for attacking China." It must withdraw all military personnel, equipment, and war matériel. At this point, however, Beijing remained cautious, preferring continued material assistance rather than a direct military involvement.[8]

Despite the warnings about China, the pressure for U.S. military escalation proved relentless. No one set out the strategic steps by which additional firepower would ensure the insurgency's defeat; victory would somehow derive from the mere presence of U.S. military might. In Diem's office in early January 1962, McGarr urged approval of the "Campaign Plan," a military strategy developed before Taylor's visit by a joint Vietnamese and MAAG study group that recommended having 278,000 South Vietnamese in uniform by the end of 1963. When McGarr inquired about the status of the Border Control Plan, Diem claimed that the ongoing battle for the Mekong Delta had prevented him from fielding a requested ranger force of 5,000, but he intended to send a smaller contingent to the Laotian border.[9] In practical terms, a massive influx of U.S. soldiers could have done little more than inconvenience Vietcong infiltration, merely causing the cadres to relocate their paths through the jungle. But it could also have brought an escalated Vietcong reaction built on tapping either the economic and military goods or the mammoth manpower resources of Communist China as well as North Vietnam.

The inherent difficulties in maintaining restraints on U.S. military actions became clear when the naval command approved measures that spread the fighting beyond South Vietnam. To stop Vietcong infiltration by water, Felt in late January recommended the immediate dispatch of patrol ships north of the seventeenth parallel but remaining outside Communist territorial waters. Already, he complained, more than fifty enemy vessels had eluded interception by turning north on spotting the patrol. Rigid adherence to the seventeenth parallel could become "a real fence in political-military thinking." Felt's response left the decision to naval officers on the scene. Even though they still had authorization to patrol only the area below the seventeenth parallel, "it was not intended that a barrier be erected to steaming north of this parallel for the purpose of identifying and interrogating suspicious craft and ships."[10] His approval of such inspections had heightened the chances for maritime encounters that expanded the U.S. military involvement.

Growing U.S. military participation in the war also became evident in the air. American planes, piloted by U.S.–South Vietnamese crews, inadvertently crossed the Cambodian border on several occasions and, in one instance, caused an incident that the White House tried to conceal. Early in the morning of January 21, 1962, American B-26s and T-28s manned by U.S. and Vietnamese crews bombed and strafed Vietcong sites in the village of Binh Hoa, located close to the Cambodian frontier and less than twenty miles from Saigon. Due to navigational error, these Jungle Jim planes attacked the Cambodian border village of Bathu that same day, killing one and injuring three. The government in Phnom Penh accused the Diem regime of border violations and termed the assault an "act of war." Washington responded with a cover-up. If the press made an inquiry, instructed the state department, the South Vietnamese government should accept full responsibility for the error. Saigon's leaders apologized and offered indemnification to the victims (which the state department secretly reimbursed), without mentioning the United States.[11]

Military escalation had proved particularly risky because of the process's innate capacity to feed on itself. After the planes had struck Binh Hoa, a large ARVN force swarmed into the area, only to discover that the Vietcong had pulled out. Hilsman, who was in Vietnam at the time, praised Saigon's military operation but declared it the wrong response. The air strikes had combined with the arrival of ARVN troops to alert the Vietcong. Its forces had dispersed, but numerous innocent villagers died in the skirmish, "recruiting more Communists than were killed."[12]

By the time Harkins arrived in Vietnam in February 1962, the situation demanded immediate attention. Fighting had been under way since 1959 in forty-three different provinces that amounted to what he termed "forty-three wars going on." An eerie sense of fear permeated the country, augmented by stern security measures. "You couldn't do anything. All the windows had steel blinds on them, and all the curtains were pulled down. . . . Even the house I lived in had steel shutters closed tight." Harkins's first instruction was simple: "Let's open this up and get some daylight in here." He had to convince the Vietnamese to take the offensive. They had constructed nearly 16,000 forts at crossroads, canals, and other pivotal points, which they manned at night while confining their patrols to daylight hours. The Vietcong simply conducted its activities at night, knowing that the South Vietnamese were inside the forts—a surety because the soldiers' families were there as well. Harkins got rid of most of the forts, although he left about 6,000 of them at canal crossings in the delta and on important roads. Other changes were in order. The Vietnamese "were still having siestas in the afternoon, which I stopped. . . . You couldn't fight a war and go to sleep from twelve to three and then not expect the enemy to do something." He also extended the fighting week from five or six days to every day.[13]

Harkins thought it impossible to close off infiltration, particularly from Laos. "When you have nine hundred miles of jungle and then a few soldiers and just tiger paths and elephant paths, it's pretty hard to defend a whole front like that." Laos was "a camp for the Vietcong." The Vietnamese easily circumvented the state department directive barring Vietnamese patrols from crossing the border into Laos. The border between South Vietnam and Laos "wasn't marked at all. It was just watershed, really, at the top of the hills. There are two or three roads that go, and they'd pick up the road sign and take it with them and put it back when they came back." No Americans could accompany them, and planes could not fly within a mile or two of the border. "If the Vietcong came over and made a raid, say up around Pleiku and places like that, and you got the division to chase them back, you couldn't follow them. You weren't allowed to. So it was a sanctuary for them."[14]

As the military prognosis worsened, Diem attempted to refurbish his government and military establishment. He approved five MAAG advisers per battalion, authorized the newly created National Economic Council to meet, and, in an effort to establish closer contact with his people, spent Christmas of 1961 in the countryside, even visiting two remote ARVN posts and an island for the first time. He also raised the salary of village leaders, and, in a move that the American news corps heartily approved, he appointed the popular and respected Dang Duc Khoi as liaison with the press. The Vietnam Task Force hailed the appointment as Diem's best recent move to improve his image abroad. Diem also recognized the need to build a village infrastructure aimed at providing stability and reducing the threat of Vietcong terrorism. Resettlement of the people to secure areas was the prime prerequisite, he asserted.[15]

But the outward signs of improvement again proved misleading, according to the firsthand observations of Wesley Fishel of Michigan State University, a political science professor who had accompanied Diem to the Geneva Conference in 1954 and established a warm friendship during his stay afterward. After returning home from two weeks in Vietnam, Fishel submitted a highly negative report in late February 1962 that reached President Kennedy. The report noted that Diem's sagging popularity had undermined the chances for reform. From 1955 to 1962 most members of Fishel's university group trained Diem's government figures in police work and public administration. Among Fishel's more than fifty advisers, however, were at least five CIA operatives who trained South Vietnam's mountain tribes in paramilitary actions. In the early part of this period, nearly 90 percent of the people he talked with had strongly supported the premier. But now, outside Saigon, nearly everyone detested the Nhus. Of 100 Vietnamese questioned, only three favored Diem, asserted Fishel, and two of them had deep reservations.[16]

In a statement confirming Galbraith's negative assessment, Fishel declared that religion had become a divisive issue, but he insisted that it was not nearly as explosive as hatred of the Nhus. Thousands of South Vietnamese military officers had converted to Catholicism as a means of career advancement—information that came from Diem's own Father-Confessor and one of the premier's strongest supporters. Indeed, one member of his cabinet had become Catholic. A major recounted his conversion, bitterly calling this the only way to succeed. Much of this so-called religious activity occurred in the interest of promotion, Fishel allowed, even though the impression of widespread preferential treatment for Catholics was far different from the reality. The intense dislike for the Nhus overrode all other matters. Two administration members had tearfully described the rampant decline in governmental control, insisting that they had stayed on board only because their departure would ensure the Ngo family's remaining in power.[17]

Fishel's dismal observations rested primarily on the insidious influence of the Nhus. Diem had canceled Michigan State University's contract with the Saigon government because of what he considered to be unjust criticisms of his regime. Fishel believed that Diem's decision derived almost exclusively from the Nhus' influence and that other members of the government, led by Vice President Tho, thought the university's work worthy of continuation. When Fishel complained to Diem, the premier accused the professors of using their "privileged position" to secure government materials and then to attack his regime.[18]

Fishel lamented that Diem had fallen prey to "evil influences" led by his brother and his wife, along with Thuan. Nhu's cold, seemingly noncaring policies had undermined popular support for the regime, while his wife was "as brilliant, vivacious, bitchy, and brutal in her Borgia-like fashion as ever." With "(charitably) the purest of intentions," Madame Nhu had sponsored "an assinine bill" that passed through the National Assembly on the back of a manufactured majority. The "Social Purification Law" banned birth control, prohibited dancing, and imposed regulations on numerous everyday activities such as displays of affection and manner of dress. Fishel called it a "silly" piece of legislation that she had secured in the name of "austerity" and "mobilizing the population." Vietnamese critics denounced the law as Catholic creed forced on the people. In the meantime Thuan, "a shifty, ambitious, clever, and unscrupulous—but able—administrator," surreptitiously sought the presidency and had cultivated American supporters who considered him more pliable than Diem. And yet, warned Fishel, Thuan had aroused as much hatred as had the Nhus and would be a probable target for assassination by either the Communists or numerous others who detested him for climbing over friends to the top.[19]

Fishel doubted South Vietnam's ability to survive. Diem adhered to the philosophy of "personalism," which taught that every man had the right to develop to his fullest capacity; and yet a great number of qualified young men had become so disenchanted that they had dropped out of public view— some even leaving the country. Diem's government was "not malicious or predatory or vicious or particularly oppressive." But it was "clumsy and bumbling" in failing to implement reforms essential to survival. "Unless the situation can be changed for the better, we are in for a very bad period in Vietnam." Only "a major and favorable psychological shock" would turn matters around. When asked the meaning of that statement, Fishel refused to reply—probably because of his long-time closeness to Diem.[20]

Colonel J. R. Kent from the defense department offered a similarly negative assessment of Diem. His regime was not as corrupt as others in the region, but it was authoritarian, inefficient, and unpopular, primarily the result of his "aloof paternalism" and standoffish mandarin background, but also because of his suspicious nature. Compromise was out of the question because he considered himself omniscient and under "divine guidance." Although Diem had no military background, he insisted on splintering military authority and holding it himself—a divisive tactic that had saved his regime more than once. Not recognizing the importance of staff work, he sought recommendations from selected officers or met with all of them at one time—the latter approach putting the "face" of generals on the line and leading to sweeping decisions based on little or no facts. Diem's reluctance to accept U.S. advice was also attributable to his belief that the central problem was internal security and not external aggression.[21]

Diem's opposition to reforms over the past five years made it unlikely that he would ever change. The recently established National Security Council seemed encouraging, but a similar body had existed sometime before MAAG's chief made a formal recommendation to Diem in April 1960. Even then, one of the participants described the meetings as places where "ministers assembled to take notes and not to talk." Regarding reforms, the general

opinion was that Diem would not succumb to Washington's pressure because he knew how valuable South Vietnam had become to U.S. interests.
The Vietnamese press had interpreted President Kennedy's message to
Diem after the Taylor mission as an ultimatum. If so, Diem's resistance to
change guaranteed trouble.[22]

Harkins, however, liked Diem and placed primary blame on his military advisers. "I'm the only one he spoke English to." The premier was
honest and was not storing away the country's treasure for himself. He had
only two suits, a white one to meet visitors and a brown one when he went
into the field. In the rural areas, he distributed money to the honor guard
or province or village chief, and he taught villagers how to sow seeds and
transplant rice. Diem had personally appointed all nineteen ARVN generals. "Yet some of them were opposed to him, and I couldn't understand
that." General Tran Van Don had blurted out on meeting Harkins, "We're
not going to get anyplace until we get rid of Diem." General Minh had
helped Diem quash the sects in the mid-1950s and yet occupied a meaningless desk job in Saigon as his security adviser. Harkins went into the
field every day, but he could never convince Minh to accompany him. When
Minh reported to Diem, the president would ask, "Why don't you go out
like General Harkins?" Minh would usually mumble that he did not have
the plane or the personnel. "As a military adviser," Harkins remarked, "I
don't know what he did, as a matter of fact, because he didn't know what
was going on."[23]

The chief danger in this touchy situation was the U.S. temptation to
assume full direction of the war. Sound strategy dictated a wide-sweeping
approach that cut off infiltration from the north while putting down the
insurrection in the south. But the points of entry along the borders were
too numerous to close without a gigantic infusion of men and matériel that
Diem did not have. Harkins insisted that U.S. advisers did not engage in
combat, but his argument was not convincing. They went on patrols with
the South Vietnamese, though they were under orders not to shoot unless
shot at first. Americans also piloted the planes in the Farmgate program. A
narrow margin for error put the Americans at risk, virtually assuring their
participation in combat both on the ground and in the air.[24]

II

To PROMOTE counterinsurgency strategy, the Vietnam Task Force proposed an intricate mixture of political, economic, psychological, and military correctives. In relatively secure areas code-named "white," the Vietcong
engaged in harassment activities that the Saigon government should counter
with paramilitary measures. "Pink" areas signaled ongoing battles for con-

trol between the government and the Vietcong, which found the former holding the upper hand by day and the latter by night. The more volatile "red" areas were under Vietcong dominance and thus the focus of the government's military efforts. The Diem regime should maintain constant pressure on the Vietcong in the pink and red areas by employing the "amoeba principle," which sought to safeguard one geographical area after the other by establishing a security ring around Saigon that gradually extended outward.[25]

President Kennedy kept the emphasis on counterinsurgency by establishing the Special Group (Counterinsurgency) in an effort to unify the U.S. military part of the program without raising the chances of combat. Its chair was General Taylor in his capacity as Military Representative of the President. To highlight the importance of this committee, its membership included Robert Kennedy, who, after every session, reported to the president. Other members were the deputy undersecretary of state for political affairs, deputy secretary of defense, chair of the Joint Chiefs of Staff, director of the CIA, special assistant to the president for National Security Affairs, and administrator of the Agency for International Development. The president had been frustrated by a recent flurry of demonstrations and stonings of U.S. embassies, and his brother had expressed concern that Communists around the world regularly launched protests while the United States did nothing to mobilize opinion against them. The Special Group's mission, according to President Kennedy, was to ensure that everyone in the U.S. government understood that "wars of liberation" were insurgencies and hence "a major form of politico-military conflict equal in importance to conventional warfare."[26]

The state department's Bureau of Intelligence and Research meanwhile suggested several changes designed to promote counterinsurgency warfare. More than a few personnel had been with the Saigon mission too long, some harboring old frustrations that made them susceptible to the country's dissidents and prophets of defeat. Most leaders, trained only in conventional warfare, lacked an understanding of the antiguerrilla strategies needed at the working level. Furthermore, the agencies had become embroiled in bitter conflicts that spilled over into the war effort. The report recommended easing the pressure on Diem to grant reforms that were not basic to the central objective of keeping the Vietcong out of the villages. Most help should be at the local level in providing sergeants, lieutenants, and Civic Action teams that included police trainers and public administrators working with the government's officials in the villages and its troops in the field. In accordance with the Taylor report, Americans must live and work in the villages and demonstrate "technical competence, imagination, and human sympathy."[27]

Counterinsurgency received a major boost with the "Delta Plan" outlined by British counterinsurgency expert Robert Thompson, who was in
Saigon as part of a six-member "British Advisory Mission" invited there by
Diem (after CIA prodding) in the fall of 1961. Based on his counterinsurgency experiences in Malaya and the Philippines during the 1940s, Thompson emphasized the importance of destroying the link between the villages
and the guerrillas. He failed to note, however, that the ties between the Vietcong insurgents and the Vietnamese peasants were more difficult to sever
than were those between the insurgents in Malaya, who were primarily Chinese, and the Malays, who worked closely with the British. How would pacification of the populace undermine the Vietcong? "More kills," brusquely
responded Thompson. The Diem regime must first construct a large number of strategic hamlets to protect the villagers from the Vietcong. Once the
government won the people's confidence, they would furnish intelligence
on Vietcong movements. "The killing of communist terrorists will follow
automatically from that." This lengthy process required the cooperation of
the Self-Defense Corps (including the Republican Youth), the Civil Guard,
and army regulars serving in a support role. Thompson insisted that the
primary conflict was between the Communists and South Vietnamese villagers and not between Diem's regime and the Vietcong. The essential ingredient to victory was a civil defense force that stopped terrorism.[28]

Military figures in the Kennedy administration strongly opposed most
of Thompson's recommendations. McGarr was infuriated by the cavalier
British attitude. "Following Mr. Thompson's medical analogy . . . we have
the case of a doctor called in for consultation on a clinical case, actually
performing an amputation without consulting the resident physician—and
without being required to assume the overall responsibility for the patient."
Thompson's emphasis on the delta, the general insisted, contrasted sharply
with the need to focus first on War Zone D in the central part of the
country, followed by the region around Saigon. The Delta Plan would
take too long to develop, permitting the Vietcong to make rapid advances
against an enlarged police force that came with a reduced ARVN.[29]

The military's argument, however, failed to overcome the support that
the Delta Plan received from Diem and Nhu, as well as from the CIA and
Nolting. The key element in Thompson's counterinsurgency program was
the erection of strategic hamlets. No village groups should become vulnerable by their isolation, which meant that the strategic hamlets must go up
in areas first secured by military sweeps and then into the less secure areas
as defended hamlets. To protect the people inside the hamlets, government officials would issue plastic identification cards to loyalists, maintain
checkpoints, and enforce curfews by shoot-on-sight authority. The U.S.
Operations Mission established the Office of Rural Development, which
oversaw economic aid to the strategic hamlets and came under the direc-

tion of Rufus Phillips, a former CIA operative and Lansdale's associate in the Saigon Military Mission during the 1950s. After serving in Laos, Phillips left the CIA and returned to Vietnam in 1962, where he became an expert on the strategic hamlet program. Thuan declared that the counterinsurgency plan would go before the National Security Council for approval.[30]

What becomes clear in this push for counterinsurgency is the erroneous public impression left by its military orientation. It *appeared* that U.S. aid had become exclusively military. Even the Delta Plan's focus on strategic hamlets could not hide the central objective of killing the Vietcong. President Kennedy recognized that military correctives were a necessary prelude to nonmilitary measures. But the military assistance grabbed more attention and encouraged the hard-liners to believe that they were winning control of the program. In truth, they were—if only because of the momentum resulting from military actions that fed on each other. The president's policy of flexibility and restraint threatened to slip from his control, meaning that the U.S. commitment would become military in thrust and reversible only at the high cost of credibility.

Diem reacted quickly and favorably to the call for counterinsurgency by issuing in early February, on his sixty-first birthday, a decree proclaiming the Strategic Hamlet Program as national policy. Shortly afterward, he established the cabinet-level Inter-Ministerial Committee for Strategic Hamlets, whose purpose was to plan and implement the program. His brother, Ngo Dinh Nhu, would head the effort even though holding no official title and maintaining a low public profile.[31]

This apparent progress encountered severe problems with the American journalists, who complained of a U.S. embassy "blackout" on information that prevented them from covering U.S. participation in military operations. They were correct. In the previous November of 1961, the White House had issued instructions to the Saigon mission that substantiated their suspicions. "Do not give other than routine cooperation to correspondents on coverage [of] current military activities in Vietnam. No comment at all on classified activities." In a tense meeting with Nolting, the correspondents angrily complained about being barred from helicopter missions. Some information, Nolting told them, must remain secret. Caution was essential to the security of both the U.S. servicemen and the news correspondents themselves.[32] No argument could ease their indignation.

The director of the Vietnam Task Force, Sterling Cottrell, had urged greater restrictions on the American press. Nolting was correct, Cottrell declared to state department public affairs adviser Carl Rowan, in seeking authority for the Task Force to determine which military operations and equipment arrivals the correspondents could observe. News coverage of such activities had cast a negative image on the assistance effort. Cottrell enclosed an article from *U.S. News and World Report*, which claimed that a "curtain of secrecy" had fallen over Vietnam that "looks like a U.S. Embassy effort to confuse and disguise the situation." To undermine these charges, Nolting should seek the military's view on which operations were acceptable for viewing and then "provide the newsmen with appropriate guidance." He must emphasize that the United States was not taking over the war. He could not reveal numbers that provided the Vietcong with military information and Hanoi with evidence it could present to the International Control Commission. Washington "[did] not want coverage of civilian casualties as a result of government military operations."[33]

Cottrell's memorandum to Rowan went through Harriman, who regarded it as a red flag. If uncovered, the veteran diplomat warned, it would substantiate the media's worst fears. The presence of so many soldiers in Vietnam made news leaks unavoidable. "We couldn't give out stuff." The war was South Vietnam's to fight. "We were there to advise them, and we couldn't be the news." The war was also difficult to report. "The interesting news was when the Vietcong attacked, and nobody knew when that would happen." When it did, the news correspondents became angry that "they weren't there and covered themselves up and blamed the Americans." They could not accompany the U.S. soldiers on the helicopters. "We were most anxious to reduce the visibility of the Americans, and every time you took anybody in a helicopter it was the Americans' war, and it increased the visibility of the Americans." Typed at the top of Cottrell's memo was a revealing directive: "Harriman said burn this." Along the border was a warning in Harriman's handwriting and addressed to Rowan: "I believe our press will build this assistance to Vietnam as our participation in this war—a new war under President Kennedy—the Democratic War [?] Party, so skillfully avoided by the Republican President Eisenhower. The Press do not belong on these aircraft but can be kept fully informed by briefings in Saigon by our military or Embassy. [signed] WAH."[34]

Rowan supported the administration's position but warned that press censorship would cause a domestic firestorm over the "undeclared war" in South Vietnam. The secret directives, he charged, aimed to "prevent American newsmen from telling our people the truth about US involvement in that war." American reporters expected to function as war correspondents, which meant to accompany U.S. soldiers on military operations. And yet, he conceded, the embassy and military commanders in Vietnam were justified in wanting to block correspondents from situations where their presence might endanger Americans. Rowan recommended a flexible policy that authorized the ambassador to determine which military operations the journalists might witness. Nolting must brief them on the problems in South Vietnam and stress the need for secrecy.[35]

The Kennedy administration, for both domestic and foreign considerations, continued to hide its growing military activities. It emphasized that the assistance program included both economic and military goods. But the White House had made military correctives a prerequisite to reforms. Instead of admitting to this change, however, the U.S. government and military denied the obvious, causing a bitter fight with American news correspondents. With MACV's advent, the press concluded that a new joint command network had become the operational headquarters of a greatly escalated military effort.[36] The White House reacted furiously to these stories, hoping to conceal these actions from the American public and from Hanoi in an effort to avert a wider war. The result was a further deterioration in trust between U.S. officials and the American press in South Vietnam that impeded the assistance program and intensified the hard-liners' demand for a military solution.

III

HILSMAN TRIED to put the growing U.S. military presence in perspective by terming it an integral first step in a sound counterinsurgency program. The "liberal press," he derisively declared after a visit to South Vietnam in early 1962, must realize that the existence of an insurgency did not necessarily mean that the government was bad. Admittedly, Diem's unpopularity had hampered the most important remedy, which was a civic action program aimed at building ties between the villages and the Saigon government. But the immediate priority was military. "We have to put the Viet Cong in a meat grinder."[37]

The problem lay more in appearance than reality. President Kennedy still preferred counterinsurgency tactics, but Washington's conspicuous efforts to implement the military part of the aid program had seriously distorted the situation, encouraging Diem's critics to believe that America's patience had run out and that its remedy was military measures alone. U.S. military advisers meanwhile added to this mistaken impression by reiterating their arguments for combat troops. The U.S. course of action had become more muddled, primarily because the White House never achieved the vital balance between military and nonmilitary measures. The problem lay less in the lack of a strategy than in the administration's failure to make that strategy clear. Several competing strategies appeared to be at work in tandem, all differing in direction and none of them taking priority.

The division within the administration over chemical destruction of crops exemplified the confusion. President Kennedy had reluctantly approved chemical deployment on an experimental basis, emphasizing the necessity of confining defoliants and herbicides to areas containing only Vietcong. Soon, however, their use became regular. In characteristic fashion, the president insisted on limitations, forbidding any action without

White House approval. McNamara acknowledged that Communist radio in Moscow, Beijing, and Hanoi had blasted the "U.S.–Diemist clique" for waging chemical warfare against the people of South Vietnam, but he assured the president that the chemicals were part of a weed-killing program that was "not injurious to human beings, animals, or the soil." The chemicals cleared the ARVN's supply routes along with potential ambush spots in heavily forested areas around air bases and ammunition dumps. MAAG emphasized that only South Vietnamese piloted their helicopters over targeted areas. Furthermore, the Diem regime wanted to expand the use of chemicals and had grown impatient with U.S. restrictions. Soon these restrictions disappeared. In mid-December 1961, huge drums containing hundreds of thousands of gallons of defoliants began their journey out of California and toward South Vietnam, all labeled civilian supplies to avoid detection by the International Control Commission. As the defoliants arrived in Saigon, Americans noted that the pungent fumes emanating from the barrels stored at Tan Son Nhut Airport began to kill the surrounding greenery.[38]

Hilsman shared the president's doubts about defoliants and preferred the use of napalm, which cleared entire areas instead of just crops. Vietcong ambushes came more often under cover of terrain than foliage. Indeed, with the vegetation removed, Hilsman maintained, the insurgents gained a clearer field of fire. But Diem strongly favored crop destruction through defoliants. When Taylor agreed with Diem, Hilsman warned that this method could not be effective until the strategic hamlets had locked the Vietcong out of the villages. Once the Saigon government had seized control of the major rice-growing areas, it could drop napalm on the Vietcong's paddy fields in the mountain valleys. The objective was not to kill the Vietcong, but to reduce them "to hungry, marauding bands of outlaws devoting all their energies to remaining alive." Taylor found no difference between napalm and defoliants, to which Hilsman replied that the latter was subject to the charge of germ warfare. President Kennedy had already approved the jelly-like gasoline that, used in incendiary bombs, exploded in fire and spread like water. Harkins had no qualms. Napalm, he declared, "really puts the fear of God into the Viet Cong. And that is what counts."[39]

The growing air war particularly alarmed Harriman. While in Honolulu, he admitted to Edwin Martin, political adviser to CINCPAC, that the Jungle Jim support of ground operations was acceptable but warned that other kinds of air strikes might turn the people against both South Vietnam and the United States. Martin admitted that the South Vietnamese chose the targets, but the U.S. Air Force validated the selections and refused to conduct those operations that the South Vietnamese were able to perform. The implication was striking. In certain instances, one may presume, U.S. pilots conducted those missions the South Vietnamese were *not* able to perform. The guidelines for interdiction actions were clear although difficult to follow because of poor boundary markings: Jungle Jim operations could not take place closer than five miles from the Laotian and Cambodian borders by day and ten miles at night. Nolting asserted that air-ground support measures were safer than interdiction strikes. Coordination with ground forces would conceivably avert air assaults beyond the borders of South Vietnam. Harriman seemed satisfied with these explanations and agreed on the need for daily planning in Saigon, not in Washington or Honolulu.[40]

Cottrell noted a "veil of secrecy" settling over the U.S. military involvement in Vietnam. To the press on February 14, President Kennedy suggestively declared, "We have not sent combat troops in the generally understood sense of the word." The Vietnamese "are doing the fighting." Technically speaking, the president had told the truth. U.S. ground forces had not engaged in combat, even though only a thin line maintained the distinction between taking the offensive and acting in self-defense. U.S. advisers regularly conferred with South Vietnamese military leaders on operations and strategy. In addition, U.S. soldiers accompanied the ARVN into the jungles; U.S. pilots flew bombing and strafing missions; U.S. naval vessels entered waters above the seventeenth parallel; and U.S. counterinsurgency tactics had veered into a military direction. For security reasons, Kennedy opposed any disclosure of the numbers and types of equipment used in the growing conflict. Secrecy became the chief means for sidestepping the Geneva Accords. But the reality had become more difficult to disguise. The insurgents had killed five Americans and wounded twelve since 1955.[41]

The White House veil of secrecy proved highly transparent when the state department confronted a Senate inquiry. In an executive session of the Foreign Relations Committee, Democrat Wayne Morse of Oregon, no friend of the administration, expressed "grave doubts as to the constitutionality of the President's course of action in South Vietnam." Did he have the power to put the lives of U.S. servicemen at risk by authorizing them to transport ARVN soldiers into battle, return fire against the North Vietnamese, patrol South Vietnam's coasts, and fly over guerrilla areas? A war in Vietnam would tear the United States apart, particularly when "ships start coming back to the West Coast with flag-draped coffins of American boys." Democrat Albert Gore of Tennessee quoted Attorney General Robert Kennedy's recent assertion in Saigon: "We are going to win in Viet-Nam. We will remain here until we do win." Gore felt "uneasy about the public commitments which seem to be with us with respect to the presence of and the purposes for U.S. military personnel in Vietnam." And finally, the chair of the committee, Democrat J. William Fulbright of Arkansas, twice inquired about alternative leadership in Vietnam. Harriman retorted that Diem "is the head of the government, and I would not have thought that it was a proper function of the U.S. to attempt to make or break governments."[42]

The state department made a major attempt to justify the nation's deepening involvement in Vietnam. Article II of the Constitution made the president commander-in-chief of the armed forces. The case of *United States* v. *Curtiss-Wright* in 1936 called him the "sole organ of the nation" in foreign affairs and upheld his authority to dispatch military personnel abroad. The Foreign Assistance Act of 1961 empowered the president to provide military aid abroad by "assigning or detailing members of the armed forces of the United States . . . to perform duties of a noncombatant nature, including those related to training or advice." On December 23, 1950, the United States and Vietnam signed the agreement for Mutual Defense Assistance in Indochina by which "each Government agrees . . . to receive within its territory such personnel of the United States of America as may be required for the purposes of this agreement." The White House recognized in early 1961 that expanded U.S. activities in South Vietnam would put its military personnel in danger. Hence the president authorized them to fire in self-defense.[43]

The state department insisted that U.S. military forces in Vietnam were noncombatants and repeated the president's fuzzy February 14 assurance to the press that the administration had "not sent combat troops in the generally understood sense of the word." The state department admitted that the type of conflict waged in Vietnam determined U.S. military actions. There was no physical "front," which meant that fighting could break out anywhere and require U.S. military personnel to defend themselves. Violence in Vietnam had escalated since 1955, leading to 26,000 casualties, including the seventeen Americans mentioned earlier.[44]

Senator Morse remained dubious. Did not these U.S. actions violate the Geneva ban on the "introduction of fresh troops, military personnel, arms and munitions, military bases"? The state department pointed out that the United States was not a signatory of the accords, even though it opposed any effort to break them. North Vietnam, however, was a party to the accords and had broken them first by aiding the insurgency in the south. International law, the state department declared, recognized that "a material breach of a treaty by one party entitles the other at least to withhold compliance with an equivalent, corresponding or related provision until the other party is prepared to observe its obligations."[45]

The state department stood on shaky legal ground. Neither the United States nor South Vietnam was a party to the accords, and yet Washington had justified violating them as retaliation for a previous violation by the signatory nation of North Vietnam. Indeed, the administration's strongest argument for defending the South Vietnamese was the independence it commanded from *not* being a signatory nation. But even that stand was less than convincing—particularly because the United States had promised in 1954 not to disturb the settlement, and because it had a long tradition of respect for international law and treaties. Finally, it had been unable to prove Hanoi's participation in the insurgency and thereby justify the inherent right of self-defense.

The state department nonetheless asserted that its chief commitment to South Vietnam's defense rested on the SEATO Treaty of 1954. Article IV declared that in the event of an armed attack against South Vietnam, the United States would take action in line with its constitutional processes. If the threat came from any means other than an armed attack, the signatories to the treaty would consult about remedial measures. The state department thought it unlikely that the North Vietnamese would intervene on a massive scale. Not only did they fear Free World retaliation, but they did not want to provide the Chinese Communists with a pretext for intervention. Hanoi preferred the freedom of action afforded by playing off Moscow and Beijing. The Soviets might increase assistance to North Vietnam, but the region was not vital to their interests and they would probably call for a conference similar to the one over Laos. Hence, the North Vietnamese had sought to avoid a confrontation with the United States by engaging in a low-pressure resistance to Saigon that depended on infiltration and insurgency. Only U.S. intervention could prevent South Vietnam's fall to communism.[46]

The Senate committee's probing questions reflected the public's opposition to a deepened military involvement in Vietnam and led the White House to impose the long anticipated restraints on the embassy's relations with the press. The day following Harriman's testimony, Rusk instructed Nolting to avoid transmitting information to journalists that might have "harmful press repercussions on both [the] domestic and international scene." U.S. officials must "appeal to [the] good faith of correspondents," and the ambassador should stress that this was not an American war. "It [is] not repeat not in our interest . . . to have stories indicating that Americans are leading and directing combat missions against the Viet Cong." That in mind, "Correspondents should not be taken on missions whose nature [was] such that undesirable dispatches would be highly probable." They should impose "self-policing machinery" similar to those voluntary practices followed by reporters during World War II. "Sensational press stories about children or civilians who become unfortunate victims of military operations are clearly inimicable to [the] national interest." U.S.–South Vietnamese cooperation was vital, meaning that "frivolous, thoughtless criticism of [the] GVN [Government of Vietnam] makes cooperation difficult [to] achieve." Journalists must recognize that "articles that tear down Diem only make our task more difficult."[47]

The administration had little hope of quieting the press criticism of what was becoming an Americanized war. The president's press secretary, Pierre Salinger, later admitted that the White House "was not anxious to admit the existence of a real war in Southeast Asia." So the Saigon embassy, according to John Mecklin, its public affairs officer and a correspondent in Vietnam during the early 1950s, practiced "excessive classification" that "denied newsmen access to whole segments of U.S. operations in Vietnam." The central problem was that "much of what the newsmen took to be lies was exactly what the Mission genuinely believed, and was reporting to Washington." The mission operated "in a world of illusion." It was "stuck hopelessly with what amounted to an all-or-nothing policy, which might not work. Yet it *had* to work," making U.S. support for Diem "an article of faith" and dissent "reprehensible."[48]

The Senate and the press were correct in their concern that the escalating U.S. military involvement had the potential of widening the war. McGarr warned Vice President Johnson that the struggle would be long and must not become an American conflict. MAAG was in the process of putting together a sweeping and coordinated program of squelching the insurgency; swift and dramatic victories were impossible in this kind of war. McNamara had called for the creation of "Civic Action–Rural Reconstruction" teams, whose responsibility was to build a village and hamlet infrastructure that protected the people from the Vietcong and laid the basis for an intelligence-gathering program. Indeed, the combination of these social, political, economic, psychological, and military measures made up "the crux of the Pacification Problem." Counterinsurgency strategy continued to guide the Kennedy administration, but its military thrust had left the impression that the United States intended to take over the war.[49]

IV

THE DEBATE OVER combat troops intensified when advocates proposed SEATO Plan 7, which called for outside air and naval help to South Vietnam, followed by the deployment of a SEATO ground force. Such a move, the argument went, would enable the ARVN to take the offensive and close the border. Opponents declared the plan unduly provocative in light of what they insisted was an improved military situation in Vietnam. Vietcong incidents had declined steadily over the past month to 241, the lowest number since August 1961. After a late February meeting in Honolulu with Felt, Nolting, and Harkins, McNamara reported that South Vietnamese forces had blunted the Communist advance but would need years of concentrated effort to put an end to guerrilla warfare. Rather than "winning the war" in the traditional military sense, Nolting reminded his superiors, the objective in Vietnam should be "pacification of the country and winning the allegiance of the people."[50]

But the attempt to construct an image of imminent success suddenly lost credibility when South Vietnamese pilots in two American-built propeller planes bombed and strafed Independence Palace with rockets and napalm at 7:20 in the morning of February 26, 1962. The CIA station in Saigon reported that the air assault had destroyed one wing of Diem's quarters, setting parts of it afire and raising questions about whether the ruling family had been hit. Were the pilots Vietcong supporters? Was this another coup attempt? Harkins had barely arrived in Saigon for his new responsibilities at MACV when in the morning, before he had shaved, he heard the explosions and looked out his hotel window to see the palace burning. Within fifteen minutes, Diem's forces responded with antiaircraft guns, downing one plane in flames as it disappeared over the horizon. The other aircraft escaped into Cambodia. As the fire engines put out the blaze at the palace, a truck carrying wounded palace guards roared off to the hospital while two tanks and a number of jeeps armed with 50-caliber machine guns cruised the smoke-filled streets. The Saigon government announced that the assault had resulted in thirty-four casualties, including four dead. The U.S. embassy estimated the wounded at perhaps forty, many of them hit by falling antiaircraft fire. The only member of the palace family injured was Madame Nhu, who sustained several scratches from flying glass.[51]

Assessments of the reasons for the attack varied. Nolting initially informed the White House that the palace had come under assault from four AD-6s, probably from a squadron at Bien Hoa. General Minh attributed the assault to "disgruntled pilots." There was no sign of hostile troop movements, and Diem and his entourage were safe. The Civil Guard remained loyal to the premier, who ordered his airborne forces to take over Tan Son Nhut Airport. Trueheart thought the pilots' attempt to kill Diem had no connection with other coup efforts. Harkins, however, reported to President Kennedy and Admiral Felt that the action was part of a larger coup plan that did not transpire. He rushed to the palace and found Diem in his office. "Well, we captured one of them," the premier boasted. "I shouldn't have put him in the air force, because I had put his father in jail years ago." After a pause, "If I'd realized what I'd done to his father, I wouldn't have made him a pilot." A short time later, Diem remarked to Harkins that this was the second coup attempt. "Sometime I'm going to get shot right in the back of the neck. Sometime they'll get me that way."[52]

The incident more than likely grew out of animosity toward Diem and his family, not from an attempt to overthrow the government. Only two planes were involved, Nolting later reported in correcting his earlier claim. Authorities captured both pilots, who termed the operation the signal for a general uprising that involved "everyone"—including Americans. To support their specious claim of U.S. complicity, one of the pilots referred to critical articles in the press, especially *Newsweek*, which reinforced Diem's hostility toward journalists. Nolting concurred with Diem that the two pilots had acted on their own in an attempt to assassinate the premier and the Nhus and that the attack was not part of a revolution in either the army or air force. All other military personnel remained loyal during the thirty-five-minute assault, including the armor and supporting units, the air force in its pursuit of the two AD-6s, and those manning the navy's antiaircraft barrage. Since the Vietcong had made no effort to exploit the ensuing confusion, Nolting called it a "limited-scope, anti-Communist assassination attempt." Diem castigated the press, refusing to take blame for the pilots' unhappiness and denouncing the news writers for raising false hopes among political dissidents. In the margin next to Diem's indictment, an adviser in the Saigon embassy scribbled a telling comment: "Never learns."[53]

The attack on the palace further convinced Diem not to permit the political opposition inherent in a democracy. One Vietnamese official put it succinctly, "We don't even talk about freedom of the press or ask for other liberties any more." Diem had "completely surrounded himself in a protective oligarchy." Nhu once remarked, "There's always going to be an opposition. If we take these people in, there will be another opposition springing up, because they are controversial men." His wife agreed. "You open a window to let in light and air, not bullets. We want freedom, but we don't want to be exploited by it." Another Diem loyalist asserted, "We're faced with a highly dangerous situation and we can't tolerate dissension."[54]

The assault on Independence Palace heated up the controversy over combat troops and raised searching questions about Diem's tenure in office. Rusk assured an anxious press gathering that the United States had no plans to send combat personnel. As for negotiations, the only basis for such a move would be to resolve "the root of the trouble," which he defined as the Communist violations of the Geneva Accords. So far, Rusk dourly observed, Hanoi's behavior had not encouraged any talks. From his post in India, Galbraith again warned the president against sending troops. The first few men in uniform would lead to a cry for more, and soon the South Vietnamese would stand aside and leave the Americans to do the fighting. The Russians would be pleased to see the United States expending billions "in these distant jungles where it does us no good and them no harm." The administration must keep the door open for a political settlement by maintaining communication lines to Hanoi through India and the Soviet Union. Admittedly, any attempt to pull out would draw widespread criticism, but a deeper involvement would be worse. Politics was the art of "choosing between the disastrous and the unpalatable." One close U.S. observer reported that the palace bombing had set off "full-scale plotting against Diem." Three groups stood ready to take over South Vietnam at the first opportunity: political leaders, including Diem's brother; secondary political and military figures; and leaders of the armed forces, the most important being the army's field commander, General Minh. Doubtless aware of these rumors, Galbraith remarked that any alternative to Diem was progress: "When the man in power is on the way down, anything is better."[55]

Veteran news correspondent Howard Sochurek supported Galbraith's cautionary views, warning President Kennedy against Diem and asserting that this "Dirty War" was "rapidly becoming ours." The ARVN's generals were frustrated with the Ngo family but still liked Diem on a personal basis. The "people around him" were at fault. If the government did not respond to this growing animosity, the army, which Sochurek considered the "real base of power," would seize control. Counterinsurgency warfare offered the only solution. Felt and McNamara erroneously considered the war conventional in nature. Only recently had McGarr realized that the political solution was inseparable from the military. Numerous MAAG officers with long experience in Vietnam believed in the necessity of winning popular support and pressuring the South Vietnamese army into taking the offensive. Military officers insisted on a change in rule; key ministers and other able government figures had resigned, Sochurek insisted, because of "the general decay and corruption." Diem's bitterness toward the United States and refusal to grant reform had driven him into a "blind loyalty" to a self-centered and corrupt family. His "lack [of] administrative ability and leadership" had alienated his own people. His anticommunism was not enough to save South Vietnam. "We cannot win with Diem."[56]

These appeals against military escalation now seem wise, for, even though unknown in Washington at the time, the Beijing government had urged Hanoi to exercise restraint. Chinese leaders emphasized the broader view, promoting peaceful coexistence with capitalist enemies and calling for a reassessment of their assistance to national liberation struggles. Wang Jiaxiang, a Central Committee member of the Chinese Communist Party who dealt with foreign Communist parties as director of the International Liaison Department, advocated a reduction of foreign animosities that would permit his government to concentrate on economic problems at home. In late February 1962 he warned the government's foreign policy leaders, Zhou Enlai, Deng Xiaoping, and Chen Yi, of their country's dwindling resources. In Vietnam, the Chinese Communist party must "guard against a Korea-style war created by American imperialists" that might climax in "Khrushchev and his associates dragging us into the trap of war." China should pursue a conciliatory policy in foreign affairs.[57]

But the NLF had refused to buckle under to the U.S. challenge and shifted its emphasis to a "General Uprising." Its First Congress was secretly under way in northern Tay Ninh Province, where in early March of 1962 its leaders concluded that a continued social movement would not achieve victory without a successful armed struggle. A diversified gathering of 150 people and organizations from all levels of society and political and religious beliefs in the south declared that the Diem regime had "scrapped the Geneva Agreements of 1954" and that the NLF's purpose was "to achieve an independent, democratic, peaceful and neutral South Viet Nam, advancing to the reunification of the Fatherland." The NLF must unite all people in South Vietnam against the "U.S. imperialist aggressors" and overthrow the "Diem ruling clique" as their "lackey." The cochairs of the Geneva Conference of 1954 must disband the "U.S. Military Aid Command" and secure a U.S. withdrawal.[58]

In mid-March 1962, Diem's problems mounted even as he implemented the highly heralded Strategic Hamlet Program. To avoid the errors that had plagued the short-lived agroville system, the Saigon regime arranged the construction of strategic hamlets that were smaller than the agrovilles and located them nearer the fields to ease the peasants' uprooting process. But the planners failed to consider the mental and physical hardships imposed on people unceremoniously torn from their homes. The financial compensation granted for the relocation remained insufficient, forcing the peasants to dismantle their dwellings and use the matériel to reconstruct their domiciles within the new complex. The government did not provide the credit or goods necessary for agricultural development. The sparse funds allotted for social services (coming from the United States) rarely made it to the peasants, usually disappearing into the deep pockets of shady government officials. Incredibly, the government refused to pay laborers building the strategic hamlets, and the workers who lived outside the hamlets derived no benefits from the program. Seldom did the two stages of the counterinsurgency effort—the military clearing of an area, followed by the hamlets' construction—come together in a coordinated fashion. Only after "Operation Switchback" began in late 1961—when the military assumed responsibilities from the CIA for arming and training the local forces—did any real cooperation take place.[59]

More important than these flaws in the strategic hamlet system was Diem's distinct conception of the plan. The Americans regarded security as the chief objective and called for governmental reforms along with an ARVN offensive that first cleared the area of Vietcong; Diem wanted his military forces to take over civic action projects as a major means of establishing control and ensuring popular loyalty to his regime. Diem fell short on the political objectives of the war: instituting administrative reforms, uniting the non-Communists against the Vietcong, and winning rural support for his government. In sum, he failed to meet his counterinsurgency mandate by coordinating the political, economic, psychological, and military elements necessary to establish security and win the war.[60]

Despite these problems, the Strategic Hamlet Program breathed life into the stumbling counterinsurgency effort. Thompson recommended that

the construction begin where success was most likely—in areas lightly populated with Vietcong—and then, under the "oil blot" principle, expand into
more dangerous areas. But Nhu preferred the erection of defended hamlets in strategically important regions all over the country. "That would of
course kill everything," Hilsman complained. The government's forces were
unable to protect all the dwellings. But Nhu's wishes prevailed. The initial
undertaking in the Delta Plan therefore began in March 1962 with "Operation Sunrise," the construction of a string of strategic hamlets in Binh
Duong Province above Saigon—a pivotal area heavily penetrated by the
Vietcong and flanked by enemy concentrations on both sides. Despite warnings from Nolting, Harkins, and Hilsman that certain failure here would
undermine the entire program, Diem gave his approval and the military
sweep was soon under way.[61]

The Kennedy administration had no choice but to publicly praise the
program. Nolting lauded the Delta Plan as a major step toward beginning
the operational phase of the counterinsurgency program. Cottrell lauded
the strategic hamlets, noting that the Saigon government planned to build
8,000 of them within the next two years. The Vietnam Task Force agreed
with this assessment, as did Marine Major General Victor "Brute" Krulak,
the joint chiefs' newly appointed Special Assistant for Counterinsurgency
and Special Activities (SACSA). Krulak had led nighttime amphibious assaults in the Pacific during World War II. In one instance, a landing craft
(the hull designed by him) with about thirty of his men on board hit a reef
and started sinking. A young PT-boat commander named John F. Kennedy
saved those men and won Krulak's thanks. Years later, Krulak visited the
new president in the White House and swapped World War II stories.
Kennedy appointed Krulak as SACSA, where he headed the covert actions
recommended by the Special Group (Counterinsurgency) and employed
the same social, political, economic, psychological, and military measures
used by the Vietcong.[62]

But the U.S. military buildup so integral to counterinsurgency strategy had drawn so much public attention that the White House stepped up
its efforts to hide the process. Earlier, in mid-February, India's representative on the International Control Commission warned that the United
States's open violations of the Geneva Accords had put the watch group in
a terrible position. The commission had authority only to investigate infractions, and yet it had undergone bitter criticism for events over which it
had no control. If it withdrew in protest, a war could break out that would
encourage Chinese intervention. North Vietnam had likewise violated the
agreements, but it had concealed those actions while the United States had
committed "daylight robbery," forcing the commission to "juggle words
or ignore what is openly taking place." A little over a month later, the
Indian and Canadian members of the International Control Commission

denounced the open importation of U.S. military matériel into Saigon as a blatant violation of the Geneva Accords and urged Americans to "avoid flaunting [their] deliveries." The Joint Chiefs of Staff offered assurances that they would "henceforth avoid open and flagrant introduction of personnel and equipment." This was an empty promise: Saigon's only dock was in front of the Imperial Hotel and in full public view. In light of the Commission's complaints, the United States would, according to Ball in the state department, "play [the] game partly their way" by maintaining a "decent veil [of] hypocrisy." The joint chiefs arranged the use of other ports for off-loading those heavy military goods that were impossible to conceal.[63]

In the meantime, reports arrived that enemy planes had penetrated South Vietnamese air space, prompting the Kennedy administration to authorize reprisals that further suggested a U.S. takeover of the war. South Vietnamese officials had picked up unidentified radar blips in the Central Highlands, raising suspicions that Communist planes were supplying the Vietcong with matériel or men. Nolting asked the Saigon government to prepare an aide-mémoire requesting the use of U.S. interceptors equipped for night fighting. That done, the state department approved their dispatch but warned against any incursions into Cambodia and insisted on basing the planes outside Saigon. From Geneva, Rusk concurred in the decision to shoot down "hostile aircraft over South Vietnam." The president likewise approved the action. Accordingly, the joint chiefs declared that U.S. planes might, "where means of deviating or bringing the aircraft under control are not practically possible, engage and destroy hostile aircraft within the geographical limits of South Vietnam."[64]

The Kennedy administration devised an elaborate scheme intended to conceal its new air war policy. The directive reversed the January 1962 order, by which CINCPAC barred U.S. aircraft from taking action against hostile planes over South Vietnam. To minimize publicity, Ball explained, field personnel would declare that any downed Communist plane had crashed, lessening the impact of American involvement in "active hostilities." If U.S. action brought down an enemy plane and the news leaked, credit should go to the Vietnam Air Force if it seemed plausible to assert that a South Vietnamese plane on a routine training mission had destroyed an unidentified but hostile plane. To make this plan work, South Vietnamese–piloted Farmgate T-28s should be airborne each time American F-102 night fighters went on a mission. If the story was not plausible, the claim was to be that the intruder had accidentally crashed. If a U.S. plane went down, the official explanation was to be an accident while on a routine orientation flight. As the president's cover story to the press, he would attribute the presence of F-102s to the Saigon government's request for night interceptors. In any case, Ball asserted to Rusk, the White House will send a "loud and clear" message to the Communists.[65]

The yearly turnover of American servicemen coming home from Vietnam led the Kennedy administration to issue directives that likewise aimed at camouflaging U.S. participation in the war. Returning Americans were to say that they had acted only as advisers and instructors in helping the South Vietnamese in matters relating to training, logistics, communications, and transportation. "U.S. personnel," according to a defense department statement, "are not in a combat status and are instructed not to fire unless fired upon." Americans continued to receive direction from the Saigon government. "This is not a U.S. war and personnel being interviewed should not imply the U.S. is fighting this war."[66]

BY THE SPRING of 1962 the United States had joined the war in every sense except the use of combat troops. U.S. advisory assistance reached down to the ARVN's battalion level, U.S. planes engaged in bombing and strafing missions, U.S. naval patrols extended into the waters above the seventeenth parallel, and U.S. advisers regularly entered the vaguely defined battle zones, authorized to fire in self-defense. Counterinsurgency remained the overriding U.S. strategy, but it had tilted so dramatically to the military side that the United States appeared to be on the verge of taking over the war. Galbraith could not understand the White House's obsession with Vietnam. "Who is the man in your administration who decides what countries are strategic? I would like to have his name and address and ask him what is so important about this real estate in the space age."[67] Not chastened by these admonitions, the Kennedy administration pursued its objective of saving South Vietnam from the Communists, particularly mindful of the impact of a setback on U.S. credibility in the Cold War. But U.S. participation in the guerrilla war had reached a more dangerous threshold. In expanding its military assistance program, the White House had threatened its credibility at home by attempting to hide its warlike activities from the American press and people.

8

DE-AMERICANIZING
THE SECRET WAR

[We must] be prepared to seize upon any favorable moment
to reduce our involvement, [though] recognizing that the
moment might yet be some time away.

> President John F. Kennedy, April 6, 1962

[Victory would come when the Vietcong] could be eliminated
as a disturbing force.

> Robert McNamara, July 23, 1962

THE APPARENT PROGRESS in the war encouraged the first talk of reducing the U.S. military involvement to its original level of January 1961. Best estimates were that the South Vietnamese government would bring the insurgents under control in three years and that a scaled withdrawal could meanwhile begin in proportion to its military's gradually improving performance. Pacification would proceed apace, spurred by the success of the Strategic Hamlet Program. Counterinsurgency tactics would triumph, destroying the myth of Vietcong invincibility and leading the peasants to depend on the Saigon government for security. Whether or not the president and his advisers really believed their optimistic pronouncements, they held to their paradoxical strategy of escalating the U.S. military involvement as the primary step toward de-Americanizing that conflict. At the president's bidding, McNamara and others in a tight inner circle began devising a plan aimed at cutting back the U.S. commitment and counting on the Diem regime to restore domestic order after the bulk of American soldiers went home.

I

BY EARLY APRIL 1962 the pressure for U.S. combat troops began to ease as the situation in South Vietnam appeared to improve. The Delta Plan had resulted in a coordinated military–civilian operation that sought to safeguard the Mekong River villagers on an area-by-area basis. Operation Sunrise would clear the Vietcong from Binh Duong Province, just twelve miles above Saigon, and then relocate its inhabitants in an ever-widening ring of secured strategic hamlets. Its vital ingredient was civic action projects, intended to resolve what Hilsman called "the essentially political nature of the problem in South Vietnam." The key to success, Rusk emphasized, was an integrated civil and military program.[1]

Meanwhile, complications resulted from the tension between the foreign press and the Saigon regime. Diem had ordered the expulsions of Homer Bigart of the *New York Times* and François Sully of *Newsweek*, only to retract the edict after Nolting's urgings. The ambassador did not always agree with the stories but warned Diem that ejecting the writers would undermine the aid effort by alienating the American public and Congress. Diem especially disliked Sully, who had criticized the Ngo family. The premier accused both correspondents of "unfriendly and inaccurate reporting" and, instead of expelling them, refused to renew their visas.[2]

Relations between the Kennedy administration and the press likewise were strained, primarily because of the stories implying that the United States had taken over the war. The U.S. role was advisory, insisted the White House. America's involvement had become so flagrant, however, that it seemed to have assumed control. Even the names of military operations—Farmgate and Sunrise—were American in origin. On April 1, Bigart wrote in the *New York Times* Sunday edition that a large contingent of U.S. colonels and civilians had recently inspected a stockade in Operation Sunrise as part of a military action. As evidence for this assertion, Bigart referred to a U.S. officer involved in planning the operation. These misleading reports, Harriman and Rusk complained, might turn White House supporters against the aid program, while the Vietcong exploited the growing U.S. presence to remind the Vietnamese of their French nightmare.[3]

The Kennedy administration's complaints about Bigart's story were justified, Nolting asserted. The South Vietnamese had devised the code words "Binh Minh" for the operation, which translated as Sunrise and only appeared to be of American origin. U.S. advisers were making a special effort to ensure the indigenous character of future names. Nolting admitted that about a dozen Americans had inspected a stockade as representatives of both civilian and military agencies, but it was a ceremonial dedication of a strategic hamlet. The Saigon government had invited more Americans, but the embassy had limited the number to minimize U.S. visibility.[4]

The appearance of progress in South Vietnam did not ease Galbraith's fears, and he again warned the president against a deeper involvement. The Saigon government remained weak and ineffective, led by a man who had gone "beyond the point of no return." If the United States continued its present path, it would "bleed as the French did." Admittedly, effective pacification necessitated the relocation of villagers, but the Diem regime's draconian measures would alienate these people and force a further escalation of America's involvement. A political firestorm would break out over "the new Korea."[5]

Galbraith repeated his recommendation for a U.S. military withdrawal, followed by a multilateral effort to end the war. The White House should scale down its commitment and encourage the establishment of a non-Communist government that was free from outside dictation. Galbraith had learned on a confidential basis that the International Control Commission would soon produce a report that held both sides responsible for the conflict, the North Vietnamese for subverting South Vietnam and the Americans for exceeding the manpower and matériel limitations prescribed by the Geneva Accords. Harriman should ask the commission to inquire whether Hanoi would restrict Vietcong actions in exchange for a phased U.S. withdrawal, liberalized commercial relations between North and South Vietnam, and the assurance of reunification discussions. "We cannot ourselves replace Diem. But we should be clear in our mind that almost any non-Communist change would probably be beneficial." Above all, the United States must not commit combat troops.[6]

Similar warnings came in a memo to the president from Bowles. Just returned from the sensitive area, he was convinced that the United States needed "an effective but unprovocative military presence capable of deterring an overt attack by Communist forces." But he also knew that the presence of combat troops so close to Communist China might serve as a "magnet for Communist pressures." Bowles favored training and arming natives against the insurgents, but only in conjunction with the construction of schools, clinics, roads, and bridges. The United States should replace SEATO with a series of bilateral treaties on an interim basis, followed by "great-power guarantees" of Southeast Asia's safety.[7]

But neither outright withdrawal nor a multilateral involvement ever became serious discussion points inside the Kennedy administration. U.S. credibility in the Cold War remained the decisive consideration, prohibiting any perceived retreat in Vietnam. Internationalization of the war aroused only cautious support from Harriman and Rostow, who conceded California Congressman D. S. Saund's recent argument that a greater role by neighboring countries would reduce the number of Americans required. Harriman, however, saw problems. U.S. military leaders did not favor the idea. Not only did the joint chiefs want to control the war, but they recognized the command and logistic difficulties that accompanied a multilateral intervention. And yet, a continued unilateral U.S. involvement was not a viable option because, as Rostow darkly warned, "we are likely to be in Viet-Nam for a long period of time."[8]

Perhaps due to the perception of progress, but also because of the danger of a deeper entanglement, President Kennedy began to inch toward paring down the U.S. involvement. He agreed with Galbraith, Harriman, and Rusk that the United States must reduce its visibility without forgoing its commitment. But how to do this without risking the collapse of South Vietnam and dealing a devastating blow to American prestige? Harriman thought Diem "a losing horse in the long run" and yet could suggest no replacement. He also opposed the neutralization of South Vietnam. Although Harriman was pushing that outcome for Laos, he realized that the United States could not similarly abandon South Vietnam without a stunning loss of credibility. The White House should "support the government and people of Viet-Nam, rather than Diem personally." Before his congressional briefing on Laos, Harriman told the president that "the more flexible policy in Laos is best understood in terms of our stronger strategic position in Vietnam." Saigon's leaders had long feared a Laotian solution imposed onto them, despite repeated U.S. assurances against such a move. To a U.S. embassy official, Vice President Tho warned that if the war continued, the "Lao solution could be catching." The president found himself trapped between the two equally unattractive options of neutralization, which would leave an image of another U.S. retreat, and a total U.S. withdrawal, which would constitute an outright defeat. Searching for a safe middle ground, Kennedy told Harriman that "[we must] be prepared to seize upon any favorable moment to reduce our involvement," though "recognizing that the moment might yet be some time away."[9]

White House expectations of total victory had virtually disappeared. Gone was the cocksure attitude of those advisers who before the Cuban Bay of Pigs debacle had boasted that the mere threat of U.S. military action ensured a rollback of enemy forces. The joint chiefs and other hardliners remained supportive of a military solution, but even some of them began to see that military measures might better serve as the means to an end rather than the end itself. At first the U.S. involvement promised to be short and decisive. How could a small band of peasants withstand American firepower? But now, after more than a year of steadily deepening military commitment, the timetable for even a limited "victory" had threatened to stretch beyond the president's term in office. And what a burden Vietnam would be in the 1964 reelection campaign! It made sense to regard South Vietnam's survival as the chief measure of success and arrange a partial withdrawal that progressed in harmony with Saigon's capacity to stand on its own.

The idea of a sharply diminished U.S. commitment attracted the interest of more than just the president, particularly after British counterinsurgency expert Robert Thompson warned that Americans were becoming too visible and that the war might last another six years. Cottrell asserted that the longer the United States remained involved, the greater the chances of its having to send combat troops and totally Americanize the war. "Vietnamese should kill Vietnamese, but never foreigners killing Vietnamese." The Vietcong "would love to get the Americans more committed to combat in Viet-Nam because they could then wrap themselves in the cloak of Nationalism and recruit more Vietnamese for the fight against the foreign devils." The U.S. military presence must be minimal. This was Saigon's "war against Vietnamese terrorist intruders."[10]

The White House had to resolve a host of problems in Vietnam before scaling back its involvement. Nhu's recent actions as head of the Strategic Hamlet Program had inflated hopes for success. In a highly publicized declaration, he called for the erection of 12,000 strategic hamlets throughout the country within the next eighteen months on the principle of more secure to less secure areas. This approach set off an ill-managed construction race among the provincial chiefs that inflicted great personal hardships on the villagers. Security measures remained inadequate, virtually inviting Vietcong raids that had seriously damaged a dozen hamlets in recent days. Government forces must communicate warnings among the villages, whether by gongs, flares, or drums. They had to stop Vietcong movements along the delta's waterways and close their sanctuaries in Cambodia, Laos, and North Vietnam. They must become familiar with central Vietnam's mountains by relying on the native Montagnards. The rangers could severely hamper the Vietcong's actions by spending more time in the jungle. Vietcong casualties must escalate.[11]

Despite the certainty of a long war, the president's advisers insisted that a negotiated U.S. withdrawal was not acceptable. The defense department rejected Galbraith's plea on the ground that the move would undermine U.S. credibility. "South Vietnam is a testing ground of U.S. resolution in Asia," according to a military adviser's memo to the president. The Communists would ignore the terms in Galbraith's withdrawal plan, leaving the United States with the unappealing choice of either raising its involvement to a more dangerous level or engaging in a retreat. Nolting likewise opposed a negotiated withdrawal. Cambodian Prince Norodom Sihanouk's recent public call for an international conference would suggest the imminence of neutralization and undermine South Vietnam's confidence in America. The United States, Nolting argued, must convince North Vietnam that its infiltration tactics could not bring down the Saigon government. Once the insurgency shrank to a level manageable by South Vietnam's forces, the United States could begin a scaled withdrawal aimed at restoring the low-key advisory and assistance program of early 1961.[12]

Pressure for a negotiated withdrawal nonetheless continued. In mid-April 1962, North Vietnamese Deputy Nguyen Van Vinh accused the United States and Diem of violating the Geneva Accords and sought to reconvene the Geneva Conference in an effort to help all Vietnamese people achieve the independence promised in 1954. Vinh's call for an international conference appeared to be Hanoi's official policy. He was chair of the National Reunification Commission, which held ministerial rank in North Vietnam's Council of Ministers, and he was major general and vice minister of National Defense. Hanoi's "Voice of Vietnam Radio" meanwhile welcomed Sihanouk's proposal for an international conference. Galbraith criticized the White House for opposing negotiations and insisted that the nation's vital interests were *not* at stake in South Vietnam. The United States must not subordinate its policy to the wishes of any regime. "This leads us to the absurdity that any action, however sensible, may undermine confidence if it doesn't fit the particular preferences of the government we are supporting." If the only way the United States could win trust was to fight wars, it "ought to get Dulles back to take charge."[13]

The Kennedy administration faced a multitude of problems in trying to cut back involvement. Lack of unity in the American aid effort ensured continued uncertainty. Diem's recalcitrance posed an ongoing obstacle. The only constant was the attempt to protect U.S. credibility in the Cold War, which dictated a continued commitment to South Vietnam. That commitment, however, would dramatically diminish after that government was able to survive on its own. To reach that threshold, the White House had to convince Hanoi to stop infiltration, which necessitated a heightened aid program. Hence the conundrum: The only way out of Vietnam was to go in deeper.

II

COUNTERINSURGENCY STRATEGY remained the key to a partial withdrawal, even though its strong military orientation encouraged a deeper involvement. The U.S. embassy officer in charge of Vietnam affairs, Theodore Heavner, warned against increasing the United States's military visibility. His April tour of five provinces convinced him that success depended on building more strategic hamlets and squelching North Vietnamese infiltration. But these measures entailed greater U.S. interference in South Vietnam's internal matters. American advisers were rarely welcome, primarily out of fear that they would take over all local responsibilities. But these same provincial officers also distrusted their home government. "I spend more time doing this," one South Vietnamese official said while pressing his palms together and bowing his head, "than this"—firing a gun at the Vietcong—"and so do all officials who want to keep their jobs."[14]

For the Strategic Hamlet Program to work, U.S. and South Vietnamese officials had to upgrade the Self-Defense Corps (SDC). Such measures included improvements in pay, equipment, training, medical attention, and disability and retirement provisions. One provincial official complained that the SDC received such poor compensation that its people had to steal chickens and pigs for food and, in so doing, had alienated the populace. The most important problem, however, was the government's decision to construct so many strategic hamlets that it lacked sufficient SDC personnel for their defense. In some instances, as few as six SDC personnel were responsible for protecting up to 3,000 villagers. With sparse provisions and in such isolated conditions, the SDC attempted to defend the hamlets while the Civil Guard and the ARVN took the initiative in ambushes, sweeps, night patrols, and other offensive actions. If the program continued, Heavner nonetheless declared, it should succeed within two years.[15]

McNamara, too, considered the Strategic Hamlet Program the "decisive battle ground" for "the hearts and minds" of the Vietnamese people. After a recent visit to Southeast Asia, he noted about 14,000 hamlets in South Vietnam, only 1,579 of them considered strategic hamlets and another 1,230 planned for completion that year. Most of them involved no population resettlement because they were in areas already under government control. Pacification would succeed, he declared, if the government made plain to villagers why relocation was essential, provided competent administrators, instituted efficient construction measures, installed a warning system, and trained and equipped local defense groups. The "National Assembly for Strategic Hamlets" would open in mid-May with a class of 500. Victory would come through programs already in place and, "hopefully, it will not take fifteen years to consummate it."[16]

The reality again was different from the appearance. There was no systematic scheme of development. Nolting complained that Nhu's attempt to construct strategic hamlets all over the country had caused provincial chiefs to build them in a "helter-skelter fashion." Thompson's plan had assigned priority to the more seriously threatened delta provinces because the government's security forces were unable to support pacification all over the country. The Diem regime, however, wanted to establish control over its people by erecting strategic hamlets in every province. This sweeping approach threatened to undermine the entire program by putting up more strategic hamlets than the government could staff.[17]

Nhu, however, defended his conception of the Strategic Hamlet Program as "the democratic system in action." Freedom and justice for the individual would spread as locally elected committees administered civic action programs that benefited everyone. The overall success of the effort rested on the "two thirds concept—meaning that if two-thirds of the populace in any given area could be assured security the other one-third would automatically fall in line." Imposition of democracy from the top in an underdeveloped country brought anarchy followed by dictatorship. The institution of democracy at the local level helped to stamp out privilege and unite the people. Free elections by secret ballot provided the key to success. Thus the so-called defended hamlet did not work because that system called for only selected areas of construction and therefore uprooted people by moving them to centralized locations. A better approach was to persuade young families to establish local hamlets defended by commando groups trained in guerrilla tactics. The time required for success, Nhu thought, was three years. War was necessary to implement this "revolution for democracy." The Vietnamese people realized that "this was their war."[18]

Diem rejected the more restrained British and American approach to building strategic hamlets in the delta and supported Nhu's argument for constructing them throughout the country. Thuan thought the government could complete the program within six months. Trueheart remained dubious. Diem's failure to incorporate the military into the planning and execution of the program meant no assurances of village security. "This was to fight with one hand tied behind your back," Trueheart declared. "Many hamlets in exposed areas were going to be overrun."[19]

Regardless of the approach, the development of strategic hamlets necessitated a massive relocation of families with all its attendant hardships. Primary among these was the uprooting of a tradition-bound people who had formed ancestral loyalties and familial ties to their home villages over generations. Faith in the program could come if the peasants became convinced that safety lay in relocation, if the Saigon government provided sufficient assistance for them to make the move, if the transplanted villagers knew that they could return to their homes in the foreseeable future, if the hamlets promoted a democratic revolution (and not simply Diem's control), if the villagers felt secure—the "ifs" could go on indefinitely. Neither the Diem regime nor U.S. officials could guarantee anything to the villagers except a change in environment for an undefined period of time. Indeed, the inclusion of schools and hospitals in the Strategic Hamlet Program implied a lengthy displacement of families into an alien environment.

Newsweek's account of a strategic hamlet in Cu Chi confirmed these doubts but nonetheless failed to shake White House confidence in the program. In this group of four villages just twenty-five miles northeast of Saigon, more than 6,000 local peasants were protected by eight miles of moats filled with bamboo spears and planks with eight-inch-long nails sticking up. To leave nothing for the Vietcong, the government's forces had torched the houses of more than 140 families from the forests and then forcefully relocated them into this hamlet with the promise of new land. On the door frames of each hut was a list of all legitimate occupants. Before leaving for the fields each morning, the villagers had to submit to a search to make sure they carried no extra food for the Vietcong. At nightfall, a curfew bell summoned them back inside the fortress. They had no choice. Anyone remaining outside was subject to being shot by the night patrol. When a U.S. officer suggested that Diem's forces should have distributed pamphlets explaining the program beforehand, a Vietnamese soldier disagreed. "We wanted to achieve a surprise. If the peasants had been told in advance, they would have bolted into the woods." Despite the peasants' unhappiness, Hilsman was exuberant over the strategic hamlets. "I thought it likely before that Diem would beat the Viet Cong, but now, with the new program, I think it will be easy."[20]

Despite the two distinctly different directions taken by South Vietnam and the United States in the Strategic Hamlet Program, the Kennedy administration insisted that harmony characterized the counterinsurgency effort. Before the Detroit Economic Club in late April 1962, Undersecretary of State George Ball praised the administration's strategy and assured a continued U.S. commitment to South Vietnam. Success would come from "the long, slow arduous execution of a process" aimed at winning freedom "village by village" against "a carefully planned and mounted campaign of subversion and insurgency—equipped and directed from Hanoi." The Strategic Hamlet Program would destroy the guerrillas' "mystique of success" by shattering the Vietcong's "aura of invincibility." Victory would "be won or lost in the villages and cities and in the minds and hearts of men."[21]

Ball inadvertently underlined the administration's central enigma when he denied any U.S. intention to take over the war while emphasizing the need for more direct involvement in the region. "The United States has *no* combat units in Viet-Nam. We are not fighting the war, as some reports have suggested. We are not running the war, as the Communists have tried assiduously to argue." The United States furnished matériel and trained personnel—at Diem's request. Admittedly, Americans were exposed to combat. Yes, the commitment would be long. "We should have no illusions. It took eight years in Malaya." But the United States had to honor a SEATO pledge to preserve South Vietnam's independence as a vital part of the global conflict between freedom and communism. Vietnam was strategically important because it was the gateway to Indonesia and Malaya and it controlled the mouth of the Mekong River, which was the main artery of Southeast Asia. South Vietnam's collapse would have tragic repercussions throughout Asia and the South Pacific.[22]

Ball's speech drew a spirited press reaction. In the *New York Herald Tribune*, Marguerite Higgins wrote that "American retreat or withdrawal from South Viet-Nam is unthinkable, according to Mr. Ball. The American commitment, moreover, is now irrevocable." To McGeorge Bundy, Ball called her comments "strong language" and an erroneous rendition of what he had said. Ball cited two other press accounts that were more accurate. Russell Baker in the *New York Times* termed the speech a response to Republican allegations that the United States was in a shooting war. Baker did not suggest that the United States had made an irreversible commitment, as Higgins claimed. Warren Unna in the *Washington Post* also characterized the speech as focusing on the White House attempt to reduce the nation's involvement. "This, of course," Ball noted with satisfaction, "is what was intended."[23]

The Kennedy administration approved Ball's speech as highlighting the move toward a scaled withdrawal from Vietnam. McGeorge Bundy implied a strong White House interest in a partial pullout when he declared that Ball's speech had a "tone and content that we would not have cleared, simply from the point of view of maintaining a chance of political settlement." The administration would not negotiate South Vietnam's neutralization, but it would reduce the U.S. involvement in conjunction with the ARVN's improved field performance. Forrestal praised the speech though also implying an even more imminent reduction in involvement by noting Ball's failure to make clear that it was South Vietnam's war. Rusk likewise pointed toward a major withdrawal. "If the communist authorities in North Viet-Nam will stop their campaign to destroy the Republic of Viet-Nam, the measures we are taking to assist your defense efforts will no longer be necessary." Harriman called for the same approach taken by the Truman administration in Greece: Help the indigenous population to determine the war's verdict, and then, after the government's forces proved themselves capable of controlling the guerrillas, cut back the U.S. involvement.[24]

But great risks lay in the White House belief that it had guided events in Greece and could do the same in Vietnam. The analogy was flawed. Whereas the Greek army had been large enough to drive the guerrillas into the barren mountains of northern Greece, it was doubtful that the South Vietnamese army would ever reach sufficient numbers to expel the insurgency. The Diem regime had failed to close the country's extensive borders, resulting in heightened infiltration and continued places of refuge outside South Vietnam. Rostow had repeatedly declared that the ARVN must be at least ten times the size of the Vietcong, which meant that the present ARVN force of less than 170,000 was already too small to deal with 25,000 Vietcong—a figure that was growing by a thousand a month.[25]

The Kennedy administration failed to recognize the entangling nature of its involvement. In seeking to restore the Geneva division at the seventeenth parallel, it had argued for a withdrawal through escalation. The infectious spirit of foreign intervention had not become clear to Washington's strategists, who believed it possible to conduct a limited war. Cottrell asserted that U.S. strategy aimed at inflicting "graduated punishment" on North Vietnam in an effort to stop its aiding the Vietcong. The White House could do this, he implied, without internationalizing the conflict. But his argument was unsound. In Greece, the threat of direct Soviet intervention had been less likely than that of a direct North Vietnamese involvement in the present conflict. And what about the Chinese Communists? Mao Zedong had carried out his threat of armed intervention in Korea during the early 1950s and was now even better equipped to conduct a similar action in Vietnam. And yet, the black memories of the Chinese intervention in the Korean War did not faze Cottrell. A Chinese "scrap" with U.S. forces would present the opportunity to reunite the Vietnams under Diem's leadership. "If we had to destroy both the Chinese and DRV [Democratic Republic of Vietnam] war making capability," he cavalierly remarked, "it would be rather silly to return the DRV to Commie control."[26]

<h1 style="text-align:center">III</h1>

DESPITE THE SIGNS of an imminent reduction in U.S. involvement, a growing number of Kennedy advisers had become impatient with Diem and called for stronger action. Diem had encouraged a showdown over the need for administrative changes by rejecting the U.S. Operations Mission's request to bypass the Saigon ministries in dealing with provincial authorities. A partial withdrawal was out of the question until the Saigon government proved itself capable of running the country. But when (if ever) would the Diem regime reach this plateau? Rostow thought the time right to "force a confrontation" over Hanoi's actions in Southeast Asia. Otherwise, the North Vietnamese (and probably the Chinese Communists) would seize northern Laos and increase infiltration into South Vietnam. Further delay would necessitate combat troops.[27]

Rostow sought to take advantage of present troubles within the international Communist front. The United States should firmly reiterate to the Soviets its condemnation of Hanoi's recent joint assault with Pathet Lao forces on the provincial capital of Nam Tha (a mere twenty miles from China) as a violation of the previous year's cease-fire agreement. If the North Vietnamese failed to respond to the U.S. attempt to restore the Geneva Accords, the White House must take "direct retaliatory action" by dispatching carriers into the South China Sea just below the seventeenth parallel, launching air attacks on transportation facilities and power sources in North Vietnam, and mining Haiphong harbor. "I believe that if we are bold enough, lucid enough in our communications, and make it clear that Hanoi cannot any longer safely be used as a Communist catspaw without paying a direct price, we have a fair chance that we can foreshorten both the Laos and Vietnam crises." The timing was good: North Vietnam and Communist China had serious domestic problems; the United States and the Soviet Union had a "relatively favorable balance of nuclear strength"; and the Soviets and Communist Chinese had fallen out over numerous issues. A strong policy could avert "an indefinitely prolonged US commitment."[28]

Nolting appealed to the so-called replacement argument to justify send-ing more matériel. One goal of the Geneva pact of 1954 was to maintain a military balance between the Vietnams. The French withdrawal of the mid-1950s, he argued, had altered the balance in North Vietnam's favor. To counter Hanoi's subversion and aggression, the Saigon government had requested U.S. assistance. Article 17b of the accords stipulated that "war material, arms and munitions which have been destroyed, damaged, or worn out or used up after cessation of hostilities may be replaced on basis of piece-for-piece of same type and with similar characteristics." The Inter-national Control Commission, Nolting insisted, recognized the replace-ment principle in 1958 when it credited the Saigon government with goods exported under its auspices. Neither the United States nor South Vietnam sought to restore a military capacity matching that of the French in 1954; they wanted to build a military base capable of resisting the guerrilla threat sponsored by Hanoi.[29]

The Indian government (with its representative one of three on the commission) flatly rejected Nolting's argument, insisting that Hanoi's vio-lations of the Geneva Accords did not justify similar U.S. actions: "Two wrongs do not add up to a right." Despite the self-restraints promised by U.S. officials, the replacement principle would result in a total breakdown of the Geneva Accords and a call for a new international conference. If India permitted the Americans to send more goods, it would expose itself to Communist charges of capitulation to Washington's pressure. The U.S. embassy in New Delhi (where Galbraith was ambassador) had strongly advised against the replacement argument.[30]

Further complicating the matter was Hanoi's taking the moral high ground on the Geneva Accords. In a recent interview with British and Aus-trian Communist newspapers, North Vietnamese prime minister Pham Van Dong emphasized that his government sought reunification by "peace-ful means on the basis of the 1954 Geneva Agreements" and called for negotiations engineered by the cochairs of the Geneva Conference. "Our struggle against US Imperialist aggression," he continued in what Nolting termed "typical upside-down Communist terminology," was "precisely aimed at maintaining peace and stability in the Southeast Asian area and actively contributing to [the] preservation of world peace." North Vietnam's position proved difficult to refute. Observers were unable to see Hanoi's hand in the Vietnamese struggle but could not miss Washington's military presence.[31]

In early June 1962 the International Control Commission released its findings for the period from February 1, 1960, to February 28, 1961, and declared that the situation in Vietnam had markedly deteriorated as each side accused the other of violating the Geneva agreements of 1954. Saigon had charged Hanoi with subversion and aggression; Hanoi had accused

Saigon of illegally accepting U.S. military assistance. The commission concluded (with the Polish delegate dissenting from the Indian and Canadian
delegates) that "armed and unarmed personnel, arms, munitions and other
supplies" had gone from the northern sector of Vietnam to the south with
the aim of "supporting, organising and carrying out hostile activities, including armed attacks," against the south. Hanoi had permitted use of the
northern zone for "inciting, encouraging and supporting hostile activities"
in the southern zone, "aimed at the overthrow of the Administration in the
South." On the other side, Hanoi had accused the United States of "direct
military intervention" in South Vietnam by sending "war material" and
"military personnel." Evidence included a bilateral military agreement; the
introduction of 5,000 U.S. military personnel and an expected increase to
8,000; the arrival of four aircraft carriers bringing in helicopters, other
aircraft, military equipment, and personnel; the importation of jet fighters,
fighter-bombers, and transport planes, accompanied by military vehicles
and other goods; well-publicized visits by U.S. military figures, including
Taylor, Felt, and Lemnitzer; and the establishment of MACV with a four-
star general, Paul Harkins, in command.[32]

The International Control Commission had been "persistently denied
the right to control and inspect" affairs in South Vietnam since December
1961; consequently, its teams could see the "steady and continuous arrival
of war material, including aircraft carriers with helicopters on board," but
they were unable "to determine precisely the quantum and nature of war
material" brought into South Vietnam. On December 9, 1961, the commission received a note from Saigon declaring that in light of Hanoi's violations of the Geneva agreements, the South Vietnamese government had
exercised its right of self-defense in asking the United States for additional
personnel and matériel. "These measures can end as soon as the North
Viet-Nam authorities will have ceased the acts of aggression and will have
begun to respect the Geneva Agreement." From December 3, 1961, through
May 5, 1962, the commission had itself observed the passage into the south
of military personnel, helicopters, jets, fighter bombers, reconnaissance
aircraft, jeeps, tractors, howitzers, armored carriers, radar equipment, and
warships.[33]

The International Control Commission came up with a mixed conclusion. It refused to recognize Saigon's claim to credits for certain goods;
Article 17b of the Geneva pact stipulated only war matériel identical to the
original pieces. As for Hanoi's charge that the United States had set up
MACV in violation of Article 19, the South Vietnamese Mission's letter of
March 15, 1962, asserted that MACV was "not a military command in the
usual sense of the term, and that its only function is to supervise and manage the utilisation of American personnel and equipment." The commission declared, however, that South Vietnam had violated Articles 16 and

17 in "receiving the increased military aid from the United States of America in the absence of any established credit in its favour." It also asserted that, despite the lack of a formal military alliance, "the establishment of a U.S. Military Assistance Command in South Viet-Nam, as well as the introduction of a large number of U.S. military personnel beyond the stated strength of the MAAG (Military Assistance and Advisory Group), amounts to a factual military alliance," which the Geneva Accords prohibited. Furthermore, both parties had shown no disposition to permit the commission to conduct its functions, resulting in "ever-increasing tension and threat of resumption of open hostilities."[34]

The International Control Commission's report, as Galbraith had said earlier, blamed both Hanoi and Washington for the war, but it left room for the White House to attribute primary cause to North Vietnam. The state department told the press that the commission had highlighted North Vietnamese policies aimed at overthrowing the Saigon government. Admittedly, South Vietnam had imported military equipment and personnel that exceeded the Geneva limits, but these moves were a necessary part of Saigon's defense against outside aggression that began in 1955 and increased to such intensity that Diem had requested U.S. military assistance in 1961. North Vietnam's aggressions had justified U.S. military aid under the universal right of self-defense, its violations of the Geneva agreements, and SEATO's "protective 'umbrella'" over Vietnam, Laos, and Cambodia. If U.S. defensive help constituted a military alliance, the state department indignantly declared, then Soviet and Communist Chinese assistance to the North Vietnamese was an "aggressive military alliance."[35]

The NLF responded with vicious countercharges. That same month of June 1962, it published a booklet accusing the United States and Diem of pursuing a "bloody war" over the past eight years that had led to "the most barbarous murders" in their effort to enslave the people of South Vietnam. The NLF's evidence included graphic descriptions of rapes, sexual violations, tortures, cannibalism, mutilations, burnings, massacres, dissections, whippings, facial stabbings, drownings, the use of poison gas, victims with barbed wire threaded through their palms and hanged alive in the sun, and the use of statues of Christ for target practice.[36]

To achieve a partial pullout from a conflict that was spiraling upward in intensity, the Kennedy administration tried to downplay the focus on South Vietnam by placing it within the context of the entire region's troubles. In late June 1962, Rusk issued a directive creating the Task Force on Southeast Asia, whose mandate was to plan and coordinate programs for the area. Chaired by Harriman, it replaced the Vietnam Task Force, which became the Vietnam Working Group. The new Southeast Asia Task Force included Cottrell as deputy chair of representatives from the defense department, Joint Chiefs of Staff, CIA, Agency for International

Development, and U.S. Information Agency.[37] Such a diffusion of the problem would establish the importance of the region as a whole and thereby encourage the chances of scaling down the U.S. involvement in Vietnam.

Once determined upon partial withdrawal, the administration found it easier to interpret battle assessments as favorable. To Harriman, Hilsman highlighted several factors that a hopeful White House could regard as optimistic. "It can be said that [the enemy] is now meeting more effective resistance and having to cope with increased aggressiveness by the Vietnamese military and security forces." Lost in the selected reading of this document was the assertion that the Vietcong had continued to grow in numbers and performance while systematically undermining Saigon's authority in the countryside. In another important section, the report noted the "encouraging signs of popular support for the government," which obscured the succeeding concession that there had been "no major breakthrough in identifying the people with the struggle against the Viet Cong." The ambivalent thrust of the report continued with the finding of "no evidence to support certain allegations of substantial deterioration in the political and military situations in Vietnam"; it then cited "evidence of heartening progress in bolstering the fighting effectiveness of the military and security forces." To predict success in this "war of national liberation" would be "premature," but "the chances are good, provided there is continuing progress by the Vietnamese Government." Final victory would take "some years" and result more from "a steady erosion of Communist strength" than from "dramatic military successes." As Thompson and McNamara had recently declared, the most likely prognosis was six years.[38]

By mid-1962, however, the highly visible U.S. military presence in Vietnam had obstructed the attempt to shift the emphasis to Southeast Asia as a whole. Covert action continued, along with a U.S. airlift of ARVN troops. Operation Farmgate had become a growing enterprise of planes and advisers. In the meantime, a joint junk patrol of the South Vietnamese Navy worked with the U.S. Navy's Seventh Fleet to curtail infiltration by water. The United States had provided more than 700 craft to patrol inland waterways and facilitate the ARVN's mobility in the delta. MACV had more than 9,000 military personnel engaged in operational and training duties. MAAG had assigned advisers to all provinces.[39] U.S. military escalation in South Vietnam obscured the effort to focus on the entire region.

The outward show of military force seemingly guaranteed victory in the traditional military sense, but more than superior firepower was necessary, as Lansdale reminded McNamara. On a piece of graph paper, the defense secretary had compiled a lengthy column of computer entries that focused on manpower, casualty, and weapons statistics. Lansdale gazed at the list and remarked, "You're going to fool yourself if you get all of these figures added up because they won't tell you how we're doing in this war."

McNamara looked puzzled. "Your list is incomplete," Lansdale explained. "You've left out the most important factor of all."

McNamara glanced down at the penciled notations and finally asked, "What is it?"

"Well," Lansdale responded, "it's the human factor. You can put it down as the X factor."

McNamara still seemed perplexed but scribbled it onto the paper. "What does it consist of?"

"What the people out on the battlefield really feel; which side they want to see win and which side they're for at the moment. That's the only way you're going to ever have this war decided."

Seemingly interested, McNamara replied, "Tell me how to put it in."

Unfortunately, Lansdale declared, "I don't think any Americans out there at the moment can report this to you." McNamara had failed to grasp the meaning of Lansdale's message and prepared to erase the item from his list. "No, leave it there," Lansdale said, intending to try again to make his point.

A week later Lansdale handed McNamara a long list of questions that MACV should ask U.S. military personnel intimately familiar with Vietnam. How did the ARVN treat civilians on a daily basis? Did the villagers, particularly the children, welcome the troops with smiles or resentment? Did the Vietcong seek reprisals for the ARVN's forceful extraction of information from villagers? What was the number of civilian casualties in military operations? How effective were civilian actions after the ARVN had secured an area from the Vietcong? How did the ARVN treat Vietcong prisoners? Did ARVN capabilities compare well with the Vietcong?

In the note's margin, McNamara praised the questions as the "kind of info I need & am not receiving." But his interest was more apparent than real. "Thank you," he curtly remarked to Lansdale and showed him the door. "I've got something else to do now."[40]

Lansdale's efforts had had no impact. His intangible considerations were not susceptible to measurement in numbers, making them incomprehensible to a statistician such as McNamara. And yet, as Lansdale realized, the attitudes that civilians and soldiers had toward each other were more important than military power in determining the outcome of this shadowy conflict.

IV

PRESIDENT KENNEDY UNDERSTOOD the importance of nonmilitary factors in achieving an honorable reduction of U.S. involvement. He recognized the danger in emphasizing military considerations. He assured Diem again that the United States did not seek to neutralize South Vietnam along with

Laos. The South Vietnamese people, Kennedy asserted, had demonstrated a willingness to fight for independence. Laos, however, was landlocked and less defensible, and its domestic conditions were worse than those in South Vietnam. A Laotian government committed to neither east nor west might curtail Vietcong assistance from Hanoi and lead to peace in Vietnam. More than military measures were necessary for success.[41]

In early July, the Associated Press published a highly critical account of the U.S. military involvement in Vietnam. Datelined Fort Leavenworth, Kansas, the story claimed that U.S. Army officers on nearly all levels believed that the attempt to save South Vietnam from the Communists was, "to put it mildly, fouled up." Major General William Rosson, chief of the U.S. Army's Special Forces, was "downright angry" over the "waste of manpower" resulting from "the misuse of his highly trained specialists in South Viet-Nam." Americans, he insisted, must work with "indigenous personnel (native forces) in company and battalion sized groups," who then "should go into the 22 Viet Cong areas nobody has been into for 15 years." The South Vietnamese should destroy the Vietcong's training and supply bases in North Vietnam. Numerous U.S. army personnel had declared that Diem had divided his government and undermined the military effort. One officer argued that Diem opposed a centralized command structure because provincial leaders would wield too much power. Others reported that the U.S. military advisory group had become "so top-heavy and unwieldy that its efficiency has been imperiled." For every soldier in the field training and advising the Vietnamese, at least five remained in the rear. Most officers thought the South Vietnamese should fight the bulk of the war; all seemed certain that the conflict would become a decade-long war of attrition with heavy American casualties.[42]

The AP allegations drew bitter retorts from the U.S. Army. Chief of Staff General George Decker insisted that the account did not reflect official army assessments. Rosson declared that he was not upset over the use of the Special Forces, that the ARVN's performance had improved because of a better intelligence system, and that most American soldiers were engaged in advising, training, and supporting the South Vietnamese in counterinsurgency actions. MACV admitted that Communist infiltration had increased since May 1962, but it attributed this buildup to the cease-fire in Laos that had freed Vietnamese Communists in that country for use in South Vietnam. The U.S. embassy feared that the Laotian agreement would open a corridor through Laos for further Vietcong infiltration and that South Vietnam would also become subject to neutralization. But President Kennedy remained determined not to let that happen.[43]

The U.S. opposition to a negotiated settlement should have been clear, and yet when the long-anticipated neutralization of Laos took place in late July 1962, Hanoi thought the same outcome possible in South Vietnam.

Le Duan encouraged party leaders in the south to maintain the struggle because the United States had withdrawn from China and North Korea short of a military triumph and would do so again in Vietnam. Hanoi's officials began contacting neutralist sympathizers in Saigon and in France about the possibility of U.S. interest in a tripartite government in the south. But White House support for a coalition government in Laos had rested on the belief that the Soviet Union would convince Hanoi to stop infiltration into the south, the bulk of which came through Laos. Until the Laotian agreement took effect in October and infiltration showed signs of letting up, the White House refused to consider negotiations over South Vietnam.[44]

Ho had become concerned about a U.S. attack on North Vietnam in the summer of 1962 and joined General Nguyen Chi Thanh in a visit to Beijing to seek additional military assistance. The timing of the U.S. military escalation in Vietnam proved advantageous to Hanoi's request. Beijing feared two wars, one with Taiwan because of Chiang Kai-shek's seemingly imminent assault on the mainland, and the other with India because of mounting border troubles. Furthermore, Sino-Soviet relations had become raw because of a recent Kazakh uprising in Chinese Central Asia. By early August the Chinese military had made emergency preparations for a U.S. and Nationalist assault from Taiwan and a war along the Indian border. Mao needed to shore up allies. He approved the dispatch of sufficient rifles and guns to meet the needs of 230 infantry battalions in South Vietnam—all weapons provided free of charge.[45]

In a mid-July Associated Press (AP) article from Saigon, the unidentified writer brought further focus to the Vietcong's expanding activities by noting its desperate effort to secure medical supplies—particularly antibiotics—in killing the infections from wounds that spread rapidly in the jungle climate. Chinese and Soviet medical equipment came through Laos, but this was not sufficient to deal with mounting casualties. The Vietcong tried to smuggle antibiotics from Saigon and other urban areas into its "liberated areas," and it looted all the medicine found in hamlets and outposts. At one point, Vietcong forces raided a leper colony 160 miles northeast of Saigon, seizing bone saws, antibiotics, and other surgical equipment. They also kidnapped an American doctor, Dr. Eleanor Vietti of Houston, Texas, and took her from hamlet to hamlet to treat the wounded. "In the long war of attrition," the writer declared, "lack of medical facilities may be a decisive factor."[46]

The NLF then launched a massive campaign to undermine the Strategic Hamlet Program. In a pamphlet to cadres, it called on the South Vietnamese people to resist "the whole system of imprisonment" instituted by Diem and the Americans. The strategic hamlet was "a jail" with barbed-wire fences and guard towers. Destroying the "government of the hamlet or the village, punishing the spies and policemen, the evil persons in the strategic hamlets to prevent the repairing of the oppression machine by the enemies, is similar to the killing of a snake by striking at his head." On July 20, 1962, the eighth anniversary of the Geneva Conference, the NLF proclaimed four conditions for peace: U.S. withdrawal from Vietnam; a cease-fire; a national coalition government of all groups followed by free general elections to select a democratic National Assembly; and a foreign policy of peace and neutrality.[47]

Despite this surging Vietcong activity, General Harkins remained optimistic, arguing that victory lay in a relentless ARVN offensive. Rather than assign six or seven battalions to a wide swath of land, he wanted to deploy small battalions acting on sound intelligence regarding Vietcong locations and moving with speed and secrecy. Larger forces required a departure the day prior to a planned mission and therefore alerted the enemy. He liked the idea of General Nguyen Khanh, Chief of Staff of the General Staff, who called for reorganizing the ranger companies into battalions with Montagnards serving as scouts, "somewhat like the American Indians of yore." They must not go out and return on the same day. "The only way to win," Harkins insisted, "is to attack, attack, attack."[48]

Diem agreed with Harkins but emphasized that the general must convince ARVN officers that the United States was "not running the war." Their French experience made them wary of any U.S. action that appeared to be a command. Harkins emphasized that his responsibility was "to advise only, not to command." French strategy had rested on the "Maginot Line concept" of constructing a powerful fortress and hoping to entice a conventional attack. "The only effect produced by this is that the enemy knows where you are." ARVN units must be in the field for weeks at a time. "Every unit needs to have a few victories under its belt. It has to get out and kill the enemy."[49]

Intrigued by Harkins's proposal, Diem presented an idea referred to as "Cutting the Forest," which called for the establishment of small, specially trained units that would trek through the jungle for at least a month at a time to ambush Vietcong. The marauding bands, Diem declared, could be more effective in setting ambushes during rainy days than in dry weather. During the wet season, the Vietcong found it difficult to preserve foods, and with the constant pounding of the rain and the unending monotony of the dreary, mind-numbing atmosphere, morale plummeted as thoughts turned to home and family. The Vietcong's habits were well known. They arose at 4 A.M., ate breakfast, engaged in physical exercise, and then went into the field. They returned around 8 P.M. and, after having their meal, closed the day with a series of political indoctrination sessions. The time to attack was four in the morning or eight at night.[50]

Harkins and Diem had moved closer together in strategy by emphasizing the necessity of taking the battle to the enemy and destroying his image of invincibility. The number of men required for such special expeditions would drain other units, but the proposal deserved a trial. Harkins recommended volunteers. Special Forces already had the training to conduct such operations. Rangers should also go out on lengthy missions. ARVN soldiers, he insisted, must learn that Vietcong forces were not "12 feet tall," an exaggerated image of the Vietcong's abilities that Diem blamed on the Western press. The priority was to destroy all Vietcong "safe havens."[51]

Buoyed by Diem's new sense of cooperation, Harkins presented a glowing report on the war at the Sixth Secretary of Defense Conference in Honolulu on July 23, 1962 (the day following the neutralization agreement in Laos), which pushed the Kennedy administration a major step closer to a partial withdrawal. The fifteen-month-long Geneva Conference on Laos had ended with a fourteen-nation agreement to neutralize the country, freeing the United States from that entanglement and bringing greater focus on the need to extricate itself from Vietnam as well. The United States was on the winning side, Harkins proclaimed. Nearly 2,400 of 6,000 strategic hamlets should be ready for occupancy by the end of the year, and about 115,000 Montagnards had fled the mountains in quest of government assistance against the Vietcong. Defoliation operations were well under way at the only approved site of Bien Hoa, and the priority for crop destruction was in areas evacuated by the Montagnards. McNamara agreed that the South Vietnamese had made "tremendous progress" in the past six months, but he then asked the most penetrating question: How long would it take before the Vietcong "could be eliminated as a disturbing force"? Harkins did not flinch. One year *after* the South Vietnamese armed forces, Civil Guard, and Self-Defense Corps were "fully operational."[52]

Encouraged by Harkins's upbeat assessment, McNamara followed President Kennedy's directive to present a formula for a phased withdrawal of American military forces. The defense secretary called for a long-range program that focused on heightened training, equipment, and advice, and rested on the premise that it would take three years to bring the Vietcong under control and permit a U.S. military cutback. American personnel would have dropped from an expected 12,000 in 1964 (the number actually reached 23,000 by December, with more soldiers en route) to 1,500 staff members at MAAG headquarters by the end of the process in fiscal year 1968. Military aid funds would meanwhile plummet from $180 million to $40.8 million by fiscal year 1969. But how to maintain U.S. domestic support in the interim—particularly as American losses began to climb? To ease political pressures on the White House, McNamara recommended a well-publicized comprehensive plan of partial U.S. withdrawal from Vietnam that began with the gradual reduction of MACV over the next three years. The primary need was an ambitious training program intended to establish a South Vietnamese Officer Corps capable of managing military operations.

By the end of this period, the Saigon government should be in the position to assume control of the struggle against the Vietcong. U.S. involvement in Vietnam in the period afterward would stand at 1,500 MAAG personnel, a level much closer to what it was when Kennedy first became president.[53]

The Kennedy administration had moved toward this major policy change for several reasons, but its chief concern was to avert an American war. Opposition to a land war in Asia remained a cardinal principle of U.S. foreign policy. Negotiations were never an option, both because of the president's staunch opposition but also because of a recent secret meeting in Geneva, during which Harriman talked with North Vietnam's foreign minister and became convinced that he would settle for nothing less than a reunified Vietnam.[54] Furthermore, the Diem regime would not accept neutralization. Nor would the president send U.S. combat troops. And yet, despite the recent outcome of the Korean War, hard-liners in Washington continued to call for an all-out involvement in Vietnam.

Just as the Cold War had provided an international atmosphere conducive to America's deepening involvement in Vietnam, so too might it furnish a means for bringing that dangerous level of involvement to an end. To facilitate the force reduction, the White House placed South Vietnam within the context of the Cold War by insisting that Berlin and Cuba were much more critical to U.S. interests in Western Europe and the Western Hemisphere than was Vietnam to Southeast Asia. Indeed, Laos loomed as a greater flash point than did South Vietnam. Thus in a highly suspect effort to reverse the many public pronouncements about Vietnam's importance to regional and world security, the White House intended to argue that a move toward disengagement in Vietnam would not mar U.S. credibility, and that the threatened cutback might force Diem into reforms and a greater war effort. America's phased-down involvement in Vietnam would ease domestic and foreign criticism of the Kennedy administration by demonstrating its capacity to fight a limited war. Only the South Vietnamese, the president repeatedly emphasized, could resolve this conflict.[55]

Harkins won McNamara's support for the Strategic Hamlet Program. The problem remained of persuading the Diem regime to establish priorities in building these village fortresses. The U.S. Country Team in Vietnam believed the key region was the delta, followed by the coastal area and then the central sector of South Vietnam. To influence the Saigon government, the Country Team authorized U.S. assistance in only those areas deemed crucial by American officials. McNamara was highly receptive to Krulak's argument that the Saigon government should treat the Montagnards with great care—that they, along with the village defense forces, Civil Guard, and Self-Defense Corps, were "the decisive factor in the war." The government must provide salaries, pensions, and other forms of support. MACV reported that each village averaged four hamlets and that about 2,500 villages and 17,000 hamlets were in South Vietnam. Every village package consisted of four squads of twelve men each who were armed with carbines, shotguns, pistols, and flares. Felt emphasized that improving the Civil Guard and Self-Defense Corps freed the ARVN to take the offensive. McNamara guaranteed the funds necessary for the civil projects and for arming the villagers.[56]

To promote the final stage of the U.S. military experience in Vietnam, McNamara recommended a continued policy of subterfuge aimed at concealing the deepened involvement. In response to Nolting's question regarding press inquiries about the money spent in South Vietnam each year, the defense secretary declared that it was not U.S. policy to publicize those figures. Regarding the need for more helicopters, he hoped to circumvent an accusation by the International Control Commission that the United States was violating the Geneva Accords by operating on the "basic principle" that all equipment taken into the country belonged to South Vietnam. Knowing that this approach would not prove convincing, he instructed Admiral Luther Heinz "to work with the military departments to package and deliver items in an inconspicuous manner."[57]

Three days after the Honolulu conference opened, the Joint Chiefs of Staff instructed CINCPAC to draft a "Comprehensive Plan for South Vietnam" that incorporated McNamara's July 23 decisions. Within three weeks, CINCPAC had directed Harkins to lay out the steps by which the South Vietnamese government would by the end of 1965 develop the capability of controlling its own affairs "without the need for continued U.S. special military assistance."[58]

V

SOUTH VIETNAM'S PERFORMANCE in the war had not improved, leading to more talk of a coup. Diem maintained his opposition to reform, causing Forrestal to recommend putting more pressure on the premier. "I sense, without having the facts, that we have been pussy-footing with Diem for too long. I don't think we have much time to decide whether to stay with SVN on our terms or get out."[59]

The sense of urgency became prevalent when more evidence appeared of Hanoi's involvement in the insurgency. University of London Professor Patrick Honey, in London's *Sunday Telegraph* in late July 1962, reported that the Vietcong had "fallen under the direct control of agents from Communist North Vietnam." At the previous week's Geneva conference on Laos, a North Vietnamese official had indiscreetly declared that the Vietcong worked under the control of the Lao Dong party of North Vietnam, which was "operating secretly in the South." The following September, Honey published two "top secret" documents dated 1951, which demonstrated through the establishment in that year of the Workers' Party or Lao Dong party in Vietnam that the North Vietnamese Communists had organized and directed the Vietcong's armed revolution in South Vietnam. The instructions to party members emphasized the necessity of concealing the fact that the Workers' Party was Communist for fear of alienating property owners and undermining national unity. The NLF was a front for hiding North Vietnam's role. When announcing the creation of the People's Revolutionary Party in South Vietnam in January 1962, Hanoi radio explained that its membership consisted of "representatives of Marxist-Leninists in the South." As one earlier instruction noted, "show the national flag only, never the Party one." In May 1962 the South Vietnamese Liaison Mission with the International Control Commission in Vietnam submitted captured "top secret" Vietcong documents to the International Control Commission that the Lao Dong party had sent to Communist leaders in Ba-xuyen Province. The objective of the People's Revolutionary Party, said one of the documents, was "to isolate the Americans and the Ngo Dinh Diem regime and to rebut their accusations about the invasion of the South by the North. It is a move which will permit us to sabotage the Geneva agreements, to advance the plan for invading the South, and will, at the same time, permit the Front for the Liberation of South Vietnam to recruit new members and to win the sympathy of the non-aligned states of South East Asia. . . . The independent existence of the People's Revolutionary Party is only apparent. In reality, the Party is the Vietnamese Workers' Party, united in North and South, under the direction of the Party Central Committee whose chairman is President Ho."[60]

Washington's fears of a Chinese involvement in Vietnam were likewise justified, for it now seems that Beijing was approaching an active role. Wang Jiaxiang's call for peaceful coexistence drew a bitter retort from Mao at the August 1962 Central Work Conference in Neidaihe. Mao denounced "revisionist" tendencies in the country's domestic and foreign policies that appeased enemies while reducing assistance to national liberation movements. Had the promise of big summer harvests encouraged an aggressive foreign policy that threatened to expand China's role in Vietnam?[61]

Not aware of this growing danger, the Kennedy administration had already begun contingency preparations for a possible leadership change in Saigon's government. The previous June, Senator Mansfield's legislative assistant in Washington had a lengthy conversation with South Vietnamese ambassador Tran Van Chuong, who insisted that Diem was in deep trouble. The assertion was not news to the state department; it had already instructed Nolting to inquire into Diem's probable successor. The most likely candidates were Vice President Tho and Secretary of State Thuan, but with the base of power resting in the military. Tho would be the constitutional successor as well as an acceptable civilian head, if he received General Minh's support.[62]

But an ominous note came from counselor Joseph Mendenhall in the Saigon embassy, who feared that Nhu would engineer a government take-over that left him in control. "A reliable American source," Mendenhall reported, had spoken of Tho's fear that if a coup occurred, Nhu would have him assassinated during the ensuing confusion. The vice president's elimination would open the succession to a person susceptible to Nhu's direction.[63]

By mid-August, Mendenhall, who had stepped down as embassy of-ficer, urged the White House to take the lead in changing the Saigon lead-ership. "Get rid of Diem, Mr. and Mrs. Nhu and the rest of the Ngo family," he declared. The best alternative was a two-headed government led by Tho as the constitutional successor to the presidency and the highly popu-lar General Minh as commander of the armed forces. Tho was a capable politician and flexible in his ideas, which meant that U.S. advisers would work with both the civilian and military members of the new administra-tion. Mendenhall recognized the importance of concealing the U.S. hand in such a plot—about which a state department official wrote in the mar-gin: "Sounds like a very complicated job & hard to keep secret before-hand." During the tumultuous transition from Diem to a new president, U.S. military forces would have to prevent the Communists from expand-ing their influence in South Vietnam. In the coup's aftermath, however, the United States must not leave the impression that the fledgling regime was a "puppet." But no matter how careful its actions, the United States would encounter suspicions of complicity—just as in the November 1960 coup attempt and the February 1962 palace bombing. The "cardinal rule" was to avoid a public admission to involvement.[64]

Mendenhall outlined the steps that U.S. officials must take in such a venture. They should discreetly inquire of Tho and Minh if they would par-ticipate in a coup that received U.S. support at the appropriate moment. Americans could advise on the plan's formulation, but the Vietnamese alone must carry out its implementation. The coup would have a greater chance for success if Diem and the Nhus were out of the palace at the time and if brothers Archbishop Thuc of Hué and Ambassador to the United Kingdom Ngo Dinh Luyen were out of the country. To prevent counterplotting, the coup makers should incarcerate both Thuan (secretary of state) and Dr. Tran Kim Tuyen (head of the secret police). It was also necessary to secure prior assurances of support from key military figures. Evacuation of American de-pendents before the coup was vital to preventing the Diem government from seizing hostages as leverage for securing assistance against the coup leaders. U.S. combat forces would be necessary to prevent Communist expansion during the interim. Throughout these events, the White House must maintain an official position of neutrality.[65]

Mendenhall's August 1962 memorandum offered the first detailed call for a White House–supported coup against Diem, but it contained no exploration of the inherent problems and profound ramifications of such a move. Although recognizing that the United States would undergo charges of complicity, Mendenhall failed to recommend any precautionary measures to avoid suspicion. He also did not consider the signals that would reverberate from placing Thuan and Tuyen in custody and evacuating Americans from the country. What if the conspirators assassinated Diem or other members of his family? Did Tho and Minh offer a significantly better alternative to Diem that would offset the certain public accusations of U.S. complicity? Could the United States control events once the coup was under way? How could its involvement remain secret? What if the coup failed? Could U.S. relations with Diem return to normality? It should have become clear that the United States as Diem's protector would draw blame for a coup, regardless of its outcome.

Perhaps a coup would prove unnecessary. In mid-August 1962, McNamara announced a three-year timetable for ending the United States's special military aid program. Colonel Howard Burris, Vice President Johnson's military aide, noted that the proposal provided a realistic assessment of the time required for success. "Under present circumstances we appear to be just about turning the corner." To "drive [the Vietcong] underground," Harkins recommended the establishment in each corps of a "Quick Reaction Strike Force," which would be a battalion of airborne or regular ARVN troops or rangers, supported by helicopters and C-47 or C123 aircraft. "One year would be enough to achieve victory." If intelligence did its job over the next five months, "the enemy could be pinpointed and hit everywhere at once." Government forces must "keep the VC moving everywhere, all of the time. If they were kept moving constantly for two weeks they would be so tired that they would have to rest and they could all be killed."[66]

Forrestal likewise assured the president that the political and military situation in South Vietnam was "somewhat bullish." Even the usually skeptical British expressed "cautious optimism." Enemy losses were the highest since September 1961. Casualties stood at 2 to 1 in favor of the Saigon government and 4 to 1 in troops killed. The price of rice had fallen for the first time in fifteen years, and successful clearing operations had permitted increased exports from the delta. Village morale had also risen because of the Strategic Hamlet Program. But problems remained, many caused by the South Vietnamese forces. Cottrell expressed concern about protecting villagers from extortion, stealing, rape, and violence by the ARVN, Civil Guard, and Self-Defense Corps. "Should the SDC, which is considered

the worst of all, receive the same pay as the Civil Guards, in order to reduce its exactions on the people?"[67]

The assistance program had also impressed Taylor, who returned to
South Vietnam in the fall of 1962 and reported considerable progress since
his October 1961 visit. The Strategic Hamlet Program counted about 5,000
encampments already fortified or in the process of becoming so. Better
training had improved the performance levels of the army, Civil Guard,
and Self-Defense Corps, which had freed more ARVN battalions to take
the offensive. Statistics—"for what they are worth"—showed growing
Vietcong casualties, fewer weapons lost to the enemy, and more people
and territory liberated from the Vietcong.[68]

The Kennedy administration's optimism remained unshaken, despite
problems reported by the CIA and U.S. Army officers advising ARVN
soldiers in the countryside. Infiltration continued through Laos and Cambodia, in sharp contrast to the great reduction in men and matériel arriving
by sea that had resulted from enhanced naval patrols. The only plan known
to reduce overland entry was the organization of tribesmen along the border to watch the trails and report violations to reserve forces close by. The
Saigon government still lacked a national plan of military coordination.
Another problem was the proliferation of paramilitary forces, who needed
centralized direction. The flaws in the counterinsurgency program were
evident to any observer, and yet, before the National Security Industrial
Association in Washington in late September 1962, General Lemnitzer,
chair of the Joint Chiefs of Staff, happily proclaimed that U.S. aid was
"beginning to tip the scales in favor of the Free World." Years afterward,
however, he admitted that the situation had become "quite bad" by October because the Vietcong had moved into "the period of the terrorism"
and South Vietnam's armed forces had been ineffective.[69]

In the midst of these reports, Diem again endangered the U.S. aid
program when he reversed his position by expelling Sully and then moved
toward banning *Newsweek* magazine itself. Shortly after his departure, Sully
filed a report alleging that the Nhus had quietly wrested control from Diem.
The premier had put on weight and no longer had the stamina of the mid-
1950s. His face had become bloated and red, he had lost his sense of humor, and he was out of touch with everyday life in Vietnam. Diem's secret
police scrutinized the private lives of Vietnamese and foreign officials in a
"terribly amateurish" way. The real power behind these police was Nhu, a
"vicious political in-fighter with an unquenchable thirst for power." But
"the most extraordinary personality in the Ngo dynasty" was Madame Nhu,
"a beautiful, gifted, and charming woman" who was "also grasping, con-
ceited, and obsessed with a drive for power that far surpasses that of even
her husband." She regarded the Ngo family as a dynasty. "It is no exaggeration to say that Madame Nhu is the most detested personality in South

Vietnam." She complained that too many Vietnamese praised Diem for saving the country. "Don't they know that we saved him from the Binh–Xuyen revolt" in 1955? Diem, Sully declared, did not recognize that "Ngo Dinh Nhu has executed a quiet coup d'etat that puts him and his wife in control." Nhu traveled throughout South Vietnam like a viceroy, confusing the peasants with his "aristocratic, low-keyed Annamese royal-court accent." A village official wryly commented: "If the effect of all this were not so disastrous, it would be hilariously funny."[70]

Nolting tried to persuade Diem to change his mind. The ambassador warned that Sully's expulsion would worsen relations with all journalists and leave the impression that the regime was too weak to undergo criticism. The American public would consider a news blackout an admission to a cover-up of government inefficiency or worse and question the wisdom of continuing the U.S. commitment to Saigon. Nolting's entreaties had no impact on the premier.[71]

Another problem arose when South Vietnam declared its intention to break diplomatic relations with Laos over its recent decision to establish relations with North Vietnam. Before the July 1962 neutralization of Laos at Geneva, South Vietnam had threatened to walk out of the negotiations. Just after the decision, Diem had stormed at Harriman, "If you put that government in Laos, and put a communist government next to my borders, I'm going to withdraw my ambassador from Vientiane." Harriman argued, unconvincingly, that it was a non-Communist government with three figures, two of whom were Communist. Diem withdrew his ambassador. In late September his government bitterly declared that in view of Laos's agreement to receive an ambassador from Hanoi, it was "obliged to revise its whole diplomatic position and all its international commitments regarding Laos."[72]

Diem eased his position, but only after U.S. warnings that his action threatened to undermine the delicate international program for peace in Laos and endanger the war effort in South Vietnam. The twelve other signatories of the neutralization pact, including the United States, would have to take sides on the matter. Diem's decision, Cottrell angrily warned Thuan in Washington, "would produce a head on collision with a firm determined US policy on Laos." Nolting spent two days with Foreign Minister Vu Van Mau, registering the Kennedy administration's concern. President Kennedy told Thuan that South Vietnam's abandonment of the Geneva Accords would permit the Soviet Union to accuse the United States of violating them. Faced with such pressure, Diem finally consented to maintain a chargé in Vientiane as long as Hanoi's representative did not hold the same rank. By the end of the month, Hanoi had agreed to the stipulation, and Diem did not break relations with Laos. In the meantime, Nolting appealed to the foreign minister to seek harmonious relations with

Laos and Cambodia in an effort to promote regional peace and prevent South Vietnam's certain "diplomatic isolation."[73]

That issue resolved, still another problem erupted when the White House, as part of its push toward a diminished involvement, expanded the use of defoliants. The joint chiefs, state department, Felt, and Harkins called for spraying herbicides over a sixty-mile mangrove area that concealed Vietcong overland routes in the delta region of South Vietnam. President Kennedy approved the operation with the virtually impossible stipulation that it destroy no food crops. Such selective care did not assuage Edward R. Murrow, director of the U.S. Information Agency, who warned that the use of defoliants raised cries of chemical and biological warfare that would appall people all over the world. As fate would have it, Rachel Carson was publishing a series of articles in the *New Yorker* magazine, which graphically depicted the devastating effect of insecticides on the balance of life and human health in general. Both friends and enemies would criticize the United States for this antienvironmental decision, encouraging the Communists to launch a far-reaching propaganda campaign.[74]

More than a few White House advisers considered the crop destruction program a step toward a partial U.S. withdrawal. Hilsman recommended this proposal by MACV and the U.S. embassy despite heavy political liabilities. Admittedly, other nations would react more strongly against crop destruction than defoliation. The first program aimed at taking lives through what critics termed germ warfare; the second sought to eliminate the Vietcong's ambush areas and hidden passageways through the jungles. The joint chiefs approved a trial program in eight heavily populated Vietcong areas totaling 2,500 acres. Both Harriman and Alexis Johnson opposed the idea as an infamous illustration of the white man's weaponry against Asian food. But the Diem government favored crop destruction. McNamara recommended that the president approve a pilot program that focused on the heavily Vietcong populated Phu Yen Province, and that worked in coordination with the Hai Yen II clear-and-hold operations and resettlement of Montagnards already under way in this area. Rusk, however, warned the president that the action would subject the United States to Communist propaganda denouncing food destruction as the prelude to its using poison gas and other means of chemical warfare against Asians. Lemnitzer showed no remorse. It was "strange that we can bomb, kill, and burn people but are not permitted to starve them."[75]

In early October, President Kennedy drew mixed support when he approved the crop destruction program. Spraying would occur only on specific targets suspected of housing large numbers of Vietcong. Forrestal informed McGeorge Bundy that the president had authorized the measure "over the mild objections of Averell [Harriman], Roger Hilsman, and myself; but with the strong approval of Secretary McNamara, General Taylor, the field, and just about everybody else you could think of. I believe his main train of thinking was that you cannot say no to your military advisors all the time, and with this I agree."[76]

President Kennedy's decision to approve crop destruction suggested several revealing features of his administration. Although he had given in to the military's wishes, he did so under narrow conditions intended to keep the effort under tight executive control. As Forrestal observed, the president could not maintain any semblance of reasonableness if he rejected every request by the military. But if he could choose the most advantageous times to support the military—when the move did not prove too costly—he could maintain unity in the administration. In actuality, his decision strengthened his position regarding any future confrontation with the military because it demonstrated his apparent willingness to accept the arguments of everyone. Most important, in selecting his battles carefully he could say no on other matters (such as combat troops) that had greater ramifications. In an ironic fashion, his support of the crop destruction program advocated by the military reiterated his distrust for its spokesmen that had emanated from the Bay of Pigs fiasco. More than that, the move constituted another step toward a phased withdrawal.

THE KENNEDY ADMINISTRATION, however, had not yet gained the initiative in the war. Rostow asserted that the situation had improved but added that victory was impossible without an end to infiltration. When the neutralization of Laos went into effect in October 1962, Hanoi did not honor the provisions stipulating a halt to Vietcong movements through Laos. In the midst of the Cuban missile crisis, Rostow urged Rusk to warn the Soviet Union that if it broke its promise to Harriman about convincing Hanoi to adhere to the Laotian agreement, Southeast Asia would also become an international issue. Perhaps, Rusk wondered years afterward, Kennedy would have forced North Vietnam to rethink its position if he had sent 100,000 troops into South Vietnam when learning in the fall of 1962 that the Laotian agreement was a failure. But the president did not want to widen the war by pulling in either the Soviet Union or China. This was sound reasoning. The Kremlin remained concerned that the Vietnam conflict might develop into an international struggle, but it had charted a careful course of sending token military aid to the NLF in the hopes of undercutting Chinese influence. Instead, the small amounts of military hardware sent by the Soviets alienated Hanoi and had no impact on China, whose leaders had already decided to limit its military assistance to North Vietnam. A military delegation led by Vo Nguyen Giap had arrived in Beijing in early October to request more military assistance. Zhou Enlai, however, continued to emphasize a broader approach, reminding his visitors that the two countries' mutual aid agreements included political and economic assistance as well as military matériel. Weapons, he insisted, were supplementary to the greater importance of capable party leaders and properly indoctrinated soldiers.[77]

When the president asked for a status report in South Vietnam, the state department declared that whereas the Vietcong was winning the war in the fall of 1961, it was *not* winning a year later. Admittedly, the morale of the government's forces and people had risen and the Strategic Hamlet Program had provided the peasants with greater social services and a taste of democracy at the local level. The Saigon government reported that by the close of the summer of 1962, it had constructed 3,225 of the planned 11,316 strategic hamlets and that one-third of the nation's people were in them. The Vietcong had lost some of its momentum and perhaps part of its claim to having the "mandate of heaven."[78] The White House had moved closer to formulating a three-year plan aimed at de-Americanizing the conflict. But it was chastened by the realization that a premature withdrawal would cause the collapse of South Vietnam.

9

FROM ESCALATION
TO DISENGAGEMENT

[The U.S. government's clandestine actions violated] the
right of the American people to be informed of the facts on
which the policies of their government are based, and on the
activities of U.S. military personnel committed to combat.

John Mecklin, November 27, 1962

Democracy here cannot come before security. It will take at
least ten years.

Province chief in South Vietnam, c. December 1962

AND SO THE IRONY remained: The secret war escalated as the
Kennedy administration steered toward a major disengagement.
While U.S. advisers pushed for governmental reforms in South
Vietnam, they urged the ARVN to clear out Vietcong strongholds. The
Vietcong, in turn, heightened its attempt to undermine the Diem regime
by intimidating village and provincial leaders, recruiting a following by
threatening the families of draftees, spreading rumors of government corruption, kidnapping or killing the opposition, and advising the peasants
against paying rent because, under squatter's rights, the land was theirs.
The Vietcong's favorite targets were teachers and village health workers
because they promoted a favorable image of the national government. Kidnapped schoolteachers numbered more than 250, thirty of whom were dead
and another hundred missing. Since early 1962, the Vietcong had kidnapped
more than 3,000 people and killed a similar number. The Saigon government meanwhile increased the emphasis on the Strategic Hamlet Program.[1]

The result was still another irony about the U.S. entanglement in Vietnam: Each success or failure necessitated another notch upward of American aid followed by a matching escalation by North Vietnam. A quagmire
was in the making, a nightmare experienced by the French that had forced
their humiliating withdrawal less than a decade earlier.

I

REFUSING EITHER to negotiate a settlement or to approve a total withdrawal, the Kennedy administration expanded its military presence as the central step toward reducing that presence. Nearly 11,000 American military personnel were in South Vietnam by the fall of 1962 (about 8,500 more than at the year's beginning), all playing a nominal advisory role. Military aid had ratcheted upward to include radar, sentry dogs, chemicals, helicopters, special forces training, sophisticated communications matériel, and intelligence and civic action advice. Despite the concentrated U.S. effort, the Vietcong killed eleven Americans and wounded thirty-two from January 1961 through September 1962, making the war's resolution more elusive.[2] Furthermore, in October the threat of nuclear war with the Soviet Union over the Cuban missile crisis relegated Vietnam to secondary importance. The road to victory in Vietnam no longer seemed straight and narrow, particularly since the most optimistic forecasts set a three-year timetable for success. Instead of a quick turnaround that freed more Americans to come home, the promised victory remained uncertain, causing frustrated U.S. policymakers to harden the commitment. How compelling the temptation to play one more card. How exhilarating to inch as close as possible to a full-scale military involvement without crossing the line. The only feasible way out of Vietnam, it seemed, was to wade in farther.

The positive signs of America's deepening involvement were deceptively encouraging. Although one-sixth of the Montagnards had fled the Vietcong-dominated mountainous regions, a large number of them requested governmental training and arms to facilitate their return home where they intended to resist the Vietcong and provide intelligence on its locations. Since July 1962, the Saigon government had expanded its control over the rural peasants by 2 percent to about 49 percent, whereas the Vietcong could claim only 9 percent of the countryside. On the surface, counterinsurgency tactics appeared effective. The number of Vietcong attacks had declined, though still averaging more than a hundred per week. Many White House advisers were willing to support social, economic, and military pressures until the enemy recognized the futility of its cause. The greatest deterrent to infiltration, they argued, was Hanoi's fear of conventional war. But Washington's hard-liners had become impatient with the lead-like restraints placed on the interventionist effort and called for accelerated military pressure to break the North Vietnamese support line to the Vietcong. The ensuing victory would show undeveloped nations that Americans working with peasants could shatter the Communist "mystique" as the "wave of the future."[3]

Despite White House concern over the aid program, Congress stood behind the president. William Bundy expressed surprise at there being so little opposition to the administration's Vietnam policies. The most common inquiry focused on whether or not the aid program had brought progress. No one asked the most piercing questions: "Isn't this a very risky enterprise? Should we be in this deep?" House and Senate leaders raised few objections to the appropriations; indeed, some congressional members advocated stronger action. Before the House Foreign Affairs Committee, Georgia Democrat J. L. Pilcher from the Far East Subcommittee expressed no apprehensions about advisers participating in the war. "I am in favor of it," he declared. "That is a hot war. . . . It is not a cold war. When you send those boys over there, they are going to shoot back." Wisconsin Democrat Clement Zablocki, chair of that same subcommittee, asserted that U.S. advisers must join the war and that Americans throughout the country would be supportive. Democratic Senators Hubert Humphrey of Minnesota and Wayne Morse of Oregon likewise favored the counterinsurgency effort. In Vietnam, Humphrey confidently proclaimed that "the tide may well have turned for the forces of freedom against the Communist guerrillas of the north. . . . A number of striking successes have been achieved." The United States must "put out these brush fires" all over the world. Morse concurred. "Unfortunately, a good many of the soldiers of freedom have not been in a position where they could successfully combat guerrilla warfare." The Communists must know that Americans "can meet them on every front—Cuba, Berlin, southeast Asia, Africa. We must let them know that wherever they threaten freedom, we will stand firm and protect freedom."[4]

Congressional acquiescence in the Kennedy administration's Vietnam policy also stemmed from the rapid expansion of presidential leadership in foreign affairs during World War II and afterward. In the fall of 1961, Fulbright complained in the *Cornell Law Quarterly* that the Constitution "hobbled the President" in foreign policy "by too niggardly a grant of power." To combat communism, the United States must not "leave vast and vital decision-making powers in the hands of a decentralized, independent-minded and largely parochial-minded body of legislators . . . . I submit that the price of democratic survival in a world of aggressive totalitarianism is to give up some of the democratic luxuries of the past." The following June of 1962, Mansfield told a large commencement audience at Michigan State University (invited at the behest of Professor Wesley Fishel) that there was nothing wrong in publicly discussing presidential policy in Southeast Asia. U.S. military commitments to Thailand and Vietnam had dangerously deepened "an already deep involvement on the Southeast Asia mainland." The time had come to reassess U.S. policy. "Is a permanent policy of that kind justified on the basis of any enduring interests of the people of the United States in Southeast Asia?" But then, drawing back in a manner similar to that of Fulbright, Mansfield added, "In this, as in all cases of foreign policy and military command, the responsibility for the direction of the Nation's course rests with the President."[5]

Other factors help to explain congressional acceptance of Kennedy's Vietnam program. The secrecy surrounding the administration's war program clouded the lack of success and undercut any cause for alarm. The Senate Foreign Relations Committee, according to Chief of Staff Carl Marcy, "did not pay much attention" to Vietnam. Most reports pointed to imminent victory and, during an election year, the Democrats had no desire to raise issues that might threaten their present control of both houses. Republicans likewise seemed to approve policy. In relation to other problems, of course, Vietnam bore secondary significance—even to Laos during the first half of 1962—and most certainly to Berlin and Cuba in the last quarter of the year. Indeed, Congress in the fall of 1962 overwhelmingly approved open-ended resolutions authorizing the president to take whatever military action he deemed necessary to stop Communist aggression in Berlin and Cuba.[6]

Pressure nonetheless mounted to end the war in Vietnam, causing the White House to recommend manpower other than Americans. In an early October 1962 meeting in Honolulu, Harkins presented another optimistic appraisal of the Vietnam situation and enthusiastically supported an enlarged Vietnamese Air Force and the employment of a B-26 unit flown by South Vietnamese pilots. Vietcong strikes at the battalion level had declined, he happily reported, almost in correlation with the rising number of ARVN battalion-sized operations. U.S. pilots were flying a hundred hours a month but, he and Air Force General Roland Anthis agreed, could not maintain this grueling pace without additional planes and personnel. The United States was assuming too much of the combat burden, McNamara concurred, but he supported the argument for enhanced air action. To do this without sending more Americans, he suggested expanding the Vietnamese Air Force to 10,000 and then assigning South Vietnamese C-47 pilots to the American B-26s and Chinese pilots to the South Vietnamese C-47s. The U.S. objective was to help the South Vietnamese fight the war, not fight it for them. "If you really want more US pilots," McNamara added in a steel-like tone, "make recommendations, but they will be received cooly."[7]

Harkins then unveiled his strategy for winning the war: an "explosive type operation" that had already won Diem's approval. Whether the United States was correct in estimating an enemy force of 20,000 hard-core Vietcong, or South Vietnam was correct, with its count at 30,000, the ARVN was vastly superior in number, with fifty-one trained divisions, or close to 300,000 men. That in mind, Harkins advocated a nationwide, simultaneous offensive against all Vietcong strongholds. Preparation for such a broad-scale operation required saturation bombing of all Vietcong locations, particularly in the heavily

infested Zone D above Saigon, followed by the explosive phase, which consisted of massive coordinated attacks at every level climaxing in sweeping
cleanup operations. In response to Taylor's question, Harkins admitted
that Saigon's forces might have to repeat the action several times. And yes,
the operation necessitated a dramatic bulge in South Vietnam's defense
budget over the next three years and a hefty expansion of its armed forces.
Most important, it required substantial increases in U.S. military help.[8]
The premise was clear: A major reduction in the U.S. involvement in Vietnam depended on a greatly enhanced program of U.S. military assistance.

Unknown to the White House, its military buildup had already had
serious repercussions in Beijing. Chinese leaders had watched the escalation with great alarm. In early October 1962, Giap met with Mao, who
declared that "in the past several years, we did not think much about whether
or not the imperialists might attack us, and now we must carefully think
about it." He offered Hanoi enough military assistance to arm 230 additional battalions.[9]

Soon after the Honolulu meeting, Harriman expressed concern about
the pitfalls of overoptimism and criticized Harkins's "explosion" scheme as
offering no guarantees of success. Although the situation had improved over
the past year, the unfortunate tendency to focus on sporadic military tri-
umphs obscured the reality of persistent failures. Harriman was especially
worried about arms making it to the villages quickly enough. McNamara
emphasized that the United States had plenty of rifles and carbines, but he
admitted to great difficulty in getting them into the villagers' hands. Harriman
also opposed strafing and saturation bombing but supported a defensive move
that would surely escalate the fighting: arming the helicopters. The success
of Harkins's plan, Harriman keenly noted, depended on the element of
surprise. And yet the news of such an extensive assault would predictably
leak to the Vietcong beforehand, permitting its people to evacuate the targeted areas. Furthermore, the use of so many military forces at one time
would result in a horrendous number of innocent casualties. And what would
be the outcome? South Vietnamese forces would have expended themselves while the Vietcong hunkered down, waiting for the assault to cease
before returning to their old locations.[10]

Nolting saw value in Harkins's proposal but likewise raised questions
about its feasibility. The very nature of guerrilla warfare placed the enemy
in close proximity with civilians and hampered the widespread strafing and
bombing so essential to the operation. Arming of civilians in the hamlets
had gone slowly because of the difficulties in determining who to trust.
Despite the obstacles, however, a semblance of order had developed in the
hamlets. Several council elections had taken place by secret ballots. Most
heartening, many strategic hamlets went up in areas that did not necessitate uprooting families. In those cases, workers constructed fences around

a settlement and villagers continued to till their land nearby. Relocation, however, did occur in those Vietcong-held areas engaged in heavy combat—part of Operation Sunrise, for example.[11]

More reservations about the strategic hamlet approach came from the U.S. consul in Hué, John Helble, who advocated instead a program called "Popular Force" that Diem's brother, Ngo Dinh Can, had developed in that city. The Saigon government had continued to deteriorate, Helble argued, suggesting that the heralded Strategic Hamlet Program was "mostly pure façade." A strategic hamlet usually consisted of "a very inadequate fence around one-quarter of the hamlet." If Can was correct in assuming that the Vietcong had deep roots in the villages—that a third of the males helped the enemy—then the critical consideration was not the number of strategic hamlets but the presence of so many Vietcong cadres in the villages who intimidated the people into refusing to help their government. To remedy this problem, Can had created a Popular Force of volunteers in Hué who underwent rigid training similar to that of U.S. Marines in boot camp. Those who survived the program became part of 150-man crack units assigned to villages for six months to work during the day and devote most of the night to defense patrols and hit-and-run tactics. This full-time involvement in village life had aroused popular support, instilled a sense of security, and encouraged the development of an effective intelligence network. The Popular Force usually accomplished its mission within the six-month period and then moved to another troubled area.[12]

Whether strategic hamlets or Popular Forces, the primary prerequisite for success was loyalty to the nation. At Gia Long Palace in late October, Nhu put his finger on the most profound problem confronting the U.S. aid effort when he suggested that the lack of nationalist sentiment was a root cause of South Vietnam's trouble. "The government in Saigon," Nhu told Nolting, "could be changed 36 times and the people would never know it." Diem had traveled throughout the country for eight years but remained incapable of "organizing the masses." A revolution had to occur—and not just in social, economic, political, and administrative reforms. An American journalist once warned Nhu that the revolution he advocated would lead to his own demise—to which Nhu blithely responded that "unless the seed die, there can be no new harvest." Real change must take place at the hamlet level. All of Southeast Asia needed "an economic and social revolution." No governments could survive "unless they themselves carried out this revolution."[13]

The chances of an inspirational leadership developing in Saigon seemed minuscule. No popular mandate for Diem's rule had become clear; indeed, the exact opposite feeling prevailed, despite the Kennedy administration's attempts to refurbish the premier into a charismatic and dynamic leader. Diem had lost the aura of sound leadership he possessed when first taking office in the mid-1950s. His image of a warm and progressive leader had steadily deteriorated into the reality of a cold and reactionary ruler, seemingly oblivious to his people's needs. A sense of national loyalty had little prospect of flourishing when the premier advocated a creed of "personalism" that appeared to exalt himself and his family over the national good. Under these circumstances, Diem would have a difficult time exerting a centralized direction from Saigon over a people who revered local control. One family's rule could never prevail over the concept of family rule.

II

IN THE MEANTIME, the feud between Saigon and U.S. newsmen had intensified, further complicating the aid effort. Diem had announced a ban on *Newsweek* as part of a crackdown on all the press. Saigon also did not honor its assurances of holding daily press briefings on military affairs, and it had barred newsmen from T-28 aircraft and from access to Special Forces without a permit from the Director of Central Intelligence. Furthermore, the government informed AP correspondent Malcolm Browne that it planned to terminate his employer's contract at the end of the year for budgetary reasons and would rotate United Press International (UPI) and AP on an annual basis afterward. Since the Saigon regime controlled AP circulation through the country's wire service, the Vietnam Press, this move would effectively deny AP's access to news. Not by coincidence did this action follow a series of stories by Browne that had criticized government figures.[14]

The culmination came during the Independence Day celebrations on October 25, 1962, when the Diem regime ordered NBC correspondent James Robinson out of the country. Technically, he had violated a rule by entering South Vietnam with a transit visa and failing to apply for a regular visa within seven days. But Nolting had learned that the real reason stemmed from Robinson's "insulting" broadcast in May that had belittled the family "clique" running the government. Diem had also become infuriated following a long interview that Robinson had not even used. Diem, Robinson had snidely remarked, could not be much of a president if he had that much time to "waste" on reporters. Nolting and Trueheart talked with Diem for over an hour on the morning of October 29, trying to dissuade him from expelling Robinson. Nolting urged Diem to recognize that this move, coming just after the expulsion of Sully and the banning of *Newsweek*, would suggest to Americans that the regime had something to hide. Diem remained rigid in his stand, pulling out a dossier of Robinson's broadcasts that included one strongly criticizing the Ngo family. This type of news reporting, Diem spat out, was "intolerable" because it showed no respect for a chief of state. Robinson had even quipped to a Saigon government official that in the course of a long interview his exalted premier had "taken a great deal of time saying nothing." Diem, Nolting lamented, was "unwilling or unable to subordinate to other considerations, however important, his canons of correct behavior, and what he regards as his primordial obligations to his family."[15]

Robinson's expulsion order had deeply divided the Saigon government. The Director General of Information, Phan Van Tao, and his deputy, Dang Duc Khoi, angrily burst into the U.S. embassy's Public Affairs Office on the night of the order. Nhu, they asserted, had originated the order and they had spent the past hour and a half trying in vain to change his mind. Follow-up discussions with both Nhu and Diem had likewise failed. Not giving up, Khoi publicly expressed opposition to the expulsion of newsmen and leaked several details of government maneuvering—including Diem's talk with Nolting. On the evening of October 27, Tao and Khoi hosted a dinner for foreign news correspondents, including Robinson. Although at first considering a boycott, the journalists decided to attend and found Madame Nhu as guest of honor. She charmed the visitors, fending off their complaints by calmly attributing the government's press policies to wartime exigencies.[16]

Newsmen sent Diem a formal protest on Robinson's behalf on October 31. NBC's vice president termed the expulsion "incomprehensible" and sought an explanation. The U.S. embassy agreed that the expulsions of Sully and Robinson would lead to others. The affair also demonstrated that Nhu and his wife had contrived this policy "in [a] bitter spirit of revenge." But the embassy could do nothing, and Robinson left for Hong Kong.[17]

The battle of the press had serious ramifications. Robinson had told his NBC home office that other U.S. news correspondents in Saigon were alarmed that the Kennedy administration did not vigorously protest his expulsion. Indeed, the timing of Diem's action was unfortunate in that the ongoing Cuban missile crisis had prevented a prompt White House reaction to the press furor in Vietnam. The Washington news director for NBC, Bill Monroe, expressed satisfaction with the embassy's firm stand but, in a surprising twist, declared that Robinson's actions did not merit unqualified support from NBC. The director of the Vietnam Working Group, Chalmers Wood, felt that the journalism profession had been less spirited about the expulsions of Sully and Robinson because "they are not perhaps among the more outstanding members of the Fourth Estate." But the problem was that the Diem regime had become convinced that it could ignore U.S. wishes.[18]

The press controversy ran deeper than the expulsions of either Robinson or Sully. Schlesinger was partly correct in alleging that no one had lied: The reporters believed their own negative stories and U.S. embassy officials believed their own positive assessments. Mecklin, who was the ambassador's chief liaison with the press, concurred with this observation. "The root of the problem was the fact that much of what the newsmen took to be lies was exactly what the Mission genuinely believed, and was reporting to Washington." Without question, however, some Americans in Saigon attempted to deceive their superiors in Washington into believing that the reporters had interfered with the aid effort. Sully's expulsion had upset Nolting and the embassy only because of its potential impact on U.S. aid policy. The correspondent's criticisms of the Diem regime had irritated Americans as well as Vietnamese. Sully's lower-class background did not appeal to either Nolting or his chargé and long-time friend, William Trueheart, both of whom were, in David Halberstam's words, products of the "Virginia-gentleman school of the foreign service." At one point Halberstam himself had so exasperated President Kennedy that he tried in vain to persuade the *New York Times* to recall its reporter. The correspondents had raised questions about the U.S. aid program that the White House could not easily dismiss. They criticized Diem and his family as oriental despots who had no interest in democracy. They ridiculed the Strategic Hamlet Program as a sham that the Ngos exploited in trying to establish authoritarian rule. They repeatedly rejected the U.S. mission's attempts to cast a favorable light on the ARVN and came to suspect Harkins and Nolting of either lying or naively twisting reality into the illusion of success. To the tune of *Twinkle, Twinkle, Little Star*, the U.S. advisers mocked their leaders in words that the journalists regarded as truth:

> We are winning, this we know.
> General Harkins tells us so.
> In the delta, things are rough.
> In the mountains, mighty tough.
> But we're winning, this we know.
> General Harkins tells us so.
> If you doubt this is true,
> McNamara says so too.[19]

Saigon's independent treatment of the press threatened to set a precedent for acting unilaterally in other matters. Mecklin warned that the measures taken against Sully and Robinson were part of a new anti-American policy engineered by Nhu and his wife, which included "a deliberate new campaign of harassment" of all correspondents. In a taped radio interview on the morning of November 27, Madame Nhu derisively remarked that U.S. newsmen were "intoxicated by communism." Some correspondents in Saigon complained of being followed on a regular basis. Others reported threats of reprisals if they criticized the Diem regime. In a move that several journalists angrily attributed to palace behest, General Le Van Ty (with Nhu's approval) ordered field commanders to communicate with reporters only through written questions and answers. Most infuriating was the forced removal of correspondents from U.S. helicopters. The week before, the Saigon government had declared the new military operation in Zone D off-limits to newsmen. Nearly forty U.S. helicopters were involved in the huge operation north of Saigon—which, combined with unit advisers, meant that upward to 150 American soldiers had entered a combat area. Among the journalists banned from the hot area was Neil Sheehan of UPI, whose ensuing story stirred up a controversial MACV inquiry that failed to change the situation and angered the newsmen even more. The ban from Zone D, Mecklin asserted, turned them against the U.S. mission more than any other action during its stay in Saigon.[20]

Sheehan joined Halberstam in calling on their home offices to file formal complaints in Washington over their exclusion from Zone D. When MACV defended the act as essential to protecting classified information, Halberstam indignantly denounced that response as "an insult to the patriotism" of the correspondents. He scribbled an angry letter while in Mecklin's office and slammed it on his desk, declaring that "you can do any damn thing you want with it." Just days earlier he had traveled with the junk forces, where a U.S. Navy officer briefed him on the operation, only to be rebuked by the South Vietnamese commander and told to ask Halberstam not to use the information. Mecklin declared that "Halberstam was literally shaking with anger" when he returned to Saigon.[21]

The central issue in the press controversy was Diem's resentment over the journalists' criticisms of his rule and his family, but the ongoing battle brought in a number of other matters as well. Americans had hoped that once Saigon's military situation improved, it would relax its strictures on news correspondents. Instead, Mecklin asserted, the Diem regime had engaged in "blind vindictiveness for past criticism." The bitter exchanges took on the visceral tone of a personal vendetta. Saigon's censorship campaign aimed at stopping all news leaving the country except for official communiqués, which Mecklin denounced as "notoriously unreliable, including news about activities of US personnel in Vietnam." Nhu was Machiavellian enough to take advantage of the explosive situation by trying to destroy U.S. credibility and hoping either to solidify his brother's rule or to facilitate his own rise to power. Such underhanded actions threatened to wreck the Kennedy administration's policy in the entire region. They violated "the right of the American people to be informed of the facts on which the policies of their government are based, and on the activities of U.S. military personnel committed to combat."[22]

The press issue opened a deep fissure in the Saigon–U.S. relationship that could expand into other matters because of the rapidly growing influence of Nhu and his wife. White House failure to take resolute action following the expulsions of Sully and Robinson not only angered the journalists, but it also encouraged Nhu and other leaders in Saigon to pursue policies that were independent of U.S. concerns in Southeast Asia. Such an autonomous path posed a great danger to the Diem regime. If it succeeded in squelching the correspondents, it would be in a position to imperil America's overall mission and thereby invigorate those in the Kennedy administration who were already urging a reassessment of its commitment to Diem. Only when the South Vietnamese government raised the quality of its performance in the war would its public image improve. The strong presence of the Nhus—whose contemptuous attitude toward Americans made them easy to despise—heightened the appeal of alternative leadership in Saigon.

III

THE UNITED STATES'S problems in Vietnam meanwhile continued to mount, this time over Diem's renewed threat to break relations with Laos. Despite Hanoi's earlier agreement to send only a chargé to Vientiane, it had upgraded its diplomatic representative to that of ambassador. If Diem cut diplomatic ties with his neighbor, Harriman assured Nolting, the move would constitute a major "diplomatic defeat" for the United States, both in Vietnam and throughout Southeast Asia. "Diem's stubbornness and personal feelings are understood, but there comes a time when being a good ally requires laying them aside and cooperating to make joint policies work." Nolting, however, chided Harriman for attempting to dictate Diem's policies. "Whatever success we have had to date rests in [an] important sense on our ultimate respect for [the Government of Vietnam's] sovereignty, including its right in [the] final analysis to make decisions in [the] field of foreign policy." Harriman hotly declared that Nolting was "not on the same wavelength" and insisted that President Kennedy's credibility was at stake because of his personal letter to Diem and the integral relationship of a Laotian settlement to U.S. objectives in South Vietnam. "From your messages," Harriman proclaimed to Nolting with heightening exasperation, "I gained the impression that you do not consider Diem's attitude towards Laos of prime importance."[23]

The United States failed to dissuade South Vietnam from severing relations with Laos. In response to Nolting's entreaties, Thuan agreed only to maintain a consul in Laos if Hanoi's ambassador received accreditation. But this move was not satisfactory, Nolting emphasized; consuls exerted no influence in diplomacy. Diem responded that he could not ignore a move by the Laotian government that so blatantly helped Hanoi. He remained infuriated over Laos's neutralization in the spring. His anger with

Harriman had become so rancid that South Vietnam's pundits had changed the name of the Vietcong's infiltration route from the north to the "Averell Harriman Memorial Highway." After North Vietnam's ambassador presented his credentials to the Laotian government on November 8, the Diem regime announced that its embassy in Vientiane would "cease to function."[24]

Having failed to dislodge Diem from his Laotian course, the Kennedy administration attempted to handle the issue within the broader context of maintaining harmony within the entire region. It remained greatly concerned about Cambodia's publicly expressed interest in receiving assistance from the Communist Chinese if its chief of state, Prince Norodom Sihanouk, detected a threat from either South Vietnam or Thailand. Sihanouk had denounced Diem as a "bloody dictator," Thuan complained to Nolting, making an accommodation extremely difficult. Thuan then warned that Laotian General Phoumi Nosavan remained bitter toward the United States for supporting the neutralization of his country. The Eisenhower administration had installed Phoumi's right-wing government during the 1950s and then provided military assistance in its civil war against neutralists and Communists. The 1962 decision to neutralize Laos had so alienated Phoumi that any reduction in his forces would drive him into the camp of the Communist Pathet Lao.[25]

The Kennedy administration's Laotian policy encouraged its South Vietnamese ally to act without regard for U.S. interests. In a late November discussion with Mecklin, Nhu spoke derisively of Americans, doubting their capacity to "understand" communism, the Third World, and Cold War realities. Nhu then made what Mecklin termed a "reckless (and psychotic?) remark"—that the United States should hit Beijing with an atomic bomb.[26] How bitterly ironic that the Kennedy administration had worked to safeguard South Vietnam's independence, only to see that country's leaders promote their own interests in a manner detrimental to its protector. Whatever its motivations, the Diem regime's autonomous actions underlined the most fundamental maxim in foreign relations: To survive as a nation, its government must pursue its own perceived interests. From the U.S. point of view, cooperation among Laos, Cambodia, and South Vietnam was essential to cutting off North Vietnamese infiltration and ending the Vietcong threat. But the Diem regime feared that Laos and North Vietnam had established a closely knit relationship that posed a danger more immediate to South Vietnam than continued infiltration and subversion. The West's neutralization of Laos had already borne its first bitter fruit: a regime in Vientiane that leaned toward the Communists and welcomed diplomatic relations with North Vietnam. Despite U.S. efforts to the contrary, Laos could become the launching pad for a North Vietnamese assault on South Vietnam.

In the meantime, the Strategic Hamlet Program continued to draw criticism. A rash of Vietcong attacks on the strategic hamlets throughout the country had raised disturbing questions about their effectiveness and further undermined popular support for the Diem regime. Provincial chiefs remained notoriously inept in implementing the program. The government had still not established a viable intelligence network as well as an effective nocturnal defense system. The program's administration was suspect, particularly since the fiscal year 1964 allotment contained no provision for strategic hamlet kits (barbed wire, weapons, and medicines) in either the Military Assistance Program or the Agency for International Development.[27]

Taylor, nevertheless, thought that the Strategic Hamlet Program would overcome its problems. Contrary to critics, he argued that the rising number of Vietcong attacks did not reflect the hamlets' weakness but their strength. Indeed, Taylor was not entirely wrong, when seen from the North Vietnamese point of view. Ho Chi Minh considered the strategic hamlets a major threat to the revolution and called for an assault based on heightened terrorist tactics. "We must figure out a way to destroy them," he told the Politburo in November 1962. "If so, our victory is assured." Ho had attributed too much credit to the strategic hamlets, for they suffered from internal problems. Although Diem had announced the program in February 1962, he did not formally approve it until early August, during which time a large number of provinces had competed for support but lacked planning and coordination. The results were predictable: poorly constructed and defended hamlets with little regard for either the quality of administrators or the needs of the people. Of nearly 11,000 areas designated for strategic hamlets, the government had completed less than a third, and no more than 600 of these met the minimum qualifications of efficiency and safety. Diem nonetheless told a journalist that the strategic hamlets were vital to safeguarding the countryside. The program stretched beyond national needs, Nhu said in an interview. It was a "revolutionary system" intended to help underdeveloped countries achieve "freedom and democracy within a system of order and respect for duly constituted authority." Although the program was stronger in potential than reality, Taylor preferred to give it a chance.[28]

Nolting likewise supported this cautionary assessment and noted Harkins's admonition to "whistle while we work" in an effort to maintain morale. Sufficient shotguns, carbines, Springfield rifles, and grenades were available, although government and local officials had been reluctant to turn them over to villagers before proper screening and training. Nhu, in fact, feared that a large arms supply in a village made it enormously attractive to Vietcong attack. No more than a dozen arms should go to a hamlet, he asserted; if a Vietcong assault proved too powerful to repel, the villagers should hide their arms and disband. Nolting had opposed this idea, and plans now called for providing arms to two or three squads of about twelve men each.[29]

Nolting's measured optimism seemed accurate. In late November, the ARVN captured a number of Vietcong documents during the An Lac operation that suggested government progress in the war. Among them were letters from Vietcong officers describing a serious shortage of resources in the high plateau area that had undermined morale, increased desertions, and heightened fear of a government attack. Diem urged his military leaders to maintain pressure throughout the highlands.[30]

As fate would have it, however, the White House received more disheartening news about Vietnam in early December 1962, just as the Comprehensive Plan for South Vietnam neared its final draft. Hilsman concluded a lengthy analysis marked by a startling warning: "Elimination, even significant reduction, of the Communist insurgency will almost certainly require several years." The Communists had grown in number and resolve, despite the expanded U.S. military involvement. Indeed, the bombing and crop destruction "may well contribute to the development of militant opposition among the peasants and positive identification with the Viet Cong." The Strategic Hamlet Program offered hope, but it was too early for an assessment. The only saving factor Hilsman saw was that Diem's growing unpopularity held out the prospect of a coup. In that event, the Kennedy administration must work with the coup makers in establishing a new regime before a power struggle erupted to interfere with the war effort.[31]

Hilsman's conclusions appeared accurate. At a December 1962 Politburo meeting, Ho Chi Minh encountered strong opposition to his emphasis on caution and a negotiated settlement. Party leaders had called for heightened political and military actions. A secret directive dispatched to the south, probably written at the behest of Le Duan, warned that the struggle would soon escalate and that the sole solution was force. The only question was timing. The culmination would be a widespread popular uprising accompanied by a massive offensive by the People's Liberation Armed Forces. Le Duan dismissed Ho's wariness as naïve. "Uncle [Ho] wavers," Le Duan bitingly remarked, "but when I left South Vietnam I had already prepared everything. I have only one goal—just final victory."[32]

Following Hilsman's prognosis came a similar assessment from another quarter: President Kennedy's long-time friend, Senator Mansfield. Kennedy had asked the majority leader to head a delegation from the Foreign Relations Committee to evaluate U.S. policy in Vietnam as well as in Berlin and Southeast Asia. This trip would mark Mansfield's fourth to Vietnam, although the first in seven years. He was accompanied by Republican Claiborne Pell and fellow Democrats J. Caleb Boggs and Benjamin Smith.[33]

On the day of their arrival in Saigon, the senators met with Nhu in Gia Long Palace, where he praised the Strategic Hamlet Program. All strategic hamlets would be in place within three years, Nhu assured his visitors, and two-thirds of the people would be living in them by January 1, 1963. To resolve the problems endemic to underdeveloped nations, South Vietnam had devised an elaborate governing system based on a combination of authoritarianism and democracy—the very essence of the strategic hamlet. The program had initiated the social, political, economic, and military revolution essential to defeating communism and building a democratic state. It provided the means for both organizing and protecting the populace against the Vietcong. Before the advent of strategic hamlets, Nhu declared, "the population was against the soldiers, the soldiers were against the generals, the generals were against the government, and the government was dissatisfied with United States effectiveness." This widespread unhappiness had prompted the Strategic Hamlet Program. "The freedom which one acquires oneself," Nhu emphasized, "is more precious than the freedom that is given by Santa Claus."[34]

If Mansfield was not impressed by Nhu's rhetoric, he was struck by the worn-out condition of his old friend Diem. Mansfield remained loyal to the premier, declaring at the embassy that "apparently Diem's ultimate aim is to provide the people with more freedom and a greater voice in their government." Diem "has had a rough road to follow. He is a man of great integrity and honesty, . . . and he is obviously devoted to Viet-Nam." But Mansfield was concerned that the premier was "very withdrawn, very secluded. He was not the Diem I knew. So the only conclusion I could come to—it was at best a guess, an estimate—was that he had fallen under the influence of his brother and his wife and they were taking control. . . . I think he was gradually being cut off from reality." As a result, America's chances for success "may be a little better than 50-50." The peasants were weary of war, wanting "to be left alone, go their own ways and live their own lives."[35]

The senators' three-day visit uncovered deep division among the Americans over the disposition of South Vietnam. Harkins promised victory in one year; Nolting was more circumspect in affirming the possibility of bringing the insurgency under control if all the "various elements mesh together toward this end." Borrowing a French phrase uttered just before their defeat at Dienbienphu in the mid-1950s, Nolting asserted that "we can see the light at the end of the tunnel but we are not yet at the point of emerging into the sunlight." The most glaring exception to this optimism came from Trueheart. Senator Pell, a former Foreign Service officer whom Trueheart had known for years, asked, "What do you think, if there were an election in Vietnam today, how would Diem come out?" Nolting surprisingly turned to Trueheart and remarked, "Why don't you answer that,

Bill?" While Nolting and other embassy officials in the room laughed, Trueheart responded, "Well, you know, I'm not sure that's a meaningful question because I honestly think that if you really went out in the boon-docks of this country I'm not sure that half the people know who Diem is." Pell was clearly agitated, refusing to believe such an assertion. "Diem has been head of this country for a long time." The delegation became visibly irritated with Trueheart's statement because he appeared to have given it in a flippant manner. But Mansfield used that assessment as the starting point for a number of penetrating questions that led him to conclude that Nolting and most of his colleagues harbored false illusions of success.[36]

The Mansfield delegation leaned toward the journalists' pessimistic view. In the course of a five-hour meeting, Halberstam, Sheehan, Browne, and Peter Arnett (AP) lambasted both the U.S. aid effort and the Diem regime. "What was clear," Halberstam asserted, "was that Mike Mansfield was really listening. He wanted to know." The next day, as the delegation gathered at the airport in preparation for departure, Mansfield broke from the press and walked across the room to shake Trueheart's hand. "I think you're right," Mansfield declared, admitting to Diem's unpopularity. The senator then offered to the assembly of dignitaries a lukewarm assessment of the situation that praised only Diem's integrity. The U.S. embassy, Halberstam derisively noted, had acted "with incredible arrogance and stu-pidity" in giving Mansfield a statement to read that lauded Diem and the assistance program. Mansfield had refused to do so.[37]

Mansfield had fallen under the influence of American reporters, Nolting complained years later. Diem had not become isolated. He was "not popu-lar because that's the wrong impression out there. No political leader is popular. He was respected in the sense of a good mandarin." Good politi-cal leadership in South Vietnam depended on "whether the man is just and whether he rules well. It's not whether he reflects popular opinion. This doesn't mean anything to them. They think that's silly, reflecting popular opinion. They want a just person, a person who doesn't steal and make crazy decisions and involve them in unnecessary difficulties and wars and things." Mansfield had committed "a great mistake" in making a judgment that would "knock the legs from under U.S. policy, which ought to have been supported by the leader of the Senate."[38]

Mansfield's visit threatened to become a turning point in U.S.–South Vietnamese relations. Nolting was perhaps correct in asserting that the Vietnamese people preferred a leader they could respect more than one they liked, but Mansfield recognized that Diem had lost touch with his people and had fallen under the influence of his impolitic brother and sis-ter-in-law. Mansfield also realized that for U.S. aid to continue, Diem had to purvey the image of democrat, whether or not it was accurate. Nolting tried to console Diem, who had become aware of the gloomy cast of

Mansfield's conclusions. "Mr. President, I'm awfully sorry. Something must have gone wrong here. I don't know what it was but those were rather discouraging remarks." Diem was deeply hurt and puzzled but remained resilient. "I have been a friend of Senator Mansfield and he has been so good to me for so many years that I'm not going to let that stand in the way of our friendship." The *New York Times* happily declared that Mansfield's refusal to read the embassy statement made him the "first high ranking official in a year who did not go out of his way to assert that considerable progress was being made against the guerrilla or Vietcong." Joseph Buttinger, a longtime supporter of Diem who had recently become disenchanted with his leadership, termed the senator "one of the few not sucked in by official self-delusion." Mansfield's negative assessment, Nolting observed, "really drove the first nail in Diem's coffin." Harkins agreed that the senators' visit was the "crucial turning point" in Diem's demise. Rumors of the expected gloomy contents of Mansfield's report further spread the talk of a coup.[39]

IV

SUPPORT FOR MANSFIELD's dismal findings came in mid-December 1962, when Theodore Heavner of the Vietnam Working Group in Washington submitted a lengthy report that made its way to President Kennedy. Heavner had just returned from a forty-day visit to Vietnam, inspecting the strategic hamlets in seventeen provinces. The program, he concluded, would ultimately bring the Vietcong under government control and permit the United States to reduce its military aid, but the process would take several years. During the past year, the situation had progressed to the point that the enemy was no longer winning the war but now found itself deadlocked with government forces. It would be misleading, however, to expect either to eliminate the Vietcong or to institute democracy.[40]

Heavner declared that democratic elections in the hamlets were highly unlikely. Hamlet officials did not hold their positions by virtue of a democratic process. Rather, they were subject to the social pressures of having to deal on a daily basis with friends, neighbors, and relatives. The political procedure was eminently practical: The village or district chief informally signified which candidate he preferred and the peasants voted for him. One provincial chief affirmed the necessity of controlling the elections: "Democracy here cannot come before security. It will take at least ten years." A missionary added that the Vietnamese found political confrontations "repugnant" because they involved loss of face. "Of course the elections are decided in advance. The people would be very uncomfortable if they were not." In most cases, the old hamlet chief won reelection. As a matter of fact, many of them had already been doing the job before winning election. Provincial officials noted that most hamlet charters did not stipulate a term of office. "We will have new elections when they are necessary," one curtly declared.[41]

The fundamental objective of the Strategic Hamlet Program was to isolate the people from the Vietcong, Heavner insisted. Elections could come later. The most urgent need was to identify capable local administrators who could work with the Saigon government in meshing the peasant into the hamlet's welfare as the chief means toward achieving security. To make the system work, the hamlets must have budgets that enabled their officials to enforce local law while not having to deal with village or district chief control. The training and motivation of hamlet chiefs must improve; they were "prime targets for VC assassination."[42]

Heavner noted some progress. Villagers were now alerting government officials of impending Vietcong attacks. Government forces had stepped up night patrols and ambushes in an effort to show that "the night no longer belongs only to the VC." U.S. advisers had reduced the number of Vietcong prisoners killed by the ARVN during interrogation. In one instance, an American turned his own weapon on a South Vietnamese officer to stop him from killing a prisoner. Several times U.S. advisers called in helicopters to transport prisoners for questioning elsewhere. The CIA and the U.S. Special Forces had worked with the Montagnards to close Vietcong infiltration through the high plateau. Although most ARVN officers regarded the primitive, mountain-dwelling Montagnard as subhuman, they nonetheless recognized his value in combatting the Vietcong. Heavner praised the Self-Defense Corps as a local force whose personal ties to villagers had provided the bulwark of hamlet security. A better trained and armed Self-Defense Corps would be effective, particularly if it worked closely with U.S. advisers.[43]

Problems remained, however. Heavner dismissed U.S. Consul John Helble's upbeat assessment of the Popular Force in Hué, asserting that it was under the control of a provincial committee that answered only to Diem's brother, Ngo Dinh Can, and had made no notable contributions to security. Indeed, the Popular Force seemed to be Can's own secret police rather than a government weapon against the Vietcong. Heavner also noted a major problem in military command: Officers feared demotion resulting from heavy casualties among their men. U.S. military advisers reported that Vietnamese commanders hesitated to take the initiative in situations certain to cause numerous losses. Thus another irony of the U.S. experience in Vietnam: Although successful in battle, ARVN officers could face demotion because of Diem's concern over casualties.[44]

Hilsman also raised disturbing questions about the Strategic Hamlet Program. In a marked reversal of his earlier enthusiasm, he asserted that the great publicity surrounding the effort left a misleading positive impression. Many times the so-called strategic hamlet was only an area enclosed by a barbed wire or bamboo fence. Few hamlets had actually provided

security and benefits to the peasant. Instead of emphasizing small-unit assaults, patrols, ambushes, and intelligence gathering, the ARVN relied on
artillery, air power, and crop destruction. The result of such heavy-handed
tactics might be "a militant opposition from the peasants and their positive
identification with the Viet Cong."[45]

If Heavner's and Hilsman's analyses saw faint hope for the U.S. assistance program, Mansfield's conclusions drove home the point. His final report, submitted to the president a week before Christmas, warned against
deepening the U.S. involvement in Vietnam. Seven years after his initial
visit to Vietnam, he noted that "it would be well to face the fact that we are
once again at the beginning of the beginning." Instead of standing on its
own, the Saigon government had become more dependent on the United
States. "If Vietnam is the cork in the Southeast Asian bottle then American
aid is more than ever the cork in the Vietnamese bottle." Without massive
U.S. assistance, South Vietnam could not survive. The strategic hamlets were
the heart of the effort to provide security and build loyalty, but also important were the greatly enlarged U.S. economic assistance program, the deployment of thousands of U.S. military personnel, and the hundreds of U.S.
Special Forces now training the Montagnards. While U.S. and South Vietnamese officials predicted success in a year or two, Mansfield rejected that
forecast. The accuracy of Vietcong casualty counts was questionable in light
of its estimated rise in strength to 20,000—which marked the highest since
the Geneva agreements of 1954. Admittedly, the Montagnards were invaluable in helping to close infiltration routes. But their role was "peripheral" to
winning the support of the Vietnamese people.[46]

The Strategic Hamlet Program, Mansfield insisted, offered no assurance of success. The essential task of attracting peasant support necessitated an "immense job of social engineering, dependent on great outlays of
aid on our part for many years and a most responsive, alert and enlight-
ened leadership in the government of Vietnam." And yet the Vietcong
would probably develop new methods of countering the strengthened hamlets along with the increasingly mobile government forces. "It would be
unwise to underestimate the resourcefulness of any group which has managed to survive years of the most rugged kind of warfare."[47]

Mansfield urged a withdrawal from Vietnam. "Our planning," he insisted, "appears to be predicated on the assumption that existing internal
problems in South Vietnam will remain about the same and can be overcome by greater effort and better techniques. But what if the problems do
not remain the same?" What if the North Vietnamese raised the infiltration level? What if they sent regulars? One option was "a truly massive
commitment of American military personnel and other resources—in short
going to war fully ourselves against the guerrillas—and the establishment
of some form of neocolonial rule in south Vietnam." But that approach
guaranteed an immense loss of American lives and treasure similar to what

the French experienced. Hanoi could inject more cadres; it could send General Vo Nguyen Giap's 300,000 regulars. Worse, the Chinese Communists might intervene. The White House must consider whether the national interest required a position of power on the Asian mainland. If not, Mansfield advised, the wisest course was a diplomatic settlement in Southeast Asia aimed at greatly reducing the U.S. involvement.[48]

Such a policy reversal would come at heavy cost. An abrupt U.S. withdrawal from Southeast Asia, Mansfield admitted, might lead to the collapse of many governments and invite Chinese Communist intervention. Still, the Kennedy administration must determine whether its commitment to the region was vital. Such a process must take place within the dictates of "the greatest realism and restraint" possible. "We may well discover that it is in our interests to do less rather than more than we are now doing." Mansfield favored negotiations aimed at neutralizing the area.[49]

The day after Christmas, Mansfield joined President Kennedy at a pool party in Palm Beach, Florida, to discuss the report. The two men exchanged pleasantries as Kennedy seemed more interested in a flirtatious game of exchanging sunglasses with a swimsuit-clad young woman. But soon the president became serious. "Let's talk alone," he grimly declared, leading his visitor from the group to take a cruise on his yacht. Two hours of detailed questioning by the president confirmed Mansfield's conclusions. The president "had a tremendous grasp of the situation. He didn't waste much time. He certainly never wasted any words." He raised some points that disagreed with the report, "but at least he got the truth as I saw it and it wasn't a pleasant picture that I had depicted for him," Mansfield later noted.

Kennedy, by then red-faced, angrily asked, "Do you expect me to take this at face value?"

"You asked me to go out there," Mansfield just as tartly replied.

"This isn't what my people are telling me," the president sharply retorted. Then, after a moment's reflection: "Well, I'll read it again!"

The president's wrath stemmed from the damning nature of the report, particularly since he thought it accurate. After Mansfield left the meeting, Kennedy explained to aide Kenneth P. O'Donnell, "I got angry with Mike for disagreeing with our policy so completely, and I got angry with myself because I found myself agreeing with him."[50]

In all the above assessments, the crucial determinant was the Saigon government's inability to improve its wartime performance to a level that would allow the United States to dismantle its recently upgraded military assistance program. A dual sponsorship bedeviled the Strategic Hamlet Program, resulting in two distinctly different and competing objectives. The Kennedy administration sought peasant support through reforms that promised safety from the Vietcong; the Diem regime wanted to establish centralized control over its people without ensuring the amenities of life. All proponents of the strategic hamlets recognized the necessity of isolating the peasants from the Vietcong; but the Americans warned that failure to provide the daily needs of those villagers inside the barbed-wire compounds might lead them to regard the fortifications as prisons intended to keep them in rather than the Vietcong out. Herein lay the central problem confronting the counterinsurgency effort: winning the people's trust.

WITH THE WAR'S END nowhere in sight, the Kennedy administration again escalated its involvement as the way toward a major withdrawal. After meeting with Diem and Nolting, along with numerous other Vietnamese and American officials, Alexis Johnson from the state department concluded that the most optimistic hope for the war's end—expressed by Thuan—was three years.[51]

Nolting had grave doubts about Harkins's "explosion" plan but seemed willing to give it a try. The general admitted that the Vietcong could hide but would never again be as effective because of the strategic hamlet and clear-and-hold programs. He assured his colleagues that the government operation was not a one-time event. Nolting thought this idea the best way to force a showdown with the Vietcong. The term "explosion" was unfortunate, but its purpose was valid in seeking to hit all Vietcong strongholds at once and leave the enemy with no avenue of escape.[52]

But the explosion strategy faded into the background as the president chose the less provocative move of using defoliants and napalm. McNamara reported that the defoliation tests in South Vietnam's mangrove forests had proved almost 95 percent effective, while those aimed at evergreens and tropical scrubs were 60 percent. The July spraying operation in the Bien Hoa Air Base area had increased ground visibility from five to fifty feet and vertical visibility by nearly 90 percent. The ensuing military campaign would not include crop destruction and would be subject to field decisions based solely on restricting Vietcong activities. An area's inhabitants would receive ample warning before the operation began, and pilots were to avoid hits near the Laotian or Cambodian borders. On the use of napalm, Harkins was to focus on "high priority targets" in Zone D that contained heavy Vietcong installations. He must have state and defense department approval in operations having political ramifications.[53]

Pressure grew on the president to increase U.S. air support in South Vietnam. Felt had sent two requests, one to expand Farmgate and the other to talk with Saigon about using up to thirty Chinese Nationalists to pilot South Vietnamese C-47s. Greater reliance on air power had already become clear from the realization that South Vietnamese fighter planes flew 620 combat sorties in September 1962, compared with only 150 the previous January. Forrestal and Harriman concurred in the overall proposal. President Kennedy approved the requests.[54]

And so the war's escalation continued, even as the White House worked toward a major disengagement.

10

END OF THE TUNNEL?
A Comprehensive Plan for South Vietnam

So we don't see the end of the tunnel, but I must say I
don't think it is darker than it was a year ago, and in some
ways lighter.

> President John F. Kennedy, December 12, 1962

On balance, the war remains a slowly escalating stalemate.

> Central Intelligence Agency, January 11, 1963

As THE WAR escalated, so did the president's interest in a partial
withdrawal. The Mansfield report was deeply troubling not only
because it contradicted most previous assessments but because it
came from a close friend. Like the recommendations of another friend and
confidant, John Kenneth Galbraith, the Montana senator called for a U.S.
withdrawal from South Vietnam followed by its neutralization. These sobering analyses weighed heavily on President Kennedy as he tautly responded
to a press conference question in mid-December 1962, "So we don't see the
end of the tunnel, but I must say I don't think it is darker than it was a year
ago, and in some ways lighter."[1] The White House remained outwardly
optimistic, but deep inside its halls the realization had begun to sink in that a
total defeat of the enemy was not possible. The only attainable success was a
diminished Vietcong threat that the South Vietnamese themselves could
control. Only then could the United States reduce its military presence to
the level it had occupied before the present crisis. But how to accomplish a
massive deescalation without sacrificing American honor?

The White House again rejected the two extremes of total withdrawal
and total immersion in the war and searched for a middle ground aimed at
saving South Vietnam without losing U.S. credibility. Best estimates were
that the insurgency would last another three years. The centerpiece of the
counterinsurgency program remained the strategic hamlets, despite serious
doubts about their effectiveness. The heavy tilt toward military measures
had not curtailed guerrilla activity. The use of defoliants, crop destruction,

and napalm had subjected the United States and South Vietnam to charges of inhumanity. Nearly 500 cadres a month slipped through South Vietnam's borders, making a mockery of its efforts to halt infiltration. Nolting publicly denied U.S. involvement in combat while privately referring in his dispatches to the presence of thousands of American combat units. Accusations of a U.S. takeover of the war drummed on, raising concern among Americans and South Vietnamese that the Kennedy administration sought total control.

In the meantime the U.S. military involvement became more tangled. Farmgate had surged beyond its advisory and training functions to become the linchpin of an expanded air campaign. As the White House pondered South Vietnam's requests for U.S. jets, it condoned bombing and strafing operations, and, in a potential policy change that promised serious repercussions, it considered whether or not to authorize helicopter pilots to fire first when threatened. Several advisers advocated stepped-up covert action against North Vietnam; a few contemplated the impact of Diem's removal from office. And all the while the military escalation spiraled upward, leading to more analyses, inspiring louder rhetoric, and increasing the vagueness over the definition of victory and its timetable for success.

A crucial test of a democracy—how long it can sustain a war—threatened to become an issue. The United States had recently fought a four-year war with the greatest commitment—a fevered tenacity that had risen from the Japanese attack on Pearl Harbor. But the conflict in Vietnam was profoundly different in that no "day of infamy" had occurred that could mobilize the American people and Congress into seeking a declaration of war. Whereas the Japanese had defined themselves as America's chief antagonist in 1941, the North Vietnamese had blurred their involvement in the present struggle, averting any inflammatory event around which Americans could rally. In this uncertain atmosphere, and in the nervous aftermath of the Cuban missile crisis, President Kennedy and a few White House advisers edged closer to scaling down the nation's involvement in Vietnam.

I

ON RECEIVING Mansfield's dreary report, President Kennedy dispatched Hilsman and Forrestal to Saigon to compile their own findings. From December 31, 1962, through January 9, 1963, they investigated the situation, interviewing participants in the war and forwarding preliminary reports to the president. By January 2, a series of memoranda from Hilsman had reached the Oval Office that further muddled the situation. The new information confirmed many of Mansfield's negative observations but quixotically rejected total withdrawal and predicted victory over a long period of time.

The Hilsman–Forrestal team expressed great skepticism about Nolting's and Harkins's airy claims of progress. Despite CINCPAC's questionable assertion that the South Vietnamese had killed 18,000 Vietcong over the past year, the enemy's strength had risen from 18,000 to perhaps 24,000. The CIA's ill-advised decision to retrieve arms from the Montagnards for distribution to less secure villages had seriously weakened the jungle tribes, whose knowledge of the terrain was critical to ending infiltration. CINCPAC meanwhile sought to take command of the war's plans and operations. Felt, for example, assumed control over equipment requests and often interfered in tactical planning. The basic problem in Vietnam was a lack of coordination between military and political operations. No single plan steered policy; at one point six proposals were on the table. MACV's narrow guidelines restricted its actions, and Harkins lacked direct communication with the joint chiefs. The requested increase in Farmgate posed problems, particularly since the U.S. air liaison officer at the division level had no role in choosing enemy targets. General Roland Anthis, chief of the U.S. Air Force Advisory Group in Vietnam, saw the danger and warned against "indiscriminate bombing."[2]

The early negative disclosures from the Hilsman–Forrestal mission gained greater credibility when, on January 2–3, 1963, a huge ARVN and Civil Guard contingent suffered what Hilsman termed a "stunning defeat" at Ap Bac in the Mekong Delta, a bare thirty-five miles southwest of Saigon. South Vietnam's forces had set out to destroy a guerrilla radio transmitter wrongly believed to be at Ap Tan Thoi, less than a mile away, but they had compounded that error by mistakenly landing near the village of Ap Bac. Lieutenant Colonel John Paul Vann, senior U.S. adviser, had drawn up the plan of attack and, once under way, intended to circle the battle area in a spotter plane, encouraging the South Vietnamese to surround the target and close in with superior numbers and firepower. He had wanted to strike on January 1, but South Vietnamese commander Colonel Bui Dinh Dam had refused to advance until the following day, lamely declaring that U.S. helicopter pilots needed sleep after the raucous New Year's Eve celebrations. More than 1,200 of Diem's forces had arrived in U.S. helicopters and M-113 armored personnel carriers (virtual tanks), giving them what they erroneously thought was a ten-to-one manpower advantage (according to faulty intelligence) and supported by artillery, fighter-bombers, and napalm. The Vietcong commander was so sure of defeat that he recorded in his diary, "Better to fight and die than run and be slaughtered."[3]

The U.S. plan went awry from the beginning and worsened as the day progressed. The first sign of trouble came in the early morning ground fog of January 2. To soften resistance, a band of T-28 fighter-bombers first sprayed the area with napalm and rockets and then strafed the smoking, burning remains. Fifteen American-piloted helicopters soon thundered in, ten of them H-21 transports carrying Vietnamese troops and the other five choppers serving as heavily armed turbo-propped escorts. The huge dark green and banana-shaped H-21s (dubbed "Angle Worms" by the Vietcong) arrived in waves, well silhouetted in the sun as they landed, off-loaded the troops, and took off as quickly as possible. They encountered no resistance during the first three landings, leaving the impression that the Vietcong had fled before massive force. But as the fourth wave hit the ground, about 400 Vietcong armed with automatic weapons opened a murderous assault, bringing down five of the helicopters in five minutes and leaving the infantrymen pinned to the ground. Only one helicopter escaped without damage.[4]

The counterattack was a debacle. Civil Guard battalions became easy targets for the Vietcong forces, who were dug into clay bunkers and foxholes along a canal nearly hidden by trees and shrubs and who had a clear and direct fire line across sweeping rice fields. Brigadier General Huynh Van Cao refused to order his ARVN forces to advance, preferring to await U.S. firepower. A Catholic from Hué and a fervent Diem loyalist, he had recently undergone a severe rebuke for losing a large number of troops in battle and hesitated to put them at risk again. An American, Captain Kenneth Good, charged the enemy by himself, vainly calling for the South Vietnamese forces to follow. Cut down by enemy fire, he was left to bleed to death by an ARVN officer who did not report the injury.[5]

The ARVN's failure to close the ring at Ap Bac had left the Vietcong with an avenue of escape. The Americans captured thirty-two Vietcong forces, but only after Vann had led a makeshift pursuit force of U.S. maintenance and communications personnel, about sixty U.S. advisers, a water purification worker, and a cook. Claiming that his only objective had been to protect a U.S. officer sent to meet the Civil Guard, Vann declared, "I am not trying to fight these people's war for them." By the time General Cao relented to U.S. entreaties and ordered his men to charge, dusk had fallen. In the smoky haze South Vietnamese forces fired on each other, providing a suitable requiem for this disaster.[6]

Casualties were significant on both sides. That night the Vietcong stole away from the battlefield, having lost a hundred dead, according to MACV, although only three bodies were found. The Vietcong actually had incurred fifty-seven casualties, including eighteen killed, but they had taken most of their comrades' bodies with them. Even then, these numbers were remarkably low in view of the fiery torrent of bullets, artillery shells, napalm, bombs, and rockets. The South Vietnamese sustained eighty dead and a hundred wounded; the U.S. casualty list included three dead crewmen and eight wounded aboard the downed helicopters, raising the American death toll in combat to thirty. An embittered American helicopter pilot afterward penned the words to this parody, sung to the tune of *On Top of Old Smoky*:

We were called up to Ap Bac
On January two;
We'd never have gone there,
If we'd only knew . . .

The VCs start shooting
They let out a roar;
We offload the ARVN's
Who think it's a bore.

An armored battalion
Just stayed in a trance
Our captain died trying
To make them advance . . .

The paratroops landed,
A magnificent sight
There was hand-to-hand combat
But no VC's in sight . . .

All pilots take warning
When tree lines are near
Let's land those darn copters
One mile to the rear.[7]

President Kennedy learned of the battle on the morning of January 3, when in Palm Beach he received a secret four-page memo from the joint chiefs.[8]

Ap Bac was not the only disturbing news in early 1963, for in the High Plateau above Pleiku in the north, Vietcong forces attacked Plei Mrong, a recently constructed U.S. Special Forces training camp for village defenders. At 1:30 on the morning of January 3, the Vietcong launched a withering assault in the darkness while the major striking forces were on patrol, threatening to overrun the camp after an ally on the inside had cut the barbed-wire barriers. TNT explosions shook the ground as grenades, a recoilless rifle, and automatic weapons took their deadly toll amid the guerrillas' piercing screams. At the center of the camp, five U.S. Special Forces fought back as a sixth American radioed for help. But neither reinforcements nor an air strike came until after the Vietcong had withdrawn at dawn. By then the hundred-yard trench surrounding the camp lay strewn with bloody and mangled bodies, many of them missing heads, arms, and legs. The Vietcong had wounded thirty-four (including four of the American Special Forces) and killed thirty-five, captured seventy-four South Vietnamese, and seized more than a hundred weapons. Traces of the Vietcong onslaught were found on both sides of the barbed wire: rusted ammunition, a cartridge that misfired but was refilled and hit with a nail, unexploded homemade grenades with bamboo handles, and a ragged medical kit. With these crude materials, the Vietcong had nearly destroyed a heavily defended camp.[9]

For a few days afterward, Vietnamese troops snaked through the jungles, looking for the enemy. An artillery unit and a bevy of T-28 fighter-bombers pummeled the forests, and a string of helicopters off-loaded six companies of Vietnamese soldiers to pursue the Vietcong. They saw no one. A U.S. helicopter pilot perhaps offered the best explanation for this failure. "Yesterday, I dropped a whole bunch of those Vietnamese troops into a field. Today I went back to the same field with another load and you know what I saw? That first group was still there in the field, tents up and cooking lunch. They hadn't moved a damn inch." Similar stories arose from the battle at Ap Bac. Several U.S. military officers shared the senti- ment of an army colonel: "I wish I had those damn Viet Cong fighting for me." A U.S. major declared that "the ARVN doesn't hate the VC. They know the VC believes in something. The VC [has] a cause."[10]

The battle of Ap Bac had a greater impact than that at Plei Mrong in that the Vietcong had, for the first time, stood their ground and fought. About 400 guerrillas, whose biggest weapon was a small 600-mm mortar that had been of no use, had held off an army three times larger and sup- ported by armor, artillery, helicopters, and fighter-bombers. The Vietcong's resiliency demonstrated that the war would be long and difficult with no guarantee of victory, according to military specialist Hanson Baldwin in the *New York Times*. The U.S. Army Command in the Pacific called Ap Bac "one of the bloodiest and costliest battles" of the war and admitted that the enemy had gained a "morale-building victory." Vann attributed the failure to South Vietnam's poor training, inept command, and lack of battlefield discipline; its officers' unwillingness to risk casualties; and the absence of coordination between ground and air forces. Captured Vietcong documents supported this judgment, although they also highlighted the victors' highly motivated, well-trained, and tightly disciplined small units. The victory, according to Hanoi's official assessment, showed the ineffec- tiveness of helicopter and armored personnel carrier attacks, as well as the "special warfare" engineered by the "American imperialists." Ironically, asserted a *New York Times* editorial, Americans in Vietnam had *wanted* to lure the Vietcong into an open battle.[11]

The state department noted nationwide newspaper complaints that the American people were not "getting the facts" on Vietnam, even as American casualties were growing. Less than a week after the battle, the *Washington Post* carried Neil Sheehan's front-page story declaring that "an- gry United States military advisers charged today that Vietnamese infan- trymen refused direct orders to advance during Wednesday's battle at Ap Bac and that an American Army captain was killed while out front pleading with them to attack."[12]

Sheehan's article failed to dampen Harkins's ardor. South Vietnam's forces made a number of mistakes at Ap Bac, the general conceded, but they resulted more from courage than timidity. The major problem lay in field leadership, political interference, and promotions based on loyalties to Diem. The soldiers had fought well. In fact, the Diem regime was correct in calling the outcome a "Vietnamese victory." The South Vietnamese had "taken the objective" and deserved praise. "It took a lot of guts on the part of those pilots and crews to go back into the area to try to rescue their pals." He then tried to put the battle in perspective. "Like any engagements in war, there are days—and there are days. This day they got a bear by the tail and they didn't let go of it."[13]

The battle of Ap Bac did nothing to change U.S. strategy. The ARVN continued to emphasize conventional warfare, and American officials declared that the war was going better than a year earlier.

In the face of widespread skepticism, Harkins blandly asserted: "I believe anyone who criticizes the fighting qualities of the armed forces of the Republic of Vietnam is doing a disservice to the thousands of gallant and courageous men who are fighting so well in defense of their country." The problem, *New Republic* writer Jerry Rose declared in reluctant agreement with Harkins, was not the Vietnamese soldier. He had the same ethnic and cultural background as the guerrilla. "The difference of fighting quality between the two lies partly in *motivation*, partly in *leadership*." The guerrillas followed the strategy and tactics of the Indochina War. At Ap Bac, they sat in well-camouflaged and well-entrenched positions and withstood a devastating air bombardment similar to that at Dienbienphu.[14]

Infiltration from North Vietnam had continued to grow in number along with that of local recruits, as evidenced by the Vietcong battalions at Ap Bac—or "My Aching Back," as Harkins called it. The Americans dropped a parachute regiment in the fields to surround the Vietcong, but its cadres disappeared in the jungle and the swamps. The Vietcong took Ap Bac, but U.S.–Vietnamese forces retrieved it the next day, only to see the Vietcong seize it again the following day. "We lost the city for a day and then we took it back," Harkins later observed. "That's war."[15]

Nolting did not regard the outcome at Ap Bac as "all that serious" and thought the press had exaggerated the results. "I don't think the South Vietnamese army ought to be indicted for cowardice." The ARVN mishandled the affair by failing to move in quickly. "The worst thing that happened was Colonel Vann's spilling his guts to the American press and having it spread all over the headlines that the South Vietnamese Army, despite all that the Americans had done to train and supply them, were basically cowards and they couldn't win. I don't believe that." Regarding the allegation that Diem had ordered his commanders to avoid casualties, Nolting did not recall such orders but admitted that Diem had urged his commanders to minimize losses on all sides in an effort to give pacification a chance. The objective was not to wipe out dissenters but to attract them to the government's side by an array of amnesty programs. In Vietnamese, French, and English, the word was pacification. But Nolting said, "I don't remember a single case in which a reporter didn't translate pacification into 'war.'" The South Vietnamese had fought as capably as had the enemy, despite the battle at Ap Bac. "I think it was the disastrous ones, the bad ones from our point of view, which hit the headlines, and very seldom the good ones. Or if they did, they weren't featured because, why, we expected to be winners."[16]

The journalists were infuriated with these slurs on their integrity because they had talked with U.S. helicopter pilots on their return from Ap Bac, whereas no military or state department information officers had sought firsthand accounts. The day after the battle, Sheehan and Nick Turner of Reuters drove to My Tho in an effort to ferret out more details about the battle. Halberstam flew to the command post at Tan Hiep airstrip, where he found Vann in a state of absolute dejection. "A miserable damn performance," Vann moaned, "just like it always is." Halberstam accompanied Arnett in a helicopter to the battle scene, where they gazed down in shock at parachutes sucked into the rice paddies, bodies scattered all over, and the wide tracks of M-113s that had left the area all too early. Sheehan and Turner were already there, questioning Brigadier General Robert York. "What happened?" asked Sheehan. "What the hell's it look like happened, boy?" York snapped back. "They got away—that's what happened." While York, Sheehan, and Turner awaited a helicopter ride back to Saigon, a storm of artillery fire opened just above their heads, forcing them to hit the ground. A panicky provincial chief had ordered a barrage on a nearby village, which narrowly missed the Americans but killed five of his own men and wounded fourteen others.[17]

Back at the command post, the reality of defeat failed to dent the phony facade of victory. Halberstam and Arnett returned to witness a nattily dressed honor guard paying homage to the bravery of General Cao, who had refused to fight. Harkins proudly snorted to Arnett and Halberstam as he hurriedly prepared to leave for Saigon, "We've got them in a trap, and we're going to spring it in half an hour." While the two baffled reporters stared at him in disbelief, they wondered how Harkins could have formed such an ill-informed conclusion in light of the Vietcong's disappearance from the field and the realization that the South Vietnamese were in such disarray that a province chief shelled his own forces and soldiers were too scared to gather their comrades' bodies.[18]

Felt shared Harkins's upbeat assessment. Two days after the battle, the admiral arrived at Saigon's airport, primed to defend the government's military performance. "I'd like to say that I don't believe what I've been reading in the papers," he pointedly remarked to a group of journalists and U.S. officials. "As I understand it, it was a Vietnamese victory—not a defeat, as the papers say." Turning to Harkins for affirmation, the general replied true to form: "Yes, that's right. It was a Vietnamese victory. It certainly was." When Harkins identified Sheehan in the crowd, Felt glared at him before remarking, "So you're Sheehan. I didn't know who you were. You ought to talk to some of the people who've got the facts." Sheehan refused to cower. "You're right, Admiral, and that's why I went down there every day." Not even fazed by this sharp response, Felt later declared that this "bad news about American casualties [was] filed immediately by young reporters representing the wire services without careful checking of the facts." He insisted that "there is good news which you may not read about in *The Washington Post*." The U.S. cause suffered "when irresponsible newsmen spread the word to the American public that GVN forces won't fight and, on the other hand, do not adequately report GVN victories which are occurring more frequently." The South Vietnamese had won the battle because the Vietcong had fled the field. When Arnett disagreed, Felt shot back, "Get on the team."[19]

Perhaps the most revealing aspect of Ap Bac was Arthur Krock's column in the *New York Times*, summarizing a perspective on U.S. military aid in Indochina that President Kennedy had offered while a senator nearly a decade earlier. "I am frankly of the belief," Kennedy asserted in April 1954, "that no amount of American military assistance in Indochina can conquer an enemy which is everywhere, and at the same time, nowhere, 'an enemy of the people' which has the sympathy and covert support of the people." Only their own fight for freedom could motivate them into action. Without this prerequisite, Kennedy asserted, U.S. policy was "doomed to failure." The South Vietnamese, Krock declared, did not make that "heroic effort" at Ap Bac, and no degree of U.S. military assistance could make the difference to people "not willing to die for it." The ARVN's refusal to fight for its country's independence necessitated a White House review of its policy toward South Vietnam.[20]

II

AT THIS SENSITIVE POINT in the war, the CIA contributed an unsettling assessment that raised disturbing questions about imminent victory. Although the South Vietnamese were making headway, "the tide has not yet turned." The counterinsurgency program had little chance for success in view of Diem's refusal to make political changes. The number of ARVN attacks had increased, but the Vietcong had repeatedly escaped beforehand. It was also misleading to gauge the Vietcong situation by its small-scale assaults; every movement further wore down the government's will in what was swiftly becoming a deadly war of attrition. The Vietcong's casualties had admittedly climbed, but so had its strength. "This suggests either that the casualty figures are exaggerated or that the Viet Cong have a remarkable replacement capability—or both."[21]

The root of the trouble, according to the CIA, was the Diem regime. ARVN promotions rested more on loyalty than ability. The absence of specific orders from the top caused unit commanders to hesitate in taking the initiative. Inept and heavy-handed provincial administrators deeply alienated the peasants. Corruption marred the regime's public image. The NLF attracted widespread peasant support by welcoming all political views. As of December 1, 1962, nearly one-third of South Vietnam's villages had come under Vietcong control, raising serious skepticism about the Strategic Hamlet Program. Most Vietcong recruits came from rural South Vietnam, which suggested that *Diem* was the problem.[22]

The CIA then noted a marked upsurge in the enemy's war effort, further refining the Kennedy administration's choice of either matching that escalation or reducing its involvement in Vietnam. The Communists expected a long conflict and had recently begun a new program of infiltrating North Vietnamese army regulars through Laos and into South Vietnam. The Communists' strategy thus looked toward ultimate conventional warfare. They were far from that stage, but, with North Vietnam's help, they had successfully upgraded the Vietcong's military performance. In late September 1962, a contingent of 400 regulars from the People's Army of Vietnam (PAVN) had entered South Vietnam, providing an effective core of cadres, commanders, and technicians. Their firepower included Chinese Communist weapons; indeed, from January through November 1962, Vietcong ground-fire had hit 115 American aircraft and brought down nine. "On balance," the CIA dourly concluded, "the war remains a slowly escalating stalemate."[23]

The most realistic analyses had finally found their way into the hands of Washington's policymakers. In addition to Mansfield's warnings and Heavner's sobering prognosis, both the CIA conclusions and the preliminary findings of the Hilsman–Forrestal mission pointed to a long and costly war. The CIA had referred to the Vietcong's fighting a war of attrition, citing the influx of army regulars and matériel from North Vietnam along with the growing number of recruits from the south. Was the arrival of PAVN soldiers merely the first installment from an enormous manpower resource? The White House had already considered a ten-to-one ratio necessary to defeat an insurgency, meaning that with the continued growth of the Vietcong alone the chance for achieving this numerical advantage had virtually vanished by early 1963. If the CIA was correct in calling the war a stalemate, would not the injection of North Vietnamese regulars tip the balance? Now, with the first tangible signs of Hanoi's direct military involvement, success no longer seemed possible without a full-scale

Americanization of the war. The most prudent U.S. action was a major military disengagement, but the prerequisite was a victory in the field that could afford a graceful exit. The battle of Ap Bac had raised serious doubts about this ever happening without drastic changes in Saigon.

The gloomy aftermath of Ap Bac caused some observers to believe that the United States should take over the war. Sunday's *Washington Post* carried a London *Times* story dated January 12, in which news correspondent Richard Hughes in Hong Kong cited recent ARVN failures as a reason for U.S. officers to assume combat command. The Kennedy administration, he declared, should acknowledge that its military forces were already so deeply involved in the war that they needed either to direct its operations or to pull out. Diem had not instituted political and social reforms, providing a disquieting reminder of China's turn to communism in 1949. Without these changes, the only alternative to withdrawal was another decade of fighting on behalf of "a reactionary, isolated and unpopular regime."[24]

Despite pressure for more resolute action, the Kennedy administration maintained restraints on the war effort. After a lengthy debate, it leaned toward denying South Vietnam's request for four American T-33 training jets. Approval of this measure, the White House asserted, would violate Article 17 of the Geneva Accords. More important, the move would increase the chances of planes entering Cambodia's air space and provide the Communist regimes with an excuse to furnish Hanoi with jets that would further expand the war. The administration also tried again to persuade Laos to close the Laotian Panhandle to infiltration. But its prime minister, Prince Souvanna Phouma, had been unable to do so. A military adviser warned that the U.S. failure to react "to these breaches of faith in the name of supporting Souvanna is jeopardizing our military position in SVN."[25]

Confusion within the U.S. military command threatened the president's wish to maintain parameters on the involvement, particularly when MACV asked for a moderate increase in the Farmgate campaign and aroused suspicions of its being a precursor to a much larger request. Without clearing the matter with the U.S. embassy, MACV secured the joint chiefs' approval for ten B-26s, five T-28s, and two C-47s. On learning of the arrangement, members of the Vietnam Working Group assumed that the request had come through the defense department and that the ambassador had concurred. When they discovered that this was not the case, they were furious. Harkins assured that this would not happen again. Nolting at first dismissed the request as small. But he soon learned that MACV had told CINCPAC of the need for 173 additional aircraft, including transports and strike planes, to underwrite Harkins's explosion scheme, now officially called the "National Campaign." Felt concurred, insisting that the South Vietnamese could not win without a greater U.S. military commitment. Nolting ultimately agreed to the transport planes but staunchly opposed the strike aircraft because of the certain questions about whether the Kennedy administration intended to take over the war.[26]

In this uneasy atmosphere, Hilsman and Forrestal handed the president their final report, which found the situation so precarious as to warrant making contact with Diem's "meaningful opposition." Diem refused to change his policies. "No one man is in charge," making U.S. efforts "fragmented and duplicative." The enemy had grown in number, now counting 23,000 regulars along with 100,000 militia and untold thousands of sympathizers. Even if U.S.–South Vietnamese forces closed off infiltration, the insurgents received assistance from villagers. American journalists were "bitter and will seize on anything that goes wrong and blow it up as much as possible." In a secret annex intended only for the president, Hilsman and Forrestal urged him to replace Nolting with someone of military background who would seek to reduce the Vietcong cadres to their "die-hard nucleus and isolate them in areas remote from the basic population." Once this occurred, the job would become that of "killing Viet Cong, of simple elimination." The South Vietnamese were "probably winning, but certainly more slowly than we had hoped." One fact loomed above all else. "No matter how one twisted and turned the problem," Hilsman declared in a conclusion similar to the CIA's findings, "it always came back to Ngo Dinh Diem."[27]

Years later, Forrestal had second thoughts about the forecast of ultimate victory contained in his and Hilsman's report. "The fact of the matter is we were wrong. We were wrong in our report. We may have been misled, but that was our own damn fault if we were." Their visit to Vietnam had deluded them into believing that success was imminent. With the "proper tactics," they had argued to the president, "sooner or later the Diem government would find its feet, would be able to carry on alone, that there would be a decline of assistance rather than an increase." But we "badly underestimated" the Vietcong's capacity to wage a counterguerrilla war, and we "underestimated the capability of the city-bred people" running the Saigon government to pursue a counterguerrilla campaign, Forrestal later admitted. We also "vastly overestimated" America's ability to supervise a small country so many miles away.[28]

The gloomy anticipation of a long war that permeated the Hilsman–Forrestal report greatly disturbed the president and provided further impetus for a major withdrawal. The battle of Ap Bac had confirmed the negative assessments of advisers and journalists. "More or less beginning then," Forrestal later recalled, Kennedy "began to get worried" about Vietnam. "It was a reaction of extreme nervousness—this thing is getting out of hand, and what am I going to do about it?" U.S. military forces, Kennedy became convinced, had gotten entangled in a civil war by assuming the role of "an elephant trying to kill a fly." In pillaging and burning villages, the ARVN had alienated the very people whose loyalty was vital to winning this political war. The president tried to cut back on the ARVN's use of napalm, herbicides, and mines but ran into MACV's opposition. The Vietnam Working Group in Washington had already urged Harkins to refrain from publicly assuring victory within a year. The insurgencies in Greece, Malaya, and the Philippines had each lasted close to a decade. "If we can win in five years," according to the group's director, Chalmers Wood, "we will be doing twice as well as was done in the others." Success did not lie in negotiations but, as was the case in the other insurgencies, in amassing enough power to cause the Communist guerrillas to "lie low."[29]

President Kennedy found himself in the middle again when the joint chiefs submitted a report that promised victory through a better use of the military measures already in place. Four days after the battle of Ap Bac, their chair, General Earle Wheeler, led an inspection team of senior service and joint staff representatives into South Vietnam. Their eight-day visit culminated in a late January report declaring that with the guidance of America's "first team," South Vietnam's military forces could defeat the Vietcong. As far south as the delta, the ARVN had captured heavy Chinese infantry weapons. More than half a million people had come under government control in 1962 alone. The number of elections had increased. About 145,000 Montagnards had emerged from the mountains to seek government training in countering Vietcong infiltration. Improvements in the Self-Defense Corps and Civil Guard had freed the army to begin the National Campaign. The joint chiefs now called for a number of measures, including the unification of the U.S. command by integrating the tasks of MAAG with those of MACV, authorized helicopter fire on Vietcong targets, and increased air and naval actions. To establish a better relationship with the press, they recommended "a series of sponsored visits to Vietnam by mature and responsible news correspondents and executives." Air and ground reconnaissance missions in Laos would stop infiltration. "We are winning slowly on the present thrust," and there was "no compelling reason to change."[30]

But the joint chiefs did advocate one major upgrade: The United States "should do something to make the North Vietnamese bleed." One possibility was a preemptive strike on North Vietnamese targets; another was to continue the CIA's "minor intelligence and sabotage forays." A "more reasonable course" was to have MACV work with the CIA in launching psywar operations on North Vietnam from within the South Vietnamese military forces. Covert actions would interfere with Hanoi's efforts to help the insurgency. The United States would secretly conduct "the anti–North Vietnam campaign as a powerful military endeavor rather than as an ancillary to the Central Intelligence Agency intelligence program." The proper program was in place for "sabotage, destruction, propaganda, and subversive missions against North Vietnam."[31]

The joint chiefs' recommended assault on North Vietnam reflected the predominant thinking in Washington: that the way out of Vietnam lay in a larger U.S. commitment in Vietnam. Previous analyses had warned of a Chinese Communist intervention if U.S. forces struck above the seventeenth parallel, and yet the joint chiefs never gave this matter serious consideration. Furthermore, would anyone believe U.S. denials of covert activities in North Vietnam? But despite the differences between the joint chiefs' report and the findings of Hilsman and Forrestal, they were much alike in a most important way. Like the Hilsman–Forrestal report, the Vietnam Working Group, and the counsel of numerous other U.S. advisers, the joint chiefs insisted that the first step to partial extrication was to expand the U.S. military effort.

The joint chiefs' proposals drew a bitter retort from Kennedy's White House advisers. Within a week of receiving their report, the president met with Wheeler, McNamara, Taylor, and CIA Director John McCone to discuss the recommendations. Forrestal flatly opposed stronger measures, even apologizing to the president for his meeting with Wheeler as "a complete waste of your time." The meeting was supposed to focus on the report that he and Hilsman had compiled. But Wheeler's "rosy euphoria" had ignored the harsh realities in Vietnam. If the president approved, Forrestal would quietly work with Harriman in establishing a direct communication line between Harkins and the joint chiefs that would give Americans in Saigon more authority. Forrestal also urged a replacement for Nolting when his two-year term ended in April, along with increased pressure on the South Vietnamese government to pursue a more aggressive policy and a more independent U.S. posture in Vietnam based on distancing Americans from Diem's actions.[32]

The most important outcome of this baffling mix of assessments was a further boost to a U.S. military withdrawal by the "Comprehensive Plan for South Vietnam." As a result of the Secretary of Defense Conference in Hawaii on July 23, 1962, Harkins had worked with the South Vietnam Country Team in drafting a plan aimed at developing South Vietnam's capacity to bring the insurgency under control by 1965. Pivotal to this effort, he believed, was the National Campaign, which would keep the Vietcong on the move until it had to fight or surrender. Also important was the Strategic Hamlet Program, which provided the civil–military steps necessary to local security. Law and order would come through the Civilian Irregular Defense Group program, which aimed at clearing and holding regions liberated from the Vietcong. During the period 1963 to 1965, the paramilitary groups would grow in accordance with current needs, permitting the main phasedown of America's special military assistance to take place between July 1965 and June 1966, but with earlier withdrawals occurring in proportion to South Vietnam's improved performance on the battlefield. The plan had the ambassador's approval.[33]

On January 19, 1963, Harkins submitted to the joint chiefs the "Comprehensive Three Year Plan for South Vietnam," which was, the Saigon-based team decided, "a generally sound basis for planning the phase-out of United States support." The United States would provide $405 million in military assistance for fiscal years 1963–64 and $673 million for fiscal years 1965–68. South Vietnam's armed forces would peak in fiscal year 1964 at 458,000 men, allowing the ARVN to assume military control by the end of 1965. In the meantime, U.S. military personnel would drop from its high of 12,200 in 1965 to 5,900 in 1966. The ongoing decrease in U.S. support personnel would leave only 1,500 in MAAG by 1968.[34] The plan deviated from the joint chiefs' call for expanded covert action against North Vietnam. But both groups agreed on the central objective: a major reduction in U.S. military forces.

Thus the Kennedy administration continued to move toward a withdrawal program that less than a decade later became known as "Vietnamization." Victory did not lie in destroying the Vietcong but in bringing it under Saigon's control and permitting the United States to pull out its special military forces. The first step was to batter the Vietcong with the National Campaign. To facilitate this broad offensive, however, the White House first had to enlarge its commitment in the form of advisers and matériel. President Kennedy remained adamantly opposed to sending U.S. combat forces and thereby Americanizing a war he still insisted was South Vietnam's alone to win or lose. Counterinsurgency remained the heart of the program. To underline the administration's effort to reduce its visibility in Vietnam and thereby lay the basis for a major cut in involvement, President Kennedy issued a directive against unscheduled visits to Vietnam by senior U.S. military and civilian officials. Press reports of such visits left the impression that the United States was deepening its commitment. "This is exactly what I don't want to do."[35]

The familiar pattern nonetheless persisted: As the interest grew in partial disengagement, so did the level of military involvement continue to rise. The White House rejected Saigon's requests for jets but expanded the bombings of Vietcong communication lines and passageways into South Vietnam as well as enemy locations inside its borders. It condoned continued defoliation and crop destruction, even as Communist spokesmen publicly accused the United States and South Vietnam of using poison gas. But instead of the National Campaign signaling "the last big push" of the war, it merely meant another military escalation.[36] The press criticized the Kennedy administration's failures, while advisers and military leaders emphasized its successes. Amid this confusion, the withdrawal plan continued to wind through the bureaucratic maze.

In an intriguing twist, the Comprehensive Plan for South Vietnam appealed to all sides of the interventionist issue: to those who wanted to cut U.S. losses and regarded partial withdrawal as the first step toward total extrication, to those who sought to prop up Diem long enough for the United States to pull out its special military forces and leave him with the responsibility of policing the Vietcong, and to those who believed it possible to win the war by killing Vietcong and refashioning their client into the American image. A major U.S. disengagement loomed as more than a possibility as the warm spring weather of 1963 swept through Washington.

III

GENERAL WHEELER ASSURED the press in mid-February 1963 that the United States was "on the right road" toward winning "a classic guerrilla war." The ARVN's intelligence, communications, and mobility had improved, and the Diem regime was reaching its people's hearts and minds through the strategic hamlets. An additional half a million people had come under government protection in the past year, Wheeler declared, the result of more than 4,000 strategic hamlets. U.S. advisers were now among the ARVN's battalions, who had taken the offensive and were inflicting significant losses on the Vietcong. But the process required more time. "It's a nasty, tough little war—a series of forays, ambushes and murders designed to terrorize the population."[37]

Calling now for decisive action, U.S. military leaders advocated a change in the rules of engagement that would allow their helicopters to fire on the Vietcong without waiting for an initial attack. Wheeler had learned during his visit to Vietnam that local officials had interpreted those rules to mean that only those U.S. aircraft in the Farmgate operations could fire on enemy forces. The joint chiefs never intended for the directive to be that exclusive, he declared. Such a restriction jeopardized the right of self-defense. They therefore authorized CINCPAC to approve helicopter fire on clearly identified Vietcong who posed a threat.[38]

President Kennedy approved the joint chiefs' decision to alter the rules of engagement for helicopters, but it quickly became an embarrassment after a news leak revealed that the measure had not gone through the state department. The *Washington Daily News* of February 25 carried the startling headline: "New Order to American Troops in Viet Nam . . . 'SHOOT FIRST.'" Mecklin called the story a "spectacular leak" because it "leaked so rapidly that stories appeared in the press before the new rules had even taken effect." Still, he conceded, the leak was predictable: "The order had to be circulated among something like a thousand persons, most of them young, embittered helicopter crewmen who had lost buddies to V.C. fire, and many of whom were close personal friends of newsmen." The joint chiefs claimed that they had gone out of channels because the attorney general had wanted the matter before the president as soon as possible.[39]

The story underlined the growing fear of a U.S. war in Vietnam. Continued Vietcong infiltration had combined with the ballooning U.S. military presence to arouse suspicions about the claims to progress in Vietnam. Diplomatic or political attempts had failed to halt infiltration through Laos and Cambodia because the United States lacked leverage in those two countries.[40] Searching questions had emerged. If the strategic hamlets were working, how could the Vietcong recruit so successfully among the peasantry? Was the recent contingent of PAVN soldiers merely the first installment?

To stem infiltration, Nolting declared, the White House must pursue a combination of political and quasimilitary measures. It should make clear to Western allies that no international conference on South Vietnam could take place. It should warn the Russian cochair of the Geneva Conference that continued infiltration guaranteed a dangerous escalation of the war and then demand action by the International Control Commission. It should invoke support from SEATO and the United Nations. And, in a move consonant with the joint chiefs' call for extending operations beyond South Vietnam's borders, the White House must authorize air reconnaissance of the avenues in Laos, approve anti-infiltration measures outside South Vietnam, and intensify harassment and sabotage in North Vietnam. In the "unlikely event of overt intervention" by Hanoi, Nolting called for aerial interdiction of Laotian supply routes, air strikes against North Vietnamese targets, the injection of U.S. "combat units" into South Vietnam, and a naval blockade of North Vietnam.[41]

The problem in taking the U.S. case before the International Control Commission, Nolting explained, was that there was no documentation of infiltration after mid-1962, largely because it took up to six months for information to reach MACV. The only way to improve border surveillance was for the Vietnamese to work more closely with the Montagnards; but the two groups detested each other. Hanoi had established a special infiltration training center at Xuan Mai Ha Dong, located about twenty-five miles southwest of the city. So far, those selected for the school were former residents of South Vietnam. The training center enrolled 3,000 men who studied political and military doctrine for three months in hundred-man groups known as training battalions. To facilitate infiltration, the Vietcong had set up way stations and processing procedures. The North Vietnamese had the capacity to train and infiltrate about 500 cadres a month, and they had enough manpower to maintain this rate for the next five years. Vietcong trails wound invisibly through thick forests, which wrapped around virtually unending mountains that connected to deep and hidden valleys. "They could put the Fourth Route Army through here," a U.S. officer remarked, "and we wouldn't know it until they hit somewhere."[42]

Those who perceived progress in Vietnam bitterly criticized the Hilsman–Forrestal report for its mixed findings. Felt insisted that the Comprehensive Plan and the National Campaign Plan constituted a unified strategy. Imminent triumph would come from U.S. military support combined with the growing coordination of the aid program. Closing the Laotian–Vietnamese border would force the Vietcong to rely on local resources that were difficult to attain because of the strategic hamlets. Thompson concurred, assuring Felt that the Vietcong had lost the initiative. "One year ago we were neither winning nor losing. Now we definitely are winning." All members of the British Advisory Mission, he asserted, believed that the South Vietnamese were "beginning to win the shooting war against the Viet Cong." If present progress continued, he told McNamara, the United States could withdraw a thousand men in a highly publicized move that would "dramatically illustrate [the] honesty of U.S. intentions."[43]

President Kennedy meanwhile continued his move toward gradually reducing U.S. military forces. At a White House breakfast with congressional leaders, he expressed annoyance with Mansfield's recommendation for ending the U.S. military involvement. The president's irritation stemmed more from ambiguous reports from his advisers than from Mansfield's candid assessment. Kennedy knew that the senator was right, but his negative assessment had put the administration in a precarious position. An immediate withdrawal could come only at great political expense, and it would cause another witch hunt similar to that following China's conversion to communism in 1949. Kennedy invited Mansfield to the Oval Office. With presidential aide Kenneth O'Donnell in the room as well, the president admitted to Mansfield that his call for a total military withdrawal was correct. "But I can't do it until 1965—after I'm reelected." Otherwise, there would be a "wild conservative outcry" in the election campaign that would have severe political repercussions. After Mansfield left the meeting, Kennedy confided his intentions to O'Donnell. "In 1965, I'll become one of the most unpopular Presidents in history. I'll be damned everywhere as a Communist appeaser. But I don't care. If I tried to pull out completely now from Vietnam, we would have another Joe McCarthy Red Scare in our hands, but I can do it after I'm reelected. So we had better make damned sure I *am* reelected."[44]

Thus no major U.S. withdrawal would take place within the coming year. When asked at a March 6, 1963, news conference about Mansfield's appeal for diminished U.S. assistance to Southeast Asia, the president responded that, short of withdrawing and conceding the entire area to the Communists, "I don't see how we are going to be able . . . to reduce very much our economic programs and military programs in South Viet-Nam, in Cambodia, in Thailand." The entire area would collapse, allowing communism to spread into the Middle East. "I don't see any real prospect of the burden being lightened for the U.S. in Southeast Asia in the next year." The president's spring 1963 remarks both in the White House and at the press conference suggested that he was inching closer to a partial withdrawal that fell within the confines of the Comprehensive Plan slowly making its way through the Washington bureaucracy.[45]

The withdrawal effort ran into another snag when a heated debate broke out within the administration over the issue of expanding the U.S. air commitment to halt infiltration. In early March 1963, the joint chiefs approved Felt's request for a temporary enlargement of the air corps that would play an integral role in the National Campaign. Farmgate's pilots and maintenance crew would double in size, with 111 aircraft and 1,200 personnel joining the program. Harriman opposed any expansion of interdiction bombing. "U.S.-piloted combat fixed-wing aircraft" already flew a thousand sorties a month, with about 530 in support of ground combat and more than 300 engaged in interdiction missions. Such targets, he pointed out, were often inhabited by innocent people. Another problem was the growing U.S. military visibility. The American presence provided substance for Communist propaganda denouncing Diem as a puppet engaged in a neocolonial war that loyal Vietnamese should oppose in the name of independence.[46]

Harriman insisted that bombing would drive the peasants into the Vietcong camp. U.S. participation in interdiction missions "badly stretches, if it does not actually break, the mandate under which American air power was first engaged in the Viet-Nam conflict." The White House had approved uniformed Americans "for air reconnaissance, photography, instruction in and execution of air–ground support techniques, and for special intelligence." But the high number of interdiction strikes had already exceeded "air–ground support techniques." The administration must avoid the impression that this was America's war. "We are already getting too close to such a position."[47]

Little did the White House know that its military escalation had pushed the Communist Chinese deeper into the North Vietnamese camp. In February 1963, Ho Chi Minh appeared before a Politburo meeting in Hanoi, arguing for negotiations aimed at the establishment of a neutral regime that included NLF participation. He still felt confident that the United States's only concern was to save face. But recent U.S. military measures had forced the North Vietnamese into a harder position. The following month, Hanoi leaned toward China in its ongoing dispute with the Soviet Union. Le Duan spoke before the Nguyen Ai Quoc (one of Ho's pseudonyms) Party School, praising the Chinese for exemplifying the party's principles and asserting that the revolutionary struggle in South Vietnam sought peace by undermining U.S. imperialism. That same month, the chief of staff of the People's Liberation Army of China, Luo Ruiqing, visited Hanoi to assure support if the United States attacked North Vietnam.[48]

The international focus on the U.S. involvement continued to swell as North Vietnam formally accused the United States of using poison gas. The NLF had published a pamphlet claiming that chemicals used in Ben Tre and My Tho provinces had hit twenty villages and caused asphyxia, headaches, colic, diarrhea, skin problems, and other irritations. Indeed, the toxic materials had killed several women and children, along with crops and livestock. Harkins and Nolting nonetheless supported defoliation and crop destruction, along with the use of herbicides. At a press briefing on the morning of March 20 in Saigon, Director of General Information Phan Van Tao and his assistant, Dang Duc Khoi, denied these accusations that General Giap had recently made to the International Control Commission. Tao noted that the chemicals constituted one part of an overall program intended to deny food to the Vietcong. When Halberstam asked for evidence of the spray's value, Khoi admitted the difficulty in measuring success but noted that the "VC propaganda reaction was one good indication of effectiveness." To demonstrate that the spray was not harmful to humans, an ARVN officer applied the chemicals to his arms. As newsreel and photo cameramen took pictures, Tao invited newsmen to visit the sprayed areas. Halberstam accepted the offer, later joining Sheehan in considering the Vietcong's allegations unfounded.[49]

In early April 1963, however, Hanoi's Foreign Ministry asked the co-chairs of the Geneva Conference of 1954 to put an end to the use of chemicals. Its spokespersons insisted that many of those 20,000 people in the affected areas had died. The purpose of the program, Hanoi charged, was to drive the peasants into the strategic hamlets where they were easier to control. These actions were a "loathsome crime" against mankind, violations of both the Geneva Agreements and the international prohibition against wartime use of toxic chemicals and bacteriological materials. Criticisms of herbicide use also came from the Polish Red Cross, Radio Pathet Lao, and the Burmese and Cambodian press.[50]

Hanoi intensified the attack by blasting the "Washington cannibals" along with "the hangman Ngo Dinh Diem." According to the South Vietnam Liberation Red Cross, "the U.S. imperialists and their lackeys" had admitted using the poisons "2-4-D" and "2-4-5-T," the first light pink and gray and smelling like chloroform, the second (or "acid 2-4-5") dissolved in light kerosene. Small doses killed weeds, but large quantities harmed mankind, cattle, fruit trees, and vegetation. Hanoi claimed that these were the only chemicals the United States acknowledged using, all part of a transparent effort to provide a "smokescreen" to hide its "monstrous crimes." Among the many substances used were 2-4 dinitro phenol (DNP), which was light yellow and smelled like gunpowder, and dinitro orthocresol (DNC), which also had the odor of gunpowder but was orange in color. DNP and DNC turned wet skin dark yellow and caused inflammation before eating the flesh.[51]

Accusations of inhumanity likewise came from the Soviet Union. Foy Kohler of the U.S. embassy in Moscow reported a story in *Pravda* under the headline, "Advocates of Poison—Some Information for Staff of U.S. Embassy in Moscow," which attacked America's use of herbicides in Vietnam in the "widest distribution any Embassy press bulletin has ever received." The story's evidence rested on quotes from the March issue of *New Republic*, which referred to Giap's March protest to the International Control Commission. The Soviet story also cited an article in the York, Pennsylvania, *Gazette and Daily*, which remarked that if Washington was so sure the herbicides were not lethal, its officials should swallow some as proof. Along with the *Pravda* article, Kohler noted, was a "highly retouched photo or drawing" from the French newspaper *L'Humanite*, showing a poisoned Vietnamese peasant surrounded by weeping women. On the same page of the Soviet paper was a reference to a recent note from Moscow to London, urging the cosigners of the Geneva convention to investigate the use of poisons in Vietnam.[52]

Despite these public accusations, the Kennedy administration continued its chemical program. The joint chiefs agreed with the Country Team in supporting the regularized use of herbicides. Both the state department and the joint chiefs wanted to continue the present policy of chemical defoliation and crop destruction with one exception: The Saigon embassy should make decisions pertaining to crop destruction just as it did on defoliation or weed killing. Approval for chemical drops must still come from Washington. Forrestal and Hilsman believed that chemical defoliation had military value in destroying food for the Vietcong, but they opposed granting the embassy exclusive power to grant authorization. Washington must maintain control over the program.[53]

The Kennedy administration remained concerned that press criticisms of the assistance program could likewise delay the planned reduction in U.S. involvement. Official policy remained advisory, but also official was the White House effort to conceal its unofficial role in combat. Nolting insisted that no one in the embassy thought the press was deliberately trying to sabotage the U.S. aid program; the central problem lay in the reporting system. The average reporter in Vietnam was twenty-seven years of age and rarely double-checked each story for accuracy. Only UPI, AP, and the *New York Times* maintained full-time staff correspondents in Saigon, and even then, they were the caliber of those assigned to a "routine stateside police beat." Older and more experienced journalists preferred service elsewhere because the Vietnam conflict did not qualify as a "big story." Favorable accounts often failed to appear in the newspapers; bad news dominated page one. The "peculiarities" of the Ngo family always drew the interest of news correspondents searching for ways to "dress up" a story. Jorden, a former journalist himself, reminded the White House that the Diem regime treated foreign correspondents as "a kind of fifth column in their midst." There was no way to prevent thousands of Americans scattered throughout Vietnam from talking with reporters.[54]

As the criticisms mounted, Chester Bowles repeated his call for a negotiated withdrawal. The undersecretary of state, now also the president's special representative and adviser on African, Asian, and Latin American affairs, had long urged the formation of neutral and independent states that included South Vietnam as well as Laos, Burma, Cambodia, Malaya, and Thailand. Their sanctity would rest on assurances given by China, India, Japan, Russia, and the SEATO member nations. Russia, according to his reasoning, would support this neutrality axis as a way of stopping Chinese expansion into Southeast Asia. But the proposal never caught on, largely because it would have left the impression that the United States had abandoned those countries in exchange for meaningless guarantees by Beijing and Moscow. There was no choice, Bowles argued. The confidence expressed by Americans in Saigon was a reminder of the French optimism before their collapse at Dienbienphu in 1954. "Nine years have passed, and now it is we who appear to be striving, in defiance of powerful indigenous political and military forces, to [ensure] the survival of an unpopular Vietnamese regime with inadequate roots among the people." As was the case with the French prognosis in 1954, U.S. military officials predicted victory within three years. These assurances rested on "a dangerously false premise" that the Communists would not escalate their military involvement. But, he warned, their counteractions would grow in proportion to the effectiveness of U.S.–South Vietnamese programs. The result would be "increasing Communist opposition, growing U.S. casualties, and rising public resentment in the United States, followed, as in the days of Korea, by politically inspired demands that we either 'admit our error' and withdraw, or go after 'the real enemy, which is China.'"[55]

The call for withdrawal contained in the Mansfield report kept alive the talk about overthrowing the Diem regime. After lunch with Forrestal in Washington in early March, South Vietnamese Ambassador Tran van Chuong expressed concern that Mansfield's recommendation would force the Kennedy administration to terminate support to his country. Diem was a dictator, Tran declared; worse, he was incompetent. Adding to the problem was the influence of Nhu—who was, ironically, Tran's son-in-law by virtue of marrying his daughter, Madame Nhu. Tran held Nhu primarily responsible for forcing qualified people from their jobs and into

Professor John Kenneth Galbraith conferring with Senator John F. Kennedy at the Democratic National Convention in 1960. *Courtesy John Kenneth Galbraith.*

President John F. Kennedy meets with Secretary of Defense Robert McNamara and Secretary of State Dean Rusk in the White House Oval Office. *Courtesy John F. Kennedy Library.*

(*Above*) President John F. Kennedy meets
with National Security Affairs adviser
McGeorge Bundy in the White House Oval
Office. *Courtesy John F. Kennedy Library.*

(*Right*) Roger Hilsman, one of President
John F. Kennedy's chief advisers on
Southeast Asia. *Courtesy U.S. News and
World Report collection, Library of Congress.*

White House adviser Walt Rostow.
Courtesy Lyndon B. Johnson Library.

President John F. Kennedy and W. Averell Harriman at Hyannis Port,
Massachusetts. *Courtesy John F. Kennedy Library.*

President John F. Kennedy meets with members of the Joint Chiefs of Staff.
From left to right: Air Force General Curtis LeMay, Admiral Arleigh Burke,
Army General George Decker, Chair General Lyman Lemnitzer, and Marine
Corps Commandant General David Shoup. *Courtesy John F. Kennedy Library.*

Vice President Lyndon B. Johnson at Saigon's Tan Son Nhut Airport, reviewing Vietnamese marines with South Vietnamese Vice President Nguyen Ngoc Tho during the welcoming ceremonies for the American visit, May 11, 1961. *Courtesy Lyndon B. Johnson Library by U.S. Information Agency.*

Vice President Lyndon B. Johnson at Independence Palace, Saigon, with South Vietnamese President Ngo Dinh Diem and U.S. Ambassador Frederick Nolting, May 12, 1961. *Courtesy Lyndon B. Johnson Library by U.S. Information Agency.*

(*Top*) Vice President Lyndon B. Johnson at Gia Long Palace, Saigon, with Ngo Dinh Nhu at reception given by the vice president, May 12, 1961. *Courtesy Lyndon B. Johnson Library by U.S. Information Agency.*

(*Middle*) Vice President Lyndon B. Johnson at the Hotel Caravelle, Saigon, with Madame Nhu at luncheon given by South Vietnamese Vice President Nguyen Ngoc Tho, May 12, 1961. *Courtesy Lyndon B. Johnson Library by U.S. Information Agency.* Photo by Yoichi Okamoto.

(*Bottom*) President John F. Kennedy and Soviet Premier Nikita Khrushchev at the opening of the Vienna Conference, June 1961. *Courtesy John F. Kennedy Library.*

President John F. Kennedy and Green Beret Brigadier General William P. Yarborough at the U.S. Army Special Warfare Center in Fort Bragg, North Carolina, October 12, 1961. *Courtesy U.S. Army.*

General Paul D. Harkins (on right), Commander, Military Assistance Command, Vietnam, and General Earle G. Wheeler, chair of Joint Chiefs of Staff. *Courtesy U.S. Army.*

President John F. Kennedy and John McCone, Director of the CIA, November 29, 1961. *Courtesy John F. Kennedy Library.*

U.S. Undersecretary of State George Ball testifying before the Senate Armed Services Subcommittee, February 27, 1962. *Courtesy National Archives, Washington, D.C.*

Montana senator Mike Mansfield and Illinois senator Everett Dirksen. *Courtesy Lyndon B. Johnson Library.*

From left to right: David Halberstam of the *New York Times*, Malcolm Browne of the Associated Press, and Neil Sheehan of United Press International. *Courtesy AP/ Wide World Photos.* Photo by Horst Faas.

President John F. Kennedy and South Vietnam's Secretary of State Nguyen Dinh Thuan in the White House Oval Office, September 25, 1962. *Courtesy John F. Kennedy Library.*

Ho Chi Minh. *Courtesy U.S. Army.*

General Edward Lansdale, 1963. *Courtesy U.S. Air Force.*

President John F. Kennedy and Attorney General Robert F. Kennedy in discussion outside the White House Oval Office, March 1963. *Courtesy John F. Kennedy Library.*

Xa Loi pagoda in Saigon after a rally. *Courtesy AP/ Wide World Photos.*

Buddhist Monk Quang Duc immolates himself in Saigon, June 11, 1963. *Courtesy AP/Wide World Photos.* Photo by Malcolm Browne.

President John F. Kennedy and Henry Cabot Lodge, U.S. Ambassador to South Vietnam, in the White House Oval Office, August 15, 1963. *Courtesy John F. Kennedy Library.*

U.S. military advisers, armed with M16 rifles and other weapons, accompanying ARVN soldiers in search of Vietcong during the "secret war," August 22, 1963. *Courtesy National Archives, Washington, D.C.*

President John F. Kennedy on CBS television with Walter Cronkite in Hyannis Port, Massachusetts, September 2, 1963. *Courtesy John F. Kennedy Library.*

President John F. Kennedy confers with General Maxwell Taylor and Secretary of Defense Robert McNamara in the White House Oval Office on October 2, 1963, following their trip to Vietnam. *Courtesy John F. Kennedy Library.*

Lucien Conein of the CIA, U.S. liaison with the coup conspirators. *Courtesy U.S. Army.*

South Vietnamese General Tran Van Don in July 1963, one of the leaders in the coup that overthrew Ngo Dinh Diem. *Courtesy AP/Wide World Photos.*

South Vietnamese General Duong Van Minh in July 1963, less than four months before he ordered the assassinations of Ngo Dinh Diem and Ngo Dinh Nhu. *Courtesy AP/Wide World Photos.*

The body of Ngo Dinh Diem, in M-113, November 2, 1963. *Courtesy Archives Photos.*

M-113 armored personnel carrier similar to that in which the assassinations of Diem and Nhu took place. *Courtesy U.S. Army.*

Buddhist monk Tri Quang (on left) and two companions leaving the U.S. Embassy in Saigon after having received political asylum there, November 4, 1963.

Secretary of Defense Robert McNamara at presentation of the Distinguished Service Medal to Admiral Harry D. Felt, U.S. Navy, standing before the Color Guard in the White House Cabinet Room, July 7, 1964. *Courtesy Lyndon B. Johnson Library.* Photo by Cecil Stoughton.

President Lyndon B. Johnson with Michael Forrestal in the White House Oval Office, July 9, 1964. *Courtesy Lyndon B. Johnson Library.*

exile. Pressures on Diem to reform his regime had failed because "running a totalitarian regime was like riding a tiger—you could not get off its back." Within six months, it would become clear that the Diem government could not win the war and that a U.S. withdrawal would promote the collapse of all Southeast Asia to communism. The only recourse "was to bring about a change in government, which could probably only be done with violence."[56]

The partnership between Saigon and Washington became more strained as Diem angrily denounced Mansfield's call for disengagement. From Saigon's perspective, the Kennedy administration appeared to be on the verge of leaving South Vietnam, much as it had already deserted Laos. Numerous high-ranking Vietnamese officials, including Vice President Tho, cynically interpreted the senator's report to mean that "the less US involvement in [Southeast Asia], the better for US interests." One result of this embittered reaction was Nhu's withdrawal of support from the joint counterinsurgency effort. U.S.–South Vietnamese relations had taken a negative turn, he complained, largely because of the Mansfield report, but also because of press criticisms and wavering U.S. support for Diem.[57]

As another part of withdrawal through escalation, the White House stepped up its covert actions. Once the Vietcong lost popular support, Hilsman argued, it would have to turn exclusively to North Vietnam for assistance. At that point, U.S. and South Vietnamese forces would conduct clandestine operations against selected infiltration points and training areas. They would make no direct move against North Vietnam until the counter-insurgency program had brought political stability to the south; otherwise, the Communists would interpret the offensive as a desperate attempt to avoid defeat. Covert action, Hilsman insisted, would signal Hanoi that the United States did not seek a wider war.[58] The exact opposite interpreta-tion seemed more likely: Heightened aggressive action could draw an equivalent response by providing notification of a final push toward mili-tary victory.

Opposing assessments of the war made the withdrawal plan more at-tractive. Optimists perceived victory within reach and urged a powerful offensive to close the deal; pessimists narrowed the definition of victory and supported an offensive aimed at securing a stronger bargaining posi-tion before reducing the U.S. involvement. Thompson insisted that the situation in Vietnam had improved enough for the United States to. deescalate the war. He emphasized to President Kennedy that Diem had significant support in the countryside and that the Vietcong would prob-ably win within six months if he lost his governing position. The war was "moving in our favor" and should veer sharply toward victory by mid-1964. Rusk likewise claimed progress. Before the New York Economic Club in late April 1963, he declared that nearly seven million Vietnamese lived in more than 5,000 strategic hamlets and that another 3,000 would be ready for occupancy by the end of the year. About half a million people once under Vietcong control were now under Saigon's protection. The previous week, on the first anniversary of the Strategic Hamlet Program, Diem proclaimed an amnesty plan called "Chieu Hoi," or "Open Arms," that authorized clemency, aid, and employment to Communist deserters. The Communists no longer were, "in Mao's figure of speech, fish swimming in a sea of peasants." Rather, Rusk declared, "Every bush is no longer their ally. They are getting hungrier. To the Viet-Namese peasant they look less and less like winners." Not everyone shared this optimism. The CIA, along with the intelligence divisions of the state and defense departments, the army, navy, air force, and the National Security Agency, concurred with a National Intelligence Estimate: The Vietcong intended to wage a war of attrition, hoping that a mixture of military pressure and political deterioration would bring down the Diem regime. "The situation remains fragile."[59]

On March 7, 1963, the Joint Chiefs of Staff approved the Comprehensive Plan for South Vietnam submitted by CINCPAC. The plan authorized a phasedown of U.S. military forces, accompanied by the necessary military assistance and matériel for South Vietnam to run the counterinsurgency program on its own after 1965. Success depended on the parallel development of the National Campaign, the strategic hamlets, and the Civilian Irregular Defense Group Program. The latter two programs, according to the joint chiefs, comprised the key to providing security and winning popular support. "It is intended that the successful prosecution of these two mutually supporting national programs will result in 90 per cent of the population pledging allegiance to the Government of Vietnam. The attainment of such a goal is inseparable from the success of the CPSVN [Comprehensive Plan for South Vietnam]."[60]

Nolting recommended White House approval of the three-year plan but warned that the United States must keep its withdrawal intentions from Diem. By the end of 1965, Nolting hoped, the Saigon government could assume greater control over domestic security and the United States could begin reducing its involvement. The three-year plan appeared to be the best estimate for winding down the insurgency and permitting an end to "special US military assistance." In addition, the U.S. Operations Mission projected a three-year action plan for the counterinsurgency effort that rested not only on the Comprehensive Plan (which called for the construction of 7,500 strategic hamlets by the end of fiscal year 1963 and 11,000 by July 1964) but also on continued progress in the war. To conceal the plan from the Diem regime, Nolting urged the White House to tie the heightened U.S. involvement to the climactic National Campaign.[61]

De-Americanization of the war was about to commence in early May of 1963. The long process initiated at the July 1962 meeting in Honolulu had culminated in a plan aimed at reducing U.S. military personnel to about 1,500 MAAG advisers by the close of 1965. The Comprehensive Plan for South Vietnam, Wood incisively declared from his post in Saigon, sought to "assure the capability of the GVN to exercise permanent and continued sovereignty over SVN at the end of CY65 [calendar year 1965] without the need for continued US special military assistance." The United States should be able to withdraw a thousand men by the end of 1963. More than 13,000 U.S. military personnel were in Vietnam, but state department authorization was already in place to raise the total to 15,600. Of the 13,000, about 10,000 were troops and the rest advisers. The massive cut would consist of troops, not advisers.[62]

THE IMAGE OF PROGRESS in Vietnam that the Kennedy administration sought to convey was considerably different from the reality. Diem was not the accomplished leader that Americans read about at home. The war's verdict remained uncertain. The temptation to encourage a coup was high, chastened by the CIA's assertion that Nhu was Diem's likely successor. The two brothers accused the White House of seeking to establish a protectorate over South Vietnam; Madame Nhu instructed the Women's Solidarity Movement to denounce U.S. attempts "to make lackeys of Vietnamese and to seduce Vietnamese women into decadent paths." And all the while, the counterinsurgency effort faltered as infiltration now included North Vietnamese regulars to augment growing numbers of Vietcong recruits from South Vietnam. Furthermore, the chances of Communist China's military involvement had risen. Its head of state, Liu Shaoqi, visited Hanoi in May and told Ho Chi Minh, "We are standing by your side, and if war breaks out, you can regard China as your rear."[63]

A war of attrition had begun, confirming the CIA's conclusion that the fighting had developed into a stalemate in which the danger of all-out war had heightened as each side attempted to match the actions of the other side. Most alarming was the certainty that the ten-to-one manpower ratio believed necessary to defeat the insurgency would force a dramatic jump in numbers as the Vietcong increased in size. At some point in this upward spiral, according to theory, the Vietcong would have to fight conventionally and thus throw the advantage to South Vietnam. In view of several considerations—the ongoing Cold War, the inability to demonstrate significant progress in the assistance program, and the perceived threat of an ultimate Chinese Communist intervention in Vietnam—the Kennedy administration appeared ready to withdraw the bulk of its military forces and leave behind the semblance of a stable South Vietnamese government.

On May 6, 1963, the president's advisers met in Honolulu at the eighth Secretary of Defense Conference to draft the details of a withdrawal. A chart, entitled "U.S. Comprehensive Plan Vietnam Phase-Down of U.S.

Forces," specified that the level of MACV and Special Assistance Units would drop to zero by the end of fiscal year 1967. Only 681 MAAG and support personnel would remain (slightly below the 685 set at Geneva in 1954), although that number would rise to 729 by the end of both fiscal years 1968 and 1969. The Military Assistance Program costs would drop from $107.7 million at the end of fiscal year 1966 to $40.8 million in 1969.[64]

Harkins exuded optimism at the conference. South Vietnam was winning the war, he triumphantly declared. Phase I of the National Campaign Plan had nearly reached completion; Phase II should begin in July. McNamara had reservations. U.S. assistance figures were too high, the disengagement process too slow, and the buildup of South Vietnam's armed forces flawed by the need to train and support too many men in the use of overly sophisticated weapons. But he noted with confidence that after the plan underwent further study and revision, South Vietnamese forces would break the insurgency's will by the end of 1963 and permit a U.S. withdrawal that would reach the desired minimum level of involvement by early 1965. Assuming continued progress of the counterinsurgency campaign, the joint chiefs asserted, the first contingent of 1,000 U.S. military personnel could pull out by the end of 1963.[65]

How upbeat was the administration in the spring of 1963 as it unknowingly approached its most serious crisis in Vietnam.

11

MANDATE FROM HEAVEN?
The Buddhist Crisis and
the Demise of De-escalation

I couldn't say that today the situation is such that we could look for a brightening in the skies that would permit us to withdraw troops or begin to by the end of this year.

President John F. Kennedy, May 22, 1963

URING THE EARLY EVENING of May 8, 1963, violence broke out in the imperial capital of Hué, when peaceful celebrations over Buddha's 2,527th birthday degenerated into a raucous, full-scale confrontation between Buddhist followers and government officials in front of the city's radio station. The day before, the deputy province chief in charge of security, a Catholic named Major Dang Sy, had invoked a previously ignored 1958 law known as Decree Number 10, which prohibited the display of religious flags without special permission from local authorities. His action aroused bitter resentment because, just the week before, he had permitted the city's Catholics to wave their white and gold papal streamers in honor of the twenty-fifth anniversary of Diem's brother, Ngo Dinh Thuc, as archbishop. On that May 7, thousands of the multicolored Buddhist flags were already prominently waving above homes and pagodas, in open defiance of the law. The regime, Consul John Helble in Hué wryly noted, had "never observed" the law forbidding such flags until Diem suddenly demanded enforcement on the most important Buddhist holiday of the year. John Mecklin from the Saigon embassy termed the decree equivalent to "a presidential proclamation in the United States outlawing carol singing at Christmas." Nhu later moaned, "Why did my brother insist on sending such a stupid order about the flags? Who cares what flags they hang out?"[1]

In the midst of this tumult, the Kennedy administration's move toward de-escalation suddenly stalled, for events quickly escalated into a crisis that endangered the U.S. aid program as well as the Diem regime. Violence soon spread from Hué to Saigon and other cities as Buddhist monks protested against alleged religious "discrimination" and "terrorism" by the Catholic-dominated government and claimed to have a "mandate from heaven" to launch a revolution aimed at securing religious freedom. Only three to four million South Vietnamese were practicing Buddhists, but, combined with the many nominal members of the faith, they made up nearly 80 percent of the population. The struggle would not be easy, however. Although the Catholics comprised barely a tenth of the population, they counted among their members the ruling Ngo family, more than half of the National Assembly, and most landholders.[2]

The Buddhist upheaval baffled most Americans. Not only were Buddhist beliefs alien to American thinking, but so was their traditional lack of political interest. In early 1963, the head of the General Association was its superior bonze, Thich (Venerable) Thien Khiet, who stressed personal salvation and adhered to the low-key social activist position of the Theravada (Hinayana) strain of Buddhism in the Mekong Delta. But by mid-1963, the Diem regime's severe measures had pushed the Buddhist center of control into the hands of the more politically active Mahayana monks, including those émigrés who had departed North Vietnam after the Geneva Accords of 1954 and who drew a wide following in Hué and the northern areas of South Vietnam. Despite weighty numbers, however, Vietnam was not a Buddhist nation. Over its long history, it had become a veritable collage of religious and philosophical beliefs that included Buddhism (self-denial permits one's soul to reach Nirvana, a release from earthly pain), Confucianism (ethical teachings incorporated into Chinese religion), animism (all life results from spiritual forces), and Taoism (Chinese emphasis on selflessness).[3] Now, however, the new generation of young Buddhists began to shift from social criticism to political activism.

The Buddhist revolt pushed the Comprehensive Plan for South Vietnam into the background, ruling out an immediate de-Americanization of the war. The disengagement process had barely come into being before grinding to a standstill. On May 9, 1963, before the impact of the burgeoning crisis had made itself known, the Joint Chiefs of Staff directed CINCPAC to set up the procedure for pulling out 1,000 men by the end of the year. The removal would take place by units and not by individual soldiers, with the units replaced by specially trained South Vietnamese forces. Two days later, CINCPAC approved the MACV withdrawal plan, which directed that the thousand men would come from logistic and service support positions, thereby averting any adverse effect on military operations.[4] But the outbreak of violence brought this program to a halt. The Buddhist uprising of 1963 became the flash point of a profound crisis in Vietnam that threatened to force Diem's collapse and to transform America's secret war into America's own war.

I

ON THE EVENING of the violence in Hué, the police convinced Dang Sy to lift the flag ban, but his decision did not ease the situation. News of the suspension failed to reach all security personnel, leading the police to tear down the flags and set off a firestorm of protest as dawn lit the city's skyline on the warm morning of May 8. More than 500 Buddhists had filed across the bridge over the Perfume River to criticize the government in a mass demonstration at Tu Dam pagoda. Nearly 3,000 participants soon flocked into downtown Hué, waving banners that called for religious equality in both English and Vietnamese, only to find themselves quickly surrounded by eight armored cars, a company of civil guardsmen, and a host of armed security officials. Leading the Buddhists was the chief bonze of Central Vietnam, Thich Tri Quang, a tawny-skinned, charismatic, and mystical monk in his early forties who had become an activist while in Ceylon. A former lawyer, he had a well-established reputation as an independent Vietnamese nationalist having no ties to the government. Indeed, he had demonstrated his resilience by spending part of his youth in jail, ridiculously accused by the French of being a Communist when his views were as far to the right as the Communist ideology was to the left. The CIA termed him "an ambitious, skillful, ruthless, political manipulator and born demagogue."[5]

Diem, Tri Quang vehemently charged, was the source of all the trouble. In a private meeting with U.S. officials in Saigon, Tri Quang delivered a prophetic warning: "The United States must either make Diem reform or get rid of him. If not, the situation will degenerate, and you worthy gentlemen will suffer most." Gazing intently into the eyes of each of his stunned hosts, he made the piercing accusation: "You are responsible for the present trouble because you back Diem and his government of ignoramuses." Despite several meetings with this Buddhist monk, the Americans were thoroughly mystified by his Asian mysticism. "You'd ask as tactfully and diplomatically as possible the obvious questions about Buddhist intentions," Helble later remembered, and Tri Quang would "sort of look off to the top of his little room in the pagoda where I'd meet him, and the answer would come out something like, 'The sky is blue, but the clouds drift across it.' And I'm just not very good at interpreting this kind of stuff." Now, in Hué and with Dang Sy present, Tri Quang skillfully exhorted the boisterous crowd by dramatically reading aloud each protest banner and then castigating the government for religious repression and preferential treatment to Catholics. "Now is [the] time to fight!"[6]

Tri Quang's challenge found a ready audience. The Buddhists had suffered more from religious discrimination than persecution by the central government, perhaps best shown by lingering French laws that considered Catholicism a religion and Buddhism an "association" that was therefore ineligible to acquire property for its pagodas. But regardless of the accuracy of the Buddhists' charges against the government, they thought the time had come for a showdown. That they had written their banners in English suggested a well-conceived strategy of catching the attention of Western photographers and attracting American sympathy for their cause. Tri Quang directed his people to meet outside the local radio station for a huge rally that evening.[7]

Tension swelled throughout the day as the demonstrators chanted their protests and waved their antigovernment banners. As darkness fell, several thousand Buddhists crowded onto the grounds in front of the radio station, demanding that the station director cancel the regularly scheduled religious broadcast and instead air Tri Quang's speech. The director refused to do so without authorization from the censor and, as the crowd threatened to get out of hand, he telephoned Dang Sy for help. Fearing a riot, Dang Sy arrived with a gun- and grenade-wielding company of men in five armored cars.[8]

Not surprisingly, violence broke out. "The crowd," Helble later recalled, "surrounded the armored vehicles and some of the troops, jostling them and shouting." A short distance from the point of confrontation, two explosions suddenly shook the ground, shocking both sides. Helble noted "an immediate reaction on the local ground commander's part bordering on panic, and shots were fired." While the demonstrators stood momentarily frozen in stunned disbelief that the government's forces had resorted to bombs, Dang Sy thought the Vietcong had launched an assault similar to a recent one on a police station and fired three times in the air as the signal for his men to employ their grenades. Government forces sprayed fire hoses into the crowd to break up the gathering as newly arrived ARVN troops ordered the people to disperse. When the bonzes refused to evacuate the area, civil guardsmen fired carbines into the air and Dang Sy's men hurled more than a dozen grenades into the throng, their shattering sounds and pellet-like debris causing a mad rush from the smoke-filled scene. One of the grenades exploded on the porch of the radio station, killing a woman and four children. Fifteen more demonstrators suffered a range of injuries that included mutilations and decapitations. By the time the violence subsided, eight had been killed and four severely wounded. Two of the dead— both children—lay mangled in the streets, crushed by armored vehicles.[9]

How had the violence become lethal? The government claimed that its forces had carried percussion grenades, designed only to stun their victims, and *not* deadly fragmentation grenades. Its spokesmen insisted that a Vietcong agent had thrown the bombs and that the panicked crowd had fled the scene, unfortunately trampling those in the way. But most people remained dubious. The sheer force of the explosions raised questions about whether the Vietcong's well-known plastic bombs could have caused that much destruction. Vietcong members then and years afterward denied involvement. A highly respected Buddhist layman, Dr. Le Khac Quyen, examined the bodies and, in a controversial finding that resulted in his incarceration as an enemy of the regime, found no evidence of plastic bombs. One story, never substantiated, tied the deaths to a high-powered explosive device known to only a select few inside the CIA. Had one of its agents detonated the device during the chaos, hoping to bring down the regime?[10]

Whatever the truth, perception rendered the final judgment. Nolting's attempt to spread the responsibility attracted little agreement. The tragedy belonged to all parties, he insisted, the demonstrators for trying to take over the radio station, the government for sending the army, the army for firing into the crowd, and the "agitators" for throwing the explosives. Some time later, however, films of that day's events showed security officials shooting at the people. And yet, when the government's report on the episode did not assign culpability for the deaths, Nolting called it "objective, accurate, and fair." Although such so-called evidence did not account for all casualties, it was conclusive for those already inclined to condemn the government. Lest there be doubt, Tri Quang rode through Hué's streets all that night, trumpeting his accusations over a loudspeaker. The Diem regime faced the very crisis of its fate.[11]

At 11 o'clock the next morning, Dang Sy announced to nearly 800 youthful demonstrators that "oppositionist agitators" had forced the troops to take severe measures in maintaining order. The Vietcong had caused the violence. But his accusation convinced no one. The government's response to the protests suggested either a callous attitude or an obtuse grasp of events, infuriating the Buddhists and their sympathizers. A large group of militant youths had set the tone for the day by marching defiantly around the old citadel section of Hué, chanting "Down with Catholicism" and "Down with Diem government." A student banner welcomed martyrdom: "Please Kill Us!" Most telling, a progovernment organization called the National Revolutionary Movement and headed by Nhu attracted no one to a public meeting it had called for the afternoon of May 9 to condemn the "Viet Cong terrorist act" of the previous day.[12]

The Buddhists' central demand was religious equality. Before the demonstrations, Tri Quang had traveled throughout the country, urging fellow Buddhists to join the campaign. He had sent telegrams to Diem on May 8, protesting the government's use of Decree Number 10 to take down the Buddhist flags. He now called on all Buddhists in Central Vietnam to attend a mass funeral for the victims in Hué, scheduled for the following day, May 10. Such a public spectacle, he knew, would draw thousands and place additional pressure on Diem to grant reforms. The government, however, rigidly opposed any changes and armed all personnel in Hué after assigning them to twenty-four-hour duty in an effort to "prevent VC infiltration." But Tri Quang persuaded the people to lay down their flags and go home. That evening, government officials rode through the streets with loudspeakers, warning the people to abide by the nine o'clock curfew and stay in their homes.[13]

The next morning, however, the atmosphere intensified anew. About 6,000 Buddhists attended a meeting at Tu Dam pagoda with Dang Sy present and ARVN troops and police hovering nearby. A sea of banners waved above the crowd, all aimed at the government: "Kill us." "Ready sacrifice blood." "Buddhists and Catholics equal." "Cancel Decree Number 10." "Request stop of arrests and kidnapping." "A Buddhist flag will never go down." Tri Quang repeated his pleas against violence, appealing instead to the power of martyrdom. "Carry no weapons; be prepared to die." "Follow Gandhi's policies," he shouted to a crowd roaring in agreement. The chair of the Government of Vietnam Buddhist Association, Mat Nguyen, exhorted the government to compensate the families of those slain in the bedlam and demanded punishment of the official who had ordered his men to fire on the crowd. Dang Sy eased the tension by expressing sorrow for the aggrieved and drew a rousing cheer when he likewise called on the government to assist the families. The hour-long meeting ended peacefully after the Buddhists formally blamed Emperor Bao Dai for the decree banning the flags.[14]

In Washington, the Kennedy administration was preoccupied with the ongoing civil rights crisis in Birmingham, Alabama, and had not yet grasped the danger in the Buddhist uprising. Indeed, the ensuing calm in Vietnam after the initial outbreak of violence had appeared to mark the end of the trouble rather than what it was: the eye of the storm. The Saigon embassy reported that even though government forces had fired into the crowd, most of the casualties resulted from a bomb, a grenade, or the "general melee." The White House urged the Saigon government to make peaceful gestures to the Buddhists. Make assurances against repressive actions. Sympathize with the bereaved. Pay funeral expenses. But the government's relations with the Buddhists had been raw for too long, and Washington's suggested remedies met a stony silence. It seems safe to say that the Diem regime believed what it said—that the Vietcong was using the Buddhists to achieve its own ends and that the cry of religious oppression had no basis in fact. But these misguided beliefs revealed the depths of the Ngo family's own personal tragedy in failing to see the seeds of its own destruction. The White House just as naïvely assumed that the problem had passed.[15]

The so-called peace lasted a bare three days. On May 13 in Hué, the Buddhist clergy handed a government official a list of five demands contained in the "Manifesto of Vietnamese Buddhist Clergy and Faithful." The Diem regime, according to the Buddhists, must (1) rescind the order against displaying their flag; (2) permit them the same legal rights allowed to Catholics; (3) halt arbitrary arrests and intimidation of the Buddhists; (4) allow them religious freedom; and (5) compensate the families of those killed and punish the perpetrators. Although the signatories of the declaration couched their demands in the form of "requests," they expected compliance on all five points. The government figure keenly noted that their declaration bore the tone of an ultimatum.[16]

Two days later, on May 15, an eight-member Buddhist delegation delivered the manifesto to Diem, who angered his visitors by fending off their demands with carefully worded qualifications. On the question of revoking the prohibition against displaying Buddhist flags, he coolly observed that Catholics as well as Buddhists were guilty of the "disorderly use" of religious flags. Decree Number 10, the Buddhists complained, did not affect Catholics, who still enjoyed special privileges left over from French rule. Diem promised to inquire into what he dismissed as administrative mistakes. As for ending arbitrary arrests, such a move would help subversive groups. Regarding freedom of worship, the Constitution already guaranteed this right, but he assured punishment to any governmental authorities found guilty of an infraction. Last, Diem guaranteed financial assistance to families of victims at Hué, but even then, he colored the assurance by derisively pointing out that Catholics and other non-Buddhists were among those killed. The Buddhists, Diem blurted out, were "damn fools" for demanding religious freedom when the Constitution already made that guarantee. And, as he reminded them without hesitation, *he* was the Constitution. After the meeting, Diem ill-advisedly approved a government communiqué that included his calling the Buddhists "damn fools."[17]

Diem failed to recognize the seriousness of the Buddhists' threat and feared that any concessions would lead to more demands. Had he not held on to power by using force against the dissident religious sects of the 1950s? Had he not used the same tactics against the generals during their aborted coup of November 1960? According to mandarin principles, a ruler must never make a concession under duress, and he must not admit to a mistake. Only by a magnanimous gesture could he extend an apology or approve reparations. Support for Diem's position came from only one of his two brothers in Hué. Archbishop Thuc recommended a severe government clampdown. Ngo Dinh Can sharply disagreed. Can ran the city like a warlord with an army and his own secret police, but, surprisingly, he urged the premier to make a deal. Diem's popularity in Hué, Can insisted, had declined so much that not even a cat would come out to welcome him. Compromise with the Buddhists before their protests united all dissatisfied groups, he urged. Diem scoffed at this advice and accused Can of caving in to the pressure of office. *Time*'s bureau chief in Hong Kong, Charley Mohr, was blunt. "It's the same old story. Diem can't admit he's wrong, and so the Government will pretend it didn't happen, and they'll lie and make a hell of a lot of people angry."[18]

The government's callous reaction to the events in Hué ensured more trouble. The Buddhists at first appeared confused over what steps to take. Their religious leaders counseled moderation, which rested on Buddhist principles of nonviolence and adhered to Tri Quang's call for restraint. Some lay leaders, however, insisted on a fresh round of demonstrations. The Saigon government, they hotly complained, had not satisfied their grievances and continued to blame the Vietcong for all the trouble. The manifesto went unheeded, making the Buddhists more determined. "We do not fear arrest," one Buddhist asserted; "we have no wives, no beautiful things." If the government arrested their leaders, the struggle would go "underground." Diem did not intend to meet their demands.[19]

The Buddhists intensified their pressure. They held a press conference at Xa Loi, an ornate, three-story structure that was the premier pagoda in Saigon, where they resumed their verbal assault on the Diem regime. Proving themselves master propagandists, they produced and mimeographed fiery pamphlets for distribution, organized mass meetings and hunger strikes, compiled daily news items that kept followers enraged, and stirred up unrest among their relatives in both civilian and military groups. More than merely presenting their case to the Vietnamese people, the Buddhists adeptly used these methods and a succession of press conferences to cultivate a following both inside and outside the country.[20]

Nolting conceded that the Saigon government had acted too slowly in accepting responsibility for its harsh measures. Diem, Nolting insisted, understood the dangerous consequences of ignoring the Buddhists' complaints. Yet his government held the Vietcong responsible and concentrated on stopgap measures intended to suppress the Buddhists and restore order. Diem should publicly affirm the constitutional guarantees of religious freedom, accept responsibility for events in Hué, and compensate the victims' families. Diem, however, agreed to provide only nominal indemnification. Nolting made a suggestion that he must have known would spark no interest: Diem should appoint a commission of inquiry headed by a prominent Buddhist. Perhaps this move would prevent further violence during the demonstrations recently announced for May 21.[21]

The possibility of reform was minuscule, primarily because both Diem and Nhu considered the Buddhists an instrument for promoting the Vietcong cause. The Buddhists, according to the Ngo brothers, supported neutralism in foreign affairs and would seek an accommodation with the Communists if the regime fell from power. The Buddhists had already made great gains in Cambodia and Ceylon, two countries intensely disliked by the Diem government. Prince Sihanouk in Cambodia had taken a middle position between the Communists and the West and might persuade the Buddhists in Vietnam to do the same. Ceylon, as well, had advocated neutrality in the East–West struggle and could work with the Vietnamese Buddhists in attempting to neutralize South Vietnam. Laos had fallen to the same fate and was now providing refuge and passageways to the Vietcong. The Diem regime concluded that political power was more important to the Buddhists than their high-principled call for religious equality.[22]

In a lengthy meeting with Nolting in Gia Long Palace on May 18, Diem again demonstrated his failure to grasp the ramifications of the Buddhist problem. For two hours they discussed the issue without any sign of a breakthrough. Diem expressed confidence that once the Buddhists had had time to reconsider their rash behavior, they would realize that the government had done nothing wrong. Regrettably, Nolting concluded, Diem was sincere in blaming the Buddhists for the violence in Hué, accusing the Vietcong of causing the deaths, and asserting that Buddhist leaders sought political objectives. Five years afterward, Nolting still maintained that Diem dealt fairly with the Buddhists, even allotting scarce funds to help underwrite the pagodas' expenses. To Nolting on one occasion, Diem expressed regret that one of his generals had converted to Christianity as a means for advancing his career. "If these fellows would only go ahead and be good men and stop trying for promotions by taking on a faith which they may or may not really believe in, it would certainly help this country." During the crisis, Buddhist bonzes in the outlying provinces wrote Nolting many letters, denying involvement in the propaganda generated by "the central organization of the agitators," the General Association of Vietnamese Buddhists. And yet the press interpreted Buddhist actions as a revolt against religious persecution, which Nolting insisted was not the case. The Buddhist protesters worked behind "a religious mask" in "a very clever political ploy" that "exactly paralleled the number one tactical objective of the Viet Cong, which was to overthrow the Diem government and thereby bring about political chaos in South Vietnam." Many of them "had just come into the pagodas; they'd just shaved their heads and put on saffron robes and had become monks, bonzes." Although he had no hard evidence, he denounced their protest effort as a Vietcong plot. Historical perspective had made him more certain. "I believe now without any question that it was."[23]

The CIA conceded that the Saigon government could truthfully deny any formal suppression of religious freedom, but it failed to realize that its repressive actions had left that impression and alienated the Buddhists. As Forrestal recalled years afterward, Diem "was getting tired" after governing for nearly a decade and had gotten "a lot of bad advice" from Brother Nhu. Diem, in fact, had begun "to retire a good deal from the public scene in Saigon." Because of his growing isolation, he had lost touch with reality and now attacked the very groups whose support he needed to continue governing. "And as those elements began to counterattack him, he found himself forced or convinced to use some pretty harsh methods against them. The harsher the methods he used, the more the reaction was."[24]

Diem never comprehended the enormity of the Buddhists' challenge to his rule and stubbornly attributed the unrest to the Vietcong. This lack of understanding proved deadly to his regime, for he ignored any chance of a peaceful settlement at the outset of the crisis. Diem's support in the United States meanwhile plummeted, increasing White House sentiment to find a new head of state. That Diem failed to recognize the impending collapse of the world as he knew it constitutes the central tragedy of his regime.

II

WORLDWIDE SYMPATHY for the Buddhists made it difficult for the Kennedy administration to support Diem, particularly after Nhu publicly called for a drastic reduction in U.S. military forces in Vietnam. In a front-page story in Sunday's *Washington Post* of May 12, 1963, Nhu told visiting news correspondent Warren Unna that South Vietnam wanted half of America's 13,000 military forces to leave. Unna considered Nhu the real power in Saigon and claimed that he had urged the withdrawal five months earlier because those forces were no longer necessary and their continued presence fueled Communist propaganda. Nhu did not think the time had come to launch a major offensive. The first step to victory was to deny sustenance to the Vietcong through the strategic hamlets rather than by killing its forces on the battlefield. "Military people," Nhu snidely remarked, "like to have big operations, but we prefer to use local [paramilitary] forces for small actions and keep the regular army as a striking force for strategic reasons later on." Once the Strategic Hamlet Program was in place, ARVN and U.S. forces could exterminate the Vietcong. In a statement implying U.S. proximity to combat if not actual involvement, Nhu asserted, "Many of our American friends who died here are cases of soldiers who exposed themselves too readily."[25]

Although Nhu's conclusions were precisely what the Kennedy administration itself planned, compliance with his call for a quick and massive withdrawal would have undermined U.S. strategy by taking place before South Vietnam's military forces could stand on their own. Furthermore, Nhu's emphasis on low-key military confrontations could convince Americans that his only concern was to save the ARVN for warding off a coup. Had not a similar pattern developed in pre-Communist China during World War II? Nationalist leader Chiang Kai-shek had hoarded Western military goods for meeting the threats of Mao Zedong and his Communist followers, and not for fighting the Japanese. If, as Nhu asserted, "half the Americans in Vietnam should leave and the other half should not expose themselves to enemy fire," and if, "after nearly a decade of hostilities the time to take up the offensive had not come yet," then, as the *Post* asked, "How much longer must the United States help President Diem to lose his war and waste its money?" Two days after the story broke, the House Foreign Affairs Committee conducted an investigation of America's involvement in Vietnam that brought Hilsman to the stand. Congressional reaction to Nhu's interview, Hilsman soon cabled Nolting, was "very strong" and could cause "considerable domestic criticism and opposition" to the administration's policy in Vietnam. Nhu's actions required a protest in the "strongest possible language." His declaration could arouse domestic pressure in the United States for a premature withdrawal.[26]

Then, in a surprising twist, Nolting assured Washington that its concerns were unfounded. Just before his departure for a sailing vacation in the Aegean, Nolting had met with Nhu and came away with a sense of relief. Nhu denied being either anti-American or xenophobic and asserted that anything he said or did became subject to attack. His "lectures" to South Vietnamese officials, he admitted, stirred up resentment and anger. He attributed his unpopularity to his people's failure to understand the necessity of South Vietnam's becoming self-sufficient. That independent stance, he argued, was consistent with the U.S. intention to reduce its involvement as his own government improved its performance. When an ARVN general recently complained about U.S. interference, Nhu asked how often *he* had visited the ARVN's training centers. When he was told "never," Nhu pointed out that Harkins and other U.S. officers were continually there. Firsthand involvement was laudatory, Nhu implied, but only a fine line separated advising from assuming control. U.S. advisers must act as "diagnosticians rather than physicians," meaning that they should analyze a problem and report it to Saigon rather than cause hard feelings "by end-running the province chief." Nolting thought Nhu sincere but capable of emotional outbursts that probably explained his ill-considered replies to Unna's questions. Nolting believed the crisis had passed, allowing him to leave Saigon for a few days.[27]

At a May 23 press conference in Washington, President Kennedy reacted to a question regarding Nhu's interview in a manner that highlighted the growing U.S. entanglement. He first hinted at an imminent reduction of U.S. involvement when he dealt with Nhu's charge that too many American troops were in South Vietnam. "We would withdraw the troops," the president declared, "any number of troops, any time the Government of South Viet-Nam would suggest it. The day after it was suggested, we would have some troops on their way home. That is number one. Number two is: we are hopeful that the situation in South Viet-Nam would permit some withdrawal in any case by the end of the year." But he then qualified the second assertion by adding, "[W]e can't possibly make that judgment at the present time." There was "still a long, hard struggle to go." Indeed, "I couldn't say that today the situation is such that we could look for a brightening in the skies that would permit us to withdraw troops or begin to by the end of this year. But I would say, if requested to, we will do it immediately." Kennedy then backpedaled by declaring his hope to begin the process at the close of the year. "But we couldn't make any final judgment at all until we see the course of the struggle the next few months."[28]

This uncertain environment revived talk in Washington of finding an alternative to Diem. In a contingency plan presented to the White House on May 23 and approved in just two weeks, the Saigon embassy proposed a course of action should Diem fall from power. To avoid Vietnamese accusations that the United States sought to establish a puppet regime, the White House would discreetly clarify its conditions for recognizing a new government. In preparation for a governmental change, the embassy would construct a file of biographical sketches of those people likely to play a role in those events.[29]

The Saigon embassy considered Vice President Tho the most attractive successor. Born in 1908 as the son of a rich landowner in the south, Tho served the French as a low-profile provincial chief. He became Minister of the Interior in 1954, before accepting the position of South Vietnam's first ambassador to Japan in 1955. Despite spending most of his time in bed with a fractured hip, he secured reparations for World War II. The government recalled him to Saigon in May 1956 to deal with the Hoa Hao, a political and religious sect in the delta whose private army refused loyalty to the Diem regime. While the ARVN's field commander, General Duong Van Minh, led the military effort, Tho helped quash the sect by buying off warlords. Diem made Tho vice president the following October in an effort to widen the regime's popular appeal. But the two leaders hardly ever appeared in public together, and Nhu, irritated by Tho's nondeferential attitude, had once ordered a bodyguard to slap him. Tho's ascension to power would be constitutional, and he would have widespread support from his place of origin, the highly important delta. The military would endorse him, especially since he had befriended Minh years earlier by securing his release from a filth-ridden French jail. Tho was less than inspiring, and he seemed reluctant to play a political role, but he was experienced and had the additional advantages of detesting Nhu and having no close association with Diem.[30]

Buddhist unrest mounted as the Diem regime maintained its resistance to reform. The Buddhists planned a series of hunger strikes and four weeks of memorial services to highlight their plight. Indeed, Tri Quang could soon be in serious physical condition as a result of his fasting and might become a martyr. Tempers flared when a *New York Times* story by David Halberstam quoted Diem's dismissal of the Buddhists as "damn fools" at the May 15 meeting. Two weeks later, the semiofficial wire service of South Vietnam, the Vietnam Press, fueled the growing anger by publishing a government declaration confirming the existence of religious freedom and emphasizing the supremacy of the country's flag. Flag regulations were necessary to symbolize national unity—not to discriminate against any religion.[31]

The Buddhist crisis threatened to have profound repercussions. The Saigon embassy noted that the problem involved more than religious freedom; it offered all dissidents an opportunity to attack the Diem regime. Secretary of State Nguyen Dinh Thuan accused the Vietcong of exploiting Buddhist unrest and declared that Diem could not make concessions without giving rise to more demands. Only a hard line would work, according to the reports from Hué that Diem regarded as correct. Government officials in the city told Diem's equally recalcitrant brother, Archbishop Thuc, "Don't coddle the bonzes. Take a strong stand and they will come crawling on all fours." Colonel Do Cao Tri, head of ARVN forces in Hué, promised to stifle the Buddhists. To a Saigon embassy official on the morning of June 1, Thuan expressed fear that the Buddhists would demand a negotiated peace with the Vietcong. Indeed, he proclaimed, they lacked a governing framework capable of acting on their behalf. Diem had discussed matters with Buddhist leaders for hours only to meet with other groups who likewise claimed to be the real leaders.[32]

If Diem's government could have defused the crisis by immediately accepting responsibility for the violence at Hué, that moment had passed. At one time, according to Rufus Phillips, Diem considered visiting Hué to talk with Buddhist leaders; but he did not do so and the problem worsened. No one in the embassy thought the Buddhist outbreak would develop into a crisis. In Trueheart's words, it "simply became a handy umbrella under which all the latent opposition to Diem could gather." The chargé repeatedly warned the premier that the troubles were undermining the U.S. aid program. He must admit government wrongs and compensate the victims. His reaction: "Just blank. No argument, no nothing." Diem's pious and patronizing statements affirming the existence of religious freedom had exasperated the Buddhists. His government found itself in a political maelstrom. Continued trouble forced its civil servants, many of them Buddhists, to take a stand on the religious issue that further divided the country. Most military figures were likewise Buddhist, causing a sharp division within the ranks that threatened to wreck the counterinsurgency program. Buddhist militancy could cause another clash with the police that would escalate both domestic and foreign sentiment against the Diem regime. In central Saigon on May 30, more than 500 bonzes squatted in the streets, averting a bloody confrontation with governmental authorities only by leaving on their own. "We will fight until we win," observed one monk—"not violently, of course."[33]

The government's May 29 affirmation of religious freedom had not quieted the Buddhists, nor did the National Assembly's approval of the declaration just two days later. The bonzes in Hué had begun a forty-eight-hour hunger strike to bring public attention to their demands, and the ensuing protests continued to swell despite a government announcement on June 1 that it would dismiss the three major officials involved in the incident at Hué: the province chief, the deputy province chief, and the government delegate for the Central Region of Vietnam. Diem had actually ordered their removals because of their failure to keep order in the city, but the news took on the appearance of concessions to the Buddhists.[34] These cosmetic changes were too little and too late.

Large groups of Buddhists gathered in Hué by 10:30 A.M. on June 1, prepared to launch demonstrations all over the city. One contingent descended on the offices of the province chief and provincial delegate, where the former had promised a government response to the Buddhists' demands. Another crowd expected to reach 10,000 in number had begun gathering at the Tu Dam pagoda. No trouble had broken out yet, but rumors had spread that the Buddhists no longer intended to remain passive. Large numbers of police and paratroopers stood ominously nearby, armed and ready with American M-113 vehicles (virtual tanks) as support. But again cooler heads prevailed. By 5:30 in the evening, the Buddhist demonstrators in Hué had dispersed without incident, in response to the bonzes' directions to go home. The Buddhists continued the hunger strike, but their tracts calling for peaceful actions now seemed hollow attempts at restraint. Tri Quang had earlier pronounced the situation beyond compromise and, in a startling statement that the Diem regime would cite in making its accusations, urged his people to accept help from anyone—*including the Vietcong*.[35]

Danang also threatened to become a hot spot when sixty bonzes and twelve Buddhist nuns carrying flags marched toward the mayor's office around eight in the morning of June 1. As they lingered across the street from his office, some standing and others sitting, the atmosphere took on a ghostly aura as the only other people in a three-block radius were police and soldiers who had cleared the area of civilians. Within an hour about 2,000 onlookers had collected near the isolated area, soon dispersed by the arrival of more troops wearing steel helmets and wielding submachine guns.[36]

The Kennedy administration found it difficult to maintain close ties with Diem in this gathering storm. It urged him to maintain communication with the Buddhists, but he stubbornly refused to make any peace overtures. Confusion reigned. Although the Buddhists comprised a great bulk of the population, they had splintered into several groups with various levels of fervor. Which group, if any, spoke for the majority? Diem repeatedly insisted that the Buddhists' call for religious freedom provided a guise for their collaboration with the Vietcong. The White House rejected this argument, insisting that legitimate political and religious issues lay behind the unrest. It feared that the presence of American M-113s and other heavy weaponry would promote more violence and that both the South Vietnamese and U.S. governments would draw blame. "Is it true," the state department asked, "that M-113's ran over bodies after [the] May 8 incident [in] Hué?" No, the Saigon embassy assured its home office; the Diem government used only armed British and American scout cars in putting down the trouble. An examination of the bodies offered no conclusive evidence regarding the cause of their deaths.[37]

Attention then turned back to Saigon, where at noon on June 3 about 500 Buddhists, mainly youths, gathered in front of the Government Delegate's office while 300 troops stood by. Several members of the crowd shouted at the soldiers, accusing them of wanting to incite violence. A West German doctor drew cries of support when, through an interpreter, he announced himself as a Catholic who could not begin to understand the Buddhists' anguish but urged them to pray rather than resort to violence. At that moment, a government car arrived on the scene, its loudspeaker blaring orders for the people to go home and warning that the government would not be responsible if trouble developed. The soldiers intended to kill the protesters, yelled someone in the crowd. The Vietcong among them sought trouble, roared the government official in response. This angry exchange ensured violence. Security forces trained their weapons on the crowd, only at the last second raising their gunsights above the people's heads. "Stupid killers!" shouted someone above the ugly din. Sensing imminent trouble, the troops fixed bayonets, donned gas masks, and moved toward the crowd. Some ran out of their path while others stood and prayed as the soldiers hurled tear-gas grenades that crashed onto the street and spewed brown clouds of choking smoke. As the Buddhists retreated, the soldiers threw more grenades, releasing another torrent of tear gas. Its victims screamed at the troops, now only shadowy silhouettes in the sun-glistened but thick and bitter-smelling chemical fog.[38]

At this dangerous moment, a representative of the Buddhist Association ran onto the scene, urging his people either to go home or to seek refuge in the pagoda. Most of them moved toward the pagoda, while some of the youths, nearly blinded by the tear gas, stumbled into its dispensary. The German doctor, obviously prepared for the situation, administered medicine to those with burning eyes. But the evacuation failed to stem the chaos. The throng of Buddhists heading to the pagoda found their passage blocked by barbed wire. Shocked and infuriated, many in the crowd, primarily Boy and Girl Scouts, sat and prayed. By now, after almost three hours of bitter confrontation, a troop spokesman gave the crowd three minutes to disperse or face another round of tear gas. Someone threw a rock at the soldier, forcing him to drop his tear gas grenades to protect himself. More troops moved in, all wearing gas masks and adding a surreal cast to these events as they forcefully scattered the crowd. No one fired weapons, but the situation had worsened.[39]

In Hué on the same day, violence erupted anew when the army, taking the place of the police, had to break up a huge crowd near Ben Ngu bridge six times, each occasion marked by the use of tear gas and other chemical irritants. Sound trucks boomed above the bedlam, urging the Buddhist demonstrators, most of them high school and college students who had arrived on bicycles, to go home but drawing only jeers in blaming the trouble on the Vietcong. The worst scene developed at 6:30 in the evening, when the security forces scattered a crowd of 1,500 by emptying glass vials of brownish red liquid on the heads of praying Buddhists. No evidence supported the rumors of three deaths, but sixty-seven of those doused in the murky solution went to the hospital, suffering from severe blisters and respiratory ailments. The people had shouted vulgarities at the soldiers for using tear gas; they became incensed over the suspected resort to poison gas. *Newsweek* reported that the police had lobbed canisters of blister gas into the crowds. Reliable sources claimed that the Saigon government was ready for a military showdown. In a statement never proved, the police chief in Central Vietnam assured an American that the three leading bonzes in Hué were Vietcong "without doubt."[40]

By midnight, Hué was under martial law and quiet though tense. U.S. Consul John Helble believed that the South Vietnamese troops had used tear gas and "possibly another type of gas which caused skin blisters." He had not yet identified the substance, but the blistering and respiratory problems were not common with tear gas and raised state department concern about whether government forces had used either blister gas or poison gas. If so, the Diem regime must disavow the action and punish those responsible. Failure to do so could force the United States to distance itself from Diem by issuing a public declaration of disapproval.[41]

U.S. officials in Saigon had finally come to understand the real danger in the Buddhist uprising. To them and to Diem, the central issue was his regime's survival against a host of dissatisfied groups anxious to exploit any unrest aimed at the government. The Buddhist crisis was about to become an American crisis.

III

THE DIEM REGIME was in a highly precarious position. Some army commanders were reluctant to repress the demonstrators because their predominantly Buddhist troops might refuse to obey orders. Members of the non-Communist opposition denounced the government. One high official in the information service declared himself part of a secret group that intended to seize control if violence broke out in Saigon. A few important military leaders were reportedly ready for such an opportunity. The government's brutal measures had breathed new life into Communist propaganda. On May 29, Ho Chi Minh announced his conditions for peace in an interview that appeared in Moscow's *New Times*. "Foreign intervention must cease," Ho asserted. "The forces and the weapons of the interventionists must be withdrawn. The 1954 Geneva Agreements must be respected and U.S. pledges not to violate these agreements by force or threat of force must also be respected." The strategic hamlets must come to an end, followed by a cease-fire and a free election in South Vietnam.[42]

Other developments threatened Diem's rule. An NLF booklet appeared in June 1963, asserting that most South Vietnamese opposed the strategic hamlets as Diem's effort to undermine the liberation movement by forcibly resetting farmers. Indeed, the Vietcong launched a major campaign during the summer to destroy the program. The Central Military Party Committee of the Communist party meanwhile met in Hanoi, where it decided to intensify its efforts to build a modern army for defending North Vietnam and to send more cadres to the south. The Kennedy administration could not have known this, but also in June, Mao Zedong assured Hanoi of assistance. Do not borrow from the Russians, he told a Vietnam Workers' Party delegation in Wuhan; "they will press for payment of debts and you will find it hard to handle. Don't worry when you borrow from China. You can pay the Chinese debts whenever you are ready and it is all right even if you do not pay." Diem's repressive actions, the CIA concluded, had transformed a local incident into a "potential political crisis" that could undermine his regime.[43]

The state department recognized that the Buddhist crisis threatened not only the South Vietnamese government but U.S. interests as well. Rusk wanted Diem to replace the troops with police or gendarmes. It was "most unlikely" that the chief bonzes were Vietcong. Diem must not identify the demonstrators as "automatically VC." He must meet with Buddhist leaders and discuss their grievances. Rusk instructed the embassy to urge Diem to do so.[44]

Just before lunch in Saigon on June 4, the day following receipt of Rusk's directives, Trueheart (in charge of the embassy while Nolting was on vacation) met with Thuan for fifteen minutes and came away only slightly encouraged. Diem had approved his cabinet's recommendation to establish direct communication with the Buddhists and had already asked Nhu to meet with their leaders from Hué. What about the alleged use of blister gas in Hué? Thuan's astounded reaction was real, Trueheart thought; Thuan even asked what a blister was. Blistering and respiratory difficulties,

Trueheart explained, were symptoms of mustard gas. But whatever the gas used, the Saigon government must disavow the action; otherwise, the White House would publicly denounce the act. On the possibility of replacing the troops with police, Thuan noted that the police in Hué lacked riot control training similar to that provided in Saigon. Trueheart then emphasized the difficulties caused by the government's insistence that the Vietcong had caused the agitation. Thuan promised an immediate inquiry, particularly into the charges relating to blister gas.[45]

The Saigon government had finally shown signs of wanting to resolve the issue without further violence. Follow-up investigations attempted to exonerate the Diem regime of the most serious allegations. Security forces in Hué, the report concluded, had used only tear gas, suggesting that government authorities were correct in theorizing that the blisters had been skin burns resulting from proximity to the exploding canisters. A commission led by General Tran Van Don supported this conclusion. The tear gas, left by the departing French in the 1950s, came in glass containers in the form of a liquid that transformed into a gas upon activation by acid. Even though some of the grenades had failed to explode, they sprayed enough acid on their targets to raise blisters. U.S. Army chemists in Maryland confirmed that the tear gas had come in canisters from French stocks dating back to World War I. To replace the troops, the Saigon government requested an American airlift of 350 military police from Vung Tau into Hué. But the United States refused to become involved. To deal with the Buddhist crisis, Diem appointed an Interministerial Committee headed by Vice President Tho and including Thuan and Minister of the Interior Bui Van Luong.[46]

Hope for a settlement came from a surprising turn toward a truce. Before breakfast on June 5, Thuan contacted Trueheart to invite him to his house for an early meeting to tell him of the new developments. Thuan explained that he had been involved in a series of secret discussions in Saigon the previous day with Diem, Nhu, and a bonze from Hué named Thich Thien Minh, who was Vice President of the Buddhist Association of the Central Region and a member of the Committee of General Association of Buddhists of Vietnam. Most important, Minh represented a group of forty leading monks and a number of laymen now fasting in Tu Dam pagoda in Hué and cut off from the outside world by the government's barbed wire and road blocks. The group inside the pagoda included Tri Quang (sick from fasting) and the chair of the General Association, the eighty-year-old Thich Tinh Khiet, who was the real force behind the May 8 demonstrations. To facilitate a truce, the Buddhists agreed to call off all demonstrations if the government removed its troops and uniformed personnel from the pagoda areas. They would also stop distributing tracts in exchange for the government's halting radio and press propaganda that urged Buddhists in the outlying provinces to support the Diem regime. Minh had to return to Hué on June 5, leading Trueheart to suspect that the Buddhists regarded their proposals as an ultimatum.[47]

The June 4 agreement was heavy with reservations, but it suggested progress toward satisfying the five Buddhist demands of mid-May. First, the Buddhists agreed to recognize the superiority of the national flag by flying it outside their pagodas on official, nonreligious holidays. On religious holidays they would display both the national and religious flags outside the pagodas. Inside, they were free from government restrictions. Second, the government disclaimed responsibility for Decree Number 10, which had gone into effect under Emperor Bao Dai, and it recommended that the Buddhists ask the National Assembly to rectify the situation. Third, Diem agreed to a statement assuring "no religious discrimination or persecution," although he derisively remarked that this was not necessary because the Constitution guaranteed religious freedom. Fourth, Diem and Nhu denied that government forces had arbitrarily arrested Buddhists in Hué, but they promised an investigation. And fifth, in a move that one could interpret as implicit acceptance of responsibility for the May 8 casualties in Hué, the government agreed to compensate the victims' families. Thuan insisted, however, that this was an "ex gratia payment" and not an admission of guilt.[48]

The Buddhist crisis seemed on the road to resolution. Thuan felt confident that Diem would approve the pact. The manner of implementation was not clear, but the premier wanted the process to take place quietly. Thuan believed that Minh represented the Buddhist center and that those in the south would accept the terms. Thuan and the government's investigative commission met with Minh and Thich Thien Hoa, the latter representing the southern Buddhists. A six-hour session resulted in a settlement containing the same terms found in the Minh–Thuan agreement. Thuan meanwhile announced that the troops had left the pagodas and that military officials were to avoid unnecessary shows of force. In the most promising sign, Diem delivered a radio address to the people in Hué on the evening of June 6, astonishing them by calling for reconciliation and admitting that his officials had made mistakes.[49]

But then, just as the truce terms appeared ready to go into effect, a series of events combined on June 7 to undermine the settlement and escalate the crisis. From government airplanes over Hué came a shower of leaflets attacking both Tri Quang for instigating the trouble and the elderly Khiet for failing to make clear who led the Buddhists. Government spokesmen accused extremist monks in Saigon's Xa Loi pagoda of subverting the truce by circulating tracts urging demonstrations against the Diem regime and, in an attempt to turn the outside world against Diem, by seeking International Red Cross assistance for their fasting brethren in Hué.

Nhu then compounded the explosive situation by joining the National Revolutionary Movement in urging all South Vietnamese people to unite behind Diem and to recognize the national flag as preeminent in South Vietnam. The Constitution guaranteed religious freedom, according to the declaration. Buddhists sought *special* treatment, and they supported communism. The Buddhists were infuriated.[50]

The significance of another event on June 7 did not become clear until the following day, when Madame Nhu spoke through the Women's Solidarity Movement in issuing an inflammatory resolution to the press that likewise threatened the potential truce. On June 8, the Central Committee of the Women's Solidarity Movement accused the Buddhists of neutralism, a brand of insult in Saigon that equated them with the Communists. It then urged "bonzes of good faith" to stop helping the Vietcong. If not done, Vietnamese Buddhism would stand before the world as a "small antinationalist branch of a dubious international association, exploited and controlled by communism and oriented to the sowing of the disorder of neutralism." The government should "immediately expel all foreign agitators whether they wear monks' robes or not." And finally, in a statement aimed at the United States, the committee warned the Diem government to "keep vigilance on all others, particularly those inclined to take Viet Nam for [a] satellite of [a] foreign power or organization."[51]

The state department expressed alarm that Madame Nhu would risk alienating both Congress and the American people. In a conversation with Halberstam, she refused to retreat, blasting the Buddhists with the acidic remark that it was "embarrassing to see people so uncultured claiming to be leaders." Washington authorized Trueheart to renounce such declarations publicly if this might prevent her from doing this again. He also was to urge Diem to take remedial action, perhaps using his emergency powers to repeal the controversial law allegedly discriminating against the Buddhists. The state department also wanted to know whether Madame Nhu's statement, which carried a semi-official tone, had received government clearance.[52]

Diem met with Trueheart on June 8 at 5 P.M., only minutes after the chargé had requested an interview. Diem appeared at ease, even allowing Trueheart to interrupt a number of times. He first presented a copy in French of the Women's Solidarity Movement Resolution, which Diem read carefully, as if this was the first time he had seen it. Trueheart expressed deep disappointment with the resolution because it violated the truce on propaganda. Would it not be wise for Diem to disavow the resolution? If he refused, Trueheart warned, the White House would probably "disassociate" itself from the regime's actions. But Diem declared that he could not do so. His people must know that extremists had exploited the tense situation for personal gain.[53]

Diem's attitude remained uncompromising. Although willing to negotiate with the Buddhists, he was convinced that no lasting settlement was possible until they "found themselves isolated." The Buddhists had violated the propaganda truce by distributing tracts and other information to the foreign press. Minh had publicly boasted that the government had capitulated to his demands. The Buddhists "had been negotiating in bad faith." The initial problems in Hué derived not only from the "ineptitude" of local government officials, but also from their encouragement to "certain" Buddhists. Would the government, Trueheart asked, resort to sterner actions if the problems erupted again? Diem promised to take all "necessary measures" to restore order, and he objected to Trueheart's calling it "Madame Nhu's statement." In a telling observation, however, Trueheart noted that the "latter remark was made (and received) with a smile."[54]

From the White House perspective, the Buddhist unrest had the potential of fomenting other dissident groups to hold protests that could combine with the government's sputtering war against the Vietcong to bring down the Diem regime and wreck the U.S. aid effort. Before the Buddhist crisis erupted, Forrestal declared, the Kennedy administration felt that it had reached "the high point, the high water mark, of our success in Vietnam." Taylor likewise thought that the Buddhist revolt had halted progress and that the press was "magnifying everything that took place." Confirmation came from the U.S. Operations Mission in Saigon, where Rufus Phillips considered the outbreak of violence as the "watershed" in Diem's regime, for in trying to put it down he alienated the army. Hilsman insisted that sometime in the spring of 1963, during the Buddhist revolt, President Kennedy decided that the Vietnamese could not win the war. "Remember Laos," he said repeatedly to his staff. "Keep it down, no more advisers, we're going downhill. We've reached the peak. From now on, we're going to cut the advisers back. If the Vietnamese win it, okay, great. But if they don't, we're going to go to Geneva and do what we did with Laos."[55]

ON JUNE 10, 1963, deceptively encouraging news came from Hué: Buddhist laymen at Tu Dam pagoda had terminated their fast and were returning home. The police, in turn, withdrew from the troubled scene, leaving the appearance of calm. But if peace still had a chance, that hope quickly faded the next day. A little after 11 A.M. in downtown Saigon, nearly 500 bonzes and nuns were among thousands of spectators jammed into a bustling intersection, frozen with horror as an elderly bonze burned himself to death to dramatize the Buddhists' cause.[56] Not only did this signal event lead to myriad discussions about toppling the Diem government, but it introduced the Kennedy administration to a new and more dangerous world that necessitated a hold on de-escalation.

12

THE FIRE THIS TIME

Who are these people?

President John F. Kennedy, June 1963

We had zero knowledge of Buddhism.

William Trueheart, July 1989

LAMES WERE COMING from a human being," wrote *New York Times* correspondent David Halberstam; "his body was slowly withering and shriveling up, his head blackening and charring." At the epicenter of this gruesome sight in downtown Saigon was Thich Quang Duc, a seventy-three-year-old bonze from an outlying province who had arrived just moments before 10 A.M. with two other monks in an old gray Austin sedan. Halberstam had joined thousands of spectators at the busy intersection of Phan Dinh Phung and Le Van Duyet streets, in anticipation of another Buddhist demonstration, but they were stunned by what transpired. From the car emerged its chief passenger, his yellow robe and shaved head glistening in the hot sun. Quang Duc eased down on the pavement in the lotus position, crossed his legs, and quietly stared straight ahead. His two companions had hurried after him, carrying a five-gallon container of gasoline mixed with diesel fuel that they emptied over his head and body as he clutched his prayer beads and repeated the sacred words, "*nam mo amita Buddha*," or "return to eternal Buddha."

In the midst of an eerie silence, Quang Duc struck a match handed to him and touched the tiny fire to his robe, now drenched with the highly combustible pink liquid. Instantly, black and yellow flames shot upward, consuming his clothing before licking into his flesh. The air became heavy with black, oily smoke and the stench of burning skin as the flames danced high. "As he burned he never moved a muscle," Halberstam continued, "never uttered a sound, his outward composure in sharp contrast to the wailing people around him." Police were unable to break through the ring of bonzes surrounding the burning monk. A fire truck could not move because of monks lying down before its wheels. In less than five minutes, the fire had burned out, and Quang Duc's blackened and smoking body twitched and crumpled forward as if he had completed his prayer. No one moved, all transformed into horrified witnesses of a surreal event in which the clock had turned backward but without a corresponding change in the contemporary physical setting. "All around this scene of medieval horror were the signs of modern times: a young Buddhist priest with a microphone saying calmly over and over again in Vietnamese and English, 'A Buddhist priest burns himself to death. A Buddhist priest becomes a martyr.'"[1]

Halberstam's words graphically captured the essence of an event that made an indelible stamp on America's collective consciousness and rudely awakened the Kennedy administration to the gravity of the Buddhist crisis. Malcolm Browne of the Associated Press had also appeared on the scene, like Halberstam alerted that something important would take place that morning on the road outside the Cambodian legation and near Xa Loi pagoda.[2] Browne's most telling photograph, taken just as the flames engulfed Quang Duc, immortalized the event that shocked the world. Not that this was the first Buddhist immolation; but to millions of people all over the globe this particular instance brutally exposed them to a gory spectacle that converted the Buddhist protests into international news.

This apparent time warp did more than traumatize observers. John Mecklin from the U.S. embassy next door declared that Browne's photograph "had a shock effect of incalculable value to the Buddhist cause, becoming a symbol of the state of things in Vietnam." Buddhists had long regarded themselves as the moral and intellectual guardians of Confucian values against misguided or corrupt rulers. On several occasions in Vietnam's history, they had sought to restore the will of heaven by inspiring a peasant uprising aimed at overturning a deceitful or mendacious government. This time the implications extended beyond domestic concerns. The well-choreographed atrocity of Quang Duc's violent death signified the wide chasm that had opened between the moral ideal and the immoral reality, greatly increasing the chances of a coup.[3]

I

IN THE AFTERMATH of this macabre scene in Saigon, Buddhist leaders called an abrupt halt to the chanting. As the dazed crowd stared in silence, a small delegation of monks threw yellow robes on the corpse and lifted it off the melting asphalt. Others had brought a coffin, but Duc's charred bones would not bend, forcing them to ease the body into the wooden box with a smoking arm jutting outward. A lengthy procession of about 400 bonzes solemnly carried the casket the short distance to Xa Loi pagoda near the U.S. Operations Mission building to await a funeral. There, the bonzes deposited the ashes in a glass bottle that became emblematic of Quang Duc's supreme sacrifice, inspiring the legend that he had departed this world with his mission unfinished but searing the image of religious persecution into the consciousness of people all over the globe. By 1:30 in the afternoon, close to a thousand bonzes had squeezed into the pagoda, while on the outside a large swarm of pro-Buddhist students had formed a cordon around the building to block further entrance. Students hoisted a makeshift banner proclaiming in English, "This Buddhist priest cremated himself for five items demanded of the government." The impromptu meeting inside the pagoda soon ended and all but about a hundred bonzes slowly left the scene. Nearly a thousand bonzes and lay people filed back to the cremation site while just as many police lingered nearby, ready to keep order. The bonzes waved banners in English and Vietnamese asserting, "A Buddhist priest burns himself for our five requests."[4] The manifesto so brazenly ignored by Diem had become the cause cèlébre of the Buddhists' protests.

Diem's road to ruin had begun a long time before Quang Duc struck the match that ignited the Buddhist revolution, but the fire from that single glow did more than any other event to engulf the regime. William Colby from the CIA later noted that the Saigon government "handled the Buddhist crisis fairly badly and allowed it to grow. But," he added, "I really don't think there was much they could have done about it once that bonze burned himself."[5] Diem now had to deal with the Buddhists' demands, which were consistent with a central theme of Vietnamese history: the restoration of the basic moral and social values of a Confucian society that, in this instance, the Ngo family had corrupted beyond repair. Heaven had mandated a revolution requiring Diem's demise.

The Diem regime reacted to the heightened crisis in a brusque manner that again demonstrated its failure to comprehend the great changes under way. Around 6 P.M. that nervous June 11, Saigon police arrested thirty nuns and half a dozen bonzes for refusing to move a prayer meeting from the street into nearby Xa Loi pagoda. The police encircled the pagoda, blocking public passage and leaving the impression that they were about to lay siege. In a nationwide radio address at 7 P.M., Diem pleaded for peace and then made the unfounded claim that he had already made significant progress toward resolving the Buddhist issue. In another ill-advised statement, he emphasized the role of personalism in government and thereby fed the fast-growing resentment for his rule. Extremist groups had twisted the facts, he insisted, but the Buddhists "can count on the Constitution, in other words, me."[6]

The moral magnitude of that fiery suicide in Saigon had not yet been registered by either American or South Vietnamese officials, both of whom simplistically defined the problem as politically inspired. Early assessments attached significance to the burning's taking place in front of the Cambodian embassy, which suggested that the Buddhists had staged the spectacle to attract that country's support. Trueheart thought so, as did another member of the Saigon embassy, Charles Flowerree, who linked the episode to the troubled relations between South Vietnam and Cambodia. In a speech on May 22, Prince Sihanouk had accused Diem of mistreating both Vietnamese and Khmer Buddhists. On June 9, the *Times of Vietnam*, which often spoke for Diem, had published an article pointing to the role of Cambodian bonzes in encouraging the Buddhist crisis in South Vietnam. This was, the writer angrily accused, all part of Cambodia's insidious policy to force neutralism on Vietnam. Flowerree reported that the Saigon government was "ready and eager to see a fine Cambodian hand in all the organized Buddhist actions."[7] Every criticism of the regime, its supporters insisted, was politically motivated, aimed at undermining Diem and facilitating a Vietcong conquest through the establishment of a neutralized South Vietnam.

The Saigon event had blindsided the Kennedy administration. "How could this have happened?" the president stormed to Forrestal. "Who are these people? Why didn't we know about them before?" U.S. advisers had not foreseen such profound repercussions of the Buddhist crisis. This was "one of my big mistakes, big misfortunes," Nolting lamented years afterward. Troubles had eased after the May 8 events in Hué, making it appear safe for him and his wife and two children to join their other two children in Greece for a long-postponed vacation. They departed on May 23, with Nolting intending to conclude his holiday with a consultation session in Washington. "During that period all hell broke loose in Vietnam." Nolting blamed the state department and Trueheart, "because they both knew exactly where I was every day and could have notified me if they had wanted me back as a mediator." But Harriman, according to Nolting, wanted him "out of there so that Diem would have enough rope to hang himself." Harkins agreed that Trueheart "wanted to get rid of Diem." Americans and South Vietnamese in responsible positions nonetheless expressed surprise at the depth of the trouble. Democratic Senator Frank Church from the Foreign Relations Committee showed no awareness of the repeated instances of self-immolation in Vietnamese history when he theatrically declared, "Such grisly scenes have not been witnessed since the Christian martyrs marched hand in hand into the Roman arenas." Years afterward, Trueheart made a revealing confession: "Nobody guessed the Buddhists had such an important role to play. We had zero knowledge of Buddhism." When the Nhus later attributed the monk's burning to his use of drugs, President Kennedy asked his advisers if that were so. Hilsman shallowly responded, "Religious fervor was an adequate explanation."[8]

The White House failed to see that the Buddhist revolt was attributable to a broadly based philosophy that considered worldly and other-worldly matters to be inseparable. Lacking any understanding of these people, U.S.

observers attempted to explain their motives in terms that were meaningful to Westerners. Hilsman was partially correct in detecting religious inspiration, but he did not grasp its vital relationship to temporal goals. Trueheart was equally accurate in citing political objectives—especially as the trouble escalated and Buddhist leaders sought changes in laws and government. But neither explanation by itself was adequate. The overwhelming number of Buddhists claimed no interest in political power and demanded changes in Saigon's leadership because it had violated the moral and ethical precepts of a just and orderly Confucian society. The name of the ruler did not matter. *Diem* would have been acceptable had he personified Heaven's virtues.

Regardless of the Buddhists' intentions, the immolation further hardened the regime and sorely tested the patience of the Kennedy administration. Ironically, the evening before, Diem had reasoned that the Buddhist matter was nearing resolution and stood prepared to issue a public pronouncement stating his government's final word on the matter. He had called an emergency cabinet meeting for 11:30 on the morning of June 11 to discuss the growing crisis. Indeed, Trueheart again had intended to urge Diem to make some "dramatic conciliatory gesture." But if Diem's attitude had ever been flexible, Trueheart declared, it was "drastically changed by [the] self-cremation of [the] bonze in Central Saigon." After news of the immolation reached Gia Long Palace, Diem canceled the cabinet meeting, choosing to confer with his ministers individually before calling them together in special session that afternoon. Trueheart had warned Thuan of the desperate need for concessions. Washington considered the situation "dangerously near the breaking point" and expected Diem to meet the Buddhists' demands. "No government in Viet-Nam can survive without their support." Unless Diem resolved this crisis "within the next few days," Rusk warned the Saigon embassy, the White House would publicly announce that it could no longer "associate itself" with the regime.[9]

The Buddhist crisis had pushed the Kennedy administration closer to ending its support of Diem and, paradoxically, into a more tangled involvement in Vietnam. The White House could not continue its normal supportive relationship with the present regime; and yet to cut off assistance would leave the impression that it was manipulating domestic affairs in an attempt to foment a coup. Diem's successor would owe his position to the Kennedy administration and take on the image of an even greater puppet than his predecessor. Hanoi had already boosted its propaganda campaign by sarcastically dubbing the Saigon government as *"My Diem,"* or American Diem. The premier had tried to cultivate an appearance of independence. But if he fell from power following the termination of U.S. aid, and if his successor entered office with the assurance of U.S. aid, the picture of U.S. domination would be complete. The White House had taken another step toward a deeper involvement that, as during its military buildup, aimed at reversing the American commitment but had instead made it larger and more direct. Rusk pointedly told Trueheart: "If Diem does not take prompt and effective steps to reestablish Buddhist confidence in him we will have to reexamine our entire relationship with his regime."[10]

President Kennedy recognized the extent of the danger but angrily demanded more caution than did his advisers. He was upset about more than the turn of events. In an astounding move, Rusk had not informed the president of the threatened break with Diem. Kennedy learned of this pivotal action only after it appeared in CIA summary form on the President's Intelligence Checklist—*two days after the directive had reached the Saigon embassy.* On reading that the state department had authorized a threat of disassociation, he became irate that his advisers had made this monumental move without consulting him. From now on, he hotly declared in a White House meeting, "[I want] to be absolutely sure that no further threats are made and no formal statement is made without [my] own personal approval."[11]

A Buddhist delegation from Hué had meanwhile boarded a plane for the 400-mile trip to Saigon, hoping to open negotiations shortly after its scheduled arrival at 1:15 on the afternoon of June 12. Thuan expressed concern about another public spectacle. Did the Buddhists plan another demonstration? Thuan also remained apprehensive about Diem's response to the peace overture. Would the premier further delay remedial action and inflame the already tense situation? Among the Buddhists were the elderly head monk Thich Tinh Khiet and the youthful activist monk Tri Quang. Thuan regarded Tri Quang as a gifted demagogue and "the real spark plug" of the trouble in Hué. Nolting thought him a "communist agent." According to most accounts, Tri Quang had long advocated South Vietnam's neutralism in an effort to remove it from Cold War struggles. Thuan feared another outbreak of trouble; word had reached the Saigon government that the Buddhist delegation intended to stir up popular excitement by walking from the airport into the city.[12]

Diem had underestimated the Buddhists' tenacity. The tension had eased following the past week's discussions, leading him to believe that he could resolve the problem by reaffirming minor concessions already made. Even the immolation had failed to awaken the regime to the danger. No major protests had occurred in its wake, suggesting that the monk's death constituted the Buddhists' final shot. After all, they had called for negotiations, which Diem considered a sign of weakness. Trueheart had correctly warned that the renewed calm would cause the government to "again conclude that it can get out of this affair on the cheap." He offered to meet with Diem before his instructions went to negotiators. Thuan recommended that Trueheart "talk as tough" to Diem as he had to him. Encouraging news came that the Buddhists had not dramatized their arrival. Their delegation had ridden by car from the airport and was now in Xa Loi pagoda.[13]

In meeting with Diem that day, Trueheart dutifully warned that without major concessions to the Buddhists, the Kennedy administration would publicly repudiate his government. Such a statement, Diem countered, would wreck the negotiations. Trueheart pleaded for a ban on all public religious processions. Diem could not do this. The next day, June 13, was the Fete de Dieu (Corpus Christi), which was the only ceremonial day on which the Catholic liturgy called for processions. A ban at this time would alienate the Catholics. Trueheart argued that the move would placate the Buddhists. Diem refused to bend.[14]

Problems clouded the negotiations as soon as the Buddhists contacted the palace. In response to their recent letter asking "to proceed rapidly to a satisfactory arrangement," Vice President Tho proposed a meeting with the Interministerial Committee on June 13, the day following the Buddhists' arrival; but they requested a delay because of Khiet's weak physical condition, worsened by the flight. The Buddhists agreed to meet on June 14, provided that the Saigon government accepted in advance their version of the June 4 agreement. In particular, they demanded revocation of the stipulation that only local officials could authorize flag displays. The pagodas, for centuries regarded as communal property in the hamlets, must come under Buddhist administration. Rather than wait for the National Assembly to amend Decree Number 10, as earlier agreed, they wanted the change immediately enacted by presidential decree. Thuan argued that the Buddhists' interpretation of terms differed from that of the government. Consequently, the Interministerial Committee refused to approve the above as a prerequisite to a meeting. It would assemble at three that afternoon to draft a reply incorporating the government's understanding of the agreement along with a proposal to meet with the Buddhists the following day. That same June 12, the National Assembly established a committee to determine how to revise Decree Number 10.[15]

Trueheart agreed that the government's view of the agreements fitted that given him at the time of the June 4 negotiations, but he did not believe this issue should obstruct a meeting with the Buddhists. They had presented a paper claiming the government's total acceptance of the five points. Diem, however, had made no commitment to these terms—as shown by Thich Minh's insistence on returning to Hué to present the matter before his superiors. But a hard-line reply to the Buddhists at this sensitive moment would give them an excuse to break off talks if that was their aim. Trueheart recommended that the Interministerial Committee accept the Buddhists' position in a "spirit of amity" and then meet with them to clarify the issues. Thuan liked the suggestion and would try that afternoon to win Diem's approval.[16]

The outlook appeared promising despite nagging problems. Not surprisingly, Diem rejected Trueheart's conciliatory approach as an implied acceptance of the Buddhists' demands. The Interministerial Committee thereupon drafted a reply that quoted from an earlier Buddhist letter asserting that no agreement had resulted from the June 4 negotiations, and calling for a meeting at nine the next morning, on June 14. The Buddhists accepted the proposal, sending a strong signal that they wanted a settlement. By lunchtime on June 14, the two parties had reached agreement on the most difficult of the five demands, that relating to the flag, and they seemed on the way to resolving the other four issues. Khiet issued a nationwide order urging all Buddhists to avoid any action that could endanger the talks. Diem directed government officials throughout South Vietnam to remove all barriers around the temples. That evening, the two sides agreed on revisions to Decree Number 10.[17] Once again, the antagonists seemed to have taken a major step toward resolving their differences. But this appearance, once again, proved illusory.

II

THE KENNEDY ADMINISTRATION's troubles with the Diem regime had meanwhile become a public issue, enhancing pressure on Washington to halt aid. "U.S. Warns South Viet-Nam on Demands of Buddhists," trumpeted the headline of a June 14 front-page story by Max Frankel in the *New York Times* that Rusk immediately forwarded to Saigon. In the "bluntest terms," Frankel wrote on the basis of information leaked by high government officials in Washington, U.S. diplomats had severely criticized Diem's government for not recognizing the legitimacy of the Buddhists' grievances. General Harkins had ordered his 12,000 military advisers and support personnel to deny assistance to ARVN units taking action against the demonstrators. In the past two weeks, the crisis had escalated into a widespread political protest that drew the support of Diem's other opponents as well. And yet his government remained "less than candid" in assuring remedies. Consequently, the White House had threatened to publicly disavow Diem if he did not negotiate a settlement. Three days later, a *New York Times* editorial proclaimed that if Diem "cannot genuinely represent a majority then he is not the man to be President."[18]

The seeming imminence of Diem's fall from power opened a spirited debate within the Kennedy administration over what its reaction should be. Some advisers wanted to implement the May 23 contingency plan by secretly notifying Vice President Tho that the White House supported his ascension to power—*before* Diem's government had collapsed. Hilsman went so far as to outline the procedure for informing Tho. "In view of the present precarious situation it would seem worthwhile to run the risk of delivering such a message now, assuming Tho would not likely consider it in his interest to inform anyone else." Tho, however, did not appeal to everyone. Taylor found Tho "unimpressive," as did a state department official who dismissed him as a "nonentity."[19]

On June 16, the Saigon government reached a formal agreement with the Buddhists that Trueheart nonetheless doubted could save the regime. "If we find Diem in a mood to freeze up, rather than move forward, then I think his days are indeed numbered and we must begin to make moves." One source had recently notified the embassy that Vietnamese Air Force Chief of Staff Lieutenant Colonel Do Khac Mai (a Buddhist) had joined other senior officers in thinking that Americans in Vietnam had a splendid opportunity to overthrow the government. In addition, the embassy continued to receive a steady barrage of unsubstantiated information regarding a coup threat. "It is to be expected in such circumstances that one is never in contact with the people (if any) who really mean business, but we have all the lines out that we know how to put out and have had for some days." Trueheart urged the White House to put pressure on Diem to accept the Buddhist uprising as a "blessing in disguise" and use the June 16 settlement as a step toward making concessions to other dissatisfied groups as well. His regime must regain popular support before the parliamentary elections in August.[20]

Trueheart's caution seemed wise. The Saigon government had reached an agreement with the Buddhists on all five demands, but the terms were vague and, smugly asserted Diem, contained nothing that he had not already accepted. According to the "Joint Communiqué," the national flag "should always be respected and be put at its appropriate place." The National Assembly would consult with religious groups in an effort to remove them "from the regulations of Ordinance No. 10," and it would establish new guidelines appropriate to their religious activities. The two parties agreed to form an investigative committee to "re-examine" the Buddhists' grievances, and Diem promised to pardon those who had participated in the protests. No longer was government approval needed for "normal and purely religious activities" within either the pagodas or the headquarters of the General Association of Buddhists. An inquiry would follow into the incidents after those in Hué, with punishment meted to government officials held responsible. In a face-saving effort, Diem signed the agreement just below a paragraph declaring that "the articles written in this joint communiqué have been approved in principle by me from the beginning."[21] Again Diem missed the point. A wide gulf remained between approval in principle and implementation into practice.

The two sides had negotiated the Joint Communiqué against a background of renewed violence at Xa Loi pagoda. That same day of June 16, a riot broke out shortly after nine in the morning when about 250 Buddhist students among a crowd of 2,000 charged the police still ringing the area, pelting them with rocks and retreating only when hit with tear gas, fire hoses, clubs, and shots fired in the air. By 11 A.M. the police had restored order, but at the cost of one death and a host of injured Buddhists and policemen. Moderates from both camps urged calm. The government blamed "extremist elements," an assessment that drew surprising agreement in a Buddhist announcement broadcast over loudspeakers. An Associated Press story described the riot as "the most violent anti-Government outburst in South Viet-Nam in years." U.S. embassy officers at the scene absolved the police of blame for the violence, suggesting that popular resentment for Diem's regime had swelled beyond the settlement's capacity to contain.[22]

Other signs indicated, however, that both sides preferred a peaceful solution. Not only did this episode wind down without further trouble, but no disturbances had occurred during the highly publicized June 19 funeral for the martyred bonze. Both government and Buddhist leaders had worked to restrain their followers' anger. No large crowds gathered either at the pagodas, along the route of the procession, or at the cemetery. Buddhist leaders had directed their people to stay away, and government radio had also helped to keep attendance down. Other than the barricades for the funeral route, Saigon appeared normal.[23]

But now, in a strange twist of logic, White House advisers became concerned that the Buddhist settlement exposed weaknesses in the Saigon government that could undermine its war against the Vietcong. Diem's ability to keep domestic order, they surmised, had come only after he made major concessions to a splintered movement of religious zealots. Like the Diem regime, U.S. advisers still underestimated the power of the Buddhists. President Kennedy's confused reaction to the monk's immolation on June 11 had signified his own advisers' failure to grasp the fervor of the Buddhists. Even the most loyal of Diem's supporters in Washington now admitted to the futility in hanging on to a sinking government. The White House continued to believe that a broadened commitment to Vietnam provided the quickest avenue to a reduced involvement. This time, however, the administration was prepared to go farther than a military escalation; it now sought to manipulate the leadership of the host regime. Such a step raised the possibility of either retreating at the cost of credibility and losing the war or advancing at the risk of taking over both the government and the war.

The Buddhists' success in the negotiations had led Hilsman to call for a "very hard-hitting approach to Diem." Until the May 8 incident at Hué, he declared, the U.S. government and public were confident that the Diem regime would defeat the Vietcong. "This favorable trend has now been dangerously reversed," putting the White House into the uncomfortable position of having to defend its Vietnam policy before a hostile Congress. Diem's blunt assertion that *he* was the Constitution had aroused angry indignation in the United States. What happened to the democracy that the Kennedy administration had made synonymous with Diem's rule? Any attempt by his regime to renege on the agreements would have "grave effects." The Buddhists "are well organized and have not permitted the Communists or political opposition elements to take control. They are a disciplined and peaceful people who must be treated without suspicion." Madame Nhu's continuing stream of critical statements had deepened Washington's concern about relations with South Vietnam. Diem must show his people that he headed a "reasonable Government dedicated to assisting, not harassing them and to preserving law and order without employing means so strong or so irritating as to cause divisions and dissensions." He must act soon. The entire aid program was "in jeopardy."[24]

Years afterward, Nolting regretted this stern action. "All of this I think could have been resolved." Instead, the United States "all of a sudden began to hammer the table on hotheaded instructions from Washington, burned into action by the American press, to get on with it and tell this guy to apologize and eat crow and do things that he couldn't possibly afford to do as president of the country, which also would not have done any good." By this time, the Buddhist movement had fallen into the hands of militants, who sought only to overthrow the government. And this was, of course, "the exact objective of the Vietcong." The two groups were "absolutely parallel" in their goals. "Whether they were united is a question which I've never been able to determine."[25]

A state department intelligence study included in the president's weekend reading file warned that the Diem regime was in mortal danger. Domestic stability hinged on Diem's implementing the June 16 agreements. Not all Buddhists were free of political aims. Some called for non-Communist and even Communist support in toppling the regime. No evidence suggested that the Communists or any other political group had caused the unrest; but the Communists were "waiting expectantly in the wings for a propitious moment to capitalize on developments." The Saigon government had instructed local officials to regard the agreements as a "tactical retreat" that bought time for Diem to regain a firm position before squelching the Buddhists. If the concessions were a ruse, the protests would break out anew, posing a greater threat to the regime than the insurgency itself. "Vietnamese Buddhism, however diluted with Confucianism, animism, and Taoism, and institutionally fragmented, is deeply set in the social and cultural consciousness of the Vietnamese people." Any threat to Buddhism, especially coming from a "non-Buddhist minority," could draw "a more personal and spontaneous response from the ordinary Vietnamese peasant than Viet Cong political propaganda."[26]

The study, as Kennedy learned, found a coup likely and even desirable. Ill feeling ran rampant in both the bureaucracy and the army over the leadership's mishandling of the Buddhists and, combined with widespread popular dissatisfaction with Diem, could lead to a coup. If masterminded by upper-level civil and military officials, a coup had a good chance for success: They were themselves predominantly Buddhists and strong supporters of the counterinsurgency program. The saving factor in this volatile situation was that Diem's greatest threat lay among those whose chief motive was to win the war. His successor would probably come from either a military junta or in the person of Vice President Tho, who would work with the army in seizing control. Tho had good rapport with the military and was "also competent and widely respected in and outside the government."[27]

America's interventionist policies had put the Kennedy administration in a precarious position, for any stance it took toward Diem would determine whether a coup took place. Both the coup conspirators and those still undecided about which side to support looked to Washington for guidance. White House action or inaction constituted a signal to everyone involved. Silence or even an assertion that the revolt was a domestic matter best left alone by the United States would appear to be an endorsement of the coup. Any indication that the administration did not uphold Diem would encourage a coup. If the government collapsed, the White House would have considerable influence over the selection of Diem's successor. On the other side, U.S. support for Diem would discourage a coup. But such a move, the state department study warned, would come at a heavy price. "A victory in these circumstances would greatly reinforce Diem's view that he is indispensable, that he knows best what the situation requires, and that he cannot trust anyone outside his immediate family."[28]

Diem remained stubbornly self-righteous and blindly loyal to family, and he hesitated to implement the peace settlement. Although "slightly heated" at Trueheart for claiming that the Nhus sought to sabotage the June 16 agreements, he attributed this accusation to the exorbitant political pressure on President Kennedy. Diem asserted that his government was releasing prisoners as quickly as processing allowed, but he refused to free known Communists. Diem also groused about discharging those who had thrown rocks at the police. Trueheart urged him to look at the larger issue of a potential break with the White House. Diem recognized the danger, but refused to compromise.[29]

The White House saw no alternative to adopting a hard-line position toward Diem that it knew could encourage a coup. The Buddhists had negotiated a peace based on their five demands. The Diem regime had accepted the agreement, only to withhold its implementation. American domestic opposition to the aid program had grown, threatening to inflict a serious blow to the Kennedy administration's foreign policy. The Cold War had meanwhile intensified because of the rapidly growing East–West rivalry over Berlin. U.S. credibility was again on the line, dictating that the White House could not survive another setback similar to those reverses already sustained in Cuba and Laos. The dire situation in South Vietnam had a bright side, however: Respectable military and civilian figures had become associated with coup rumors. A leadership change in Saigon now appeared to be the only way to restore domestic peace and win the war.

These realities necessitated a change in U.S. policy that began with the appointment of Henry Cabot Lodge, Jr., as new ambassador to South Vietnam. A dashing and debonair Boston Brahmin, Lodge was a Republican who had lost the 1952 Senate race to Kennedy and then had run as vice president under Richard Nixon in 1960, only to lose again to the Kennedy ticket. Lodge then spent the year 1962 on active duty as a brigadier general in the Army Reserves, writing policy papers on Vietnam. Not the least of Lodge's attractions was his affiliation with the Republican party. If the U.S. program failed in South Vietnam, it made good sense to the president that the opposing political party should share in that failure. And the prospects were not good. In his mid-June meeting with Lodge, Kennedy glumly referred to the infamous picture of the Buddhist monk on fire in Saigon. The Diem regime, according to the president, had entered its "terminal phase."[30]

Lodge agreed to serve both as ambassador and, in a pivotal move, as the president's "personal representative." Lodge would report directly to Kennedy rather than to Rusk. Indeed, the head of the CIA, John McCone, believed that Lodge had private instructions from President Kennedy to warn Diem that if he failed to get rid of his brother and change his government, the new ambassador was to "use his influence to bring about a change in the top leadership." Why else would Kennedy make an ambassador his personal representative other than to ensure secrecy regarding his involvement in an overthrow?[31]

Lodge's appointment greatly disturbed Diem, who trusted Nolting and preferred that he stay. "Does your departure mean that the American government has changed its policy from what you and I agreed two and one half years ago?" "No, Mr. President, it does not," Nolting answered. In a remarkable display of either naïveté or the art of lying, the outgoing ambassador maintained the fiction of White House loyalty to the premier. Diem was not convinced. When Nolting presented a telegram from Rusk affirming a continuation of policy, the premier cryptically noted, "Mr. Ambassador, I believe you, but I don't believe the telegram that you have received."[32]

The appointment of a new ambassador, combined with growing U.S. pressure for reforms, made Diem suspicious that the United States intended to unseat him. Diem's fears rested on a firm foundation. Changes in diplomatic posts usually signaled a change in policy. For too long, Diem complained, the Kennedy administration had called for democratic reforms that he as a mandarin could not deliver. Furthermore, to institute such changes in wartime was to invite disaster. Not only might he lose the war, but he would also lose office. "They can send ten Lodges," Diem hotly proclaimed to Thuan, "but I will not permit myself or my country to be humiliated, not if they train their artillery on this Palace." Diem's stubbornness, Thuan moaned to Trueheart, guaranteed "head-to-head confrontations." The state department tried to reassure Diem that Nolting had completed his agreed two-year term in Saigon and that Lodge's name had been under consideration since late April—*before* the May 8 incident in Hué. Lodge's appointment, the Kennedy administration insisted, ensured bipartisan support for its Vietnam policy. These statements were true, but they did not reflect reality. The White House believed that Nolting had become too close to Diem, whom the mild-mannered George Ball later termed "a weak, third-rate bigot."[33]

Diem was correct in regarding Lodge's appointment as a threat. The administration's chief defense of the new appointment suggested a hidden agenda. The White House had chosen someone from the opposition Republican party, signifying the need for bipartisan support for an imminent shift in strategy toward South Vietnam. Lodge would have a direct pipeline to the president, implying Kennedy's intention to bypass the state department in shaping a new policy. Given the spate of coup rumors, the president and his advisers knew that a change in ambassadors would encourage Diem's opposition to believe that the United States no longer stood with him. Lodge's appointment set in motion a chain of events that pointed to Diem's demise.

III

WHITE HOUSE CONCERN about a coup was warranted. In addition to the constant flow of rumors, a CIA contact in Saigon had learned on June 25 that the Dai Viet, a non-Communist opposition group in the central provinces, had met that day with "leading Buddhist officials" and won their support for a coup. The Dai Viet, a tightly organized and long-time conspiratorial society, had splintered into several factions after collaborating with the French before their departure from South Vietnam during the mid-1950s. Its members had vainly resisted Diem in 1955 and then participated in the abortive coup of November 1960. At the outset of the Buddhist crisis, the Dai Viet had conferred with its activist leaders and then with CIA agents about securing U.S. support for a coup that, according to the society, had ARVN backing. Indeed, several Dai Viet members were influential army officers who had provided the information that fueled Halberstam's criticisms of the regime. The CIA unofficially recommended that the Dai Viet contact the U.S. mission in Saigon. When one of its representatives did so that same day, the mission's spokesperson followed Washington's directives in affirming support of Diem. The Dai Viet hotly called this the "last chance for a non-Communist political solution." Embassy officials believed there was "substance to the plot" but that the Dai Viet's leaders remained hesitant because of their inability to secure U.S. and ARVN support.[34]

The Dai Viet scheme might have stalled, but it provided further proof that Diem was in deeper trouble than at any other time during his checkered reign. As the CIA asserted, the Buddhist crisis had catalyzed the growing unrest over his "Catholic-oriented regime." Only circumstantial evidence substantiated Diem's charge that the Communists had instigated the Buddhists' protests. It seemed certain, however, that both Hanoi and the Vietcong had exploited the turmoil. Communist propaganda insisted that all religious groups had joined youths and students in supporting the disturbances. On June 16, the day of the Joint Communiqué, church dignitaries read a pastoral letter in all Roman Catholic churches of the Saigon Archdiocese that supported the Buddhists' call for religious freedom. The Buddhist clash had divided the government along religious lines. Vice President Tho and three other cabinet members were avowed Buddhists, as were numerous generals and an overwhelming majority of the soldiers. Continued government focus on the Buddhists would further divert its attention from the war.[35]

Diem was engaged in his own war for survival. The open door in Laos was a great boon to the Communist insurgency in South Vietnam, making it vital that he tighten domestic control. Diem could not approve political and social reforms at this critical juncture. Pleas for a broadened government that included members of the opposition, appeals to remove his brother Ngo Dinh Can along with Nhu and his wife from positions of prominence, the acceptance of opposition delegates in the National Assembly—these and other proposals Diem flatly rejected. He would not turn against family and he could not ignore the powerful groups these people controlled: Can's tightly organized "Movement of National Revolution" that allowed him to run the central provinces like a virtual warlord; Nhu's veritable "praetorian guard," the Republican Youth Organization, and his darkly secretive Can Lao party; and Madame Nhu's highly spirited Women's Solidarity Movement, "a paramilitary organization of 25,000 blue-uniformed amazons," according to Newsweek. Still another brother, Ngo Dinh Thuc, was Archbishop of Hué, where he wielded arbitrary power both as church leader and as head of major businesses. Diem was in a perilous position. Granting reforms would invite his enemies into the government and lead to his downfall. Refusal to make changes would cost U.S. support. Much of his opposition considered his overthrow as critical to winning the war.[36]

Through it all, Diem demonstrated an uncanny inability to recognize realities. In a two-and-a-half-hour evening meeting with Trueheart and Thuan in late June, the premier spoke of democratizing South Vietnam from the bottom up and pointed to the Strategic Hamlet Program as the chief instrument for achieving this revolution. Within three years, Vietnam would become "a model of democracy for all of Southeast Asia." Diem ignored Trueheart's entreaties to reaffirm support for the June 16 agreements before the Buddhists renewed their demonstrations. Trueheart referred to the full-page denunciation of the Diem regime in the June 27 edition of the *New York Times* that he had given to Thuan the night before. Twelve prominent U.S. clergymen, including Dr. Reinhold Niebuhr, had affixed their signatures beneath a copy of Browne's lurid photograph of Quang Duc burning himself alive in Saigon.[37]

The surging crisis led Forrestal to urge the president to approve an earlier arrival of Lodge. Nolting should return to Saigon immediately and close out his tenure, allowing Lodge to assume his duties in early August rather than September. "We all believe one more burning bonze will cause [a] domestic U.S. reaction which will require [a] strong public statement despite [the] danger that this might precipitate [a] coup in Saigon."[38]

The most exasperating aspect of America's involvement in Vietnam was the long list of contradictory assessments that continued to baffle the president. Although negative reports kept pouring in from the CIA, the Saigon embassy, and others on the scene, the military maintained its forecast of victory. Krulak praised the counterinsurgency campaign, insisting that the Strategic Hamlet Program had pacified villagers and thereby undercut the Vietcong. Anti-Diem groups had attempted to exploit the Buddhist crisis as a "Buddha-sent opportunity" to attack the premier. But the internal troubles had not hampered the war effort. The "shooting part of the war" was moving to a climax, leading Harkins to believe that the army could go ahead with the administration's plan to remove the first thousand U.S. military forces by the end of the year.[39]

At the same time, however, President Kennedy's civilian advisers had called for an *immediate* change in ambassadors, even if the move suggested an imminent severance of relations with South Vietnam. Diem could not survive another Buddhist uprising. A U.S. break with Diem would constitute the first step toward the installation of a new premier, a fact well known to the president and his advisers. Most important, Diem was aware of this fact. Trueheart repeated his assertion that a threat of disassociation would have no impact on Diem; his government had just made the outlandish charge that Quang Duc had committed suicide while under the influence of drugs. Tho feared that the Vietcong had infiltrated the Buddhists and had pushed them into seeking political objectives. Minister of the Interior Bui Van Luong alleged that all government ministers had received threatening letters, mostly anonymous, and that he had not had a "family life" for more than two months. Trueheart would try to see Nhu after talking with Diem but expected "another outburst." Ball agreed that a stern warning to Diem might harden his resistance to change. "If he is so incapable of rational consideration of what we believe are the extreme dangers of the Buddhist crisis, and can only behave emotionally, then we have no confidence in his ability to lead an effective fight against the Viet Cong."[40]

President Kennedy recognized the necessity of sending Lodge to Saigon without delay. He agreed with his advisers—Ball, Harriman, Hilsman, Forrestal, and McGeorge Bundy—that getting rid of the Nhus was not possible. Hilsman noted that the Buddhists might push their demands to the point that Diem's fall became certain. The next four months, he predicted, would see a number of coup attempts. President Kennedy believed it important that Lodge finish his briefings and his counterinsurgency course by mid-August.[41]

The president's haste was justified. On July 3, the CIA reported a plot to kill the Nhus, even though it "should be taken with a considerable amount of reserve." According to "an alleged opposition group," unnamed military leaders had planned to assassinate the Nhus, perhaps during a strategic hamlet inspection, and then to convince Diem to work with them in constructing a broadly based regime. They claimed to have close ties with Buddhist figures, particularly the president and the secretary of the delegation who had negotiated with the Saigon government. The next day in Saigon, Lucien Conein, a veteran of the Office of Strategic Services (forerunner of the CIA) in World War II and now a CIA agent who had served under Lansdale's command in Vietnam during the mid-1950s, learned that a coup was in the works and that its makers were the most respected military figures in the country. General Don, Acting Chief of Staff of Vietnamese Armed Forces, and his brother-in-law, General Le Van Kim, had already discussed the necessity of a coup with ARVN field commander General Minh and the Army Chief of Staff, General Tran Thien Khiem. The CIA informed Washington that the new regime "might be initially less effective against the Viet Cong but, given support from the U.S., could provide reasonably effective leadership for the government and the war effort."[42]

Pressure for Diem's overthrow received another impetus when, immediately after a Buddhist ceremony at Saigon's Chantareansey pagoda on the Sunday morning of July 7, an altercation broke out between plainclothes police and U.S. journalists. July 7 was Double Seven Day, the seventh day of the seventh month, and it marked the anniversary of Diem's ascension to the premiership. Instead of a day of gala celebration, it turned ugly. The night before had started in a festive mood as thirteen military officers received decorations at an awards ceremony. But the atmosphere abruptly changed the next day, when several of those on the scene—including Browne, Sheehan, and Halberstam, along with mission personnel—affirmed that the Buddhists had alerted the press of the ceremony beforehand. Indeed, CBS had mounted a camera and lights in the window of the pagoda. After an hour-long session, the Buddhists filed out of the pagoda and through a narrow alley toward the street, where the plainclothes police abruptly moved in their path and ordered them to stop. The Buddhists, Trueheart declared, put up no serious protest. AP reporter Peter Arnett and others began photographing the confrontation, whereupon the plainclothesmen punched him in the face, knocked him to the ground, and smashed his camera. Halberstam, about eight inches taller than the police, jumped into the fray, swinging at them and screaming, "Get back, get back, you sons of bitches, or I'll beat the shit out of you!" The police ran away but not before Browne, having climbed up a power pole, snapped a picture of Arnett's bloody face and circulated the photo in the United States. Trueheart asserted that the uniformed police had "tacitly" helped the plainclothesmen, but he also had "no doubt that [the] reporters, at least once [the] fracas had started, acted in [a] belligerent manner towards [the] police." They hotly accused the Saigon regime of provoking this incident and, in a stormy meeting that same day in the U.S. embassy, demanded that it deliver a formal protest to Diem. Trueheart declined to do so, infuriating his visitors by blaming both sides for the incident.[43]

The journalists angrily demanded Diem's removal. Browne joined Halberstam, Sheehan, and Peter Kalischer of CBS News in writing a letter to President Kennedy, complaining that the regime had begun an all-out intimidation campaign against reporters. As Diem's police became more aggressive, the correspondents sought U.S. protection. Since the embassy had refused to file a protest, the signatories asked the president to do so.[44]

The situation worsened when Diem issued a proclamation on Double Seven Day, blithely announcing that the "problems raised by the General Association of Buddhists have just been settled." Then he capitalized this baseless claim by firing a round of inflammatory rhetoric. Lingering troubles he attributed to the "underground intervention of international red agents and Communist fellow travelers who in collusion with fascist ideologues disguised as democrats were surreptitiously seeking to revive and rekindle disunity at home while arousing public opinion against us abroad." The "ideologues" undoubtedly referred to the Dai Viet, who had been his long-time enemies, but his wide net of castigation included all those who had berated him. Diem trusted no one but family and now considered himself a martyr.[45]

The White House did not know what to do. The deadline for implementation of the agreement with the Buddhists had expired. One Buddhist charged the government's secret police with forcing his people to sign confessions that they were Communists or under their influence. In this tense atmosphere, the Diem regime sent a ringing message to its critics. It put to trial nineteen ARVN soldiers accused of participation in the coup attempt of 1960. In the course of the trial, the prosecution charged in closed session that the United States had been involved in the plot. The U.S. embassy immediately denied complicity. Its members appeared so indecisive that the current joke in Saigon was that the American mission was like a log drifting downstream covered with ants, each one thinking he is steering.[46]

The highly sensitive political situation had spawned several coup plots but, most important, one engineered by the military because of the failing war effort. According to the CIA, the Buddhist protest "may well have transformed itself into an entirely new political force whose aims transcend the basically religious purposes for which it was originally set in motion." Tri Quang had assumed a greater leadership role and now claimed that he would not stop until the government fell. He intended to call for "suicide volunteers." Three coup groups were working together in exploiting the Buddhist crisis: one led by Lieutenant Colonel Pham Ngoc Thao, former chief of Kien Hoa Province and Nhu's special investigator for the strategic hamlets; a second organized but not led by Tran Kim Tuyen, former head of presidential security and, according to a CIA analyst, a master of "dirty tricks"; and a third that was primarily military in makeup and included Generals Minh and Don. In June of 1963, Minh and Don had visited Thailand to observe SEATO exercises, where they fully grasped the international furor over the Diem regime's repression of the Buddhists. On returning to Vietnam, the two generals began building support for a coup. They planned a palace revolution, asserted the CIA, that hinged on the assassination of the Nhus and the "elimination" of Diem "by less forceable means if possible, but by assassination if necessary." Their goal was to install a military ruler who would actually be under the control of an advisory committee of three. Elections would take place within six months of the takeover. The military found it necessary to take decisive action before the Vietcong won the war.[47]

Truth can be stranger than fiction, as shown by a CIA report that *Nhu* had presented a coup plan to the army's leadership. Before a meeting of all fifteen ARVN general officers on July 11, Nhu criticized their handling of the Buddhist crisis and questioned their loyalty to the regime. The Vietnamese must win the war on their own, he told the senior officers. In a bitter allusion to the United States, he warned that it might push for a negotiated settlement that granted victory to the Communists. Nhu then astounded his listeners by promising his support if the army launched a coup. "All general officers" must stage a "lightning fast" coup at night that would probably amount to only a "show of force" and then, the following day, hand over governmental control to the civilians. The government, he declared, had made no progress in the war, and the general officers had been humiliated. To regain respect, they must engineer a coup. Nhu insisted that he did not agree with his brother or his administration, but he had no power to change matters. Rapid action was necessary since the new U.S. ambassador would soon arrive, authorized to make policy changes in accordance with a successor government that would favor American interests. The army must lead a coup and stop the "ringleaders" of the Buddhist uprising who "had used their religion to further their own ambitions and designs."[48]

For good reason, the CIA was dubious about Nhu's sincerity. Nothing in the record suggests a schism between Nhu and Diem that could pit brother against brother. But it would not be surprising to see the two siblings conspiring against the military in a charade intended to uncover which officers promoted a coup. Nor would it be out of character for Nhu, though still not trying to unseat his brother, to pursue such clandestine activity without informing him beforehand. The CIA thought Diem unaware of Nhu's discussion with the generals and, in fact, "a complete prisoner of his brother." The generals were suspicious of Nhu. About five of them seemed to favor his remarks, but only "because they owed their advancement personally to Nhu." Most of them reacted negatively, primarily because "Nhu had treated the generals as though they were children." One considered the proposal "another Nhu maneuver" and acidly remarked, "Why did he hold such a meeting now, after years of criticizing and undermining army leadership?" General Nguyen Ngoc Le told Nhu: "You say that you do not agree with the government but the people say that you are concerned with all decisions made." Le remarked the next day that the Nhus wanted only to save themselves and that the generals should proceed without Nhu. The CIA tended to agree with its agents and the U.S. embassy in declaring that if the generals went along with Nhu's proposal, it would be "a temporary marriage of convenience." Rusk thought that any move by the generals to cooperate with Nhu in a coup "would most likely be [a] tactical maneuver . . . intended [to] neutralize Nhu with [the] objective [of] disposing of him at [the] moment [of] their own choosing." The CIA concluded that Nhu sought to "entrap the generals" and perhaps with Diem's knowledge.[49]

Whatever the truth of this bizarre episode, the rush of events had outpaced the Saigon regime's capacity to cope with either the Vietcong or the domestic troubles. Diem's own military was riddled with dissension, some officers so brazen as to talk openly of a coup as vital to winning the war.

His closest advisers were also deeply divided. The Nhus opposed the June 16 agreements; Thuan and Tho supported them. Further repression of the Buddhists, Diem's more moderate cabinet officials feared, would provide his enemies with a pretext for conspiring against him. Failure to take strong action would attract foreign criticism from those peoples already inclined to sympathize with the Buddhists. Moreover, the Buddhists might interpret conciliatory offers as a sign of weakness and make further demands. Most important, Diem's brusque temperament and stiff mandarin training prohibited concessions; U.S. pressure was not likely to change his mind.[50]

Diem's waning chances for survival posed an enormous dilemma for the White House. Harriman and Hilsman warned against confusing U.S. interests with those of Diem's: The White House must support him if he seemed likely to prevail but drop him if he appeared likely to fall. Forrestal advocated a policy of "fence sitting, realizing of course that such a policy constitutes something less than full identification between our own interests and those of President Diem." Nolting (who returned to his post on July 11) must prod Diem into adopting reforms. "It is, perhaps, the last effort we can make in this direction and should be taken if only for that reason." The war against the Vietcong was "the part of the iceberg which is under water."[51] The White House intended to pursue a hands-off policy, still not realizing that neutrality toward a coup sent a signal of support for that coup.

U.S. intelligence saw little hope. In a Special National Intelligence Estimate put together by the CIA and a mix of intelligence groups from the state and defense departments, the army, navy, air force, and the National Security Agency, its investigators echoed the familiar refrain: Diem's failure to implement the June 16 agreements guaranteed more demonstrations and the likelihood of a coup.[52]

IV

AS IF A SELF-FULFILLING PROPHECY, the Buddhist demonstrations erupted anew, culminating again in violence in Saigon. More than a hundred bonzes gathered in front of the U.S. embassy at nine on the morning of July 16, in support of a bonze's plea for U.S. help in persuading Diem to comply with the June 16 agreements. The Buddhists, shouted the bonze in English, were not Vietcong; they were anti-Communists who had vehemently protested against the government's program of terror. With both the local and international press present, the Buddhists chanted while waving signs proclaiming, "Buddhist flag must be for all Buddhists"; "Request government keep its promises faithfully"; "Free world and USA are expected to do anything possible for Buddhist problem." More human sacrifices would follow if Buddhist demands went unmet, the bonze warned a crowd of nearly 500 spectators, including a substantial number of uniformed police and plainclothesmen. By 11 A.M. the spirited gathering had dispersed without incident, with the bonzes and nuns entering Xa Loi pagoda to begin a two-day fast. The next morning, however, renewed demonstrations escalated into a near riot in the Chinese district of the city known as Cholon. At Giac Minh pagoda, Americans observed the police, with no provocation from the Buddhists, kick, slug, and club bonzes and lay persons before arresting many of them and forcing them onto trucks, only to continue the beatings as the captives cowered on the floors of the vehicles. The police then stripped the loudspeaker and banners from the pagoda and sealed off the area with barbed wire.[53]

Once again, confronted by the specter of spreading violence, Diem appeared ready to make concessions. Nolting insisted that radicals had seized control of the Buddhist movement and sought Diem's overthrow. The Buddhists might not have had any connection with the military's coup talk, but they were certainly aware of it. The CIA described Diem as "considerably disturbed" that Lodge's appointment signaled the beginning of a "big stick" policy. Diem finally agreed to make a general appeal for calm and to guarantee religious toleration and implementation of the June 16 agreements. If Diem carried out these assurances, Nolting asserted, the regime might survive its "two-headed crisis" of "Buddhist agitation and coup plotting."[54]

At the behest of the Interministerial Committee, Diem delivered a nationwide radio address on July 18 that was received with skepticism. He issued the following directives: (1) that flag display regulations apply to all sects that adopt the same flag; (2) that the Interministerial Committee work with the Buddhist delegation in resolving all grievances relating to the June 16 agreements; and (3) that everyone in Vietnam cooperate in promoting a settlement. Nolting recommended that the state department approve Diem's broadcast as a step in the right direction. The Buddhists, however, refused to accept anything less than the terms already promised in the June 16 agreements. Diem's curt two-minute address was so cold and his words so empty that it undermined any favorable impact his minor concessions might have had on easing the tense situation.[55]

The Kennedy administration praised Diem's announced intention to carry out the June 16 agreements but emphasized that he *must* put them into practice. Mixed signals continued to perplex the White House. Diem removed the barricades from the pagodas in Saigon, but, in a sharply provocative action, he barred the bonzes from Xa Loi pagoda. Nolting urged Diem to release all those incarcerated following the July 17 demonstration, indemnify those injured by the police on that day, and institute peaceful measures for dealing with demonstrations. But Diem again froze into silence. Hilsman informed Nolting that "alternatives to Diem seem to be emerging," although it was "not yet clear who and what they are." The CIA reported General Minh's unhappiness with Diem along with his warning that if Nhu took control, the people would turn to the Vietcong for support. The state department resumed its course of "watchful waiting."[56]

The administration's concern over Madame Nhu continued to grow, as shown by its decision to reject her request for a visit to the United States during this particularly touchy period. She had written a letter to Vice President Johnson, seeking his assistance in arranging what would have been a second tour. This was "the worst possible time," Forrestal fumed. "The last thing we want to have is this woman coming around." But how to tell her? Johnson had the task of denying the request. Forrestal wrote a draft response that explained the administration's reasons and took it to the Executive Office Building for the vice president's reading.

"Who wrote this?" Johnson asked after a few moments.

"I wrote it," Forrestal replied. "I drafted it."

"In that case I suppose there's no point in me trying to change it, is there?"

"Mr. Vice President, why, of course, you can change it any way you want."

Reading the note again, Johnson declared, "Well, I don't think it's a particularly charming letter that you've drafted." After a pause, he continued, "That's all right. Go show it to President Kennedy."

Forrestal took it to the White House, where he found the president in the steam bath. After reading the note, Kennedy expressed the same reaction as that of Johnson. "This is not the kind of a letter that you write a charming lady. It's got to be more gentle and more. . . ." The president began revising the note, ending with a flourish that expounded on her beauty and charm and asserted that they preferred her coming some other time. Forrestal returned to the Executive Office Building, where Johnson read the redraft.

"Well, now, did you make these changes, Forrestal?"

"No, sir."

"Well, I can guess who did. It's pretty good. Pretty good. Type it up and I'll sign it."[57]

American press coverage also continued to pose problems for the administration. On July 25, an AP story by Arnett claimed that U.S. helicopters had assumed a "full combat role" because of changed rules of engagement that permitted them to take the offensive. Rusk countered that "US personnel fire only when threatened." At the behest of the president, Robert Manning from the state department's public affairs division had earlier visited Vietnam to compile a report on the press situation. He found the correspondents in a "sullen Alice in Wonderland miasma." They were young and of little experience for the most part, and they contained "no journalistic giants." Most of them were stringers or freelance writers who supported the U.S. involvement but held unanimous contempt for the Diem regime. Mecklin was correct in insisting that they were probably better than most of those "in such boondocks assignments." They were not irresponsible, although they had made damaging errors. On numerous occasions, they had withheld information that would have hurt U.S. interests. Several "shabby incidents" had occurred between U.S. military personnel and Saigon's police, including a few months earlier a homosexual American civilian official who was attacked and hurt badly by his "Vietnamese partner." U.S. officials had gone too far in presenting a "rosy picture," and the press believed that they had lied to them. The embassy gave the press only "the most transparently desirable stories," which had hurt its credibility. The U.S. embassy and MACV must begin "a concerted effort to woo individual reporters." Lodge's arrival afforded this opportunity.[58]

A furor then developed in both Saigon and Washington when Nolting asserted in a UPI interview in late July that the Diem regime had not mistreated the Buddhists. "I myself, I say this very frankly, after almost two and one half years here, have never seen any evidence of religious persecution; in fact I have the feeling that there is a great deal of religious toleration among Vietnamese people at all levels." The Intersect Committee for the Protection of Buddhism unleashed a scathing attack on Nolting. On August 1, "a group of Vietnamese patriots" questioned the ambassador's integrity and his understanding of the Buddhist situation in an open letter given both to him and the news media at Xa Loi pagoda. On behalf of the Intersect Committee, Khiet sent President Kennedy a telegram of protest. Harriman was infuriated and called for the ambassador's immediate recall. He finally withdrew this demand, largely because Nolting was due home in less than two weeks, anyway. Instead of a reprimand, Nolting received a note directing him to seek Washington's counsel *before* making public statements.[59]

Meanwhile, violence threatened again in South Vietnam. In an August 3 speech before a Women's Paramilitary Youth training class, Madame Nhu blasted the Buddhists as "seditious elements who use the most odious Communist tactics to subvert the country." Her husband then threatened to destroy Xa Loi pagoda as a hotbed of coup talk. The next day, in Binh Thuan Province and with no correspondents or photographers present, another monk burned himself to death. The state department became convinced that the regime had dropped all thoughts of conciliation. If Nhu "crushed" Xa Loi pagoda, the U.S. government would publicly denounce the action, and thereby lay the basis for severing relations.[60]

A coup had become likely in what Hilsman termed the "tense, volatile and potentially explosive" atmosphere in Saigon. Odds for such an attempt in the next few months were even—as were the chances of success. Either Nhu could seize power or civil war could break out among the numerous non-Communist groups. The state department stood ready to implement its May 23 contingency plan mandating U.S. influence behind Tho and the military if a coup attempt seemed likely to succeed. Furthermore, U.S. officials in Saigon were trying to contact Diem's opposition, both military and civilian. "With all that is at stake in Viet-Nam," Hilsman cautioned, "we obviously cannot afford to back a loser but we are not yet in a position to pick a winner with any confidence."[61]

The White House needed time to make a proper assessment, but time was in short supply. The administration had become deeply mired in its third year of a steadily expanding commitment to a regime that had shown no signs of improvement. Indeed, the situation had worsened almost in direct proportion to America's growing involvement. On August 4, the Defense Intelligence Agency reported rising Vietcong activity over the past three weeks.[62] Was the Vietcong finally exploiting the Buddhist crisis? The president realized the dead weight he would carry into his reelection campaign if South Vietnam continued its regression. And yet he also recognized the heavy costs to U.S. credibility of failure in Vietnam. America's prestige rested on maintaining at least the semblance of success. Only then could the White House implement its withdrawal plan.

At this sensitive moment, Madame Nhu all but put the finishing touch on the Diem regime. On August 8, after attacking the United States on the front page of the *Times of Vietnam*, she callously asserted that all the Buddhists had done on June 11 was "barbecue a bonze." Indeed, she offered them gasoline and matches for more such spectacles. "Let them burn! And we shall clap our hands."[63]

No other statements could have repulsed so many people. Madame Nhu was "out of control of everybody," the genteel Nolting bitterly exclaimed. Even Diem conceded that "she ought to take a rest." Nolting insisted that Diem erase the image of "schizophrenia" from his regime by taking corrective action against her. He must also support his ambassador in Washington, Tran Van Chuong—Madame Nhu's father, who, with his wife, South Vietnam's observer at the United Nations, was estranged from his daughter. Through the Voice of America in Vietnam, Chuong denounced the venomous remarks. Nolting raised the possibility of a "leave of absence" for Madame Nhu in discussions with several government figures. Had not Diem in the early years of his regime banished her to a convent in Hong Kong? Nonetheless, Nolting's efforts failed and Madame Nhu remained in the country.[64]

Who was this Madame Nhu, suddenly the flash point of the Buddhist crisis and not so affectionately dubbed the "Dragon Lady," the "Queen Bee," "Joan of Arc," and "Lucretia Borgia." In a letter of August 14 to the *New York Times*, she wrote: "I may shock some by saying 'I would beat such provocateurs 10 times more if they wore monks' robes,' and I would clap hands at seeing another monk barbecue show, for one cannot be responsible for the madness of others." The world was under some "mad spell" cast by the Buddhists. The *Times* and others needed "an electroshock" to bring them back to reality.[65]

Madame Nhu's real name was Tran Le Xuan, translated as either "Tears of Spring" or "Beautiful Spring," who at eighteen had married the raspy-voiced and tightly wired Ngo Dinh Nhu. Educated in Saigon and in Hanoi, she was known as a tomboy who had fourteen servants and loved ballet and piano, once dancing solo at Hanoi's National Theater. Her mother was a cousin of Emperor Bao Dai and daughter of a former imperial family. After the Communist uprising in Hanoi in December 1946, the Vietminh buried Diem's oldest brother alive and forced Nhu and another brother, Ngo Dinh Can, to run for their lives. The Communists, however, captured Madame Nhu, her infant daughter, and her mother-in-law. They blew up her piano because they thought it a radio for communicating with the French and kept her four months in a remote village, barely keeping her alive by giving her two bowls of rice a day. After French troops took back the area, she reunited with her husband in the mountain resort town of Dalat, where they worked to arrange Diem's return from exile.[66]

Now the virtual first lady in Vietnam, Madame Nhu rode in a chauffeur-driven black Mercedes and wore a small diamond crucifix to symbolize her conversion from Buddhist to Catholic. She also wore form-fitting apparel so tight that one French correspondent suggestively described her as "molded into her . . . dress like a dagger in its sheath." On formal occasions, she wore red satin pantaloons with three vertical pleats, which was the mark of the highest-ranking women of the imperial court in ancient Annam. When Diem once criticized her apparel, she snapped: "It's not your neck that sticks out, it's mine. So, shut up."[67]

Her cutting comments about the Buddhists had thoroughly disgusted her parents. After hearing of the barbecue remark, her mother moaned: "There is an old proverb in my country which means 'one should not make oneself or one's family naked before the world.'" She continued: "I was sick. . . . Now, nobody can stop her. . . . She never listened to our advice . . . never, never, never." When her father criticized her calloused words, she shot back: "He is a coward." Chuong warned that the Diem regime had alienated "the strongest moral forces."[68]

Diem's power rested heavily on the support of his brother and wife. Madame Nhu and her husband controlled the country through a network of secret police and private organizations loyal only to them. She had already alienated a large segment of the South Vietnamese population by securing a stronger position than men in marriage and property matters and by imposing a new morality on the city once known as the "Paris of the Orient." As a member of the National Assembly, Madame Nhu had strong-armed the passage of a series of blue laws that prohibited polygamy and contraceptives, declared adultery a crime subject to prison, made divorce illegal except through a presidential exemption, and virtually banned night life by outlawing cafés, dancing, and prostitution. Indeed, she had secured an order for U.S. embassy personnel to stop the "immoral" practice of dancing, even in their own homes. Nolting, according to Homer Bigart in the *New York Times*, had even agreed to a "surrender on square dancing." So disliked was she in her own country that on a cocktail napkin in a Saigon café, a patron had scrawled, "No Nhus is good news."[69]

Nolting conceded that the premier had entered his final days. On the night of August 11, Thuan had secretly visited the ambassador's home to say that he and most cabinet members considered this Diem's "11th hour" as president. The following morning, Nolting met with Diem and noted that the premier was deeply torn between public duty and family loyalty. Nolting urged Diem to resolve the Buddhist crisis and bring Nhu and his wife under control. When Diem strongly denied that they had usurped his presidential prerogatives, Nolting urged him to remove that public impression by repudiating Madame Nhu. Diem would not consider such a suggestion. Instead, he complained that the bonzes' actions had hurt the war effort and asserted that "good people" in the provinces had urged him not to give in to the "false monks." The Buddhists had fabricated the religious issue in their effort to topple his government. If Diem did not implement conciliatory measures, Nolting warned him one last time, he would lose U.S. support.[70]

The state department continued to receive mixed signals from Saigon. On August 13, news arrived from Hué that a third monk had become a fiery martyr. Diem finally agreed to a "policy of conciliation." In a press conference that same day, Vice President Tho claimed that Madame Nhu's public declarations were the "personal opinions" of a key member of the National Assembly—quite similar to those critical but unofficial remarks made earlier by Senator Mansfield about South Vietnam. That same day, Diem arranged for Madame Nhu to leave South Vietnam for an undetermined period. But then, in the early morning of the following day, Nolting reported that Diem "slipped back into postponement and vacillation." At 11 A.M., just following Nolting's farewell ceremony, Diem complained that neither the U.S. press nor government grasped either the magnitude of the Buddhist problem or the extensive contributions made by the Ngo family to Vietnam's independence. Nolting warned Diem that if he did not renounce Madame Nhu, "it would be impossible for the U.S. government to continue our present relationship." At the end of what Nolting termed "a rather strenuous goodbye," Diem promised to issue such a proclamation, perhaps before his friend departed for home the following day.[71]

Hysteria seemed about to consume South Vietnam, finally convincing Diem to offer public assurances of conciliation that, predictably, drew only cynicism from the United States. Khiet had banned further suicides "unless necessary," but a nun burned herself to death near Nha Trang on August 15, just days after a young girl tried to cut off her hand as a sacrifice to Buddha. Then, again in Hué, an elderly monk on August 16 immolated himself in another savage reminder of that June 11 morning in Saigon.[72]

White House advisers remained dubious about Diem's sincerity. First, it took tremendous pressure from Nolting to convince Diem to go this far. Second, although his statement implicitly repudiated Madame Nhu, it took the form of a reply to a news correspondent's question and was subject to disavowal. Washington did not expect Diem to change his policies.

As the situation continued to deteriorate, the president met with Lodge in the White House on August 15, just before his departure for Saigon. Kennedy was not in a good mood, having just read an article questioning military progress in the delta that his nemesis Halberstam had written in that day's *New York Times*. Under the title of "Vietnamese Reds Gain in Key Area," Halberstam asserted that the Vietcong had used captured U.S. weapons in attacking South Vietnam's regulars. That same day the president received a petition bearing the signatures of 15,000 clergymen across the nation who protested U.S. policy in Vietnam. The Ministers Vietnam Committee, as they called themselves, demanded that he terminate military assistance to the Saigon government and that he stop the "immoral spraying" of chemicals and the "herding" of villagers into "concentration camps" euphemistically called "strategic hamlets." The United States was helping an "unjust, undemocratic, and unstable" regime, all under the "fiction" of a struggle for freedom.[73]

The Diem regime's repressive actions had fostered a move toward a coup that, if not carefully managed, could result in Nhu becoming premier. On that same day of August 15, Nhu met with general officers and other government dignitaries to announce a major change in South Vietnam's policy. He referred to the recently signed Partial Test Ban Treaty to show that the Kennedy administration had adopted "a policy of appeasement" toward the Soviet Union and other Communist countries and warned that this could signal an impending cut in U.S. assistance. South Vietnam must prepare to stand on its own. Was Nhu about to seize command?[74]

Nhu's meeting with the generals was a ruse, the CIA believed, intended to break the back of the conspiracies that he knew existed among them. Even though Nhu was second to Diem in political power, the chances of his becoming president were poor. Educated and articulate groups in the country joined the army in despising Nhu as cold, vindictive, and power-hungry; they all considered Madame Nhu "vicious, meddlesome, neurotic, or worse." If Diem fell to a coup, the Nhus would be fortunate to survive.

Several reports had reached the CIA of a plot to assassinate them but to leave Diem in office to head a reorganized government.[75]

As Diem's impending collapse became certain, the Joint Chiefs of Staff in Washington prepared to implement the military reduction program. Just a few days earlier, the president's Special Assistant of Counterinsurgency and Special Activities (SACSA) urged the secretary of defense to ignore the recent report of rising Vietcong activities by noting that the level had fallen considerably below the average of either of the past two years. For "purely psychological purposes," however, the joint chiefs recommended no pullouts until the political and religious problems had abated. Late October 1963 appeared to be the best time to begin the retrenchment process. CINCPAC's "Withdrawal Plan" would permit the scheduled 1,000 personnel to be home by Christmas. The partial disengagement would occur over a two-month period and in perhaps four increments rather than as a one-time event. This measured approach would lessen the impact on military operations, afford a longer period for the press to publicize the event, and cause fewer problems in administration and transportation. The military personnel withdrawn would total 276, a number that included MAAG figures from the army, air force, and navy, along with a marine security platoon and various other highly visible units. Since the first withdrawal would draw the most publicity, it should contain "more colorful units, a wide spectrum of skills, and representatives from all Services."[76]

PARADOXICALLY, as the military prepared to implement the partial withdrawal plan, the White House found itself deeper in Vietnam after attaching itself to the expected coup. The Kennedy administration had implicitly notified the Vietnamese generals that it would not come to Diem's assistance in a coup when it replaced Nolting with Lodge and then assumed a stance of neutrality. Rusk was direct. As he declared, "we must surely be ready to play every effective card at decisive moments." U.S. prestige rested on the coup operation, affording the administration the right to suspend its cooperation at any point. "We continue to believe [that the] Nhus must go and [that a] coup will be needed." The June 11 immolation in Saigon had trained the world's attention on South Vietnam, starkly revealing Diem's weaknesses and forcing the Kennedy administration to find some way to change his government. "All evidence indicates to us," Rusk observed, "that removal of [the] Nhus is [the] center of [the] problem."[77] Diem's refusal to rid himself of his brother and his wife made a coup the only solution.

13

THE ROAD TO A COUP

We may deem it useful to throw our influence toward
reducing or eliminating the power of the Nhus.

Roger Hilsman, August 22, 1963

You can't have the police knocking on the door at three
o'clock in the morning, taking sixteen- and seventeen-year-
old girls to camps outside of town where they may be
molested. You can't do that in any country . . . without laying
the basis for assassination.

Henry Cabot Lodge, March 20, 1978

SHORTLY AFTER MIDNIGHT on August 21, 1963, government forces
wielding pistols, submachine guns, carbines, shotguns, grenades, and
tear gas began a brutal crackdown on Buddhist pagodas throughout
South Vietnam. Diem's proclamation of nationwide martial law just moments earlier had opened the way for truckloads of steel-helmeted combat
police in army camouflage uniforms to join Colonel Le Quang Tung's
red-bereted Special Forces in arresting more than 1,400 bonzes and charging them with possessing weapons.

The violence at Hué was a harsh reminder of the May 8 events. As the
troops stormed Tu Dam pagoda around 3 A.M., they encountered fierce resistance from monks and nuns, who put up eight hours of resistance with
stones, sharp sticks, and clubs bearing embedded nails. The battle led to the
toppling of a giant statue of Buddha and an explosion that nearly destroyed
the pagoda and brought fire trucks racing to the scene. Thousands of Buddhist sympathizers had meanwhile gathered in the streets, leading to a confrontation in which at least a hundred injuries occurred among priests,
students, and Boy Scouts, and nine policemen were hurt, five seriously. Police ransacked the building and scuffled with swarms of angry people, arresting several professors and deans of the University of Hué and confiscating
the remains of an elderly monk who had recently immolated himself. Popular indignation toward Diem in the former imperial capital spilled over to
include his protector, the United States, driving anti-American feeling to
fever pitch. Had not Tung's shock troops been CIA-trained?[1]

Shortly after midnight in Saigon, twenty-eight army trucks packed with more than a thousand uniformed personnel joined the combat police in easily overrunning those Buddhists armed with knives and rocks. ABC News reported monks screaming as they ducked behind a tree to escape a torrent of smoke and flashing lights streaming from gunfire, grenades, and tear gas bombs. Police with fixed bayonets burst through the iron-grilled gates opening into Xa Loi pagoda, accompanied by the bizarre sounds of banging pots, pans, drums, and gongs, and the sharp ringing of alarm bells coming from the Buddhist tocsins. An explosion inside the pagoda shook the entire area. Armed forces beat hundreds of priests and nuns with rifle butts and terrorized others by firing pistols dangerously close to their heads as they crouched on the floor of the building, blinded by tear gas and frantically warding off the vicious jabs of rifle butts and bayonets. Police flashlights darted back and forth through the dark pagoda until someone scaled its walls and turned on the lights to facilitate entry through the open windows. From the second floor came the sounds of soldiers smashing doors and furniture and shattering glass emblems. The III Corps Commander soon established military control over the entire Saigon district, canceling commercial flights into the city and instituting press censorship.[2]

By 2 A.M. the bell at Xa Loi pagoda had stopped tolling and an eerie silence fell over the grounds. In one of many stories disproved by a U.N. investigation, NBC reported more than a dozen dead and wounded priests and nuns inside the temple. No one had been killed, but the total Buddhist and government casualties reached thirty, including five with serious wounds. Seven police ambulances had rushed to the scene after the ninety-minute attack, while police trucks and vans hustled hundreds of prisoners to detention centers outside Saigon. As the operation came to a close just before daylight, the government's forces held all strategic points and had incarcerated more than a thousand bonzes from throughout South Vietnam. Government sources claimed that in Xa Loi, An Quang, and Theravada pagodas, the soldiers found a machine gun with ammunition, more than a dozen plastic explosive devices, numerous homemade mines, ten daggers, a submachine gun, a radio, printing equipment, and a pile of Vietcong documents.[3]

I

NO SINGLE ACTION could have done more than the raid at Xa Loi pagoda to undermine the last vestiges of U.S. support for the Diem regime. Relations with Saigon had already cooled after its initial repressive policies toward the Buddhists. That stand seemed correct in view of the South Vietnamese people's growing distrust for their government, only heightened by the pagoda raids. Many Americans ignored the evidence suggesting that Xa Loi had been a command headquarters for militants and regarded the assaults as violations of holy land.[4] Increasing numbers of government officials became more outspoken to Americans about seeing the premier's rule coming to an end. But both the U.S. embassy and the White House were perplexed by the military's role on August 21. Had it merely followed orders from either Diem or Nhu—or both? Or had the generals executed a silent coup and taken control of the government? If so, the raids had no rational justification. It was inconceivable that the military leaders, most of them Buddhists, would take such drastic action against fellow members of the faith. The Washington administration attempted to pursue a hands-off policy toward these explosive events, only to find out again that this position was impossible to maintain.

The United States got caught in the crossfire when two head bonzes escaped the government's forces by climbing over the wall around Xa Loi pagoda and finding sanctuary in the U.S. Operations Mission building next door. U.S. officials denied entry to Saigon's police chief, nattily dressed in a Republican Youth uniform, who threw up a cordon around the building and angrily ordered all Vietnamese out of the area. When the police threatened to storm the building, Foreign Minister Vu Van Mau stepped between the antagonists. A Buddhist himself, Mau had rushed to the tense scene and, to avert bloodshed, demanded that the Americans turn over the priests. Trueheart had also arrived from the U.S. embassy. Refusing to buckle under the pressure, he announced that he would take no action until instructions arrived from Washington but warned Mau against violating the United States's diplomatic immunity. Giving up the priests, Trueheart knew, would imply U.S. approval of the Saigon government's actions. Moreover, the Diem regime had refused to ensure their safety if they surrendered. The face-off ended peacefully, and the state department soon directed Trueheart not to release the two bonzes and to regard the U.S. Operations Building as having the same immunity as that of the embassy. More bonzes soon found sanctity in the U.S. embassy, which became known as "the Buddhist Hilton."[5]

Saigon resembled an armed camp. U.S. embassy officials had been caught by surprise and, along with the U.S. Information Service, their phone lines had been out and they had no communication outside the city. No one knew the fate of the hundreds of monks and nuns seized during the raids. Battle geared troops ringed the now empty pagodas, and armored cars and bayonet-fixed sentries stood watch over government buildings. The city's post office was closed, the streets were deserted in accordance with the 9 P.M. to 5 A.M. curfew, and Diem had issued shoot-to-kill orders at key installations. The 14,000 U.S. military advisers and their families throughout the country were under orders to stay in their homes, and all leaves had been canceled.[6]

The driving force behind the government's assault on the Buddhists had seemingly come from senior military commanders who had acted without consulting civilian advisers. Secretary of State Thuan and Minister of the Interior Luong appeared bewildered by the whirlwind of events. Initial impressions suggested that the military establishment had suddenly clamped down on the Buddhists because of their threat to the war effort. The military, or so the argument went, felt compelled to take action after the explosive events of August 17 and 18, which included massive student unrest in Hué, a Buddhist attack on an ARVN officer in Danang after he had fired into a procession of demonstrators, and the monks denouncing Madame Nhu and calling for a governmental overthrow before a huge and boisterous crowd at Xa Loi pagoda. But this argument made little sense, nor did the government's claim that the clampdown had occurred spontaneously. Long-time distrust had bedeviled the relationship between Diem and his generals, and the military contained too many Buddhists and their sympathizers to assume it would have acted so cold-heartedly against the bonzes. Coordinated military operations against the Buddhists in several cities, the rapidity with which banners went up in Saigon declaring the army's resolve to defeat the Communists, and the quick appearance of ARVN psywar pictures claiming to prove Vietcong infiltration of the Buddhist movement—all these developments suggested a carefully thought-out plan.[7] But by whom, if not the military establishment?

The official stance termed the nationwide action a military effort intended to put down domestic unrest as a necessary prelude to winning the war. On August 18, in reaction to the previous two days of violence, ten of the fifteen generals gathered to prepare for asking Diem to declare martial law, which would allow them to arrest alien Buddhist monks and return them to their home provinces and pagodas. On August 20, Nhu met with some of the generals and told them to take their proposal to Diem. According to Luong, Diem discussed the matter with the generals that same day, emphasizing his intention to resolve the Buddhist crisis. Later that evening, Diem approved the plan without consulting his cabinet and at midnight implemented the measure with General Don's signature in his capacity as head of the Joint General Staff. The raids started soon afterward.[8]

Trueheart disputed the government's defense. Diem, according to the chargé, recognized the value of presenting Lodge with a fait accompli upon his arrival in Saigon. In an ingenious move, the military's involvement in the pagoda raids had identified Diem with the only group the United States would have accepted as an alternative to his rule. The government's repression of the Buddhists likewise appealed to Nhu, who had long advocated force and more than once had made such an overture to military leaders. Trueheart suspected Nhu of manipulating them into absorbing the brunt of the criticisms for suppressing the Buddhists.[9]

The Diem regime's severe measures promised to have serious repercussions. A large number of South Vietnamese, particularly students, prepared to protest on behalf of the Buddhists. Although the premier rejected his brother's suggestion to shut down the schools, he approved the mass arrests of civilians whose names appeared on lists carried by the Special Forces and whom the government called "Communists in Disguise." Included in the roundup were students of all ages from grade school to college, raising the specter of parents—many of them in the military and the government—visiting their children in jail.[10]

The situation became more volatile because of a certain power struggle within the military. General Ton That Dinh, Saigon's military governor, had never been able to control either his hunger for power or his thirst for whisky. Although his antics had amused many Americans, they considered him an unstable eccentric who had provoked fellow Vietnamese by posturing loudly about his military prowess. The Buddhists, he now proclaimed over Saigon radio, were "political speculators" who had engaged in "illegal actions" and got what they deserved. The spectacle ceased to be comical when one realized that Dinh commanded an infantry division along with 5,000 paratroopers, marines, and military police.[11]

The most powerful military man in South Vietnam was Colonel Tung, the mercurial head of the Special Forces, which the CIA had paid, equipped, and trained for covert operations in Laos and North Vietnam. Tung had long been the Ngo family's guardian and now led 3,000 forces in the Praetorian Guard along with the Can Lao, Nhu's personal clique of secret terrorist agents. Short and bespectacled, Tung was a devout Roman Catholic from central Vietnam, home of the Ngo family. About forty years old, his military record was almost totally in security and counterespionage—factors considered vital to a government more concerned with survival than defeating the Vietcong. Tung had first served the French as a security officer in central Vietnam and then had worked for Diem in the military-security section in the same area. Before becoming head of the Special Forces, Tung was a high official in Nhu's Can Lao party. Tung mouthed support for General Don, but the outspoken colonel had aroused the visceral hatred of other senior officers—including Dinh and Khanh. Tung's specialty, according to one source, was following orders. "He's damn good at that."[12]

Diem's brutal assault on the Buddhists had done more than inflame the domestic scene: It infuriated Americans. In an area of the world that emphasized the importance of "face," the regime had humiliated its U.S. sponsor by ruthlessly suppressing a defenseless people. A *New York Times* editorial called for a reassessment of American policy and declared that if the situation seemed hopeless, the United States "should pull out or use its influence to seek a change of regime in Saigon." One U.S. officer put it succinctly: "Some Vietnamese Army officers are telling us that it is necessary to crack down on the Buddhists because they are influenced by the Communists, but from what I have seen, nearly all the people in Vietnam are Buddhists. If they are Communists, what are we Americans doing here at all?" In gazing at the Vietnamese troops standing at intersections to enforce martial law, an American G.I. caustically remarked that they had "their bayonets and grenades ready to shoot girls, monks and nuns. Why don't they try shooting up some Vietcong for a change?"[13]

The regime's repressive tactics had thoroughly shaken the Kennedy administration. The raids had broken Diem's pledge to seek reconciliation with the Buddhists, raising speculation about whether the military had taken over the country. Some wondered whether the Nhus had seized control. Halberstam reported reliable sources alleging that Nhu had planned the pagoda attacks without confiding in the army, and that Tung had led the operation with secret policemen wearing army uniforms. In an accompanying story, however, Szulc reported the White House belief that Vietnamese army commanders had persuaded Diem to crack down on the Buddhists and declare martial law. Confusion dominated Washington's thinking, but whatever the source of the attacks, U.S. officials were convinced that the Buddhist struggle had become thoroughly political.[14]

The pagoda raids had destroyed the final remnants of trust in the Saigon government. Diem's use of the army had stunned many contemporaries, particularly the Buddhists, who previously thought the officers critical of Diem and interested in leading a coup. "I was shocked and so were others," moaned Nolting, who had been conferring with Lodge in Honolulu when news arrived of the raids. Having been personally assured by Diem that he was making every effort to conciliate the Buddhists, the outgoing ambassador felt betrayed, cabling, "This is the first time that you've ever gone back on your word to me." Diem responded to the telegram by insisting that he had had no choice: His forces had found arms stored in the pagodas; the Buddhists had called for the government's overthrow; and Tri Quang and other leaders had refused to compromise. Nolting countered that "upstart Buddhist militants" were behind the trouble and that many bonzes had written the embassy renouncing the General Association of Vietnamese Buddhists. Trueheart, however, disagreed. He angered Nolting by calling the raids "a clear violation" of Diem's guarantees of reconciliation with the Buddhists and hence a "benchmark" event. The White House never made a "serious effort to get behind Diem again."[15]

The Kennedy administration was in the unenviable position of having either to continue its support of Diem and alienation of the Vietnamese people or to abandon his government and invite a coup. The key question was whether the great number of junior officers and enlisted men in the ARVN—most of them Buddhists—would stand by the regime and its generals. The entire world awaited the U.S. reaction to the raids. Some Americans saw only two choices: Withdraw or favor a coup. Indeed, a coup might facilitate a U.S. withdrawal.

II

THE ADMINISTRATION'S most pressing task was to determine whether the military had taken over the Saigon government. Based on information provided by Nhu, defense intelligence sources told McNamara that the army had "assumed full control" in what was tantamount to a military coup. In response to Taylor's query, however, Harkins asserted that the premier had authorized the military to take the lead. The action, Harkins continued, was "a blessing in disguise." General Don had openly declared that the military could not win the war with the Nhus in control. Diem was surely aware of these remarks and had perhaps become "a hostage of the military." With "another coup slinger," General Dinh, now in command of the Saigon–Cholon district, the situation seemed right for "a military take-over with minimum violence." In a statement showing limited understanding of the situation, Harkins blandly declared that only "a few bones were bruised as the police and military took over the main Pagodas yesterday." Hilsman agreed that the military appeared to be the chief impetus behind martial law. Krulak warned that the most important step was to identify the leaders. Was Nhu behind the move? Once this became clear, the United States should urge the Diem regime to resolve the religious crisis, arrange for the Nhus' departure from the country, and concentrate on the Vietcong. Hilsman asked William Colby, who had recently served as CIA station chief in Saigon, to ascertain Nhu's status and the relationship between Diem and his military leaders.[16]

The raids took on another level of importance when the very next day, Tran Van Chuong, Saigon's ambassador to Washington and Madame Nhu's father, resigned his post of nine years in protest against his government's Buddhist policy. His wife, a Buddhist, likewise resigned as observer to the United Nations. A Confucian, Chuong lamented that the regime had lost all virtue. The United States could never convince Diem to grant reforms, and a withdrawal of aid would hand the Communists a victory. New leadership was imperative, he insisted. There was "not one chance in a hundred for victory" over the Vietcong with Diem in power. Over CBS television, Chuong called his daughter "only the shadow of her husband," even though she was "very vocal." She "has not the power she is supposed to have." It was "nonsense" to claim that there was no alternative to Diem.[17]

Coup rumors had multiplied, raising the hopes of Diem's opponents within the Kennedy administration. Indeed, high civilian and military officials within the Saigon regime spoke openly of Diem's assassination. The CIA dampened any thoughts in Washington of this prospect when it reminded proponents that Nhu could be the successor. The White House, Hilsman told Lodge, was uncertain where power rested in South Vietnam. As the situation developed, "we may deem it useful to throw our influence toward reducing or eliminating the power of the Nhus."[18]

U.S. promotion of a coup had risen from the subject of whispered conversations in Washington's halls to the highest level of official discussion just as the new ambassador was due to arrive in Saigon. Diem's concerns about a new direction in U.S. policy seemed warranted. Ball's only restraint in seeking a government change was his caution against instructing Lodge to "eliminate the Nhus" before he had had the opportunity to assess the situation.[19]

The urgency with which President Kennedy dispensed Lodge to Saigon provided a clear indication of the raids' importance. When the trouble had erupted in Saigon on August 21, Lodge was in Tokyo, en route to his new position but first planning recreational time in Hong Kong. In the middle of the night, however, he received a phone call from the White House informing him of the Diem government's assault on the pagodas and ordering him to South Vietnam post haste. President Kennedy dispatched a military plane to pick up Lodge on the morning of August 22 for an eleven-hour, nonstop flight to Saigon.

At 9:30 that evening, Lodge arrived at Tan Son Nhut Airport and stepped out into a drizzling rain and steamy, oppressive heat. Squinting through the myriad flashing of cameras and near-blinding glare of TV floodlights, he saw a small number of U.S. military and civilian officials, including General Harkins, whom he had met while serving the military in France during World War II. Lodge also spotted about forty American journalists among the crowd. The reporters remained grouped, brought there by bus under police jeep escort because of the ambassador-select's scheduled arrival a short time after the government's curfew. Pursuant to last-minute instructions from Kennedy, Lodge focused first on improving relations with the press. On reaching the microphone, he asked, "Where are the gentlemen of the press?" After they had identified themselves, Lodge delivered a few remarks before breaking from the official party to gather with the journalists. A former correspondent himself, he praised the importance of a free press and, in doing so, took the first step toward salving their raw relations with the embassy. Trueheart remarked that he had never seen anyone take command so well. Madame Nhu likewise detected a stronger tone in U.S. policy. "They have sent us a proconsul." As much an aristocrat as Diem, Lodge instantly won the favor of crusty embassy members who boasted, "Our old mandarin can lick your old mandarin."[20]

Lodge did not assume the ambassadorial post until he presented his credentials to the government on August 26. A small crisis had preoccupied the regime when Mau suddenly resigned as foreign minister in protest against its actions. After shaving his head and announcing his intention to become a monk, Mau asked Diem for permission to go on a pilgrimage to India. Instead, the premier placed his former cabinet member under arrest.[21]

Lodge did not arrive with an open mind regarding the rapidly deteriorating situation in Vietnam. At his final briefing in the White House, he had listened as Kennedy expressed great concern about the situation, referring in particular to the AP photo of the burning monk. Vietnam, the president darkly concluded, had entered "a terminal phase." Just before Lodge departed for Vietnam, he met with Madame Tran Van Chuong, who offered an equally ominous forecast. "Unless they [the Nhus] leave the country, there is no power on earth that can prevent the assassination of Madame Nhu, her husband Mr. Nhu, and his brother Mr. Diem." The regime's arbitrary arrests, imprisonments, and executions had set off a "general reign of terror" that made assassination inevitable. Years afterward, Lodge remarked that the pagoda raids had "marked the end of the Diem regime." Firing at people in worship made it "just a matter of time before they would be through." The government's "insane policies" had converted Saigon into an armed camp. "You can't have the police knocking on the door at three o'clock in the morning, taking sixteen- and seventeen-year-old girls to camps outside of town where they may be molested. You can't do that in any country . . . without laying the basis for assassination."[22]

Lodge's immediate assessment fed the growing suspicion of the Nhus' heavy hand in the violence. Ngo Dinh Nhu, the ambassador-select reported without explanation, was taking drugs. Madame Nhu, although "giving a superficial appearance of brilliance," was not aware of how badly she had hurt the United States's standing by the adverse publicity she had generated. American support for "corrupt dictators" was palatable if the story did not get into the newspapers. "But an inefficient Hitlerism, the leaders of which make fantastic statements to the press[,] is the hardest thing on earth for the U.S. Government to support." Few South Vietnamese officers had known in advance about the anti-Buddhist measures. To preserve secrecy, special printing presses had produced propaganda materials only hours before the government made its move. Also disturbing was the probability of more trouble from Madame Nhu. In a three-hour interview with a *New York Daily News* correspondent, she expressed intense hatred for Tri Quang, whom she thought was hiding in the U.S. Operations Mission building. That hatred, Lodge thought, stemmed in part from the bonze's long-time friendship with her father, "whom she also hates." Such bitter animosity was in no small measure attributable to his resignation as ambassador and bitter denunciation of his daughter after the Buddhist assaults, but also to her belief that Tri Quang spoke for many intellectuals who had repeatedly ridiculed her. Madame Nhu demanded that the troops break in and seize Tri Quang and his companions. The government must arrest "all key Buddhists."[23]

Lodge felt certain that Diem remained in control though under his brother's inordinate influence. South Vietnamese Army radio broadcasts reeked with Nhu's abrasive tone in directing the Republican Youth to cooperate with the government. Nhu accused the Buddhists of turning their pagodas into headquarters from which to conspire against the government. The Intersect Committee, he asserted, operated under the control of "political speculators who exploited religion and terrorism." According to Lodge, Nhu's divide-and-rule tactics had split the military. At least three power groups, led by General Don, General Dinh, and Colonel Tung, existed in the army. Don did not command the allegiance of the other two; both Dinh and Tung derived their authority from the palace. The latter two men, however, detested each other but could count on support from a substantial number of loyalists in the army. If the army deposed Diem, fighting would break out within the military establishment—particularly since the army "thoroughly disliked and distrusted" Tung. To further complicate the mix, Don was tightly connected with the Nhus, and Dinh had allied with Don and the Nhus, along with the Saigon Military District Commander and other unidentified generals. The fast-growing bitterness became personal as well as professional when Nhu denounced his in-laws as "stupid and useless." Nhu, Lodge concluded, was "dynamic and a thinker" and "had no difficulty in bringing President Diem around to his way of thinking."[24]

The CIA corroborated Lodge's assertions but added an intriguing twist to the pagoda raids: ARVN officers adamantly denied responsibility. They charged that Tung's Special Forces had disguised themselves in ARVN uniforms before attacking the pagodas. Furthermore, unfounded rumors had spread within the military establishment that Americans, who had long supported the Special Forces, had helped to plan the attack. Many army officers thought changes necessary to pursue the war against the Vietcong but were afraid to say anything because of the United States's support for Diem. The problem became clear: The White House had to win the confidence of the generals without losing the allegiance of Diem. Nhu was the culprit, according to Washington, but he was attached to Diem as tightly as a Siamese twin. Not much different than in the United States, said smirking Americans in the Saigon embassy, who referred to Nhu as "Bobby."[25]

ARVN leaders did not know what to do. General Don had called a staff meeting on the morning of August 23 to discuss the impending demonstrations and the growing anger among junior officers about the pagoda attacks. General Minh ("Big Minh") admitted that the perpetual presence of armed military personnel had created an "aura of suppression" that had alienated the populace. The charismatic leader had won his colleagues' support in reducing the size of the military contingents and in recalling all arms held by civilians. Khiem asked whether the government had a plan for dealing with student demonstrations. No such plan existed. Minh grimly commented that bloodshed would only incite the movement, and General Tran Van Minh (called "Little Minh" to distinguish him from "Big Minh") warned that the matter would "get out of hand." Don noted that when he alerted Diem of trouble, the premier had rejected the use of force against students.[26]

The dominance of both Nhu and his wife continued to grow. In a three-hour meeting later that same day of August 23, Don privately met with CIA agent Lucien Conein and assured him that the army had *not* been involved in the pagoda assaults. Diem remained in control, Don insisted, but all generals had to go through Nhu to see him. Conein believed him, having become fairly close to Don after a series of nightclub jaunts with him and other generals. In early July, following the Independence Day celebrations at the U.S. ambassador's home, the two men had met at the Caravelle Hotel, where Don confided his intentions to topple Diem from power. Don then tried to explain Madame Nhu's strange hold on Diem. She had the status of a premier's wife, a veritable "First Lady." Diem had never married and was not comfortable around women. Indeed, Don suggestively remarked, "The President likes good looking men around him." For nine years, Madame Nhu had comforted him at the end of the day, consoling him, talking and arguing with him, and, like a Vietnamese wife, playing the dominant role in the household. She and the president, however, resided in separate quarters and, according to Don, had never had sexual relations. As a matter of fact, he facetiously added, Diem had "never had sexual relations." Madame Nhu had beguiled Diem with her charm and had maneuvered herself into position to shape his government policies. It would be nearly impossible to convince Diem to turn his back on the Nhus because of their special positions: Nhu as Diem's "thinker" and Madame Nhu as Diem's "platonic wife."[27]

Don insisted that *Nhu* had engineered the pagoda raids out of fear that too much power had gravitated to the generals. In a masterful display of Machiavellian tactics, Nhu had used the cover of martial law to discredit the generals by outfitting the Special Forces in army garb during the attack. Don insisted that he had not known of this scheme and was with Khiem at Joint General Staff headquarters when a call came on his command radio informing him of the assault. Police Commissioner Tran Van Tu, supported by Tung's Special Forces nearby, was in charge when the police broke into Xa Loi pagoda, intending to confiscate the charred heart of Quang Duc. But two monks had fled the pagoda with the martyr's ashes in an urn, scurrying over the backyard wall and finding safety at the U.S. Operations Mission building next door. By the time Don arrived, the police had taken the other bonzes away.[28]

Don feared that Nhu would seize control of the government and emphasized the importance of keeping Diem in office. Lest someone suspect his own motives, Don renounced any interest in power. "I'm not smart nor am I ambitious. I only took the job to keep the Generals together." When asked by Conein if he preferred Diem or Nhu, Don did not hesitate to answer. "If I have the choice between the President and Nhu, Nhu is going."[29]

III

AT ANOTHER STAFF MEETING the following day of August 24, Don informed his colleagues that Nhu was organizing a huge Republican Youth demonstration for the next day. They all scoffed at Republican Youth director Cao Xuan Vy's estimate that 800,000 demonstrators would participate. "He'd be lucky to have 5,000," Tran Van Minh snidely remarked. But Big Minh referred to "reliable information" that predicted upward to 10,000—enough to ensure trouble. Students from the Faculties of Medicine and Pharmacy had already demonstrated the previous morning, leading the government to issue riot control directives to ARVN unit leaders. Minh had asked Diem what the army should do if matters got out of hand. "The demonstrations would be all right," angrily responded the premier in reiterating his refusal to use force against students. Minh urged Don to tell Diem that the army could not guarantee order. Don said nothing but "was visibly shaken and confused." How could he admit to his inability to keep order? Further disquieting was the report of a student group who had prepared banners for a counter-demonstration against the Republican Youth activists.[30]

General Kim, Deputy for Public Relations to Don and his brother-in-law, was anxious to know the U.S. position. Nhu had cleverly weakened the army command by first dividing it among Tung, Dinh, and Don, and then dealing with each man separately. Don did not command strong loyalty from the officer corps but appealed to most other generals and senior officers. If the United States supported an attempt by the generals to dispel the Nhus, the rest of the army (except for Tung) would unite behind the effort. Kim did not personally care for Diem but would support his retention if the Nhus fell from power.[31]

Thuan likewise urged the Kennedy administration to separate Diem from Nhu. In an August 24 breakfast meeting with his long-time friend Rufus Phillips, director of Rural Affairs in the U.S. Operations Mission, Thuan insisted that there was no alternative to Diem in terms of respect and acceptability in the country. Thuan sought U.S. assistance in ridding South Vietnam of the Nhus. Phillips did not trust Thuan because of his close association with Nhu but thought the conversation had "the ring of truth." Thuan had considered resigning his cabinet post following the pagoda assaults but, after long and agonizing thought, remained in office for fear of his family's safety as well as out of personal loyalty to Diem. The premier, Thuan declared, had ordered Madame Nhu to stop making public statements and holding press conferences, and he had directed General Tran Tu Oai and the director general of information not to print any more of her acerbic remarks. Both Nhu and his wife were furious. Nhu was in "a dangerously triumphant mood," thinking himself in total control of events and openly "contemptuous" of Americans. The army, Thuan insisted, would break with Nhu if the United States clarified its opposition to a government run by him. "The Army would respond."[32]

That same day, Lodge informed the White House of further evidence of Nhu's attempt to disgrace the army. Indeed, Hilsman regarded the mode of delivery of the news to the embassy as a virtual overture by South Vietnam's generals to the U.S. government. The previous day, General Kim bitterly confided to Phillips that Nhu had tricked the army into imposing martial law and becoming his "puppet." Generals Dinh, Don, and the others had not been aware of the plans to raid the pagodas. These actions had resulted from Nhu's secret orders to Tung's Special Forces and the combat police. Nhu held control, with Don answering only to him. More than 1,400 Buddhists were in jail for harboring arms and explosives that Nhu had planted in the pagodas. His scheme had worked. The Vietnamese people had castigated the army (and its sponsor, the United States), further facilitating Nhu's rise to power.[33]

Still another source of information held Nhu responsible for the present crisis. In a conversation with Foreign Service officer Paul Kattenburg in Saigon on August 24, Vo Van Hai, Diem's personal secretary, reported that Nhu's agents had him (Hai) under surveillance and that his life was in danger. Hai insisted that Diem wanted a settlement with the Buddhists but had squandered the opportunity by lengthy delays that undermined the credibility of the older and more conservative monks and thrust the younger and more activist monks to the front. Nhu, Hai nervously contended, had "carefully stage-managed" the actions against the Buddhists, using his wife to stir up popular anger against the bonzes and shifting the blame to the generals by setting up their meeting with Diem just before the raids. In a statement confirming Trueheart's earlier observation, Hai declared that Nhu had orchestrated the action to take place just before Lodge's arrival so as to present him with a fait accompli. "It would not be difficult" for the generals to throw out Nhu if the United States offered encouragement. Please "save the boss by getting rid of Nhu."[34]

Almost every source considered Nhu the central problem, and yet Lodge remained cautious, warning the White House on August 24 that the time was not right to cast its lot with the generals. Lodge did not agree with the CIA, which called Nhu "the controlling figure, possibly without President Diem's assent." Based on the separate conversations with Thuan, Hai, Don, and Kim, Lodge asserted that Nhu ("if he did not fully mastermind it") probably had Diem's support in planning the raids. It seemed likely that the army had not participated in the pagoda strikes and that the guilty parties were the police and Tung's Special Forces. But most important, Lodge emphasized, all three officers commanding significant military strength in Saigon—Don, Dinh, and Tung—remained loyal to either Diem or Nhu. Any U.S. effort to manipulate the generals would be "a shot in the dark."[35]

At this critical juncture, General Khanh informed the CIA Station Chief in Saigon, John Richardson, on Sunday, August 25, of a disturbing development: Nhu was considering an agreement with Hanoi that would end the war. Besides dishonoring the generals in the pagoda raids, did Nhu also seek a North–South settlement that would force a U.S. withdrawal? The Kennedy administration denounced this betrayal of trust, even though a year earlier it had privately authorized Harriman to explore similar possibilities with Hanoi's representatives in Geneva. Hilsman asserted years afterward that the White House dismissed all such talk as the Diem regime's attempt to place pressure on the United States. But Khanh's allegations attracted immediate attention in the state department, which considered him "one of [the] best of Generals, both courageous and sophisticated." Most important, the ARVN generals believed the story. Khanh told a CIA officer in Saigon that they feared for their lives and "would definitely revolt" if Nhu sought an agreement with either Hanoi or Communist China that neutralized South Vietnam. Afterward, the generals realized, Nhu would turn on them. They "would go down fighting if the politicians now in power moved in the wrong direction." Because of the difference in times, the cable reporting Khanh's meeting with Richardson arrived in Washington on Saturday, August 24, at 9:30 in the morning.[36]

Khanh's story could not have been a total surprise in Washington. Nolting had reported a number of back-channel contacts made by Nhu with the Communists that his brother "knew all about." Trueheart, however, disputed the claim that Nhu was privately dealing with North Vietnam and wanted U.S. forces withdrawn. "I really think that was a lot of horseshit." Years afterward, however, Nolting recalled that "Viet Cong leaders would come into Nhu's office in the palace . . . under a gentlemen's agreement that they wouldn't be nabbed while they were there." "I knew about this," Nolting declared. "And I'm sure they said, 'Don't let the Americans get any heavier in here.' And Nhu said, 'Don't let the Chinese meddle in this one.'" Washington, Nolting noted, blasted the Ngo brothers' actions as treason. "I got into real difficulties on occasion trying to say, 'Wait a minute. Maybe this isn't so treasonable. Maybe this is the way to compose this thing. Give them a chance. They're not all that stupid, and they're not going to betray us." Nhu was trying to persuade the Vietcong "to sell out, in effect, to the government.'" The White House decided not to interfere, letting the business proceed as long as the Diem regime did not sell out to the Communists. Nolting was not sure who responded to his telegrams, but Rusk's signature was on all of them.[37]

Nolting's account fits with numerous well-founded stories in the summer of 1963 that the Polish representative on the International Control Commission, Mieczyslaw Maneli, was serving as a peace intermediary between Nhu and Hanoi. Maneli, who had survived the concentration camp at Auschwitz during World War II and was now a University of Warsaw law professor and member of the Communist party, later affirmed he met twice with Nhu. The first occasion was on August 25, at a reception in Saigon attended by a large gathering of diplomatic representatives, and the second time was in private at Gia Long Palace on September 2. The French ambassador in Saigon, Roger Lalouette, had arranged the initial meeting with the support of Indian ambassador and ICC chair Ramchundur Goburdhun, Italian ambassador Giovanni Orlandi, and the Vatican's delegate, Monsignor Salvatore d'Asta. Lalouette, according to Maneli, sought to develop a cultural and economic exchange between the Vietnamese antagonists that would lay the basis for reunification and thereby "redeem the Diem regime for France from the reckless Americans." The end of the war would permit neutralization under the direction of French president Charles de Gaulle, who intended to combine Vietnam with neutral Laos and Cambodia and make the region once again "a pearl in the 'grandeur de France.'" The timing of the first meeting between Nhu and Maneli coincided with the alarm expressed by Khanh and lends credence to his fears.[38]

When Maneli had first presented these peace plans to Hanoi in the spring of 1963, Prime Minister Pham Van Dong repeated Ho Chi Minh's earlier assertion that the North Vietnamese were ready to negotiate at any time. Foreign Minister Xuan Thuy had a list of goods that included coal and other industrial materials, which his government would exchange with the south for rice and various foodstuffs. Both North Vietnamese leaders were openly hostile to the Diem regime but nonetheless receptive to negotiations. Ho had earlier conceded to Goburdhun that Diem was "a patriot in his way" and that trade relations were possible. "Shake hands with him for me if you see him," Ho declared.[39]

In July 1963, Maneli visited Hanoi again, later claiming that Ho's interest in negotiations had shaped the NLF's decision against escalating its actions during the Buddhist crisis. Indeed, the North Vietnamese indicated that Diem could become an acceptable head of the Saigon government. Lalouette thought Diem would survive if he accepted a political settlement. "He would have had to change the system if he stayed on, but he had the government and administration, and he had good men." That summer, Ho publicly called for a cease-fire that, this time, seemed sincere in light of his government's concern over the expanding U.S. military involvement. Maneli also saw hope for Diem's staying in office—at least for a while. "If the government in Hanoi does not undertake an offensive designed to remove Diem and Nhu from Saigon, this is certainly because it wishes them to survive for a time yet—long enough to come to an agreement with them behind the Americans' backs." Based on information received in the North, Nhu had perhaps already talked with Ho "through direct emissaries of the North, with the help of the French." Maneli was correct. Years later, according to the Saigon newspaper *Hoa Binh*, Nhu met with Vietcong representatives in his home city of Hué in early 1963. He then talked with the brother of a North Vietnamese ambassador, and negotiations had begun by July, as Maneli suspected. And, in accordance with Lalouette's thinking, these secret discussions help to explain why the Vietcong did not take advantage of Diem's troubles with the United States by launching a major assault in late August.[40]

When Maneli asked Pham Van Dong and Xuan Thuy what he should say if Nhu invited discussions, they replied: "Everything you know about our stand on economic and cultural exchange and cooperation, about peace and unification. One thing is sure: the Americans have to leave. On this political basis, we can negotiate about everything." Maneli asked Pham Van Dong (with Ho Chi Minh in the room, "silent, as if intimidated") whether Hanoi would consider "some kind of federation with Diem–Nhu or something in the nature of a coalition government." The prime minister declared: "Everything is negotiable on the basis of the independence and sovereignty of Vietnam. The Geneva Accords supply the legal and political basis for this: no foreign bases or troops on our territory. We can come to an agreement with any Vietnamese." Maneli warned that the Western powers would oppose a coalition government and insist on the safety of Diem and Nhu. "Everything can be the subject of negotiations," Pham Van Dong repeated. "We have a sincere desire to end hostilities, to establish peace and unification on a completely realistic basis. We are realists."[41]

Maneli concluded in his report to his superiors in Warsaw on July 10, 1963, that both Vietnamese governments wanted to reach an agreement on their own. They sought to do this "without the participation of the Great Powers, without Moscow, Washington, and certainly without Peking [Beijing]; both governments wish for supersecret talks and the retention of a certain official façade." Hanoi had taken the initiative without first securing Beijing's approval. If Diem and Nhu wished to survive, Maneli repeatedly insisted to his government in early August, they would either have to leave the country or crush the Buddhists. Hanoi and the Vietcong had opted to "wait for a new 'civil war'" and at the first opportunity will back Diem against the Americans." Both Pham Van Dong and Ho Chi Minh had made their stand clear: "Our most important aim and task is to get rid of the Americans. And then we will see." Maneli had no doubt that "a supersecret understanding" existed between "Diem–Nhu and Hanoi"— that "as long as Diem–Nhu are engaged in a struggle against their American constituents and allies, Hanoi lets them live."[42]

Lodge's appointment as the new U.S. ambassador, Maneli asserted, set off the events that led to his first meeting with Nhu on August 25, 1963. Indeed, the White House move "spelled the end of the Diem regime" and forced it to squelch the "pro-American" Buddhists before Lodge's arrival. The premier and his brother had launched the pagoda raids, Maneli argued, to "save themselves from an American coup d'etat," but the act had instead discredited the regime before its people and the world. Now desperate, Nhu arranged to have Saigon's new foreign minister, Truong Cong Cuu, invite Maneli to a reception just four days after the raids, which included Lodge on its guest list of diplomatic dignitaries. It was a pivotal decision. Maneli's presence marked the first time that a Communist diplomat had attended such a function in Saigon. There, in an obviously staged move, Lalouette, Orlandi, d'Asta, and Goburdhun brought Maneli and Nhu together.[43]

"I have already heard a great deal about you from our mutual friends," Nhu told Maneli as the small circle of diplomats looked on. "There exists in the Vietnamese people a sensitivity about sovereignty and a mistrust not only of the Chinese but of all occupants and colonizers, all!"[44]

Was he, thought Maneli and undoubtedly the others taking in the conversation, including the Americans?

"Now we are interested in peace," Nhu asserted, "and only in peace. . . . I believe that the International Commission can and should play an important role in restoring peace to Vietnam."

All members of the commission, Maneli dutifully assured Nhu, thought it "could play a constructive role if both sides desired it."

"The Vietnamese government wishes to act in keeping with the spirit of the Geneva Accords," Nhu emphasized.

That was the only way to achieve peace and reunification, Maneli responded.[45]

Lodge had met Maneli at the reception but wheeled away in the midst of a conversation, affirming Maneli's initial assessment of the ambassador's arrogance. Had Lodge stayed a few moments instead of leaving so early in the evening, he might have noticed Maneli's discussion with Nhu. Combined with what the White House already knew about Nhu's contacts with the Vietcong and with North Vietnam, Maneli's public exchange with Nhu might have encouraged the administration to examine its political implications. Did the meeting substantiate the widely held suspicion that Maneli had become an intermediary between the Vietnams? What impact would North–South discussions have on the generals' outlook toward a coup?[46]

III

LODGE'S ATTEMPT to delay any action had no impact: His August 24 telegram had arrived in Washington at 2:05 on a Saturday afternoon, when, as fate would have it, those few advisers on duty were the most outspoken opponents of the Diem regime. Forrestal, Hilsman, and Harriman anxiously read Lodge's account, noting that it confirmed their suspicions of Nhu's underhanded tactics in the pagoda raids. Did not this news strengthen the credibility of that morning's cable from Saigon containing Khanh's allegation that Nhu was in secret negotiations with Hanoi? Perhaps even Halberstam had been correct in that day's edition of the *New York Times*, when he reported that numerous observers in Saigon called the pagoda raids the "Nhu coup." Without checking first with assistant national security affairs adviser McGeorge Bundy, Forrestal attached an "eyes only" cover letter to a telegram sent to the president at 4:50 P.M., informing him of Lodge's note and including a suggested response to Saigon, which the three advisers—Forrestal, Harriman, and Hilsman—had drafted with the approval of Ball and Felt and wanted to send that night. Lodge had recommended a "wait and see" policy until he could determine whether the military would take action against Nhu. Harriman, Hilsman, and Forrestal wanted to act now because the situation in Saigon might not "remain fluid for long." Hilsman termed Lodge's cable as "perhaps the most convincing judgment of all" that South Vietnam's military leaders were unhappy with the Nhus' treatment of the Buddhists. If Nhu remained in power, "the regime would continue to follow the suicidal policies that were not only dragging Vietnam down to ignominy and disaster but the United States as well." Harriman and Hilsman insisted that the United States "move before the situation in Saigon freezes."[47]

The truth had become undeniable: Nhu was responsible for the raids. Telegram 243, drafted by Harriman, Hilsman, and Forrestal (with Mendenhall's help), called on Lodge to publicly accuse Nhu of the assault, while Washington and Voice of America did the same once the ambassador signified the proper time to do so. Nhu had cultivated the public impression that the army was responsible for the bloodshed and had thus maneuvered himself into leadership. The "US Government cannot tolerate [a] situation in which power lies in Nhu's hands. Diem must be given

[a] chance to rid himself of [Nhu] and his coterie and replace them [with the] best military and political personalities available."[48]

But Harriman, Hilsman, and Forrestal wanted to go farther: If Diem refused to remove Nhu, "we must face the possibility that Diem himself cannot be preserved." The United States must cut off all aid unless Diem instituted a reform program that included Nhu's removal. If Diem rejected this "reasonable opportunity" to regain control of his government, "then we are prepared to accept the obvious implication that we can no longer support Diem." Lodge and the Country Team should "urgently examine all possible alternative leadership and make detailed plans as to how we might bring about Diem's replacement if this should become necessary." In a statement that Hilsman later asserted had come by phone from Rusk (then in New York at the United Nations) but that the secretary of state denied, Lodge was to assure the "appropriate military commanders" of "direct [U.S.] support in any interim period of [a] breakdown [in the] central government mechanism." Although Washington could not provide "detailed instructions as to how the operation should proceed, . . . we will back you to the hilt on actions you take to achieve our objectives."[49]

To avoid delay, Forrestal telephoned the president, who was then in Hyannis Port, seeking verbal approval of the draft response.

"Can't we wait until Monday, when everybody is back?" Kennedy asked.

Harriman and Hilsman "really want to get this thing out right away," Forrestal shot back.

"Well," replied the president, "go and see what you can do to get it cleared."

Harriman and Hilsman were in "a great sweat," Ball later recalled, when they found him with Alexis Johnson on a Maryland golf course. Ball told his three colleagues to meet him at his home. There, Ball read the cable but refused to approve its dispatch without talking first with Rusk. Ball knew that the telegram could spark a coup. "It was perfectly clear that this could be taken as encouragement and would indeed be taken as encouragement by the generals." After reading the key paragraphs to Rusk over the phone and indicating that he would seek the president's view, Rusk responded, "Well, go ahead. If the president understood the implications, [I] would give a green light."

"What do you think?" Kennedy asked after Ball went over the entire matter by phone. Harriman and Hilsman strongly supported the move, Ball replied, noting that he had "watered down" the original version but that even the revision "would certainly be taken as encouragement by the generals to a coup." Diem had become an "enormous humiliation" for the United States by behaving in "the most unconscionable and cruel, uncivilized way toward a significant minority of the population." Madame Nhu continued to make "the most outrageous statements, and Nhu was a very devious and unreliable fellow." It was "probably all right" to send the telegram to Lodge. Kennedy, according to Ball, "seemed favorable to our proposed message, although he recognized the risk that, if a coup occurred, we might not like Diem's successor any better than Diem himself."

"Where's Bob [McNamara]?" Kennedy asked.

"He's away," Ball replied.

"Get hold of Ros Gilpatric and see that it's cleared with them [the Pentagon]." If Rusk and Gilpatric approved, "go ahead."

The most noteworthy feature of this bizarre decision-making process was that no one made a decision but merely signed off on one that they all thought someone else had made. Two decades afterward, Rusk showed no remorse over his approval of the telegram. "If Ball, Harriman, and President Kennedy were going to send it out, I wasn't going to raise any questions." Gilpatric had the same reaction. Forrestal telephoned him that Saturday night at his Maryland farm, assuring him that both the president and Rusk had approved the telegram. "If Rusk went along with it and the President went along with it, I wasn't going to oppose it," Gilpatric recalled years afterward. It was a matter between the White House and the state department. "In McNamara's absence I felt I should not hold it up, so I went along with it just like you countersign a voucher." Krulak likewise cleared the telegram without showing it to Taylor. Richard Helms of the CIA did the same—not referring the matter to its director, John McCone, because, Helms later explained, he thought that Forrestal had called to advise him of a decision already made. "It's about time we bit this bullet."

Forrestal informed the president that his advisers supported the telegram. "Send it out," Kennedy responded.[50]

Telegram 243 left Washington for Saigon at 9:36 in the evening of August 24.

Kennedy's advisers had not served him well. Having the advantage of hindsight, Gilpatric later remarked, "I frankly thought it was an end run. I was suspicious of the circumstances in which it was being done. The Defense and the military were brought in sort of after the fact." Harriman's views, Gilpatric argued, largely shaped the president's attitude toward a coup. For months, Kennedy's major advisers, McNamara and Taylor, had been defending Diem, and Harriman had never taken a strong stand on the matter. But during these August meetings, Harriman suddenly became a major player. "I think in the face of a very strong statement from him, enjoying as he did the president's confidence, . . . there was nothing that those of us who had any doubts could do about it." Gilpatric sensed that the president felt that he "was sort of being reluctantly or unwillingly carried along." The outcome "wasn't something that moved or sprang from any initiative on his part or any sense of judgment on his part." Nolting agreed. The president "felt uneasy" about the telegram to Lodge but could find no way to reverse matters. "I'm not sure he really wanted to, although he gave me the impression at times that if he could find a way to get back on the old track, he would like to do it."

Nolting asked Rusk about the new policy. "Why this change?"

"We cannot stand any more burnings," the secretary replied.

Thinking this an outlandish statement, Nolting pushed the issue: "Do you think the government of South Vietnam is responsible for these burnings?"[51]

That made no difference, Rusk implied. Public opinion overwhelmingly supported a change and that's the way the White House had to go.[52]

All those aware of Telegram 243 recognized that it promoted a coup. Ball assured the president that this was the case, even while making the questionable assertion years later that the telegram did not precipitate the coup. "I think we had established the causal relation, one way or another," Ball admitted. But he spread the blame. "I think this was only one of a number of things, and to put the total focus on this, I think, was a great mistake." William Bundy, however, did not hesitate. The assistant secretary of defense for International Security Affairs insisted that the August 24 telegram had encouraged a coup. Lodge was "to go to the military and say if you want to start something new, we won't be against you." This "had the effect of setting in motion all the thinking" that pointed to a coup. Ball realized that the telegram assured the generals of the president's favorable position toward their making the move. President Kennedy understood the ramifications of his action.[53]

Support for Lodge's caution had meanwhile come from Harkins, who met with Don on August 24 and became fully aware of the confused command in Vietnam. Don insisted that the army lacked unity and that his orders, along with those to the police and Special Forces, came directly from the palace. "A neatly engineered stalemate," Don testily remarked. The United States should continue supporting Diem but press him to establish an interim cabinet of civilian and military figures during the remainder of the crisis. Thuan should stay as secretary of state, Oai should remain minister of information, and Big Minh should become minister of the interior alongside another military figure as minister of defense. Admiral Felt forwarded Don's proposal to the Joint Chiefs of Staff late on the following morning of August 25, Honolulu time.[54]

But Don's recommendations aroused little interest among Americans both in Saigon and in Washington, who preferred an alternative approach just proposed by Lodge. The day after receiving Telegram 243, the ambassador saw that it had the president's blessing and called a meeting of his top embassy officers. The recommended action, Lodge feared, was too radical. He and Harkins concurred that the "chances of Diem's meeting our demands are virtually nil." A push for reforms at this critical stage would alert the regime that a coup was in the works and provide it with time to take action against the generals. Lodge proposed that "we go straight to [the] generals with our demands, without informing Diem. Would tell them we [are] prepared [to] have Diem without [the] Nhus but it is in effect up to them whether to keep him." Ball responded that same day: "Agree to modification proposed."[55]

It is impossible to determine whether Lodge had had direct contact with the president regarding this pivotal decision to speak directly to the generals. In actuality, it does not matter. Diem had not honored the agreements made with the Buddhists. He had rejected every U.S. argument for reforming his government and expelling the Nhus. The war against the Vietcong was going badly, despite U.S. military aid and advice. Now, with Congress and the American people hardening their opposition to a government that the Kennedy administration deemed crucial in the Cold War, the only recourse was to seek a viable alternative to Diem. Lodge had gone to Saigon as the president's personal representative, presumably authorized to promote any changes that facilitated U.S. interests. Why else would he have a private connection to the Oval Office? To go around Diem and talk with the generals fitted within the parameters of such a sweeping mandate.

Despite unanimous disgust with Nhu, several senior members of the Kennedy administration hotly denounced Saturday's events in Washington on their return to the White House on the Monday afterward. President Kennedy was taken aback by the bristling complaints he encountered that morning from Rusk, McNamara, Taylor, and McCone, who all denied approving the cable. "My God! My government's coming apart," the president afterward exclaimed to an old friend. McCone had been so incensed that he had asked Colby to use a White House jet to fly to his new home in California on Sunday, where he read the text, canceled his vacation, and returned to Washington that night. Taylor felt insulted by the cable's final line asserting that only the "minimum essential people" had seen its contents. In an acrimonious exchange during a noon White House meeting, he blasted the missive as an "egregious end run" that would have failed if senior officials had been in Washington on the day of its arrival. The cable, he bitterly declared, was the work of a faction unalterably opposed to Diem. Hilsman countered that the president and representatives of all agencies concerned had cleared the cable. But this assertion was specious. Admiral Herbert Riley had approved the action, admittedly without seeing the note. Spokesmen for both the defense department and the CIA had concurred, even though neither McNamara nor McCone had seen it. Taylor was outraged. He had not received a copy of the cable until late that Saturday night and, in a statement that ignored all previous efforts to convince Diem to make changes, insisted that it did not provide the premier with enough time to comply. And yet he signed it, not knowing that it had already gone to Saigon. Years afterward, he declared that "the anti-

Diem group centered in State had taken advantage of the absence of the principal officials to get out instructions which would never have been approved as written under normal circumstances." The message reflected Forrestal and Hilsman's "well-known compulsion" to topple Diem. They had pulled "a fast one."[56]

The infighting had finally pushed the president beyond his threshold of endurance. "This shit has got to stop!" he bellowed to a confidant. Kennedy was furious with Hilsman and Forrestal for incompetence and with Harriman for his indiscretion. He flared out at Forrestal for going ahead without securing McCone's specific approval. When Forrestal offered to resign, Kennedy sharply retorted, "You're not worth firing. You owe me something, so you stick around."[57]

In this fiercely adversarial atmosphere, the administration ultimately decided not to rescind the instructions to Lodge. Ball refused to retreat, insisting that "the evil influence of the Nhus" overrode all other considerations. "I didn't know any of the [Vietnamese] personalities," he later confessed, but Diem was "an offense to America." How could the United States permit "such brutality and crass disregard of world sensitivities?" McCone fumed over the manner in which the cable left Washington but did not advocate a change in policy. Even Taylor approved the chosen path, disgustedly asserting, "Yes, it's true that I signed the cable, or I released the cable. But I thought that the President had already made up his mind. There was not anything I could do." Besides, he groused, "You can't change American policy in twenty-four hours and expect anyone to ever believe you again." Kennedy, Ball later observed, appeared "annoyed by the waffling of his top command" and buttonholed each adviser while walking around the long table. "John, do you want to cancel it? Bob, do you want to cancel it? Dean, do you want to cancel it?" No one wanted to alter the present course. As Colby later observed, "It is difficult indeed to tell a President to his face that something he has approved is wrong and to do so without anything positive to offer in its place."[58]

Kennedy chose not to change policy, thereby fostering a coup and making his approval of Telegram 243 a momentous decision. If he had any reservations, according to Hilsman, "He didn't say anything." The president, with the unanimous but ambivalent support of his advisers, had allowed a vocal minority to rush him into a judgment that should have come only after careful deliberation. He was angry, both with his advisers for pushing too fast and with himself for giving in too easily. Had he not taken the same imprudent approach to Cuba in the spring of 1961? A change in Saigon's government under these shaky circumstances would tie the United States to a cause that was in total flux. His brother had discussed the matter with McNamara and Taylor, who all thought the outcome in Vietnam unpredictable and yet felt pressured into a policy that the administration had not even "fully discussed, as every other major decision since the Bay of Pigs had been discussed." The president later admitted to a "major mistake" and attributed much of the blame to Harriman. Robert Kennedy put it bluntly: "The result is we started down a road that we never really recovered from."[59]

The Kennedy administration had authorized direct involvement in reshaping South Vietnam's government. At a noon meeting in the White House on that same Monday of August 26, Hilsman recommended pressing Diem to replace Nhu with a mix of military and civilian personnel. Buoyed by the administration's decision to go ahead with the telegram, Hilsman declared that if Diem refused, the United States should seek his removal and work in the interim with Khiem as Army Chief of Staff and Khanh as II Corps Commander in Pleiku. The president pushed the issue. What would be the outcome should a coup fail? "The prospect," Hilsman replied, "was a very gloomy one; Nhu was anti-American." If Nhu's role in the pagoda raids seemed confirmed, a number of middle level officers and noncommissioned officers would abandon the regime and "disaster would be virtually unavoidable." McNamara concurred, warning that if the coup failed, "we would be on an inevitable road to disaster. The decision for the United States would be, therefore, to get out and let the country go to the Communists or to move U.S. combat forces into South Viet-Nam and put in a government of our own choosing." No one dissented. In response to the president's inquiry, Hilsman explained that an evacuation plan for Americans was in place. Most agreed that the only forces loyal to Nhu were those under Tung's command along with a few marine battalions. This was the time to act, chimed in Harriman. Kennedy then affirmed his support for a coup while taking a jab at the press. "Halberstam was a 28-year-old kid," the president sarcastically declared, and "[I want] assurances we were not giving him serious consideration in our decision. When we move to eliminate this government, it should not be the result of *New York Times* pressure."[60]

Taylor staunchly opposed the administration's willingness to manipulate a change in Saigon. Years afterward, he admitted that Diem was "a terrible pain in the neck," but he was honest and loyal to his country. The United States should have supported him until it found "someone better—looking under the bushes for George Washington, as I used to call it." South Vietnam's military command had split three ways, Taylor reminded his colleagues, making it prudent to continue working with Diem. President Kennedy recalled Nhu's recent meeting with the generals and asked whether he sought power for himself. Hilsman referred to two August 24 phone calls from Felt, urging the administration to support the generals in throwing out Nhu. "Unless the Nhus were eliminated," Felt had warned, "the middle level enlisted men would soon lose their interest in fighting." Taylor was furious over Felt's unauthorized actions. Hilsman noted the general's hot reaction and privately recorded that "Felt will hear about it." He did. Speaking for the joint chiefs, Taylor severely reprimanded the admiral for stepping out of channels in advising Hilsman. When the president asked Taylor about the chances of a successful coup, the general snidely remarked that "in Washington we would not turn over the problem of choosing a head of state to the military."[61]

Hilsman had emerged as the most outspoken proponent of a coup. Indeed, contemporaries would later refer to Telegram 243 as the "Roger Hilsman cable." McNamara wanted a precise definition of the "general officers group" that the United States intended to contact. Hilsman listed only three—Big Minh, Khiem, and Khanh—but insisted that there were others the three refused to name. Lodge was correct, the president declared; Diem would never remove Nhu. When Rusk disagreed, Hilsman pointed out that the Country Team in Vietnam was also convinced that Diem and Nhu would stand or fall together. What if both brothers survived? asked the president. "Nhu's grave emotional instability" made this "horrible to contemplate," remarked Hilsman. The Vietnamese people blamed the Nhus for the country's plight, not the United States, but, he warned, no change in power could take place without U.S. support. Rusk reiterated the need to act quickly, agreeing with McNamara that there was no middle ground. If Diem refused to change, "we must actually decide whether to move our resources out or to move our troops in." Hilsman drew the meeting to a close with the cryptic comment: "It is imperative that we act."[62]

THUS THE REALITY: A triumvirate of hard-line advisers who happened to be in Washington when news arrived of a possible coup had tied the administration to that coup. For too long, they complained, the White House had been coddling Diem, allowing him to slide by without pressuring him into instituting the reforms necessary to restoring domestic order and pursuing the war. The premier, insisted Harriman, Hilsman, and Forrestal, must either change his government or face a coup.

What no one realized—or at least acknowledged—was that the White House as Diem's long-time protector had taken a fateful step. Whether or not the Kennedy administration intervened directly, any action (or inaction) that suggested less than wholehearted support for the existing regime would leave the impression that its benefactor welcomed a change in leadership. The United States found itself in a precarious position. Failure to protect Diem would demonstrate support for the coup conspirators; any effort to safeguard his rule might scare off his enemies and undermine any chance of reforming South Vietnam. So the administration proposed a solution that was inherently contradictory: It offered Diem an opportunity to salvage his regime by making reforms at the same time that it undercut his regime by assuring assistance to the generals if they staged a coup. These incongruities did not faze the three White House advisers who had seized the moment to call for immediate action.

14

AT THE BRINK OF
A COUP—AGAIN

[The] American official hand should not show.

> Henry Cabot Lodge, August 26, 1963

I know from experience that failure is more destructive than
an appearance of indecision.

> President John F. Kennedy, August 29, 1963

We are launched on a course from which there is no
respectable turning back: the overthrow of the Diem
government.

> Henry Cabot Lodge, August 29, 1963

A T EIGHT in the morning of August 26, 1963, Saigon time, Voice of
America made an explosive announcement over radio: "Officials
in Washington say military leaders in the Republic of Vietnam are
not repeat not responsible for the attack against the Buddhists." Nhu, the
broadcast continued, had authorized the pagoda raids by Vietnam's secret
police and Special Forces, "some disguised as Army troops, and some wearing the uniforms of the Republican Youth Corps." Then, in an unprecedented move, Voice of America announced an impending change in U.S.
policy toward South Vietnam: The White House "may" order a "sharp
reduction" in its aid program unless Diem rids himself of the "secret police
officials" responsible for the attack. The broadcast reached a great mass of
Vietnamese people, as evidenced by the Diem regime's recent edict to arrest all those who listened to the radio station.[1]

Voice of America acted without authorization. Admittedly, Telegram
243 had approved a public statement of White House policy, *but only that
part dealing with Nhu's role in the pagoda raids, and only when the ambassador
determined its timing*. The speaker had violated the directive in two ways:
Lodge had *not* approved any release of information, and the administration
had not authorized any mention of aid cuts. The broadcast had resulted
from a combination of errors. Rusk attributed the gaffe to the "failure of

machinery here over [the] weekend to carry out policy instructions which would have prevented these broadcasts." The state department expressed regret for the broadcast and assured tighter coordination with the embassy in the future. Hilsman told the president that Voice of America was "guilty of an error" in discussing possible aid cuts. "This was contrary to explicit instructions that Voice of America should not become involved in specula-tion." The only part of the "press guidance" telegram authorized for public distribution was the assertion that the ARVN had not been responsible for the raids. The U.S. Information Agency ultimately accepted blame for the broadcast, calling it a "goof." What made the error so damaging is that the statement about cutting aid *did* express official policy. But the White House had not intended to announce that major policy reversal over radio.[2]

The timing of the radio proclamation could not have been worse. The fallout interfered with the U.S. embassy's intention to approach the gener-als quietly about keeping Diem without Nhu's suspecting an attempt to oust him from power. Trueheart termed the broadcast "an open invitation to the army to take over." The element of surprise was gone, Lodge an-grily told the White House. Its publicly acknowledged involvement in South Vietnam's internal affairs marked the "kiss of death" to America's "friends." He was especially apprehensive about the reactions of Diem and Nhu. They might seize him or some other high U.S. official as a hostage at his creden-tials ceremony scheduled for that same day. So concerned was Lodge that he followed Trueheart's recommendation and directed Harkins and Richardson not to attend. "If they try any funny business," Lodge explained, "it might be better if one of us were on the outside."[3]

Voice of America publicly retracted its statement about a possible aid cut, but that made matters worse. Nhu regarded the broadcast as further evidence that the Kennedy administration sought to keep only Diem in power. The premier interpreted the message as the first step toward bring-ing him down along with the entire regime. The episode created two in-congruous problems, both in need of immediate rectification: The original radio transmission signaled Diem that the White House was on the verge of abandoning him; its retraction suggested to the rebel generals that they would *not* receive U.S. support.[4]

I

THE UPROAR OVER the Voice of America broadcast did not stop the Kennedy administration's covert encouragement of a coup. In accordance with Washington's instructions, Lodge met with Harkins and the embassy staff on that same tumultuous morning to devise a strategy aimed at concealing U.S. involvement. The CIA would serve as a clandestine intermediary with the conspirators. Lucien Conein would make the initial contact with General Khiem, and a second CIA agent, Al Spera (posing as embassy adviser to the ARVN's Joint General Staff), would talk with his long-time friend, General Khanh. Conein could also discuss the matter with Don, if Khiem thought this approach advisable. No other general was to learn of the plan, even though this stipulation proved impossible to enforce. As noted earlier, Don had already approached Conein in early July about the generals' interest in unseating Diem. And just the day before Lodge's directive went into effect, Khanh told Spera in his Saigon home of the generals' plan to overthrow the government but refused to reveal the identities of other conspirators. Spera, however, specifically inquired about Khiem's stance, leading Khanh to clench his hands together and declare, "We are like this." But when Spera informed Khanh the next day that another U.S. emissary was discussing the matter with Khiem as well, the general angrily blasted the Americans' inability to maintain secrecy. "The U.S. government," he charged, "is endangering the entire plan." Although *Khanh* was responsible for exposing Khiem's sentiments, he blamed the embassy and cut off contact.[5]

The generals' apprehensions over U.S. support were justified because the White House had made clear that it would become involved only in the event of success. Indeed, Lodge had directed that the "American official hand should not show." The Nhus must leave the regime, but the generals could decide whether or not to retain Diem. The United States would furnish logistical support to military leaders in the field during the interim period between the collapse of the existing government and the installation of its successor. In the initial stages of the coup, however, the United States would provide no help to the generals. It was "entirely their own action, win or lose." They could not "expect [to] be bailed out."[6]

The generals' response to Lodge's noncommittal overtures laid open their lack of unity. Khiem was receptive to Conein's assurances but dared not take the matter to Don because his staff included some of Nhu's supporters. Khiem arranged for Conein to meet with Big Minh instead. Khanh seemed hesitant. No one should make a move against the regime, he told Spera, until Nhu contacted Hanoi about his treasonous plan for settling the war and thereby provided legal justification for deposing the government. Khanh also hoped that a U.S. aid cut would force Diem to dismiss Nhu and eliminate the need for a coup. If Nhu left the government, what countermeasures might Diem take? Would the United States provide refuge and support to families if the generals failed to overthrow the regime? Khanh, Spera observed, was having second thoughts about a coup.[7]

Conein's meeting with Big Minh was more productive. Khiem had accompanied Conein to the Joint General Staff's headquarters, informing him en route that Minh headed a committee of generals who wanted a coup within a week. The committee seemed impressive, including Khanh, Kim, Oai, Nguyen Ngoc Le, and Pham Xuan Chieu. Don was also a member of the committee but could do nothing because he was surrounded by Diem's supporters. One of the coup committee's first acts would be to disable Tung and his Special Forces. Vice President Tho supported the plot and was the generals' choice to head the successor government. The new regime would not be a military junta, although the projected cabinet included military figures.[8]

In these tense moments, Lodge demonstrated his strong support of a coup. Vietnamese from all parts of society were angry that U.S. military equipment had provided Diem with the means for repressing the Buddhists. If the current crisis continued, the vocal criticisms of the United States could escalate into outright hostility. Some Vietnamese had already equated the U.S. "hands-off" policy toward the Buddhist crisis with White House approval of Diem's oppressive actions, which, Lodge warned, was "only one step removed from placing [a] share of [the] blame on US shoulders." The "strong implication in these comments (and frequently overtly stated)" was that the "Diem government and family must go."[9]

Edward Lansdale now briefly returned to the scene, forwarding information to the White House that further suggested the wisdom of a coup. Although assigned to special operations toward Cuba, he had accepted an invitation to the Vietnamese embassy in Washington from Madame Chuong. On the evening of August 27, she and her husband told Lansdale that the United States must "act firmly and quickly to replace both Diem and Nhu with a new government." The Vietnamese people, the Chuongs insisted, were sickened by the brutal repression of the Buddhists by the Special Forces, then armed with U.S. weapons, and would turn against the United States unless a change in government took place. Madame Chuong urged Lansdale to warn Diem and the Nhus to leave the country. "The people hate them and they shouldn't stay for the people to kill them." Diem and his family were "cut off from reality." The United States had told Syngman Rhee to leave the Republic of Korea. "Why not Diem and Nhu?" Forrestal did not regard Lansdale's news as "hard stuff," but it reinforced the administration's interest in a coup.[10]

The subject of the coup had so consumed the White House that the president met daily with his advisers in a practice similar to that of the Cuban missile crisis of October 1962. At the first meeting on August 26, 1963, McNamara recommended the preparation of biographical sketches of the key people involved in overthrowing the government. According to Gilpatric, the state department tried to bar Nolting from White House meetings having anything to do with Diem. Harriman, Hilsman, Mendenhall, and others "were trying to take over jurisdiction in this area. The President came to resent the pressure, particularly when he found that General Krulak and the people from the Defense Department didn't go along and when Ambassador Nolting, for whom President Kennedy had a very high regard, was being excluded." When the president suggested inviting Nolting to the next day's meeting, Hilsman balked, warning that the former ambassador's views were "colored" because he was "emotionally involved in the situation." "Maybe properly," the president sharply retorted in insisting on Nolting's presence.[11]

The following day, August 27, the administration's coup advocates confronted considerable opposition. Colby informed his colleagues that CIA officials had talked with two Vietnamese generals the day before, one of whom thought the atmosphere favorable for a coup within a week. The other, however, gave a "jumpy answer" to the CIA query. In response to the president's question, Nolting thought the generals a poor bet for a coup. They were divided, had no leadership, did not control the military, and lacked the "guts of Diem or Nhu." McNamara seemed to agree, referring to a list of coup generals who were scattered throughout the country and had a small following. Loyalist generals held the advantage in that they were in Saigon. Nolting insisted that the unrest caused by the Vietcong was confined to the cities and that the peasants wanted only personal security. Diem was a man of integrity who should receive an "E" for effort. Kennedy was puzzled. Did not your August 13 report highlight Diem's promises to "oust Madame Nhu" and conciliate the Buddhists? Was Hilsman correct in calling Diem a liar? Diem had asked Australia to take Madame Nhu, Nolting explained. But Diem and Nhu had changed tactics the day following the report, calling conciliation a failure and resorting to force. Now, however, they were trying to defuse the situation by quietly releasing the monks.[12]

President Kennedy was not persuaded by Nolting's defense of the regime, and yet he saw no sense in a coup that had little chance for success. Did it have military support? No, insisted Nolting. Numerous generals would back a coup aimed at Nhu, but not at Diem. This created an impossible situation. "Diem and Nhu were Siamese twins who could not be forced apart." If the generals acted against Nhu, Nolting insisted, "Diem would go down with him in the palace." If Diem escaped, he would return to lead a countercoup. The only way to separate the brothers was to convince Diem to send Nhu out of the country. Nolting wryly noted that "the circle had nearly been completed in a three-year period." Ambassador Durbrow had told Diem three years earlier that Nhu had to leave the government. Diem had refused to follow the suggestion, and Durbrow lost his post. President Kennedy saw the irony in Nolting's recent removal from Saigon and smiled. This was not the time to act, Nolting declared. "We will take our lumps because of the actions of Diem and Nhu, but if they succeed, we will have preserved a base for the fight against the Viet Cong." CIA "agents had already told some generals to undertake a coup. If we go back on these generals now," Nolting admitted, "we will lose them." But "why should we jump unless we have some place to jump?" The president countered that the administration had not gone too far and that it could delay a signal to the generals, who had requested a sign over Voice of America. "We should send no signal if there is no real coup planning."[13]

The president remained uncertain, given his advisers' conflicting assessments. Hilsman preferred prompt action. "The longer we wait the harder it would be to get Diem out." What was Harkins's position? asked the president. Taylor asserted that "General Harkins had never been asked for his views. . . . [H]e merely got orders." Rusk insisted that the crucial consideration was whether the domestic unrest interfered with the war. "If Vietnamese opposition to Diem is great, it is very hard for us to support Diem." The president wanted a cable sent to Lodge and Harkins, asking for their prognosis regarding a coup. Nolting thought that a White House threat to reduce assistance might convince Diem to make changes in his government. The president pondered what impact a decision "to cut our losses" would have on a coup. He closed the meeting by repeating Nolting's admonition that "the generals interested in the coup were not good enough to bring it about."[14]

By the time the president and his advisers gathered at noon on August 28, they had found themselves immersed in a coup plot that was no longer secret and that was fast spinning out of control. Before the meeting could begin, Colby had to clear up a furor resulting from a commercial telegram sent by an unknown source in California, who had urged Lodge to overthrow the Saigon government and trick Diem into thinking that the instruction had come from President Kennedy. Hilsman called the writer a "crackpot," and Robert Kennedy recommended that the CIA discredit the cable by having several more messages sent from the same person. Did *everyone* know of the coup?[15]

The advice continued its contradictory course, even though interest in a coup remained steady. Nolting warned again that Diem and Nhu were probably aware of U.S. contacts with the generals. The "good faith of the U.S. is involved" and it should not go ahead. Hilsman called General Dinh "the key to the situation. We must find out whether he could be corrupted and, if so, attempt to get him to go against Diem." Ball declared that the United States could not accept Nhu in power. "We had no option but to back a coup. We are already beyond the point of no return. The question is how do we make this coup effort successful." McNamara, however, doubted that the generals could overthrow Diem and warned that we could not be pushed into this. "If we decided to back a coup we should go in to win." The president noted that both Lodge and Harkins thought the United States should go ahead. Nolting expressed surprise at Harkins's support, but President Kennedy asserted that the White House had asked him twice and received approval both times. "If a coup is not in the cards," the president noted, "we could unload." Ball had no reservations about moving ahead. If we did nothing and the generals failed, "we have lost as well." That left one option: "We decide to do the job right. There is no other acceptable alternative. We must decide now to go through to a successful overthrow of Diem. We had no option but to back a coup." Harriman agreed. Colby noted, "The point of no return had been reached." Ball briskly added, "We are already beyond the point of no return."[16]

II

MOMENTUM FOR A COUP continued to build, overriding any thought of holding back U.S. support. Treasury Secretary Douglas Dillon warned that "if anything starts it will be labeled as a U.S. show from the very beginning. If we decide to back the rebel generals we must do whatever is required to be certain they succeed in overthrowing Diem." The president concurred. "We should decide what we can do here or suggest things that can be done in the field which would maximize the chances of the rebel generals. We should ask Ambassador Lodge and General Harkins how we can build up military forces which would carry out a coup." Kennedy, however, expressed concern about the generals. "At present, it does not look as if the coup forces could defeat Diem." Dillon interrupted to say, "Then don't go." But Kennedy persisted. Lodge had requested authority to divert all economic and military assistance from the regime to the coup generals. In a preposterous suggestion, he wanted to make a public announcement that the United States was helping those interested in overthrowing Diem. Ignoring this idea, the president asked what the state department had done to attract support from those generals who remained undecided. "Suitable discreet comments about the US attitude towards the Nhus," Hilsman responded, along with leaks about the presence of U.S. military forces, including the Seventh Fleet.[17]

Harriman railed against further hesitation. "We have lost Vietnam if the coup fails. We cannot win the war with the Nhus. We have lost the fight in Vietnam and must withdraw if a coup does not take place. We put Diem in power and he has doublecrossed us. Diem and his followers have betrayed us." The United States must remove the entire family. "It was a mistake that we had not acted a long time ago." Hilsman heartily agreed. "We can't stop the generals now. They must go forward or die."[18]

The president nonetheless remained cautious. "Diem held the balance of power," and we need more information from Lodge and Harkins on the generals' strength. Robert Kennedy wondered what the U.S. reaction should be if Diem tried to destroy the coup before the generals acted. Hilsman had a ready answer: "The generals could put the Vice President of Vietnam in power and govern the country the way the generals have in Korea. Diem and Nhu would have to be exiled." Nolting called for one last attempt to persuade Diem to remove the Nhus. Harriman opposed that suggestion, insisting that "the political forces in Vietnam will rally quickly against Diem." Diem and Nhu, Hilsman asserted, were probably aware of the coup plotting and the generals had no choice but to go ahead or flee the country. President Kennedy argued that he "was not sure that we were in that deep." In a statement revealing no small measure of naïveté, he declared that, according to his understanding, "only two contacts by two CIA men had been made with two Vietnamese generals."[19]

President Kennedy's dilemma became more difficult because of Taylor's backstage tactics in seeking to halt the coup involvement. World opinion criticized Diem along with the United States for supporting him, the president noted, and yet the margin of coup support in South Vietnam remained extremely narrow. Taylor saw the opening and emphasized that Diem's loyalists outnumbered the coup units about two to one in the critical area of Saigon. Admittedly, the coup's proponents had the upper hand outside the city. But on balance, the president was correct in observing that the generals held only a thin advantage. Further disturbing was the arrival of conflicting messages from Saigon. Lodge remained optimistic about a coup; Harkins, however, had suddenly surprised everyone by doubting the generals' capacity to succeed. What had caused Harkins's transformation? A follow-up investigation revealed that he had responded in tune to a private telegram from Taylor, who had planted a leading question indicating that the administration was "now having second thoughts." Whereas Harkins had been silent before, he now found fault in Telegram 243, telling Taylor that it was "a bit contradictory" in that "it gave Diem a chance yet at the same time it told [the] military to go ahead." The key, Harkins insisted, was to eliminate the Nhus. "By elimination I do not mean destruction. I hope that we could even pay for a protracted leave of absence from the post to someplace where their voice of authority could not be heard." To President Kennedy's puzzled query about Harkins's markedly changed views on a coup, Taylor asserted, "We thought he was for the coup plan, but General Harkins apparently thought that a decision had been made in Washington to back a coup and that his task was to carry out a decision communicated to him." Finding that the White House had not made such a decision, Harkins now spoke his mind.[20]

Hilsman suspected Taylor of underhanded behavior. To balance Felt's support for the telegram, Taylor had played "dirty pool" in going "behind the back door" to reshape Harkins's response. Had Harkins shifted his position only because, as loyal team player, he thought the White House had done so? The president called Taylor into the Oval Office, or "into the woodshed," as Hilsman happily remarked, and gave him "a verbal spanking." Indeed, Hilsman added, this was probably the point at which both Kennedys saw Taylor "in a quite different light."[21]

The president must have recalled strikingly similar events during the spring of 1961 as he had stood at the brink of another coup—in Cuba. Surely, he grasped the irony of the combined civilian and military pressure on his office as he made the observation now, more than two years later, "Both Ambassador Lodge and General Harkins had recommended that we go ahead." Yet Kennedy had learned from the 1961 disaster that he must not feel compelled to take a similar action in 1963 just because he had come this far. How pivotal this moment must have seemed as he sat in silent rumination over the global consequences of a move that bore remarkable resemblance to that time not so long ago—when the clock had loudly monitored the new administration's ill-fated attempt to remove Fidel Castro from office. Kennedy's civilian and military experts in both instances had professed to know much more than they did, advocating risky military interventionist schemes for which they (then and now) could escape blame because, as Harry Truman publicly declared, the buck stopped with the president. And now, as in the final days before the Bay of Pigs invasion, the United States's clandestine involvement in the coup effort in Vietnam had threatened to become public as the result of a reporter's assiduous work. In the *New York Times* on August 28, Tad Szulc (who had likewise revealed the 1961 coup effort) published a story entitled "Long Crisis Seen on Vietnam Rule," which now exposed the White House's intention to remove Nhu and, if necessary, his brother, by a military coup.[22] Kennedy might well have recalled a statement he made while admonishing himself in the aftermath of the 1961 debacle: that victory had a hundred fathers, but defeat was an orphan.

This time, however, the president felt confident that the U.S. hand would remain hidden; after all, its secret CIA contacts with the generals were plausibly deniable. He recognized that more than a few of his civilian and military advisers were uncertain about a coup's success. But he also knew that, unlike the United States's direct participation in the Cuban fiasco, it would play no direct role in Diem's overthrow. The generals *must* take the first step; only after they seized control of the government would the United States become visibly involved—and then only by extending aid to the successor regime. Comforting was the notion that U.S. action was contingent on success and therefore subject to cancellation at any time. Like McNamara and Nolting, however, Kennedy had nagging doubts about the generals' will. But the web-like affair became more entangled. Ball noted that the only U.S. connection with the generals had been through two CIA officials, and he recommended that American military leaders leave no doubt of the U.S. position by talking directly with them. "Until our military officers contact the generals, several generals who we now consider doubtful would not shift to supporting the group planning to overthrow Diem."[23]

As the White House debate continued, it became clear that the administration could not evade responsibility for a coup. McGeorge Bundy tried to distinguish between taking "operational control of a coup," which they were *not* trying to do, and "merely telling the generals that we understand how they feel about Diem and that we can't live with the Nhus." In the din and confusion of a coup, would that distinction prove convincing? Hilsman wanted to surge ahead. Failure to act would undermine U.S. influence throughout Asia by leaving the impression that it had condoned Nhu's "desecration of the temples." After a pause, he darkly asserted, "There were some things we could do in which the U.S. hand would not show."[24]

In retrospect, Dillon had offered the wisest insight into the growing imbroglio. Regardless of the administration's clandestine actions, the treasury secretary had warned, it could not escape the public perception of U.S. involvement in a coup. If Diem failed to survive, everyone would assume that the White House had been instrumental in the outcome, either by facilitating his collapse or by doing nothing to stop it. Hanoi had gained a great propaganda victory in calling Diem America's puppet, meaning that if he lost his position as premier the widespread belief would be that the United States had cut the strings. If he held onto his office, the popular assumption would be that his protector had made this possible. Consequently, the only satisfactory form of involvement in a coup was to go all the way and succeed while preparing to sustain major criticisms; to go halfway raised the likelihood of a defeat whose onus would fall on the United States.

The CIA believed that the situation in Saigon had "reached [the] point of no return." The Ngo family had "dug in for [a] last ditch battle" from which the generals could not retreat. Conein's meeting with Khiem had revealed that the great majority of officers favored swift action. "Unless the generals are neutralized before being able to launch their operation," the CIA claimed, "we believe they will . . . have [a] good chance to win." At the outset of the revolt, its leaders must capture Dinh and Tung. Should the Ngos hold on, "they and Vietnam will stagger on to final defeat at the hands of their own people." If the generals failed, the Saigon government, Americans at home, and the international community would demand a drastically reduced U.S. presence in South Vietnam. The generals must succeed "without apparent American assistance." But "whatever needs to be done on our part must be done." If the generals failed, the CIA concluded, "we believe it no exaggeration to say that Vietnam runs [the] serious risk of being lost over the course of time."[25]

The road to a coup remained uncertain as the pressure threatened to rip apart the Kennedy administration. At the third White House meeting, in the early evening of August 28, the tension reached fever pitch when Harriman laced into Nolting's unbending loyalty to Diem. "You've been wrong from the beginning," the former New York governor bitterly charged in front of his shocked colleagues. "No one cares what you think." Harriman, Gilpatric asserted, "was very hot on Nolting and I thought very unfairly critical. Indeed, I never was present at a session with the President at which someone took the dressing down that Nolting did from Harriman. I think a lot of us were very surprised and rather shocked at Harriman's attitude, but Harriman held a unique position because of his age and prior experience." He was "very rough" and deserved his nickname of the "Crocodile," Gilpatric remarked. "He could be very, very alligatorish." Harriman "just lies up there on the riverbank," McGeorge Bundy shrewdly remarked, "his eyes half closed, looking sleepy. Then, *whap*, he bites." The grizzled diplomat and political warrior even carried his anger outside the meeting when he refused to accompany Nolting in the limousine ride back to the state department. Kennedy was both furious with Taylor's unauthorized telegram to Harkins and dumbfounded by Harriman. How could his advisers so viciously "divide almost down the middle in their opinions of what was going on in the country and what should be done about it"?[26]

Harriman was excessively blunt but not entirely wrong in his assessment of Nolting, for the ambassador had not foreseen the coming fury of the Buddhist revolt. He had left his post for a vacation at precisely the time the trouble first erupted in May 1963, never expecting the events in Hué to develop into a crisis. Now, in August, he was stunned by the pagoda raids but still supported Diem against the great majority of colleagues who were appalled by the regime's brutalities. Harriman later declared, "I never thought a great deal of Nolting." The ambassador had always been close to Trueheart, but on his return to Saigon he found that his chargé had taken a strong anti-Diem position and unfairly "put in the record that Trueheart had been disloyal to him." Harriman insisted that Nolting let personal motivations guide him. He was captivated by Diem, accepting him "hook, line, and sinker . . . I don't think he's a man that I'd give full marks for loyalty, number one, or judgment, number two."[27]

Out of these rancorous meetings came a directive to Lodge that was masterful in obfuscation. The White House indicated that his call for coup support had undergone review "at [the] highest levels" and was "most helpful." It warned that "whatever cover you and we maintain," U.S. prestige would become involved. What was the latest time at which the operation could come to a halt? The "Nhus must go and [a] coup will be needed," but the White House did not want to "bind" Lodge against his "better judgment at any stage." Its understanding was that the generals had been told that "they will have to proceed at their own risk and will not be bailed out by us."[28]

The Kennedy administration was attempting to steer between full-scale involvement and no involvement in the coup, but its longstanding public commitment to Diem left no midway point. The result was a shaky policy that ensured the perception of U.S. intervention no matter the outcome. The only way for the White House to evade responsibility for a coup was to side openly with Diem, which was out of the question, while anything less than all-out support for the regime would automatically ally the Kennedy administration with the coup makers. The president nonetheless held to the fiction that he could stop a coup and that two CIA contacts with two Vietnamese rebel generals did not constitute a signal of U.S. cooperation. Were they not two representatives of the Washington government? To speak with the rebel generals through CIA agents; to discuss terminating aid to the Saigon government in an effort to force reform; and to express interest in aiding a successor government—these actions sent signals to the generals that they would encounter no U.S. opposition to their seizure of the government. A critical snag remained, however: They could count on U.S. support only if they succeeded. If there were any principles involved in this episode, one comes to mind: Even a White House refusal to help the coup generals would not relieve it of blame.

The Kennedy administration decided to foster a coup by a group of indecisive generals against an undemocratic host government that had been a U.S. protectorate for nearly a decade but had become increasingly uncooperative. Harriman, Hilsman, and Forrestal had pushed a course of action that, whether or not successful, would tie their nation's prestige to the result. Hilsman had attempted to ease his colleagues' concerns by insisting that the generals wanted a bloodless coup and might only need a few U.S. helicopters. How could they guarantee no casualties? Would not the loan of a single helicopter constitute direct U.S. military involvement in a coup? The president had adopted a slippery policy of indirectly encouraging a coup without directly encouraging the coup makers. If the generals overthrew the Saigon regime, either with or without Diem's remaining in office after the Nhus' departure, the Kennedy administration would work with the new premier. But if the generals failed, it intended to continue supporting the Diem government as if nothing had happened.

Such a transparent two-faced policy offered no benefits to the United States. In the first scenario, a new government would come to power without direct U.S. assistance and hence feel no obligation to the United States. In the second, the Diem regime would hang on to power without having received direct U.S. support and likewise owe nothing to the United States. If there is a second principle involved in this bizarre set of events, it is that outside interference in another country's internal affairs is rarely as simple as it seems.

III

WHILE THE PRESIDENT'S ADVISERS continued their heated discussions, Lodge sought White House authority to suspend aid to the regime if such a step facilitated the coup. Big Minh had retracted his no-contact policy with Americans and asked to meet with CIA representatives the following morning of August 29 at Joint General Staff headquarters. Did that request signify the certainty of a coup? Or did it reveal deepening doubts of U.S. support and growing fears of going ahead? Vice President Tho that same morning had made a few remarks to Lodge that were consistent with coup plans. In the middle of a casual conversation, Tho's entire demeanor suddenly changed. "It can't go on in this way," he exclaimed. "We absolutely must get out of the state we are in. Emotions are rising so high that it is very dangerous." Lodge insisted that the majority of generals would back a coup if the United States offered encouragement. The coup committee was the "best group" in "ability and orientation." Khanh and Kim would unite behind Big Minh's leadership. Most of the officer corps agreed with the coup proponents, whose chances "would be greatly enhanced if at [the] critical juncture [the] U.S. publicly announced that all aid through the Diem government had ceased and would be resumed as soon as conditions warranted."[29]

Lodge felt certain that Diem was aware of his perilous position. In compliance with Rusk's note of the day before, Lodge arranged a meeting with the premier on the afternoon of August 28, during which he "talked largely to himself" for three hours and evidenced a "growing neurosis." At one point, Diem personified the funereal tone of their conversation when he emotionally declared: "I'm ready to die, at once, if [the] sweat and blood of [the] last nine years [is] now to be sacrificed to [a] small group of agitators in Buddhist disguise, whom [the] population [in] any case despises." Communists had infiltrated the Buddhist leadership, he charged. The generals had unanimously called for the pagoda assault, convincing him that "Communist controlled agitators" were responsible for the domestic troubles and that severe governmental measures were necessary. "How could [the] American press and even official broadcasts accuse Colonel Tung . . . of being responsible for [an] action which all generals [in] his armed forces had pressed on him out of [a] patriotic sense of duty and devotion to country?" But Lodge noted that Diem's "mumbling" was "largely irrelevant" and that he had presented no "real hard evidence" of Communist infiltration. When asked for proof, Diem hazily agreed to comply "when [the] inquiry is complete."[30]

Diem's fervent defense of his family confirmed Lodge's belief that the premier would never break with the Nhus. His brother, Diem declared, was a "pure intellectual, a philosopher who never raised [his] voice in debate, never sought favor for himself. [I] [w]ish [the] Americans could provide me with another like him." Diem had tried to placate Madame Nhu, but American journalists had infuriated her. The press, he angrily continued, had committed a "criminal" act by criticizing his brother Archbishop Thuc, who was a man of "total integrity and holy devotion." The Nhus had built the Republican Youth into the symbol of a "new, vital and democratic generation." Brother Nguyen Dinh Luyen, the ambassador to the United Kingdom, had effectively explained government policies to London's leaders, which was in marked contrast with the "perfidy" of Chuong, "who had never forgiven [the] fact [that] some of his ricelands [had been] taken in land reform."[31]

The Buddhist problem, Diem insisted, had been "entirely solved" but remained a burning issue only because of the Communists. Young activist bonzes had stirred up an "insane atmosphere" among the Buddhists by playing on "traditional primitive proclivities in people for irrational acts." Vietcong cadres had then elevated this "raving and noise" into a national crisis. Diem bitterly accused U.S. correspondents of distorting events and asked Lodge to correct their "constant misstatement of fact." The Vietcong "would stop at nothing, not even at organizing attacks in [the] U.S. against his government." In what Lodge termed "strong and impassioned language," Diem blamed the Vietcong for "organizing [the] U.S. press corps against him." But the government knew who these cadres were and would soon put an end to their activities. That very morning, Diem contended, he had met with members of the "Sangka," who were the "real representatives [of the] Vietnamese Buddhist clergy." They had been pushed aside by "agitators" like the young Thich Duc Nghiep, whom the American press had erroneously dignified as "venerable." The meeting had resulted in a settlement of all issues that would enable the government to resume the "principal task [of] building democracy through [the] strategic hamlet program."[32]

Lodge managed to break into Diem's monologue only once or twice, emphasizing that his image as democratic leader had suffered, both inside and outside the country. Having known Diem for ten years and "speaking frankly as [a] friend," Lodge urged him to convene the National Assembly and announce his government's resolution of the Buddhist issue. Would he hold new elections? Diem claimed to be examining the wisdom of going before the assembly but refused to comment on the possibility of elections. Exasperated, Lodge finally interrupted another long string of sentences to announce his departure. Their final exchange epitomized the hopeless situation. "Try [to] help us," Diem pleaded with "great sincerity." "Please try to do [the] same for us," Lodge solemnly replied.[33]

In light of the rumored coup, Nhu's role became more pronounced as the Saigon government tightened palace security. Particularly ominous was the installation of antiaircraft guns and the reassignment of some of Colonel Tung's Special Forces to the elite army unit already stationed inside

the walls. Indeed, these shifts in military priorities highlighted the negative impact of the Buddhist crisis on the war effort: To satisfy these demands, the army had to suspend a major military operation against the
Vietcong in central Vietnam. In the meantime, Nhu's picture appeared on
numerous public buildings, often replacing that of Diem. A million post-
ers of Nhu, dressed in his Youth Corps uniform, were in nationwide circulation, further catalyzing the army's fear that he intended to seize power.
Nhu meanwhile ordered the arrest of all potential civilian enemies, including those who had earlier gone to jail for having signed the "Caravelle
Manifesto" of April 1960, which had called for governmental reforms and
resulted in the aborted coup of November.[34]

The generals' coup interest began to wane in the midst of their growing confusion about the U.S. position. On the morning of August 29, Conein
saw Taylor's "second thoughts" telegram to Harkins and, at Richardson's
instruction, offered no advice about the coup when meeting later that same
morning with Big Minh. Had the White House retreated from the coup?
Conein's lukewarm reception alarmed the general, who smelled treachery.
Would the Kennedy administration suspend economic assistance to the
Diem government? Conein could make no assurance, further arousing
Minh's suspicions. In view of the volatile situation, Minh angrily proclaimed
that he would have no more contact with Americans and specifically barred
Conein from staff headquarters. Lodge was livid over this turn of events.
He learned on Conein's return to the embassy that he had not assured
Minh of an aid cut to Diem and demanded the reason. Taylor's telegram,
responded Conein. As a result of it, Richardson had prohibited any promises to the generals. "Why wasn't I informed of this cable?" Lodge stormed,
his words echoing loudly throughout the embassy hallways. Lodge could
do nothing until the generals initiated the action. And now, of course, they
would do nothing. His worst fears seemed justified. At a dinner that night,
according to the CIA, Big Minh, Khiem, and Khanh had expressed great
reluctance about starting a coup. Instead of a week as earlier surmised,
they appeared ready to wait for perhaps a month.[35]

Lodge, however, tried to get matters moving again after receiving a
private note from the president that related his confidence in Harkins and
in the ambassador's judgment as "personal representative." Enlivened by
this support, Lodge responded that "any course is risky," but he insisted
that "no action at all is perhaps the riskiest of all." Lodge then told the
state department, "We are launched on a course from which there is no
respectable turning back: the overthrow of the Diem government." U.S.
prestige was publicly tied to the growing opposition to his regime and would
become more prominent as the facts behind the coup leaked out. But this
was the only acceptable course of action, given Diem's poor leadership.
"We should proceed to make [an] all-out effort to get [the] Generals to

move promptly." Harkins must assure them of a cutoff in aid to the Diem regime once the coup was under way. The generals doubted that the United States had "the will power, courage, and determination to see this thing through. They are haunted by the idea that we will run out on them." An evacuation of Americans at this critical juncture would appear to mark the beginning of a total withdrawal that would "alarm the Generals and demoralize the people." Lodge opposed Harkins's recommendation to give Diem one more chance to remove the Nhus. The generals already distrusted us and might regard such a request "as a sign of American indecision and delay." In words that expressed the tangles inherent in interventionist policy, he asserted that the United States's long-time support for South Vietnam "inescapably gives us a large responsibility which we cannot avoid." The venture could cost American as well as Vietnamese lives. "I would never propose it if I felt there was a reasonable chance of holding Vietnam with Diem."[36]

As Lodge shifted the focus from the Nhus to Diem, the president met again with his advisers and delved deeper into the coup effort. Did anyone, Kennedy asked, have reservations about the proposed course of action? McNamara did. We must "disassociate ourselves from efforts to bring about a coup" but support Harkins's call to persuade Diem to get rid of Nhu. Rusk did not believe this possible. If a coup succeeded, Nhu "would lose power and possibly his life." He "had nothing to lose and we must recognize this fact in dealing with him. Nhu might call on the North Vietnamese to help him throw out the Americans." Before the coup began, the generals must demand that Diem dismiss Nhu. Nolting strongly disagreed, insisting that Lodge have a "cards-down talk with Diem" *before* any coup discussions with the generals. "If we proceed in this fashion, we would have nothing to hide."[37]

An ultimatum to Diem did not attract any interest. Rusk opposed this suggestion. "If Ambassador Lodge takes this line with Diem, telling him he must change or else, the effect will be to stimulate Nhu to immediate action. . . . We should not proceed along this line until the generals are ready to launch a coup." President Kennedy agreed. If Diem ignored U.S. demands, "there is the possibility that the generals' planning would be upset and Nhu would act against them." Taylor warned that before delivering a final warning to Diem, the White House must have a coup plan in its "hip pocket." It must not get involved in "coup planning in such a way as to prematurely commit us to an uncertain coup to be carried out by people we were uncertain about." Nolting suggested that the White House tell *both* Diem and the generals that it would cut economic and political help until changes took place. President Kennedy rejected that idea. If Diem refused, "there would be no way in which we could withdraw our demand." McNamara and Rusk opposed a stoppage in aid. Wait until the generals had set up a new government, then extend recognition and transfer the aid to it. McGeorge Bundy warned against that proposal. "Prompt recognition of a new government and an announcement that we were continuing U.S. aid to them would convince everyone that we had been in cahoots with the Vietnamese generals."[38]

Each proposed step forward exposed new pitfalls. Nolting expressed concern about a U.S. military involvement. What if the ARVN generals requested military assistance against the government? Hilsman's response again ignored the power of perception: "Our objective was merely to reassure the generals of our support. These generals want to have a bloodless coup and will not need to use U.S. equipment with the exception of possibly U.S. helicopters." U.S. assurances would pull over those generals "on the fence." Bundy likewise maintained the fiction of U.S. noninvolvement. The coup was "their show," and "we should stick with our plan, which was to support the Vietnamese effort."[39]

The president approved several measures, all designed to provide contingent support to a coup that he thought he could reverse at any time. Harkins was to back the CIA's approaches to the generals; Lodge would announce an aid suspension but only when Washington considered the time right; the White House would not publicize the movement of U.S. military personnel to the area for evacuation purposes. "We do not want the Vietnamese to conclude that we are getting in a position to intervene in Vietnam with U.S. fighting forces." Lodge would oversee both overt and covert operations. Hilsman was to have a list to the president that afternoon of covert actions to take place in the event of a military coup. This was a "high risk" situation, warned Rusk. "Shooting of and by Americans would almost certainly be involved. Before any action is over, American troops would be firing their weapons and American citizens might be killed." His forecast seemed accurate. An evacuation force of more than 7,000 marines was ready to enter Saigon.[40]

The Kennedy administration's interventionist policy seemed irreversible. Rusk informed Lodge that the White House had "reaffirmed [its] basic course" of indirectly encouraging a coup. In response to Lodge's recommendation, Harkins could divulge CIA information with Vietnamese generals carefully selected by Lodge. The White House "supports the movement to eliminate the Nhus from the Government," but before reaching any "specific understandings" with the generals, it must know the names of those involved in the coup, their resources, and their plan. The administration "will support a coup which has [a] good chance of succeeding but plans no direct involvement of U.S. Armed Forces." In an impossible directive, Harkins could establish contact with the coup leaders and review their plan, but he was not to "engage directly in joint coup planning." How did this approval constitute a distinction between direct and indirect involvement? What if he made a recommendation? Or did not? How could he deny complicity when he knew both the participants and their plans beforehand and did nothing to stop the coup? Taylor's missive to Harkins did not reveal any concern about these pivotal questions. "Let me say," the joint chiefs chair wrote, "that while this operation got off to a rather uncoordinated start, it is now squarely on the track and all Washington agencies are participating fully in its support."[41]

Not restrained by the dangerous ramifications of these instructions, Rusk authorized Lodge to decide when to announce an aid suspension to the Diem regime. In another impossible directive, Lodge was to leave no appearance of a collaboration with the generals that could spark an "unpredictable and disruptive reaction by [the] existing government." But, one may ask, would not Harkins's overture to the generals constitute an official contact that implied U.S. assurances? "Our own view," Rusk nonetheless wrote, "is that it will be best to hold this authority for use in close conjunction with [a] coup, and not for [the] present encouragement of [the] Generals, but," in a remarkable assignment of power, he declared that "[the] decision is yours." Rusk considered the Nhus the "greater part of the problem in Vietnam, internally, internationally and for American public opinion." He still thought it possible to separate Diem from the Nhus by threatening aid sanctions. Only this measure "would be taken completely seriously by a man who may feel that we are inescapably committed to an anti-communist Vietnam." The premier still might "move against the generals or even take some quite fantastic action such as calling on North Vietnam for assistance in expelling the Americans." It therefore seemed prudent to delay pressure tactics until the generals were ready to launch their coup. At that point, the question would arise as to whether the generals or the Americans should demand the Nhus' expulsion. "This might be the means by which the generals could indicate that they were prepared to distinguish between Diem and the Nhus." Such action "would tend to protect succeeding Vietnam administrations from the charge of being wholly American puppets."[42]

President Kennedy held to his dubious belief that he could cancel America's involvement in the coup at the last moment. Although privately assuring Lodge of total support of all measures designed to "conclude this operation successfully," he warned that he might change his mind. "Until the very moment of the go signal for the operation by the Generals, I must reserve a contingent right to change course and reverse previous instructions." He understood Lodge's warnings against inaction, but in an obvious allusion to the Cuban debacle of April 1961, he added, "I know from experience that failure is more destructive than an appearance of indecision." Kennedy accepted "full responsibility for this operation and its consequences" and urged Lodge to tell him if the "current course begins to go sour." If the United States acted, "we must go to win, but it will be better to change our minds than fail." To Lodge, the president privately wrote: "I have approved all the messages you are receiving from others, and I emphasize that everything in these messages has my full support."[43]

Lodge understood the president's prerogative to change policy at any time. But he also knew that events would at some time reach a point of no return. "To be successful," he replied the next day, "this operation must be essentially a Vietnamese affair with a momentum of its own." For that reason, the "go signal" must come from the generals and "you may not be able to control it."[44]

<h1 style="text-align:center">IV</h1>

BUT THE DAYS crawled by with no action, causing Lodge to become frustrated with the generals' "inertia" and "timidity." The wisest U.S. strategy was to wait for the generals to remove the Nhus and decide whether or not to retain Diem. "It is better for them and for us," Lodge wrote Rusk, "to throw out the Nhus than for us to get involved in it." But this outcome seemed remote. Lodge anticipated no further discussions with Diem. "I am sure that the best way to handle this matter is by a truly Vietnamese movement even if it puts me rather in the position of pushing a piece of spaghetti."[45]

On August 30, the White House advisers met again, this time in the state department and without the president there. Rusk warned that President Kennedy was not clear on "who we are dealing with and we were apparently operating in a jungle." The coup makers had proved disappointing. "Last Saturday the view was that the Vietnamese generals were ready to act and would do so without the U.S. hand showing. One week later there does not appear to be much gristle." Dillon asserted that the generals would take no action against Diem "unless we pushed it." Rusk declared that no one favored changing the instructions to Lodge, but all wanted to tell him that "we were dealing with shadows and not reality insofar as the Vietnamese generals were concerned." In words that best expressed the administration's situation, the secretary of state groaned: "Everyone here and in Vietnam is in the dark."[46]

Most unsettling was the growing certainty that the generals had never had a plan and that along with that realization came the unavoidable corollary: that only U.S. leadership could initiate a coup. McNamara admitted that the coup conspirators had always talked of developing a plan once the United States promised support. It now looked as if the generals "were either backing off or were wallowing." Rusk lamented that a coup that seemed so certain a week before now seemed to be just as uncertain. The generals, he moaned to Lodge, appeared to have "no plan and little momentum." Rusk felt sure "that if there is to be a change, it can only be brought about by American rather than Vietnamese effort."[47]

At this crucial time, the French again tried to exert their influence. Just the day before, August 29, President de Gaulle proposed a meeting in Paris to bring about a reunified Vietnam with a neutralized government. McGeorge Bundy warned President Kennedy that the French had interfered in these matters in an effort to restore their imperial influence. "We do best when we ignore Nosey Charlie." William Bundy termed the proposal "impractical if not mischievous." The talk of neutralization moved the Kennedy administration closer toward welcoming a coup, for it feared that Diem or Nhu might enter negotiations with Hanoi.[48]

The amorphous plot against the Diem regime further unraveled when the French pointedly warned the United States against coups and argued that Diem was better off with the Nhus by his side. Ambassador Lalouette wanted to retain Diem so that he could negotiate a North–South rapprochement that promoted French interests in the region. Nolting adamantly insisted that Nhu was too strongly anti-Communist to negotiate with Ho, but Colby thought it possible that out of self-preservation Nhu had already talked with North Vietnam through the French. Lalouette now told Lodge that Diem was "the best Chief of State in Southeast Asia," but, unfortunately, he was not politically astute and needed Nhu as adviser. Diem's war against the Vietcong had floundered in the face of chronically inept military performance and the incessant barrage of press criticisms. His regime had gone a long way toward rectifying matters with Buddhists by quietly releasing those held captive, preparing to repeal Decree Number 10, and making reparations for the damaged pagodas. Madame Nhu would be out of the country for the next several months. What would make the United States happy? "Get rid of the Nhus," Lodge sharply retorted. "This is impossible," Lalouette declared, "but it might be possible to bring in someone with title of Prime Minister and reduce Nhu's role."[49]

Lalouette insisted that the guerrilla war could be over in a year or so. Vietcong and North Vietnamese morale was down, according to the French mission in Hanoi. Once the war ended, the South Vietnamese might be able to establish commercial relations with the North in rice and coal. "This might lead towards a unified Vietnam with South Vietnam the dominant element." As Lodge rose to leave, Lalouette asserted: "Let me say two things—first, try to calm American opinion and, second, no coups."[50]

The French involvement in these events continued to grow. On the night of September 1 (August 31 in Washington), Maneli received a phone call from the French embassy, inviting him to join Lalouette there for a cup of coffee. Thinking something serious had happened, Maneli arrived within half an hour and saw the West German ambassador's black Mercedes in the driveway. Lalouette's chief of residence, Mademoiselle Sophie de Passavant, ushered Maneli into the library, where she warned that he was under continual watch. "All of your conversations, especially over the telephone, are listened in on from three sides: the Saigon government, the Americans, and the Vietcong." This news did not surprise him, but he was puzzled about why she made the remark. A few moments later, Lalouette entered the room.

"I understand that you are to see Nhu tomorrow. . . . I doubt very much whether the meeting will take place. . . . Tonight the Americans are to carry out a coup d'etat."

Trying to stay calm, Maneli responded: "We have expected this for a long time. Since Lodge's arrival, the regime's days have been numbered."

"The situation is tragic," Lalouette remarked. "It is difficult to defend the Diem-Nhu regime since the raid on the pagodas. They are discredited, but nevertheless I feel that only Diem can conclude peace with the North and come to an agreement with the Front. . . . You are not the only person to whom I have told this. . . . I have said the same thing to Ambassador Lodge. I insisted that Diem's removal by force would be a mistake impossible to repair, that the last—small, it is true—chance for peace would be lost. . . . If Diem and Nhu are removed, all our plans designed to end the fighting and bring about agreement with the North will come to naught."

"We could not be sure that Diem and Nhu would really like to become engaged in any serious talks," Maneli responded. "They were carrying on such a complicated and many-sided game that one could not be certain about the direction in which they were heading. Their departure from power might nullify some possibilities for peace, but others could emerge."

"Unfortunately," lamented Lalouette, "It is difficult to say anything good about Diem and Nhu; what they have done lately is terrible, but nevertheless it is only them who can now stand up to the Americans. Any other government will be even more dependent on the Americans, will be obedient to them in all things, and so there will be no chance for peace."[51]

French concern proved premature, for on the morning of August 31 the state department received word from Saigon that the generals had scrapped their coup effort. "This particular coup is finished," reported the CIA station in Saigon to its home office in Washington. Harkins had talked with Khiem that morning, belatedly assuring U.S. support. "If the generals were ready to remove Diem," Harkins promised, "the United States government would back them." This eleventh-hour assurance came too late. Big Minh, Khiem replied with great reluctance, had already called a halt to coup proceedings. "All concerned had such a respect for Big Minh [that] they followed his direction." Don had won his colleagues' support in proposing to Diem that he appoint generals to the key cabinet positions of Interior, Defense, and Director General of Information. Nhu could become "Chief of Cabinet or a government coordinator." Indeed, the generals were considering a proposal to Diem that Nhu take charge of the cabinet in "a kind of prime ministerial role." The generals, Harkins declared, "could not achieve [a] balance of forces favorable to them." He concluded on a somber if rapier-like note: "So we see we have an 'organization de confusion' with everyone suspicious of everyone else and none desiring to take any positive action as of right now. You can't hurry the east."[52]

In despair, Lodge recommended that the White House return to its former policy of pressuring Diem to implement reforms. "Our record," he questionably asserted, "has been thoroughly respectable throughout and we have shown our willingness to put ourselves on the line." Despite the setback, some other coup group will emerge "and we can contemplate another effort." In the meantime, Diem suspected the United States of instigating his overthrow. This suspicion, Lodge believed, had received greater impetus from his "strictly correct" behavior as ambassador in not seeking either to "flatter or cajole" the Nhus. "I am reliably advised that Nhu is in a highly volatile state of mind and that some sort of gesture through Nhu to North Viet-Nam is not impossible." The only way to change the government was through an effort "which the U.S. could mount itself and, of course, that is out of the question." In a telling epitaph, the *Pentagon Papers* declared years afterward that the Kennedy administration had "found itself . . . without a policy and with most of its bridges burned."[53]

The U.S. commitment to South Vietnam had not diminished, as shown by the administration's strong reaction against a withdrawal. Kattenburg warned Rusk that, on the basis of ten years' experience with the regime and his recent time in Saigon as director of the Vietnam Task Force, Diem would never make meaningful changes. "While there is no doubt [Diem] is in full possession of his faculties, [the] impression of [a] growing neurosis cannot be escaped." Better to withdraw now in honor. Kattenburg's recommendation drew so much flack in Washington that he never attended another meeting on Vietnam and the state department abruptly transferred him to the fledgling country of Guyana. McNamara concurred with Rusk, who stubbornly insisted that "we will not pull out of Vietnam until the war is won, and . . . we will not run a coup." There was "good proof that we have been winning the war." Vice President Johnson supported this hardline stance, asserting that he had "great reservations himself with respect to a coup, particularly so because he had never really seen a genuine alternative to Diem." He had not become aware of U.S. actions taken the previous Saturday until the following Tuesday meeting in the White House. He had never supported the idea of changing the Saigon government by "plotting with Vietnamese generals." Now that they had failed to engineer a coup, the United States "ought to reestablish ties to the Diem government as quickly as possible and get forward with the war against the Viet

Cong." Withdrawal was not an option. "It would be a disaster to pull out." We must "stop playing cops and robbers and . . . once again go about winning the war."[54]

Rusk agreed with Lodge's recommendation to resume pressure on Diem to institute governmental changes. Still making the specious argument that promotion of a coup did not mean complicity, the secretary of state asserted that the White House would support a Vietnamese coup attempt, but it "should not and would not mount and operate one." In an equally shaky attempt to distinguish between U.S. motives and U.S. actions, Rusk declared that Diem must understand that the United States sought "to improve [his] government not overthrow it." The House of Representatives had recently cut its aid program, "largely due to [a] sense of disillusionment in [the] whole effort in Viet-Nam." If no governmental changes resulted, the United States might have to suspend all assistance. Diem must prove to Congress and the public that "we are not asking Americans to be killed to support Madame Nhu's desire to barbecue bonzes." Firm tactics now had a chance to work, given that Diem "might have had a scare during these recent days too."[55]

The unpredictability of the Vietnam situation continued to baffle the White House when, on September 1, Lodge had a two-hour meeting with Nhu, in which he surprisingly agreed to resign from the government as a signal of its success in the war. In the presence of the Italian ambassador and the papal delegate, Nhu declared that he no longer was needed and would retire to Dalat after the Saigon government lifted martial law. His stunned visitors listened as Nhu sarcastically asserted that he preferred to wait until "certain U.S. agents" who were still advocating a coup against his family had left the country. "Everybody knows who they are." Madame Nhu would leave on September 17 for the Interparliamentary Union meeting in Yugoslavia, followed by a trip to Italy and possibly to the United States, where she had an invitation to speak before the Overseas Press Club of New York. The papal delegate would facilitate Archbishop Thuc's departure from the country. Nhu refused to leave the country, however, because of his contacts with Vietcong cadres, who had become demoralized by insufficient support from North Vietnam and were ready to give up their resistance.[56]

Lodge surely recognized that Nhu had not been truthful about walking away from the government and that he had hidden motives. What evidence was there of ARVN success? What contacts had Nhu made with the Vietcong? What about his rumored talks with Hanoi? The CIA called it an "open secret" in Saigon's diplomatic circles that Nhu had communicated with Hanoi and that the French sought a North–South rapprochement. Nhu had recently told all fifteen generals at ARVN headquarters not to worry about U.S. threats to terminate aid; he "had contacts with Northern brothers and could get [a] breathing spell by having [the] North direct Southern guerrillas [to] ease off operations while negotiating [for a] more permanent settlement." He accused the CIA of wanting him "out of way" and working with "secret elements" in the U.S. government to overthrow the Diem regime. Only Lodge offered hope, Nhu asserted in a statement that revealed his own illusions. "We can manage him—he will fully agree with our concepts and actions."[57]

Nhu's erratic behavior continued when, unknown until years afterward, Maneli met with him on September 2 in the midst of a furor over a front-page story in the *Times of Vietnam* that exposed the breach between the Diem regime and the United States. "CIA financing planned coup d'etat," read the caption. Written by Nhu, the original version of the article had mentioned the names of prominent CIA officials behind the plot, including the CIA station chief, Richardson himself. Madame Nhu, some later claimed, had removed his name from the published piece. Maneli arrived at the palace, where he joined Nhu at a small table in a room cluttered so badly that it "looked like a junk heap." Nhu quickly began a monologue so laced with Marxist language and ideas that it dumbfounded Maneli.[58]

"I am carrying on a war to end war forever in Vietnam; I am really combating Communism in order to put an end to materialistic capitalism. I am temporarily curtailing freedom to offer it in unlimited form. I am strengthening discipline to do away with its external bonds. I am centralizing the state in order to democratize and decentralize it. . . . The strategic hamlets are the basic institutions of direct democracy. When they develop and flourish, they will become the real nucleus of national organization, and then the state itself—as Marx said—will wither away."[59]

Nhu saw Maneli's astonished look and repeated his statement. "That is right. I agree with Marx's final conclusion: the state must wither away—this is a condition for the final triumph of democracy. The sense of my life is to work so that I can become unnecessary. I am not against negotiations and cooperation with the North. . . . Here, the International Commission—and you personally—could play a positive role."[60]

Maneli repeated his earlier assurance to Nhu that the International Control Commission would do everything possible to end the war, noting that Saigon was abuzz with rumors of secret negotiations. Maneli believed that Diem and Nhu thought that if they broke with the United States, they might be in the position to arrange a settlement with Hanoi. They therefore used this widespread fear "to frighten and blackmail their anti-Communist allies."[61]

Later that day, Maneli talked with Lalouette, who emphasized again that the only way to peace in Vietnam was through the Diem regime. Maneli had never accepted this proposition. "There was no doubt," he later wrote, "that the French government, and de Gaulle personally, decided to seize the chance, to take control of the Diem government, make it dependent on the help of the French government, and somehow oust the Americans."[62]

Nhu remained the great enigma for the United States. If Diem removed him, the chances of a coup would markedly diminish. But the premier refused to do so, raising the likelihood of a forceful change in leadership. Nhu realized the stakes involved and sought to manipulate Maneli and the International Control Commission, the French and their interest in regaining global status, and the coup makers, who feared that Diem was no longer running the government. Certainly, Nhu had not lost his hatred for the Communists; but now the issue was personal survival. If his negotiations with North Vietnam succeeded, he would gain strong leverage for demanding a U.S. withdrawal that would permit the Vietnamese to settle their problems by themselves. His actions left the Kennedy administration in a state of indecision, which made a coup more problematic because the White House could offer no encouragement to the generals.

The impetus for a coup had fizzled. In this critical period, the generals had refused to proceed without some sign of U.S. support. That sign never came. The generals questioned the trustworthiness of the CIA, particularly when one of its most visible members was Lansdale, the long-time friend and protector of Diem. Their suspicions of the CIA had also grown because Richardson had followed Washington's orders so well in cultivating a close relationship with Nhu that they found it difficult to dismiss his claim to having the Kennedy administration's support. The generals also realized that some of their colleagues remained lukewarm toward a coup. And, of course, Khanh's report of Nhu's negotiating with Hanoi had raised the risk factor.

That the coup did not take place during this peak time of discussion and planning provides ample proof of the conspirators' need for U.S. support. When that help did not come, the coup talk failed to materialize into action. Lodge gloomily informed Rusk that the U.S. mission was no longer in contact with the generals. Khiem canceled a meeting with Conein and, probably for security reasons, explained that he was "too busy" to take a phone call from Harkins. To signal U.S. intentions, Conein complied with Khiem's request by turning over a complete ordnance list and a sketch of Camp Long Thanh's weapons locations.[63] But this move did not snap the generals out of their so-called inertia.

On September 2, the CIA reported General Kim's explanation to Phillips and Conein that the coup had not transpired because Nhu had been aware of the generals' intentions and put Tung's Special Forces on full alert. Big Minh emphasized, however, that the coup planning continued. "Under no circumstances would Nhu be acceptable." The generals did not lack will, Kim declared; "at [the] moment they lacked the means." The Americans had been their own worst enemy. They had furnished the

Diem regime with so much military matériel over the years that the rebel generals were unable to mount effective action in just a few days. Most important, however, they remained uncertain of U.S. support. The Americans, Kim emphasized, must "indicate by actions, as well as words, that they do not support [the] Nhus or their creatures."[64]

DIEM HAD SURVIVED another crisis, although, according to the CIA, he was not "out of [the] woods." Coup possibilities remained, as indicated by Kim's conversation with Phillips. But Diem and the Nhus realized that the U.S. government had encouraged a coup and now understood that the White House was serious about turning its back on the regime. The ultimate outcome of these events still depended on whether Diem implemented reforms. The prognosis did not look good. The atmosphere of repression became increasingly evident. Police searched the handbags of American soldiers' wives as they entered the U.S. commissary. Government officials arrested thousands of students, many of high school and junior high school age, and sent them to indoctrination camps. Those youths who resisted were knocked from their bicycles and thrown into trucks furnished by the United States and bearing the clasped hands emblem of the U.S. aid mission. Authorities gradually released the captives to the custody of their parents, but the mothers and fathers, many of them influential middle-class members of the bureaucracy and more than a few of the men in ARVN uniform and of Buddhist faith, had to appear at the police stations to claim their offspring. No more poignant proof could have demonstrated how deeply the government had isolated itself from its people.[65]

In the meantime, the White House ordered the destruction of all cables between Washington and Saigon that related to a coup. Not that this move, even if it had succeeded, signified the end of such strategy. Hilsman wrote Lodge (with Rusk's concurrence), "To use your metaphor, when the spaghetti was pushed, it curled; now we must try pulling."[66]

15

TOWARD A PARTIAL WITHDRAWAL

> In the final analysis, it is their war. They are the ones who
> have to win it or lose it. We can help them, we can give them
> equipment, we can send our men out there as advisers, but
> they have to win it, the people of Viet-Nam, against the
> Communists.
>
> President John F. Kennedy, September 2, 1963

IN AN INTERVIEW ON TELEVISION with CBS Evening News anchorman Walter Cronkite on September 2 in Hyannis Port, President Kennedy reiterated his commitment to Vietnam while insisting that Diem could not win the war without reforming his government and building a base of support at home. During the past two months, the Diem regime had sunk to a new popular low. "Do you think this government has time to regain the support of the people?" Cronkite asked. "I do," the president emphatically responded. But Diem must change both his policies and his personnel. "We hope that he comes to see that, but in the final analysis it is the people and the government itself who have to win or lose this struggle. All we can do is help, and we are making it very clear, but I don't agree with those who say we should withdraw. That would be a great mistake. That would be a great mistake."[1]

The president's comments revealed his intention to cap his nation's escalating involvement in the war, to continue pressing for Nhu's removal from government, and, indeed, to return to the partial withdrawal plan. A *New York Times* editorial, however, missed the central thrust of Kennedy's remarks. Four days afterward, it warned of an expanded U.S. military role by declaring that the president considered the war in Vietnam "our war—a war from which we cannot retreat and which we dare not lose."[2] The administration, according to the *Times*, stood on the verge of a far more dangerous involvement that had no end in sight. The heralded newspaper, as events would show, was correct in its dark prognosis of events but wrong in its analysis of this White House's objectives. Kennedy had not changed his position. He opposed a total withdrawal from Vietnam, just as he resisted an Americanization of the war. Frustrated by the generals' failure to launch a coup, the president publicly emphasized again the importance of ridding the nation of the Nhus and helping the South Vietnamese do a job that was theirs alone. Meanwhile, he revived the move toward a scaled-down involvement, which meant turning the clock back to early 1961.

The key to success lay with the Vietnamese, but that outcome remained elusive. Seemingly encouraging was Taylor's recent report to the president that the ARVN had improved its performance. Vietcong casualties had risen and the number of strategic hamlets had reached 8,227 of the 10,592 projected. Most important, about 76 percent, or 9,563,370, of the rural people were now within the protective confines of the hamlets.[3] But these figures were misleading. Rather than reflecting a growing sense of security, the heightened enemy casualties and the greater number of inhabitants in the strategic hamlets more realistically suggested a swelling Vietcong offensive that had exposed the regime's inability to safeguard its people.

The continued threat of a coup had resurrected the Kennedy administration's interest in a partial withdrawal. Indeed, such a move might signal the generals that the White House would do nothing to help the regime if they launched a coup. Diem must either grant reforms and perhaps preserve his rule or continue to oppose change and face a coup. The chances of his removing the Nhus and instituting governmental changes were nearly nonexistent. According to the U.S. withdrawal plan, by the end of 1965 the ARVN would stand virtually on its own—as would Diem.

I

THE WHITE HOUSE continued to work toward improving South Vietnam's military performance to the level that it could wind down the insurgency without special U.S. military assistance. To reach that coveted point in the war, Diem must resolve his domestic problems before concentrating on the Vietcong. The task of convincing him to make the necessary changes had become more difficult. The Kennedy administration's clumsy encouragement of a coup had heightened Diem's suspicions about his partner, making it impossible for the White House to resume its lame policy of simply urging him to make changes. Diem became certain that the U.S. call for reforms was a mere guise for undermining his rule. Particularly touchy was the U.S. interest in removing the Nhus not just from office but from the country. Hilsman, Forrestal, and McGeorge Bundy emphasized to Lodge that Nhu must *not* remain in the hillside retreat at Dalat because he "could still be [the] power behind [the] throne." Madame Nhu's forthcoming foreign tour could actually enhance her prestige at home unless she stayed away for an extended period. Furthermore, Lodge must not talk with Nhu, for to do so suggested his legitimacy. These were not the administration's only expectations. Diem must go beyond expressing good intentions toward the Buddhists and take specific actions, including fulfilling the June 16 agreements and appointing Thuan as prime minister and at least two generals to cabinet positions. The momentum toward U.S. involvement in a coup had given way to a restrained approach that paradoxically rested on a greater and more direct involvement in South Vietnam's domestic affairs. On the surface the White House appeared to have dropped the previous week's conspiratorial policy by reasserting its aim of improving the Saigon government.[4]

And yet the White House had not closed the door on fostering a coup. Its proponents still wanted the generals to take the step, insisting that the administration's ambivalent stance had caused them to cancel the August effort. Washington's coup advocates had perhaps lost the lead, but the fact remained that the generals would interpret any U.S. move toward either exerting pressure for governmental reform or shaving its commitment to the regime as a sign of support for their cause. Even a decision *not* to coerce Diem into changes could leave the impression that the White House had abandoned his regime.

Although Washington's moderates had regained control, the administration's flirtation with a coup had maintained the interest of President Kennedy and others still skeptical about converting Diem to reforms. Most of the president's advisers joined McNamara in opposing only the *initiation* of contacts with the Vietnamese generals. The United States, he insisted, must refrain from trying "to unscramble the confused situation among the generals in Vietnam." The president intended to listen to any promising plan. If the generals wished to revive coup discussions, he asserted, they must take the first step by communicating with either Lodge or Harkins. "When they come to us we will talk to them," President Kennedy declared, realizing that this would send a signal that his loyalty to Diem remained in question. "We should avoid letting the generals think that the U.S. had backed off."[5]

The moderates confronted a new problem when Madame Nhu publicly accused the CIA of planning a coup in which Lodge intended to have her either removed from the country or murdered. In a September 2 front-page article in the *Times of Vietnam*, she accused the British, Filipino, and Australian military attachés of conniving with Lodge and the CIA in planning a generals' coup. At a luncheon the next day, Hilsman strongly denied the charge. To Peter Lisagor of the *Chicago Daily News*, Hugh Sidey of *Time*, and Marguerite Higgins of the *New York Herald Tribune*, Hilsman insisted that the United States was not trying to "play God" by "plotting and pulling strings on puppets" in Vietnam. *Nhu* was the culprit. In an effort "to tar the Army" and the United States, he "beat up the Pagodas without the Army knowing about it" and now sought "to lead the US around by the nose to demonstrate to all of Viet-Nam that we were controllable." The United States was not a "Diem–Nhu" puppet. In a curiously suggestive statement, however, Hilsman argued that the Kennedy administration's exoneration of the ARVN did not constitute an "invitation to rebellion in exactly that sense." The White House wished "to put all concerned on notice that it was winning the war . . . and that if the Vietnamese chose to change their government, we were not committed to Diem."[6]

The continued suspicions of Nhu's clandestine negotiations with Hanoi further complicated the moderates' slippery position. After his surprising September 2 statement about leaving the government, Nhu had suddenly reversed himself and now obstructed every attempt by the Italian ambassador and the papal delegate to facilitate his departure. Nhu dismissed their warning that the United States would suspend aid to the regime and angrily asserted that he would "formally" resign though remain in the country. Furthermore, he denied having talked with Hanoi, indignantly pronouncing it "immoral" to do so without informing the United States. Nhu insisted that he had rejected North Vietnam's overture and that he had become a "scapegoat" for his country's troubles. There was reason to believe his denials. Nhu hated the Communists, and not only because they had tortured and killed one of his brothers, but also because of ideological differences. But there was an even stronger reason *not* to believe him: Nhu's survival depended on either reaching a settlement with Hanoi or blackmailing the United States into maintaining support for the regime. What about the long-standing French interest in reestablishing their influence in the region? Had not President de Gaulle attempted to intervene by publicly calling for Vietnam's neutralization and reunification, conveniently just after the first rumors of Nhu's secret contacts with Hanoi? Nhu was not telling the truth. North Vietnamese premier Pham Van Dong had authorized Maneli to act as Nhu's intermediary in constructing a peace. The CIA argued that Nhu sought to amplify his power by reducing the U.S. presence in South Vietnam.[7]

Lodge remained skeptical about reform in light of the Ngo family's failure to grasp the concept of democracy. False hopes came from Archbishop Thuc's acceptance of the papal delegate's invitation to leave Vietnam on September 7 for a lengthy visit in Rome and Madame Nhu's departure from the country just two days later. The reality was continued student arrests, followed by numerous accounts of torture by government officials. In one instance, Saigon's combat police broke up a demonstration and threw 800 teenagers in jail, including 200 girls. As the trucks pulled away, the youths yelled: "President Kennedy supports Ngo Dinh Diem beating and arresting students." Nhu's resignation would mean nothing, Lodge asserted, and Madame Nhu had fanned emotions by predicting "a triumphant lecture tour." Indeed, Lalouette had attested to Nhu's intentions to negotiate a deal with the Vietcong that hinged on a U.S. troop withdrawal. When the White House appeared to have second thoughts about continuing to underwrite the war at the amount of $1.5 million a day, one foreign diplomat caustically remarked, "I only wish that the Administration would have its second thoughts first." The Ngos, Lodge complained, did not see the political importance of building a constituency both at home and outside the country. They were "essentially a medieval, Oriental despotism of the classic family type, who understand few, if any, of the arts of popular government."[8]

Diem's Buddhist policy had heightened congressional opposition to the U.S. assistance program. Hilsman spent a grueling two hours in executive session with the Senate Foreign Relations Committee, defending the administration's support of Diem. The White House faced huge obstacles in maintaining Senate approval of a government that violated fundamental democratic principles by brutally repressing the Buddhists. Democrat Frank Lausche agreed with President Kennedy's call for changes in both Vietnamese policy and personnel. Republican Frank Carlson joined Democrat Frank Church in threatening to suspend aid unless Diem instituted reforms. Church soon secured the signatures of twenty-two other senators in warning that if Diem did not halt his repressive tactics, the United States would terminate *all* aid. According to Lodge, several influential people (unnamed) in South Vietnam had told the Nhus to let matters cool down by staying out of the country for at least six months. "This will open the way for my showdown conference with Diem," Lodge remarked.[9]

Given President Kennedy's interest in a reduced commitment, one can reasonably ask why he did not welcome a congressionally mandated aid cut that would take the pressure off the White House. The answer was simple: The Diem regime might suddenly collapse, leaving a power vacuum that would open the door to a Vietcong victory. The Democrats had already borne the political brunt of "losing" China to communism in 1949; they were not about to lose South Vietnam—particularly so close to the presidential election of 1964. Blame would gravitate to the White House, not to Congress. A fine line existed between cutting off assistance because the Diem regime had become hopeless and using the measure to stimulate reform. The Kennedy administration was not willing to take that risk. No one else had demonstrated the capacity to rule, and until someone stepped forward it was more practical to support Diem.

The White House remained concerned that Diem's domestic policies would impede the war effort. Even if Taylor's upbeat report was accurate, the Buddhist crisis continued to block the military's concentration on the Vietcong. Like a house of cards crumbling from within, the Diem regime had followed a path of self-destruction by alienating students, civil functionaries, the educated elite, and key sectors within the military establishment. The CIA reported that Tri Quang, still in political asylum in the U.S. embassy, had captured the "imagination" of the urban populace. Lodge agreed, warning that Tri Quang should leave the country because his public call for overthrowing the regime had made him its chief enemy. Tri Quang demonstrated a "complete mastery of crowds" but was also "self-assured to [the] point of conceit." Although the charismatic young bonze had denied political interests, embassy figures were skeptical of his richly acclaimed altruism. The real peril, warned the CIA, lay in the Vietcong's infiltration of the Buddhists. Diem had never been in such danger.[10]

The rapidly growing problems with the Diem regime emphasized again the Kennedy administration's ironic position: Its interest in a reduced involvement still depended on escalated military actions, but these tactics now included the possibility of *fomenting* a coup. At a morning meeting of the National Security Council on September 6, Rusk opened the proceedings before the president arrived by issuing a chilling warning. If the situation continued to deteriorate, the only alternative would be "a massive U.S. military effort." In response to Robert Kennedy's question, Rusk declared that victory was not possible with the Nhus in power. "We have to be tough," the president's brother agreed. Diem "must do the things we demand or we will have to cut down our effort as forced by the U.S. public." The attorney general, according to Forrestal, had "serious doubts" about the U.S. involvement. If we decided that the war was not winnable, Kennedy declared, "it would be better to get out now rather than waiting." Rusk now tied together a U.S. withdrawal with U.S. support of a coup. If the United States decided to pull out, it "might want to consider promoting a coup" beforehand. Indeed, he somberly added, any movement toward withdrawal "might well make a military coup probable."[11]

The Nhus' entanglement deeply confounded the situation. Thus, President Kennedy (who had just joined the meeting) was encouraged to accept Taylor's suggestion to authorize another special commission to South Vietnam. We need to get "the grass roots military view" about Diem's chances of survival, the general argued. Kennedy raised the touchy subject of Madame Nhu, starkly demonstrating how great an irritant she had become to the administration. Couldn't we ask Diem to bar her from making public statements? McGeorge Bundy felt so strongly about her that he would accept her husband in Saigon in exchange for her departure. In a decision suggesting that Madame Nhu had somehow become a threat to U.S. security, the National Security Council approved a directive to Lodge that he seek her removal from the country. That business settled, the focus of the meeting turned to the special mission. At its head would be Marine Major General Krulak from the Joint Chiefs of Staff and Joseph Mendenhall from the state department's Far Eastern Affairs division. The mission was so important that its members left Washington that same day for the 10,000-mile trip, with Mendenhall to talk with the embassy about Vietnamese civilian morale and Krulak to work with MACV in assessing the ARVN's progress in the war.[12]

As the Kennedy administration privately pondered a direct intervention in Saigon's domestic affairs, it publicly expressed intentions that were predictably different though not convincing. Two days after this high-level meeting in Washington, the administrator of the U.S. Agency for International Development, David Bell, assured state department correspondent John Scali on ABC's television and radio broadcast of *Issues and Answers* that the White House sought only to guarantee self-determination in South Vietnam. "We are not in the business of conducting military coups or trying to establish leaders in those other countries that we pick. It is for the people of those countries to decide their own leadership."[13] These statements were far from the truth. The White House had moved from a willingness to support a coup after the generals took the first step to itself considering the initiation of a coup and, if Rusk would have his way, sending U.S. soldiers to close the deal. The official rhetoric of partnership remained the same, whereas the actual policy revealed a U.S. readiness to manipulate South Vietnam's governmental affairs.

The likelihood of U.S. collaboration in a coup grew in almost direct proportion to the increasingly remote chances of Nhu's leaving the regime. Lodge learned from an unnamed source that the talk about suspending aid had shaken Nhu and that pressure from within his own country (again, its source unknown) had intensified for his resignation and immediate departure from the country for six months. "There was nothing to haggle over," Nhu lashed out at the Americans to an unidentified acquaintance. Fiercely agitated and strutting rapidly back and forth, he frantically asserted, "I'm the winning horse—they should bet on me. Why do they want to finish me?" Then, in an astonishing assertion of his thirst for power, he blurted out, "I want to be—not the adviser to Pres[ident] Diem—but the adviser to Henry Cabot Lodge." Nhu emotionally warned that his departure from the country would undermine the Strategic Hamlet Program. The military would seize control of the government and the CIA would work with the U.S. Information Service to "sabotage the war effort." Nhu refused to leave Vietnam.[14]

And Diem just as stubbornly refused to remove his brother. In response to Lodge's recommendation that Nhu vacate the regime until at least the end of the year—after Congress had voted on whether to continue assistance to South Vietnam—Diem insisted that Nhu stay to manage the strategic hamlets. Nhu stood unfairly accused, Diem asserted. "He was always the influence in favor of a flexible solution of the problem. . . .

If American opinion is in the state that you describe then it is up to you, Ambassador Lodge, to disintoxicate American opinion."

"I would be only too glad to do so," Lodge crisply retorted, "if [you] would give me something with which to work."

Ignoring Lodge's efforts to shift the focus of the conversation to Nhu's departure, Diem launched a tirade against the Buddhists that suggested a severe loss of self-control. His representative in New York, Diem self-righteously proclaimed, would soon show "that the pagodas had been turned into bordellos, that they had found a great deal of female underwear, love letters and obscene photographs. That the virgins were being despoiled there." One priest "had despoiled 13 virgins" in the Buddhists' crude attempt to resolve their "crisis of growth." Indeed, Diem claimed, the U.S. Information Service had circulated propaganda designed to stir up the Buddhists into supporting the Communists and taking over the cities to counter the overwhelming success of the strategic hamlets in the countryside.[15]

It would be easy to attribute these baseless charges to neurotic behavior but, in fairness to Diem, his suspicions of White House deceptions were justified. Lodge's appointment had substantiated Diem's worst fears about a change in U.S. policy. And yet, Diem's refusal to accept blame for his troubles lacked credence. His rigid opposition to change had virtually ensured his self-destruction at home followed by a Vietcong victory. The differences between the Saigon and Washington governments had become irreconcilable. Each side in this strained partnership believed it was correct, making a breakup more certain.

Despite the collision course that the Diem regime seemed determined to take, the Kennedy administration had maintained its public commitment to South Vietnam as an integral part of Cold War policy. The previous June of 1963 the president had stood before the Berlin Wall, promising that the Free World would not permit West Germany's fall to communism. Freedom was indivisible, he proclaimed; the Communists must not prevail anywhere. In an interview for NBC-TV's *Huntley–Brinkley Report*, Kennedy explained his dilemma in South Vietnam. A cutoff in aid might force Diem into governmental changes, but it might just as easily undermine that government. When asked whether he doubted the domino theory, Kennedy firmly replied: "No, I believe it. I believe it. I think that the struggle is close enough. China is so large, looms so high just beyond the frontiers, that if South Viet Nam went, it would not only give them an improved geographic position for a guerilla assault on Malaya, but would also give the impression that the wave of the future in Southeast Asia was China and the communists. So I believe it." Americans should not expect South Vietnam and other recipients of U.S. aid to do everything in accordance with American wishes. "We can't make everyone in our image, and," he incisively added, "there are a good many people who don't want to go in our image. . . . We can't make the world over, but we can influence the world." Total withdrawal from Vietnam was out of the question. "I think we should stay. We should use our influence in as effective a way as we can, but we should not withdraw."[16]

As in the days before the Buddhist eruption in early May 1963, the Kennedy administration focused on a partial withdrawal. It remained open to a coup that ensured a new government amenable to reforms and determined to defeat the Vietcong. At that pivotal moment, U.S. manpower reductions could begin in earnest. The U.S. commitment to South Vietnam stood unbroken even while its support for Diem had become more shaky.

II

FROM SAIGON CAME a steady stream of mixed assessments regarding a coup that reaffirmed White House suspicions that the generals would not act without direct U.S. assistance. Several generals had contacted Thuan about a coup, but he feared that they were agents for Nhu. General Dinh, however, could be "had" for liquor, women, and money. And even though many ARVN officers remained personally loyal to Diem, they recognized the futility of the war effort and looked to the United States for guidance. The CIA, however, insisted that the generals "were not unified, determined, or emotionally geared up." The absence of a coup following Telegram 243 had "exploded [the] often-held assumption that certain general officers and other dissidents would move quickly if given [the] green light and adequate assurances by appropriate U.S. officials."[17]

If Kennedy had expected the Mendenhall–Krulak mission to resolve his dilemma, he was sorely disappointed. The two men had engaged in a four-day whirlwind visit. Mendenhall talked with long-time Vietnamese acquaintances in Saigon, Hué, Danang, and other cities, whereas Krulak traveled to all four corps areas, conferring with Lodge, Harkins and his staff, nearly ninety U.S. advisers, and more than twenty Vietnamese officers. When Mendenhall and Krulak returned to Washington, they would bring with them two firsthand observers of the troubled Vietnamese scene: John Mecklin, director of the U.S. Information Service and a former news correspondent who had covered the French military effort in the 1950s, and Rufus Phillips, who headed the U.S. Operations Mission's rural programs and was responsible for economic aid to the strategic hamlets. "It was a remarkable assignment," Mecklin later wrote, "to travel twenty-four thousand miles and assess a situation as complex as Vietnam and return in just four days. It was a symptom of the state the U.S. Government was in." Nor was it a harmonious mission. Mendenhall and Krulak disliked each other, speaking only when they had no choice. Krulak and Mecklin got into a spat over the latter's decision to bring back television film that the Diem regime had censored and the general thought a violation of its sovereignty. A lengthy and embittered exchange took place on the plane, reaching a climax when Krulak angrily ordered Mecklin to leave the film in Alaska during a refueling stop at Elmendorf Air Force Base and even suggested that Mecklin remain with the film.[18]

Predictably, the assessments by the two mission leaders contradicted each other. Mendenhall was a Foreign Service Officer who had worked in Vietnam under Durbrow and had long urged political reforms. Krulak was a small-bodied and fiery marine who had earned his nickname of "Brute" while a wrestler at Annapolis. Gilpatric remarked that Mendenhall was regarded "with great suspicion on the Virginia side of the river," whereas Krulak was "universally liked and trusted in the Pentagon, both on the civilian and on the military side." Mendenhall reported a governmental "reign of terror" in Saigon, Hué, and Danang. Residents of those cities hated the Nhus but had begun to turn against Diem as well. His brutal treatment of the Buddhists had led many Vietnamese to assert that they might as well submit to the Vietcong. Krulak concluded that numerous Vietnamese officers were unhappy with Diem but did not call for concerted action against the government. Although favorable to Nhu's departure, "few officers would extend their necks to bring it about." One officer revealed his Catholic wife's complaint that Madame Nhu talked too much. Three ARVN advisers strongly criticized the Nhus, one declaring that they should leave the country and another warning that Madame Nhu's possible presence before the United Nations in New York would result in a public relations fiasco. Krulak ignored all these warning signs and insisted that the war was going well.[19]

In a National Security Council meeting on the morning of September 10, the two men presented their diametrically opposed conclusions, touching off a spirited debate that starkly illustrated the president's dilemma. Krulak praised the war's progress, maintaining that it did not matter who headed the regime. Mendenhall insisted that the war was not winnable under present rule and predicted a collapse of the Saigon government followed by a vicious religious war or a massive Vietcong offensive. "The two of you did visit the same country, didn't you?" bluntly retorted the president in a faint stab at humor that could not hide his utter disbelief. Krulak tried to account for the discrepancy by noting that Mendenhall had focused on the urban areas while he had gone into the countryside, "where the war is." The political issues that weighed so heavily on the Saigon government, he argued, had *not* interfered with military progress. "We can stagger through to win the war with Nhu remaining in control." Hilsman told the president that "it was the difference between a military and a political view."[20]

Mendenhall later elaborated on his report to the president, convincingly asserting that the Saigon government had experienced "a virtually complete breakdown" following the pagoda raids. Thuan felt useless. Thanh sat in his office reading detective stories. Vietnamese officials feared being seen with Americans. On one visit to a Vietnamese official, Mendenhall had to remain quiet while his host crept around his office, searching for hidden microphones before speaking. "Saigon was heavy with an atmosphere of fear and hate," Mendenhall declared. The people feared the government more than the Vietcong. Numerous officials no longer slept at home because of the growing terror of night arrests. The mass incarceration of students had infuriated both civilian and military leaders who, in many cases, were parents of those in jail. Indeed, the government's oppressive policies had forced many officials to spend the bulk of their time negotiating their children's release. The war against the Vietcong was no longer the priority. One Vietnamese citizen hotly declared that his prime concern was the "war" against the Diem regime.[21]

The Saigon government's so-called conciliatory measures toward the Buddhists, Mendenhall concluded, were a sham that only the United States could correct. Those provincial bonzes released from prison were under orders to return to homes, but government officials retained their identification papers. When the freed bonzes attempted to leave Saigon, government forces arrested them as Vietcong because they lacked proper identification. The story of such tactics spread quickly throughout Saigon, causing a number of bonzes to seek refuge in the city—some in the homes of army officers. Most anger focused on Nhu, although many Vietnamese, particularly the students, blamed Diem. A growing number of students supported the Vietcong as a viable alternative to the government. The United States, Mendenhall insisted, bore the chief responsibility for this state of affairs. It had put the Ngo family into power and supported its reign with arms and other types of aid, and now the regime was using those arms against its own people. The United States must rectify matters. In a penetrating statement that revealed the no-win situation in which the Kennedy administration had found itself, Mendenhall declared that "a refusal to act would be just as much interference in Viet-Nam's affairs as acting."[22]

When someone at the National Security Council meeting noted that Phillips had just been on the battle scene, Kennedy asked for his take on the situation. "Well, I don't like to contradict General Krulak," Phillips first said, "but I have to tell you, Mr. President, that we're not winning the war, particularly in the Delta. The troops are paralyzed, they're in the barracks, and this is what is actually going on in one province that's right next to Saigon." The only way to save Diem was to arrange the Nhus' departure. "They were the chief source of the problem." In a statement reflecting his CIA experiences with Lansdale, Phillips asserted that only one person could get them out, and that was the old psywarrior himself. Diem might work with Lansdale in making needed changes. Doubtless realizing the furor such a move would arouse in Washington, the president passed over the suggestion and asked what steps the administration should take. Phillips recommended three measures: Terminate aid to Colonel Tung as an expression of U.S. disapproval of the Nhus; cut funds to the Motion Picture Center for producing films that praised the Nhus; and pursue covert actions aimed at dividing and discrediting Dinh and Tung. Kennedy seemed skeptical. What if Nhu withdrew funds from the war and blamed the United States for the ensuing defeat? The army, Phillips replied, would not permit that to happen, primarily because so many of its personnel were on the Vietcong's "assassination list." The money going to the provinces belonged to the United States, and Americans alone controlled its dispersal. "If worse came to worst, we could take our piasters out to the provinces in suitcases."[23]

The atmosphere of the meeting became testy when Krulak interrupted Phillips to assert that U.S. military advisers in South Vietnam had rejected that negative assessment. Phillips admitted that the general fighting level had progressed, but *not* in the critical delta, where "the strategic hamlets are being chewed to pieces by the Viet Cong." He had just returned from Long An province, where the provincial military adviser had moaned, "We're in bad shape." The Vietcong had overrun 200 hamlets during the past week at night, forcing the villagers to tear down the barbed wire fences and to destroy their own houses. McNamara shook his head the entire time, finding it difficult to believe a report that so radically differed with the steady stream of positive accounts from military advisers. Krulak derisively remarked that he placed more faith in Harkins's assertion that "the battle was not being lost in a purely military sense." Harriman could contain himself no longer. You're "a damn fool" for believing Harkins, the crocodile snorted to Krulak. You've missed the point, Phillips chimed in a little more diplomatically to the stunned general. "This was not a military war but a political war. It was a war for men's minds more than battles against the Viet Cong." Asked his opinion by the president, Mecklin agreed with Phillips and bemoaned the loss of America's image among the politically astute people in Vietnam. "US prestige was at stake."[24]

Before emotions calmed, Mecklin caused another divided reaction by advocating the use of U.S. combat troops in "unseating" the regime and winning the war. "The time had come for the U.S. to apply direct pressure to bring about a change of government, however distasteful." Diem was gone. "We must be ready to use US combat forces." The first step was "to remove the whole government, including Diem, since the Nhus are a symptom, not a cause. Then we might compromise and let Diem stay." What would the U.S. troops do? asked the president. Mecklin declared that "if we cut aid there would be retaliation so we would have to go in as we did in Lebanon" during the 1950s.[25]

Mecklin wanted the United States to take over the war. He later wrote Edward R. Murrow, radio and TV commentator and then head of the U.S. Information Agency, insisting that U.S. soldiers would "accept an engagement comparable to Korea if the Communists choose to escalate." On the long plane trip from Vietnam to Washington, Mecklin had composed a memo asserting that the presence of U.S. combat forces would demonstrate America's willingness to depose the present government and fight the Vietcong. "It would be vastly wiser—and more effective—to make this unpalatable decision now." If the United States did not provoke a coup by cutting aid, it must engineer that coup. Should the attempt fail, the administration would still have "plentiful excuses" for using its military forces to restore order and protect American citizens. "And once U.S. forces had been introduced into Viet-Nam, it would be relatively simple—on the invitation of the new regime—to keep them on hand to help, if needed, in [the] final destruction of the Viet Cong." The United States must show that it "means business."[26]

Nolting later expressed surprise that Phillips and Mecklin had spoken so negatively about the U.S. effort. Phillips had been in Vietnam for only about six months, and his pessimistic account "surprised the hell out of me. I couldn't believe my ears." Mecklin's gloomy attitude was explainable. His wife had left him, and he "had been brainwashed by his roommates, David Halberstam and . . . Neil Sheehan." Phillips's assault on the American effort was a different story. "I've seen him since and I've asked him, and he said, 'Oh, did I go that far?' and I said, 'You just ruined it.'"[27]

Once again, the two pivotal questions of promoting a coup and sending U.S. troops had come before the president's chief advisers, and once again they sharply disagreed. McNamara admitted that present strategy encouraged Diem's overthrow without offering a viable successor. Harriman remained adamant, insisting that the administration could not turn back the clock: "Diem had created a situation where we cannot back him." Hilsman called for enhanced pressure to force the regime into compliance. He warned, however, that "if we started down this path we would have to be prepared to contemplate the use of U.S. forces on the ground in Vietnam." Taylor maintained his opposition to U.S. troops, "either against the Diem government or against the Viet Cong."[28]

Rusk expressed apprehension about applying pressure to the Saigon regime. "We do not underestimate the capacity of Diem and Nhu to pull the temple down around their heads and ours if they won't buy what we demand. . . . Nhu may turn to the northern Vietnamese and make a deal with them." A cut in U.S. aid would hurt both the war effort in Vietnam and the Vietnamese people, who needed American goods. Gilpatric warned that suspension of any part of the military assistance program would have an adverse effect on the war. McCone insisted that selective aid cuts were impossible—that Hilsman's idea of withdrawing assistance to Tung's Special Forces could not work. "Aid to the Special Forces was so interlaced that we could not stop some forms of aid without affecting others." Rusk backtracked from his earlier inclination toward military force and now agreed with Taylor. "If we do go in with U.S. combat troops," Rusk asserted, "the Vietnamese will turn against us."[29]

Madame Nhu's actions added to the Kennedy administration's frustrations. McGeorge Bundy exploded in anger at a White House Staff meeting on September 11 when word arrived that Diem's brother, Archbishop Thuc, had left Rome that day for the United States to make arrangements for her highly publicized visit. "Already wobbly," the meeting's note-taker observed, "this was close to the last blow for Bundy." The national security affairs adviser blurted out that "this was the first time the world had been faced with collective madness in a ruling family since the days of the czars." In another meeting that same day, President Kennedy read the ticker-tape report of Madame Nhu's interview with the press in Belgrade: "President Kennedy," she bitingly charged, "is a politician, and when he hears a loud opinion speaking in a certain way, he tries to appease it somehow." Bundy found one consolation in her remarks: "The worse Madame Nhu becomes the easier it is to argue that she must get out of the Vietnamese government." Kennedy was indignant. "How could we continue to have her making anti-American comments at the same time she is one of the leaders of a government we are supporting?" He saw the problem in writing Diem a letter, asking him to silence her over "what, in effect, was a family matter." And publication of the letter, of course, would cause great complications. Lodge should make an oral request.[30]

Faced with deepening division among his advisers, the president became more supportive of a partial withdrawal. He had kept his views to himself while his experts presented theirs, but when he reiterated his resistance to combat troops, no one could have been surprised. His long-time insistence that only the South Vietnamese could win the war constituted his implicit and unbroken opposition to U.S. soldiers. Once the first combat forces entered the fight, it would be extremely difficult to limit the numbers. The only acceptable policy was a retrenchment. Continue to advise and assist the South Vietnamese, hoping to improve their civilian and military performance to the point that their government could stand on its own while the United States systematically shrank its involvement. But confronted with mounting evidence that a South Vietnamese victory was highly unlikely, his opposition to combat troops implied that without a successful coup, U.S. disengagement could come only at a lethal political cost. The situation had become "impossible," Kennedy complained after meeting with his advisers. "We can't run a policy when there are such divergent views on the same set of facts."[31]

The split within the administration over the issue of combat troops again stymied both camps, leaving selective aid cuts as the only feasible avenue to either governmental reforms or an outright coup. Sentiment for military force lost some of its glitter because of Phillips's insistence that the war was going badly. Forrestal thought Phillips's analyses of Vietnam "as good as any we have." He had "first hand—long term knowledge of the situation both in Saigon and in the field." Hilsman nonetheless refused to rule out troops. At a state department meeting later that same day, he urged his colleagues to ignore the dangerous ramifications of pressuring Diem into making changes. Lodge added to the sense of urgency, arguing that the time had come to suspend aid in an effort to force the present government to either change its ways or face collapse. The government's response to the threat of more student demonstrations was to defend its moribund policies while "privately thumbing its nose at the US." Lodge was dubious about the military's optimistic assessment. If the war effort faltered, "will not the popularity of the US inevitably suffer because we are so closely supporting a regime which is now brutalizing children, although we are clearly able, in the opinion of Vietnamese, to change it if we wanted to?" The United States must make overtures to a potential new leader—Big Minh, perhaps. In a striking metaphor, Lodge warned that the "ship of state" was "slowly sinking" in Vietnam.[32]

Intelligence sources reinforced Lodge's belief that the time for decisive action had come, particularly because of repeated reports that Nhu was negotiating with Hanoi, "with or without French connivance." De Gaulle had recently repeated his assertion that only the neutralization of South Vietnam could thwart a Communist takeover. He was not without selfish interests. Such an approach would present an opportunity to restore his country's stature in the region. Indeed, de Gaulle's ambitions stretched beyond Vietnam. He had drawn widespread domestic support for establishing France as the chief power broker in easing Cold War tension. A neutralist government in Vietnam would enhance his influence as world leader and, combined with his support for China's admission to the United Nations, inflict major setbacks on U.S. policy in Asia and Europe. De Gaulle knew that the mere existence of talks between Nhu and Hanoi would legitimize the National Liberation Front and build pressure for an international conference on Vietnam that the French might host. The Soviet Union would be supportive, as would China if the attendant nations called on the United States to leave South Vietnam. Lodge insisted that Nhu's sole chance for survival lay in securing an arrangement with North Vietnam that stipulated a U.S. departure. Both McCone and Harriman were aware of Thompson's warning that "the only trump card Nhu had was the withdrawal of the U.S. For this," the British adviser argued, "North Vietnam would pay almost any price."[33]

The CIA also considered it likely that the Diem regime, Hanoi, and the French had been pursuing a North–South rapprochement. Admittedly, Vietnam's unification was not a viable alternative in light of present animosities. But a cease-fire could bolster Hanoi's demand for a total U.S. withdrawal from Vietnam, followed by the establishment of a national coalition government in the south that welcomed all political groups, including the Vietcong. The French sought to act as Hanoi's liaison with the West. Although Nhu would confront stringent opposition from the ARVN generals to any agreement with the north, he might think the feat possible with French support. Columnist Joseph Alsop's September 18 article in the *Washington Post* added to White House concern. In a piece entitled "Very Ugly Stuff," Alsop charged that, for the first time, Nhu had admitted to making contacts with Hanoi.[34]

If so, Nhu's actions promised serious consequences for U.S. policy. He recognized that a North–South settlement was a risk, but one worth taking. How could he be sure that he (and his brother) would survive the new arrangement? The CIA insisted that immediate reunification was unlikely, because Hanoi had publicly proclaimed its intention to absorb South Vietnam. But the North Vietnamese were eminently patient and would find it preferable to wind down the war before the United States stepped up its involvement. Saigon would probably accept a cease-fire and some form of neutralization out of self-preservation. Nhu had made his position clear. Both publicly and privately, he accused the United States of reducing South Vietnam to colonial status. On the other side, however, his claim to having U.S. support worked to undermine his opposition at home while enhancing his prestige. Nhu's megalomania became evident in his boast that only he could save South Vietnam. I am the "unique spine" of the anti-Communist battle, he boasted to Alsop. "Even if you Americans pull out, I will still win the war at the head of [my] great guerrilla movement." Both Thuan and Hai (Diem's secretary) declared that Nhu had been smoking opium the last two years, helping to explain his delusions of grandeur.[35]

The whirlwind of events made the fall of 1963 a critical period in Vietnam. The Diem regime had lifted martial law on September 16, but its repressive Buddhist policies continued. In a radio broadcast of that same day, the NLF denounced the Diem regime for its severe treatment of the Buddhists and the "warlike U.S. clique" for moving "into the endless tunnel." All South Vietnamese should rise against "the U.S. aggressors and their running dogs—the Ngo Dinh Diem family." Both U.S. intelligence sources and the Country Team in South Vietnam concluded that Nhu's opposition pervaded all levels of government as well as the military and the

urban elite. MACV insisted that most high ranking ARVN officers rejected Nhu's leadership "under any conditions."[36] If these assertions were
accurate, the more actions Nhu took, the closer he came to ensuring his
fall from power.

III

AT THIS CRITICAL JUNCTURE, the administration's concern over the Nhus
became entangled with the coup issue. On September 16, Madame Chuong
telephoned Paul Kattenburg, director of the Vietnam Working Group,
who was then in Washington, inviting him to her home that evening to
discuss a "vital matter." In what Kattenburg termed hushed, "conspiratorial tones," she asserted that "many Vietnamese of all parties" had asked
her husband to head a government of national unity. He had always shunned
"exile politics" but now sought Kattenburg's advice as a long-time friend.
When Kattenburg refused to offer counsel and sought only clarity on the
proposed government, Madame Chuong abruptly lashed out at her daughter. She had told the Vietnamese community in New York and Washington that when the "wife of Nhu" arrived, they should "run her over with a
car" and, failing that, pelt her with eggs and tomatoes. She herself had
organized the recent White House picket demonstration of Vietnamese
against this "monster." After a pause, Madame Chuong gravely concluded,
"There is only one solution; get rid of both Diem and Nhu." Diem was "an
incompetent" and Nhu was "*un barbare.*" Why was the United States waiting? As Kattenburg's memorandum of the meeting wound its way to the
Oval Office, Forrestal scribbled in the column, "Family life in Vietnam"
and, next to her call for running over her daughter, mockingly wrote,
"Mother love."[37]

The Nhus' public outbursts had meanwhile encouraged Lodge to propose that Lansdale mastermind a coup. In a letter regarded as so secret that
Lodge typed it himself, arranged for its delivery by a special messenger,
and asked Rusk to show it to the president personally, he sought the removal of the present CIA station chief in Saigon, John Richardson, who
had worked so closely with the regime in the war effort that many Vietnamese "suspected him of being pro-Diem." Lansdale should replace him,
accompanied by a full staff whose ostensible duty would be to oversee all
U.S. relations with a new government. The ambassador's real purpose,
according to McCone, was to initiate a coup "through General Don with
MACV."[38]

A risky venture it was, but the full measure of the administration's desperation became clear when President Kennedy invited Lansdale to the White
House to discuss the proposal. Soon after Lansdale accepted the invitation,

McNamara showed up in his limousine at the Pentagon and offered him a ride to the meeting. The defense secretary escorted Lansdale into the room and took a chair. The meeting would be about Cuba, Lansdale must have guessed, for his most recent work for the president had been to head the secret program code-named "Operation Mongoose" (terminated in late 1962, after the Cuban missile crisis). Robert Kennedy was also party to the effort to remove Castro from power, even if by assassination. The president, however, surprised the general by raising an entirely different matter.

Would you return to Vietnam and attempt to persuade Diem to remove his brother and sister-in-law from the country?

Yes, Lansdale replied. At long last, the administration had come to realize what he had known for a long time: The Nhus were the problem, not his old friend Diem.

The president had much more in mind, however. "But if that didn't work out—or I changed my mind and decided we had to get rid of Diem—would you be able to go along with that?"

A deafening silence. Although McNamara sat in the room, Lansdale could not have been aware of anyone but the president. Was he thinking exile, Lansdale must have asked himself. If so, Lansdale realized that bloodless coups were rare. He also knew that Diem would choose death over leaving his country. Exile was not a viable option. Was the president proposing Diem's assassination?

President Kennedy's words were purposely vague in meaning, and Lansdale's long experience with the CIA had taught him not to ask for clarification in instructions. "No, Mr. President," shaking his head slowly. "I couldn't do that. Diem is my friend."

The meeting was over. The president tried to smooth over what had transpired, but his small talk did nothing to erase the pall of the underworld that had just visited the room.

Lansdale would not be going to Vietnam.

In the limousine afterward, McNamara angrily lashed out at Lansdale as they returned to the Pentagon. "You don't talk to the President of the United States that way. When he asks you to do something, you don't tell him you won't do it."[39]

Is this story credible? According to both investigative reporter Seymour Hersh and to A. J. Langguth, a *New York Times* correspondent in South Vietnam during the 1960s, Lansdale related these events to Daniel Ellsberg, the defense department official who later leaked the secret documents that became known as the *Pentagon Papers*. Ellsberg's unpublished memoir, Langguth asserted, contained this account of Lansdale's clandestine meeting with the president. Langguth believes Lansdale, arguing that President Kennedy had become desperate by the fall of 1963. Ellsberg likewise considers the story valid. But in an interview of McNamara conducted by

Langguth years afterward, the former defense secretary alleged that he did not recall the meeting.[40]

McNamara's claim to a memory lapse was not surprising, for he could not remember other meetings he had attended while in office, some of which dealt with the subject of assassinations. During the mid-1970s, the Church Committee of the U.S. Senate investigated assassinations of the previous decade and asked McNamara about Operation Mongoose. The former secretary and now president of the World Bank had come under media fire for his alleged participation in a special committee discussion on August 10, 1962, regarding the assassination of Castro. McNamara could not recall being at such a meeting. "I'm not suggesting that I wasn't, but I have no recollection of it. I do seem to recall that there was such a group, [but] I doubt very much if I was a member of it." Indeed, he vehemently denied any knowledge of assassination plans either before or during his time in office. "I believed then," he told the committee, "that the U.S. Government should not undertake or encourage assassination openly or secretly as an instrument of national policy against people with whom we are not at war." Assassination "is totally inconsistent with my moral standards now and then." Indeed, McNamara objected to a committee member's assertion that the Kennedy administration had authorized "a program to overthrow the Castro regime," arguing instead that the administration had approved "a program to weaken the Castro regime with the hope that it would be overthrown."[41]

The evidence amassed by the Church Committee raised serious questions about the veracity of McNamara's testimony. Particularly damaging was a memo of August 14, 1962, in which William Harvey, chief of the CIA Task Force dealing with Cuba, claimed that at a meeting of the Special Group (Augmented) in Rusk's office on August 10, *McNamara* raised the question of assassination, "particularly of Fidel Castro." The senior administration members comprising this committee were shocked that the defense secretary had used the word "liquidation" in a formal meeting. The consensus of those present was that "this is not a subject which has been made a matter of official record." McCone, according to an observer, "got rather red in the face" and made known his intention "to stop any such proposals, suggestion or any discussion thereof at that meeting within that forum immediately." He joined Murrow from the U.S. Information Agency in hotly declaring the subject out of order, and the secretary at the meeting did not mention the topic in his minutes. McCone felt so strongly that he telephoned McNamara later that same day, stressing the importance of not raising the matter again.

But the issue would not go away. Just three days later, Harvey received a memo from Lansdale, asking him to prepare study papers dealing with a number of correctives to the Castro problem, "*including liquidation of lead-*

ers." Harvey, a hard-nosed former FBI agent, became irate over "the inadmissibility and stupidity of putting this type of comment in writing in such a document." The CIA, he stormed, "would write no document pertaining to this and would participate in no open meeting discussing it." Lansdale deleted the words from the copies sent to the state and defense departments and to the U.S. Information Agency.

The matter rose again a year later. On April 23, 1963, McNamara attended a top-level meeting where, according to the note-taker, he "made clear his belief that the elimination of the Castro regime was a requirement." At that meeting, Attorney General Robert Kennedy proposed the compilation of "a list of measures we would take following contingencies such as the death of Castro" and the development of "a program with the objective of overthrowing Castro." Sorensen then listed seven objectives of the meeting, including "a program to get rid of Castro."

A special CIA Commission during the mid-1970s concluded that "the CIA was directly involved in plans to assassinate Fidel Castro of Cuba." Although it could not determine whether the impetus came from the White House, several pieces of evidence suggest presidential involvement. According to Richard Helms, then ambassador to Iran but in the CIA during the 1960s, "President Kennedy" had ordered "a flat-out effort" to "unseat the Castro government," and his brother was "the principal driving force" behind the program. Although Helms could recall no specific plans about "eliminating Castro," there were "conversations about it." McCone testified to the Church Committee that he had opposed assassination. "I think it was generally understood within the Agency that I would not tolerate planning, or the authorization, of assassination, on moral grounds. I didn't think it was proper from the standpoint of the US Government and the Central Intelligence Agency." In an interview of mid-1975, Richard Goodwin, Latin American specialist in the state department during the 1960s, told members of the Select Committee that at a Cuban Task Force meeting after the Bay of Pigs episode, McNamara suggested "getting rid of Castro." When someone from the CIA asked if he meant by "Executive Action" (the euphemism for assassination of foreign leaders), the secretary affirmed that he did.[42]

This brief digression from Vietnam suggests that McNamara was not telling the truth about President Kennedy's meeting with Lansdale. Was there a pattern to McNamara's behavior? It is difficult to believe that he forgot all these discussions about eliminating Castro. How could the defense secretary fail to recall his own recommendations for assassination? Better yet, is it likely that he would forget McCone's admonition—not once, but twice—about raising the subject in formal discussions? *Cuba* dominated much of the administration's thinking after the Bay of Pigs humiliation. The records show that McNamara attended many of these meetings relating to Mongoose. Lansdale claimed that the secretary was present at the 1963 conference with the president. Lansdale asserted that McNamara had accompanied him to and from the White House. The former CIA operative was devious and manipulative by trade, but it is incomprehensible that he would fabricate a clandestine meeting that tied the secretary of defense and the president of the United States to an assassination proposal. Perhaps Lansdale misread President Kennedy's intentions about how to remove Diem from power. But it is likely that the meeting took place, despite McNamara's inability to remember the event.

Evidence of the White House meeting is admittedly shaky, but it fits with other features of this sensitive period. Lodge had a direct connection with the White House as the president's "personal representative," which implied a special status that could cover the exchange of delicate information. Telegram 243 had established a policy declaring that if Diem refused to remove his brother, the White House would support the elimination of the premier. That policy remained in force. Lodge had urged the White House "to use what effective sanctions it has to bring about the fall of the existing government and the installation of another." How exasperating it must have been in Washington to read his account of the Saigon police abusing children and then hauling them off to detention camps in trucks bearing the U.S. insignia. But just two days after calling for an aid suspension on September 11, Lodge expressed concern that if the United States did not act quickly, Nhu would negotiate a pact with North Vietnam that stipulated either a U.S. departure from Vietnam or a drastic reduction in manpower. Later that same day of September 13, Lodge wrote the note recommending to the president that Lansdale head the CIA station and, quite clearly, promote a coup. McCone recognized that Diem would not remove his brother and that the ambassador's real intention was to initiate a coup aimed at the premier. Lodge was not naïve; he was certainly aware of Lansdale's propensity to stray beyond the parameters of orders.[43]

The chances of such a scheme taking form were minuscule, and not only because of Lansdale's long friendship with Diem. Rusk opposed bringing the mercurial Lansdale into the picture and warned Lodge against "coup plotting" until Washington made a final decision. McCone had no confidence in Lansdale and refused to assume any responsibility for such a venture led by "someone from the outside." The CIA director's opposition deeply disappointed Lodge. But he would not give up on his efforts to promote a coup. "You can be sure I will continue to do my very best to carry out instructions even if I must use persons trained in the old way." "It is really a pity," he lamented to Rusk. "Had my request been granted, I believe the coup might have been pulled off."[44]

Unknown to everyone except McNamara (and Lansdale), however, the president had been willing to give Lodge's proposal a chance.

Coup prospects nonetheless remained alive, as evidenced by the rumblings of discontent that continued to come from the generals. The call for governmental reforms had gone unmet. In response to their request for military control over the departments of defense, interior, psychological warfare, and education, Diem refused to make any decision until after the elections. By mid-September, Khiem found his colleagues mortally concerned over reports of Nhu's negotiating with Hanoi. Indeed, Nhu had sent an unmistakable warning to potential rebel generals of the danger that awaited them if they tried a coup. He approached Big Minh and other generals (not including Khiem) with Pham Van Dong's proposal for ending the war and establishing commercial relations between North and South Vietnam. Maneli was ready on a moment's notice to fly to Hanoi with Nhu's response. French ambassador Lalouette, according to Nhu, had also offered his services. Would Nhu's warning drive away the coup supporters? Or would it push them into a coup? A North–South arrangement, the generals realized, would preserve the regime and mean deadly retribution to its domestic opposition, given Nhu's knowledge of their coup activities.[45]

III

THE KENNEDY ADMINISTRATION had meanwhile opted for a series of escalating pressures ostensibly designed to force governmental reforms but that it knew had the capacity to encourage the generals to launch a coup. Lodge soon received a White House directive to exert pressure on Diem. "We see no good opportunity for action to remove [the] present government in [the] immediate future; therefore, as your most recent messages suggest, we must for the present apply such pressures as are available to secure whatever modest improvements on the scene may be possible." But the administration hoped for a coup. "Such a course is consistent with [a] more drastic effort as and when means become available." In an intriguing statement, it asserted that "we will be in touch on other channels on this problem."[46]

To persuade Diem to make changes, President Kennedy dispatched another special mission to Saigon in mid-September. Headed by McNamara and Taylor, it was a military mission that included Forrestal, Colby, William Bundy, and William Sullivan from the state department. "Clear the air," the president instructed Lodge, by convincing Diem to make the first "dramatic, symbolic move" of removing Nhu and then to get everyone involved in the war effort. Lodge remained dubious. The special mission would result in his accompanying the emissaries in a highly publicized visit to the palace that Diem could herald as a restoration of friendship and an end to U.S. pressures on the regime. The Ngo family was already promoting the idea that the only matter open for discussion was that of winning the war, and it could boast that the military mission confirmed U.S. support for the regime. To avoid this impression, the president recommended a strategy aimed at encouraging the rebel generals to act. The White House and Saigon embassy were to state publicly that the visit did *not* signify favor for Diem. McNamara would "speak some home truths" and emphasize that the White House was not "open to oriental divisive tactics." The mission's sole purpose was to promote victory in the war. "The whole cast of the visit," Kennedy told his defense secretary, "will be that of military consultation with you on the execution of the policy which you and I have determined."[47]

An objective appraisal seemed unlikely. As the mission's plane was en route to Vietnam, Bundy and others on board received huge binders of materials, including a draft of the report they were to write afterward. Forrestal asserted years later that the conclusions had already been "carefully spelled out, [with] all the statistics to back them up." It was a "dreadful visit" in which everyone tried to fill the mission members with "phony statistical" evidence of success.[48]

The timing of the McNamara–Taylor mission proved pivotal because of the dismal military prognosis and the widespread coup talk. Big Minh had recently assured Lodge that 80 percent of the Vietnamese people had no reason to support the Diem regime and that the government's curtailment of martial law was merely "eyewash for Americans." The two guardhouses outside his headquarters were jammed with prisoners, many of them students who had joined the Vietcong's cause out of desperation. The army's middle-ranked officers now favored a coup. When Minh approached Diem about military problems, the premier either referred him to Nhu or called Nhu into the meeting. Every district and province chief was a member of the shadowy Can Lao party, the semisecretive arm of the regime through which the Ngo brothers maintained control over the police, army officers, and civil servants by distributing kickbacks from U.S. assistance designated for the rural populace. Minh left the impression of having seriously considered a coup but gave no sign of planning one. Any coup, he indicated, would have to take place quickly and result in total success; a drawn-out civil war would benefit the Vietcong.[49]

Nhu's behavior had continued to raise Lodge's apprehensions, further driving his interest in a coup. At a dinner on September 18, he found Nhu very outspoken about his role in creating the strategic hamlets and doing anything to win the war. His departure from the country, Nhu warned, would undermine the morale of the Republican Youth Corps and hinder victory. Lodge remained unconvinced. "Frankly," he reported to Washington, "I am not impressed by his statement that he is willing to do anything because actually he isn't." Nhu was "a striking figure," handsome, highly intelligent, but ruthless and possessing a "cruel face." Yet "one feels sorry for him. He is wound up as tight as a wire. He appears to be a lost soul, a haunted man who is caught in a vicious circle. The Furies are after him."[50]

But the generals were the key to a coup, and doubts remained about their capabilities and their willpower. Harkins admitted to Minh's leadership qualities but insisted that he had not contributed to the war effort. "In fact, he has done nothing but complain to me about the government and the way it is handled ever since I have been here." Harkins's assessment was ill founded. Minh had never received a troop command because he had remained under governmental suspicion since the 1960 coup attempt. Almost every time coup rumors circulated, his name appeared on the list of suspects. Harkins nonetheless had no confidence in Minh's ability to engineer a coup. He was also skeptical about Minh's claims that the great masses of Vietnamese people were disenchanted with the government, that large numbers of students had turned to the Vietcong, and that middle-ranked officers were ready to overthrow the regime. The CIA confirmed Harkins's concerns about the generals, reporting that they were wavering on a coup for fear of failure and certain execution.[51]

In the course of the mission's ten-day stay in Vietnam, McNamara spent two hours with Richardson, who argued that the situation was rapidly deteriorating. A "climate of suspicion" blanketed the country, the CIA station director gloomily declared. He did not think there was anyone of sufficient moral authority to replace Diem but warned that keeping him and his family in power ensured disaster. "Diem is devoted to his country but wed to his family." Most people blamed Nhu for the pagoda raids and detested his wife for her cruel remarks. The night arrests had caused the greatest resentment. Many cabinet members wanted to resign, but if they did, they had to leave the country or go to jail.[52]

On that somber note, the mission members met with Diem on September 29. With Thuan at his side, the premier passionately defended his administration. For more than two hours, Diem talked nonstop while chain smoking and moving animatedly around the room to consult maps. When he finally paused, McNamara interjected his government's concern over the political repression that threatened both the war effort and continued U.S. support. Diem's foreign minister had resigned, his ambassador in Washington had either resigned or had been recalled, and Saigon University was closed. Americans at home doubted the wisdom of assisting a highly unpopular government that had little chance of inspiring the national unity so vital to winning the war. McNamara's remarks implied an imminent end to U.S. support, and yet Diem ignored the warning. "In two or three more years," Diem insisted, "Viet-Nam will be a model democracy." The rapid growth of the strategic hamlets had brought a sense of security that encouraged wider participation in recent elections. This last assertion particularly irritated Lodge. The enlarged vote, he derisively returned, had resulted from the great number of soldiers who had driven around in army trucks on election day, voting over and over for the regime.[53]

McNamara broke the uncomfortable silence by complaining about "the ill-advised and unfortunate declarations of Madame Nhu." From his pocket he pulled out a newspaper clipping quoting her recent allegation that younger U.S. officers in Vietnam were "acting like little soldiers of fortune." Such "irresponsible behavior," she asserted, had deeply offended Americans on the scene and caused senior U.S. officers to pursue "a confused policy." These public remarks hurt the aid program, McNamara snorted. The "American people would flatly refuse to send out the best of their young officers to face mortal perils to support an effort that had such irresponsible spokesmen." One American in the delegation lost his composure and demanded of Diem whether "there were not something the government could do to shut her up."[54]

Stunned and deflated by this acerbic remark, Diem suddenly appeared tired and on the defensive. Perhaps for the first time he had grasped the thrust of the visit—especially when Lodge pointedly charged that Madame Chiang Kai-shek had played a major role in losing China to the Communists in 1949. But if Diem had for a moment betrayed silent acquiescence in McNamara's arguments, he quickly regained composure and showed no interest in making changes. His problems he attributed to "inexperience and demagoguery" within the country along with U.S. failure to understand the situation because of the distorted American press attacks on the government, himself, and his family. McNamara insisted that the real problem was "a crisis of confidence in the government of Viet Nam both in Viet Nam and in the United States." Diem seemed to dismiss this fear as imaginary and then abruptly switched the subject back to Madame Nhu. Her membership in the assembly afforded her the right to express her sentiments both as a member of government and as a citizen of a free country. "Furthermore," Diem snidely remarked, "one cannot deny a lady the right to defend herself when she has been unjustly attacked."[55]

Now just as deftly back on the offensive, Diem shocked his visitors by asserting that his many kindnesses toward the Buddhists had helped to bring on the trouble by encouraging them to demand more than they deserved. Indeed, he had extended "so much assistance that the number of Buddhist temples in the country had doubled during his administration." For twenty minutes he repeated the lurid charge that sexual orgies took place in the pagodas on a regular basis. The core of the problem, he derisively remarked, was that "anyone could become a bonze who shaved his head and acquired a yellow robe." Diem then alleged that "some American services in Saigon" were plotting against the regime and that he was gathering information on the matter. Most Buddhists, he insisted to his befuddled visitors, supported the government and opposed the small minority of extremists causing the trouble.[56]

The U.S. special mission had failed to convince Diem of the necessity for change. Indeed, the premier came away from the confrontation apparently satisfied that he had cleared up all misunderstandings. Lodge could not have been surprised by Diem's stoic reaction to the thinly veiled warning. Too many times the ambassador had encountered the same lifeless expression and had thrown up his hands in despair. Taylor later remarked that Diem had not grasped the seriousness of the mission's warning. "You could just see it bouncing off him."[57]

The mission's visit then took a comical twist when Big Minh expressed interest in talking with McNamara and Taylor, either alone or together. Was the ARVN general preparing for a coup? That same day, after an intricate series of discretionary arrangements, Taylor joined Big Minh in a game of doubles on the tennis court of the Saigon Officers Club. With McNamara watching in quiet anticipation, Taylor played the match, anxiously searching for any sign of a response from Minh to "broad hints of our interest in other subjects which we gave him during breaks in the game." But Minh revealed nothing, leaving McNamara and Taylor thoroughly bewildered as they left the court. "I sat on the sideline two feet from Big Minh for over an hour and I couldn't get a damn thing out of him," McNamara snorted some time afterward to President Kennedy. "I got a tennis game out of it, that's all," Taylor recalled. In frustration, he had asked one of the tennis players, Colonel Raymond Jones, to contact Minh that same night about the situation. The following day, Minh sent a bland response that reflected the generals' bitter disenchantment with the Kennedy administration's restrained reaction to their initial coup overtures. He cagily expressed confusion about the events on the tennis court, thinking it merely a game of tennis, but offered to discuss the military situation at any time.[58]

In a later conversation with Vice President Tho, the two leaders of the mission and Lodge gained a far different perspective on the strategic hamlets than that related by Diem. Tho cited widespread dissatisfaction in the villages as well as in the cities, much of it stemming from villagers having to make forced payments of excessive taxes to the village agent and another tax to the Viet Cong. This should not be the case in a well-fortified hamlet, Taylor indignantly observed. "Why, General Taylor," Tho responded in feigned surprise at Taylor's naïveté, "there are not more than 20 to 30 properly defended hamlets in the whole country." Warming up to the baffled look on his visitors' faces, Tho asked: "Why do you gentlemen think that the Viet Cong is still so popular?" Just two years ago, its forces numbered perhaps 30,000; in the past two years the ARVN had killed a thousand a month. And yet the Viet Cong was larger today. "Why is this true?" When Taylor attributed the growth to forced recruitment, Tho agreed only in part. "Intimidation can make them join, but it cannot stop them from running away. While some of them do run away, there are many who stay. Why is this?" The Viet Cong could promise "neither food nor shelter nor security." Seeing that his visitors had no answer, Tho insisted that those in the Vietcong stayed "because they want to, and the reason they want to is their extreme discontent with the Government of Vietnam."[59]

Negative reports continued to reach the U.S. mission. A group of university professors from Dalat, Hué, and Saigon complained to McNamara that Diem's government had transformed South Vietnam into a police state. Large numbers of people had undergone torture because they opposed the regime. With no help from either the church or the United States, the professors declared, more South Vietnamese had turned to the Vietcong in hopes of toppling the regime and ending the war. They preferred "the devil we do not know to the one we do." If Nhu emerged triumphant, he would order the United States to leave and then negotiate a deal with the Communists that made him "boss of all of Vietnam." Supporting evidence came from the U.S. embassy, which had received word from the French chargé and the Canadian and Indian members of the International Control Commission that Nhu and Ho would probably reach an agreement in the next three or four months. Nhu sought to drive out the Americans and "beat the Communists at their own game." Big Minh lamented that his country was "in chains with no way to shake them off."[60]

Many wondered how McNamara could continue making strong statements about progress in the face of so much contradictory evidence. At one point in a week-long guided tour, he attempted to justify his optimism in a government "open arms" camp near Tam Ky. From a pile of arms captured from the Vietcong, he pointed to a weapon and triumphantly asked, "Is this Chinese?" "I'm afraid I have to say," replied his embarrassed Vietnamese guide, "that this is a regular American 57-mm. recoilless rifle which they captured earlier from us." In the Mekong Delta, the Vietcong had overrun two major towns in An Xuyen Province. Despite the U.S. Army's claim that the Vietcong numbers had risen there by 15 percent the past year, senior officers gave McNamara what news correspondents derisively termed the standard "glossy" briefing. A junior officer overheard the favorable assessment and later admitted, "We were in tears." More doubts arose in a meeting with junior U.S. Army officers in Can Tho. As McNamara and Bundy looked on, Taylor asked a young major and provincial adviser to assess the situation. "Lousy, General." "What do you mean by that?" Taylor asked. The young army officer set out the details "very convincingly," Forrestal remembered, encouraging others to speak out. "All hell broke loose."[61]

Other revelations convinced the advisers that the war was far more complex than imagined. McNamara had talked with Thuan, Diem's minister of defense, and with British journalist Patrick Honey, who had lived in Saigon for years, and their negative analyses fitted those of the army officers. Bundy's discussions with Halberstam and Sheehan likewise confirmed these findings, causing him to realize "for the first time of how immensely diverse the war was in itself." Particularly alarming was the Vietcong's control over the well-populated province of Long An, just outside Saigon. "I was left, as I think McNamara was, with a lasting skepticism of the ability of any man, however honest, to interpret accurately what was going on. It was just too diffuse, and too much that was critical took place below the surface." Most of the mission members concluded that "an unchanged Diem regime stood only a small chance of holding South Vietnam together and carrying the conflict with the Viet Cong and Hanoi to a successful conclusion. What Diem and Nhu were doing was not merely repugnant, but seemed calculated to end in chaos."[62]

Forrestal declared that the McNamara–Taylor report, written hurriedly on the plane home to Washington, was a "mishmash of everything." It asserted that the "military campaign has made great progress" while admitting that the Diem regime had become "increasingly unpopular" and that its repression of the Buddhists had endangered the military campaign. The United States must express its disapproval of Diem's political efforts and suspend food assistance (which the regime sold on the local market to amass money to pay its civil servants). It must also end the special $200,000 a month earmarked as salary for Diem's Special Forces unless those units moved their operations out of Saigon and into the countryside. The latter action, as Forrestal noted, would encourage the generals advocating a coup. "It was the first sign the generals had . . . that maybe the United States was serious about this." Bundy admitted that the report demonstrated a "clear internal inconsistency" between its claim that South Vietnam could win the war if the government granted political reforms and its follow-up assertion that Diem would probably reject them. After only two hours' sleep during the twenty-seven-hour flight home, Bundy was exhausted. "Neither draftsmanship nor judgment is likely to be at its best under such working conditions." And yet this report would provide the Kennedy administration's plan of action in the forthcoming critical days.[63]

The McNamara–Taylor mission noted mild progress in the war but saw no wisdom in maintaining the present level of U.S. commitment. Indeed, McNamara recommended an acceleration of the phased withdrawal program aimed at yielding results six months earlier than planned. The military effort was in jeopardy because of the growing political instability in Saigon and the government's rising unpopularity. A successful coup appeared unlikely, although the assassination of Diem or Nhu seemed conceivable. Some high-ranking officers leaned toward a coup; others had relatives who had participated in the government's repression of the Buddhists and were reluctant to break with Diem. Resentment of Nhu permeated the highest military echelons and probably the mid-level officers as well. It was doubtful that the United States could pressure Diem and Nhu into making changes.[64]

PARTIAL U.S. DISENGAGEMENT resurfaced as the sole feasible choice—but only after the regime demonstrated the capacity to control the insurgents. To achieve military success in the northern and central areas by the close of 1964 and in the delta a year later, static missions must end and all combat troops must be in the field about twenty of every thirty days. The ARVN must focus on "clear and hold operations" rather than broad sweeps. An improved Vietnamese military performance should permit "the bulk of U.S. personnel" to withdraw by the end of 1965. In the meantime, the defense department should announce plans to withdraw the first thousand U.S. military forces by the close of 1963. This move would constitute the initial step in a long-range program designed to replace U.S. soldiers with Vietnamese in conjunction with their improved performance. In a statement that reflected the president's long-time belief, the mission asserted that this was "a Vietnamese war and the country and the war must, in the end, be run solely by the Vietnamese."[65]

The withdrawal plan forced into the background by the Buddhist crisis had come to the fore again. But whereas the initial move in that direction had rested on the firm belief that the South Vietnamese would put down the rebellion and win the war, the second attempt was more restrained and less optimistic in tone. Victory, according to the McNamara–Taylor report, consisted of reducing the insurgency "to proportions manageable by the national security forces of the GVN [Government of Vietnam], unassisted by the presence of U.S. military forces."[66]

16

PRESIDENT KENNEDY'S
DECISION TO WITHDRAW

We need a way to get out of Vietnam.

Robert S. McNamara, October 2, 1963

Mr. President, it ought to be very clear what we mean by
victory or success. That doesn't mean that every Viet Cong
comes in with a white flag, but that we do suppress this
insurgency to the point that the national security forces of
Vietnam can contain [it].

General Maxwell D. Taylor, October 2, 1963

All planning will be directed towards preparing RVN forces
for the withdrawal of all U.S. special assistance units and
personnel by the end of calendar year 1965.

General Maxwell D. Taylor, October 4, 1963

ON OCTOBER 2, 1963, President Kennedy made the decision to withdraw the first contingent of U.S. military forces from Vietnam,
the initial step toward a major disengagement. This action resulted primarily from the conflicting military assessments that had dogged
the administration for months. But the timing was also attributable to political considerations. The president must first win reelection in 1964 before implementing the rest of the phased withdrawal plan. Otherwise, the
public outcry over the loss of Vietnam could cost him a second term and
bring in a hard-line advocate of military victory.

Kennedy's decision to withdraw was unconditional, for he approved a
calendar of events that did not necessitate a victory. Indeed, the meaning of
success had virtually melded with the reality of failure to produce the call for
a meltdown of Vietcong resistance to the point that Saigon could police the
situation on its own. The White House, of course, defended its decision as
honorable in that the withdrawal would take place in harmony with South
Vietnam's improved battlefield performance. But this plan was *not* contingent on success. President Kennedy never deviated from his belief that only

the South Vietnamese could win the war, and it had become increasingly clear by the summer and fall of 1963 that the war was not winnable in a traditional military sense. Indeed, as Galbraith insisted years afterward, Kennedy "had learned by that time to second guess the military establishment and his mind was made up as regards the Vietnam disaster." Withdrawal was the only option. "Implicit" in all his conversations with the president was "the realization that victory was not possible."[1]

As McNamara wrote in his postwar account, President Kennedy made the "decision on October 2 to begin the withdrawal of U.S. forces." Three days later, the president made the formal decision to remove the first 1,000 American soldiers, and on October 11 he signed off on NSAM 263, which authorized an unpublicized completion of the initial stage of the withdrawal by December 31, 1963. Kennedy had set into motion the beginning of a massive military disengagement designed to return the U.S. involvement to the low-key advisory level of January 1961.[2]

I

THE McNAMARA–TAYLOR MISSION recommended several ways to gain leverage over the Diem regime, all vulnerable to the charge of promoting a coup but defensible as an effort to bring about reforms aimed at facilitating a U.S. military withdrawal based on progress in the war. Economic pressure received top priority. Suspension of the Commodity Import Program, which with the PL 480 program provided nearly 70 percent of Vietnam's imports, would set off an inflationary spiral. Withholding funds for two AID projects—the Saigon-Cholon Waterworks ($9 million) and the Saigon Electric Power Project ($4 million)—would signal U.S. disapproval of Diem's policies. Termination of assistance to other programs was possible, including Colonel Tung's Special Forces. U.S. civilian and military representatives in Saigon were to follow Lodge's policy of "coolness" toward all Vietnamese except those whose contact was essential to military operations. William Bundy insisted that the White House had *not* adopted these measures to force Diem into reforms. Its "coolness" toward Diem "would encourage other elements, and specifically the military, to take some action to overthrow him."[3]

It should have been clear (and it doubtless was to the president and his advisers) that any stance taken by the United States would affect the likelihood of a coup. McNamara and Taylor had arrived in Washington on the morning of October 2 and proceeded to the White House to brief the president on their findings. After setting out three alternative policies—reconciliation with the regime, "selective pressures," and active promotion of a military coup—the McNamara–Taylor report recommended option two. Reconciliation would signify approval of Diem and alienate the generals; initiating a coup was inadvisable "at the present time" in view of the conspirators' reluctance to act. The only choice was a program of "selective short-term pressures" that were primarily economic and all conditioned on the regime's improved performance. This stand posed a major dilemma. It sought to achieve the mission's central objective of a phased withdrawal. "I think," McNamara told the president, "we must have a means of disengaging from this area, and we must show our country that means." In reality, however, this step was the one most coveted by the generals as a quiet signal of U.S. interest in a coup. "We should work with the Diem government," the authors of the report asserted, "but not support it." We must establish contacts with "an alternative leadership if and when it appears" but not encourage a coup under present circumstances. "[W]hether or not it proves to be wise to promote a coup at a later time, we must be ready for the possibility of a spontaneous coup, and this too requires clandestine contacts on an intensive basis."[4]

Sullivan had refused to sign the report because, he complained to McNamara, its call for withdrawal based on progress in the war was "totally unrealistic. We're not going to get troops out in '65. We mustn't submit anything as phony as this to the president." The war "was going to be a long, grinding sort of thing," and the administration should not raise false hopes. Indeed, Sullivan later recalled, "It looked to me as though it was going to be just the opposite: We were going to be putting in more people by the end of 1963." McNamara, according to Sullivan, had appeared to agree until he talked with Taylor. "Well, goddammit," the general declared, "we've got to make these people put their noses to the wheel. . . . If we don't give them some indication that we're going to get out sometime, they're just going to be leaning on us forever. So that's why I had it in there." Taylor regarded the withdrawal as a means for pressuring Diem into making changes. Sullivan saw through the subterfuge and warned that "if this becomes a matter of public record, it would be considered a phony and a fraud and an effort to mollify the American public and just not be considered honest."[5]

Harriman defended his assistant, agreeing that the mission's leaders had ignored the harsh reality of the war because of their "desire to have good news come out." Sullivan thought that the mission's leaders had dropped the withdrawal call from the report and was surprised that it appeared in the recommendations sent to the White House. "Bill Sullivan wasn't taken in, and therefore I wasn't taken in," exclaimed Harriman. The problem stemmed from the military's control over policy. Its soldiers were trained to paint the "best face" on every situation to maintain morale and "were taken in by their own statements." The civilian advisers were not fooled. Sullivan, Forrestal, and Hilsman knew the truth. "I would say this clearly shows the blunder of Dean Rusk surrendering the State Department leadership."[6]

Harriman contended that the military had gotten caught up in the "numbers racket" and was unduly optimistic. Nhu's strategic hamlets snaked down roads and canals, leaving vast areas in which the Vietcong could operate. Thompson warned that the strategic hamlets would collapse. No one either checked back on their status after construction or followed up on the clear-and-hold operations. According to statistics, Harriman declared, "very real progress was being made, but on a very, very weak foundation." The problem "was misjudging the information that was available." The president was never aware of Sullivan's opposition. Taylor had won the full confidence of both Kennedys, as he was "very earnest, sincere, very close to Bobby—and, you know, the president." Taylor had no political understanding, however. "He followed the advice of Harkins, General Harkins. Accepted it, and none of us did. We didn't believe it; we didn't think it was true."[7]

Later that same morning, President Kennedy met with the mission leaders and other advisers in the Oval Office to discuss the report. Taylor admitted to uncertainty about Vietcong strength but was sure of the rising number of its deaths. "They're now actually counting the bodies."

The president asked whether the initial reduction of a thousand men rested on the assumption "that it's going well."

"Yes sir," replied McNamara. The ARVN could complete the military campaign by the end of 1965. "If it extends beyond that period, we believe we can train the Vietnamese to take over the essential functions and withdraw the bulk of our forces." The point was clear. "We need a way to get out of Vietnam. This is a way of doing it."

Taylor agreed. Mission members had talked with more than 170 U.S. and Vietnamese officers, and all American officers expressed confidence that they would "reduce this insurgency to little more than sporadic itching" by 1965.

If we fail to meet that date, McNamara asserted in supporting Taylor, "we nonetheless can withdraw the bulk of our US forces according to the schedule we've laid out, worked out, because we can train the Vietnamese to do the job."

In that respect, Taylor interjected, "it ought to be very clear what we mean by victory or success. That doesn't mean that every Viet Cong comes in with a white flag, but that we do suppress this insurgency to the point that the national security forces of Vietnam can contain [it]."

McGeorge Bundy sought clarification. "That doesn't quite mean that every American officer comes out of there, either."

"No, no," emphatically responded Taylor.

"You're really talking about two different things," Bundy noted. "What you're saying is that the US advice and stiffening function you may want to continue, but that the large use of US troops who can be replaced by properly trained Vietnamese can end."

The president agreed that the policy statement should say that "while there may continue to be a requirement for special training forces, we believe that the major United States part of the task can be completed by the end of '65."[8]

McNamara later noted that the president had endorsed the mission's recommendation for a withdrawal of 1,000 Americans without explaining his reasoning. To prevent others from pressuring him into a change, the secretary urged him to make a public announcement. "That would set it in concrete."[9]

At an early evening meeting of the National Security Council on that same October 2, the president saw a consensus among his advisers and sought to get the report approved. "To cut off completely would not be wise, unless the situation really begins to deteriorate more." After some discussion, he continued: "My only reservation about it is, . . . if the war doesn't continue to go well, it will look like we were overly optimistic. And I'm not sure what benefit we get out at this time by announcing a thousand."

"Mr. President," McNamara responded, "we have the thousand split by units. So that if the war doesn't go well, we can say that these thousand would not have influenced the course of action."

"And the advantage?"

"And the advantage of taking them out is that we can say to the Congress and the people that we *do* have a plan for reducing the exposure of US combat personnel to the guerilla actions in South Vietnam—actions that the people of South Vietnam should gradually develop a capability to suppress themselves. And I think this will be of great value to us in meeting the very strong views of Fulbright and others that we're bogged down in Asia and we'll be there for decades."

"All right," answered the president. For public release, "I think we ought to say that as of tonight, we have a policy, and this is what we're hanging on to. And more than that. It's not only that statement to obey but also the report, the essence of the report was endorsed by all." Facing the press would not be easy. "The more difficult question is what means are we going to use to bring pressure to change the political atmosphere."[10]

President Kennedy had approved the phased withdrawal. Whether or not he believed the report's optimistic conclusions, they fitted with his inclination toward reducing the U.S. military involvement. The president, Gilpatric asserted, "made it clear to McNamara and me that he wanted to not only hold the level of U.S. military presence in Vietnam down, but he wanted to reverse the flow and that's when this question of bringing back some of the U.S. military personnel came up. But it was in keeping with his general reluctance to see us sucked in militarily to Southeast Asia." It also constituted a signal to Diem and his generals that the United States intended to play only "an accessory advisory role." Lodge assured Rusk that Thompson's negative prognosis had made "a profound impression on President Kennedy." Sullivan later conceded that the scaled down commitment "may have reflected more of President Kennedy's thinking than I was aware at the time." Gilpatric likewise noted that the president had become "particularly restive" during the summer and fall of 1963 about the "exit point." McNamara assured Gilpatric that the October withdrawal "was part of a plan the president asked him to develop to unwind the whole thing."[11]

The administration considered it necessary to issue a public announcement of the imminent withdrawal. Otherwise, according to the *Pentagon Papers*, "the formal and classified planning process would have seemed to be nothing more than a drill." The president objected, however, to stating publicly that an expected improvement in the Vietnamese training program would enable the United States to pull out a thousand military personnel "by the end of the year." If such an improvement failed to transpire, the administration would come under severe attack. McNamara, however, wanted to maintain the declaration in an effort to counter critics at home who insisted that the United States was unable to get out of Vietnam. "The sentence reveals that we have a withdrawal plan." The result was a compromise in which the withdrawal schedule remained in place, but as part of the anticipated improvements highlighted in the McNamara–Taylor report and not a rose-colored prediction by the president. A CIA report confirmed Kennedy's caution by recommending the following qualification: "If present military progress continues, we believe that the US part of the task might be completed by the end of 1965." As McNamara left the meeting to speak with journalists, Kennedy instructed him to "tell them that means all of the helicopter pilots, too."[12]

Despite the White House attempt to play down the withdrawal, the matter drew nationwide attention as a major turnaround in the war's fortunes. At a news conference immediately following the National Security Council meeting of October 2, White House spokesman Pierre Salinger reported on the McNamara-Taylor mission, inadvertently leaving the erroneous impression that South Vietnam's field performance had improved so dramatically that the United States could soon withdraw the great mass of its military forces. Few listeners recognized that the administration's definition of victory had come under severe constraints. In trying to create an atmosphere conducive to a major disengagement, Salinger declared that the present level of U.S. military support would continue "only until the insurgency has been suppressed or until the national security forces of the government of South Viet-Nam are capable of suppressing it." Secretary

McNamara and General Taylor had concluded "that the major part of the U.S. military task can be completed by the end of 1965, although there may be a continuing requirement for a limited number of U.S. training personnel." By the end of 1963, "the U.S. program for training Vietnamese should have progressed to the point where 1,000 U.S. military personnel assigned to South Viet-Nam can be withdrawn." This was risky policy, for nothing would stem the profound disappointment resulting from failure to satisfy what one member of the National Security Council termed the certain "Bring-the-boys-home-by-1965" euphoria released by this announcement. The day following the news, the usually astute *New York Times* showed no awareness of the subtleties contained in the withdrawal plan. The journal's headline blared: "VIETNAM VICTORY BY END OF '65 ENVISAGED BY U.S."[13]

Thus, without any appreciable upsurge in South Vietnam's performance, either at home or on the battlefield, the Kennedy administration had publicly specified a date for winding down its military involvement in Vietnam. Indeed, it had returned full circle to the push for disengagement that had preceded the Buddhist outbreak in early May 1963. And yet, with the present regime still floundering, the possibility of a withdrawal taking place within the boundaries of honor was highly improbable. Nothing had altered Diem's disastrous course toward defeat by the Vietcong, and it seemed certain that nothing could do so short of a coup. If anyone in the White House still believed that selective economic pressures might force Diem into reforms, no one counted on his removing the central nemesis to the entire aid program: Nhu himself. One state department adviser urged Hilsman to cooperate with the unhappy "Vietnamese Establishment" of military and business leaders in overthrowing Diem. There was no middle ground. McNamara warned his colleagues that their program would either "push us toward a reconciliation with Diem or toward a coup to overthrow Diem."[14]

On October 4 Taylor sent a memorandum to his joint chiefs colleagues, setting out the withdrawal recommendation as one of President Kennedy's "Approved Actions for South Vietnam." Training of Vietnamese forces would accelerate to the point that those duties "now performed by U.S. military units and personnel . . . can be assumed properly by the Vietnamese by the end of the calendar year 1965." This was not a plan contingent on military victory; it was unconditional. "All planning will be directed towards preparing RVN [Republic of Vietnam] forces for the withdrawal of all U.S. special assistance units and personnel by the end of calendar year 1965. The U.S. Comprehensive Plan, Vietnam will be revised to bring it into consonance with these objectives, and to reduce planned residual (post 1965) MAAG strengths to approximately pre-insurgency levels." The administration would "[e]xecute the plan to withdraw 1,000 U.S. military personnel by the end of 1963. . . . The action will now be treated in low key, as the initial increment of U.S. forces whose presence is no longer required because (a) Vietnamese forces have been trained to assume the function involved; or (b) the function for which they came to Vietnam has been completed." To maintain pressure on South Vietnam, the United States would evaluate progress on a quarterly basis, thereby providing "continued leverage on the GVN [Government of Vietnam] to maintain the required rate of progress." President Kennedy, as this document attests, had decided on a major disengagement that rested on a greatly restricted definition of "victory"—so restricted, in fact, that it was tantamount to an admission of defeat.[15]

Barring a successful coup, the only solution was to adjudge the South Vietnamese army as sufficiently improved to control the insurgency by itself. The United States could then roll back its military presence to its early 1961 level. McNamara saw no basis for staying there once the administration had determined that the Vietnamese could handle the Vietcong on their own. But he also believed that a Diem government could never accomplish this objective. The sticky question lay in deciding when, if ever, the ARVN had reached that elusive performance level. The president was well aware of the continuing military failures of the Diem government and knew that he would experience great difficulties in convincing the public that the withdrawal had resulted from success. Indeed, he was prepared to pull out even if the act acknowledged failure. Robert Kennedy recommended downplaying the withdrawal. The president saw his brother's point and at a cabinet meeting on October 5 directed that there be no formal announcement to Diem of "our decision" to remove a thousand Americans by December. "Instead the action should be carried out routinely as part of our general posture of withdrawing people when they are no longer needed." He was emphatic. "Let's just go ahead and do it, without making a public statement about it."[16]

This the Kennedy administration intended to do, even as Madame Nhu threatened to embarrass the United States by her visit, as her husband pursued secret negotiations with the North Vietnamese, and as the movement toward a coup resumed among the generals.

II

MADAME NHU'S VISIT to the United States had the potential to inflict severe embarrassment on the White House. Her twenty-two-day itinerary presented countless opportunities to attack the Kennedy administration. It listed two private interviews with *Time* and Knight newspapers along with twenty-nine major public appearances that included ten television programs, two radio shows, six major press and public affairs gatherings, and eleven university visits. There was an added feature to this public relations extravaganza. After Madame Nhu bitterly attacked the Buddhists and U.S. policy toward the Diem regime, her father and former ambassador to the United States followed her on the circuit, disputing her accusations and thereby drawing more attention to this bizarre episode. Furthermore, on the day following her arrival in the United States on October 7, the U.N. General Assembly authorized an inquiry into the charges against Diem of brutally mistreating the Buddhists.[17]

The White House had tried to circumvent certain trouble. Before her arrival, Harlan Cleveland from the state department had asked South Vietnam's new ambassador to the United States, Buu Hoi, if the Diem regime had taken any steps "to tone down Madame Nhu's public utterances" while she was in the United States. Buu Hoi declared that he had sent in five reports on this matter alone and that the government had privately instructed her to "quiet down." He admitted that her previous outbursts had caused considerable damage. Her use of "barbecue" had been particularly unfortunate, Buu Hoi told Cleveland. "She did not even know the word, which would not be as colorful in the French language, but had picked it up from 'an English language publication in Saigon'"—presumably, the *Times of Vietnam*. Madame Nhu was a hot new item, Cleveland reported to the White House. The problem was "press magnification of quotable comments by a lady who is unfortunately too beautiful to ignore." Bui Hoi recognized that major issues were at stake. In a conversation at the United Nations in New York, he told Rusk in the presence of others that Madame Nhu "must clearly be eliminated."[18]

The administration found it impossible to parry the rapier-like remarks of its Vietnamese visitor. President Kennedy had dismissed a recommendation to deny her a visa. Vice President Johnson emphasized to Madame Nhu that Americans no longer believed the Diem regime responsive to its people or capable of winning the war. Her scathing attacks on the U.S. government and the president had hurt relations between the countries and jeopardized the aid program. Madame Nhu refused to cower, calling herself a "scapegoat" for America's failures and berating the White House for betraying the Diem regime. "I refuse to play the role of an accomplice in an awful murder," she bitterly declared. "According to a few immature American junior officials—too imbued by a real but obsolete imperialist spirit, the Vietnamese regime is not puppet enough and must be liquidated." These same "junior officials" had sabotaged her nation's policy by "briberies, threats and other means," all to destroy the Ngo family because they "do not like" it. Why is it, she sneered, that "all the people around President Kennedy are pink?" The president grumbled that her actions would "make this whole pot boil again." McCone thought the only person who could quiet her was "her damn husband." Kennedy was dubious. "How do you tell a fellow to keep his wife home?" He was "either scared or he must be stupid because she's been running around making inflammatory statements." The press would "eat her alive."[19]

Meanwhile, resurgent violence in Saigon bolstered the president's interest in withdrawal. McNamara assured him that the Buddhist protests had moved beyond a religious issue to become a sweeping program of political opposition. The government's forces had eased the pressure, apparently intending to allow the university to reopen though retaining a few Buddhists in custody and occasionally raiding a pagoda. But sporadic disturbances kept emotions high. Shortly after noon in early October, Buddhist bonze Thich Quang Huong duplicated the June 11 immolation by arriving alone in a cab in front of the Saigon Central Market and dousing himself with gasoline before setting himself afire. Among the small group of spectators were Halberstam and two NBC journalists. Police tried to stop them from taking pictures of the burning bonze and then grabbed at their cameras. During the scuffle, plainclothes policemen threw the three correspondents to the ground and kicked them. In another part of the city, someone tossed a propaganda grenade into the compound of the Philippine embassy, which exploded and ejected a dozen Buddhist flags without harming anyone. Meanwhile, at least a hundred Buddhists (bonzes and laymen) in Saigon expressed a willingness to commit suicide in an effort to expose their problems to the world. Only a police crackdown had prevented at least three Buddhist demonstrations while McNamara and Taylor were in the country.[20]

In this highly charged atmosphere, the chances of a coup had regained momentum. On October 2, at Saigon's Tan Son Nhut Airport, Conein (allegedly by chance) encountered General Don, who said he had been trying to contact his old CIA friend for some time. Could they meet that night at his quarters in Nha Trang? Yes, responded Conein, not hesitating to make the 200-mile trip to a spot northeast of Saigon. In an hour-long session, Don emphasized that the generals "now have a plan." Big Minh wanted to meet with Conein at Joint General Staff Headquarters in Saigon.[21]

At this point Conein emerged as the central figure in all contacts between the U.S. embassy and the generals. "I was a liaison between my government and the people who were plotting the coup," he later explained. "My job was to convey the orders from my Ambassador and the instructions from my Ambassador to the people who were planning the coup, to monitor those individuals who were planning the coup, to get as much information so that our government would not be caught with their pants down." When he met with Lodge, the ambassador was very cautious about revealing anything that came from Washington. He "would fold a piece of paper and what pertained to you for instructions he would let you read that, and that alone so that you didn't know who was sending it or where it came from." Afterward, he would remark, "Those are the instructions. Do you understand them?" "Yes, sir." "All right, go carry them out."[22]

Conein had excellent credentials for the shadowy task, including a sense of humor and a wealth of self-confidence. Born in France but raised in the United States, he joined the French army at the outset of World War II, only to desert after its surrender in 1940. He returned to the United States, where he volunteered for the Office of Strategic Services. After further training with the Special Operations Executive in England, he parachuted behind enemy lines in France in 1944 and worked with the resistance. The following year he went to the China–Burma–India theater for a short time before transferring into French Indochina to form a base of operations in the north against the Japanese. When the war ended, he returned to the United States and soon joined the fledgling CIA. He served in Germany until 1953, soon afterward joining Lansdale in conducting psywar operations in North Vietnam. After Diem became premier of South Vietnam in October 1954, Conein relocated in Saigon to help the new government. He soon left the CIA to join the army's Special Forces, only to retire in 1961 and return to Vietnam as, again, a CIA agent. The CIA, he once said in a bullhorn voice so often laced with obscenities, stood for "criminals, idiots, and asses." It was a "cookie factory" because "there's nothing but fruits and nuts in the goddamn place." But he could not resist the adventure. Lansdale's secretary remarked that Conein thought himself a daring and strikingly handsome buccaneer. "He never saw a mirror he didn't like."[23]

As a cover for his clandestine activities, Conein operated under the code name of Black Luigi or Lulu and wore a military uniform signifying the rank of lieutenant colonel. Colby had asked him to serve as liaison with the Ministry of the Interior on the Strategic Hamlet Program. In reality, his assignment was to travel all over South Vietnam, amassing evidence of anti-Diem sentiment. The task was dangerous. One slip and Nhu could have had him killed and blamed the Vietcong. But Conein was a gifted undercover agent. Indeed, he was the only American *not* on a list of suspected coup makers once shown by Nhu to Don. Conein's movement throughout the provinces and his meetings with military personnel raised no eyebrows. In the city, he often met with coup conspirators in a dentist's office, even having work done on his teeth as a cover. Conein accumulated so much information that the White House feared that the generals were setting him up as a "patsy" and once considered replacing him with General Richard Stilwell from MACV. But Don refused to talk with anyone else.[24]

Three days after the meeting with Don, Conein had Lodge's approval (*without* Harkins's knowledge, which further embittered their relations over the ambassador's repeated refusals to share information from the White

House) to meet with Minh for what turned out to be more than an hour. A coup was about to take place, the general emphasized, and he did *not* want it to be "American sponsored." But he needed an assurance of U.S. military and economic assistance afterward. In a response that Colby later termed a "green light" to the generals, Conein promised that the United States would not obstruct a coup and would provide help following success. Big Minh explained that he and his accomplices—Don, Khiem, and Kim—recognized that the rapidly deteriorating war effort had necessitated a leadership change. Minh claimed to speak for all the generals except perhaps, he said while laughing, Dinh, in alleging that they had no political ambitions and wanted only to win the war.[25]

The generals intended to leave Diem in office as a figurehead but to assassinate those they considered to be the three most dangerous men in South Vietnam—his two brothers, Nhu and Ngo Dinh Can, along with Ngo Trong Hieu, a former Communist who still harbored Communist sympathies. According to one well-placed source, the generals hated Can more than Nhu. What about Tung? asked Conein. Minh shrugged off any concern about the colonel by asserting, "[I]f I get rid of Nhu, Can and Hieu, Colonel Tung will be on his knees before me." The alternatives to assassinating Diem's brothers and keeping the premier in office, Minh declared, were either to launch an ARVN offensive against Tung's Special Forces or to encircle Saigon with rebel military forces. In both cases, the result would be a long civil war that benefited the Vietcong. Swift action was necessary because several other military leaders were devising coup plans.[26]

For the first important time, the possibility of assassination arose as an integral part of the coup. As fate would have it, Lodge succeeded in having Richardson removed from the CIA station on October 5, leaving his deputy, David Smith, as acting chief. That very day, Smith took matters into his own hands. He recommended to Lodge that "we do not set ourselves irrevocably against the assassination plot, since the other two alternatives mean either a bloodbath in Saigon or a protracted struggle which could rip the Army and the country asunder." In a later conversation with Trueheart, however, Smith remarked that Minh was "naïve" to think that he could eliminate Nhu and Can while retaining Diem. The premier would never cooperate with his brothers' assassins.[27]

McCone was livid over Smith's unauthorized action and shot off two cables to Saigon directing him to withdraw his recommendation to the ambassador. Any "assassination discussions need more careful handling." The "best line is no line." The White House must bear "no responsibility for [the] actions of any of [the] various contending Vietnamese groups." It "cannot be in [the] position of stimulating, approving or supporting assassination, but on [the] other hand, we are in no way responsible for stopping every such threat of which we might receive even partial knowledge.

We certainly would not favor [the] assassination of Diem." But "taking [a] position on this matter opens [the] door too easily for probes of our position." The White House was "naturally interested in intelligence on any such plan," but it "cannot be in [the] position [of] actively condoning such [a] course of action and thereby engaging our responsibility therefor." The "best approach is hands off." Lodge agreed.[28]

McCone's stand ignored the reality of U.S. involvement in all events relating to a coup. It was naïve to chart a hands-off policy and expect anyone to believe him. Colby wrote the cable reprimanding Smith's action and doubtless was correct in later asserting that McCone personally opposed CIA involvement in assassinations. But that stance by no means curtailed the generals' intentions. Minh got exactly what he wanted. The United States would not initiate a coup, but it would do nothing to stop one and it guaranteed aid afterward. Most important, McCone's position against assassination did not reach Minh at this critical moment—and perhaps never did. Colby thought the message expressing Washington's opposition to assassinations never went beyond Don. Conein did not learn of McCone's cable until almost three weeks afterward, when Lodge informed him that the White House would not condone assassinations. By that time, the generals had moved forward in the knowledge that they would encounter no U.S. resistance. As Colby noted, the "option as to how they conduct their coup was left to the generals."[29]

McCone later insisted that the White House approved his hands-off attitude toward assassination. President Kennedy called him to the White House, where Robert Kennedy joined them to discuss the matter in private. "I felt that the President agreed with my position, despite the fact that he had great reservations concerning Diem and his conduct. I urged him to try to bring all the pressure we could on Diem to change his ways, to encourage more support throughout the country. My precise words to the President, and I remember them very clearly, were that 'Mr. President, if I was manager of a baseball team, I had one pitcher, I'd keep him in the box whether he was a good pitcher or not.' By that I was saying that, if Diem was removed we would have not one coup but we would have a succession of coups and political disorder in Vietnam and it might last several years." McCone asserted that he did not discuss assassination with the president. Instead, they talked about "whether we should let the coup go or use our influences not to."[30]

The Kennedy administration's reaction to Conein's revelations remained consistent though impossible to implement: Welcome a coup without promoting it. This tactic had already proved to be a meaningless charade in light of the selective aid cuts. Conein's instructions were inherently contradictory. He assured Minh that the United States would not interfere with the generals' efforts but then asked to see all plans other than those dealing with assassinations. Furthermore, he guaranteed White House assistance to any government that seemed capable of winning the war.[31]

The administration had taken subtle but major steps toward promoting a coup. President Kennedy directed Lodge to take "no initiative" in giving "any active covert encouragement to a coup." But, in a move that encouraged the conspirators, the ambassador should make an "urgent covert effort . . . to identify and build contacts with possible alternative leadership as and when it appears." Such a move must be "totally secure and fully deniable." This was "not to be aimed at active promotion of [a] coup but only at surveillance and readiness." To ensure "plausibility to denial," Lodge was to issue these instructions orally to the CIA's Acting Station Chief, who would report to Lodge alone.[32]

The White House continued to play out the make-believe drama of removing all obstacles to a coup while denying that it was encouraging a coup. It had recalled Richardson to Washington, confirming Harkins's belief that Lodge was "a maverick, a loner," who had secured the CIA station chief's removal and would now push for a coup. Ironically, Richardson had laid the basis for his own demise by doing his job so well. He had followed Washington's instructions to cultivate good relations with Nhu, only to become the victim of changed circumstances that dictated Nhu's removal. Richardson's departure proved more far-reaching in consequences than anyone could have imagined. It opened the door to a coup by sending a message to both Diem and the generals that the regime had lost its closest supporter.[33]

III

PRESIDENT KENNEDY MEANWHILE moved toward activating the selective pressures advocated by the McNamara–Taylor mission. He approved the existing aid suspension to the Commodity Import Program, postponed loans for the Saigon–Cholon Waterworks and Saigon electric power project, and halted support to Colonel Tung's forces until they came under Joint General Staff control. But the president remained perplexed over how to suspend aid in a manner that hurt Diem and Nhu without damaging the economy. Lodge was to continue his policy of "cool correctness" in an effort to make Diem approach him for assistance. Thus, the White House pursued the impossible task of imposing economic cuts while denying any intent to instigate a coup. All actions should take place quietly, leaving "no public impression of a package of sanctions and a package of demands."[34]

No one in the Kennedy administration expected Diem to make the desired changes; but all recognized that the economic sanctions had bought time to initiate the withdrawal process called for in the McNamara–Taylor report. Lodge agreed with the mission's dark prognosis. The Joint Chiefs of Staff, in harmony with Harkins, approved the mission's recommendations for South Vietnam, each one aimed at concluding the military campaigns in the north and center by the end of 1964 and in the delta by the end of 1965. "All planning," the joint chiefs asserted in echoing Taylor's October 4 memorandum, "will be directed towards preparing RVN [Republic of Vietnam] forces for the withdrawal of all U.S. special assistance units and personnel by the end of calendar year 1965." That objective in mind, they intended to withdraw the initial 1000 U.S. military personnel by the end of 1963. Rather than making this move a media event, "the action will now be treated in low key" and in conjunction with the improved performance of the Vietnamese military forces. The White House considered two more years of U.S. military involvement in Vietnam a reasonable period before withdrawing most of its forces.[35]

If a difference existed between promoting a coup and doing nothing to stop one, that distinction was narrow—particularly since the major player on the scene was the United States. South Vietnam had a government, thanks primarily to the U.S. aid program. Continued assistance to the Diem regime meant a continued commitment to that government and necessary opposition to its enemies, just as a reduced commitment to the regime meant automatic favor to its challengers. The Kennedy administration had inadvertently undermined the generals' August coup plans by refusing to stop assistance to Diem and to guarantee them aid; it now had cut assistance to the regime and promised economic and military help to the generals once they took over the government. The president and his advisers realized that this assurance was the trigger to the coup. Furthermore, the White House had expressed no opposition to Minh's assassination plan. In remaining silent, it avoided an admission to awareness of the plot, but (and this was the crucial point) it had thereby lost any potential control over events. The official silence regarding the generals' assassination proposal tacitly left the door open for them to kill Diem's brothers. And, in the heat of the moment, could the assassins guarantee no harm to Diem? The White House could not claim plausible denial of a coup involvement, regardless of its action. Colby put it best years afterward when he declared that the cables back and forth between Washington and Saigon carried "this nice theory . . . that it's really the generals who are going to decide, and not us, about the removal of Diem." He added, "There's an unreality to it when you think of the enormous importance of the American position."[36]

Concern grew among the president's advisers that the administration had tied itself too closely to the coup talk. At a White House meeting, President Kennedy announced that Big Minh had inquired about the U.S. position toward a coup.

"Mr. President," Taylor declared, "we're wasting our time with Big Minh." He and McNamara had seen him while in Vietnam, and he said nothing about a coup.

McNamara was equally disgusted. "Two people on Big Minh for an hour, and I couldn't get a damn thing out of him." He complained about U.S. policy. "This is a very, very unsophisticated approach to overthrowing a government, and I think it's cost us a lot already. It's all become known to the press, there and here. It's really disgraceful when you look back on what happened to message 243 and the actions that we took to carry that out." Conein in particular worried the secretary. "It's taken as gospel now that this government tried to overthrow Diem's government and used Conein for that purpose."

The president looked puzzled. Who is Conein?

"Conein," McNamara replied, "is the man who is the contact with General Minh."

"What's his status?"

"He's a former colonel in one of the military services. . . . He's under contract to CIA."

"What does he do?"

Colby explained, "He's in the MACV, sir. That's his cover."

"He's an American?" Kennedy asked.

"Yes, he's American," McCone replied. "He's one of our agents, under cover."

"He's a colorful figure," McNamara sarcastically added. "He's a Lawrence of Arabia type. He's well known to all the reporters in Vietnam. He's well known to the Vietnamese government. And here he is contacting an individual that's known to be a dissident and a probable coup leader. It's open as though we were announcing it over the radio. To continue this kind of activity just strikes me as absurd."

After McGeorge Bundy asked whether Conein should maintain his contact with Big Minh, McCone asserted, "Our preference would be to have Conein make only one contact, and then to establish at that time a completely new channel." The purpose of the single contact would be "[t]o set things up."

Colby opposed bringing in someone else. "It might be harder for someone who's outside the country even to get anywhere near Minh without arousing more attention than a fellow who lives actually in the country. . . . The advantage of Conein is that he's been working with administrative superiors, working on strategic hamlets, and this and that and the other, and he has natural access to a lot of people."

Colby's argument prevailed.

The president then summed up the administration's position on a coup. "We'll listen to what they have to say." But the White House "will not join" until it received satisfactory information regarding the coup makers' prospects and plans for a government.[37]

The White House continued inching closer to precipitating a coup. The president authorized a CIA cable to Lodge, informing him that even though the administration did not want to cause a coup, it did not wish "to leave [the] impression that [the] U.S. would thwart a change of government or deny economic and military assistance to a new regime" if it seemed capable of winning the war and willing to cooperate with the United States. Lodge was to walk a fine line between welcoming information about potential new leaders and avoiding any activity that might "identify [the] U.S. too closely with [a] change in government."[38]

Nhu's public outbursts against his opposition further encouraged the movement toward a coup. His recent interview with Italy's illustrated weekly *Expresso* (much of which the *Times of Vietnam* repeated) was a veritable diatribe against the United States. American troops, including the highly exalted Special Forces, knew nothing about guerrilla warfare. The use of helicopters was his own "invention," and specially trained Vietnamese pilots should fly them. If the United States forced him out of office, the Strategic Hamlet Program would collapse. The Civil Guard and Self-Defense Corps were "mere functionaries" who had alienated the people by stealing chickens and engaging in other forms of stupid behavior. The United States should treat South Vietnam as it treated Yugoslavia—furnish funds without seeking to influence the government. The Americans stood in the way of the revolution so essential to victory and should withdraw. Nhu also lashed out at his father-in-law, former Ambassador Chuong. If he were to "come to Saigon, I will have his head cut off. I will hang him in the center of a square and let him dangle there. My wife will make the knot on the rope because she is proud of being a Vietnamese and she is a good patriot."[39]

Further suspicions of Nhu's unbalanced state of mind came from reports that he was plotting to assassinate Lodge and other Americans in Saigon. One story, which the CIA regarded with skepticism, claimed that Nhu and Tung planned to stage a student demonstration in front of the U.S. Embassy Chancery as a cover for an attack. During the commotion, their agents would assassinate Lodge and other U.S. officials, along with Tri Quang, and then burn down the Chancery. Lodge blasted any such attempt as "unbelievably idiotic" but reminded Washington that Nhu was not a reasonable person. Nhu was furious with Lodge for advising him to leave the country and appeared to be under the dizzying influence of opium. Veteran embassy officials considered assassination a definite possibility. That in mind, Lodge developed a contingency plan. He ordered the embassy's gates closed when a crowd formed in the streets, and he placed the marine guard into a continual state of readiness. He also directed the CIA's acting station chief to assure the Saigon government that the U.S. Marines' reaction to an invasion of embassy grounds would be similar to that of World War II—swift and "awful beyond description." Surely, the Diem regime would not invite "such a horrible and crushing blow."[40]

In reasonable times, the likelihood of an attempt on Lodge's life was extremely slim; but these were not reasonable times. The Diem regime was under siege at home, faltering in the war, and about to lose its U.S. ally. Diem remained insulated from reality and thereby certain that all was not as bad as it seemed. Nhu publicly attacked the Kennedy administration, conspired with confidants inside South Vietnam, and pursued secret talks with Hanoi that had raised the anxieties of the generals already plotting a coup. Harriman dismissed the possibility of Lodge's assassination as "far-fetched" and called his response "rather hysterical." The CIA remained dubious about an assassination attempt, thinking that the regime had circulated the story to intimidate the United States and keep it uncertain about what to do.[41] But both skeptical assessments failed to consider the possibility of an unreasonable act engineered by two brothers in Saigon who had lost contact with the real world. Reason lay behind Lodge's so-called hysteria.

The U.S. withdrawal plan meanwhile moved closer to fruition. On October 11, the White House issued NSAM 263, in which the president "directed that no formal announcement be made of the implementation of plans to withdraw 1,000 U.S. military personnel by the end of 1963." The White House soon approved leaks to the press that specified the total number of U.S. military forces in Vietnam as 16,500. This marked the first official announcement of actual figures, which were massively higher than the 888 military advisers authorized by the Geneva Accords of 1954. In the fall of 1961, when the administration approved additional troop injections, it had dodged the Geneva issue by not publicizing the numbers. Now, with the figures no longer concealed, the International Control Commission in Saigon would surely cite the United States for violating the accords and then call for further withdrawals aimed at reducing the level to the authorized limit. The White House would emphasize that a decline in North Vietnamese aggression had permitted U.S. compliance with the Geneva regulations and allowed most of the remaining soldiers to withdraw by 1965.[42]

Coup talk likewise moved toward action. On the night of October 20, a U.S. Army lieutenant colonel from MACV received word of an imminent coup. Two long-time Vietnamese acquaintances (not named), along with a third, Air Force Colonel Nguyen Khuong, informed the American that "a small, powerful group" of military officers was ready to assassinate Diem and install a new government. The conspirators had felt compelled to move. Nhu might succeed his brother and seek a neutralist solution to the war that resulted in a reunified Vietnam and retribution to dissatisfied generals. Khuong identified four generals and at least six colonels involved in the plot, including Generals Minh, Nghiem, and Kim, and Colonels Nguyen Van Thieu, Pham Van Dong (not to be confused with the North Vietnamese leader with the same name), and himself. They sought no assistance in the coup but wanted assurances of U.S. recognition and support afterward. The lack of cohesion among the generals had again become evident. Minh had already secured these guarantees from Conein.[43]

Three days later, Don notified Conein that the generals planned a coup during the week of the October 26 National Independence Day holiday. Don feared that Harkins might learn the generals' plans from Khuong, who would, Don declared, receive a reprimand for confiding this information to the MACV officer. Indeed, Harkins had become aware of the coup and, at a British embassy party on October 22, urged Don to hold off because the war was going well. Harkins's remarks led Don to believe that the White House intended to stand by Diem. Don immediately contacted Conein, angrily asserting that the generals had canceled the planned coup and denouncing the Kennedy administration's mixed signals. Conein assured Washington's support for a coup and asked for proof of its leadership and the existence of a plan. But when the two men met in the airport on the morning of October 24, Don failed to produce the evidence. He promised, however, to provide details of the operation and the makeup of the new government two days before a rescheduled coup took place. At this point Conein warned Don that the White House opposed assassinations. "All right, you don't like it," Don replied, "we won't talk about it anymore." The generals, Conein suspected, had already decided to do it their own way. The next day, Don informed Conein of alarming news. Diem had learned of Khuong's overture to the MACV officer and had ordered two key army divisions who supported the coup to remain stationed outside Saigon, separated from their coconspirators.[44]

Lodge tried to ease Washington's concern over the lack of hard information pertaining to the plot. Conein had been a friend of Don's for eighteen years, and the general refused to talk with anyone else. The conspirators' reluctance to disclose all information stemmed from their apprehension over a leak. If the coup failed, the United States's indirect involvement through Conein remained "within the realm of plausible denial." Indeed, Lodge told the White House, the CIA had privately authorized him to disavow Conein at any time. The United States must not stand in the way of a coup. No new government could "bungle and stumble as much as the present one has."[45]

A White House meeting on October 25 further unraveled the threat of events. Harkins had exposed the president's hand in the plot. Furthermore, the rebel generals suspected that the general had betrayed their intentions to Diem. Harkins talked too much, McCone angrily charged. Conein's account had caused the furor: "General Don stated that General Harkins had reiterated the fact that he had misunderstood a presidential directive, that Ambassador Lodge was aware of and controlling Conein's contacts with Don, and that Conein was the proper person with whom to speak." Harkins later denied having made any statement tying President Kennedy to the coup, but Conein's report proved otherwise.[46]

McCone wondered whether Don was working for Diem. "If such is the case," he told the president, "the manner in which the contacts have been made—and the attribution to you, and to General Harkins, and to Lodge—put us in a situation where the government just cannot plausibly deny implication."

Robert Kennedy expressed concern about his brother's culpability, whether or not Don was working both sides. "If some of these people are caught, and they talk about the conversations they had with the United States . . . you're in a good deal of trouble."

McCone was disenchanted with Conein. He was "perfectly overt. . . . He was not an undercover person at all." Everyone knew he was CIA. His military uniform and phony identification card fooled no one.

McGeorge Bundy was dumbfounded. "What we've got to find is a man that really is regarded as highly professional by the agency . . . that also Lodge will take and use as his own. And that man doesn't exist."

"We're just like a bunch of amateurs," McNamara complained. "I hate to be associated with this effort, uh, dealing with Conein. He's an unstable person. . . . We're dealing through a press-minded ambassador and an unstable, uh, uh, Frenchman."

But there was no way to find an alternative contact with the coup plotters. Robert Kennedy insisted that no one from the embassy have contact with the generals.

The president disagreed. "They want to have a conversation with an American, uh, to understand what the American governmental policy will be."

RFK: "Somebody should really find out where it's going."

JFK: "How they gonna find out unless they have a conversation?"

RFK: "Well, somebody can have the conversation initially."

JFK: "Well, then, he will be the representative of the American government."

RFK: "Well, I don't know that that's necessarily true." The coup plotters don't "have to know where he's from or who he's from."

McGeorge Bundy disagreed. "They really have to know if they're gonna tell him the coup plans."

RFK: "Well, I don't know. A person comes in and . . . he's not seen around the embassy all the time. . . ."

"But who do [the plotters] think they're talking to?" asked Bundy, incredulous at this suggestion.

RFK: "Well, they just, they think they're talking to somebody that's, uh, probably somehow associated with the United States. But they're not sure. And they can't identify who it is, exactly."

The president finally put an end to this foolish discussion. "I don't think we can set up any satisfactory contact other than Conein between now and November 2nd. There's this reservation about Lodge's conduct, but he's there. . . . We can't fire him."[47]

The Kennedy administration's central concern, as McGeorge Bundy phrased it, was that an abortive coup, "however carefully we avoid direct engagement, will be laid at our door by public opinion almost everywhere." The president therefore reserved the right to oppose any plan that offered little hope of success. Harkins, however, continued to argue against investing U.S. prestige in a coup, regardless of Don's assurances that it would remain "purely Vietnamese." The United States "should go along with only a sure thing." The coup groups had revealed "no batting order." They had "no one with the strength of character of Diem, at least in fighting communists." The United States had supported him for eight years, making it "incongruous now to get him down, kick him around, and get rid of him." But Harkins's protests had no impact on events. Lodge told him that the White House favored a coup that began at the generals' initiative. The National Security Council prepared for a coup by examining the wisdom of keeping Lodge in Saigon. If he stayed, could he present a "plausible denial"? As a contingency, the defense department intended to safeguard Americans by instructing Felt to "preserve cover but move substantial forces to within easy range of Saigon."[48]

The critical factor in determining the likelihood of a coup was the generals' success in winning the support of General Dinh, whose vanity had provided them with the opportunity. Only with Dinh's support, Conein asserted, could a coup begin. The Ngos' trust in Dinh ranked second only to that in General Huynh Van Cao. Both commanders were responsible for protecting the government from an overthrow, with Dinh in charge of the northern sector of Saigon and Cao in the south. Dinh was showy and flamboyant, wearing a tailored paratrooper's uniform and a red beret at an angle, and accompanied by a tall Cambodian bodyguard. Nhu had assigned Dinh the task of planning the August 1963 pagoda raids. Afterward, Dinh bragged that he had "defeated" Lodge, who "came here to hold a coup. But I, Dinh, have conquered him and saved the country." In a news conference, he denounced "foreign adventurers," indirectly referred to the CIA as "crypto-Communist," and blasted the Buddhists as Communists. Sharp questions followed, and at several points, Vietnamese reporters for government-controlled newspapers broke out in laughter over his wild accusations. He was furious. He was a "hero of the republic," a monument to patriotic courage, and he had lost face both inside and outside his country.[49]

Generals Minh, Don, and Kim decided to exploit Dinh's damaged pride. They flattered him as a great historical figure, and they bribed an astrologer to foresee a great leadership role for him. He was a national hero, abused by the regime and made to look like a fool. Don baited him into asking Nhu about becoming Minister of the Interior as a just reward for his bravery. Could the government also find new positions for military personnel? Diem would never permit military officers into his cabinet and was furious with this brash request. He lectured Dinh on his impropriety and then ordered him to take a "vacation" at Dalat. "Stay out of politics and leave the politics to me," Diem snarled to his outraged visitor.[50]

Dinh had become even more susceptible to Don's Machiavellian tactics. After a few days of seclusion at Dalat, Dinh returned to Saigon and, in an effort to save face, told journalist Stanley Karnow, "I decided to give Diem another chance." Don cultivated Dinh's hurt and embarrassment by surrounding him with coup supporters, including Dinh's own deputy, Colonel Nguyen Huu Co.[51]

IV

SOMETIME IN MID-OCTOBER, Dinh became the centerpiece of a bizarre plan devised by Nhu to root out all opposition to the regime: a phony coup that he dubbed "Operation Bravo." According to the plan, Colonel Tung would stage a "revolt" with a few carefully chosen police forces that would drive Diem and Nhu from the palace and to a place of refuge at Cap St. Jacques, a seaside resort east of Saigon. General Dinh's loyalists would meanwhile wait in Saigon's outskirts as mobs ransacked the city and the "traitors" killed choice Buddhist and student leaders and perhaps a few Americans. Tung would announce a "revolutionary government" made up of Diem's opponents and headed by Madame Nhu's father, Tran Van Chuong (without his approval), who had become an arch-critic of the regime after resigning his ambassadorial post in the United States. Saigon radio would meanwhile attack the United States and all neutralists, appealing for nationwide support against the Communists. After twenty-four hours, Dinh's loyalist troops would enter the city and put down the rebellion. Diem and Nhu would return to power, proclaiming that their opponents were anti-Americans, neutralists, and pro-Communists. Enemies of the regime had been unable to control the mob, whose anger had focused on Americans. The army had remained loyal, demonstrating that only the Diem regime could run the country.[52]

But the rebel generals had their sources and learned of this strange scheme. The junior officers decided to launch a real coup before the phony one and set it for October 24. The senior officers, however, insisted that they could not succeed without the help of Dinh and his troops and sabotaged the initial effort by ordering one of the essential rebel regiments into the field against the Communists. The senior generals had to move quickly, both to placate the juniors and to undercut Nhu's plan. They bought Dinh's allegiance by assuring him many things, including the prize position of Minister of Interior. They also agreed to kill him if he betrayed the coup.[53]

With Dinh a convert, the generals on October 29 played out their charade by leaking the coming of the coup to Nhu. As part of the plan, Dinh sent his deputy, Colonel Co, to the Seventh Division's headquarters in My Tho, a town forty miles southwest of Saigon, to talk with the officers about the necessity of overthrowing Diem. The Seventh Division's support was critical, for it had saved Diem in the abortive coup of 1960 and was now quartered in the Mekong Delta, where it could cross the river and enter Saigon. Co announced to the officers that a coup was about to occur in Saigon, and he revealed some of the leaders' names. General Dinh, Co asserted, was "not yet involved" but would probably come over. All generals at the meeting joined the effort but Cao.[54]

As Dinh had suspected, an informer was present who immediately warned Diem and Nhu. The next day, they summoned Dinh to the palace and informed him that one of his officers was a traitor. In a convincing piece of theatrics, Dinh broke down and wept. "This is my fault," he sobbed. "Because you have suspected me, I have not really gone to work for the last 15 days but have stayed at home because I was sad. But I am not against you. I was sad because I thought I was discredited with you. So Nguyen Huu Co profited from my absence to make trouble." Should he arrest his deputy and have him shot? No, said Nhu; he wanted to interrogate him about the others involved. Dinh's performance had so reaffirmed the brothers' trust that Diem promoted him on the spot to major general. Dinh had now become a double agent, whose task was to penetrate the coup circle and twist it into a countercoup. He was to do this on November 1—All Saints' Day, during which participants prepared for the following day, All Souls' Day, the saddest on the Catholic calendar, known as the Day of the Dead—when Saigon's offices were closed and the troops could move easily through the primarily deserted streets. Nhu triumphantly dubbed this phase of his plan "Operation Bravo II."[55]

Now at least visibly ensconced in the loyalist camp, Dinh emphasized that this countercoup depended on a massive show of force. They must use tanks "because armor is dangerous." Fresh soldiers were essential, he told Colonel Tung in an effort to isolate him from the coup scene. "If we move reserves into the city, the Americans will be angry. They'll complain that we're not fighting the war. So we must camouflage our plan by sending the Special Forces out to the country. That will deceive them." Diem approved the action the following day, not knowing that he had opened the way for Dinh to use his rebel forces in the coup. Also unknown to Diem and Nhu, the coup makers set Friday, November 1, at 1:30 P.M. as the time of the coup. Thus had developed the two-staged plan known as "Operation Bravo

I and II," which to the Ngo brothers was a show of force designed to un-dermine the coup but to the rebel generals was a major step toward the coup. As Halberstam noted, Diem's approval of the plan had "legalized the groundwork for a coup d'etat."[56]

The movement toward a coup now took on a momentum of its own. At 7 A.M. on Sunday, October 27, Lodge had met with Don at the Saigon air-port in a secret arrangement made by Conein at the general's request. Don had a question. Did Conein speak for the White House in supporting the generals' intention to overturn Diem? Yes, Lodge responded; when would the coup take place? Don again refused to disclose any information, inad-vertently providing Lodge with a "plausible denial" of U.S. involvement.[57]

Diem's last chance for stopping a coup came, unbeknownst to him, in the afternoon of that same Sunday, when at his villa in Dalat he enter-tained Lodge and his wife on the day following the National Indepen-dence Day celebration. Lodge tried to determine whether the premier had changed his attitude toward White House demands. He urged Diem to cooperate with the recently arrived U.N. team of inquiry and stop the bar-rage of anti-American criticisms still coming from the Nhus and the *Times of Vietnam*. Did he plan to release the Buddhists and students from jail? Reopen the schools and halt discrimination against the Buddhists? Stop the government's attacks on American journalists? Madame Nhu was in the United States making derogatory remarks about the Kennedy admin-istration that put public pressure on the president to suspend all aid. Si-lently gazing at Diem for some response, Lodge sullenly sat through another demonstration of the premier's mastery in the art of obfuscation. "When it was evident that the conversation was practically over," Lodge recounted with deep frustration, "I said: 'Mr. President, every single specific sugges-tion which I have made, you have rejected. Isn't there some one thing you may think of that is within your capabilities to do and that would favorably impress US opinion?' As on other previous occasions when I asked him similar questions, he gave me a blank look and changed the subject."[58]

In the evening of October 28, Conein accepted Don's invitation to meet in downtown Saigon. The generals had no political ambitions, Don assured his friend; their sole objective was to win the war and restore the prestige of the country and army. "The only way to win before the Ameri-cans leave in 1965 was to change the present regime." Conein noted that Lodge was about to return to Washington on October 31 and should know the generals' intentions before his departure. Lodge would have the plans before the coup, Don promised, but instead of the previously planned forty-eight-hour notice, he could assure only four hours. Don pushed for the exact time of Lodge's departure and warned that any change in schedule would arouse suspicion. Nothing would take place within the next forty-eight hours.[59]

Don explained that he would leave the next morning for a secret meeting with Tri and Khanh to "perfect the planning." He asked Conein to stay in touch by remaining at home from Wednesday evening on. General Dinh, Don repeated, was not part of the planning and was surrounded by coup supporters who would eliminate him if he did anything to compromise the coup. General Le Van Kim was doing the political planning, and others (Lodge presumed Big Minh) were doing the military planning. The coup's strength included half of the airborne brigade; two marine battalions; all of the air force, except its commander, Colonel Huynh Huu Hien; three and a half army divisions; some units of the presidential guard; and at least four tanks. Neither the navy nor the Special Forces was involved, but the combat police and parts of the national police in Saigon might join the coup after it began. Joint General Staff headquarters would serve as the command post because of its proximity to the airport and Special Forces Headquarters. The generals were aware of the two underground escape tunnels from Gia Long Palace. The moment the coup began, they would cut off the phones. Don closed the meeting by assuring Conein that he would contact him again within forty-eight hours. Lodge should not forewarn the U.S. community, and Americans must not arouse suspicions by stocking up on food. Either step would alert the Diem regime.[60]

The palace atmosphere was chaotic. Phillips delivered a report on the strategic hamlets to Diem and found that everyone knew that something was about to happen. One story in the *Times of Vietnam* (run by Nhu) claimed that Phillips had pushed Richardson aside and wanted to head the CIA station in Saigon. "Nhu was going bananas at this point, plotting counter coups," while a "crazy brother" of Madame Nhu was in the palace declaring in panic, "We've got an assassination list." He gave this list to Australian correspondent Denis Warner, who passed it to Phillips. "Oh, you talk about—I did it, in a way, for fun, because I knew this guy was a nut, but I sent it on down to the embassy, anyway, and Jesus, you ought to see the—everybody went aagh!" Mecklin's name was on the list. "But part of the irony was that they put Richardson on the damn list, and Richardson had been very close to Nhu. . . . It was a nutty period."[61]

During Phillips's visit to the palace, Diem revealed his suspicions of an impending coup attempt.

"Are the military planning a coup?"

"Yes, sir, I think they are."

Phillips had based his response on "a feeling, and the news, and . . . friends." Conein was one of his friends. Diem asked no more questions. "He knew pretty well what was happening to him. It was just sad, it was pathetic. I really went away feeling just down in the dumps."[62]

Lodge still held to the fiction that only the Vietnamese were responsible for the certain coup. Despite his assurance to Don that the White

House stood behind Conein's call for deposing Diem, Lodge insisted that the United States bore no culpability. He assured Rusk that "we are not engineering the coup," although he intended to avoid thwarting it and he termed Conein's long-time friendship with Don "a real help." Lodge knew that the United States would draw blame for the coup, regardless of its outcome. Indeed, the imminent event had long passed the U.S. capacity to control. The embassy would have only four hours' notice before the uprising began, thereby denying the United States sufficient time to influence events.[63]

White House preparations for the coup continued. In two late afternoon meetings on October 29, the president and the National Security Council weighed the dangers of participating in Diem's overthrow. That same day, CINCPAC in Hawaii directed a naval and air task force to hover off South Vietnam's coast, ready to evacuate American dependents and civilians. To protect Americans, the United States could move a marine battalion into Saigon by air from Okinawa within twenty-four hours if Tan Son Nhut Airport were available. Rusk emphasized the necessity of averting a long, drawn-out civil war that could help only the Vietcong. Both sides in the coup would seek our assistance, he warned. If the United States tried to save Diem, it would have to take a stand against the generals who were fighting the war against the Vietcong. If it supported the rebels, it must guarantee their success. President Kennedy insisted that the coup leaders call off the coup if they realized they could not succeed—as if it were possible that, having taken the critical first step, they could reconsider and turn back without suffering mortal consequences.[64]

At 4:30 P.M., the president and the National Security Council discussed the chances for the coup's success. Colby reported the CIA's estimate, complete with pointer and maps, that the military forces for and against Diem were about even, with about 9,800 on each side and another 18,000 considered neutral. "The key units come out about even. There's enough, in other words, to have a good fight."

"Thank you for your decisive point," remarked McGeorge Bundy amid raucous laughter.

What had Diem learned from the aborted coup attempt of 1960? asked the president.

Diem, Colby responded, had established tighter communications with military forces outside Saigon for immediate call-up if trouble developed.

Taylor cautioned against "looking at the Vietnam situation as if it were a football game. A few key people are crucial to the success of a coup and are more important than total numbers."

Who were these "key people"? asked the president.

"Who of our officials in Saigon are in charge of the coup planning?" asked McNamara in seeking clarification before dealing with the question.

Trueheart should work with Harkins and the acting CIA chief to determine the actions of "our agent Conein."

McCone opposed such a "troika," insisting that the CIA officer should take direction rather than be part of a decision-making group.

Robert Kennedy was deeply concerned. Diem "has sufficient forces to protect him from key figures against him in any kind of coup."

"I think he has," observed Colby.

The president did not share his brother's concern over the apparent power balance. "I'm sure that's the way it is with every coup. It always looks balanced, until somebody acts. Then support for the coup is forthcoming."

The attorney general was not dissuaded. "The situation now is no different than that of four months ago when the generals were not able to organize a coup." There was a lack of sufficient information. "We have a right to know what the rebel generals are planning. We can't go half way. If the coup fails, Diem will throw us out." The younger Kennedy knew he was expressing an unpopular view. "I may be in the minority. I just don't see that this makes any sense, on the face of it. We're putting the whole future of the country—and, really, Southeast Asia—in the hands of somebody we don't know very well. . . . [Diem]'s a determined figure who's gonna stick around and, I should think, go down fighting. If [the coup]'s a failure, I would think Diem's gonna tell us to get the hell out of the country. . . . He's gonna have enough, with his intelligence, to know that there's been these contacts and these conversations, and he's gonna capture these people. They're gonna say the United States was behind it. I would think that we're just going down the road to disaster."

Robert Kennedy opposed a coup, although he had limited credibility because he did not attend all meetings and had not read all relative documentation. He conceded his lack of understanding of events in Vietnam, but he had raised the concern of his brother and others that the White House seemed ready to place South Vietnam's future in the hands of someone no one knew.

Rusk, however, remained supportive of a coup. "If we say we are not for a coup," he warned, "then the coup-minded military leaders will turn against us and the war effort will drop off rapidly."

Taylor agreed with the attorney general. "Even a successful coup would slow down the war effort because the new central government would be inexperienced." Indeed, the victors would have to remove all the province chiefs. Pressed by President Kennedy on this point, Taylor noted that "as Diem appointees they would be loyal to Diem, and, therefore, not trusted by the rebel generals who had overthrown Diem."

McCone concurred with Taylor and pointed to a no-win situation. "The failure of a coup would be a disaster and a successful coup would have a harmful effect on the war effort."

"The important question," Rusk declared, "was whether the rebel generals could achieve quick success." Remaining supportive of Diem would ensure failure.

Harriman heartily concurred. "We cannot predict that the rebel generals can overthrow the Diem government, but Diem cannot carry the country to victory over the Viet Cong."

The president altered his position, insisting that perhaps the time was not yet right. "With, with our correlation of forces, uh, th-they're almost even in the immediate Saigon area. If that is true, then, of course, it wouldn't make any sense to have a coup. Unless [Lodge] has information—and he can produce information—which would indicate that the balance of force quite easily is on the side of the, uh, rebels, then it seems to me that he should discourage it at this time." He instructed Bundy to draft a message to Lodge. With Saigon militarily divided, the president remarked, "There is a substantial possibility that there [will be] a prolonged fight."

"Or even defeat," Bundy added.

"Or even defeat," the president repeated. "This being true, we think it would be disastrous to proceed unless they can give us evidence that, uh, indicates" a success. A failure "could in one blow defeat our whole effort in South Vietnam." The coup should proceed only if there was a guarantee of success. If the military forces on both sides of the question were about equal, "any attempt to engineer a coup is silly." If Lodge thought this so, "we should instruct him to discourage a coup."[65]

After a half-hour recess, the president and his advisers reconvened at 6 P.M., this time more cautious about supporting a coup. "The burden of proof," emphasized the president, "should be on the coup promoters to show that they can overthrow the Diem government and not create a situation in which there would be a draw." Lodge had compared a coup "to a stone rolling down hill which can't be stopped. If this is so, then no one can say that we are to blame for the coup, no matter what we do." Pausing a moment, the president solemnly observed, "If we miscalculated, we could lose our entire position in Southeast Asia overnight." Lodge should travel to Washington by military plane so that, if necessary, he could return to Saigon on a moment's notice. These directives immediately went to the ambassador.[66]

So certain was Lodge that the coup was coming that he canceled his trip to Washington. Don's October 28 assurance of at least forty-eight hours' notice had set the earliest target date as that very day in South Vietnam, October 30. Lodge could make no predictions of success. "Should the coup fail, we will have to pick up the pieces as best we can at that time." If a protracted civil conflict developed, the United States should make its good offices available to resolve the dispute. Yes, a miscalculation could damage U.S. interests in Southeast Asia. But, he darkly added, "[w]e also run tremendous risks by doing nothing."[67]

That same day in Washington, the president implicitly gave his final approval for the coup. Although the words specifically authorizing U.S. involvement did not appear in his note to Lodge, it is critical to recognize that Kennedy issued no directive to oppose the coup. The United States, the White House message made clear, would not intervene. No U.S.-controlled aircraft or matériel was to go to either side. Lodge was to "explicitly reject any implication that we oppose the effort of the generals because of preference for [the] present regime." He was to "maintain [a] clear distinction between strong and honest advice given as a friend and any opposition to their objective." It was not in the U.S. interest "to be or appear to be [the] instrument of [the] existing government or [the] instrument of [a] coup." If the conflict proved indecisive, the United States would remain neutral. It would provide sanctuary along with other embassies doing the same. In a key statement, however, the White House made clear that "once a coup under responsible leadership has begun, within these restrictions, it is in the interest of the U.S. Government that it should succeed."[68]

The United States had become an accomplice in the tangled events leading to a coup. Although still denying having taken any initiative, it had provided the critical spark by refusing to stand in the way of the generals (thereby signaling no help to Diem) and by assuring them support in the key period after their success (thereby terminating the U.S. commitment to Diem). The president still held to the illusion that his administration would do nothing to foster Diem's overthrow.

Only in a narrow sense was Don correct in calling the planned coup a Vietnamese affair. Americans were not to be involved in the coup itself, but the White House had promoted the attempt by exerting economic pressures on Diem and then assuring his enemies of help in a successful aftermath. The White House feared that if it impeded a coup, it might lose the only opportunity for changing the Saigon government and facilitating a withdrawal. If South Vietnam's "best generals" failed, how could anyone else succeed? Lodge recommended that the embassy and other U.S. installations grant asylum to coup participants if need be, particularly since they had done so for Tri Quang. If the generals succeeded and requested funds to buy off remaining opposition to their rule, the White House should comply in a discreet manner. Recognition of the new regime and distribution of aid should resume on the condition that it continued the war against the Vietcong. If the coup proved indecisive and a long power struggle ensued, the United States should make its good offices available in attempting to end the domestic unrest and return the focus to the war. U.S. mediation would not be popular, but it was preferable to a lengthy stalemate that left the country vulnerable to the Vietcong. The United States was trying to move this "medieval country into the 20th century," Lodge declared with exasperation.[69]

Lodge was correct in asserting that no American could have stopped the generals from launching a coup. Powerful forces impelled them into action, most notably the Kennedy administration's selective aid cut, Lodge's unmistakable support for the coup, and the certain deadly consequences for them of any deal made between Nhu and Hanoi. Dinh later justified the coup in several ways, the most immediate being Nhu's recent contact with Vietcong General Van Tieng Dung through the Polish representative on the International Control Commission. Nhu appeared to be close to an arrangement that would end the war, preserve the Diem regime, and culminate in death sentences for the coup conspirators. The crucial moment had arrived when the rebel generals perceived a greater mortal danger in holding back on a coup than in going ahead.[70]

BY THE END of October 1963, a coup had again seemed imminent. Lodge reported at least ten groups talking of a coup, but the main one, of course, was the ARVN's senior generals. This time was vastly different from the August experience. The Kennedy administration had signaled support, Big Minh and his fellow officers had a plan, and Nhu's threatened negotiations with Hanoi had removed their hesitation. The White House maintained its August policy of supporting the generals if they triumphed and never knowing them if they failed. But domestic and foreign matters had deteriorated so radically during the past two months that a coup became the only feasible avenue for the Kennedy administration to extricate its military forces from Vietnam. Only with a government change could the United States proclaim sufficient progress in the aid effort to justify a return to the low-key advisory and assistance level of early 1961. A U.S. naval and air task force had maneuvered into position off Vietnam's coast to evacuate Americans. Lodge was under orders to turn down any appeals for help from either side in the course of a coup. Nhu was seemingly ready to negotiate a settlement with Hanoi. It was now or never for the generals.[71]

17

FALL OF THE HOUSE OF NGO

Whoever has the Americans as allies does not need any
enemies.

> Madame Nhu, November 2, 1963

We didn't plot Diem's downfall. But we certainly created the
climate and state of mind that inspired his opponents to
overthrow him.

> Unidentified U.S. diplomat in Saigon, c. November 4, 1963

We should not overlook what this coup can mean in the way
of shortening the war and enabling Americans to come home.

> Henry Cabot Lodge, November 4, 1963

[Even though the coup was a] Vietnamese effort, our own
actions made it clear that we wanted improvements, and
when these were not forthcoming from the Diem
government, we necessarily faced and accepted the possibility
that our position might encourage a change of government.

> President John F. Kennedy, November 6, 1963

[The end of 1965 was] the terminal date for our withdrawal.

> U.S. Department of State, November 15, 1963

IN THE AFTERNOON of November 1, 1963, the generals launched their
long-anticipated coup. To eliminate a paper trail, they alerted the
embassy a bare four minutes beforehand, not four hours as promised.
Don telephoned MACV headquarters at 1:45 P.M., reaching Harkins's
deputy, Major General Richard Stilwell. The generals had decided to stage
a coup, Don declared. When? Immediately, responded Don. Notify Harkins
at once. Harkins was dubious but called Lodge, who had just learned that
rebel marines had taken over the Ministry of the Interior. In the meantime, the CIA reported their seizure of the police station. Troops from
both sides were in motion all over the city. The Diem regime had entered
its final hours.[1]

I

THE COUP had actually begun at 1:15 P.M., about halfway into *ngu trua* (siesta) time on All Saints' Day. Droves of Catholics and Buddhists had attended morning prayer sessions before returning to their homes after the airport siren signaled the three-hour noonday break. The weather was hot and humid as they made their way down the broad, tree-lined boulevards. Most of Saigon's 1.5 million residents—including many of the presidential guards in the palace, along with Diem and Nhu—were already resting, many of them under their white mosquito nets. That quiet suddenly ended with the sound of guns in the downtown area. Caught in the crossfire were the Rue Catinat and the Caravelle Hotel, the latter providing the headquarters for the U.S. correspondents.[2]

Preparations for the assault had begun hours earlier. All the previous night and into the early morning, marines and armored cars had converged on the city, while paratroopers at a seaside resort seventy miles outside Saigon met up with infantry units marching in from the north and southwest. By lunchtime, thousands of combat-ready rebel troops had amassed on the city's outskirts, checking their equipment and weapons as they listened to last-minute orders. Three battalions of U.S.-trained rebel marines in tanks and armored cars had moved toward the center of town to spearhead the revolt, and the Seventh Division had arrived from the south to block the main road to Tan Son Nhut Airport. To hide the coup from the soldiers, the senior officers announced that they were putting down a revolt by the police. One lieutenant among the paratroopers was suspicious. When they approached a command post in the suburbs, a colonel pinpointed their objective as the Cong Hoa Barracks of the presidential guard. "Who is the enemy and who our friend?" asked the lieutenant. "Anyone who opposes us is the enemy," came the curt response.[3]

The rebel generals had neutralized the opposition in a carefully staged operation at the military's weekly noon luncheon. In the Officers' Club of the Joint General Staff Headquarters, they had arranged for some special guests, including Colonel Tung and other loyalist officers. Once everyone was seated, General Minh stood and announced the coup. Instantly, military police armed with submachine guns burst into the room and covered all strategic points. Those officers willing to join the coup were to stand. The bulk of them did so as Minh declared that they were free to move around the compound but could not leave. The few who remained in their chairs were taken away and placed under armed guard. Tung was among them. Pulled from the room, he bitterly shouted at the generals, "Remember who gave you the stars you're wearing."[4]

Once the loyalists were gone, Minh had a tape recorder brought into the room. He read the coup proclamation and its objectives onto the tape and then had everyone sign the proclamation. Afterward, they took turns at the recorder, stating their names and pledging support for the coup. Minh had several copies made of the original, intending to play one of them over the radio that day. The others he had hidden in various places throughout the city so that, in the event of failure, no one could claim that he had been forced into the coup.[5]

The insurgents had also guaranteed that the Seventh Division would not save Diem again, as in 1960. Diem had ordered Colonel Lam Van Phat to take command of that force on the previous Thursday, the day before the coup. According to tradition, Phat could not do so until paying a courtesy call on his new corps commander, General Dinh. In a carefully conceived plan, Dinh refused to see the colonel, telling him to come back the next day, Friday, at 2 P.M. Dinh then arranged for the transfer of the Seventh Division to his deputy, Colonel Nguyen Huu Co, who immediately traveled by helicopter to My Tho to seize command. Co telephoned the Fourth Corps commander in the Mekong Delta, General Nguyen Van Cao, who, like Phat, was a southerner. Co disguised his central highlands accent, fooling Cao into thinking that he was talking with Phat and that he had taken control. Cao heard in mid-afternoon of the troop movements in Saigon but informed the Seventh Division officers of Nhu's assurances that this was a fake coup led by loyalists, who intended to wipe out all dissidents. When Cao finally realized that this was the real coup, he radioed My Tho, shocked that Co answered. Co could not resist taunting the general. "Didn't you recognize my accent?" All ferry boats had been moved to the Saigon side of the Mekong River, he told Cao, and if he tried to cross he would die. Shortly before 10 P.M. that evening, Cao announced his support for the coup.[6]

The rebels outnumbered the loyalists and struck quickly and effectively. Speed and a minimum of hand-to-hand combat were vital, for the generals knew that both sides would have to forget their differences and reunite after the coup. Indeed, Minh intended to reinstate his military opponents "in grade" on the sole condition that they agreed to fight the Vietcong. Furthermore, a drawn-out conflict would benefit the Vietcong. Moreover, few rebels relished the thought of a pitched battle for the palace that led to Diem's death. They isolated Saigon from the airport, set up defenses against a possible counterattack from outside the city, blew up government buildings, and seized the post office, radio stations, naval headquarters, and other important installations. Four AD-6 fighter-bombers thundered overhead, adding to the wild din of noise and confusion. Local radio went off the air around 2 P.M., abruptly severing outside communication. To block escape routes, tank and artillery contingents stationed themselves fender to fender in readiness for pounding the presidential guard barracks near the palace. Armored cars jammed with rebel troops wielding machine guns raced toward the palace, where they would join their allies in confronting loyalist marines armed with artillery, mortars, and machine guns. Rebel leaders meanwhile forced Tung from his place of custody to order his Special Forces to cease fire, which left only the presidential guard to protect the premier.[7]

Gia Long Palace was the prize, a well-fortified and lavishly furnished mansion that had once served as the French governor general's residence and now housed the premier and his family. The Ngos had moved there in February 1962, shortly after two turncoat pilots bombed their official home in Independence Palace, which was the former domicile of Emperor Bao Dai. For protective purposes, the streets around Gia Long Palace were regularly blocked off at night, and beneath the sprawling building were extensive bunkers and an intricate tunnel system that included a half-block-long passage connecting with the City Hall. Loyalists had sometime earlier sealed off the National Police Headquarters, which accommodated Nhu's secret police, and on the very morning of the coup Diem had tightened palace security with additional troops and barbed-wire barricades. Inside its seven-foot-high cream-colored stucco walls were 150 members of the Palace Guard, referred to as "Diem's Angels." Gia Long Palace was a veritable citadel, defended by machine guns and antiaircraft guns, and cordoned by pillboxes, dug-in tanks, and 20-mm cannon mounted on half-tracks. A siege seemed probable.[8]

The coup forces met little resistance in the critical first moments of the city-wide assault, thanks primarily to Diem and Nhu's mistaken assumption that Operation Bravo was under way. The central police called Diem, informing him that the marines rolling into Saigon did not appear friendly. Diem ordered his military aide to call Dinh. But Dinh was not there. Diem was not alarmed, however; this was the phony coup. When security police first noticed the troop movements, a frantic young officer telephoned Nhu. "It's all right," he calmly replied. "I know about it." The generals, according to Conein, had "double bumped" Nhu into believing this the fake coup.[9]

The rebels had converted Joint General Staff Headquarters near the airport into an operations center and, in an ingenious move, brought Conein there to witness events. Just before noon, Don's military aide arrived at Conein's home, telling him that the general needed him now. Why the change in plan? asked Conein, knowing that this did not fit previously made security arrangements about their next meeting. The aide replied that he was only following orders and left. As Conein dressed into his military uniform, a second emissary arrived—the dentist whose office Conein and Don had used for secret meetings. He eased Conein's suspicions by confirming the aide's message, and then informed him of the coup. The generals wanted him to "bring all available money." Conein used voice codes to radio news of the coup to the embassy and the CIA station in Saigon before grabbing his two radio sets. He then pulled several packages of piasters from his safe and stuffed all that would fit into a diplomatic pouch—about $42,000 in American money. The CIA had provided a short-range contingency fund for distribution to the rebels; the Vietnamese had no insurance programs and would need cash for food, medical costs, and death benefits.[10]

Conein also packed a short-nosed .38 revolver for self-defense before boarding a military jeep. Although his weapon had an effective range of only a few feet, his driver was a Vietnamese sergeant who carried a .45. At Conein's house was a team of Special Forces who remained throughout the coup to guard his family, including his three-month-old daughter. If the Diem government discovered his involvement in a conspiracy, Conein later explained, "I probably would have a very efficient Vietcong incident—in other words, I would be blown up or assassinated or something like that and it would be blamed on the Vietcong."[11]

By the time Conein arrived at rebel headquarters, the coup was well under way. At approximately 3:30 P.M., in the midst of a fiery exchange between the rebels and a Special Forces unit, he made his way into the building.

General Minh quickly confronted him. "What are you doing here?" He doubtless recalled how CIA agents had persuaded the rebel generals in 1960 to negotiate with Diem, enabling him to abort the coup.

"I was told to report here," Conein shot back.

"In case we fail," Minh remarked, "you're going with us."[12]

Conein recognized his precarious situation. "I was part and parcel of the whole conspiracy, so if something went wrong, they would go down the drain with me. We were all going down the drain together."[13]

Conein supplied the embassy and Washington with invaluable minute-by-minute information on the coup. Don had arranged telephone communications with both the U.S. embassy and Conein's home. After notifying his superiors in Saigon of his safe arrival, Conein followed the generals' directive in emphasizing to the embassy that no Americans were to participate in the coup. According to Lodge's special assistant and interpreter, Frederick Flott, Conein provided "excellent blow-by-blow accounts of what was going on," all "timely and accurate." He noted a number of prisoners, including Tung, the police commissioner, and the commanders of the air force, marines, and civil guard. Captain Ho Tan Quyen of the navy was missing. In what Conein termed a premature action, Quyen's young deputy had shot him in an isolated spot along Bien Hoa Highway. The naval commander was dead, assassinated a little before noon by what the *Pentagon Papers* later called a "trigger-happy escort" who had joined the coup.[14]

Mortars and heavy firepower rocked the city. A young and cocksure lieutenant colonel from the air force, Nguyen Cao Ky, ordered two T-28 fighter-bombers into action. Swooping over the palace, they fired two rockets in the midst of sporadic black and white puffs of antiaircraft fire. Both rockets missed their targets, with the second missile hitting an unoccupied U.S. Marine barracks. Huge clouds of dust swirled upward from rebel artillery shells then flattening the presidential guard barracks, a scant five blocks from the palace. Diem's tanks returned fire, blasting the avenues around the palace. The small number of civilians who had braved the streets now sought safety in buildings and doorways after abandoning their motor scooters and other vehicles.[15]

Shortly after Conein's arrival, the generals telephoned an ultimatum to the palace: If Diem resigned immediately, he and Nhu would receive safe passage out of the country. A refusal would set off an air and armor attack within the hour. There was no room for discussion; Diem must say either yes or no.

No response came from the palace.[16]

Diem had finally realized a coup was under way, but he was not yet aware of Dinh's perfidy. The premier had tried to call Dinh a second time, only to learn that he still was not there. Dinh's aide could hear Diem muttering in the background, "Dinh must have been arrested."[17]

A little after 4 P.M., Diem telephoned Joint General Staff Headquarters and spoke with Don. "What are you generals doing?"

"Sir," Don declared, "the time has come when the army must respond to the wishes of the people."[18]

A heated exchange ensued, during which Diem expressed interest in granting reforms and suggested "consultations" in the palace. "All you officers must come here if you want to negotiate." Diem's proposal, Dinh later asserted, "proved he wanted to stall for time." Don rejected the offer as a ploy, designed to buy time for reinforcements—just as Diem had done in quashing the coup of 1960.[19]

At 4:30 P.M., the generals announced the coup over the radio at five-minute intervals and demanded the resignations of Diem and Nhu. A large number of the officers identified themselves. The generals also played the tapes of those who had pledged themselves to the coup, and air force transports dropped leaflets calling for popular support. They had already broadcasted Minh's words: "The day the people have been waiting for has come. For eight years, the people of Vietnam have suffered under the rotten and nepotic Diem regime, but now the armed forces have come to their rescue." Almost surrealistically, these radio announcements were interrupted by twist and cha-cha records—all banned by the Diem regime.[20]

Also at 4:30 P.M., Diem telephoned Lodge. The premier shouted his words in French, forcing the ambassador to hold the receiver away from his ear and making the conversation audible to his aide, Frederick Flott, then seated nearby. "Some units have made a rebellion," Diem proclaimed, "and I want to know: What is the attitude of the U.S.?"

"I do not feel well enough informed to be able to tell you," Lodge replied. "I have heard the shooting, but am not acquainted with all the facts. Also it is 4:30 A.M. in Washington and [the] U.S. government cannot possibly have a view."

"But you must have some general ideas. After all, I am a chief of state. I have tried to do my duty. I want to do now what duty and good sense require. I believe in duty above all."

"You have certainly done your duty," Lodge agreed. "As I told you only this morning, I admire your courage and your great contributions to your country. No one can take away from you the credit for all you have done. Now I am worried about your physical safety. I have a report that those in charge of the current activity offer you and your brother safe conduct out of the country if you resign. Had you heard this?"

"No. (pause) You have my telephone number."

"Yes," Lodge replied. "If I can do anything for your physical safety, please call me."

"What would be your advice?"

"Well, you are a chief of state," Lodge noted. "I cannot give you advice, but personally, and as a friend, and as somebody who is concerned about your health, my suggestion would be you think seriously of getting away. Now, if I can be of any help on that, I'm prepared to send my driver with an officer of mine to escort you to safety. And we can get you on my jet aircraft, and I'm sure I can deliver on that. One of my officers will ride in the front seat of my limousine with the chauffeur."

Lodge had devised a plan to assure Diem's safe departure from the country. Flott was to go to the palace, riding in an old Checker Cab that prominently displayed several American flags. Flott was well known in the palace as an interpreter and would try to gain entrance into the compound to negotiate Diem's evacuation.

But Diem rejected Lodge's offer. "No, I cannot agree to fleeing, because this is all a tempest in a teapot; it's a couple of hothead generals who don't speak for the army, and I know that the real troops are loyal to me and will soon have this all straightened out."

"Well, Mr. President, that is your decision, certainly. I cannot advise you one way or the other. But as I've said, if I can ever be of any assistance in looking after your security, I would certainly do so."

Diem misinterpreted this assertion as an offer of U.S. military help. "Well, I want you to tell Washington that this is being done, and that I want them to land the BLTs [battalion landing teams], the two marine BLTs on the aircraft carriers offshore. I want them to land and protect the palace."

Lodge deflected the request: "Well, you know, it's four o'clock in the morning in Washington; we can't do that."

Diem now had proof of Lodge's complicity in the coup. "I am trying to re-establish order," Diem insisted as he curtly ended the call.[21]

The rebels repeatedly telephoned the palace, demanding a surrender. At 4:45 P.M., Minh talked with Nhu, who bitterly asserted that Diem was not there. In a show of strength, all generals were present. Colonels Lam, Khang, and Khuong all spoke to Nhu, and Tung was forced at gunpoint to declare himself a prisoner and to inform him that his Special Forces had laid down their arms. Nhu refused to surrender. Diem had five minutes to resign, Minh warned; otherwise the generals would launch a massive artillery and air assault on the palace. Not waiting for a reply, he slammed down the phone.[22]

The military showdown that Minh had tried to avoid now loomed ahead. Less than a half hour later, he called again, asking for Diem. But the premier refused to talk with him and hung up the phone. Minh was furious over this loss of face. At 7:15 P.M., he tried one last time, warning Nhu that if Diem did not surrender, the rebel forces would "blast him off the face of the earth." Diem would not come to the phone. Minh could wait no longer. His credibility as leader was on the line. His colleagues expressed concern that further delay would work to Diem's advantage. Had he not risen from the ashes in 1960? Conein warned Minh, "If you hesitate, you will be lost."[23]

To diminish the chances of a countercoup, Minh decided to dispose of Tung. The colonel had failed to secure a surrender, and he still commanded the loyalty of his men. This decision aroused no opposition from the other generals; it was Tung, after all, who had connived with Nhu in framing them for the pagoda raids. Minh ordered his bodyguard, Captain Nguyen Van Nhung, to execute Tung and his brother, who was second in command of the Special Forces. Nhung had their hands tied behind their backs before throwing the two men into a jeep. The driver took them to a desolate area near the outer edge of the command base and stopped next to two newly dug holes. There, the brothers were shot and buried.[24]

Minh had no choice but to lay siege on the palace. In command of the rebel forces was a young colonel, Nguyen Van Thieu, who had only recently abandoned the premier and could now prove himself by directing the assault. Moreover, Thieu was a Catholic, and the Buddhist generals thought it made eminently good sense that he should lead the attack on fellow Catholics. As dark approached and a light drizzle fell, rebel tanks, artillery, cannons, and troops bearing machine guns and rifles advanced toward the palace grounds. A little before 10 P.M., infantry forces began the attack, covered by a massive tank and artillery pummeling that reduced the Palace Guard barracks to rubble. While demolition experts set charges to blow up the palace, rebel flamethrowers sprayed buildings near the target, transforming them into fiery infernos. Palace guns retaliated, hitting two rebel armored vehicles and setting them ablaze. Red tracer bullets shot through the bright moonlight, some of them penetrating the frosted glass of a domed structure on top of the palace and giving it an eerie radiance. The fighting around the palace was, according to one observer, like "two boxers fighting in a closet." When a member of the U.S. embassy ran downstairs to tell Tri Quang that the coup was under way, he responded: "Do you think I am deaf?"[25]

Fighting had also erupted in the vicinity of the U.S. embassy. Trueheart observed artillery shots soaring over the chancery and into the palace yard. Harkins's wife heard gunfire near their home. The general frantically called his wife, telling her to seek shelter under one of the big concrete archways downstairs. "All hell broke out," he moaned after a frenzied rush to her side. "The soldiers had gone through my place, the people on the roof of the palace were shooting down at the soldiers in the streets and several of the bullets were coming into my house, in the front yard, particularly. All I can say is there is never a dull moment here in Saigon."[26]

While the battle raged under a full moon that Friday night, much of the city continued its normal activity, seemingly oblivious to the pivotal events under way. U.S. servicemen in civilian clothing wandered around the restaurants and bars, noting that after the fiery exchanges had begun, shopkeepers and other merchants methodically folded up their sidewalk stalls, pulled down steel shutters, or put up grills over the windows and doors. Rebel troops swarmed over the red tile roofs near the palace, while soldiers armed with machine guns stood guard at intersections as tanks and other armed vehicles continued to rumble into town. Service went on in a leading hotel, however slowly, because some of the help had left.[27]

The opening moments of the Day of the Dead turned out to be the lull before the storm. The city had become still after midnight, deserted and quiet except for the occasional barking of a dog. But shortly after 3 A.M., the cannon boomed again, lofting heavy shells that softly hissed through the air before hitting a building behind the city's telecommunications center. The rebel leaders adjusted their sights and, just as the cathedral's bells tolled at 4 A.M., Colonel Thieu ordered the climactic phase of the siege to begin. Large balls of white smoke rolled upward into low-hanging rain clouds as mortars, artillery pieces, and tanks lobbed their deadly payloads onto the palace. Flares cast a ghostly red light on the target as red-and-white tracer bullets zig-zagged across the skyline, shattering store windows and ripping into trees. Spectators jumped off rooftops as bullets whistled by.[28]

The premier remained resistant to the end. Before the siege had begun, he had used a special transmitter in the palace to seek help from his provincial officers. No one responded. Nhu telephoned the Republican

Youth and paramilitary women's groups. Again, no response. Diem had finally realized that Dinh had switched sides. Shortly after midnight, he had reached Dinh—at rebel headquarters. To showcase his loyalty to the generals standing by, Dinh blasted Diem and his brother with a string of obscenities. At 6 A.M., Diem talked with Dinh again, lashing out at him and demanding that *he* surrender. Half an hour later, Diem once more called rebel headquarters, agreeing to speak with Minh for the first time. Diem would surrender in exchange for a full-scale ceremony with military honors, followed by a flight out of the country. Minh could barely contain his rage. I will make no guarantees while "Vietnamese [are] still killing one another." Diem finally agreed to order a cease-fire and to accept an unconditional surrender.[29]

At 6:37 A.M., a white flag waved from the south wing of the blackened fortress. On hearing the news, Minh dispatched an M-113 armored personnel carrier and four jeeps to transport Diem and Nhu to the command post. The general likewise rushed to the fiery scene, choosing a shorter route and riding in a sedan with his aide, Captain Nhung. News of the surrender raised cries throughout the city of "Freedom" and "Long Live the Junta." Jubilant crowds cheered the steel-helmeted marines as they crossed the open yard of the palace grounds to gather prisoners. The fighting had come to an end, about seventeen hours after the coup had begun.[30]

Flott was among the first contingent of Vietnamese marines who entered the palace after the cease-fire. But he was not among the first inside the building. Coming down the marble staircase was David Halberstam, dragging a ten-foot-long ivory tusk as a souvenir. Flott grabbed a couple of ashtrays as part of the general looting going on by the victorious soldiers—including those carrying bottles of Nhu's whiskey and others triumphantly waving his wife's negligees.[31]

II

THE GENERALS INTENDED to consign Diem and Nhu to exile. Shortly before Diem's last call to rebel headquarters, Minh and Don asked Conein to secure an aircraft that would take the premier and his brother out of the country. But Conein ran into unexpected obstacles when he called the U.S. embassy. Two days before the coup, Lodge had alerted Washington to the possibility of such a request and recommended Saigon as the point of departure. This could not have been an easy decision: Provision of a plane would publicly tie the Kennedy administration to the coup. After a ten-minute wait, the acting chief of station, David Smith, came back to the phone with a response to Conein's query. The U.S. government would not consent to land the aircraft in any country other than one willing to grant Diem asylum.

It became clear that Washington did not want Diem and Nhu to form a government in exile and therefore preferred a government some distance from Vietnam. But the nearest plane capable of a long-range flight was in Guam. It would take twenty-four hours to make all the arrangements.[32]

Minh was astounded. "We can't hold them that long," he stammered. Conein did not suspect any purposeful delay by the U.S. embassy, but a U.S. Senate investigative commission in the early 1970s raised a provocative point: "One wonders what became of the U.S. military aircraft that had been dispatched to stand by for Lodge's departure, scheduled for the previous day."[33]

After Minh's departure from rebel headquarters, Generals Don, Khiem, and Kim remained behind to complete preparations for the final moments of the Diem regime. Conein watched as their men took down Diem's pictures, covered his statue in front of the building, and cleaned up the entire area. They then brought in a large table covered with green felt. The generals feared that their new regime would not win foreign recognition unless they engineered a legal changeover in government. Vice President Tho would become the new premier, and then Diem and Nhu would move into secure housing on the base until their evacuation from the country. The rebel leaders had arranged for the press to cover Tho's acceptance of Diem's resignation. As movie cameras and other communications equipment arrived, Don told Conein, "Get the hell out, we're bringing in the Press." Conein realized the implications of an American's presence at a press briefing announcing Diem's capitulation. Worn out, in need of sleep, but most of all scared of being seen by newsmen and linked to the coup, he made a quick exit for home.[34]

Minh meanwhile arrived at Gia Long Palace at 8 A.M., resplendent in full military dress uniform and ready to supervise the transportation of Diem and his brother to command headquarters for the surrender ceremony. According to Conein, the generals expected to take Diem and Nhu peacefully. Most of the officers, including Minh, wanted Diem to have an "honorable retirement" from office followed by exile. At about six that morning, just as dawn approached, Conein had been on the patio of the Joint General Staff Headquarters as the generals discussed what to do with the premier. General Nguyen Ngoc Le, a former police chief under Diem during the mid-1950s, strongly advocated killing Diem. But Le attracted no support. Never in Conein's presence did the generals suggest assassination. Their overriding concern was an orderly transition in government that would win international acceptance of the coup.[35]

The victory was special to Big Minh. His career had risen and fallen at Diem's bidding. Captured by the guerrillas in 1954, Minh won his freedom by strangling a guard and overpowering others. The following year, he led government forces in crushing the crime-ridden underworld organization

known as the Binh Xuyen. When Minh arrived in his jeep before the reviewing stand sometime afterward, Diem embraced him and kissed both
cheeks. Known as "Beo" or fat boy, Minh was a prime candidate for national favor. He graduated from the Ecole Militaire in France and attended
the Command and General Staff School at Fort Leavenworth, Kansas. An
American acquaintance remarked that Minh reminded him of "a high-school
football hero who never grew up." He always flashed a broad smile, showing only the single tooth that remained from Japanese torture during World
War II. Little did he know that his military fortunes had peaked. Minh
became field commander in 1959, but he had no power. Three years later,
Diem abolished the command and made him military adviser in charge of
three telephones that, Minh complained, led "nowhere." Minh's popularity had been his undoing. He had become, as Diem feared, a magnet for
dissidents.[36]

Minh's moment of retribution had finally arrived. He intended to personally escort Diem and Nhu back to command headquarters, where, with
full press coverage, they would all sit at the green-covered table while Diem
relinquished power to Vice President Tho. After the ceremony, Diem would
ask for asylum in a fully broadcasted event. The generals would grant the
request, stipulating that Diem and Nhu must remain in custody until the
aircraft whisked them out of the country.[37]

None of this happened. The brothers were not in the palace. Minh
was livid and humiliated. Diem and Nhu had fled.

An intriguing story soon began to unfold. Sometime earlier, in anticipation of a coup, Diem had arranged for the digging of three tunnels that
snaked away into remote areas outside the palace. Around eight o'clock on
the night of the coup, with the praetorian guard under siege and the palace
encircled by rebel forces and armor, Diem and Nhu hurriedly packed a
briefcase with American currency. Accompanied by a servant and a military aide, they left the palace through a subterranean tunnel that "was so
far down," Harkins later explained after gazing down the stairway, that "I
didn't want to go down to walk up the thing. It really went down to the
depths." The brothers emerged in a wooded spot close to the Cercle Sportif,
the city's sporting club, where they jumped into a waiting car. Taking the
back roads to evade rebel checkpoints, they raced to the home of Ma Tuyen,
a Chinese merchant and friend in Cholon who reportedly served as Nhu's
main contact with the Chinese syndicates involved in the opium trade.
Failing to secure asylum in the Chinese Nationalist embassy, Diem and
Nhu stayed the night in Ma Tuyen's clubhouse. It was from there that
they frantically telephoned numerous ARVN officers in a vain attempt to
secure help. They also talked with the coup generals, who did not realize
that the brothers were no longer in the palace. Mortified before his peers,
Minh was furious that Diem and Nhu had stolen away in the night.[38]

The generals proceeded with their planned announcement of a provisional government. The central body was the Military Revolutionary Council, which consisted of twelve generals with Minh as chair and Don as deputy. This group deposed Diem and abolished the governing system, suspended the constitution of 1956, dissolved the recently elected National Assembly as, the generals declared, "dishonest and fraudulent," and assembled a new cabinet made up of anti-Communist, pro-Western civilians. General Kim thought the changeover from a military junta to civilian leadership would be rapid. Tho would serve as prime minister of a government comprised of members chosen by him with the Council's approval. The coup leaders imposed martial law, announced a curfew, and ordered the release of all jailed monks and students. At a press conference that same morning of November 2, the Military Revolutionary Council issued a statement asserting that the government intended to revise the constitution and establish "Democracy and Liberty." In place of the abolished legislature would stand an advisory group known as the Council of Notables. Senior U.S. officers praised the new administration. "They're putting some young tigers in command, and they could make an all-out effort to finish off the Viet Cong."[39]

The coup results had exceeded the wildest expectations. Casualties were surprisingly light: nine insurgents killed and forty-six wounded; four dead and forty-four wounded from the Palace Guard; twenty civilian deaths and 146 wounded. The governmental transition had been amazingly smooth, leading to widespread anticipation that the new regime would restore domestic stability and more effectively pursue the war. Although Beijing and Moscow denounced the coup for bringing in a U.S. "puppet" government, expressions of hope came from all over the world that the new regime would end the Buddhist persecutions and concentrate on defeating the Communists.[40]

The coup had surprised the Vietcong. Radio Hanoi summed up events without comment, suggesting North Vietnam's initial uncertainty about events. On the one side, party leaders were disheartened because they could no longer exploit Diem's unpopularity. And yet, on the other side, they felt confident that the new government would fall apart and thereby facilitate the revolution. On the night of November 1, Vietcong radio in South Vietnam had urged the Vietnamese people, the NLF, and ARVN loyalists to resist the coup. But the generals' rapid success had precluded any joint counteraction. What did the Military Revolutionary Council intend to do? What would the U.S. reaction be? Within a week of the coup, however, the Vietcong had regained direction and launched more than a thousand attacks. A spokesperson for the Vietnamese Communists in Paris expressed shock to an American that his government had undermined one of the strongest opponents they faced, and the leader of the National Liberation

Front, Nguyen Huu Tho, termed the coup a "gift from Heaven for us." In mid-November 1963, the NLF announced a list of demands that included a cease-fire, U.S. withdrawal, and the establishment of a coalition government—all aimed, according to the NLF's first public declaration to this effect, at reunifying Vietnam.[41]

In a stand that belied all evidence to the contrary, the White House disclaimed responsibility for the coup. Harriman was emphatic. "There was nothing we did that I know of that encouraged the coup." Taylor concurred. "We couldn't have done anything about it had we known it was about to occur." Hilsman agreed. "We never manipulated any coup, we never planned any coup." But, he admitted, we "were perfectly aware that our public opposition to Diem's Buddhist policy would encourage the plotters." Diem "made the decisions, we didn't. We were forced to do what we did." Lodge's removal of Richardson, Hilsman insisted, was "terribly important" in signaling displeasure with the regime, for the CIA station chief had openly supported Nhu. "This was probably the most significant thing that was done, but we didn't know that."[42]

The coup could *not* have surprised the administration. On the precoup morning of November 1, Lodge and Felt met with Diem at the premier's request, only to sit through another unconvincing monologue assuring compliance with U.S. demands. As Felt and Lodge prepared to depart, Diem called the ambassador aside and for twenty minutes repeatedly asked what the United States wanted him to do. This was a ploy, for he and his brother were poised to launch the counterfeit coup. The feigned sincerity did not fool Lodge. He had told Diem countless times what the White House expected. More than that, Lodge knew of the imminent coup. Felt, however, was not aware of impending events and hurried to meet his noon departure time at the airport. Indeed, he first held a press conference with Don standing nervously by his side as coup forces gathered around Saigon. The rebels kept the air strip open until Felt's plane took off. On learning of the coup soon afterward, Harkins called him: "The airfield's closed. Don't try to come back because they're having a coup."[43]

Lodge made no effort to expedite the report of his morning conversation with Diem to Washington. Indeed, his cablegram did not leave Saigon until 3 P.M., arriving in the state department long after news of the coup. The account of Diem's alleged submission appeared near the end of the lengthy telegram: "If [the] U.S. wants to make a package deal, I would think we were in a position to do it. In effect he [Diem] said: tell us what you want and we'll do it." Either Lodge attached no importance to these words, or he ignored them in light of his preference for a change in government. Probably his reaction was a combination of both. "We believe that Vietnam's best Generals are involved in directing this effort. If they can't pull it off, it is doubtful other military leadership could do so successfully."[44]

The White House was elated over the coup. In a staff meeting the day afterward, the advisers praised the generals for what Forrestal triumphantly called a "well executed coup, much better than anyone would have thought possible." Colby detailed the events, captivating his colleagues by tracing the order of battle on a map. Rusk happily observed that the rebels had support throughout the military. "If the generals hold together, the coup forces will prevail." McGeorge Bundy noted with relief that Diem remained alive, demonstrating that "no one wanted to go in for the kill" and that the generals simply wanted him to leave the country. "This was an example of the acceptable type of military coup." In this immediate afterglow, Rusk emphasized the need to show publicly that the coup was not the result of a "few scheming officers" but of the "virtually unanimous determination of [the] military and civilian leadership of his country." Since these events had taken place during a civil war (a slip of the tongue?), "this amounts to a national decision."[45]

To clinch the point, Rusk wanted the generals to make a public announcement that one of their major reasons for the coup was Nhu's "dickering with [the] Communists to betray [the] anti-Communist cause." Less than two hours later, Lodge replied that this "point has been made to [the] Generals." Dinh told the press that Nhu had "entered negotiations" with North Vietnam through the Polish representative on the International Control Commission. As Halberstam observed, the generals feared that a neutralist Vietnam would culminate in the deaths of them and their families. Dinh insisted that he and his cohort had no choice but to overthrow the government.[46]

The White House fostered the impression that the Vietnamese alone had engineered the coup. "The plot itself was news to us," blandly declared an unidentified administration source. Mike Mansfield was convinced. The Democratic Leader of the Senate asserted that "the news of the coup came as a complete surprise to me and I am quite certain a surprise to the Administration." Despite the rumors of White House involvement, "this appears to me to be a purely Vietnamese affair which the Vietnamese should settle among themselves." Rusk confirmed this assessment. "We were not privy to these plans." In an assertion that was technically true but underestimated the importance of perception, he emphasized that "Americans were not involved in the planning nor were any Americans involved in the fighting." Admittedly, the White House had urged Diem to get rid of Nhu. Yes, its selective aid cuts had failed to persuade Diem to make changes and had pushed him into a "solitude" that left him "isolated and impervious" to his people. Still, Rusk denied that Washington had had a "decisive influence" on events. Diem's overthrow was "a South Vietnamese affair." Rusk nonetheless remained concerned. "I think our press problem is likely to be pinpointed on U.S. involvement." The president wanted a public pronouncement that this was not a U.S. coup. The state department's press officer dutifully followed through: "I can categorically state that the U.S. government was not involved in any way."[47]

U.S. denials were not convincing then or now. Some administration officials were truthful, albeit years afterward. Mecklin charged the White House with putting "direct, relentless, table-hammering pressure on Diem such as the United States had seldom before attempted with a sovereign, friendly government." Trueheart admitted that the United States was well aware of the generals' actions. Conein and Spera had kept close touch with the conspirators, and Kim and others were close friends of Phillips and Stilwell. Of course, there were loyalty and ethical questions about publicly supporting a government while knowing a coup was under way; but, Trueheart added, much of this was "greatly offset by the feeling that we had been had by these people." The Diem regime no longer served the interests of either South Vietnam or the United States. "Once we had listened to these generals, then we had a commitment to them." Like Hilsman, Trueheart considered Richardson's removal a major impetus for the coup. Colby concurred, calling the move "a policy decision just to indicate the end of a close relationship with Nhu." Richardson had cultivated a closeness with Diem, and the CIA had provided both financial and technical support to Nhu's special forces. Richardson had to return home, Trueheart insisted, so that Lodge could show that *he* spoke for the White House. "This was a clear signal, the only kind of really believable signal he could give."[48]

The White House was justified in its concern over the public's perception of culpability. U.S. aid reductions and public denunciations of the Diem regime's Buddhist policies, *Time* declared in its cover story, had "set the scene for the coup" and made U.S. denials "misleading." White House pressures were "an invitation to overthrow." One U.S. official bluntly told the media: "Hell, there's been so much advance knowledge we can't possibly imagine why the Diem government didn't know, too." Below a picture of Taylor, Rostow, and Minh (on the tennis court the previous October) read the caption: "There could be no doubt that the U.S. encouraged the coup." The *New York Times* echoed that view, with Max Frankel asserting that Washington "had created the atmosphere that made the coup possible." President Kennedy's TV call for "changes in policy and perhaps with personnel" in Saigon amounted to a "virtual invitation to insurrection." Hedrick Smith concurred, declaring that the White House "had helped create the climate for the coup."[49]

From Beverly Hills, California, Madame Nhu further embarrassed the administration with her caustic comments to the press. Was the United States involved? "Definitely," she replied, peering through heavy dark glasses necessitated by minor eye surgery. "No coup can erupt without American incitement and backing." Would she seek asylum in the United

States? "Never! I cannot stay in a country whose government stabbed me in the back. I believe all the devils of hell are against us," she exclaimed as she and her eighteen-year-old daughter were escorted to a limousine. This was no less a "dirty crime" than that committed by the Communists, when they murdered her brother-in-law and his only son. "Whoever has the Americans as allies does not need any enemies."[50]

Later investigations by U.S. officials agreed with the contemporary view. The *Pentagon Papers* declared that the United States "must accept its full share of responsibility." In August 1963 and afterward, Washington's leaders "variously authorized, sanctioned and encouraged the coup efforts of the Vietnamese generals and offered full support for a successor government." In October, the White House terminated aid to the regime "in a direct rebuff, giving a green light to the generals." It then maintained secret contact with them "throughout the planning and execution of the coup and sought to review their operational plans and proposed new government." The Church Committee in the 1970s concluded in its investigation of assassinations that "American officials offered encouragement to the Vietnamese generals who plotted Diem's overthrow, and a CIA official in Vietnam gave the generals money after the coup had begun." As Diem's rule came to an end, according to the *Pentagon Papers*, "our complicity in his overthrow heightened our responsibilities and our commitment in an essentially leaderless Vietnam."[51]

With the worst apparently over, President Kennedy sought Lodge's advice on the problem of extending diplomatic recognition to the new Saigon regime. How could we "square recognition of the Vietnamese rebel government which had overthrown a constitutional government with our position of not recognizing the rebel government which had overthrown the constitutional government in Honduras?" The president wanted a paper prepared that would justify recognition. It should highlight the widespread popularity of a coup that involved the country's entire senior staff of officers and the promise of a constitutional government under Tho.[52]

In Vietnam, popular approval of the coup seemed so widespread that Lodge recommended immediate recognition and support of the provisional regime. "Every Vietnamese has a grin on his face today." Large crowds had swarmed into the streets and onto the palace grounds, wildly praising both the ARVN and the Americans. In the midst of what Trueheart termed a "Mardi Gras" atmosphere, a sea of Buddhist flags flew throughout the city while soldiers celebrated by firing their weapons in the air. Many Vietnamese cheered as Lodge's car with the U.S. flag flapping in the breeze headed for the embassy the morning after. The atmosphere was "extraordinary," according to Mrs. Lodge. "I had not realized how feared and hated the government was. . . . We have just had a marvelous experience—as Cabot was early for lunch we walked two blocks to the Xa Loi Pagoda—

Cabot was recognized—great smiles—bows—some cries of Vive Capa Lodge and out came a bonze who hurried us into the pagoda with the crowd following—they were so excited seeing Cabot they nearly squashed us. It was incredibly moving." Lodge reported that the populace had "lionized" the soldiers, giving them fruits and flowers and wrapping garlands of roses around the tanks. Young men wielding acetylene torches cut off the feet of the statues of the Truong sisters modeled in Madame Nhu's image, while others fastened a cable around the necks of the statues to pull them down. Others in the boisterous crowd broke windows, yanked down governmental flags from public buildings, and sacked and burned any structures associated with Nhu—including the home of the *Times of Vietnam*. "If the generals stay together," Robert Thompson told Lodge, "the coup should help very much to win the war." Lodge urged the administration to avoid the appearance of a payoff for the coup by quietly resuming periodic and selective commercial import payments and by extending recognition only after other nations had done so.[53]

Nolting did not share this optimism and once again came to Diem's defense. The former ambassador denounced the press accounts of street celebrations as misleading and insisted that most people had remained supportive of Diem. Years afterward, Nolting argued that "the majority were shocked and it was only the hotheads stirred up by I don't know what elements, but certainly some of them were Vietcong or Vietcong sympathizers." The Nhus were a different story. "I could understand that Madame Nhu would have been a target." She was unpopular, as was "brother Nhu, whom some Vietnamese called Bobby Nhu, in imitation of Bobby Kennedy." Seldom had anyone called Diem "unjust or cruel." No one questioned his "integrity and the reputation for honesty and trying to do good for his people."[54]

Don and Khiem, however, had criticized Diem's leadership long before the coup. After dinner in Nolting's home one evening, they launched a tirade against the premier, accusing him of interfering with the military's efforts and leading the country into ruin. Implying that a coup was in order, they called Diem "no good. He's a bad character." Nolting was indignant. "Gentlemen, you are my guests and I am an accredited diplomat to the government which happens to be headed by your president, who was elected." If they were unhappy, Nolting pointed out, "You have a chance to run for president next time. Don't give me this stuff about revolt and supporting a revolt. Why don't you do your duty as military men? The United States is not going to get into this question of a coup d'etat."[55]

Both the White House and the new leadership in Saigon denied U.S. complicity in the coup, but their arguments rang hollow amid the thunderous praise for Americans. Lodge nonetheless claimed that the Vietnamese alone had carried out the coup. Conein emphasized that no one could have stopped it. Had he expressed opposition, the generals would have drummed him out of their headquarters and cut him off from everything. Before the press almost a week afterward, Dinh maintained that the coup was entirely Vietnamese. "No Americans," he emphasized, "were in any way involved." This claim is simply not true. Those at the locus of U.S. power—Kennedy, his White House advisers, Lodge, and Conein, who spoke for all three—played a critical role in Diem's fall. As the exuberant crowds toppled the Truong monument, several Vietnamese abandoned custom and shook the hands and slapped the back of an American on the scene. The Vietnamese, perceptively warned the CIA, "are clearly expecting much, perhaps too much." Lodge did not think so. According to one observer, the ambassador looked like "an old riverboat gambler who had just won it all." Making no attempt to conceal his satisfaction, Lodge joyously hailed Conein's services as "priceless."[56] The coup had been such a resounding success that Americans did not *want* to dissociate from it.

III

SUDDENLY, HOWEVER, the atmosphere of exultation turned rancid when the news hit Washington that Diem and Nhu were dead. A little after midnight on November 2, the CIA sent word to the White House of their alleged suicides. Vietnam radio had announced their deaths by poison, taken while prisoners in an armored personnel carrier transporting them from the city to the rebel command center. Harkins, however, reported the claim of death by "self destruction," either by gunshot or by a grenade wrestled from the belt of an ARVN officer holding them under guard. "Due to an inadvertence," Big Minh explained in trying to clear up the discrepancy, "there was a gun inside the vehicle. It was with this gun that they committed suicide."[57]

President Kennedy learned of the deaths on the morning following the coup, when Forrestal rushed into the cabinet room waving a telegram declaring that Diem and Nhu had committed suicide. Taylor recorded the president's stunned reaction: "Kennedy leaped to his feet and rushed from the room with a look of shock and dismay on his face which I had never seen before. He had always insisted that Diem must never suffer more than exile and had been led to believe or had persuaded himself that a change in government could be carried out without bloodshed." Colby made a similar observation, attesting that the president "blanched and walked out of the room to compose himself." Schlesinger insisted that Kennedy was "somber and shaken" by the news. Soon afterward the president dictated a memo for his records that referred to Diem's assassination as "particularly abhorrent" but blamed himself for approving the August

24 cable. It had "encouraged Lodge along a course to which he was in any case inclined." The *Pentagon Papers* was doubtless correct in concluding that the deaths had unsettled the president, "particularly in view of the heavy U.S. involvement in encouraging the coup leaders."[58]

The president's revulsion toward the deaths did not draw sympathy from everyone in his administration. At a meeting the next day with the CIA's top officials, McCone recounted Kennedy's look of horror. The president had ignored CIA opposition in promoting the coup, insisted one indignant participant. Coups were notoriously uncontrollable. How could he have been surprised at the outcome? Richard Helms was astounded that Kennedy had failed to comprehend the enormous implications of his decision to condone a coup. He had approved the August 1963 cable that put the White House in the coup makers' camp. When the coup seemed certain in late October, he assigned Lodge virtual unilateral authority—which, in view of the ambassador's well-known sentiments, was tantamount to approving the coup. The assassinations did not surprise Trueheart. Diem had rallied his forces in 1960, making the generals fear that he would do the same if they let him live. "Long before there was any idea of any involvement of the U.S.," Trueheart and others had warned of the "very strong possibility" of assassination. Rusk emphasized that the administration could not look back. Above all, the generals must not visit Lodge and leave the impression that they were "reporting in."[59]

Kennedy suspected a dual assassination. He told the National Security Council that he could not believe that the brothers as Catholics would have committed suicide. Hilsman disagreed. "It was not difficult to conceive of Diem and Nhu taking their own lives, despite their Catholic religion." They were "Asian Catholics who might have chosen to commit suicide in a spirit of 'this is Armageddon.'" McCone concurred with Kennedy's suspicions. Conein, the CIA director declared, had declined an invitation to see the bodies. "He may have known how Diem and Nhu were killed and that the suicide story put out by the new government was false. He may have decided under these circumstances to avoid learning the truth." The new government, Hilsman asserted, must not do anything to suggest any "mystery about the deaths of Diem and Nhu." The president directed his advisers to prepare a report that "would throw the least discredit on them and on us if, as it appeared likely, Diem and Nhu have been assassinated. We should try to confine press speculation crediting the U.S. with bringing off the coup. Our line should be that the aid pressures which we used against Diem were not for the purpose of overthrowing him, but for the purpose of putting pressure on him to come to terms in order to ensure the success of the war against the Viet Cong."[60]

Later that day the president and his cabinet continued to wrestle with the generals' suicide claim. "About this, this suicide," Hilsman asserted, "there is some question in some of our minds as to how much we want to know about this. It's becoming more and more clear that it is assassination. At least I think it was." Hilsman frowned on sending a just drafted cable that instructed Conein to press Minh for the truth. "There's some, uh, doubt in some of our minds whether we want to do this. Maybe we oughta just let it alone."

McCone agreed. "I would su-suggest that we not get into, into this story."

McGeorge Bundy likewise concurred. "What happens if we now ask to see the bodies, and there were a couple of bullets in the back of the, in the back of this kind? We don't gain much by that."

"If Big Minh ordered the execution," declared President Kennedy, "then, then, uh, I don't know. Do we think he meant to?"

"There's some suspicion," Hilsman noted.

"Some think he did," Bundy observed.

"Some think he did," Hilsman repeated.

Then, barely above a whisper came the president's assessment: "Pretty stupid."

A few moments later, President Kennedy inquired about the Vietnamese people's reaction to the assassination. Hilsman reported jubilation in the streets. He then related Harriman's wry comment that Lodge's stock had risen so much that he might finally become president—*of Vietnam*. Kennedy quickly remarked, "I'm not so sure about that," drawing a round of laughter. "I think," he continued over the sniggering, that it would be "interesting to know what reaction is, public reaction is. We'll hear all about this, and the assassination, and whether it will be popular or not." Silence blanketed the room.

The president finally spoke. "What are we gonna say about the, uh, death of Diem and Nhu? We're not gonna say anything, right?" No conclusive evidence has appeared. "We've already got an unfortunate event," he continued. "Nonetheless, it'd be regrettable if it were ascribed, unless the evidence is clear, if it were ascribed to Big Minh and the responsible council of generals. I don't want it wrapped around him if we can help it."

Hilsman recommended that they wait before reacting. "The information's gonna come out. It's gonna come out in the next forty-eight hours."

"His role may not," asserted the president. "I'm sure Lodge must be aware that this is an unfortunate matter, and I suppose next they're gonna make every effort to disassociate Big Minh and Conein." The president wanted Lodge to note "any extenuating circumstances which develop" regarding the assassination. "If there was not responsibility on [Minh's] part," Kennedy emphasized, "that should be made clear."

"In other words," Hilsman interjected, "get a story and stick to it."

"It ought to be a true story," Kennedy added, "if possible."[61]

If the White House had hoped that a coup would facilitate the withdrawal plan, the deaths of Diem and Nhu had severely complicated the process. Taylor considered the administration largely responsible for the chaos conducive to Diem's collapse. It "was certainly in part our doing." The coup was "a disaster, a national disaster," for both Americans and South Vietnamese. Nolting declared that contemporaries believed that "we had a great deal to do with creating the atmosphere for that coup. In fact," he emphasized, "we encouraged it." Trueheart thought the coup cost more than it gained. Colby termed the "American-sponsored overthrow of Diem" the "worst mistake of the Vietnam War." Lansdale called it "a terrible, stupid thing" that undermined the Vietnamese constitution and shattered domestic order. In the postcoup fall of 1963, according to administration adviser William Bundy, "Americans in both public and policy circles were bound henceforth to feel more responsible for what happened in South Vietnam." No one could seriously consider "withdrawing with the task unfinished."[62]

Bundy's projection of a deeper entanglement, combined with Kennedy's preference for a reduced commitment, exemplified the dilemma that had dogged the administration. No one wanted to "lose" the war, and yet no one could suggest a way to win it other than sending U.S. combat troops and hoping for the best. The deaths of Saigon's two leaders hardened the president's interest in a massive military disengagement. For only the briefest of moments, Kennedy's restraint appeared to have paid off. The generals' well-managed seizure of power had left the image of competence and thereby presented an opportunity to initiate a withdrawal. But news of the Ngo brothers' deaths had suddenly dispelled the aura surrounding the generals and their quiet American collaborators. At risk was not only the tenure of the new regime but also the future of the U.S. withdrawal plan.

The truth behind the two brothers' deaths began to seep out. After Minh had ordered a search of all areas frequented by the Ngo family, Colonel Pham Ngoc Thao learned from a captured Palace Guard officer of their escape through the tunnels and into Cholon. When Thao arrived at Ma Tuyen's house, Diem and Nhu overheard him calling his superiors and sought refuge in the nearby Catholic church of St. Francis Xavier. Just after the early morning mass celebrating All Souls' Day (the Day of the Dead), the congregation filed out and Diem and Nhu, both in dark gray suits and worn out from lack of sleep, walked through the shady courtyard and into the building. Now fugitives in a country they had headed since 1954, they prayed and took communion. It was perhaps while Diem and Nhu crossed the yard that an informant recognized them and notified authorities.[63]

A few minutes later, just before 10 A.M., two jeeps and an armored personnel carrier screeched into the narrow alcove housing the church building. In command was General Mai Huu Xuan, a long-time enemy of Diem's. Xuan sent a detachment of men into the building to bring out the brothers. Once outside, Diem requested a brief stop at the palace to gather personal items before his flight out of Vietnam. Xuan turned him down, coldly stating that his orders were to take them to headquarters. Tension built when one young officer asked to shoot Nhu. No, replied Xuan. Nhu expressed disgust at Diem's having to ride in an armored car. "You use such a vehicle to drive the president?" Colonel Duong Nghoc Lam assured the captives that the armored car was for their protection. Xuan ordered their hands tied behind their backs and shoved the brothers into the carrier. As he jumped into a jeep to head the convoy, Diem and Nhu found themselves sitting in the carrier with two men: Captain Duong Huu Nhgia, who was at the turret of the armored vehicle, and Captain Nhung, Minh's personal aide and bodyguard. According to Khanh some months afterward, Nhung was an assassin by trade who had put forty marks on his revolver, one for each life he had taken. He had executed Tung just hours earlier. Nhung's animosity toward Diem ran second only to his visceral hatred for Nhu.[64]

En route to the generals' headquarters, Nhung killed Diem and Nhu. Nghia explained what happened. "As we rode back to the Joint General Staff headquarters, Diem sat silently, but Nhu and the [captain] began to insult each other. I don't know who started it. The name-calling grew passionate. The [captain] had hated Nhu before. Now he was charged with emotion." When the convoy stopped for a train, Nhung "lunged at Nhu with a bayonet and stabbed him again and again, maybe fifteen or twenty times. Still in a rage, he turned to Diem, took out his revolver and shot him in the head. Then he looked back at Nhu, who was lying on the floor, twitching. He put a bullet into his head too. Neither Diem nor Nhu ever defended themselves. Their hands were tied."[65]

The deaths shocked the generals. Although they felt no sympathy for Nhu, they respected Diem's position and courage. One general broke down and wept. Minh's assistant, Colonel Nguyen Van Quan, crumpled down on a table, sickened by the news. Even the usually brash General Dinh later declared, "I couldn't sleep that night." The generals, Don insisted, were "truly grievous" over the deaths. They had promised Diem safe passage if he resigned. But Nhu, Don charged, had convinced Diem to reject the offer. "Once again," Lodge cynically remarked, "brother Nhu proves to be the evil genius in Diem's life."[66]

Don directed a fellow general to inform reporters that the brothers had died by an accident. Then going to Minh, Don shot out: "Why are they dead?"

"And what does it matter that they are dead?" haughtily replied the general.

Xuan burst in and, not seeing Don by the door, proudly declared in French: "*Mission accomplie.*"[67]

Conein soon became aware of the deaths. He had left rebel headquarters as the generals were making preparations for Diem and Nhu's safekeeping. On arriving home, however, he received a telephone call from David Smith at the CIA station, telling him to go to the embassy. There he learned that President Kennedy wanted him to find Diem. Conein returned to the rebels' headquarters about 10:30 A.M. and found Minh in the Officers' Club.

Where were Diem and Nhu?

"They committed suicide," Minh attested. "They were in the Catholic church at Cholon, and they committed suicide."

Conein was aghast. "Look, you're a Buddhist, I'm a Catholic. If they committed suicide at that church and the priest holds Mass tonight, that story won't hold water." Conein pushed harder. "Where are they?"

"Their bodies are behind General Staff Headquarters," Minh replied. "Do you want to see them?"

"No."

"Why not?"

"Well, if by chance one of a million of the people believe you that they committed suicide in Church and I see that they have not committed suicide and I know differently, then if it ever leaks out, I am in trouble."

Conein realized that if he saw marks on the bodies, he would not be able to deny their assassinations. To have such knowledge would endanger his safety. They had been killed, and Conein refused to view the proof. He returned to the embassy and sent his report to Washington.[68]

It gradually became public knowledge that the Ngo brothers had died by assassination. As late as November 6, Minister of Information Tran Tu Oai declared at a news conference that Diem and Nhu had died by "accidental suicide"—shot when Nhu tried to grab the gun from the officer placing them under arrest. Halberstam was dubious from the outset. "Extremely reliable private military sources," he wrote the state department, affirm that on the return to rebel headquarters, someone ordered their assassination. Sheehan reported a similar story based on "highly reliable sources." The clinching evidence came from Father Leger of the St. Xavier Catholic church in Cholon, who declared that Diem and Nhu were kneeling in the church building when soldiers burst in, took them outside, forced them into the armored car, and later shot them. Lodge had learned from "an unimpeachable source" that both men were shot in the nape of the neck and that Diem's body bore signs of a brutal beating.[69]

Meanwhile, the CIA in Saigon secured a set of snapshots that left no doubt of a double assassination. Taken around 10 A.M. on November 2, they showed the two dead brothers covered with blood on the floor of an armored vehicle, dressed in Roman Catholic priests' robes, hands tied behind their backs, faces bloodied and bruised, and stabbed repeatedly. The photographs seemed authentic, discrediting the generals' claims of suicide. The pictures of the slain leaders soon appeared all over the world, having been sold to the international press in Saigon. The caption below the picture in *Time* read: "'Suicide' with no hands."[70]

Rusk expressed deep concern about this news and directed Lodge to make inquiries of Minh. The newspaper headlines describing the deaths of Diem and Nhu—"shot and stabbed with gory details"—had already horrified Americans. The impact would worsen once the photographs appeared. Lodge must provide a complete account of the generals' arrangements for the two brothers' safe removal from the palace. "We do not think there should be any suggestion that this is just the sort of thing you have to expect in a coup." In an interesting twist, Rusk insisted that the White House opposed using aid as "leverage on [the] Generals, but you should emphasize [the] importance of immediate action to ensure as favorable [an] international image as possible."[71]

Lodge showed no alarm over the public's reaction. He met with Don and Kim in the mid-afternoon of November 3, making no effort to hide his exultation. He heartily congratulated them on their "masterful performance" and offered help to the new regime. Recognition was forthcoming. Did they intend to issue a statement denying any role in the assassinations? They had not planned to do so, but they would emphasize that they had offered safe conduct to Diem. They "deeply deplored" the assassinations but recognized that coups often led to casualties. Lodge was satisfied and told the state department, "I am sure assassination was not at their direction." The following day, on White House instructions, he and Conein met with Minh and Don, who denied that the assassinations had resulted from specific orders and seemed receptive to Lodge's request to publicly guarantee humane treatment to other members of the Ngo family. Lodge then chided the state department's "excessive preoccupation with the negative public relations problems of the coup" and its "failure to note the brilliance with which the coup was planned and executed."[72]

News of the deaths terrified Madame Nhu, who feared that the assassins would kill her children. That night of November 2, she called journalist Marguerite Higgins, who had been supportive of the regime. "Do you really believe they are dead?"

"I am afraid so."

"I could spit upon the world." Madame Nhu had telephoned Saigon, but when the operator got through, she was told, "Sorry, no one is at home in the palace." Madame Nhu's daughter was with her in Los Angeles, but her two sons and baby daughter were in Dalat. "Are they going to kill my children, too?" she sobbed.

"It's the last thing President Kennedy would want," Higgins replied, conjuring up the image of three murdered children in a land reeking with vengeance.

"Then why doesn't the United States government do something to help me get them out?"

"I'll put the question to the State Department officer in charge of Vietnam," Higgins promised.

"Hurry," Madame Nhu pleaded. She was also concerned about Diem's brother, the hated war lord in central Vietnam. "Please hurry and ask about Can," she added.

Seeing that it was 2 A.M., Higgins called Hilsman at home. "Congratulations, Roger," Higgins acidly remarked to the White House adviser, still in a semistupor. "How does it feel to have blood on your hands?"

"Oh, come on now, Maggie," recapturing his abrasive verve. "Revolutions are rough. People get hurt."

"What about Madame Nhu's children?" Higgins asked. "Are they going to get hurt?"

The White House could not let this happen. "If you will find out from Madame Nhu where her children are," Hilsman asserted, "we will have General Harkins send his personal plane to get them. If you will find out, further, where Madame Nhu wants the children sent, we will get them tickets and see that they are delivered to any address she names. The President is deeply shocked over the death of Diem and Nhu. He will do anything he can to safeguard Madame Nhu's children."

"What about Ngo Dinh Can?"

"He can have asylum if he wants it."[73]

Hilsman kept his promise regarding the children; the other one he did not keep. Late in the afternoon of November 3, Lodge assigned Flott to a special mission. Those Vietnamese army officers responsible for the three children's safety in Dalat had hidden them in the woods after the coup and then moved them to Saigon. "I prevailed upon the generals [through Conein] to get these children back to their mother. And what I want you to do is, one hour from now—you've got an hour to pack and get out to Tan Son Nhut. The children are out there. We've got General Harkins's C-54, which will fly you to Bangkok, and then I want you to fly commercial with them to Rome, and turn them over to Archbishop Thuc, the brother of Diem."

Flott accompanied the three children on the plane, sitting next to the older of the two boys—a fifteen-year-old who maintained a stoic expression throughout the ordeal. He had read an English account of the coup in a Bangkok newspaper that described his father and his uncle sustaining rifle shots and bayonet wounds and having their heads "squashed." Not understanding the word "squashed," he asked Flott in French, "What's the word for squashed?"

"*Écrabouillée*," Flott replied in French. "It means squashed, but you don't want to pay too much attention to the details, because the reporters probably didn't even see it, and it's the way they write their things." The boy betrayed no emotion, continuing his conversation with Flott the remainder of the trip.

On arriving in Rome, Archbishop Thuc met the party at the plane. He was "very hostile" and refused to speak, Flott reported. "Total distance, total ice treatment."[74]

Madame Nhu soon joined her children in Rome. Before attending an All Souls' Day mass on November 2, she had told a large gathering of news correspondents that the White House was responsible for the deaths of her husband and brother-in-law and called the affair an "indelible stigma against the United States." If "my family has been treacherously killed with either official or unofficial blessing of the American Government, I can predict to you now that the story is only at its beginning." The following day, as she prepared to board the plane, she again accused the United States of encouraging the coup. "Judas has sold the Christ for 30 pieces of silver. The Ngo brothers have been sold for a few dollars."[75]

The White House caved in to popular pressure in Vietnam regarding Diem's widely despised brother, Ngo Dinh Can. Mass graves containing nearly 200 people had been found on his land. The U.S. consul, John Helble, had personally confirmed the existence of rows of "eighteenth century type dungeons with filthy, tiny pitch black cells" in an old French arsenal on Can's property. Don assured Harkins that the graves were the burial places for many of the town's residents before Can had moved onto the land. The public, however, believed Can a murderer. On November 4, thousands of angry townspeople walked nearly two miles to his house just south of Hué (where he lived with his aged and sickly mother), surrounding it and demanding vengeance. The new government had expected trouble and had ringed Can's home two days earlier with barbed wire and armored cars. But Can had already escaped to a nearby Catholic seminary. *Newsweek* soon reported that "a shambling, obese figure in tattered clothes," stricken with diabetes and a bad heart, begged for asylum from the U.S. consul in Hué. Once "a feudal chieftain" who had ruled central Vietnam for eight years, he had all his belongings clutched tightly in his hands: a beat-up valise crammed with American dollar bills.[76]

Helble warned both Saigon and the state department against granting asylum. "Sheltering this fellow . . . was going to be a risk to the American citizens and the U.S. facility." The state department, however, rejected Helble's recommendation, explaining that more violence would hurt the new government's reputation before the world. Helble feared mob action and requested Can's removal from Hué and to the Saigon embassy. Told that Can would receive safe passage out of the country, Helble put him on a U.S. plane for the flight to Saigon.[77]

But Conein, not embassy officials, met the plane at the airport and, under Lodge's instructions, turned over Can to government authorities. The ambassador had secured Don's personal guarantee that the government would deal with Can "legally and juridically." Asylum was no longer necessary. The United States could not interfere with justice, Lodge continued, "particularly as Can is undoubtedly a reprehensible figure who deserves all the loathing which he now receives."[78]

Surely Lodge realized that Can would not escape retribution. In late November, as Can stood trial before a military tribunal, Minh left Lodge with "the distinct impression" that if sentenced to death, "there was a good chance he would get clemency." And yet, just a month earlier, Conein reported that the "majority of the officers, including General Minh," believed that Can's death "would be welcomed." Less than a week before, rebel forces had killed Can's two brothers. The timing of Can's arrest had not helped his case. The government had just freed nearly 20,000 political prisoners. Tales of torture hit the news, casting a blanket of condemnation over Can and others associated with the Diem regime. In spring of 1964, he was convicted of murder and executed by a firing squad.[79]

IV

AT A MEETING of the White House staff, McGeorge Bundy set aside his own misgivings about the manner of Diem's death to emphasize the importance of extending recognition to the new Saigon government. Indeed, Rusk had already announced the imminent action in a circular telegram to all diplomatic posts. Schlesinger warned that recognition of a government resulting from a coup could cause trouble for the administration's Latin American policy. He called for a distinction based on the United States's special responsibilities in this hemisphere. Bundy, however, feared that such an approach would leave the feeling that "if we liked people, we would say what they did was constitutional and if we didn't we would not." A consensus soon developed that recognition should depend on the existence of an effective government that had popular support. The stories and pictures of the Vietnamese people throwing roses on the tanks and their open praise for the coup leaders would clarify the distinction between Saigon and Latin America. Bundy still had misgivings over the assassinations. The photographs about to become public showed the two brothers lying in "a pool of blood with their hands tied behind their backs." This was not the "preferred way to commit suicide."[80]

The administration's worst suspicions materialized into fact when it became certain that *Minh* had ordered Nhung to kill Diem and Nhu. Lodge was convinced of Xuan's involvement as well. "Diem and Nhu had been assassinated, if not by Xuan personally, at least at his direction." But this was only part of the truth. Once Diem and Nhu had escaped from the palace, Minh decided that they had sacrificed their safe passage out of the country. Conein termed the general "a very proud man" who had lost face after arriving at the palace "in all of his splendor with a sedan and everything else." Had Diem and Nhu stayed there, Conein declared more than a decade afterward, they "would probably be alive today." There were "too many people present at the Palace" to consider killing them. But their decision to flee "was one of the things that ticked [Minh] off and he gave the order." As Nhung accompanied the convoy to Cholon, he was under Minh's orders to kill the brothers after their arrest and before their return to headquarters. Nhung shot Diem and Nhu while in the armored car, their hands tied behind their backs.[81]

There can be little doubt that Minh ordered Nhung to assassinate Diem and Nhu. The White House had surmised that the generals would try the brothers for violating the surrender agreement; it had badly miscalculated Minh's reaction. "I have it on very good authority of very many people," Conein asserted, "that Big Minh gave the order." Colby likewise held the general solely responsible for the decision. Don was equally emphatic: "I can state without equivocation that this was done by General Big Minh, and by him alone." When Thieu became general and chief of state in 1971, Minh attributed the murders to him. Thieu hotly denied the charge and issued a statement that Minh did not dispute: "Duong Van Minh has to assume entire responsibility for the death of Ngo Dinh Diem."[82]

The question of motive remains a matter of debate. Conein argued convincingly that Minh's humiliation contributed greatly to his decision to have the premier killed. But there were other reasons as well. One baffled Vietnamese loyal to Diem asked friends in the CIA, "If you felt that President Diem was inefficient I can see that you have to replace him, but why assassinate him?" The response: "They had to kill him. Otherwise his supporters would gradually rally and organize and there would be civil war." Minh told an American months afterward, "We had no alternative. They had to be killed. Diem could not be allowed to live because he was too much respected among simple, gullible people in the countryside, especially the Catholics and the refugees. We had to kill Nhu because he was so widely feared—and he had created organizations that were arms of his personal power." The most striking conclusion came from Tran Van Huong, a civilian who had gone to jail in 1960 for signing the Caravelle Manifesto that criticized Diem, and who became prime minister for a short time following the assassination. "The top generals who decided to murder Diem and his brother were scared to death. The generals knew very well that having no talent, no moral virtues, no political support whatsoever, they could not prevent a spectacular comeback of the president and Mr. Nhu if they were alive."[83]

The deaths of Diem and Nhu appalled several members of the Kennedy administration. Harriman later declared that "it was a great shock to everybody that they were killed. I think that was one of those accidents that happened, probably because Nhu insulted the junior officer. I think he probably told him if he didn't let him out that he would see that he was shot." Phillips deeply lamented the assassination as an incredibly senseless act. On the morning after the coup, he went into the palace, which "was all shot to hell." He recalled his meeting with Diem just two days earlier. "The chairs that we were sitting in were all sort of thrown all over the goddam place, with a couple of artillery holes and—sad. God, you know, I wanted to sit down and cry. And I was so upset when I heard that he'd been killed." He did not know whether Minh had given the order to kill Diem. "That is very, very obscure as to how the hell that all came about. That was a stupid decision and, God, we paid, they paid, everybody paid."[84]

Ironically, Big Minh and his inner circle of generals had masterminded a coup and then not so masterfully engineered their own destruction by assassinating Diem and Nhu. That the killings failed to make the brothers into martyrs constituted a vivid testimonial to the depth of popular hatred they had aroused. But instead of choosing the prudent step of placing Diem and Nhu in foreign exile, Minh succumbed to his own pride and insecurity to order the assassinations, opening a bitter split within the coup leadership and repulsing both U.S. and world opinion. Minh's decision to kill the two brothers had exploded the myth that the rebels constituted a distinct improvement over their predecessors and ultimately convinced Washington that even though the leaders' names had changed in Saigon, the situation remained the same.

Diem's assassination drove the initial harmony among the generals into rank discord. Stung by the internecine criticisms of the premier's death, their bitterness spilled over into fights over positions in the new government. Don abhorred the assassinations, caustically insisting that he and his cohort had furnished the armored car in an effort to *protect* Diem and Nhu, not kill them. Khanh hotly complained that his single condition for joining the coup had been that no one kill the premier. And yet, both Don and Khanh failed to recognize that even though Minh had ordered the assassinations without consulting his colleagues, all conspirators bore responsibility for the deaths by participating in the coup. Now, when decisions regarding postcoup affairs took priority, resentment over the killings meshed with the visceral competition over government posts to disassemble the new regime before it fully took form.[85]

On November 5, the generals' spokesmen in Saigon announced the composition of a new government that had civilian components but was unmistakably military in tone. Tho would be premier as well as Minister of Economy and Minister of Finance, but four generals would fill key slots: Minh as president, Don as Minister of Defense, Dinh as Minister of Interior, and Oai as Minister of Information. The result was confusion and bitterness. According to Tho's assistant, Nguyen Ngoc Huy, "Generals Don [and] Dinh . . . were both in the [Military Revolutionary] Council and in the Government. As members of the Council, they were superior to Tho, and as members of the Government, they were under Tho. So when Tho gave an order, they refused. They went into the Council and gave a counter order. This was chaos."[86]

The next day, Minh addressed the nation about the new regime, which in less than twenty-four hours had lost all semblance of order. Reports had emerged of civilian candidates "wrangling" over positions and of dissension among the coup leaders. General Kim, head of political planning, had encountered "haggling" civilians even before the fall of Gia Long Palace. General Oai did not ease growing anxieties over military rule by announcing that the new government's policy would be "democracy within discipline," a clear message that the generals intended to play a major role. Kim and Don had already admitted to Lodge that the military might have to run the country for as much as two years. Lodge had earlier observed that Minh "seemed tired and somewhat frazzled." He was "a good, well-intentioned man," but "will he be strong enough to get on top of things?"[87]

The most inflammatory issue developed over Tho's vehement opposition to Dinh's appointment as Minister of Interior. Most generals, the White House knew, considered Dinh "unstable, unprincipled, and opportunistic." Just promoted to major general, the immodest thirty-eight-year-old officer had grossly exaggerated his role in the coup during an interview with UPI that appeared in the *Washington Post* and the *New York Times*. Wearing dark glasses and waving a cigarette in a long black holder, he arrogantly asserted that he had assumed a leading role in the coup because "we would have lost the war under Diem." He promoted the coup "not for personal ambition, but for the population, the people, and to get rid of Nhu." He made the decision on "the day after the national elections" of a month ago. He went to Dalat, a mountain resort in the central highlands, to demonstrate his opposition to the government's policies. "I had been thinking about a coup all the while I was in Dalat." He was "the specialist in the *coup*." He "gave the orders in only thirty minutes." The planning had gone on for several weeks, but he "kept it all in [his] head." Big Minh finally secured a compromise whereby Dinh became Minister of Security, and the Ministry of Administrative Affairs, which was under Tho's control, assumed some of Interior's duties.[88]

Dinh's antics worried his peers, not only because he was an embarrassment, but also because he seemed poised to seize control of the government. According to *Newsweek*, he was a "vain swashbuckler in a black beret, red kerchief, and camouflage uniform," who celebrated his new position as Minister of Security by hitting Saigon's nightclubs and dancing (he had lifted the ban on dancing, grinning as he explained that "it does not constitute any threat to security"), kissing the young bar matrons, and ordering champagne for everyone. Bragging again that he had masterminded the coup, he proudly asserted, "On August 21, I was governor of Saigon and loyal to Diem; on November 1, I was again governor of Saigon and fighting Diem; maybe in the future I'll be governor of Saigon and fighting against the Americans."[89]

The Provisional Government in Saigon was a leaking sieve of inefficiency and confusion, but it was the only one that could claim any level of popular support and authority. The United States extended diplomatic recognition to the new regime on November 7, the same day as did the United Kingdom and four other nations. Malaysia had already made the move, as had Burma, Honduras, and Thailand.[90]

Lodge continued to believe that the change in Saigon's government could lead to a quicker end to the war. As one person noted about the generals, "if these men can perform like this when their hearts are in it, why isn't it reasonable to believe that they can do equally well against the Viet Cong?" More to the point, Lodge declared, "we should not overlook what this coup can mean in the way of shortening the war and enabling Americans to come home." Thompson likewise expected a vastly shortened war, while Harkins happily noted that Minh intended to step up the campaign and establish "extremely cordial and open" relations with U.S. advisers. "Nothing," Lodge asserted with great satisfaction, "could put the cause of freedom into a stronger position than for those on the side of freedom to be able to clean their own house and not be so often in a situation in which we have to put up with autocrats at the very worst or at the best with Colonel Blimps in order to avoid being taken over by communism."[91]

Lodge expressed no regrets about the United States's connection with the coup even while he continued to deny its responsibility. And yet, he stained his plea of innocence by his admissions to complicity. It was "certain," he assured the president, "that the ground in which the coup seed grew into a robust plant was prepared by us and that the coup would not have happened [when] it did without our preparation. General Don as much as said this to me on November 3." U.S. economic pressure and other actions "made the people who could do something about it start thinking hard about how to get a change of government." On the day of the coup, Vietnamese radio declared that the Diem regime had cost the country U.S. economic help and would facilitate a Communist takeover, whereas a coup would result in a restoration of U.S. aid and a greater likelihood of success in the war. Lodge asserted with immense satisfaction that the coup's outcome afforded a "useful lesson in the use of US power for those who face similar situations in other places in the future." Those who deserved credit for the outcome, he told Rusk, included the president, state department, U.S. Information Service, and CIA. "Without united action by the US government, it would not have been possible."[92]

The president likewise adhered to a dual interpretation of his administration's role in the coup. He could not deny that the selective aid policies were integral to the generals' decision to go forward, just as his rejection of such policies in August had caused the generals to cancel the coup. Even though the coup was a "Vietnamese effort," Kennedy asserted, "our own actions made it clear that we wanted improvements, and when these were not forthcoming from the Diem government, we necessarily faced and accepted the possibility that our position might encourage a change of government." The United States must take advantage of this turn of events to upgrade the ARVN's performance in the war. "This is what we must help in, just as it was ineffectiveness, loss of popular confidence, and the prospect of defeat that were decisive in shaping our relations to the Diem regime."[93]

Both Lodge and the president had deceived themselves into believing that the United States bore no culpability for the coup. By their strained reasoning, the making of a coup constituted only its actual planning and implementation and not the subtle (or not so subtle) encouragement coming from the nine-year-long protector of the government under siege. The Kennedy administration could not escape responsibility for promoting a coup at its most critical moment: when its leaders were poised to act and needed only a green light from Washington. That approval had not come in August; but it did come in late October when the White House cut back aid to the Diem regime and Lodge assured Don (through Conein) of U.S. support for Diem's overthrow. And with participation came culpability. As Don and *all* the other generals involved in the coup shared guilt for the assassinations of Diem and Nhu, so did the U.S. government's actions make it an accomplice.

Withdrawal of the U.S. military forces, however, might cover a multitude of sins, but the process ran into another snag when critics demanded an immediate and total departure based on neutralizing South Vietnam. *New York Times* columnist James Reston called for international discussions aimed at neutralization. Such public statements by reputable journalists, the president's advisers feared, might alarm the new Saigon government about U.S. intentions. To counter this proposal, Forrestal recommended that the White House restate its views contained in the president's remarks of more than a year before: that if North Vietnam halted its aggression, the United

States could begin a scaled withdrawal. Indeed, the National Security Council's statement of the previous October strongly implied that the United States would extract most of its military personnel if the South Vietnamese could ever fend for themselves. Despite the downturn of recent events, McNamara and Taylor remained confident that the disengagement process could be well under way by 1965.[94]

Halberstam likewise called for neutralization. In a front-page *New York Times* article, he attacked Harkins and, like Reston, advocated a negotiated settlement. The triumphant coup generals, according to Halberstam, considered Harkins "a symbol of the old order" and had not even entrusted him with the coup plans. Lodge, however, had won great acclaim from the generals since the coup, starkly exposing his differences with Harkins over whether to continue supporting the Ngos. On the same morning of the article, Forrestal complained to Bob Kleiman of the paper's editorial board that Halberstam was "irresponsible" and had a "personal animus" toward Harkins. Kleiman admitted that this might be the case, but he emphasized the marked differences of opinion between MACV and the U.S. embassy. The White House, he insisted, must negotiate a settlement. South Vietnam was as sound as it ever would be, providing a chance to resolve the matter.[95]

The White House rejected neutralization, charging that such hasty action would facilitate North Vietnam's takeover of the south. Hanoi would "remain exactly as it is, the Communist regime, a member of the Communist bloc, and . . . would then press for far-reaching changes, something that they call neutralization, in South Viet Nam." Rusk cynically observed that "we have run into that before, where they say 'On our side of the line nothing is to be changed, but on your side of the line something must be changed.'" South Vietnam was undergoing a relentless "attack from the outside through penetration, infiltration, arms supplies, subversive activities, matters of that sort." Neutralization would provide the North Vietnamese with "some formula by which they can bring South Viet Nam within the Communist world." Although Rusk proclaimed that South Vietnam must determine its own fate, the *Pentagon Papers* more nearly expressed the truth: "The new government would be heavily dependent on U.S. advice and support, not only for the war effort, but also in the practical problems of running the country."[96]

The White House staunchly opposed negotiations because, Forrestal declared, South Vietnam was not ready to stand on its own and would regard such an approach as "a complete sellout by the U.S." The administration looked forward to the time when South Vietnam could "deal with the North on at least a basis of equality." Both the president and the National Security Council wanted to withdraw from Vietnam as soon as the Saigon government no longer needed protection. "We had not yet reached that point, however." Rusk feared that Halberstam's article had damaged the administration's relations with the new regime by exposing divisions in the aid effort.[97]

The CIA, however, confirmed most of Halberstam's allegations. The military junta *did* consider Harkins "a symbol of the old order," which helps to explain why the conspirators had maintained little contact with U.S. military officials. The coup leaders had refused to share their plans with Harkins out of fear that he would pass them to the palace. The coup therefore surprised both Harkins and MACV. Lodge, according to the CIA, deserved a share of the blame for not working closely with the Country Team. The White House had contributed to the problem by instructing him to discuss a coup only with the CIA, shutting out Harkins from decision making.[98]

In accordance with Rusk's earlier argument, the administration used the coup's success to justify thinking about withdrawal. The defense department affirmed plans to bring home 1,000 servicemen. The president, however, refused to mention numbers. Before a press conference on November 14, he asserted that at the scheduled Honolulu Conference in six days, his advisers would develop detailed plans for the initial troop withdrawal. Did the administration still intend to bring back 1,000 troops by the end of 1963? "We are going to bring back several hundred before the end of the year," Kennedy responded. "But I think on the question of the exact number, I thought we would wait until the meeting of November 20th." Withdrawal would take place once the South Vietnamese were able to "maintain themselves as a free and independent country." Military officials were less circumspect. In Saigon on November 15, Major General Charles Timmes, MAAG's head since March 1962, announced that the first 1,000 servicemen would pull out in early December, leaving 15,500 there by the end of the year. The Pentagon expressed confidence that the Saigon government would have the insurgency under control by the close of 1965, allowing the major U.S. involvement to end. On the day the conference convened, Assistant Secretary of Defense Arthur Sylvester told news correspondents that 1,000 soldiers would be home by January 1. The first 300 men would leave Saigon on December 3.[99]

At the Honolulu Conference, Lodge recommended taking advantage of Saigon's stability to begin a military withdrawal. Before forty-five senior officials, including McNamara, Rusk, Taylor, and McGeorge Bundy, the ambassador insisted that the situation was "hopeful" but warned that the moment might not last. "If we can get through the next six months without a serious falling out among the Generals we will be lucky." The withdrawal plan had had a "tonic effect" on Saigon. The Vietnamese now had "a real chain of command, an improved fighting spirit, the commitment of troops to fight the VC." The White House must maintain the scheduled "phasing out [of] U.S. activities and turning them over to the Vietnamese." It must set dates for reducing the military aid programs. "An American presence will be wanted—and needed—in Vietnam for some time in the future. But it should perhaps be a different kind of presence from what exists—and is needed—in Vietnam today."[100]

Accepting Lodge's counsel, the advisers at Honolulu recommended approval of the withdrawal process contained in the Comprehensive Plan for South Vietnam. The initial recall of 1,000 men would take place by the end of 1963 in a "low key fashion," followed by "the withdrawal of all U.S. special assistance units and personnel by the end of calendar year 1965." Despite the sharp rise of Vietcong activity, the noticeable decline in its defections, and the failing amnesty program, the advisers insisted that by early 1966 the U.S. military aid program would have reduced the insurgency "to a level which the Vietnamese themselves could control."[101]

McGeorge Bundy drafted a National Security Action Memorandum based on the Honolulu proceedings that he expected President Kennedy to sign and that some writers have erroneously cited as evidence of his intention to escalate the U.S. military involvement. A close reading of what became NSAM 273 does not support this charge. The White House, Bundy wrote, remained committed to "the withdrawal of U.S. military personnel." The United States and South Vietnam were to focus on the Mekong Delta by "not only [a] military but [a] political, economic, social, educational and informational effort." Rather than enlarging the assistance program, "military and economic assistance should be maintained at such levels that their magnitude and effectiveness in the eyes of the Vietnamese Government do not fall below the levels sustained by the United States in the time of the Diem Government." Bundy's memorandum reiterated White House support for the troop withdrawal process approved by the president on October 2, 1963, and it assured a continued high level of military and economic assistance. It said nothing about expanding the U.S. military presence.[102]

In the late afternoon of Thursday, November 21, 1963, Forrestal spoke with the president in the Oval Office. Kennedy was hours away from leaving for Texas. Forrestal was about to embark on a trip to Cambodia, where he would reassure Prince Norodom Sihanouk of U.S. support for his country's neutrality. On his return from Cambodia, the president asserted, "I want you to come and see me because we have to start to plan for what we are going to do now in South Vietnam. I want to start a complete and very profound review of how we got into this country, and what we thought we were doing, and what we now think we can do. I even want to think about whether or not we should be there." The election campaign precluded any "drastic changes of policy, quickly," but he wanted to consider "how some kind of a gradual shift in our presence in South Vietnam [could] occur."[103]

THE ATMOSPHERE was euphoric in both Saigon and Washington as Diem's fall had taken on the image of a watershed event in U.S.–South Vietnamese relations. The predicted improvement in the war effort would provide an opportunity to begin a graceful phasedown of the U.S. military involvement.

CONCLUSION
The Tragedy of JFK

There is better assurance than under Diem that the war can be won.

U.S. Department of State, November 23, 1963

I am not going to lose Vietnam. I am not going to be the President who saw Southeast Asia go the way China went.

President Lyndon B. Johnson, November 24, 1963

[Had President Kennedy lived,] there would have been a lot of Americans alive today that aren't and a hell of a lot of Vietnamese.

Roger Hilsman, September 17, 2001

JUST AS the withdrawal plan moved closer to implementation, President Kennedy was assassinated on November 22, 1963, bringing the process to a close. His successor, Lyndon B. Johnson, assured Americans that he would continue his predecessor's domestic and foreign policies. Indeed, *Newsweek* observed that the White House intended to fulfill its October 2 decision to withdraw 1,000 troops by the end of the year. In a bitter irony, however, Johnson's pledge to continuity helped to undermine the rest of the withdrawal plan because the Kennedy administration had so carefully kept its existence from public view that any further troop reduction would appear to repudiate previous policy. Johnson, according to Ball, "would have been subject to all kinds of attack—that the moment he gets in, he turns his back on the policy of President Kennedy and gives something to the communists." The United States still intended to withdraw the first thousand troops in Vietnam by the end of the year; but the Johnson administration escalated the nation's military involvement, and the heart of the plan soon died.[1]

I

THE DIFFERENCES in style and emphasis between Kennedy and Johnson became evident just two days after the assassination, when the new president first discussed Vietnam with his national security advisers. That subject was not at the top of Johnson's agenda, but the timing of Lodge's visit home had led to the meeting. McNamara, Rusk, Ball, McCone, McGeorge Bundy, and other officials had gathered with the president on the Sunday afternoon of November 24 to hear Lodge's report on Vietnam. Contradictory assessments continued to perplex the White House. The state department had just asserted that "there is better assurance than under Diem that the war can be won." Lodge predicted substantial progress by March 1964. McCone highlighted the swelling Vietcong activity. Johnson pondered the matter for a moment before expressing "serious misgivings" about the wisdom of turning out the Diem regime. He had never been pleased with U.S. operations in Vietnam, and he abhorred the infighting among Americans in Saigon. Johnson's position should not have been surprising. His May 1961 visit to Saigon showed his willingness to escalate the military involvement, even to dropping all demands for social reforms as a quid pro quo for stronger military action by the South Vietnamese. But he had not wanted to Americanize the war. "American combat troop involvement is not only not required," he reported to Kennedy, "it is not desirable." At a National Security Council meeting on August 31, 1963, Johnson had opposed U.S. involvement in a coup. Now, no longer second in command, he clarified his stand. It was not important to "reform every Asian into our own image." He had little patience with "do-gooders" and demanded immediate results in the war. "I am not going to lose Vietnam," he told his advisers. "I am not going to be the President who saw Southeast Asia go the way China went."[2]

President Johnson's pronouncement signaled an imminent change in American policy toward Vietnam. Whereas Kennedy had been skeptical about CIA and joint chiefs' wisdom after the abortive Bay of Pigs invasion, his successor turned to them for advice. Hilsman later argued that when Johnson became president, "his mind had been made up that the people he was going to listen to were the guys with the military hard line and that he was not going to listen to any others." McNamara's repeated trips to Vietnam over the past three years had "elevated the problem" by turning the public's focus even more to military issues. At one point, Hilsman became so infuriated over another McNamara visit that he followed President Kennedy into his Oval Office to complain. "With some impatience," Hilsman noted, "as if he were dealing with some unruly child, which he was at the moment, he said, 'Look, Roger, I know that. I know that it's costly and bad to send McNamara out there. But the only way that we can keep the JCS on board is to keep McNamara on board, and the only way we can keep McNamara on board is to let him go see for himself. Now that's the price we have to pay."[3]

Kennedy, Hilsman thought, "had to make more concessions than were wise to the military because Rusk did not stand up as much as he should have." The secretary of state "did not serve Kennedy well, in the sense that he did not present the case for the political side vigorously" and just "tended to sit there." Without Rusk's support, Hilsman asserted, he, Harriman, and Forrestal faced an uphill battle in attempting to restrain the militancy of McNamara, McCone, and the joint chiefs. As long as Kennedy was alive, "we [had] Bob Kennedy on our side and we [had] the President on our side." But with the president dead, Hilsman concluded, "we [were] finished."[4]

After the advisers filed out of the hour-long meeting, one of Johnson's aides, Bill Moyers, came into the room. He found the president pensive as he sat back in his chair with feet resting on a wastebasket and sipping Scotch. Shaking the ice in his glass, Johnson asserted above the tinkling sound that the Chinese will "think with Kennedy dead, we've lost heart. So they'll think we're yellow and we don't mean what we say." The "fellas in the Kremlin," he added, will also "be taking the measure of us. They'll be wondering just how far they can go." "What are you going to do?" asked Moyers. "I told them [Lodge and McCone] that I'm not going to let Vietnam go the way of China. I told them to go back and tell those generals in Saigon that Lyndon Johnson intends to stay by our word. But, by God, I want them to get off their butts and get out in those jungles and whip hell out of some Communists. And I want them to leave me alone, because I've got some bigger things to do right here at home."[5]

Perhaps disturbed by Johnson's hard line, Lodge made a proposal that aroused no support from the new administration: a U.S. withdrawal through the neutralization of *North* Vietnam. On the basis of intelligence reports indicating Hanoi's wishes to end the war, Lodge concluded that its leaders wanted above all to see the Americans leave. The White House should seek some quid pro quo for withdrawing its troops "rather than handing it to them on a silver platter, as our present plans for withdrawal would do." If Hanoi agreed to pull out its forces, the White House should reciprocate. In a recommendation that demonstrated his failure to grasp Hanoi's resolve, Lodge urged the White House to warn the North Vietnamese of military retaliation if they continued helping the Vietcong. What Lodge wanted, Hilsman keenly noted, was to convert North Vietnam into "a Communist neutral along the lines of Yugoslavia."[6]

A change in policy became unmistakable when Johnson decided to relieve Lodge of his post. The president considered Lodge a poor administrator who leaked news to the press and encouraged discord among Americans in Saigon. To a confidant, Johnson declared that on Vietnam, "we've got to either get in or get out, or get off." We need to put someone there who knows what he is doing. But Johnson also realized that Lodge was a presidential aspirant from the opposing Republican party whose removal could set off a political firestorm capable of interfering with the new administration's domestic reform program. Johnson telephoned J. William Fulbright, his friend and chair of the Senate Foreign Relations Committee, expressing his interest in removing Lodge.

"Why did you send Lodge out there for God's sake? . . . I think he's got things screwed up good . . . that's what I think."

"Well," Fulbright responded, "that is a hell of a situation. . . ."

"What would happen if I moved Lodge? . . . Who does he satisfy?"

Important groups in the Republican party, Fulbright asserted.

Johnson asked Lodge to step down, anyway. A few days after the new president's first advisory meeting on Vietnam, McGeorge Bundy observed that Lodge was "nervous" and "didn't distinguish himself in his interview with the President." The ambassador perhaps knew that Johnson "never thought much of him." The implications of Lodge's eventual recall from Saigon were serious: Johnson had rejected the ambassador's optimistic assessment; the new president's aversion to social reforms in Vietnam meant a greater reliance on military correctives; and his interest in winning the war shelved the withdrawal plan. General Taylor became the new ambassador in the summer of 1964, a move that sent another signal of the president's military emphasis.[7]

The sharp change in direction became clear in the president's decision to revise NSAM 273 by raising the level of covert actions against Hanoi. McGeorge Bundy had drafted the original document for President Kennedy, just after the November conference in Honolulu. But whereas Kennedy had supported a reduced commitment based on a partial success at best, the new president intended to win the war. Bundy's draft (prepared for Kennedy) had sought to enhance South Vietnam's capacity to fight North Vietnam on sea and on land; the revised version (approved by Johnson on November 26, 1963) escalated the military situation by focusing on "different levels of possible increased activity" that included "damage to North Vietnam," the "plausibility of denial," and the possibility of "North Vietnamese retaliation." The covert action proposal, code-named OPLAN 34A, went to President Johnson in mid-December 1963. He approved it less than a month later without informing Congress.[8]

The *Pentagon Papers* termed OPLAN 34A "an elaborate program of covert military operations against the state of North Vietnam." The plan authorized "progressively escalating pressure" designed "to inflict increasing punishment upon North Vietnam and to create pressures, which may convince the North Vietnamese leadership, in its own self interest, to desist from its aggressive policies." In cooperation with the Studies and Observation Group, a secret organization established by MACV, the sabotage program ultimately resulted in more than 2,000 covert assaults on North Vietnam. To justify this new focus on the north, Johnson ordered another state department study similar to the Jorden report of December 1961, which had highlighted Hanoi's sponsorship of the insurgency.[9] As soon became evident, President Johnson's signature on OPLAN 34A set in motion the events that led to the Tonkin Gulf crisis of August 1964 and the ultimate decisions to bomb North Vietnam and to inject U.S. combat troops.

The Johnson White House forecast of a longer war did not interfere with the planned withdrawal of 1,000 men. Harkins announced that on December 3, the first 300 military personnel would leave Vietnam, followed by 700 more over the next three weeks. But these figures were misleading. Many of the soldiers were part of the regular turnover of more than a thousand returnees a month. Some were technicians whose jobs in many cases the Vietnamese had assumed. Others went home for medical or other reasons. South Vietnam feared that this first exodus marked the beginning of a premature U.S. evacuation of all forces. In response to concerns expressed by Tran Chanh Thanh, its ambassador to Tunisia and special representative to President Kennedy's funeral, Hilsman emphasized that the departing Americans would be "training personnel" only. "We shall keep in Viet-Nam whatever forces are needed for victory." U.S. military strength by the end of the year remained at nearly 16,000, only a little less than the 16,732 soldiers there during the peak month of October.[10]

The Vietcong's intensified activities drew a sharp response from the White House. President Johnson told both the joint chiefs and the CIA that South Vietnam was "our most critical military area right now." He wanted "blue ribbon men" on every level to take "a fresh new look" at the problem. The joint chiefs chair, General Taylor, assured the president that Harkins would receive "the best officers available." General Thomas Powers, head of the Strategic Air Command, advocated bombing *both* North and South Vietnam. American B-52s, he insisted after returning to Washington, could "pulverize North Vietnam" along with Vietcong bases in the south. General LeMay likewise argued for bombing North Vietnam. "We are swatting flies, when we should be going after the manure pile."[11]

The joint chiefs agreed with Johnson that South Vietnam was "our most critical military area at the moment." In a statement that put all thoughts of withdrawal on indefinite hold, Rusk expressed regret that a heightened war "might seriously derange our prospects for the future." President Johnson lectured McNamara on not doing everything possible to win in Vietnam.[12]

II

THE EXPANSION OF U.S. military action seemed a foregone conclusion by the end of 1963. In early December, the head of Australian forces in Vietnam, Colonel F. P. Serong, warned Lodge that "in its five weeks of existence," the

South Vietnamese government had "shown itself incapable. Meanwhile the war and the nation is disintegrating—*You* must take control of the GVN. Force it to accept policy and executive direction at all levels." Forrestal called for "larger-scale operations against selected targets in the North *provided* we carried them out in connection with a political program designed to get a practical reaction out of Hanoi." He joined Harriman and Hilsman in supporting the deployment of U.S. troops, *not* to fight the war but to discourage North Vietnamese escalation. As warnings, one U.S. division could go into Thailand and another along the Laotian border. All three advisers, Hilsman later recounted, were ready to send a U.S. division into Vietnam, "and so on."[13]

McNamara visited Vietnam in late December and came away convinced of the need for military escalation. The Diem regime had regularly falsified records to demonstrate progress in the war. The highly touted Strategic Hamlet Program was a failure. The Vietcong had raised its volume of activities in the areas near Saigon. By the end of 1963, Hanoi had sent nearly 40,000 cadres and soldiers to South Vietnam, most of them natives of the south but trained as regulars in the north. The situation in the delta had deteriorated so badly that the United States needed to send more than 300 additional military personnel to accompany South Vietnamese battalions in the field.[14]

McNamara mentioned nothing about signs of unrest among American soldiers. Shortly before his death in early 1964, U.S. Air Force Captain Edwin Shank of Winamac, Indiana, and a graduate of Notre Dame University, wrote a series of letters to his wife and family that emphasized the downward turn of the war. In excerpts that *Newsweek* published, Shank declared that the Vietcong forces were "mean, vicious, well-trained veterans" and "killers" in a "big, mean war." "We are getting beat" because we are "undermanned and undergunned." If the administration sent combat troops, Shank wrote in early December 1963, "we could win and win fast." The Vietcong was "kind of a Mafia" that terrorized people in villages where Americans had been and then sold these people "insurance" to ward off further attack. The defense secretary had just visited Saigon and returned home to manage the war with "his screwed-up bunch of people" that Shank derisively called "McNamara's Band." McNamara had infuriated the pilots when they complained about not being able to understand the air controller. They should learn Vietnamese, McNamara curtly replied. There was not enough time, one of the men responded. Then stay there for two years, he shot back. McNamara's "lucky to be alive," according to Shank. "Some of the guys honestly had to be held back from beating this idiot up." Although McNamara was second in command to the president, "as a military man, he finishes a definite and decided last—all the way last."[15]

Not deterred by this episode, McNamara called for covert actions in the north, all aimed at "maximum pressure with minimum risk" and certain to escalate the war. Then, in late 1963, an early November decision by the Kennedy administration began to have a notable impact on Johnson's policy. "Operation Switchback" had greatly enhanced the military's control over the war by transferring to it all CIA paramilitary actions. As Colby asserted, "the military wanted to do its own thing, and neither wanted nor listened to [the] CIA's political ideas of how to fight the war." He had warned McNamara at the November conference in Honolulu that covert operations in North Vietnam would fail. The secretary "listened to me with a cold look and then rejected my advice. The desire to put pressure onto North Vietnam prevailed, and there and then the United States military started the planning and activity that would escalate finally to full-scale air attacks."[16] McNamara had condoned an action that ultimately escalated the U.S. military involvement at the same time he had been urging a military withdrawal. Never did it seem more clear that Hilsman was correct in accusing the defense secretary of inconsistency.

The outward appearance of McNamara's resolve hid the reality of his inner doubts. In a strikingly ambivalent conclusion that did not slow the president's rush to stronger action, McNamara emphasized the need to "watch the situation very carefully, running scared, hoping for the best, but preparing for more forceful moves."[17]

Johnson had conceded the initiative to the military. Before becoming president, he as Senate majority leader had felt a deep-rooted animosity toward the military, largely because of its poorly prepared presentations before appropriations committees and later when its officers ignored him while he was vice president. But as a southerner, Johnson realized that it was good politics to support the joint chiefs and cultivated them at the Christmas Eve reception in the White House. "Just let me get elected," he told them, "and then you can have your war."[18]

The Johnson White House could not have known about a dark prospect that emanated from China. General Li Tianyou, deputy chief of staff of the People's Liberation Army of China, had led a military inspection team to North Vietnam in December 1963 that culminated in a Chinese decision to provide a war plan and to help build defenses and naval bases in the Tonkin Delta region. Encouraged by Beijing's assistance and yet badly divided over what to do after the coup, the Vietnam Workers' Party reached a compromise at the Ninth Plenum of the Third Congress in early December 1963: Hanoi would increase military aid to the south but send no combat units. Le Duan approved Mao Zedong's call for revolutionary war through the peasants. North Vietnam was ready to escalate the push for a revolution.[19]

The Soviet Union posed less of an immediate threat, but by early 1964 it showed more interest in Vietnam, primarily because of the growing rift with the Chinese. In late January of that year, representatives from the Lao

Dong party visited Moscow to explore its views on the fighting in Vietnam. Headed by Le Duan, the delegation (including Le Duc Tho and Hoang Van Hoan, both members of the politburo and secretaries of the central committee) informed the Soviets of the party's December decision to escalate the conflict. What was the Soviet reaction? Hanoi had inflated its role in the "world revolutionary process," Moscow charged; national liberation movements were *not* the key to success. Le Duan and his cohort defended their position, "belittl[ing] the importance of assistance the Soviet Union and other socialist countries provide[d] to the struggles for freedom and national independence." The Soviets should drop their call for peaceful coexistence with the West and work toward worldwide unity of the Communist movement. Soviet Communists and Chinese Communists must cooperate with each other. Moscow, however, extended only moral support.[20]

Bolstered by Chinese favor, the Vietcong focused its actions primarily on American advisers and their families. In the first three weeks of February 1964, terrorists launched more than a dozen assaults on Americans, killing six and wounding nearly 100 by crude bombs and homemade grenades. One bomb exploded in an American movie house, taking the lives of three U.S. soldiers and injuring forty-nine others (including women and children). Another explosive blew up bleachers at a baseball field used by Americans, killing two and wounding twenty-three. Terrorists tossed bombs in bars frequented by Americans and grenades into American homes and cars. They attacked U.S. military advisers in their quarters at night. Although American soldiers had authority to fire back, these tactics had little impact on terrorists who threw a grenade from the street or mailed a package containing a bomb. More guards were posted around military barracks, homes, and on school buses. Americans no longer gathered in large numbers. Many families evacuated the country. Such measures created the illusion that the enemy was much stronger than it was. The Communists fed on this fear, claiming credit for Diem's overthrow and declaring their intention to "throw out the American imperialists." Their weapons did not come from Hanoi or Beijing, which weakened the arguments for retaliating against North Vietnam. As one news correspondent put it, "Nothing much can be done about terrorism, you are told, except to tighten security and get on with the war."[21]

The withdrawal plan faded even more deeply into the past. *Newsweek* reported that the previous year's talk of pulling out of Vietnam in 1965 "no longer is heard" and that the war would "go on indefinitely." President Johnson told McNamara in February 1964 that he had always considered it "foolish" to speak publicly of withdrawing. "I thought it was bad psychologically. But you and the President [Kennedy] thought otherwise and I just sat silent." Now even the most inveterate optimists saw 1967 as a possibility. A senior U.S. military adviser insisted that to speak of any specific date was "meaningless."[22]

In mid-March 1964, McNamara returned to Washington from yet another trip to Vietnam, offering the president a sobering report: "The situation has unquestionably been growing worse, at least since September." Just days earlier, the defense secretary had urged Johnson "to say as little as possible" about Vietnam. "The frank answer is we don't know what's going on out there." Hanoi's increased support to the Vietcong, he now asserted, necessitated greater U.S. military and economic assistance to Saigon. For the South Vietnamese to go "on a war footing," they needed more armed forces, a guerrilla contingent to take the offensive, airplanes for bombing and strafing missions, and authorization for military actions in Cambodia and for "hot pursuit" and ARVN ground operations into Laos. Within thirty days, a program of "Graduated Overt Military Pressure" would begin against North Vietnam. The concept of a phased withdrawal based on South Vietnam's improvement remained "sound," with major reductions in U.S. military training personnel "possible before the end of 1965." But this calendar seemed unlikely. The United States must "do the job regardless of how long it takes."[23]

The atmosphere of optimism had washed away in the face of what one news correspondent termed the "drift toward defeat." Vietnamese children no longer waved at Americans; now they turned their backs. When asked how many students were willing to take the war to the north, a leading Vietnamese official tersely replied, "Not a single one." Yet most leading Vietnamese insisted that the Vietcong would not win the war because "the U.S. cannot afford to lose it."[24]

President Johnson quickly approved McNamara's recommendations, providing an appropriate requiem for the Comprehensive Plan for South Vietnam: "The policy should continue of withdrawing United States personnel where their roles can be assumed by South Vietnamese and of sending additional men if they are needed. It will remain the policy of the United States to furnish assistance and support to South Vietnam for as long as it is required to bring Communist aggression and terrorism under control."[25]

The Johnson administration seemed determined to relive the last half-decade. Jorden had reported a much higher level of North Vietnamese military and economic assistance to the south. The pattern of governmental deception continued. Although the thousand troops had left on schedule, the White House, according to the *Pentagon Papers*, had played with the numbers "by concentrating rotations home in December and letting strength rebound in the subsequent two months." A veritable "People's Republic of the Viet Cong" governed the delta, running a military center, controlling the waterways, and collecting taxes. As in late 1961, Washington's leaders planned a major military buildup to counter the rising Vietcong threat and to resuscitate America's credibility. And, as was the case with the Kennedy administration, the Johnson White House turned to Lodge, sending him back as ambassador in July 1965. The following month, in a final winding back of the clock, the administration returned Lansdale to Saigon as Lodge's assistant in charge of pacification.[26]

But there were notable distinctions between the presidents: Kennedy had maintained that only the South Vietnamese could win the war and repeatedly resisted the demands for bombing North Vietnam, sending combat troops, and taking charge of the war; Johnson adopted all three measures. Admittedly, the war had taken a more serious turn after Kennedy's death, but the most crucial consideration in assessing what he might have done was his willingness to accept an outcome other than a traditional military victory. Ironically, both presidents came to realize the wisdom of de-Americanizing the war in an approach that another president, Richard Nixon, would claim as his own under the label of "Vietnamization." And, again ironically, Nixon would join the previous two presidents in justifying military escalation as the chief step toward withdrawal. On the basis of this twisted logic, the United States became entrapped in its longest war.

III

HAD KENNEDY LIVED, would he have pursued the withdrawal plan? Were Robert F. Kennedy, Theodore Sorensen, and William Bundy correct in asserting that President Kennedy would never have pulled out of Vietnam?[27]

Nothing suggests that the president would have given up his attempt to return the military commitment to its early 1961 level. Gilpatric maintained that Kennedy's views toward Vietnam were "consistent with everything he did do and said before his death," meaning that "he would have been very reluctant to involve ourselves to the extent that the country did after President Johnson took over." Gilpatric's argument is persuasive. Never in Kennedy's thousand days in office did he stray from the principle that the war was South Vietnam's to win or lose. Nor did he ever forget General MacArthur's warning against land wars in Asia. There is no reason to believe that Kennedy would have listened more closely to the joint chiefs. The Bay of Pigs fiasco still weighed heavily on his mind. The Cuban missile crisis remained an indelible memory. The ongoing Berlin troubles caused continuous talk of war. To tone down the Cold War thrust of the nation's foreign policy, the president intended to replace Rusk with McNamara as secretary of state. Kennedy's only reservation about moving McNamara from the defense department was that the White House might lose control over the military.[28] The critical point is that Kennedy expressed interest in pulling out all special military forces (albeit after the 1964 election) short of victory.

Robert Kennedy, Sorensen, and Bundy were also correct. The young president had matured in office, realizing that military force was not always a guarantor of peace. And yet he also considered a total withdrawal to be unacceptable. The only solution lay somewhere between the two extremes—a partial disengagement. To phase out special military assistance did not constitute an abandonment of Vietnam. MAAG would maintain its advisory role as an integral part of a continuing military and economic assistance program. President Kennedy sought to reduce the U.S. involvement, not end it.[29]

The existence of a withdrawal plan has long been a matter of heated dispute, particularly to those who served in both the Kennedy and Johnson administrations and who, therefore, have the most in reputation to lose. Years afterward, Rusk insisted that no withdrawal proposal came to his attention, despite the many references in the official record and despite his presence at several discussions of the matter. McNamara recently affirmed that a withdrawal process was under consideration by the time of Kennedy's death, but he never brought this idea before President Johnson as a subject for discussion. Galbraith asserted that Kennedy had considered the war unwinnable by the spring of 1963 and sought to return the U.S. involvement to an advisory level. Hilsman, who served the new president for only a short time before resigning, insisted that Kennedy had realized during the Buddhist crisis that the Diem regime could not win the war and that the only feasible solution was to pressure South Vietnam into accepting a neutralization scheme patterned after the Laotian example. "There would have been a lot of Americans alive today that aren't and a hell of a lot of Vietnamese."[30]

If President Kennedy so clearly supported the phased withdrawal plan, why did it fail? His assassination, as noted, was a key factor, but there is more to the story.

From the beginning, President Johnson opposed a major disengagement from Vietnam. The new chief executive was in a hurry to implement reforms at home and sought victory in the war without delay. Not chastened by the Bay of Pigs fiasco, he invited advice from the CIA and joint chiefs, who advocated direct attacks on North Vietnam. Johnson at first rejected both a ground assault and major aerial support, but he ultimately changed his stance. Victory soon assumed its traditional meaning of destroying an enemy rather than reducing the Vietcong to roving, desperate bands that the ARVN could control.

Johnson's decision to escalate the U.S. military role found favor among most civilian and military advisers in Washington. In the final days of the Kennedy administration, Rusk had revealed a marked propensity for stronger action, but as a loyal team player, he continued to support the president. McNamara, too, had stood with his superior in the White House, despite having to deal on a daily basis with military leaders who demanded more stringent action. But it is noteworthy to recall that in the early days of the Kennedy administration—particularly in the aftermath of the aborted Cuban invasion—both Rusk and McNamara were among the many civilian and military advisers who, in the sanctuary of the White House, advocated military action against Hanoi. Like Kennedy, they believed that South Vietnam could not win the war on its own; but like then Vice-President Johnson, they must have privately considered the withdrawal plan an admission of defeat. Now, after the assassination, they agreed with Johnson in supporting U.S. military escalation as the primary means for achieving victory.[31]

In August 1964, during the Tonkin Gulf crisis, congressional members expressed concern over their nation's deepening involvement in Vietnam and asked McNamara about the earlier talk of withdrawal. The defense secretary explained that the Kennedy administration had made progress in Vietnam until the Buddhist eruption in May 1963 endangered the war effort and fostered an atmosphere conducive to the November coup. Political instability then engulfed the nation in the aftermath of Diem's death, followed by another governmental overthrow in late January 1964 that put the Vietcong into the position to exploit South Vietnam's political and military weaknesses. Consequently, McNamara asserted, "It is now necessary to add further U.S. military assistance to counter that Viet Cong offensive." The fall of 1963 was the turning point. "We have never made the statement since September, 1963, that we believed we could bring the bulk of the training forces out by the end of 1965, because the actions in November [1963] and January [1964] made it quite clear that would not be possible." And yet, as the presidential tapes show, McNamara urged President Kennedy as late as October 2, 1963, to pursue the withdrawal plan as "a way to get out of Vietnam." Kennedy's assassination brought the process to a halt.[32]

The plan, however, had almost ground to a stop *before* the events of November 22, 1963. Chiefly at fault was the failure of President Kennedy and his advisers to explore the enormous implications of their policies. Withdrawal through escalation had become both the strategy and the objective, which in the immediate sense seemed practical but in the long run had catastrophic potential. Always in demand was a rapid solution that, as it should have been clear, played into the hands of an enemy whose strategy of revolutionary war rested on a protracted political and armed struggle. None of the president's advisers thoroughly examined the ramifications of the two remedies most discussed: sending U.S. combat troops and becoming involved in a coup. Kennedy carefully restrained the advocates of direct military action, but he exercised no similar caution toward promoting a coup. He asked critical questions about a troop commitment that revealed its dangers. He recognized that the initial deployment would automatically require more men and thus lead to either an unlimited commitment or an embarrassing retreat. But he did not ask equally crucial questions about White House complicity in a coup. Was there a satisfactory alternative to Diem? Could the United States escape blame? What happened if the coup led to loss of life? Would the president become an accessory to murder?

Perhaps it is appropriate to return to where we began—with the Archbishop of Canterbury, Thomas Becket. In twelfth-century England, King Henry II became so irate over Becket's loyalty to the church over the throne that he reportedly shouted in the presence of advisers, "Will no one rid me of this turbulent priest?" Soon afterward, four knights killed Becket, raising profound questions about guilt and innocence.[33] Were the king's words a mere outburst of anger, not intended to incite his subjects into committing murder? Or had he beguiled them into an action for which he could deny responsibility? Knowing that the challenge had come from a king, the knights doubtless thought they were carrying out his wishes.

President Kennedy's advisers knew that he wanted Diem out of office and sought to bring this about. Like the king, the president had said nothing about assassination and, in fact, probably expected exile. But, if so, he never made this preference clear to either his advisers or the Vietnamese generals. Indeed, Kennedy's clandestine meeting with Lansdale in the fall of 1963 suggests that assassination was not beyond the realm of possibility. Surely, the king and the president recognized that as heads of state, their expressed desires were tantamount to administrative decrees.

To use another analogy, is the driver of a getaway car in a robbery an accomplice to the crime? What if someone is killed? Is a president who promoted a coup an accomplice in the act? What if someone is assassinated?

Colby later admitted that the driver in a holdup was an accomplice, although he argued (unconvincingly) that there was "a point at which you are no longer responsible for the detailed actions [the thieves] take because they begin to take a responsibility themselves for that." He nonetheless asserted that "when you support a coup through violent overthrow you have to understand that you are taking responsibility for people getting killed." Conein was with the conspirators "in the overthrow, in the coup, no question about it, and he was there with the full knowledge and approval of the Ambassador and full knowledge and approval of people in Washington." The White House was "certainly part of the overthrow . . . And if you talk about overthrows I think you have to accept the responsibility for the fact that President Diem was killed in the overthrow." Admittedly, new developments in the coup led to the decision to kill Diem, but "it is something that you have to anticipate may take place in the event of an overthrow of a government."[34]

The Kennedy administration was a party to the coup and hence to the assassinations of Diem and Nhu. The White House knew that it could spark a coup by assuring the generals of no interference with their actions and of support in the period afterward. In its defense, the White House expected the rebels to ensure the premier's safe departure out of the country, but his decision to flee the palace changed the situation. Big Minh ordered the brothers killed, making President Kennedy and his advisers not only accomplices in a coup but also accessories to murder.

The coup and the assassinations caused confusion and anger in both Washington and Saigon. The Kennedy administration spent valuable time trying to disassociate itself from the events and thereby lost an opportunity in the momentary euphoria of success to revive the withdrawal proposal. Big Minh's decision to order the assassinations, followed by the generals' falling out among themselves over myriad issues, raised questions about whether the new government was, indeed, an improvement over its predecessor. Any thoughts of withdrawal became secondary to these emotional matters. Kennedy's death in Dallas put everything on hold.

THE VIETNAM POLICY of President Kennedy was complex and deeply ironic. He was a hostage of the Cold War, a captive of history's so-called lessons, an advocate of the domino theory, and an avid proponent of intervention in the name of freedom. Vietnam would not have been a critical American issue had he been able to assess the problems in Southeast Asia without viewing them through Cold War lenses. Like Truman and Eisenhower, Kennedy (along with others after him) regarded freedom as indivisible, leading him to respond to perceived Communist challenges in an area of the world that was peripheral to U.S. security. And also like other presidents, he interpreted the West's experiences at Munich in 1938 as demonstrative of the principle that appeasement feeds aggression. Unlike them, however, President Kennedy attempted to disengage from a failing effort, only to find himself stonewalled by his own policies.

President Kennedy's central tragedy lies in his ill-advised decision to promote a coup aimed at facilitating a military withdrawal from Vietnam. His action set the administration on a path that tied the United States more closely to Vietnam, furthered the Communists' revolutionary war strategy by igniting political chaos in Saigon, and obstructed his plan to bring the troops home. No one can know, of course, what Kennedy would have done had he lived, but his assassination ended the waning prospect of withdrawal. Kennedy's legacy was a highly volatile situation in Vietnam that, in the hands of a new leader seeking victory, lay open to full-scale military escalation. President Johnson soon Americanized the war that resulted in the death of a generation.

NOTES

Introduction

1. John F. Kennedy, "America's Stake in Vietnam," *Vital Speeches* 22 (Aug. 1, 1956): 617–19.

2. Merle L. Pribbenow, trans., *Victory in Vietnam: The Official History of the People's Army of Vietnam, 1954–1975* (Lawrence: University Press of Kansas, 2002), 3–5, 86; William J. Duiker, *Sacred War: Nationalism and Revolution in a Divided Vietnam* (New York: McGraw-Hill, 1995), 137; John M. Gates, "People's War in Vietnam," *Journal of Military History* 54 (July 1990): 332.

3. Roger Hilsman, "McNamara's War—Against the Truth: A Review Essay," *Political Science Quarterly* 111 (Spring 1996): 155; author's interview with Roger Hilsman, Sept. 17, 2001; transcript, U. Alexis Johnson, 28, c. mid-1961–64, by William Brubeck, for John F. Kennedy Library (hereafter referred to as JFKL) Oral History Program.

4. Pribbenow, trans., *Victory in Vietnam*, 76, 78, 103; Douglas Pike, *Viet Cong: The Organization and Techniques of the National Liberation Front of South Vietnam* (Cambridge, Mass.: MIT Press, 1966), 31–33; Douglas Pike, *PAVN: People's Army of Vietnam* (Novato, Calif.: Presidio Press, 1986), 216–22; John Shy and Thomas W. Collier, "Revolutionary War," in Peter Paret, ed., *Makers of Modern Strategy: From Machiavelli to the Nuclear Age* (Princeton, N.J.: Princeton University Press, 1986), 817, 850, 855–56; Gates, "People's War in Vietnam," 327–28, 343.

5. There were 12,000 Vietcong "hardcore Communists" in South Vietnam by 1961, according to one study. See "Outline Chief MAAG Vietnam," mid-[?] 1961, Vice-Presidential Security File, Nations and Regions: Program for South Vietnam, box 10, Lyndon B. Johnson Library (hereafter referred to as LBJL). Arthur M. Schlesinger, Jr., believes the number to be 15,000. See his study, *A Thousand Days: John F. Kennedy in the White House* (Boston: Houghton Mifflin, 1965), 451, 452. These numbers did not reflect the many other men, women, and children who supported the insurgency and fell within its organizational structure.

6. Transcript, W. Averell Harriman, June 6, 1965, pp. 102–4 by Arthur M. Schlesinger, Jr., for JFKL Oral History Program; McNamara quoted in Thomas G. Paterson, "Bearing the Burden: A Critical Look at JFK's Foreign Policy," *Virginia Quarterly Review* 54 (Spring 1978): 203; Dean Rusk, *As I Saw It* (New York: W. W. Norton, 1990), 435.

7. Author's interview with Hilsman, Sept. 17, 2001; Hilsman, "McNamara's War," 153–54; President's press conference, March 23, 1961, National Security File (hereafter referred to as NSF), Countries—Laos, March 23–24, 1961, box 130–131, JFKL; U.S. Policy on Laos, April 7, 1961, ibid.; James N. Giglio, *The Presidency of John F. Kennedy* (Lawrence: University Press of Kansas, 1991), 241; Robert McNamara, *In Retrospect: The Tragedy and Lessons of Vietnam* (New York: Random House, 1995), 32–33.

8. Lawrence J. Bassett and Stephen E. Pelz, "The Failed Search for Victory: Vietnam and the Politics of War," in Thomas G. Paterson, ed., *Kennedy's Quest for Victory: American Foreign Policy, 1961–1963* (New York: Oxford University Press, 1989), 229; Giglio, *Presidency of John F. Kennedy*, 241.

9. Rostow to Rusk, Jan. 6, 1961, pp. 2–3, 8–9, President's Office File (hereafter referred to as POF), Staff Memoranda Nov. 1960–Feb. 1961—Rostow, box 64a, JFKL; Walt W. Rostow, *The Stages of Economic Growth, A Non-Communist Manifesto* (Cambridge, Engl.: Cambridge University Press, 1960); William J. Rust, *Kennedy in Vietnam: American Vietnam Policy, 1960–1963* (New York: Charles Scribner's Sons, 1985), 31; JFK's Inaugural Address, Jan. 20, 1961, *Public Papers of the Presidents of the United States: John F. Kennedy, 1961* (Washington, D.C.: Government Printing Office, 1962), 1; David Halberstam, *The Making of a Quagmire: America and Vietnam during the Kennedy Era* (New York: Alfred A. Knopf, 1964; revised ed., New York: Alfred A. Knopf, 1988); David Halberstam, *The Best and the Brightest* (New York: Random House, 1969); Neil Sheehan, *A Bright Shining Lie: John Paul Vann and America in Vietnam* (New York: Random House, 1988).

10. Hedrick Smith, "220 G.I.'s Leave South Vietnam as Troop Reduction Gets Under Way," *New York Times*, Dec. 4, 1963, p. 1; "South Vietnam: The Break-Even Point," *Newsweek*, Dec. 2, 1963, p. 57; Hilsman, "McNamara's War," 161.

11. Hilsman, "McNamara's War," 158; Mme. Nhu quoted in Schlesinger, *Thousand Days*, 451. For background of Diem and family, see Denis Warner, *The Last Confucian: Vietnam, Southeast Asia, and the West* (New York: Macmillan, 1963), chap. 5, and Robert Scigliano, *South Vietnam: Nation under Stress* (Boston: Houghton Mifflin, 1964), 13–24.

12. Author's interview with Galbraith, March 28, 2001; author's interview with Hilsman, Sept. 17, 2001; author's interview with McNamara, March 5, April 17, 2001.

13. Author's interview with Galbraith, March 28, 2001; Galbraith to author, Oct. 10, 2001 (letter in author's possession); Rusk, *As I Saw It*, 83; author's interview with Hilsman, Sept. 17, 2001.

14. Author's interview with Hilsman, Sept. 17, 2001; author's interview with Rostow, Feb. 20, 2001; author's interview with Galbraith, March 28, 2001; author's interview with McNamara, April 17, 2001. Hilsman thought that President Kennedy might replace Rusk with McGeorge Bundy.

15. Author's interview with McNamara, April 17, 2001; author's interview with Hilsman, Sept. 17, 2001.

16. Other historians have made this argument before me, daring to speculate about what might have resulted in Vietnam had the bullets missed Kennedy. The three most deeply researched works on Kennedy and Vietnam are: John M.

Newman, *JFK and Vietnam: Deception, Intrigue, and the Struggle for Power* (New York: Warner Books, 1992); Fredrik Logevall, *Choosing War: The Lost Chance for Peace and the Escalation of War in Vietnam* (Berkeley: University of California Press, 1999); and David Kaiser, *American Tragedy: Kennedy, Johnson, and the Origins of the Vietnam War* (Cambridge, Mass.: Harvard University Press, 2000). Logevall most directly speculates about what might have been, but he bases his thoughts on sound reasoning. President Kennedy, Logevall maintains, had always been ambivalent about the war, never wavering from his desire to win but recognizing the danger of enlarging U.S. intervention without allied support and understanding the domestic political costs involved in taking over the war. Despite Kennedy's setbacks in foreign policy, he had earned sufficient credibility to permit him to change Vietnam policy after his presumed reelection in 1964. He knew that political reforms in Vietnam were more important than battlefield victories; he had no Great Society program to implement; and, having faced a number of crises while in office for three years, he had less need than Johnson to prove himself. The dire situation in Vietnam by late 1964 would doubtless have encouraged Kennedy to reduce the U.S. commitment. See Logevall, *Choosing War*, 395–400, and his essay, "Vietnam and the Question of What Might Have Been," in Mark J. White, ed., *Kennedy: The New Frontier Revisited* (New York: New York University Press, 1998), 43–48.

17. Emmet John Hughes, "A Lesson from Vietnam," *Newsweek*, Sept. 9, 1963, p. 17.

18. T. S. Eliot, *Murder in the Cathedral* (New York: Harcourt, Brace, 1935), 44.

Chapter 1

1. JFK and Rostow quotes in Walt W. Rostow, *The Diffusion of Power: An Essay in Recent History* (New York: Macmillan, 1972), 264–65, and transcript, Walt W. Rostow Oral History Interview, I: 63–64, March 21, 1969, by Paige E. Mulhollan, LBJL; Cecil B. Currey, *Edward Lansdale: The Unquiet American* (Boston: Houghton Mifflin, 1988), 224; Richard Reeves, *President Kennedy: Profile of Power* (New York: Simon and Schuster, 1993), 46, 46 n.; Fred I. Greenstein and Richard H. Immerman, "What Did Eisenhower Tell Kennedy about Indochina? The Politics of Misperception," *Journal of American History* 79 (Sept. 1992): 568–87.

2. Khrushchev quoted in William C. Gibbons, *The U.S. Government and the Vietnam War: Executive and Legislative Roles and Relationships*, 4 vols. (Princeton, N.J.: Princeton University Press, 1986), 2: 16; Bundy to Rusk, McNamara, and Dulles, Jan. 27, 1961, NSF, Countries—Vietnam, box 194, JFKL; Bassett and Pelz, "Failed Search for Victory," 229; Schlesinger, *Thousand Days*, 253; George McT. Kahin, *Intervention: How America Became Involved in Vietnam* (New York: Knopf, 1986), 128, 129; transcript, Walt W. Rostow, April 11, 1964, p. 46, by Richard Neustadt, for JFKL Oral History Program.

3. William J. Duiker, *Ho Chi Minh* (New York: Hyperion, 2000), 509–10; Robert K. Brigham, *Guerrilla Diplomacy: The NLF's Foreign Relations and the Viet Nam War* (Ithaca, N.Y.: Cornell University Press, 1999), 4–6; Duiker, *Sacred War*, 117; Communist party member quoted in Ronald H. Spector, *Advice and Support:*

The Early Years of the U.S. Army in Vietnam, 1941–1960 (New York: The Free Press, 1985), 312.

4. Duiker, *Ho Chi Minh*, 511–12.

5. Ibid., 512–13; Pribbenow, trans., *Victory in Vietnam*, 49–50.

6. Duiker, *Ho Chi Minh*, 513.

7. Pribbenow, trans., *Victory in Vietnam*, 45, 51, 73; Duiker, *Ho Chi Minh*, 513; Gates, "People's War in Vietnam," 330, 333, 335–36, 343; John M. Gates, "Vietnam: The Debate Goes On," *Parameters: Journal of the U.S. Army War College* 14 (June 1984): 43–56; Duiker, *Sacred War*, 134–37; William J. Duiker, *The Communist Road to Power in Vietnam* (Boulder, Colo.: Westview Press, 1981), 198; Brigham, *Guerrilla Diplomacy*, x–xi; Pike, *Viet Cong*, 80; George C. Herring, *America's Longest War: The United States and Vietnam, 1950–1975*, 4th ed. (New York: McGraw-Hill, 2002), 80–81.

8. John Prados, *The Blood Road: The Ho Chi Minh Trail and the Vietnam War* (New York: John Wiley and Sons, 1999), 9–13; Duiker, *Ho Chi Minh*, 513–15; Brigham, *Guerrilla Diplomacy*, 10.

9. Ilya V. Gaiduk, *The Soviet Union and the Vietnam War* (Chicago: Ivan R. Dee, 1996), 4–6; Duiker, *Ho Chi Minh*, 515; Chen Jian, *Mao's China and the Cold War* (Chapel Hill: University of North Carolina Press, 2001), 206–7.

10. Pribbenow, trans., *Victory in Vietnam*, 51, 79–80; Duiker, *Ho Chi Minh*, 516–17.

11. Letter from the Communist Nambo (Southern) Regional Committee, 4–6, 9–10, March 28, 1960, Indochina Archives: History of the Vietnam War, Unit 5: NLF, General Materials, 1960 (University of California, Berkeley).

12. "The Viet Cong," n.d., ibid.; Pribbenow, trans., *Victory in Vietnam*, 65–66; Duiker, *Ho Chi Minh*, 523–24.

13. Gates, "People's War in Vietnam," 327–28; Duiker, *Ho Chi Minh*, 524–25.

14. Duiker, *Ho Chi Minh*, 525; Pribbenow, trans., *Victory in Vietnam*, 67–68; Truong Nhu Tang, *A Vietcong Memoir: An Inside Account of the Vietnam War and Its Aftermath* (San Diego: Harcourt Brace Jovanovich, 1985), 76–80, Tang's quote on 78; *Declaration of the First Congress of the South Viet Nam National Front for Liberation* (Hanoi: Foreign Languages Publishing House, June 1962), 30, Indochina Archives, General Materials, 1962 (University of California, Berkeley); "Text of 1960 Program," Dec. 20, 1960, pp. 1–7, ibid., General Materials, 1960 (University of California, Berkeley).

15. Duiker, *Ho Chi Minh*, 526; Ho quoted in Truong, *Vietcong Memoir*, 15; Duiker, *PAVN*, 222; Manifesto of the South-Vietnam Section of the Vietnam Labor (Lao Dong) Party on the Establishment of the NLF, Jan. 20, 1961, p. 1, Indochina Archives, Documentation (University of California, Berkeley).

16. Herring, *America's Longest War*, 54, 62; Stanley Karnow, *Vietnam: A History* (New York: Viking, 1983; revised ed., New York: Penguin, 1997), 237–39; Rust, *Kennedy in Vietnam*, 21; McNamara, *In Retrospect*, 32; Halberstam, *Best and the Brightest*, 122–24.

17. Schlesinger, *Thousand Days*, 206, 217; Seymour J. Deitchman, *The Best-Laid Schemes: A Tale of Social Research and Bureaucracy* (Cambridge, Mass.: MIT Press, 1976), 4.

18. William J. Lederer and Eugene Burdick, *The Ugly American* (New York: W. W. Norton, 1958). Lansdale had also served as model for U.S. official Alden Pyle in a British novel. See Graham Greene, *The Quiet American* (New York: Viking Press, 1956). See Reeves, *President Kennedy*, 46–47; Arthur M. Schlesinger, Jr., *Robert Kennedy and His Times*, 2 vols. (Boston: Houghton Mifflin, 1978), 1: 481; Karnow, *Vietnam*, 236.

19. Lansdale to Sec. of Defense Thomas S. Gates, Jan. 17, 1961, U.S. Department of Defense, *United States–Vietnam Relations, 1945–1967* [The Pentagon Papers], 12 vols. (Washington, D.C.: Government Printing Office, 1971) (hereafter referred to as *USVR*), Book 11: 1, 3. Lansdale's report also printed ibid., Book 2: 66–77.

20. William Bundy and numerous others in the administration were convinced that Lansdale wanted the ambassador's post in Saigon. Rust, *Kennedy in Vietnam*, 25. Lansdale had told Washington shortly after the coup effort that Durbrow had "urged Diem to give in to rebel demands to avoid bloodshed." That Durbrow had called for compromise with the rebels earlier and negotiations with them later aroused Diem's suspicions. Lansdale to Deputy Sec. of Defense James H. Douglas, Nov. 15, 1960, U.S. Department of State, *Foreign Relations of the United States* (hereafter referred to as *FRUS*), *1958–1960*, vol. 1: *Vietnam* (Washington, D.C.: Government Printing Office, 1986), 667–68; Kahin, *Intervention*, 125; Currey, *Lansdale*, 223; Lansdale to Gates, Jan. 17, 1961, *USVR*, Book 11: 3–4.

21. Lansdale to Gates, Jan. 17, 1961, *USVR*, Book 11: 4, 8–10.

22. Ibid., 5.

23. Ibid., 5–7.

24. Ibid., 6.

25. Ibid., 7.

26. Ibid., 8.

27. Ibid.; Kahin, *Intervention*, 130.

28. Lansdale to Gates, Jan. 17, 1961, *USVR*, Book 11: 11–12.

29. Summary record of White House meeting, Jan. 28, 1961, *FRUS, 1961–1963*, vol. 1: *Vietnam 1961* (Washington, D.C.: Government Printing Office, 1988), 13; Rostow to Bundy, Jan. 30, 1961, ibid., 16–19; JFK quote, Jan. 30, 1961, ibid., 14; Lansdale quote in Currey, *Lansdale*, 227; transcript, Edward G. Lansdale, July 11, 1970, p. 106 by Dennis J. O'Brien, for JFKL Oral History Program; Giglio, *Presidency of John F. Kennedy*, 239; Currey, *Lansdale*, 224–25; Kahin, *Intervention*, 130–32; Reeves, *President Kennedy*, 48.

30. Notes on meeting in Washington between Rusk and Parsons, Jan. 28, 1961, *FRUS*, 1: *Vietnam 1961*, 19; Kahin, *Intervention*, 130; Reeves, *President Kennedy*, 50; Lansdale oral history transcript, 106–7, JFKL.

31. Summary record of White House meeting, Jan. 28, 1961, *FRUS*, 1: *Vietnam 1961*, 13–14.

32. Paper prepared by Country Team Staff Committee, "Basic Counterinsurgency Plan for Viet-Nam," Jan. 4, 1961, ibid., 1–2.

33. Ibid., 2–3, 5.

34. Ibid., 6–9.

35. Ibid., 9–11.

36. Rostow to Bundy, Jan. 30, 1961, ibid., 17.

37. Summary record of White House meeting, Jan. 28, 1961, ibid., 14–15; Kahin, *Intervention*, 130; Lansdale oral history transcript, 107–8, JFKL.

38. Rostow to McGeorge Bundy, Jan. 30, 1961, *FRUS*, 1: *Vietnam 1961*, 17; Summary record of White House meeting, Jan. 28, 1961, ibid., 14; John M. Newman, *JFK and Vietnam*, 3–4.

39. Summary record of White House meeting, Jan. 28, 1961, *FRUS*, 1: *Vietnam 1961*, 15, 18; Rostow to McGeorge Bundy, Jan. 30, 1961, ibid., 19; Richard H. Shultz, Jr., *The Secret War against Hanoi: Kennedy's and Johnson's Use of Spies, Saboteurs, and Covert Warriors in North Vietnam* (New York: HarperCollins, 1999), 6–7.

40. JFK to Rusk and McNamara, Jan. 30, 1961, POF, Departments and Agencies, Department of State, Jan. 1961, JFKL; McGeorge Bundy to McNamara, NSC Action Memo No. 2, Feb. 3, 1961, ibid., box 77; Mike Gravel, ed., *The Pentagon Papers: The Department of Defense History of United States Decisionmaking on Vietnam*, 4 vols. (Boston: Beacon Press, 1971), 2: 6; Country Team Report, Annex B, cited in Reeves, *President Kennedy*, 50; Shultz, *Secret War against Hanoi*, ix, xiii, 3.

41. Hilsman quote in Marilyn B. Young, *The Vietnam Wars, 1945–1990* (New York: HarperCollins, 1991), 77; Schlesinger, *Thousand Days*, 286–87; first Mao quote on 287; second Mao quote in Paterson, ed., *Kennedy's Quest for Victory*, 13; Gibbons, *U.S. Government and the Vietnam War*, 2: vii, 17.

42. Kahin, *Intervention*, 131–32; Paul M. Kattenburg, *The Vietnam Trauma in American Foreign Policy, 1945–75* (New Brunswick, N.J.: Transactions Books, 1980), 111; Pribbenow, trans., *Victory in Vietnam*, 68, 74–76; Duiker, *Ho Chi Minh*, 527.

Chapter 2

1. Durbrow to Rusk, Feb. 8, 1961, *FRUS*, 1: *Vietnam 1961*, 29–30.

2. Memo of conversation in the Department of State between Bowles and Chuong, Feb. 13, 1961, ibid., 33.

3. Young's notes on field trip to Banmethuot and Vinh Long Provinces, Vietnam, Dec. 8, 1959, NSF, Countries—Laos, Feb. 16–19, 1961, box 130–31, JFKL.

4. Young to Rostow, Feb. 17, 1961, ibid. Diem had introduced the agroville program in the summer of 1959.

5. Ibid.

6. Rostow to JFK, Feb. 23, 1961, p. 13, POF, Staff Memoranda Nov. 1960– Feb. 1961, box 64a, JFKL.

7. Lansdale to Rostow, Feb. 23, 1961, encl.: Lecture before Counter-Guerrilla School, Special Warfare Center, Ft. Bragg, Feb. 24, 1961, ibid.; Currey, *Lansdale*, 267–71; 393 n. 30.

8. Lansdale to Rostow, Feb. 23, 1961, encl.: Lecture before Counter-Guerrilla School, Special Warfare Center, Ft. Bragg, Feb. 24, 1961, POF, Staff Memoranda Nov. 1960–Feb. 1961, box 64a, JFKL.

9. Taber and Lansdale quotes in Currey, *Lansdale*, 272.

10. Memo of conversation between Bowles and Chuong, Feb. 13, 1961, *FRUS*, 1: *Vietnam 1961*, 33; Lansdale to Gilpatric, June 30, 1961, ibid., 190; Edward G. Lansdale, *In the Midst of Wars: An American's Mission to Southeast Asia* (New York:

Harper and Row, 1972), 343, 355–56; Rostow to JFK, Feb. 24, 1961, encl.: Wolf Ladejinsky to Rostow, Feb. 24, 1961, POF, Staff Memoranda Nov. 1960–Feb. 1961, box 64a, JFKL; transcript, Lansdale Oral History Interview, 81–84, JFKL.

11. Rostow to JFK, Feb. 24, 1961, encl.: Ladejinsky to Rostow, Feb. 24, 1961, POF, Staff Memoranda, Nov. 1960–Feb. 1961, box 64a, JFKL.

12. Ibid.

13. Ibid.; Ho quoted in Roy Jumper, "Mandarin Bureaucracy and Politics of South Vietnam," *Pacific Affairs* 30 (March 1957): 47–58; and cited in Fulbright to JFK, March 24, 1961, POF, Vietnam General, 1960–61, box 128, JFKL.

14. Rostow to JFK, Feb. 24, 1961, encl.: Ladejinsky to Rostow, Feb. 24, 1961, POF, Staff Memoranda, Nov. 1960–Feb. 1961, box 64a, JFKL.

15. Ibid.

16. Rusk to Saigon embassy, March 1, 1961, *FRUS*, 1: *Vietnam 1961*, 40–42; Gibbons, *U.S. Government and the Vietnam War*, 2: 17.

17. Durbrow to Rusk, March 8, 1961, *FRUS*, 1: *Vietnam 1961*, 42 n.4.

18. McGarr to Thuan, March 13, 1961, ibid., 45; Durbrow to Rusk, March 16, 1961, ibid., 48–49.

19. Durbrow to Rusk, March 16, 1961, ibid., 50–51.

20. NIE 50–61, March 28, 1961, ibid., 58–59.

21. Memo of conversation in U.S. embassy in Bangkok, March 27, 1961, ibid., 52–53.

22. Ibid., 53.

23. Ibid., 53–54.

24. Rostow to Sorensen, March 16, 1961, quoted in Herbert S. Parmet, *JFK: The Presidency of John F. Kennedy* (New York: Dial Press, 1983), 138; Rostow to JFK, March 29, 1961, POF, Staff Memoranda March–May 1961, box 64a, JFKL. Nolting was deputy permanent representative to NATO. President Kennedy had submitted Nolting's name to the Senate on February 17, and that body approved the appointment on March 15. *FRUS*, vol. 1: *Vietnam 1961*, 46 n. 2.

25. Rostow to JFK, April 3, 1961, *FRUS*, 1: *Vietnam 1961*, 63; memo of discussion at Department of State–Joint Chiefs of Staff meeting, April 14, 1961, ibid., 71; Gibbons, *U.S. Government and the Vietnam War*, 14.

26. Gravel, ed., *Pentagon Papers*, 2: 32; Rostow to JFK, April 12, 1961, *FRUS*, 1: *Vietnam 1961*, 68; memo of discussion at Department of State–Joint Chiefs of Staff meeting, April 14, 1961, ibid., 70–71; memo for record by Chief of Naval Operations Adm. Arleigh Burke, NSC meeting on South Vietnam, April 27, 1961, memo dated April 28, 1961, ibid., 82–83; JFK to Diem, April 26, 1961, ibid., 81; Durbrow to Rusk, April 12, 1961, ibid., 72 n. 2.

27. Komer to Rostow, April 14, 1961, *FRUS*, 1: *Vietnam 1961*, 73 n. 3; Rostow to JFK, April 15, 1961, ibid., 72–73. Komer was later instrumental in establishing the Phoenix Program, which aimed at destroying the Vietcong infrastructure by a variety of methods that included assassination. See Douglas Valentine, *The Phoenix Program* (New York: William Morrow, 1990).

28. JFK quote in Theodore C. Sorensen, *Kennedy* (New York: Harper and Row, 1965), 309; Reeves, *President Kennedy*, 104; Peter Wyden, *Bay of Pigs* (New York: Simon and Schuster, 1979), 304–5; Schlesinger, *Thousand Days*, 282–83;

Lawrence Freedman, *Kennedy's Wars: Berlin, Cuba, Laos, and Vietnam* (New York: Oxford University Press, 2000), 301–2.

29. JFK quote in Maxwell D. Taylor, *Swords and Plowshares* (New York: W. W. Norton, 1972), 180; George W. Ball (Department of State observer), *The Past Has Another Pattern: Memoirs* (New York: W. W. Norton, 1982), 365; Rust, *Kennedy in Vietnam*, 42–43.

30. Taylor, *Swords and Plowshares*, 180.

31. Thomson quoted in Gibbons, *U.S. Government and the Vietnam War*, 2: 24; William Sullivan Oral History Interview (second of two), Aug. 5, 1970, p. 33, JFKL; notes on author's interview with Rusk, Aug. 16, 1989.

32. First JFK quote in Schlesinger, *Thousand Days*, 284; second JFK quote in Sorensen, *Kennedy*, 644; Galbraith to JFK, May 10, 1961, POF, Special Correspondence, Galbraith, March–Oct. 1961, box 29a, JFKL; third JFK quote in Herring, *America's Longest War*, 94; ibid., 93; Rostow Oral History Interview, 1: 66–67, LBJL; JFK to Reston quoted in Halberstam, *Best and the Brightest*, 76; James Reston, *Deadline* (New York: Random House, 1991), 291.

33. Rostow to JFK, April 21, 1961, POF, Staff Memoranda, March–May 1961, box 64A, JFKL.

34. Ibid.; Bundy quoted in Henry Fairlie, *The Kennedy Promise: The Politics of Expectation* (Garden City, N.Y.: Doubleday, 1973), 180.

35. Cabinet meeting, April 20, 1961, *FRUS*, 1: *Vietnam 1961*, Ed. Note, 74; McNamara to JFK, April 20, 1961, ibid.; Roswell Gilpatric Oral History Interview, 1: 1–2, Nov. 2, 1982, by Ted Gittinger, LBJL; Reeves, *President Kennedy*, 99.

36. Rostow quoted in Gravel, ed., *Pentagon Papers*, 2: 34; Gilpatric Oral History Interview, 1: 2–3, LBJL; transcript, Roger Hilsman, Jr., 22, Aug. 14, 1970, by Dennis J. O'Brien, for JFKL Oral History Program; transcript, Roswell Gilpatric, May 5, 1970, p. 9 by Dennis J. O'Brien for JFKL Oral History Program.

37. Gravel, ed., *Pentagon Papers*, 2:43; Currey, *Lansdale*, 231–34, quote on Department of State, 43; ibid., 43–44; Lansdale's study, April 19, 1961, in *USVR*, Book 11: 22–34; Gilpatric to JFK, May 3, 1961, *FRUS*, 1: *Vietnam 1961*, 92; memo of second meeting of Presidential Task Force on Vietnam, Pentagon, May 4, 1961, ibid., 116.

38. Gravel, ed., *Pentagon Papers*, 2: 38.

39. Lansdale Oral History Interview, 105, JFKL; transcript, Edward G. Lansdale Oral History Interview, 2: 47, Sept. 15, 1981, by Ted Gittinger, LBJL.

40. Program for Presidential Task Force on Vietnam, April 22, 1961 (circulated at first meeting on April 24), *FRUS*, 1: *Vietnam 1961*, 74–77; draft notes on first meeting of Presidential Task Force on Vietnam, Pentagon, April 24, 1961, ibid., 78; Gravel, ed., *Pentagon Papers*, 2: 39.

41. Sorensen, Bundy, and Bell to JFK, NSF, Countries—Vietnam, April 28, 1961, JFKL; draft notes on first meeting of Presidential Task Force on Vietnam, Pentagon, April 24, 1961, *FRUS*, 1: *Vietnam 1961*, 78–80; McGarr to Felt, May 6, 1961, ibid., 89.

42. Alexis Johnson Oral History Interview, 7–10, 21, JFKL; Rostow quoted in Gravel, ed., *Pentagon Papers*, 2: 42; U. Alexis Johnson, *The Right Hand of Power* (Englewood Cliffs, N.J.: Prentice-Hall, 1984), 321–25.

43. Rostow Oral History Interview, 1: 64, LBJL; Johnson Oral History Interview, 10, 20, 33–34, JFKL; Sorensen, *Kennedy*, 641; Parmet, *JFK*, 178–79. MacArthur, according to Schlesinger, declared that "anyone wanting to commit American ground forces to the mainland of Asia should have his head examined." Schlesinger, *Thousand Days*, 284. The president met with MacArthur in the general's hotel suite at the Waldorf-Astoria Towers on the morning of April 28.

44. Gravel, ed., *Pentagon Papers*, 2: 40–42; Laos Annex reprinted on 41.

45. Gilpatric Oral History Interview, 23, JFKL.

46. Memo of conversation in Department of State, April 29, 1961, NSF, Countries—Laos, March 23–24, 1961, box 130–31, JFKL; *USVR*, Book 11: 62–66; Newman, *JFK and Vietnam*, 49–51.

47. Memo of conversation in Department of State, April 29, 1961, NSF, Countries—Laos, March 23–24, 1961, box 130–31, JFKL.

48. Ibid.; *USVR*, Book 11: 62–66.

49. Memo of conversation in Department of State, April 29, 1961, NSF, Countries—Laos, March 23–24, 1961, box 130–31, JFKL.

50. Ibid.

51. Gilpatric quoted in Schlesinger, *Robert Kennedy*, 1: 469; author's interview with Galbraith, March 28, 2001.

52. Hilsman Oral History Interview, 20–22, JFKL.

Chapter 3

1. Neil Sheehan et al., eds., *The Pentagon Papers as Published by the New York Times* (New York: Quadrangle Books, 1971), 94; Schlesinger, *Thousand Days*, 284.

2. Lemnitzer quoted in Schlesinger, *Thousand Days*, 284; Roger Hilsman, *To Move a Nation: The Politics of Foreign Policy in the Administration of John F. Kennedy* (New York: Dell, 1964), 413.

3. "A Program of Action to Prevent Communist Domination of South Vietnam," May 1, 1961, encl. in Gilpatric to JFK, May 3, 1961, *FRUS*, 1: *Vietnam 1961*, 94–96.

4. Ibid., 100, 102–4.

5. Ibid., 97, 100.

6. Ibid., 108–9; Kaiser, *American Tragedy*, 71–72.

7. Sorensen to JFK, April 28, 1961, *FRUS*, 1: *Vietnam 1961*, 84; Kaiser, *American Tragedy*, 72–73.

8. "Program of Action," ibid., 107–9; Dean Rusk Oral History Interview, 2, Sept. 26, 1969, by Paige E. Mulhollan, LBJL; author's interview with Rusk, Aug. 16, 1989; Sheehan et al., eds., *Pentagon Papers*, 86, 94; Gravel, ed., *Pentagon Papers*, 2: 37–38.

9. *USVR*, Book 11: 123–24.

10. "Program of Action," *FRUS*, 1: *Vietnam 1961*, 111.

11. Ibid., 113.

12. Memo of second meeting of Presidential Task Force on Vietnam, in the Pentagon, May 4, 1961, ibid., 116; Lansdale to McNamara, May 3, 1961, ibid., 116 n. 5.

13. JFK to McGeorge Bundy, Feb. 5, 1961, quoted in Parmet, *JFK*, 137; Gibbons, *U.S. Government and the Vietnam War*, 2: 16; Sorensen, *Kennedy*, 652–53.

14. Draft memo of conversation of second meeting of Presidential Task Force on Vietnam, in Pentagon, May 4, 1961, *FRUS*, 1: *Vietnam 1961*, 116–17.

15. Ibid., 117–18.

16. Ibid., 118–19.

17. Ibid. For the U.S. military effort in the Greek civil war, see Howard Jones, *"A New Kind of War": America's Global Strategy and the Truman Doctrine in Greece* (New York: Oxford University Press, 1989).

18. Draft memo of conversation of second meeting of Presidential Task Force on Vietnam, *FRUS*, 1: *Vietnam 1961*, 119–20.

19. Durbrow to Rusk, no. 1656 (2 sections), May 3, 1961, NSF, Countries—Laos, March 23–24, 1961, box 130–31, JFKL.

20. Ibid.; draft memo of conversation of second meeting of Presidential Task Force on Vietnam, in Pentagon, May 4, 1961, *FRUS*, 1: *Vietnam 1961*, 121.

21. Komer to McGeorge Bundy, May 4, 1961, *FRUS*, 1: *Vietnam 1961*, 123–24.

22. Ibid., 124.

23. NSC reference in McNamara to service secretaries, May 9, 1961, ibid., 115 n. 3; first reference to Rusk in memo for record (presumably by Admiral Burke), May 5, 1961, ibid., 125; second reference to Rusk in memo for record by Joint Chiefs of Staff representative, May 5, 1961, *USVR*, Book 11: 67–68.

24. Reeves, *President Kennedy*, 115–16; Rostow Oral History Interview, 1: 64–66, LBJL.

25. *Time*, May 12, 1961, pp. 12–13; JFK quoted in Reeves, *President Kennedy*, 116.

26. McGarr to Felt, May 6, 1961, *FRUS*, 1: *Vietnam 1961*, 89–90.

27. Ibid., 91.

28. Lemnitzer (in Seoul) to Joint Chiefs of Staff, May 8, 1961, ibid., 126–27.

29. Ibid., 127.

30. Joint Chiefs of Staff to McNamara, May 1961, in "Nations and Regions: Program for South Vietnam," Vice-Presidential Security File, box 10, LBJL; "Outline Chief MAAG Vietnam," n.d., "Nations and Regions: Program for South Vietnam," Vice-Presidential Security File, box 10, ibid.; "MAAG Response to Vice President Johnson's Request for a Statement of the Requirements to Save Vietnam from Communist Aggression," n.d., ibid.

31. McGarr to Felt, May 10, 1961, *FRUS*, 1: *Vietnam 1961*, 129–30.

32. "The President's News Conference of May 5, 1961," *Public Papers of Presidents: JFK, 1961*, 1: 354; LBJ and JFK quotes in Reeves, *President Kennedy*, 118, 119.

33. Nolting quote in Newman, *JFK and Vietnam*, 70; Ed. Note, *FRUS*, 1: *Vietnam 1961*, 135.

34. "Saigon's Press Summary," May 1961, Vice-President's Visit to Southeast Asia, Vice-Presidential Security File, box 1, LBJL; "Appraisal of Capabilities of Conventional Forces," May 12, 1961, POF, Depts. and Agencies, Army, box 30, JFKL.

35. LBJ quoted in Reeves, *President Kennedy*, 119; Karnow, *Vietnam*, 267; Frederick Nolting Oral History Interview, 1: 2, Nov. 11, 1982, by Ted Gittinger, LBJL.

36. Rostow to JFK, May 10, 1961, *FRUS, 1961–1963*, vol. 1: *Vietnam 1961*, 131.

37. Nolting to Rusk, May 13, 1961, ibid., 136. The interpreter was Joseph Mendenhall, Counselor for Political Affairs in the embassy.

38. Gravel, ed., *Pentagon Papers*, 2: 55; quote in Rust, *Kennedy in Vietnam*, 34.

39. The president's words were: "The problem of troops is a matter—the matter of what we are going to do to assist Viet-Nam to obtain its independence is a matter still under consideration. There are a good many which I think can most usefully wait until we have had consultations with the government, which up to the present time—which will be one of the matters which Vice President Johnson will deal with: the problem of consultations with the Government of Viet-Nam as to what further steps could most usefully be taken." President's News Conference, May 5, 1961, *Public Papers of Presidents: JFK, 1961*, 1: 356. Gravel, ed., *Pentagon Papers*, 2: 11, 56. The highly dubious charge has risen that the joint chiefs purposely bypassed the White House in sending the vice president a copy of their May 10 recommendation for combat troops earlier sent to Gilpatric on the Task Force. According to the story, the message arrived in Saigon just before Johnson met with Diem on the morning of May 12 and led the vice president to engage in intrigue and deception in acting with the military against the president. For this unlikely account, see Newman, *JFK and Vietnam*, 69, 72–75.

40. Gilpatric to chair of Joint Chiefs of Staff, May 8, 1961, *USVR*, Book 11: 131; Joint Chiefs of Staff memo of May 10, 1961, in Vice-Presidential Security File, "Nations and Regions: Program for South Vietnam," box 10, LBJL; Kahin, *Intervention*, 476 n. 27; Newman, *JFK and Vietnam*, 57–59.

41. NSAM 52, encl. in McGeorge Bundy to Rusk, May 11, 1961, *FRUS*, 1: *Vietnam 1961*, 132–33; Rusk to Saigon embassy, May 20, 1961, ibid., 140; "Presidential Program for Viet-Nam," May 23, 1961, Vice-Presidential Security File, Vice-Presidential Travel, Vice-President's Visit to Southeast Asia, May 9–24, 1961, box 1, LBJL; Gravel, ed., *Pentagon Papers*, 2: 50, 51.

42. *Saturday Evening Post*, May 20, 1961, pp. 31, 69–70; Newman, *JFK and Vietnam*, 69–75.

43. Nolting to Rusk, May 13, 1961, *FRUS*, 1: *Vietnam 1961*, 136–38; memo of conversation, May 13, 1961, ibid., 139 n.2.

44. Ed. Note, ibid., 135.

45. Alexis Johnson Oral History Interview, June 14, 1969, by Paige E. Mulhollan, LBJL; LBJ to JFK, May 23, 1961, pp. 1–3, POF, Special Correspondence, LBJ, box 30, JFKL.

46. Report by Vice President, undated, but c. May 23, 1961, *FRUS*, 1: *Vietnam 1961*, 152–53.

47. LBJ to JFK, May 23, 1961, pp. 6–7, POF, Special Correspondence, LBJ, box 30, JFKL; Report by Vice President, undated, but c. May 23, 1961, *FRUS*, 1: *Vietnam 1961*, 153–54.

48. Report by Vice President, undated, but c. May 23, 1961, *FRUS*, 1: *Vietnam 1961*, 154–55.

49. LBJ to JFK, May 23, 1961, p. 5, POF, Special Correspondence, LBJ, box 30, JFKL; report by Vice President, undated, but c. May 23, 1961, *FRUS*, 1: *Vietnam 1961*, 156.

50. Report by Vice President, undated, but c. May 23, 1961, *FRUS*, 1: *Vietnam 1961*, 156.

51. Ibid., 157.

52. LBJ to JFK, May 23, 1961, pp. 4, 6, POF, Special Correspondence, LBJ, box 30, JFKL.

53. Ibid., 4–5.

54. Ibid., 8.

55. Dodd to LBJ, May 12, 1961, Vice-Presidential Security File, "Nations and Regions: Program for South Vietnam," box 10, LBJL; Dodd's and Findley's quotes in Gibbons, *U.S. Government and the Vietnam War*, 2: 46–47.

56. Young (in Thailand) to Rusk, May 20, 1961, *FRUS*, 1: *Vietnam 1961*, 143, 145–46.

57. Nolting to Rusk, May 26, 1961, ibid., 159; Robert Shaplen, *The Lost Revolution* (New York: Harper and Row, 1955, 1965), 153–54.

58. Nolting to Rusk, May 16, 1961, in Gareth Porter, ed., *Vietnam: The Definitive Documentation of Human Decisions*, 2 vols. (Stanfordville, N.Y.: Earl M. Coleman Enterprises, 1979), 2: 101–2; Rusk to various embassies, May 26, 1961, ibid., 102–3; Nolting to Rusk, May 27, 1961, ibid., 105–6.

59. Gravel, ed., *Pentagon Papers*, 2: 69; "Profiles of Diem and Nhu, Ousted Saigon Chiefs," *New York Times*, Nov. 2, 1962, p. 2.

Chapter 4

1. Summary of Conference Agreements, c. early June 1961, "Official Use Only," POF, Countries Series, Laos General, Jan.–March 1961, box 121, JFKL; Khrushchev and JFK exchange in Gibbons, *U.S. Government and the Vietnam War*, 2: 48.

2. Reston quote in Giglio, *Presidency of John F. Kennedy*, 78; JFK quote in Reston interview cited in Reeves, *President Kennedy*, 172–73.

3. Herring, *America's Longest War*, 93–94; Timothy N. Castle, *At War in the Shadow of Vietnam: U.S. Military Aid to the Royal Lao Government, 1955–1975* (New York: Columbia University Press, 1993), 38–44; Jane Hamilton Merritt, *Tragic Mountains: The Hmong, the Americans, and the Secret Wars for Laos, 1942–1992* (Bloomington: Indiana University Press, 1993), 71–112.

4. Gravel, ed., *Pentagon Papers*, 2: 63; memo of conversation in White House among JFK, Thuan, Asst. Sec. of State for Far Eastern Affairs Walter P. McConaughy, and Chalmers B. Wood, June 14, 1961, *FRUS*, 1: *Vietnam 1961*, 173; Kennedy quote ibid., 174; Ed. Note, ibid., 179.

5. Gravel, ed., *Pentagon Papers*, 2: 64; Gilpatric to Rusk, July 3, 1961, *FRUS*, 1: *Vietnam 1961*, 197–98; Lansdale to Gilpatric, June 26, 1961, ibid., 181; Gibbons, *U.S. Government and the Vietnam War*, 2: 50–51; Staley Report in *USVR*, Book 11: 182–226; Lansdale to Gilpatric, June 30, 1961, ibid., 190; Newman, *JFK and Vietnam*, 105–7.

6. Memo of conversation between Alexis Johnson and Rostow, June 21, encl. in Cottrell to McConaughy, July 8, 1961, *FRUS*, 1: *Vietnam 1961*, 201, 203; memo by Alexis Johnson of telephone conversation with Rostow, June 21, 1961, ibid.,

201 n. 2; Robert H. Johnson to Rostow, July 11, 1961, ibid., 201 n. 1; Alexis Johnson Oral History Interview, 21, JFKL; Schlesinger, *Thousand Days*, 248.

7. Rostow to JFK, June 26, 1961, NSF, Countries—Laos, box 130–31, JFKL.

8. Rostow to JFK, June 24, 1961, encl.: speech to Special Warfare School, Ft. Bragg, June 28, 1961, p. 9, POF, Depts. and Agencies, Army, 1961, box 69a, JFKL.

9. Ibid., 10–12.

10. Wood to Cottrell, July 1, 1961, *FRUS*, 1: *Vietnam 1961*, 196.

11. Rostow to Rusk, July 13, 1961, ibid., 206–7.

12. Rusk to Saigon embassy, June 16, 1961, ibid., 177; Nolting to Rusk, June 28, 1961, ibid., 186; Rusk to Saigon embassy, June 28, 1961, ibid., 187–88.

13. Diem letter in *USVR*, Book 11: 168–73; Gibbons, *U.S. Government and the Vietnam War*, 2: 50; Thuan quoted in memo of a conversation in the White House, June 14, 1961, *FRUS*, 1: *Vietnam 1961*, 173.

14. William Colby and Peter Forbath, *Honorable Men: My Life in the CIA* (New York: Simon and Schuster, 1978), 173.

15. Memo of conversation in Department of State between McConaughy and D. N. Chatterjee, chargé d'affaires of Indian embassy in Washington, June 30, 1961, *FRUS*, 1: *Vietnam 1961*, 192, 194–95.

16. Nolting to Rusk, July 8, 1961, ibid., 203; Nolting to Rusk, July 13, 1961, ibid., 204; Nolting to Cottrell, July 31, 1961, ibid.; Nolting to Rusk, May 25, 1962, ibid., 204.

17. Letter from Vietnam and U.S. Special Financial Groups to Diem and JFK, July 14, 1961, ibid., 221–22.

18. Paper prepared by Taylor, July 15, 1961, ibid., 223–24.

19. Ibid., 224.

20. William Bundy to Lemnitzer, July 19, 1961, ibid., 233–34; U.S. Department of State, Vietnam Working Group Files, minutes of Task Force meeting, July 17, 1961, ibid., 228–29.

21. Ibid., 229.

22. Komer to Rostow, July 20, 1961, ibid., 234–36.

23. Taylor to JFK, July 26, 1961, ibid., 243; Taylor and Rostow to JFK, July 27, 1961, ibid., 248; Chair of Southeast Asia Task Force, John M. Steeves, to JFK, July 28, 1961, ibid., 251.

24. Memo by McGeorge Bundy of White House discussion, July 28, 1961, ibid., 252–53; Harriman Oral History Interview, 128, JFKL; Hilsman Oral History Interview, 23, JFKL.

25. Memo by McGeorge Bundy of White House discussion, July 28, 1961, *FRUS*, 1: *Vietnam 1961*, 253–54.

26. Lemnitzer to JFK, Aug. 7, 1961, POF, Countries Series, Laos General, Jan.–March 1961, box 121, JFKL.

27. Memo by McGeorge Bundy of White House discussion, July 28, 1961, *FRUS*, 1: *Vietnam 1961*, 252–56; Rusk to JFK, July 28, 1961, ibid., 255 n. 2; Gibbons, *U.S. Government and the Vietnam War*, 2: 51–52; Rostow to JFK, Aug. 4, 1961, POF, Staff Memoranda June–Dec. 1961, box 65, JFKL.

28. Rostow to JFK, Aug. 4, 1961, quoted in Gibbons, *U.S. Government and the Vietnam War*, 2: 61; ibid., 61–62; Johnson memo, "Strategy for Southeast Asia," Aug. 14, 1961, ibid., 61 n. 151; Rostow to JFK, Aug. 17, 1961, ibid., 63.

29. Sorensen, *Kennedy*, 654–55; memo by McGeorge Bundy of White House discussion, July 28, 1961, *FRUS*, 1: *Vietnam 1961*, 255; Department of State telegram to Saigon embassy, no. 140, Aug. 3, 1961, NSF, Countries—Vietnam, box 194, JFKL; Joint Chiefs of Staff to McNamara, Aug. 3, 1961, *FRUS*, 1: *Vietnam 1961*, 258; JFK to Diem, Aug. 5, 1961, ibid., 266; Ball to JFK, c. after Aug. 4, 1961, POF, Staff Memoranda, June–Dec. 1961, box 65, JFKL; Nolting to Rusk, no. 192, Aug. 8, 1961, NSF, Countries—Vietnam, box 194, JFKL.

30. Nolting to Rusk, July 14, 1961, *FRUS*, 1: *Vietnam 1961*, 219–20; Gravel, ed., *Pentagon Papers*, 2: 439; Qiang Zhai, *China and the Vietnam Wars, 1950–1975* (Chapel Hill: University of North Carolina Press, 2000), 112.

31. White quoted in Schlesinger, *Thousand Days*, 456. The president took White's letter to Hyannis Port for "weekend reading." Reeves, *President Kennedy*, 236–37, 697.

32. Diem to JFK, June 9, 1961, in Gravel, ed., *Pentagon Papers*, 2: 60–62.

33. NSAM 56, June 28, 1961, *USVR*, Book 11: 174; first quote in Kenneth Conboy and Dale Andradé, *Spies and Commandos: How America Lost the Secret War in North Vietnam* (Lawrence: University Press of Kansas, 2000), 84; Shultz, *Secret War against Hanoi*, 19–21; Newman, *JFK and Vietnam*, 98–99.

34. Gravel, ed., *Pentagon Papers*, 2: 3, 11.

35. Nolting to Rusk, Aug. 14, 1961, *FRUS*, 1: *Vietnam 1961*, 276; Ed. Note, ibid., 300; Status Report on the Presidential Program for Viet-Nam, as of Aug. 18, 1961, NSF, Countries—Vietnam, box 202–3, JFKL.

36. Zhai, *China and the Vietnam Wars*, 112–13.

37. "The Viet Cong," *Time*, Sept. 15, 1961.

38. Cottrell to Rusk, Sept. 1, 1961, NSF, Countries—Vietnam, box 194, JFKL; Douglas J. Macdonald, *Adventures in Chaos: American Intervention for Reform in the Third World* (Cambridge, Mass.: Harvard University Press, 1992), 202; McGarr to Felt, Sept. 10, 1961, *FRUS*, 1: *Vietnam 1961*, 296–98; Gravel, ed., *Pentagon Papers*, 2: 12, 71; Rust, *Kennedy in Vietnam*, 37; ranger commander quoted in *Time*, Sept. 29, 1961, p. 33; Newman, *JFK and Vietnam*, 115–16.

39. Nolting to Rusk, Sept. 20, 1961, *FRUS*, 1: *Vietnam 1961*, 305–6; Rust, *Kennedy in Vietnam*, 37–38; Reeves, *President Kennedy*, 237.

40. Nolting to Rusk, Sept. 20, 1961, *FRUS*, 1: *Vietnam 1961*, 306; Kahin, *Intervention*, 133.

41. Bowles to Saigon embassy, Sept. 22, 1961, *FRUS*, 1: *Vietnam 1961*, 307–8.

42. Gravel, ed., *Pentagon Papers*, 2: 69; Nolting to Rusk, Oct. 1, 1961, *FRUS*, 1: *Vietnam 1961*, 316–17; Rusk to Nolting, Oct. 1, 1961, ibid., 317 n. 5. See also Reeves, *President Kennedy*, 238.

43. Nolting to Rusk, Oct. 1, 1961, *FRUS*, 1: *Vietnam 1961*, 317; Rusk to Nolting, Oct. 1, 1961, ibid., 317 n. 5. See also Reeves, *President Kennedy*, 238.

44. Cottrell to Nolting, Aug. 17, 1961, *FRUS*, 1: *Vietnam 1961*, Ed. Note, 282; Jorden to Taylor, Sept. 27, 1961, NSF, Countries—Vietnam, box 194, JFKL; Jorden to Robert Johnson (to Rostow), Oct. 3, 1961, ibid. Jorden's report was entitled "A Threat to Peace." See transcript, William J. Jorden Oral History Interview, 1: 2–3, March 22, 1969, by Paige E. Mulhollan, LBJL.

45. "Bloc Support of the Communist Effort against the Government of Vietnam," Oct. 5, 1961, pp. 1, 4–5, CIA, NSF, Countries—Vietnam, box 194, JFKL.

Nolting recommended SEATO action in the Laotian corridor. Nolting to Rusk, no. 462, Oct. 10, 1961, ibid.; Nolting to Rusk, Oct. 10, 1961, *FRUS*, 1: *Vietnam 1961*, 334–35.

46. U.S. Department of State, *Working Paper on the North Vietnamese Role in the War in South Vietnam* (1968), no. 26, pp. 1–3, 5, Indochina Archives: History of the Vietnam War, Unit 5: NLF, General Materials, External Relations, 1961 (University of California, Berkeley); Pribbenow, trans., *Victory in Vietnam*, 80, 110–12.

47. Duiker, *Ho Chi Minh*, 529.

48. Rostow to JFK, Oct. 5, 1961, Gibbons, *U.S. Government and the Vietnam War*, 2: 67; Gravel, ed., *Pentagon Papers*, 2: 12, 73; memo from Joint Chiefs of Staff to McNamara, Oct. 9, 1961, *FRUS*, 1: *Vietnam 1961*, 330–31; *USVR*, Book 2, IVB.I: 76.

49. Gravel, ed., *Pentagon Papers*, 2: 12, 73–74; Kaiser, *American Tragedy*, 96–97; Newman, *JFK and Vietnam*, 119–20.

50. Memo for Taylor: "JCS [Joint Chiefs of Staff] Study of Operation in SVN [South Vietnam]," Oct. 9, 1961, NSF, Countries—Vietnam, box 194, JFKL; Lemnitzer to McNamara, Oct. 9, 1961, *USVR*, Book 11: 297–98; Rust, *Kennedy in Vietnam*, 40–41.

51. Lemnitzer to McNamara (Appendix A attached), Oct. 9, 1961, *USVR*, Book 11: 302–3; Gibbons, *U.S. Government and the Vietnam War*, 2: 68.

52. Lemnitzer to McNamara (Appendix A attached), Oct. 9, 1961, *USVR*, Book 11: 304–7.

53. Ibid., 308.

54. Ibid., 309.

55. William Bundy to McNamara, Oct. 10, 1961, ibid., 312; U. Alexis Johnson, "Concept of Intervention in Vietnam," Oct. 10, 1961, ibid., Book 2, IVB.I: 77–78; Gravel, ed., *Pentagon Papers*, 2: 13, 74–77, 79–80; Gibbons, *U.S. Government and the Vietnam War*, 2: 69.

56. Taylor to JFK, Oct. 11, 1961, *FRUS*, 1: *Vietnam 1961*, 336–37.

57. White to JFK, Oct. 11, 1961, POF, Vietnam General 1960–61, box 128, JFKL.

58. NSAM 104, Oct. 13, 1961, *USVR*, Book 11: 328; Gravel, ed., *Pentagon Papers*, 2: 79–81; Ed. Note, *FRUS*, 1: *Vietnam 1961*, 380; Taylor, *Swords and Plowshares*, 227; Hilsman, *To Move a Nation*, 421; Schlesinger, *Thousand Days*, 457.

59. Freedman, *Kennedy's Wars*, 288; Earl H. Tilford, Jr., *Crosswinds: The Air Force's Setup in Vietnam* (College Station: Texas A&M University Press, 1993), 45–46; Robert F. Futrell, *The United States Air Force in Southeast Asia: The Advisory Years to 1965* (Washington, D.C.: Office of Air Force History, 1981), 79–80, 82; Kaiser, *American Tragedy*, 98; Newman, *JFK and Vietnam*, 127.

60. Memo for record by Gilpatric, Oct. 11, 1961, *FRUS*, 1: *Vietnam 1961*, 343–44; Bundy memo on NSAM 104, Oct. 13, 1961, *USVR*, Book 11: 328; draft instructions from JFK to Taylor, Oct. 11, 1961, ibid., 345; Lemnitzer to McGarr, Oct. 11, 1961, ibid., 343 n. 2. For "secret war" in Laos, see Castle, *At War in the Shadow of Vietnam*.

61. Gravel, ed., *Pentagon Papers*, 2: 79–81; Earl H. Tilford, Jr., *Search and Rescue Operations in Southeast Asia, 1961–1975* (Washington, D.C.: Office of Air Force History, 1980), 36; Futrell, *USAF in Southeast Asia*, 79–82; Tilford, *Cross-*

winds, 45–46; Gibbons, *U.S. Government and the Vietnam War*, 2: 70–71; Rust, *Kennedy in Vietnam*, 43; Reeves, *President Kennedy*, 241.

62. Draft instructions from JFK to Taylor, Oct. 11, 1961, *FRUS*, 1: *Vietnam 1961*, 345.

63. Taylor, *Swords and Plowshares*, 225–26; Newman, *JFK and Vietnam*, 128–29; JFK's policy approved in NSAM 52 of May 11, 1961, in *FRUS*, 1: *Vietnam 1961*, 133; JFK conversation with Krock, Oct. 11, 1961, quoted in Herring, *America's Longest War*, 97. Reeves fails to note that Taylor had written the draft instructions and that the president deleted the references to SEATO or U.S. troop introductions from the final instructions. Consequently, Reeves logically but erroneously concludes that the president "did not know what to do." Reeves, *President Kennedy*, 241, 242. Kennedy remained opposed to combat troops.

64. Memo for record by Lt. Commander Worth H. Bagley of U.S. Navy (copy to Rostow), Oct. 12, 1961, NSF, Countries—Vietnam, box 194, JFKL. Taylor (no first name given) was the U.S. Marine major.

65. Lansdale to Rostow, encl.: USAF Maj. Gen. Bela K. Kiraly to Lansdale, USAF, n.d.—Comment on "The Atlantic Report: South Vietnam," *The Atlantic*, Oct. 1961, pp. 16–22, NSF, Countries—Vietnam, box 194, JFKL; McGarr to Lemnitzer, Oct. 12, 1961, *FRUS*, 1: *Vietnam 1961*, 351–54.

66. McGarr to Lemnitzer, Oct. 12, 1961, *FRUS*, 1: *Vietnam 1961*, 355–58.

67. Taylor, *Swords and Plowshares*, 226; President's News Conference, Oct. 11, 1961, *Public Papers of the Presidents, JFK, 1961*, pp. 656, 660; Lemnitzer to Felt, Oct. 13, 1961, *FRUS*, 1: *Vietnam 1961*, 362–63.

Chapter 5

1. Rusk to embassy in New Delhi, India, no. 1094, Oct 17, 1961, NSF, Countries—Vietnam, box 194, JFKL.

2. Estimates prepared in the Dept. of Defense and other U.S. agencies, Oct. 15, 1961, *FRUS*, 1: *Vietnam 1961*, 376–79; Felt to Joint Chiefs of Staff, Oct. 18, 1961, in Ed. Note, ibid., 380; Rostow to Taylor, Oct. 16, 1961, ibid., 381; Taylor, *Swords and Plowshares*, 227–28; Rostow to JFK, Oct. 5, 1961, in Gravel, ed., *Pentagon Papers*, 2: 73, Felt's views on 84; Gibbons, *U.S. Government and the Vietnam War*, 2: 67, 72.

3. Nolting to Rusk, Oct. 16, 1961, *FRUS*, 1: *Vietnam 1961*, 383–85 (Nolting quote on 383); Hilsman, *To Move a Nation*, 421.

4. For the Taylor–Lansdale exchanges, see transcript, Maxwell D. Taylor Oral History Interview, 2: 5, June 1, 1981, by Ted Gittinger, LBJL; Lansdale Oral History Interview, 2: 41–42, LBJL; Lansdale Oral History Interview, 115–16, JFKL; Currey, *Lansdale*, 235; Newman, *JFK and Vietnam*, 131–32.

5. Currey, *Lansdale*, 237; Lansdale Oral History Interview, 116–17, JFKL.

6. Lansdale Oral History Interview, 2: 42–43, LBJL.

7. Lansdale Oral History Interview, 117–18, JFKL.

8. Ibid., 118–19.

9. Ibid., 121; Lansdale Oral History Interview, 2: 42–43, LBJL; Rust, *Kennedy in Vietnam*, 45–46; Currey, *Lansdale*, 237–38.

10. Rust, *Kennedy in Vietnam*, 45–46, Lansdale quote on 46; Hilsman, *To Move a Nation*, 421.

11. Lansdale quoted in Currey, *Lansdale*, 238.

12. Lemnitzer to Taylor, Oct. 18, 1961, *USVR*, Book 11: 324–25.

13. Ibid.; Spector, *Advice and Support*, 365–66.

14. Nolting to Rusk, Oct. 18, 1961, *FRUS*, 1: *Vietnam 1961*, 391–92.

15. Memo for record, Oct. 19, 1961, ibid., 396–98; Gravel, ed., *Pentagon Papers*, 2: 100; Herring, *America's Longest War*, 63–66; Taylor, *Swords and Plowshares*, 234.

16. Nolting to Rusk, Oct. 20, 1961, *FRUS*, 1: *Vietnam 1961*, 399–400.

17. Oka to Joseph G. Harrison, *Christian Science Monitor*'s Overseas News Editor, Nov. 2, 1961, POF, Vietnam General, 1960–61, box 128, JFKL.

18. "Suggested Contingency Plan," memo prepared in Department of State, Oct. 20, 1961, encl. in McConaughy to Nolting, Oct. 20, 1961, *FRUS*, 1: *Vietnam 1961*, 408–10.

19. Draft paper prepared by Mendenhall, Oct. 22, 1961, ibid., 416–17.

20. "Suggested Contingency Plan," ibid., 410–11.

21. "McGarr Briefing for Gen. Taylor," Oct. 20, 1961, ibid., 403 n. 2; memo for record of meeting on intelligence matters, Oct. 20, 1961, ibid., 406.

22. Lansdale to Taylor, Oct. 21, 1961, ibid., 411–12, 414.

23. Ibid., 414–15.

24. Nolting to Rusk, Oct. 18, 1961, ibid., 393; English text of Government of Vietnam letter to International Control Commission regarding North Vietnam's subversion and aggression, Oct. 24, 1961, 14–15, POF, Vietnam General, 1960–61, box 128, JFKL; Gravel, ed., *Pentagon Papers*, 2: 106.

25. Nolting to Rusk, Oct. 18, 1961, *FRUS*, 1: *Vietnam 1961*, 393–94.

26. Government of Vietnam letter to ICC, 1–3.

27. Ibid., 4–6.

28. The Saigon government cited the following arrests of Vietcong: six on a junk off the island of Ly-Son in Quang Ngai Province on January 31, 1960; five on a fishing junk on July 5, 1961, in Am-Hai Bay, Tourane (Danang); thirty-seven on seven boats on June 14, 1961, just offshore from Thuan-An in central Vietnam; thirty-six on seven boats in the same area on June 15, 1961; twenty-nine on six boats on June 17, 1961, at the mouth of the Thuan-An River; and two in May 1959 at Cat-Son security post in the southern part of the DMZ. Ibid., 6–7.

29. Ibid., 13–14; "Experiences in Turning XB Village in Kien Phong Province into a Combattant Village," 40, 42, 47–50, Vietcong Delegate to NLF interdistrict meeting (place unknown), in "Organizing a Village in the Mekong Delta," Oct. 1961, Indochina Archives: History of the Vietnam War, Unit 5: NLF, General Materials, 1961 (University of California, Berkeley).

30. NLF pamphlet entitled, *The Policy of the Southern People's Liberation Front*, 1, c. 1961, Indochina Archives: History of the Vietnam War, Unit 5: NLF, General Materials, 1961 (University of California, Berkeley); NLF handbook on military proselyting work, 1961, p. 10, ibid., Military Operations, 1961; NLF Binh Van Directive: 1961, "Political Mission for 1962," 12–13, ibid.; Duiker, *Communist Road to Power in Vietnam*, 172–84, 186–93, 196–98; Spector, *Advice and Support*, 310–16, 326–27, 329–32; Duiker, *Sacred War*, 115–37, 141; Truong, *Viet Cong Memoir*, 66–68; Pike, *Viet Cong*, 74–85.

31. Nolting to Rusk, Oct. 25, 1961, *FRUS*, 1: *Vietnam 1961*, 433–34.

32. Taylor Oral History Interview, 2: 8, LBJL; Schlesinger, *Thousand Days*, 457; Taylor to JFK, Nov. 1, 1961, *USVR*, Book 11: 332; Taylor to Rusk, Oct. 25, 1961, *FRUS*, 1: *Vietnam 1961*, 427–28.

33. Nolting Oral History Interview, 1: 4–6, LBJL; McGarr to Felt, Oct. 23, 1961, *FRUS*, 1: *Vietnam 1961*, 424–25; McGarr to Lemnitzer, Oct. 24, 1961, ibid., 426; Gravel, ed., *Pentagon Papers*, 2: 14, 101; Nolting Oral History Interview 1: 2–3, LBJL; Taylor Oral History Interview, 2: 14, LBJL; Gilpatric Oral History Interview, 26, JFKL; McGarr to Lemnitzer, Oct. 24, 1961, *FRUS*, 1: *Vietnam, 1961*, 425–27.

34. Taylor to Rusk, Oct. 25, 1961, *FRUS*, 1: *Vietnam, 1961*, 428–29; Taylor to Saigon embassy, Oct. 27, 1961, ibid., 440–41; Gravel, ed., *Pentagon Papers*, 2: 85, 86, 102; Kaiser, *American Tragedy*, 105–6; Newman, *JFK and Vietnam*, 133–34.

35. Taylor to Rusk, Oct. 25, 1961, *FRUS*, 1: *Vietnam 1961*, 429; Taylor, *Swords and Plowshares*, 228; Taylor report, Nov. 3, 1961, in Gravel, ed., *Pentagon Papers*, 2: 93.

36. Taylor to Rusk, Oct. 25, 1961, *FRUS*, 1: *Vietnam 1961*, 430; Wood to Alexis Johnson, Oct. 25, 1961, ibid., 436–40.

37. Nolting to Rusk, Oct. 25, 1961, ibid., 432; Lemnitzer to McNamara, Oct. 31, 1961, in ibid., 463–64; "If GI's Go to Vietnam—The Way It Looks Out There," *U.S. News and World Report*, Nov. 6, 1961, p. 40.

38. Memo for record by William Bundy, Oct. 25, 1961, *FRUS*, 1: *Vietnam 1961*, 434–36.

39. Cottrell to Taylor, Oct. 27, 1961, NSF, Countries—Vietnam, boxes 202–3, JFKL.

40. Taylor to Rusk, Oct. 27, 1961, *FRUS*, 1: *Vietnam 1961*, 442–43.

41. Transcript, William Trueheart Oral History Interview, 1: 8–9, March 2, 1981, by Ted Gittinger, LBJL. Rusk considered the flood control mission a "guise" for introducing troops. Dean Rusk, *As I Saw It*, ed. Daniel S. Papp (New York: W. W. Norton, 1990), 432. Felt's views in memo for record by William Bundy, Oct. 25, 1961, *FRUS*, 1: *Vietnam 1961*, 435; McGarr to McNamara, Oct. 30, 1961, ibid., 454.

42. Taylor interview with Andrew Krepinevich, quoted in Andrew F. Krepinevich, *The Army and Vietnam* (Baltimore: Johns Hopkins University Press, 1986), 61–62; Colby interview with Newman, cited in Newman, *JFK and Vietnam*, 136.

43. Gilpatric asserted that the president opposed the mission's recommendation of "a combat battalion going in under the guise of being an engineering group." Hilsman also noted that "Kennedy rejected the Taylor–Rostow recommendation" for U.S. combat troops. See Gilpatric Oral History Interview, 1: 8–9, LBJL, and Hilsman Oral History Interview, 24, JFKL. Status Report on the Presidential Program for Viet-Nam, as of Sept. 29, 1961, NSF, Countries—Vietnam, boxes 202–3, JFKL; JFK's directive in McGeorge Bundy to Taylor, Oct. 28, 1961, *FRUS*, 1: *Vietnam 1961*, 443.

44. Nolting to Rusk, Oct. 28, 1961, *FRUS*, 1: *Vietnam 1961*, 444–46; Thuan quoted ibid., 445.

45. Jorden to Taylor, Oct. 30, 1961, NSF Countries—Vietnam, boxes 202–3, JFKL.

46. Frank Child, "U.S. Policy in Viet Nam," (draft of Oct. 5, 1961), encl. in Carl Kaysen to Robert Johnson, Oct. 30, 1961, ibid., box 194. Someone had crossed

through the words "—or an assassin's bullet—are" and inserted "is" after coup. Gibbons, *U.S. Government and Vietnam War*, 2: 76, 76 n. 9. See also Child's December 1961 article entitled "Vietnam—The Eleventh Hour," in the *New Republic*. For the nearly comical aspects of the aborted coup, see Spector, *Advice and Support*, 369–70.

47. Komer quoted in Gibbons, *U.S. Government and the Vietnam War*, 2: 81.

48. Robert Johnson to Carl Kaysen, Oct. 31, 1961, cited in ibid., 2: 76; ibid., 75–76; Gravel, ed., *Pentagon Papers*, 2: 90–91, 652–54.

49. Craig report to Taylor, cited in Gibbons, *U.S. Government and the Vietnam War*, 2: 77 n. 11; Gravel, ed., *Pentagon Papers*, 2: 96, 98; Taylor Oral History Interview, 2: 8–9, 11, LBJL.

50. Lansdale first quote in Currey, *Lansdale*, 237; Lansdale second quote in Rust, *Kennedy in Vietnam*, 45; Lansdale to Taylor, Nov. 3, 1961, Taylor report, NSF, Countries—Vietnam, boxes 202–3, JFKL; Taylor quoted in Rust, *Kennedy in Vietnam*, 45.

51. McGarr to Rostow, Oct. 25, 1961, NSF, Countries—Vietnam, box 194, JFKL.

52. McGarr to McNamara, Oct. 30, 1961, *FRUS*, 1: *Vietnam 1961*, 448–49.

53. Ibid., 449–51.

54. Ibid., 454.

55. Status Report on Presidential Program for Vietnam, as of Oct. 27, 1961, NSF, Countries—Vietnam, boxes 202–3, JFKL; Nolting to Rusk, no. 575, Oct. 31, 1961, ibid., box 194.

56. Taylor to JFK (eyes only), Nov. 1, 1961, *USVR*, Book 11: 339–41; Gravel, ed., *Pentagon Papers*, 2: 14, 104.

57. Robert Johnson to Bundy, Oct. 31, 1961, NSF, Countries—Vietnam, box 194, JFKL. For the argument that Taylor's flood control unit provided an implicit U.S. commitment to send combat units if necessary, see Gravel, ed., *Pentagon Papers*, 2: 105.

58. Robert Johnson to Bundy, Nov. 1, 1961, ibid.; Rusk (in Hakone) to Department of State, Nov. 1, 1961, *FRUS*, 1: *Vietnam 1961*, 464.

Chapter 6

1. Ball, *Past Has Another Pattern*, 365.

2. Gregory A. Olson, *Mansfield and Vietnam: A Study in Rhetorical Adaptation* (East Lansing: Michigan State University Press, 1995), 8, 39–40, 66.

3. Mansfield to JFK, Nov. 2, 1961, NSF, Countries—Vietnam, box 194, JFKL.

4. Ibid.; Kaiser, *American Tragedy*, 108.

5. Galbraith's paper entitled, "A Plan for South Vietnam," Nov. 3, 1961, *FRUS*, 1: *Vietnam 1961*, 474.

6. Ibid., 474–76.

7. Author's interview with Galbraith, March 28, 2001.

8. Ibid.

9. Robert P. Martin, "If GI's Go to Vietnam—The Way It Looks Out There," *U.S. News and World Report*, Nov. 6, 1961, pp. 39–41.

10. Galbraith, "A Plan for South Vietnam," Nov. 3, 1961, *FRUS*, 1: *Vietnam 1961*, 476.

11. Currey, *Lansdale*, 239; Reeves, *Kennedy*, 256.

12. Taylor report, Nov. 3, 1961, NSF, Countries—Vietnam, boxes 202–3, JFKL; Gravel, ed., *Pentagon Papers*, 2: 15.

13. Lansdale Oral History Interview, 120, JFKL; Lansdale Oral History Interview, 2: 46, LBJL; Rust, *Kennedy in Vietnam*, 49.

14. Taylor report encl. in Taylor to JFK, Nov. 3, 1961, NSF, Countries—Vietnam, boxes 202–3, JFKL; Rostow quoted in Michael Charlton and Anthony Moncrieff, *Many Reasons Why: The American Involvement in Vietnam* (New York: Hill and Wang, 1978), 74–75.

15. Taylor report, Covert Annex, Nov. 3, 1961, NSF, Countries—Vietnam, boxes 202–3, JFKL; Taylor report, ibid.; Lansdale to Taylor, Nov. 3, 1961, ibid.; Taylor report, Appendix F: "Frontier Force, Vietnam," encl. in Taylor to JFK, Nov. 3, 1961, *FRUS*, 1: *Vietnam 1961*, 518–22; Suggestions, Taylor report, Covert Annex, Nov. 3, 1961, NSF, Countries—Vietnam, boxes 202–3, JFKL; Lansdale to Taylor, Nov. 3, 1961, Taylor report, ibid.; Taylor report, Appendix F: "Frontier Force, Vietnam," encl. in Taylor to JFK, Nov. 3, 1961, *FRUS*, 1: *Vietnam 1961*, 518–20; Taylor report, Nov. 3, 1961, p. 5 (quote on U.S. weakness), NSF, Countries—Vietnam, boxes 202–3, JFKL.

16. Taylor report, Nov. 3, 1961, pp. 11, 13, NSF, Countries—Vietnam, boxes 202–3, JFKL.

17. Memo for record by Lt. Cmdr. Worth H. Bagley, naval aide to Taylor, Nov. 6, 1961, *FRUS*, 1: *Vietnam 1961*, 532–34; Berlin quote in Alexis Johnson to Rusk, Nov. 5, 1961, ibid., 537; Bundy quoted in Gibbons, *U.S. Government and Vietnam War*, 2: 79; Nolting to Rusk, Nov. 6, 1961, *FRUS*, 1: *Vietnam 1961*, 542–43; Ball, *Past Has Another Pattern*, 366.

18. Ball, *Past Has Another Pattern*, 366.

19. Rusk to Nolting, Nov. 4, 1961, no. 545, cited in Gibbons, *U.S. Government and Vietnam War*, 2: 79; Nolting to Rusk, Nov. 7, 1961, *FRUS*, 1: *Vietnam 1961*, 546–47.

20. Gravel, ed., *Pentagon Papers*, 2: 15–16; Maj. Gen. Max S. Johnson, U.S. Army (Ret.), "Fight or Give Up in Asia? Advice the Generals Are Giving," *U.S. News and World Report*, Nov. 6, 1961, p. 42. Van Fleet headed the U.S. military assistance program in Greece during the late 1940s.

21. Special Memo: "Communist Radio Reaction to Possibility of Dispatch of U.S. Troops to South Vietnam," Foreign Broadcast Information Division, Office of Operations, Nov. 6, 1961, NSF, Countries—Vietnam, box 194, JFKL; luncheon of November 5 described in John Kenneth Galbraith, *Ambassador's Journal: A Personal Account of the Kennedy Years* (Boston: Houghton Mifflin, 1969), 246–47; Galbraith to JFK, Nov. 8, 1961, NSF, Countries—Vietnam, box 194, JFKL; M. J. Desai, India's foreign secretary and a member of the ICC, memo of conversation in Department of State, Nov. 7, 1961, *FRUS*, 1: *Vietnam 1961*, 549–50, and memo of conversation in Department of State, Nov. 9, 1961, ibid., 567.

22. Rusk, *As I Saw It*, 432.

23. Draft memo from Rusk to JFK, Nov. 7, 1961, *FRUS*, 1: *Vietnam 1961*, 551–52.

24. Bundy quotes in Gibbons, *U.S. Government and the Vietnam War*, 2: 87 (second quote in Nov. 8, 1961, memo to JFK); memo by William Bundy, "Reflec-

tions on the Possible Outcomes of US Intervention in South Vietnam," Nov. 7, 1961 (second draft), *FRUS*, 1: *Vietnam 1961*, 553–55; Bagley to Taylor, Nov. 7, 1961, ibid., 556.

25. Bagley to Taylor, Nov. 9, 1961, *FRUS*, 1: *Vietnam 1961*, 569.

26. Notes by McNamara, Nov. 6, 1961, ibid., 543; McNamara to JFK, Nov. 8, 1961, ibid., 560; draft memo from McNamara to JFK, Nov. 5, 1961, ibid., 538–40. McNamara wanted to circulate "plausible cover stories" that referred to the combat troops as reinforcements for Hawaii or for exercises in the Philippines. McNamara to Lemnitzer, Nov. 8, 1961, ibid., 559. Draft paper by William Bundy, encl. in William Bundy to McNamara, Nov. 7, 1961, ibid., 555; Gravel, ed., *Pentagon Papers*, 2: 4–5, 16.

27. Draft memo for JFK (prepared in Department of State), Nov. 8, 1961, *FRUS*, 1: *Vietnam 1961*, 562–63.

28. Ibid., 564, 566.

29. Ball quote to McNamara in Gibbons, *U.S. Government and the Vietnam War*, 2: 88; Ball, *Past Has Another Pattern*, 366–67; David L. Di Leo, *George Ball, Vietnam, and the Rethinking of Containment* (Chapel Hill: University of North Carolina Press, 1991), 56–57.

30. Ball, *Past Has Another Pattern*, 367. For a Kennedy critic, see Richard J. Walton, *Cold War and Counterrevolution: The Foreign Policy of John F. Kennedy* (New York: Viking Press, 1972). For a defender, see Newman, *JFK and Vietnam*.

31. JFK quoted in Schlesinger, *Thousand Days*, 458; Schlesinger to Di Leo, Aug. 27, 1988, cited in Di Leo, *Ball*, 228 n. 120.

32. Rusk and McNamara to JFK, Nov. 11, 1961, NSF, Countries—Vietnam, box 195, JFKL; Alexis Johnson to McGeorge Bundy, Nov. 11, 1961, ibid.; Rostow to JFK, Nov. 11, 1961, ibid.; Gravel, ed., *Pentagon Papers*, 2: 5, 16, 110–16.

33. Gravel, ed., *Pentagon Papers*, 2: 112.

34. Ibid., 16; list of questions prepared by president, Nov. 11, 1961, *FRUS*, 1: *Vietnam 1961*, 576; JFK quote in Lemnitzer's notes of White House meeting, Nov. 11, 1961, ibid., 577; Bundy quoted in Gibbons, *U.S. Government and the Vietnam War*, 2: 91–92; memo for NSC on South Vietnam, encl.: Draft NSAM to secs. of state and defense, Nov. 13, 1961, NSF, Countries—Vietnam, box 195, JFKL; Logevall, *Choosing War*, 30–33.

35. Gravel, ed., *Pentagon Papers*, 2: 16–17.

36. Taylor, *Swords and Plowshares*, 248; *USVR*, Book 11: 400–405; Rostow, *Diffusion of Power*, 278. NSAM 52 of May 11, 1961, declared the president's intention "to prevent Communist domination of South Vietnam." *USVR*, Book 11: 136.

37. Robert Johnson to Rostow, Nov. 14, 1961, NSF, Countries—Vietnam, box 195, JFKL; Harriman to JFK, Nov. 11, 1961, ibid.; Bowles to Rusk, Oct. 5, 1961, *FRUS*, 1: *Vietnam 1961*, 322–25; Bowles to Schlesinger, Oct. 7, 1961, ibid., 322 n. 1; Chester L. Bowles, *Promises to Keep* (New York: Harper and Row, 1971), 409.

38. Halberstam, *Best and the Brightest*, 189; Harriman to JFK, Nov. 12, 1961, NSF, Countries—Vietnam, box 195, JFKL.

39. Rostow to JFK, Nov. 14, 1961, NSF, Countries—Vietnam, box 195, JFKL; Symington to JFK, Nov. 10, 1961, POF, Special Correspondence, box 33, JFKL; Symington to JFK, Oct. 21, 1961, POF, Countries Series, Vietnam, box 128, JFKL.

40. JFK memo for secs. of state and defense, Nov. 14, 1961, POF, Vietnam General, 1960–61, box 128, JFKL; memo of conversation in Department of State, Nov. 9, 1961, *FRUS*, 1: *Vietnam 1961*, 568; Reeves, *President Kennedy*, 282; "Man of the Year [President Kennedy]," *Time*, Jan. 5, 1962, p. 12.

41. Rostow to JFK, Nov. 12, 1961, *FRUS*, 1: *Vietnam 1961*, 579; McGeorge Bundy to JFK, Nov. 15, 1961, NSF, Countries—Vietnam, box 195, JFKL.

42. Notes on NSC meeting, Nov. 15, 1961, LBJ Papers, Vice-Presidential Security File, box 4, LBJL.

43. Ibid.; memo of conversation in Department of State by L. Dean Brown, Nov. 13, 1961, ibid., 584–85; Rusk to Saigon embassy, No. 600, Nov. 13, 1961, NSF, Countries—Vietnam, box 195, JFKL. That same day, Rusk informed the British ambassador in Washington that U.S. combat units might become necessary in a "few weeks." Rusk to London embassy, no. 2648, Nov. 14, 1961, ibid.

44. Notes on NSC meeting, Nov. 15, 1961, LBJ Papers, Vice-Presidential Security File, box 4, LBJL; Kaiser, *American Tragedy*, 116–18.

45. Gibbons, *U.S. Government and the Vietnam War*, 2: 99–100; Rusk to Nolting, Nov. 15, 1961, *USVR*, Book 11: 400–405.

46. Hilsman to McGeorge Bundy, Nov. 16, 1961, NSF, Countries—Vietnam, box 195, JFKL.

47. Chayes to Rusk, Nov. 16, 1961, *FRUS*, 1: *Vietnam 1961*, 634–35.

48. DS circular telegram to selected embassies, no. 966, Nov. 18, 1961, NSF, Countries—Vietnam, box 195, JFKL.

49. Author's interview with Galbraith, March 28, 2001.

50. Ibid.; Galbraith to JFK, Nov. 20, 1961, *USVR*, Book 11: 406–9; Galbraith to JFK, Nov. 21, 1961, NSF, Countries—Vietnam, box 195, JFKL; Gravel, ed., *Pentagon Papers*, 2: 124. Galbraith's son James told me of his father's experiences with bombing analyses primarily of Germany. James Galbraith to author, June 24, 2001 (in author's possession).

51. Galbraith to JFK, Nov. 20, 1961, *USVR*, Book 11: 406–9; Galbraith to JFK, Nov. 21, 1961, NSF, Countries—Vietnam, box 195, JFKL; Gravel, ed., *Pentagon Papers*, 2: 122–24.

52. Rostow to JFK, Nov. 24, 1961, POF, Staff Memoranda, June–Dec. 1961, box 65, JFKL.

53. Ibid.

54. Ibid.

55. Galbraith to JFK, Nov. 28, 1961, POF, Special Correspondence, Galbraith, Nov.–Dec. 1961, box 29a, JFKL.

56. Hilsman to Rusk, Nov. 28, 1961, *FRUS*, 1: *Vietnam 1961*, 681–82; Nolting to Rusk, no. 734, Nov. 29, 1961, NSF, Countries—Vietnam, box 195, JFKL; Rostow to JFK, Nov. 24, 1961, POF, Staff Memoranda, June–Dec. 1961, box 65, JFKL; memo for record by Public Affairs Officer in embassy, John M. Anspacher, Dec. 1, 1961, *FRUS*, 1: *Vietnam 1961*, 704. Pham Van Dong should not be confused with the North Vietnamese leader of the same name.

57. Paper prepared by Robert Johnson of NSC Staff, "Possible Contingencies in Viet Nam," Nov. 28, 1961, *FRUS*, 1: *Vietnam 1961*, 684–86.

58. NSAM 111, Nov. 22, 1961, ibid., 656–57; Gravel, ed., *Pentagon Papers*, 2: 17; NASA Memo No. 115, Nov. 30, 1961, *USVR*, Book 11: 425; Alexis Johnson to

Rusk, Nov. 22, 1961, *FRUS*, 1: *Vietnam 1961*, 663 n. 1; N. Paul Neilson, Asst. Director, Far East, United States Information Agency (hereafter referred to as USIA), to Edward R. Murrow, Director of USIA, Nov. 17, 1961, ibid., 642; Rusk to JFK, Nov. 24, 1961, ibid., 663; Kaiser, *American Tragedy*, 121.

59. NSAM 111, Nov. 22, 1961, *FRUS*, 1: *Vietnam 1961*, 656; JFK memo for secs. of state and defense, Nov. 14, 1961, POF, Vietnam General, 1960–61, box 128, JFKL. According to Kahin, the president wanted strong military measures. See his *Intervention*, 136. For other critics of Kennedy, see Louise FitzSimons, *The Kennedy Doctrine* (New York: Random House, 1972), and Walton, *Cold War and Counterrevolution*.

60. Robert P. Martin, "Where War Danger Is Greatest," *U.S. News and World Report*, Nov. 27, 1961, pp. 36–37.

61. Nolting to Rusk, no. 708, Nov. 25, 1961, NSF, Countries—Vietnam, box 195, JFKL; memo for record by U.S. Embassy's Public Affairs Officer (John M. Anspacher), Dec. 1, 1961, *FRUS*, 1: *Vietnam 1961*, 704–6.

62. Memo for record by Anspacher, Dec. 1, 1961, *FRUS*, 1: *Vietnam 1961*, 704–6.

63. Nolting to Rusk, Dec. 1, 1961, ibid., 706–7; Nolting to Rusk, Dec. 21, 1961, ibid., 751.

64. Nolting to Rusk, Dec. 3, 1961, ibid., 709–10.

65. Ibid., 711–12.

66. Nolting to Rusk, Nov. 18, 1961, ibid., 642–44; Rusk to Nolting, Nov. 27, 1961, ibid., 676–77; Nolting to Diem, Dec. 5, 1961, encl.: "Memorandum of Understanding" approved by Diem on Dec. 4, 1961, ibid., 714, 716; Nolting to Rusk, no. 708, Nov. 26, 1961, NSF, Countries—Vietnam, box 195, JFKL; Gravel, ed., *Pentagon Papers*, 2: 17; Taylor, *Swords and Plowshares*, 248; Nolting to Rusk, no. 678, Nov. 18, 1961, NSF, Countries—Vietnam, box 195, JFKL, and Nolting to Rusk, Nov. 22, 1961, *FRUS*, 1: *Vietnam 1961*, 649–50; Newman, *JFK and Vietnam*, 156–57.

67. Notes of meeting in White House, Nov. 27, 1961, *FRUS*, 1: *Vietnam 1961*, 675; Rostow to JFK, Dec. 6, 1961, POF, Staff Memoranda June–Dec. 1961, box 65, JFKL; Lansdale to Gen. Samuel Williams, Nov. 28, 1961, *FRUS*, 1: *Vietnam 1961*, 687–89.

68. Gibbons, *U.S. Government and the Vietnam War*, 2: 103.

69. *New York Times* stories cited in Gravel, ed., *Pentagon Papers*, 2: 17, 126–27; Kahin, *Intervention*, 139; Halberstam, *Making of a Quagmire*, 35–36; Status Report of the Military Actions in South Vietnam contained in Sec. of Defense memorandum dated Nov. 27, 1961, Subject: "First Phase of Vietnam Program," Operations Directorate, J-3, Joint Chiefs of Staff, NSF, Countries—Vietnam, boxes 202–3, JFKL; Harriman's memo of conversation with British Ambassador David Gore, Dec. 7, 1961, *FRUS*, 1: *Vietnam 1961*, 725–26. For Jorden report, see ibid., 725.

70. Department of State delegation to NATO Ministerial Meeting in Paris, Dec. 12, 1961, *FRUS*, 1: *Vietnam 1961*, 729–30.

71. Taylor Oral History Interview, 2: 12, LBJL; Gilpatric Oral History Interview, 26–27, JFKL; transcript, Gen. Lyman Lemnitzer Oral History Interview, 20, March 3, 1982, by Ted Gittinger, LBJL; transcript, Gen. Paul D. Harkins Oral History Interview, 1: 1–4, Nov. 10, 1981, by Ted Gittinger, LBJL; Hilsman

Oral History Interview, 23, JFKL; memo for secretary and chief of staff, U.S. Army, from McNamara, Dec. 21, 1961, NSF, Countries—Vietnam, box 195, JFKL; McNamara to JFK, Dec. 22, 1961, *FRUS*, 1: *Vietnam 1961*, 756; Shultz, *Secret War against Hanoi*, 23; Kaiser, *American Tragedy*, 125–26; Newman, *JFK and Vietnam*, 182–84.

72. Lemnitzer to McGarr, Dec. 23, 1961, *FRUS*, 1: *Vietnam 1961*, 759–60.

73. McGarr to Felt, Dec. 21, 1961, ibid., 753.

74. Rostow to Harriman, Dec. 22, 1961, ibid., 755–56; Lansdale to Lemnitzer, Dec. 27, 1961, ibid., 764.

75. Duiker, *Ho Chi Minh*, 528; "The Viet Cong," n.d., Indochina Archives: History of the Vietnam War, Unit 5: NLF, General Materials, 1960 (University of California, Berkeley); Hanoi to Europe and Asia, Dec. 11, 1961, ibid., General Materials, 1961.

76. Zhai, *China and the Vietnam Wars*, 113.

77. Alexis Johnson Oral History Interview, 29, LBJL.

78. "Guerrilla Warfare," *Newsweek*, Feb. 12, 1962, p. 29; Military Personnel Records (National Archives), National Personnel Records Center, St. Louis, Mo.; Macdonald, *Adventures in Chaos*, 212; Newman, *JFK and Vietnam*, 204.

79. Gravel, ed., *Pentagon Papers*, 2: 454; Trueheart Oral History Interview, 1: 24–25, LBJL; Nolting Oral History Interview, 1: 23–25, LBJL; Lemnitzer Oral History Interview, 19, LBJL; Reeves, *President Kennedy*, 262; Schlesinger, *Robert Kennedy and His Times*, 739; Nolting to Rusk, Dec. 13, 1961, *FRUS*, 1: *Vietnam 1961*, 731; McGarr to Lemnitzer, Dec. 27, 1961, ibid., 765.

Chapter 7

1. Hilsman, *To Move a Nation*, 444.

2. Tilford, *Search and Rescue in Southeast Asia*, 37; Gibbons, *U.S. Government and the Vietnam War*, 2: 108, 109; President's News Conference of Jan. 15, 1962, *Public Papers of the Presidents: JFK, 1962*, 17.

3. Trueheart Oral History Interview, 1: 17–20, LBJL; author's interview with Hilsman, Sept. 17, 2001.

4. Transcript, Samuel T. Williams Oral History Interview, 1: 58, March 2 or 16, 1981, by Ted Gittinger, LBJL.

5. Lemnitzer to Felt, Jan. 6, 1962, *FRUS, 1961–1963*, 2: *Vietnam 1962* (Washington, D.C.: Government Printing Office, 1990), 15–16; Kennedy quoted in memo for record of meeting in Palm Beach, Florida, Jan. 3, 1962, ibid., 4; Harkins Oral History Interview, 1: 5–6, LBJL; Rusk to Saigon embassy, no. 836, Jan. 3, 1962, NSF, Countries—Vietnam, box 195, JFKL.

6. Gilpatric to Lemnitzer, Jan. 4, 1962, *FRUS*, 2: *Vietnam 1962*, 5.

7. Trueheart to Rusk, no. 276, Jan. 8, 1962, NSF, Countries—Vietnam, box 195, JFKL.

8. Press excerpts: "NLFSV Representative Welcomed by Rally," Beijing, Jan. 12, 1962, pp. 7–11, Indochina Archives: History of the Vietnam War, Unit 5: NLF, General Materials, External Relations/DRV, 1962 (University of California, Berkeley); Jian, *Mao's China and the Cold War*, 207; Zhai, *China and the Vietnam Wars*, 113–14.

9. Memo for record of meeting between McGarr and Diem, Jan. 12, 1962, *FRUS*, 2: *Vietnam 1962*, 23–24, 30.

10. Status Report of Military Actions in South Vietnam contained in Sec. of Defense memo dated Nov. 27, 1961—Subject: "First Phase of Vietnam Program," Jan. 24, 1962, encl. in L. D. Battle, executive secretary, Department of State, to McGeorge Bundy, Jan. 25, 1962, NSF, Countries—Vietnam, boxes 202–3, JFKL.

11. Battle to McGeorge Bundy, Jan. 25, 1962, ibid.; Status Report of Developments since Feb. 8, Feb. 15, 1962, ibid.; Rust, *Kennedy in Vietnam*, 67–68.

12. Hilsman, "A Strategic Concept for Vietnam," Feb. 2, 1962, NSF, Countries—Vietnam, box 195, JFKL.

13. Harkins Oral History Interview, 1: 7–9, LBJL.

14. Ibid., 6, 18.

15. Nolting to Rusk, Jan. 5, 1962, *FRUS*, 2: *Vietnam 1962*, 12–13; Vietnam Task Force to USIA, no. 6794, Jan. 5, 1962, ibid., 13; memo for record of meeting between McGarr and Diem, Jan. 12, 1962, ibid., 23–24, 30.

16. Memo of conversation in Joseph Mendenhall's residence in Saigon, Jan. 16, 1962, ibid., 45–46; memo of conversation between Fishel and Mendenhall, Jan. 23, 1962, ibid., 56; John A. Hannah, president of Michigan State University, to JFK, Feb. 26, 1962, encl.: Fishel to Hannah, Feb. 17, 1962 (from Burma), NSF, Countries—Vietnam, box 196, JFKL; Robert Mann, *A Grand Delusion: America's Descent into Vietnam* (New York: Basic Books, 2001), 262 n.

17. Memo of conversation in Mendenhall's residence in Saigon, Jan. 16, 1962, *FRUS*, 2: *Vietnam 1962*, 45–46; memo of conversation between Fishel and Mendenhall, Jan. 23, 1962, ibid., 56; Hannah to JFK, Feb 26, 1962, encl.: Fishel to Hannah, Feb. 17, 1962, NSF, Countries—Vietnam, box 196, JFKL. Huynh Huu Ngia, secretary of state for labor, had converted to Catholicism.

18. Fishel to Hannah, Feb. 17, 1962, *FRUS*, 2: *Vietnam 1962*, 148–49.

19. Ibid., 150–51.

20. Ibid., 151–52; memo of conversation in Mendenhall's residence in Saigon, Jan. 16, 1962, ibid., 45–46; memo of conversation between Fishel and Mendenhall, Jan. 23, 1962, ibid., 56.

21. Draft memo by Assistant to Director for Regional Affairs (Far East), Office of International Security Affairs, Dept. of Defense (Col. J. R. Kent), Jan. 26, 1962, ibid., 60–62.

22. Ibid., 63–64.

23. Harkins Oral History Interview, 1: 14–16, LBJL.

24. Ibid., 11.

25. Paper prepared by Vietnam Task Force, "Outline Plan of Counterinsurgency Operations," Jan. 10, 1962, *FRUS*, 2: *Vietnam 1962*, 18, 21.

26. Alexis Johnson Oral History Interview, 21–25, JFKL; Gilpatric Oral History Interview, 1: 22–23, 2: 35, 37, JFKL. In an annex to NSAM 124, President Kennedy assigned Laos, South Vietnam, and Thailand to the Special Group (Counterinsurgency). See NSAM 124, Jan. 18, 1962, ibid., 49–50.

27. Hilsman to Taylor, encl.: Bureau of Intelligence and Research, Department of State, "A Strategic Concept for South Vietnam," Feb. 2, 1962, NSF, Countries—Vietnam, box 195, JFKL.

28. Alexis Johnson to Taylor, Jan. 18, 1962, NSAM 124, Jan. 18, 1962, pp. 50–51; Col. Howard L. Burris, vice-president's military aide, to LBJ, March 30, 1962, ibid., 284–85; Kahin, *Intervention*, 478 n. 49; Gibbons, *U.S. Government and the Vietnam War*, 2: 104; Thompson plan in *USVR*, Book 11: 347–58; Kaiser, *American Tragedy*, 154.

29. Gravel, ed., *Pentagon Papers*, 2: 140–42.

30. Draft by head of British Advisory Mission in Vietnam, Robert Thompson, n.d. but c. early Feb. 1962, in Gibbons, *U.S. Government and the Vietnam War*, 2: 103–5; Trueheart to Cottrell, Feb. 12, 1962, ibid., 120; *USVR*, Book 11: 325; Rust, *Kennedy in Vietnam*, 136.

31. Ed. Note, Feb. 3, 1962, *FRUS*, 2: *Vietnam 1962*, 96; Felt to McGarr, Feb. 8, 1962, ibid., 111–12; Nolting to Rusk, Feb. 3, 1962, ibid., 95; Status Report of Developments since Feb. 8, Feb. 15, 1962, NSF, Countries—Vietnam, boxes 202–3, JFKL.

32. Nolting to Rusk, Feb. 6, 1962, *FRUS*, 2: *Vietnam 1962*, 98; Rusk to Nolting, no. 698, Nov. 28, 1961, NSF, Countries—Vietnam, boxes 202–3, JFKL.

33. Harriman Oral History Interview, 119–20, JFKL; Cottrell to Rowan, Feb. 13, 1962, *FRUS*, 2: *Vietnam 1962*, 124–26.

34. Harriman in *FRUS*, 2: *Vietnam 1962*, 124 n. 1.

35. Rowan to Alexis Johnson, Feb. 15, 1962, ibid., 129–32; Rowan to Alexis Johnson, Feb. 16, 1962, ibid., 139; Newman, *JFK and Vietnam*, 206.

36. Press Briefing Material on Vietnam, Feb. 8, 1962, POF, Cabinet Meetings, March 12, 1962, box 92, JFKL.

37. Memo of discussion at Department of State–Joint Chiefs of Staff meeting in the Pentagon, Feb. 9, 1962, *FRUS*, 2: *Vietnam 1962*, 113–15; Cottrell to Harriman, Feb. 17, 1962, ibid., 142.

38. McNamara to JFK, Jan. 2, 1962, ibid., 3; McNamara to JFK, Feb. 2, 1962, NSF, Countries—Vietnam, box 195, JFKL; MAAG to CINCPAC, no. 779, Feb. 5, 1962, ibid.; NSAM 115, Nov. 30, 1961, *USVR*, Book 11: 425; Reeves, *President Kennedy*, 282–83.

39. Memo (by Hilsman) of conversation in White House, May 1, 1962, *FRUS*, 2: *Vietnam 1962*, 367; Hilsman, *To Move a Nation*, 432, 442, 443.

40. Martin to Cottrell, Feb. 21, 1962, *FRUS*, 2: *Vietnam 1962*, 161–63.

41. Cottrell to Harriman, Feb. 17, 1962, ibid., 142, 144–45.

42. Morse, Gore, and Fulbright quoted in Gibbons, *U.S. Government and the Vietnam War*, 2: 110; RFK quote of February 18 in *New York Times*, Feb. 19, 1962, p. 1.

43. Department of State replies to questions posed by Morse to Harriman after executive session of Senate Foreign Relations Committee, Feb. 21, 1962, encl. in Frederick G. Dutton, Asst. Sec. of State for Congressional Relations, to Fulbright, March 14, 1962, *FRUS*, 2: *Vietnam 1962*, 222; ibid., 222–23; *U.S.* v. *Curtiss-Wright* in 299 U.S. 304, 318 ff.; Foreign Assistance Act in P.L. 87–195, Sept. 4, 1961; 75 Stat. 424, Section 503.

44. Letter from Asst. Sec. of State for Congressional Relations, Frederick G. Dutton, to Fulbright, March 14, 1962, encl.: Answers to Sen. Wayne Morse's Questions of Feb. 21, 1972, on Vietnam, *FRUS*, 2: *Vietnam 1962*, 225.

45. Ibid., 225–26.

46. Ibid., 227, 231.

47. Rusk to Saigon embassy, Feb. 21, 1962, ibid., 158–60.

48. Pierre Salinger, *With Kennedy* (New York: Avon Books, 1967), 394; John Mecklin, *Mission in Torment: An Intimate Account of the U.S. Role in Vietnam* (Garden City, N.Y.: Doubleday, 1965), 100, 105, 111, 115.

49. McGarr to LBJ, Feb. 22, 1962, *FRUS*, 2: *Vietnam 1962*, 165.

50. Bagley to Taylor, Feb. 23, 1962, ibid., 172–73; Nolting to Rusk, Feb. 26, 1962, ibid., 176; Press Briefing Material on Vietnam, Feb. 23, 1962, POF, Cabinet Meetings, March 12, 1962, box 92, JFKL.

51. Al Chang, a photographer for the *Pacific Stars and Stripes* (U.S. Armed Forces newspaper), joined David Pike from the U.S. Information Service in being among the first on the fiery scene. From Saigon, UPI 237, 238, 240, Feb. 26, 1962, POF, Vietnam General, 1962, box 128, JFKL; CIA station in Saigon to Rusk, Feb. 27, 1962, *FRUS*, 2: *Vietnam 1962*, 181; Nolting to Rusk, March 2, 1962, ibid., 195; Harkins Oral History Interview, 1: 16, LBJL.

52. Nolting to White House, Feb. 26, 1962 (3 messages), POF, Countries Series, Vietnam, JFKL; Trueheart Oral History Interview, 1: 26, LBJL; Harkins Oral History Interview, 1: 16–17, LBJL; Harkins to JFK and Felt, Feb. 26, 1962, POF, Vietnam General, 1962, box 128, JFKL; Clifton memo for record, Feb. 26, 1962, ibid.; memo for record of meeting at Independence Palace, March 1, 1962, *FRUS*, 2: *Vietnam 1962*, 188–90.

53. Nolting to Rusk, Feb. 27, 1962, *FRUS*, 2: *Vietnam 1962*, 181; Nolting to Rusk, March 2, 1962, ibid., 195–97; memo for record of meeting at Gia Long Palace, March 1, 1962, ibid., 188–93, 193 n. 2. Immediately after the attack on Independence Palace, the ruling family relocated in Gia Long Palace, once the residence of the French governor general.

54. See Shaplen, *Lost Revolution*, 160.

55. Rusk news conference on Vietnam, March 1, 1962, POF, Cabinet Meetings, March 12, 1962, box 92, JFKL; Galbraith to JFK, March 2, 1962, POF, Special Correspondence, 1962–63, box 30, JFKL; Burris to LBJ, April 16, 1962, *FRUS*, 2: *Vietnam 1962*, 330–31; Galbraith, *Ambassador's Journal*, 311.

56. Schlesinger to JFK, March 7, 1962, encl.: "Report from Vietnam" from Howard Sochurek, head of Time Bureau in Saigon (confidential), 1, 10–11, POF, Countries—Vietnam, 1962, box 128, JFKL.

57. Zhai, *China and the Vietnam Wars*, 114.

58. Mat tran dan-toc giai-phong mien Nam, *Declaration of the First Congress of the South Viet-Nam National Front for Liberation* (Hanoi: Foreign Languages Publishing House, June 1962), 6–7, 12–14, 18, 23, 35–36. Wason Pamphlet, Department of State Vietnam 42, John M. Echols Collection (Cornell University): Selections on the Vietnam War, or in Indochina Archives: History of the Vietnam War, Unit 5: NLF, General Materials, 1962 (University of California, Berkeley); Pike, *Viet Cong*, 157, 348–50.

59. Kahin, *Intervention*, 140–41; Gibbons, *U.S. Government and the Vietnam War*, 2: 105; Gravel, ed., *Pentagon Papers*, 2: 129–30.

60. Cabinet meetings, March 12, 1962, p. 6, POF, Depts. and Agencies, Defense, box 92, JFKL; Decree by the President of the Republic of Vietnam, March 16, 1962, *FRUS*, 2: *Vietnam 1962*, 239–41; Theodore Heavner, Officer in Charge of Vietnam Affairs, to Wood, March 19, 1962, ibid., 248.

61. Heavner to Wood, March 19, 1962, *FRUS*, 2: *Vietnam 1962*, 248–49.

62. Nolting to Rusk, March 20, 1962, ibid., 251–52; Krulak to Gilpatric, March 26, 1962, ibid., 278; Cottrell's note in Trueheart to Rusk, March 12, 1962, ibid., 273 n. 7; briefing paper for presentation by Cottrell before Special Group (Counterinsurgency), March 22, 1962, ibid., 260; Hilsman, *To Move a Nation*, 442; Shultz, *Secret War against Hanoi*, 22; Gravel, ed., *Pentagon Papers*, 2: 129, 140; memo, "Visit with General Paul Harkins and Ambassador Nolting—17 March 1962," cited in Rust, *Kennedy in Vietnam*, 68; ibid., 69.

63. Benson E. L. Timmons of U.S. embassy in New Delhi, India, to Rusk, Feb. 14, 1962, *FRUS*, 2: *Vietnam 1962*, 126–27; memo of discussion in Pentagon between Department of State and Joint Chiefs of Staff, March 23, 1962, ibid., 263–64; Ball to Saigon embassy, March 24, 1962, ibid., 274–75.

64. Status Report of Developments since March 21, encl. in memo for McGeorge Bundy in White House, March 28, 1962, NSF, Countries—Vietnam, boxes 202–3, JFKL; Trueheart to Rusk, March 21, 1962, *FRUS*, 2: *Vietnam 1962*, 254–55; Rusk to Saigon embassy, March 21, 1962, ibid., 255; Joint Chiefs of Staff to CINCPAC, March 21, 1962, NSF, Countries—Vietnam, box 196, JFKL; Ball to Rusk (in Geneva), March 24, 1962, *FRUS*, 2: *Vietnam 1962*, 274; Rusk to Department of State, March 24, 1962, ibid., 273; Ball to Rusk, March 26, 1962, NSF, Countries—Vietnam, box 196, JFKL; Joint Chiefs of Staff to CINCPAC, March 26, 1962, ibid.

65. CINCPAC to Pacific Air Force, Hickam Air Force Base, Jan. 23, 1962, but not received until March 23, 1962, NSF, Countries—Vietnam, box 196, JFKL; Joint Chiefs of Staff to CINCPAC, March 26, 1962 (two messages), ibid.; Ball to Rusk, March 26, 1962, ibid.; CINCPAC to Commander, U.S. Military Assistance Command, Vietnam, Rules of Engagement in South Vietnam, March 27, 1962, ibid.; CINCPAC to Joint Chiefs of Staff, March 1962, ibid.; CINCPAC to RUMSC/Commander, U.S. Military Assistance Command, Vietnam, March 28, 1962, ibid.; Newman, *JFK and Vietnam*, 212–15.

66. Office of Sec. of Defense: "Public Affairs Policy Guidance for Personnel Returning from South Viet-Nam," c. late March 1962, NSF, Countries—Vietnam, box 196, JFKL.

67. Galbraith to JFK, March 2, 1962, in Galbraith, *Ambassador's Journal*, 311.

Chapter 8

1. Cottrell to Harriman, April 3, 1962, *FRUS*, 2: *Vietnam 1962*, 287; Hilsman to Harriman, April 3, 1962, ibid., 291; Rusk to Nolting, April 4, 1962, ibid., 292, 304.

2. Nolting to Rusk, March 27, 1962, ibid., 279–80; Status Report of Developments since March 21, encl. in memo for McGeorge Bundy, March 28, 1962, NSF, Countries—Vietnam, boxes 202–3, JFKL. Bigart's visa expired in April and Sully's in June.

3. Harriman to Nolting, April 4, 1962, Department of State Telegram no. 1173, NSF, Countries—Vietnam, box 196, JFKL; Rusk to Nolting, April 4, 1962, *FRUS*, 2: *Vietnam 1962*, 305–6; Kaiser, *American Tragedy*, 169–70.

4. Nolting to Rusk, April 7, 1962, *FRUS*, 2: *Vietnam 1962*, 316.

5. Galbraith to JFK, April 4, 1962, ibid., 297–98.

6. Ibid. Galbraith's account of the ICC report proved accurate. In early May, the report criticized both sides and viewed negotiations as the key to ending the war. Galbraith to Department of State, May 5, 1962, ibid., 375–76.

7. Bowles to JFK (memo entitled "U.S. Policies in the Far East"), April 4, 1962, ibid., 299–300, 302.

8. Harriman to Rostow, April 5, 1962, ibid., 306–7.

9. Memo (by Forrestal) of conversation between JFK and Harriman, April 6, 1962, ibid., 309–10; memo of conversation between Mendenhall and Tho, June 26, 1962, ibid., 477; memo for JFK from Forrestal, April 17, 1962, POF, Countries Series—Laos, box 121, JFKL.

10. Bagley to Taylor, April 5, 1962, *FRUS*, 2: *Vietnam 1962*, 307–8; Cottrell to Harriman, April 6, 1962, NSF, Countries—Vietnam, boxes 202–3, JFKL.

11. Cottrell to Harriman, April 6, 1962, NSF, Countries—Vietnam, boxes 202–3, JFKL.

12. Joint Chiefs of Staff to McNamara, April 13, 1962, *USVR*, Book 12: 464–65; memo for JFK, drafted by Kent and sent to McNamara with recommendation that he sign, April 14, 1962, *FRUS*, 2: *Vietnam 1962*, 325–27; Nolting to Rusk, April 16, 1962, ibid., 329–30; John M. Newman, "The Kennedy–Johnson Transition: The Case for Policy Reversal," in Lloyd C. Gardner and Ted Gittinger, eds., *Vietnam: The Early Decisions* (Austin: University of Texas Press, 1997), 162.

13. Trueheart to Rusk, April 20, 1962, *FRUS*, 2: *Vietnam 1962*, 342; Galbraith to Department of State, April 19, 1962, ibid., 336.

14. Heavner to Nolting, April 27, 1962, ibid., 353–54.

15. Ibid., 355–58, 360, 364.

16. Dept. of Defense paper, c. May 11, 1962, ibid., 380–81, 387.

17. Nolting to Rusk, May 23, 1962, ibid., 427; Rusk to Nolting, May 22, 1962, ibid., 415; Nolting to Rusk, June 4, 1962, ibid., 435.

18. Nhu's conversation with Rufus Phillips, Special Consultant for Counterinsurgency, U.S. Operations Mission, June 22, 1962, recounted in Phillips to William H. Fippin, Acting Director of Mission, June 25, 1962, ibid., 470–71; memo for record of meeting on Sept. 11 in Saigon of Nhu, Nolting, Taylor, and Harkins, Sept. 14, 1962, ibid., 638–39, 641.

19. Memo by Trueheart of his conversation with Thuan in Gia Long Palace, May 24, 1962, ibid., 428–30.

20. "Americans in Vietnam: What Price Victory in the Jungle?" *Newsweek*, April 30, 1962, pp. 40, 43.

21. Ball's speech before Detroit Economic Club, April 30, 1962, "Viet-Nam—Free World Challenge in Southeast Asia," POF, Department of State, April–May 1962, Depts. and Agencies, box 88, JFKL, or in POF, Countries—Vietnam, 1962, box 128, JFKL; Gibbons, *U.S. Government and the Vietnam War*, 2: 122–23.

22. Ball's speech before Detroit Economic Club.

23. Ball to McGeorge Bundy, May 1, 1962, POF, Countries—Vietnam, 1962, box 128, JFKL. Newspapers enclosed in note.

24. Ibid.; Forrestal to McGeorge Bundy, May 5, 1962, encl.: statements by Rusk and JFK on Vietnam, NSF, Countries—Vietnam, box 196, JFKL. For the Greek crisis, see Jones, *"New Kind of War."*

25. Jones, *"New Kind of War,"* 214–15, 22; Howard Jones, "Mistaken Prelude to Vietnam: The Truman Doctrine and 'A New Kind of War' in Greece," *Journal of Modern Greek Studies* 10 (May 1992): 121–43.

26. Cottrell to Martin, c. late April 1962, *FRUS,* 2: *Vietnam 1962,* 365–66; discussion of Vietcong and ARVN figures, along with Rostow's reaction, in Newman, *JFK and Vietnam,* 175–76.

27. Bagley to Taylor, May 9, 1962, *FRUS,* 2: *Vietnam 1962,* 377–78; Wood to Harriman, May 11, 1962, ibid., 389; Rostow to Rusk, May 12, 1962, ibid., 393–94.

28. Rostow to Rusk, May 12, 1962, ibid., 394–95; Rostow to Rusk, May 31, 1962, ibid., 433; Rostow to Rusk, May 31, 1962, ibid., 433. Sensing a heightened demand for U.S. combat troops, President Kennedy declared before a news conference just three days after the attack on Nam Tha that the introduction of such forces would mark a "hazardous course" and that he preferred a negotiated restoration of the cease-fire in Laos. But within the week he approved the dispatch of U.S. air and ground forces to Thailand, a show of force that ultimately totaled 3,000 soldiers and that doubtless discouraged any thoughts of a North Vietnamese–Pathet Lao movement to the Mekong River. President's News Conference of May 9, 1962, *Public Papers of the Presidents: JFK, 1962,* 378; Rust, *Kennedy in Vietnam,* 73, 75.

29. Nolting to Rusk, May 17, 1962, *FRUS,* 2: *Vietnam 1962,* 402–3.

30. Benson Timmons, U.S. embassy in India, to Department of State, May 22, 1962, ibid., 415–16.

31. Nolting to Rusk, no. A-325, June 8, 1962, NSF, Countries—Vietnam, box 196, JFKL.

32. "Special Report to the Co-Chairmen of the Geneva Conference on Indo-China" (June 2, 1962), from the International Control Commission in Vietnam to Parliament, 4, 7–8, Indochina Archives: History of the Vietnam War, Unit 5: NLF, General Materials, 1962 (University of California, Berkeley).

33. Ibid., 8–9.

34. Ibid., 9–10.

35. Department of State to press on ICC report, June 14, 1962, ibid.

36. NLF booklet, *Eight Years of US–Diem Crimes* (c. 1962), 1–5, Indochina Archives: History of the Vietnam War, Unit 5: NLF, General Materials, 1962 (University of California, Berkeley).

37. Ball to McNamara and others, June 21, 1962, *FRUS,* 2: *Vietnam 1962,* ed. note, 466.

38. Hilsman to Harriman, "Progress Report on South Vietnam," June 18, 1962, *USVR,* Book 12: 479–80; Thompson cited in Bagley to Taylor, April 5, 1962, *FRUS,* 2: *Vietnam 1962,* 307; McNamara cited in Taylor, *Swords and Plowshares,* 251.

39. Final Report of Vietnam Task Force, July 1, 1962, *FRUS,* 2: *Vietnam 1962,* 490, 493–95.

40. Lansdale to McNamara, July 7, 1962, ibid., 506 n. 1, 506–10; Congressional Research Service (Library of Congress) interview with Lansdale, Nov. 19, 1982, in Gibbons, *U.S. Government and the Vietnam War,* 2: 107.

41. Memo (by Hilsman) of conversation in White House, May 1, 1962, *FRUS,* 2: *Vietnam 1962,* 367. Typed in capital letters at the bottom of the note was a statement declaring Rostow's opposition to Bowles's plan as well. Harriman to

Rusk, July 30, 1962, ibid., 565–66; JFK to Diem, encl. in Rusk to Nolting, July 9, 1962, ibid., 511.

42. Telegram 3590 from CINFO to RUMSMA/COMMACV, July 9, 1962, NSF, Countries—Vietnam, box 196, JFKL.

43. Ibid.; Hilsman to Rusk, July 16, 1962, *FRUS*, 2: *Vietnam 1962*, 522–23; Trueheart Oral History Interview, 1: 21–22, LBJL.

44. Duiker, *Ho Chi Minh*, 529–30.

45. Ibid., 531; Zhai, *China and the Vietnam Wars*, 116.

46. "Viets Wage Medicine War—Antibiotics a 'Must' in Jungle," July 16, 1962, no name on newspaper clipping, Indochina Archives: History of the Vietnam War, Unit 5: NLF, General Materials, 1962 (University of California, Berkeley).

47. NLF pamphlet entitled, "Let Us Develop the Fighting Spirit to Destroy the Americano–Diem Strategic Hamlets on the Anniversary of July 20, 1962," July 20, 1962, pp. 1–2, 4, ibid. In an essay on the subject, "On the big political attack on the occasion of July 20th," a second pamphlet issued by the Vietnam Revolutionary People's Party, Bien Hoa Affiliate, likewise called on comrades to destroy the strategic hamlets. Second pamphlet entitled, "Peace, Unification, Independence, Democracy," Vietnam Revolutionary People's Party, Bien Hoa Affiliate, by Nguyen Manh Ha, July 24, 1962, but dated as sent to comrades on July 26, 1962, ibid. NLF Central Committee Declaration on "Four Urgently Needed Policies to Save the Country," p. 1, July 20, 1962, ibid., NLF, Documentation.

48. Memo for record of meeting on July 18 between Diem and Harkins at Gia Long Palace, July 31, 1962, *FRUS*, 2: *Vietnam 1962*, 526–27.

49. Ibid., 527, 530–31.

50. Ibid., 531–32.

51. Ibid., 532–33, 536, 539.

52. Record of Sixth Secretary of Defense Conference, Camp Smith, Hawaii, July 23, 1962, ibid., 546–48; Gravel, ed., *Pentagon Papers*, 2: 174–75.

53. Record of Sixth Secretary of Defense Conference, *FRUS*, 2: *Vietnam 1962*, 549–50; Gravel, ed., *Pentagon Papers*, 2: 160, 162–63, 178–79; Logevall, *Choosing War*, 34.

54. Rust, *Kennedy in Vietnam*, 76.

55. Gravel, ed., *Pentagon Papers*, 2: 161–62.

56. Record of Sixth Secretary of Defense Conference, *FRUS*, 2: *Vietnam 1962*, 550–51, 553; Krulak to McNamara, July 30, 1962, ibid., 564, 564 n. 1.

57. Record of Sixth Secretary of Defense Conference, ibid., 554.

58. Gravel, ed., *Pentagon Papers*, 2: 162, 164, 175–76; Newman, *JFK and Vietnam*, 287.

59. Forrestal to Carl Kaysen, Aug. 6, 1962, NSF, Countries—Vietnam, box 196, JFKL.

60. Typed copy of press excerpt: *Sunday Telegraph* of London, July 29, 1962 (excerpts from story), Indochina Archives: History of the Vietnam War, Unit 5: NLF, General Materials, External Relations/DRV, 1962 (University of California, Berkeley); Patrick J. Honey, "Notes and Comment: North Vietnam's Workers' Party and South Vietnam's People's Revolutionary Party," *Pacific Affairs* 35 (Sept. 1962), 375–83, ibid.

61. Zhai, *China and the Vietnam Wars*, 114–15.

62. Mansfield's legislative assistant, Frank Valeo, to Mansfield, June 15, 1962, *FRUS*, 2: *Vietnam 1962*, 457; memo of discussion between Department of State and Joint Chiefs of Staff in Pentagon, June 15, 1962, ibid., 459–60.

63. Memo of conversation between Mendenhall and Tho, June 26, 1962, ibid., 477–78.

64. Mendenhall to Edward Rice, deputy asst. sec. of state for Far Eastern Affairs, Department of State, Aug. 16, 1962, ibid., 598–600, 599 n. 2.

65. Ibid., 600–601; Newman, *JFK and Vietnam*, 290–91.

66. Burris to LBJ, Aug. 17, 1962, *FRUS*, 2: *Vietnam 1962*, 601–3; memo for record of meeting at Gia Long Palace, Sept. 7, among Diem, Harkins, and Trueheart, Sept. 10, 1962, ibid., 624, 626–28, 630, 632.

67. Forrestal to JFK, Sept. 18, 1962, NSF, Countries—Vietnam, box 196, JFKL; Cottrell to Nolting, Sept. 11, 1962, *FRUS*, 2: *Vietnam 1962*, 649.

68. Taylor, "Impressions of South Vietnam," Sept. 20, 1962, *FRUS*, 2: *Vietnam 1962*, 660.

69. Ibid., 660–61; Shultz, *Secret War against Hanoi*, 32; Lemnitzer Oral History Interview, 29, LBJL; news release of Lemnitzer's remarks before National Security Industrial Association in Washington, D.C., Sept. 27, 1962, POF, Depts. and Agencies, Joint Chiefs of Staff, 1962–63, JFKL.

70. François Sully, "Vietnam: Two Views, Official ... and Unofficial," *Newsweek*, Sept. 24, 1962, pp. 30–31; Ball to Nolting, Sept. 25, 1962, *FRUS*, 2: *Vietnam 1962*, 672–73; Binh Xuyen in Herring, *America's Longest War*, 63–66.

71. Nolting to Rusk, Sept. 29, 1962, *FRUS*, 2: *Vietnam 1962*, 673 n. 3.

72. Schlesinger, *Thousand Days*, 432; Harkins Oral History Interview, 1: 19, LBJL; Nolting to Rusk, Sept. 20, 1962, *FRUS*, 2: *Vietnam 1962*, 663 n. 2.

73. Nolting to Rusk, Sept. 20, 1962, *FRUS*, 2: *Vietnam 1962*, 663 n.2 ; Rusk to Nolting, Sept. 21, 1962, ibid., 663–64; Nolting to Rusk (2 cables), Sept. 22, 1962, ibid., 664 n. 4; memo of conversation between JFK and Thuan, Sept. 25, 1962, ibid., 668, 668 n. 3; Nolting to Rusk, Oct. 4, 1962, ibid., 677–79. Harkins declared that the first cry to get rid of Diem came when he threatened to remove his ambassador from Vientiane if Harriman negotiated a neutralist government in Laos. Harkins Oral History Interview, 1: 25, LBJL.

74. Forrestal to McGeorge Bundy, June 26, 1962, NSF, Countries—Vietnam, box 196, JFKL; McNamara to JFK, Aug. 1, 1962, ibid.; NSAM 178, encl. in McGeorge Bundy to Rusk and McNamara, Aug. 9, 1962, *FRUS*, 2: *Vietnam 1962*, 586–87; Murrow to McGeorge Bundy, Aug. 16, 1962, ibid., 590–91.

75. Joint Chiefs of Staff to McNamara, July 28, 1962, *FRUS*, 2: *Vietnam 1962*, 561–63; Rice to Harriman, Aug. 2, 1962, ibid., 570; Wood to Nolting, Aug. 7, 1962, ibid., 580; Nolting to Rusk, Aug. 7, 1962, ibid., 582; Rusk to JFK, Aug. 23, 1962, ibid., 606–7; memo of discussion at Department of State–Joint Chiefs of Staff meeting in Pentagon, Aug. 24, 1962, ibid., 610–11; McNamara to JFK, Aug. 8, 1962, NSF, Countries—Vietnam, box 196, JFKL.

76. Nolting to Rusk, Sept. 26, 1962, *FRUS*, 2: *Vietnam 1962*, 673; memo for record, Oct. 2, 1962, ibid., 675 n. 4; Forrestal to McGeorge Bundy, Oct. 4, 1962, ibid., 675 n. 4; tape recording of White House meeting, Sept. 12, 1962, POF, Presidential Recordings Collection, tape no. 23 (one cassette), JFKL.

77. Rostow Oral History Interview, 1: 67–68, LBJL; Rusk Oral History Interview, 7, LBJL; Ilya V. Gaiduk, "Containing the Warriors: Soviet Policy toward the Indochina Conflict, 1960–65," in Lloyd C. Gardner and Ted Gittinger, eds., *International Perspectives on Vietnam* (College Station: Texas A&M University Press, 2000), 73–75; Zhai, *China and the Vietnam Wars*, 116–17.

78. "Message of the President," Oct. 1, 1962, *Times of Vietnam*, Oct. 28, 1962, p. 5. Diem declared that the strategic hamlets would lead to a social, political, and economic revolution that was the "essential revolution" for underdeveloped nations. *1962, the Year of Strategic Hamlets* (Saigon: 1963?), Echols Collection: Selections on the Vietnam War; Gravel, ed., *Pentagon Papers*, 2: 150; paper prepared in Department of State by Heavner and Wood on October 5 in response to president's request, "Developments in Viet-Nam between General Taylor's Visits—October 1961–October 1962," encl. in Heavner and Wood to McGeorge Bundy, Oct. 8, 1962, *FRUS*, 2: *Vietnam 1962*, 679–80.

Chapter 9

1. "Developments in Viet-Nam between General Taylor's Visits—October 1961–October 1962," Department of State paper prepared by Heavner and Wood on October 5 in response to president's request and encl. in Heavner and Wood to McGeorge Bundy, Oct. 8, 1962, *FRUS*, 2: *Vietnam 1962*, 680–81, 686–87.

2. Ibid., 683–84; William Brubeck, executive secretary, to McGeorge Bundy, Oct. 8, 1962, NSF, Countries—Vietnam, box 197, JFKL.

3. "Developments in Viet-Nam between General Taylor's Visits," 686–87.

4. Gibbons, *U.S. Government and the Vietnam War*, 2: 126–27.

5. Ibid., 127–28; Olson, *Mansfield and Vietnam*, 99–100.

6. Gibbons, *U.S. Government and the Vietnam War*, 2: 128–30.

7. Wood to Alexis Johnson, Oct. 11, 1962, *FRUS*, 2: *Vietnam 1962*, 688–89.

8. Ibid., 689–90; Kaiser, *American Tragedy*, 160–61.

9. Jian, *Mao's China and the Cold War*, 207.

10. Harriman to Nolting, Oct. 12, 1962, *FRUS*, 2: *Vietnam 1962*, 693–95.

11. Nolting to Cottrell, Oct. 15, 1962, ibid., 698–700.

12. Robert Johnson to Rostow, Oct. 16, 1962, ibid., 703–5.

13. Memo for record of meeting on Oct. 20 in Gia Long Palace, Oct. 21, 1962, ibid., 712–13.

14. Mecklin to USIA, Nov. 5, 1962, ibid., 723–25.

15. Nolting to Rusk, Oct. 29, 1962, ibid., 721–22; William M. Hammond, *Reporting Vietnam: Media and Military at War* (Lawrence: University Press of Kansas, 1998), 5–7; Daniel C. Hallin, *The "Uncensored War": The Media and Vietnam* (Berkeley: University of California Press, 1986), 38.

16. Mecklin to USIA, Nov. 5, 1962, *FRUS*, 2: *Vietnam 1962*, 724.

17. Ibid., 724–25. Robinson left South Vietnam on November 5, 1962.

18. Nolting to Rusk, Oct. 29, 1962, ibid., 722 n. 4; Wood to Nolting, Nov. 16, 1962, ibid., 734–35.

19. Schlesinger, *Thousand Days*, 818–19; Mecklin, *Mission in Torment*, 100; Kahin, *Intervention*, 142; Halberstam, *Best and the Brightest*, 252.

20. Mecklin to Nolting, Nov. 27, 1962, *FRUS*, 2: *Vietnam 1962*, 743–45.

21. Ibid., 745–46.

22. Ibid., 746.

23. Harriman to Nolting, Oct. 18, 1962, ibid., 707; Nolting to Harriman, Oct. 20, 1962, ibid., 716–17; Harriman to Nolting, Oct. 22, 1962, ibid., 717–18.

24. Nolting to Harriman, Oct. 25, 1962, ibid., 720; Nolting to Rusk, Nov. 9, 1962, ibid., 720 n. 5; Harkins Oral History Interview, 19, LBJL.

25. Nolting to Rusk, Nov. 21, 1962, *FRUS*, 2: *Vietnam 1962*, 741–42.

26. Mecklin to Nolting, Nov. 27, 1962, ibid., 743–44.

27. Bagley to Taylor, Nov. 12, 1962, ibid., 728.

28. Taylor to McNamara, Nov. 17, 1962, ibid., 737–38; Duiker, *Ho Chi Minh*, 530–31; pamphlet entitled *1962, the Year of Strategic Hamlets* (no author), 6, Echols Collection: Selections on the Vietnam War. The debate continues over the impact of the strategic hamlets. For a slightly favorable assessment, see William J. Duiker, "Hanoi's Response to American Policy, 1961–1965: Crossed Signals?" in Gardner and Gittinger, eds., *Vietnam*, 65–66. A strongly negative view based on the government's emphasis on security rather than reform appears in Macdonald, *Adventures in Chaos*, 218–19.

29. Nolting to Harriman, Nov. 19, 1962, *FRUS*, 2: *Vietnam 1962*, 738–39.

30. Nolting to Rusk, Nov. 21, 1962, ibid., 741.

31. Hilsman to Rusk, Dec. 3, 1962, Gravel, ed., *Pentagon Papers*, 2: 690 ff.; Gibbons, *U.S. Government and the Vietnam War*, 2: 130–31.

32. Duiker, *Ho Chi Minh*, 533–34.

33. Gibbons, *U.S. Government and the Vietnam War*, 2: 131. The delegation left Washington on November 7 and returned on December 17.

34. Memo of conversation in Gia Long Palace, Dec. 1, 1962, *FRUS*, 2: *Vietnam 1962*, 750–55.

35. First Mansfield quotes in Olson, *Mansfield and Vietnam*, 107; last Mansfield quote ibid., 108; depiction of Ngo family in Ellen I. Hammer, *A Death in November: America in Vietnam, 1963* (New York: E. P. Dutton, 1987), 82; Kaiser, *American Tragedy*, 179.

36. Frederick Nolting, *From Trust to Tragedy: The Political Memoirs of Frederick Nolting, Kennedy's Ambassador to Diem's Vietnam* (New York: Praeger, 1988), 85–86; Olson, *Mansfield and Vietnam*, 106; Nolting quoted ibid., 106–7; Trueheart Oral History Interview, 1: 28, LBJL.

37. Trueheart Oral History Interview, 1: 28, LBJL; Mansfield quoted in Olson, *Mansfield and Vietnam*, 110.

38. Nolting, *From Trust to Tragedy*, 140; Transcript, Frederick E. Nolting, 77–78, May 14, 1966, Joseph E. O'Connor, for JFKL Oral History Program.

39. Halberstam, "Mansfield Is Cool on Vietnam War," *New York Times*, Dec. 3, 1962, p. 12; Joseph Buttinger, *Vietnam: A Dragon Embattled* (New York: Praeger, 1967), 2: 1180; Olson, *Mansfield and Vietnam*, 50–52, 58, 67; Congressional Research Interview with Halberstam, Jan. 9, 1979, and with Nolting, Dec. 7, 1978, both quoted in Gibbons, *U.S. Government and the Vietnam War*, 2: 131–32; Nolting Oral History Interview, 77, JFKL; Nolting, *From Trust to Tragedy*, 98; Harkins Oral History Interview, 57, LBJL; Hammer, *Death in November*, 83; Halberstam, *The Best and the Brightest*, 208.

40. Heavner report, Dec. 11, 1962, *FRUS*, 2: *Vietnam 1962*, 763–64; n. 1, ibid., 763.

41. Heavner report, 766–67.

42. Ibid., 768–70.

43. Ibid., 771–73, 776.

44. Ibid., 772–73, 776.

45. Hilsman to Harriman, Dec. 19, 1962, ibid., 791–92.

46. Mansfield report, "Southeast Asia—Vietnam," Dec. 18, 1962, ibid., 779–80; Gibbons, *U.S. Government and the Vietnam War*, 2: 132.

47. Gibbons, *U.S. Government and the Vietnam War*, 2: 132; Mansfield report, 780–81.

48. Mansfield report, 781–83.

49. Ibid., 787; Heavner's memo for files, Dec. 27, 1962, ibid., 797–98.

50. Olson, *Mansfield and Vietnam*, 111; Reeves, *President Kennedy*, 442; Halberstam, *Best and the Brightest*, 208; Palm Beach meeting in Kenneth P. O'Donnell and David F. Powers, *"Johnny, We Hardly Knew Ye": Memories of John Fitzgerald Kennedy* (Boston: Little, Brown, 1970), 15; transcript, Mike Mansfield, 24, June 23, 1964, Seth P. Tillman, for JFKL Oral History Program; Newman, *JFK and Vietnam*, 320, 321.

51. Notes on visits to Thailand, Laos, Vietnam, and Okinawa by Alexis Johnson, Dec. 10, 1962, *FRUS*, 2: *Vietnam 1962*, 761.

52. Nolting to Harriman, Nov. 19, 1962, ibid., 739; Nolting to Rusk, Dec. 19, 1962, ibid., 788–89.

53. McNamara to JFK, Nov. 16, 1962, ibid.; McGeorge Bundy to McNamara, Nov. 27, 1962, NSF, Countries—Vietnam, box 197, JFKL; Rusk to Saigon embassy, Dec. 8, 1962, *FRUS*, 2: *Vietnam 1962*, 760; Nolting to Rusk, Dec. 5, 1962, ibid., 760 n. 2; Department of State to Saigon, Dec. 21, 1962, ibid., 778 n. 4.

54. Gilpatric to JFK, Dec. 20, 1962, encl. in Forrestal to JFK, Dec. 21, 1962, ibid., 794, 796; Forrestal to JFK, Dec. 21, 1962, ibid., 793; McGeorge Bundy to Gilpatric, Dec. 31, 1962, ibid., 797 n. 5.

Chapter 10

1. President's News Conference, Dec. 12, 1962, *Public Papers of the Presidents: JFK, 1962*, 870.

2. Memo for record by Hilsman, Jan. 1963, *FRUS, 1961–1963*, vol. 3: *Vietnam January–August 1963* (Washington, D.C.: Government Printing Office, 1991), 3–11, 16; memo of conversation between Hilsman and Anthis in Saigon, Jan. 2, 1963, ibid., 15–16.

3. Ed. Note, Jan. 2–7, 1963, ibid., 1; Karnow, *Vietnam*, 276–77; Vietcong commander quoted ibid., 278; Hilsman, *To Move a Nation*, 449; Halberstam, *Making of a Quagmire*, 71–72; Reeves, *President Kennedy*, 445–46; Rust, *Kennedy in Vietnam*, 81–83; Herring, *America's Longest War*, 106; Newman, *JFK and Vietnam*, 302–3. For a detailed account of the battle, see Sheehan, *Bright Shining Lie*, 203–65. Sheehan shows that the Vietcong had about three times the number expected, giving the South Vietnamese only a four-to-one advantage. Ibid., 205. See also David M. Toczek, *The Battle of Ap Bac, Vietnam: They Did Everything but Learn*

from It (Westport, Conn.: Greenwood Press, 2001), chap. 3; Kaiser, *American Tragedy*, 180–82.

4. Ed. Note, Jan. 2–7, 1963, *FRUS*, 3: *Vietnam January–August 1963*, 1; Sheehan, *Bright Shining Lie*, 216, 220; Jerry A. Rose, "The Elusive Viet Cong: 25,000 Guerrillas, 300,000 Sympathizers," *New Republic*, May 4, 1963, p. 10; Indochina Archives: History of the Vietnam War, Unit 5: NLF, General Materials, 1963 (University of California, Berkeley); Karnow, *Vietnam*, 277–78; Rust, *Kennedy in Vietnam*, 81–82; Halberstam, *Making of a Quagmire*, 72–74; Newman, *JFK and Vietnam*, 302–3; "A Bloody Nose," *Newsweek*, Jan. 14, 1963, p. 34; David Halberstam, "Vietcong Downs Five U.S. Copters, Hits Nine Others," *New York Times*, pp. 1, 2; Kaiser, *American Tragedy*, 182–84.

5. Sheehan, *Bright Shining Lie*, 262; Toczek, *Battle of Ap Bac*, 95–96, 121; Rose, "Elusive Viet Cong," 19–20; Hilsman, *To Move a Nation*, 448–49; Rust, *Kennedy in Vietnam*, 82; Halberstam, *Making of a Quagmire*, 73–76; Newman, *JFK and Vietnam*, 303; "Bloody Nose," 36; David Halberstam, "Vietcong Downs Five U.S. Copters, Hits Nine Others," *New York Times*, pp. 1, 2.

6. Rose "Elusive Viet Cong," 19–20; "Bloody Nose," 34, 36; Ed. Note, Jan. 2–7, 1963, *FRUS*, 3: *Vietnam January–August 1963*, 1; Sheehan, *Bright Shining Lie*, 216, 220, 262; Karnow, *Vietnam*, 277; Hilsman, *To Move a Nation*, 448–49; Rust, *Kennedy in Vietnam*, 81; Halberstam, *Making of a Quagmire*, 73; Newman, *JFK and Vietnam*, 302; "Setback in Vietnam," *New York Times*, p. 6; David Halberstam, "Vietnam Defeat Shocks U.S. Aides," ibid., Jan. 7, 1963, p. 2; David Halberstam, "Motley U.S. Force Blocks Vietcong," ibid., Jan. 5, 1963, p. 2.

7. Ed. Note, Jan. 2–7, 1963, *FRUS*, 3: *Vietnam January–August 1963*, 1; Sheehan, *Bright Shining Lie*, 262–63; Rose, "Elusive Viet Cong," 20; Karnow, *Vietnam*, 278; Hilsman, *To Move a Nation*, 448; Reeves, *President Kennedy*, 445–46; Rust, *Kennedy in Vietnam*, 82; Halberstam, *Making of a Quagmire*, 73–77, parody on 76; Herring, *America's Longest War*, 106; Newman, *JFK and Vietnam*, 302–3; "Toll Is 30 Americans," *New York Times*, Jan. 3, 1963, p. 2; "On Top of Old Ap Bac," *Newsweek*, April 1963, p. 48.

8. Reeves, *President Kennedy*, 445.

9. Col. Francis J. Kelly, *U.S. Army Special Forces, 1961–1971* (Washington, D.C.: Department of the Army, 1973), 40; Prados, *Blood Road*, 57–58; Rose, "Elusive Viet Cong," 20.

10. Rose, "Elusive Viet Cong," 20.

11. Hanson W. Baldwin, "Copters No Substitute for Men," *New York Times*, Jan. 5, 1963, p. 6; USARPAC (U.S. Army of the Pacific) to Joint Chiefs of Staff, Jan. 4, 1963, *FRUS*, 3: *Vietnam January–August 1963*, Ed. Note, 1; Toczek, *Battle of Ap Bac*, 117, 126–28; "Raid in Vietnam," *New York Times*, Jan 7, 1963, p. 10; Pribbenow, trans., *Victory in Vietnam*, 19–20.

12. Sheehan, *Bright Shining Lie*, 206, 262; USARPAC to Joint Chiefs of Staff, Jan. 4, 1963, *FRUS*, 3: *Vietnam January–August 1963*, Ed. Note, 1; Ed. Note, Jan. 2–7, 1963, ibid., 1–2; critical stories in *Washington Post*, Jan. 3, 7, 1963, and *New York Times*, Jan. 4, 1963, all cited ibid., 2; Sheehan's story in *Washington Post*, Jan. 7, 1963, ibid.

13. Ed. Note, Jan. 2–7, 1963, *FRUS*, 3: *Vietnam January–August 1963*, 2–3; Harkins on South Vietnamese victory quoted in Hilsman, *To Move a Nation*, 449;

Karnow, *Vietnam*, 279; Newman, *JFK and Vietnam*, 303; David Halberstam, "Harkins Praises Vietnam Troops," *New York Times*, Jan. 11, 1963, p. 3.

14. Toczek, *Battle of Ap Bac*, 135–36; Rose, "Elusive Viet Cong," 20; Harkins quoted ibid.

15. Harkins Oral History Interview, 1: 12–13, 49–50, LBJL.

16. Nolting Oral History Interview, 1: 11–13, 28, LBJL.

17. Halberstam, *Making of a Quagmire*, 77–78.

18. Ibid., 78.

19. Ed. Note, Jan. 2–7, 1963, *FRUS*, 3: *Vietnam January–August 1963*, 2–3; Harkins on South Vietnamese victory quoted in Hilsman, *To Move a Nation*, 449; Halberstam, *Making of a Quagmire*, 78–79; Karnow, *Vietnam*, 279; Newman, *JFK and Vietnam*, 303.

20. Arthur Krock, "In the Nation: Kennedy's Foresight of the Events at Ap Bac," *New York Times*, Jan. 8, 1963, p. 6; Krock cited in "Year of the Man," *Newsweek*, Jan. 21, 1963, p. 46.

21. Wheeler's report came before the joint chiefs by the end of the month. Ed. Note, Jan. 2–7, 1963, *FRUS*, 3: *Vietnam January–August 1963*, 3; CIA memo on war, Jan. 11, 1963, NSF, Countries—Vietnam, box 197, JFKL.

22. CIA memo on war, Jan. 11, 1963, NSF, Countries—Vietnam, box 197, JFKL.

23. Ibid.; Pribbenow, trans., *Victory in Vietnam*, 84.

24. Saigon embassy to CINCPAC/POLAD (Political Adviser), no. 688, Jan. 13, 1963, ibid. The London *Times* story first appeared on Sunday, January 12, 1963.

25. Wood to Harriman, Jan. 16, 1963, *FRUS*, 3: *Vietnam January–August 1963*, 26–27; Alexis Johnson to Henry Koren, Director of Southeast Asian Affairs of Department of State, Jan. 18, 1963, ibid., 28–29 n. 3; Bagley to Taylor, Jan. 17, 1963, ibid., 30–32.

26. Melvin Manfull, counselor of Saigon embassy, to Wood, Jan. 23, 1963, ibid., 33, 34 n. 4.

27. Eyes Only Annex: Performance of U.S. Mission, by Forrestal and Hilsman, n.d., c. mid-Jan. 1963, NSF, Countries—Vietnam, box 197, JFKL; "A Report on South Vietnam," encl. in Hilsman and Forrestal to JFK, Jan. 25, 1963, *FRUS*, 3: *Vietnam January–August 1963*, 49–53, 59; Gibbons, *U.S. Government and the Vietnam War*, 2: 134–35; Hilsman, *To Move a Nation*, 460.

28. Transcript, Michael Forrestal Oral History Interview, Nov. 3, 1969, pp. 7–8, by Paige E. Mulhollan, LBJL.

29. Forrestal interview, Oct. 16, 1978, quoted in Gibbons, *U.S. Government and the Vietnam War*, 2: 138; Wood to Harriman, Jan. 31, 1963, "Comments on Senator Mansfield Report," *FRUS*, 3: *Vietnam January–August 1963*, 70–72.

30. "Report of Visit by Joint Chiefs of Staff Team to South Vietnam, January 1963," NSF, Countries—Vietnam, box 197, JFKL; Newman, *JFK and Vietnam*, 305.

31. "Report of Visit by Joint Chiefs of Staff Team."

32. Forrestal to JFK, Feb. 4, 1963, NSF, Countries—Vietnam, box 197, JFKL.

33. Harkins to Felt, Jan. 19, 1963, encl. in Felt to JCS, Jan. 25, 1963, *FRUS*, 3: *Vietnam January–August 1963*, 35–49.

34. Gravel, ed., *Pentagon Papers*, 2: 162–63. CINCPAC reviewed this plan before it went before the joint chiefs on January 25, 1963. "Report of Visit by Joint Chiefs of Staff Team."

35. NSAM 217, Jan. 25, 1963, ibid., 63; JFK quoted by Hilsman in interview of May 15, 1984, *FRUS*, 3: *Vietnam January–August 1963*, 63 n. 2.

36. Rusk to Saigon embassy, Feb. 6, 1963, *FRUS*, 3: *Vietnam January–August 1963*, 102–3; Nolting to Thuan, Feb. 14, 1963, ibid., 115; Hilsman to McGeorge Bundy, May 1, 1963, ibid., 260–61; Wood to Trueheart, Feb. 26, 1963, ibid., 126.

37. Department of State to all posts, Feb. 15, 1963, NSF, Countries—Vietnam, box 197, JFKL.

38. Minutes of meeting in Washington of Special Group for Counterinsurgency, Feb. 7, 1963, *FRUS*, 3: *Vietnam January–August 1963*, 103; Joint Chiefs of Staff to McNamara, Feb. 16, 1963, ibid., 117.

39. Wood to Harriman, Feb. 25, 1963, ibid., 117 n. 2; Mecklin, *Mission in Torment*, 119.

40. Nolting to Rusk, Feb. 8, 1963, *FRUS*, 3: *Vietnam January–August 1963*, 109–10.

41. Ibid., 110–11.

42. Ibid., 111–12; Message from Staff Communications Office, Dept. of Army, MAC J3 1329 (prepared by Forrestal), c. mid-Feb. 1963, NSF, Countries—Vietnam, box 197, JFKL; Jorden to Harriman, March 20, 1963, *FRUS*, 3: *Vietnam January–August 1963*, 166–67.

43. CINCPAC to Joint Chiefs of Staff, March 10, 1963, NSF, Countries—Vietnam, box 197, JFKL; CINCPAC to Joint Chiefs of Staff, late March 1963, ibid.; memo of conversation in Department of State, April 1, 1963, *FRUS*, 3: *Vietnam January–August 1963*, 193; Gravel, ed., *Pentagon Papers*, 2: 225.

44. Charlton and Moncrieff, *Many Reasons Why*, 81–82; O'Donnell, *Johnny, We Hardly Knew Ye*, 16; Gibbons, *U.S. Government and the Vietnam War*, 137 n. 1; Newman, *JFK and Vietnam*, 321–22.

45. President's News Conference of March 6, 1963, *Public Papers of the Presidents: JFK, 1963*, 243–44.

46. Joint Chiefs of Staff to McNamara, March 11, 1963, *FRUS*, 3: *Vietnam January–August 1963*, 145–46; Rusk to Saigon embassy, encl.: Harriman to Nolting, March 22, 1963, NSF, Countries—Vietnam, box 197, JFKL.

47. Rusk to Saigon embassy, encl.: Harriman to Nolting, March 22, 1963, NSF, Countries—Vietnam, box 197, JFKL.

48. Duiker, *Ho Chi Minh*, 530; Zhai, *China and the Vietnam Wars*, 117, 123–24; Jian, *Mao's China and the Cold War*, 207.

49. NLF protest against spraying toxic chemicals, c. Feb. 1963, Indochina Archives: History of the Vietnam War, Unit 5: NLF, Documentation, 1963 (University of California, Berkeley); Nolting to Rusk, March 20, 1963, *FRUS*, 3: *Vietnam January–August 1963*, 163–64; Trueheart to Rusk (2 cables), March 20, 1963, NSF, Countries—Vietnam, box 197, JFKL.

50. Foreign Broadcast Information Service Daily Report: Far East, April 2 and 3, 1963, nos. 64 and 65, April 5, 1963, no. 67, NSF, Countries—Vietnam, box 197, JFKL.

51. Foreign Broadcast Information Service Daily Report: Far East, April 8, 1963, no. 68, ibid.

52. Foy Kohler of Moscow embassy to Rusk, no. 2766, April 27, 1963, ibid.

53. Joint Chiefs of Staff to McNamara, April 17, 1963, *FRUS*, 3: *Vietnam January–August 1963*, 231–32; memo prepared in Department of State, April 18, 1963, ibid., 238, 241–42; Forrestal to JFK, April 22, 1963, ibid., 245–46.

54. Rusk to Saigon embassy, Feb. 27, 1963, ibid., 128; Nolting to Rusk, Feb. 5, 1963, ibid., 98–99; Jorden to Harriman, March 21, 1963, ibid., 169–71.

55. Bowles to JFK, March 7, 1963, ibid., 136–40; Schlesinger, *Thousand Days*, 456–57.

56. Forrestal to Harriman, March 8, 1963, *FRUS*, 3: *Vietnam January–August 1963*, 142–43.

57. Helble to Trueheart, March 1, 1963, ibid., Ed. Note, 124; Nolting to Rusk, March 8, 1963, ibid.; Nolting to Rusk, March 28, 1963, ibid., 183–84; Hilsman to Frederick Dutton, Asst. Sec. of State for Congressional Affairs, April 3, 1963, ibid., Ed. Note, 124.

58. Hilsman to Rusk, April 1963, ibid., 191–92.

59. Memo of conversation in White House, April 4, 1963, ibid., 198–99; minutes of meeting in Washington of Special Group for Counterinsurgency, April 4, 1963, ibid., 202; Ball to all diplomatic posts, May 3, 1963, encl.: Rusk's speech of April 22 before Economic Club of New York on "The Stake in Viet-Nam," NSF, Countries—Vietnam, box 197, JFKL. Diem announced his amnesty plan on April 17, 1963. The U.S. Information Agency mobilized a massive effort in support of the proclamation. "Chieu Hoi proclamation," April 17, 1963, *FRUS*, 3: *Vietnam January–August 1963*, Ed. Note, 229; National Intelligence Estimate (NIE), 53–63, "Prospects in South Vietnam," April 17, 1963, ibid., 233.

60. Joint Chiefs of Staff to McNamara, March 7, 1963, *FRUS*, 3: *Vietnam January–August 1963*, 133–34.

61. Nolting to Rusk, March 26, 1963, ibid., 178–79, 181–83.

62. Wood to Hilsman, April 18, 1963, ibid., 243–45.

63. Heavner to Wood, May 2, 1963, ibid., 261–63; Nolting to Rusk, April 13, 1963, ibid., 225; Zhai, *China and the Vietnam Wars*, 117; Duiker, *Ho Chi Minh*, 531–32; Jian, *Mao's China and the Cold War*, 208.

64. Joint Chiefs of Staff, Record of the Eighth Secretary of Defense Conference, May 6, 1963, Taylor Papers, box 1, National Defense University, Washington, D.C. I want to thank James Galbraith for drawing these materials to my attention.

65. Memo of Secretary of Defense Conference in Honolulu, May 6, 1963, *FRUS*, 3: *Vietnam January–August 1963*, 265, 267–70; Gravel, ed., *Pentagon Papers*, 163, 166. For a planned U.S. troop withdrawal based on projected success, see ibid., 179–81.

Chapter 11

1. Helble to Rusk, May 9, 1963, *FRUS*, 3: *Vietnam January–August 1963*, 278; Helble to Rusk, May 10, 1963, ibid., 285; Nolting to Rusk, May 9, 1963, ibid., 278 n. 3; Mecklin, *Mission in Torment*, 153; Hammer, *Death in November*, 110; Karnow, *Vietnam*, 295; *Newsweek*, May 27, 1963, p. 49. May 8 was also the anniversary of the French defeat at Dienbienphu in 1954. "7 Reported Dead in Riots over South Vietnam Order," *New York Times*, May 10, 1963, p. 12.

2. Hammer, *Death in November*, 83–84; Gravel, ed., *Pentagon Papers*, 2: 226; *Newsweek*, June 17, 1963, p. 40; Gibbons, *U.S. Government and the Vietnam War*, 2: 143.

3. Francis X. Winters, *The Year of the Hare: America in Vietnam, January 25, 1963 – February 15, 1964* (Athens: University of Georgia Press, 1997), 30; Kahin, *Intervention*, 148. "Thich" was a title of honor much like "reverend" in the Protestant faith.

4. Gravel, ed., *Pentagon Papers*, 2: 167.

5. CIA quote in Rust, *Kennedy in Vietnam*, 100.

6. Helble to Rusk, May 10, 1963, *FRUS*, 3: *Vietnam January–August 1963*, 285; Hammer, *Death in November*, 110; Karnow, *Vietnam*, 295–96; Tri Quang quoted ibid., 296; Helble quoted in Rust, *Kennedy in Vietnam*, 100.

7. Hammer, *Death in November*, 113; Hilsman, *To Move a Nation*, 470.

8. Helble to Rusk, May 9, 1963, *FRUS*, 3: *Vietnam January–August 1963*, 277–78; Helble to Rusk, June 3, 1963, ibid., 277 n. 2; Helble to Rusk, May 10, 1963, ibid., 285.

9. Helble to Rusk, May 9, 1963, ibid., 277–78; Helble to Rusk, June 3, 1963, ibid., 277 n. 2; Helble to Rusk, May 10, 1963, ibid., 285; Helble quoted in Rust, *Kennedy in Vietnam*, 95; Gravel, ed., *Pentagon Papers*, 2: 226; "7 Reported Dead in Riots over South Vietnam Order," 12; Hammer, *Death in November*, 113–14; Karnow, *Vietnam*, 295; Kahin, *Intervention*, 148–49.

10. Hammer, *Death in November*, 114.

11. Ibid., 113–16, 135; Newman, *JFK and Vietnam*, 332; Nolting, *From Trust to Tragedy*, 106–8; Gravel, ed., *Pentagon Papers*, 2: 226; Karnow, *Vietnam*, 296.

12. Nolting to Rusk, May 9, 1963, *FRUS*, 3: *Vietnam January–August 1963*, 277 n. 2, 278 n. 3; Helble to Rusk, May 10, 1963, ibid., 284–85; Hammer, *Death in November*, 81, 142; *Newsweek*, May 27, 1963, p. 49.

13. Helble to Rusk, May 9, 1963, *FRUS*, 3: *Vietnam January–August 1963*, 278; Helble to Rusk, May 10, ibid., 285. Decree Number 10 was actually Decree Number 189.

14. Helble to Rusk, May 10, 1963, ibid., 285–86.

15. Nolting to Rusk, May 9, 1963, ibid., 277 n. 2, 278 n. 3; Rusk to Saigon embassy, May 9, 1963, ibid., 283.

16. "Manifesto of Vietnamese Buddhist Clergy and Faithful," May 10, 1963, ibid., 287–88, 288 n. 3.

17. Nolting to Rusk, May 18, 1963, ibid., 309–10; William Prochnau, *Once upon a Distant War: David Halberstam, Neil Sheehan, Peter Arnett—Young War Correspondents and Their Early Vietnam Battles* (New York: Random House, 1995), 305.

18. Hilsman, *To Move a Nation*, 468, 473; Prochnau, *Once upon a Distant War*, 16, 303–4; Mohr quoted in Halberstam, *Making of a Quagmire*, 104, 107.

19. Nolting to Rusk, May 18, 1963, *FRUS*, 3: *Vietnam January–August 1963*, 311; Buddhist quoted in "Diem under Pressure," *Newsweek*, May 27, 1963, p. 48; Karnow, *Vietnam*, 295.

20. Hammer, *Death in November*, 117; Karnow, *Vietnam*, 295; Hué consulate to Rusk, May 13, 1963, *FRUS*, 3: *Vietnam January–August 1963*, 288 n. 3.

21. Nolting to Rusk, May 18, 1963, *FRUS*, 3: *Vietnam January–August 1963*, 312.

22. Hammer, *Death in November*, 140–42.

23. Nolting to Rusk, May 22, 1963, *FRUS*, 3: *Vietnam January–August 1963*, 314; Nolting Oral History Interview, 18–20, 76, JFKL.

24. CIA Current Intelligence Memorandum, OCI no. 1561/63, June 3, 1963, NSF, Countries—Vietnam, box 197, JFKL; Forrestal Oral History Interview, 9–10, Nov. 3, 1969, LBJL.

25. Interview of Nhu by Warren Unna in *Washington Post*, May 12, 1963, cited in *FRUS*, 3: *Vietnam January–August 1963*, 294 n. 2; Hammer, *Death in November*, 122.

26. Rusk to Saigon embassy, May 13, 1963, *FRUS*, 3: *Vietnam January–August 1963*, 294–95; Hilsman to Nolting, May 16, 1963, ibid., 295 n. 4; Rusk to Saigon embassy, May 17, 1963, ibid., 308; Hammer, *Death in November*, 122–23.

27. Nolting to Rusk, no. 1056, May 23, 1963, NSF, Countries—Vietnam, box 197, JFKL; Nolting, *From Trust to Tragedy*, 108.

28. President's News Conference of May 22, 1963, *Public Papers of Presidents: JFK, 1963*, 421; *Washington Post*, May 23, 1963, quoted in Hammer, *Death in November*, 124.

29. Contingency Plan in event of Diem's fall from power, drafted by Chalmers B. Wood, Director of Vietnam Working Group, encl. in Nolting to Hilsman, May 23, 1963, *FRUS*, 3: *Vietnam January–August 1963*, 317–18.

30. Ibid., 321; Hammer, *Death in November*, 124. On Tho, see "Revolution in the Afternoon," *Time*, Nov. 8, 1963, p. 32; "The Fall of the House of Ngo," *Newsweek*, Nov. 11, 1963, pp. 29–30; and "Vietnam's Provisional Premier Is Noted as a Genial Mediator," *New York Times*, Nov. 3, 1963, p. 24.

31. Rusk to Saigon embassy, May 29, 1963, *FRUS*, 3: *Vietnam January–August 1963*, 335, 335 n. 3, 336; Trueheart to Rusk, May 30, 1963, ibid., 336–37; Trueheart to Rusk, June 3, 1963, ibid., 344; Trueheart to Rusk, June 4, 1963, ibid., 347; *New York Times*, May 29, 1963, p. 5; "Tear Gas and Daggers," *Newsweek*, June 17, 1963, p. 40; Prochnau, *Once upon a Distant War*, 154; Rust, *Kennedy in Vietnam*, 96.

32. Trueheart to Rusk, May 31, 1963, *FRUS*, 3: *Vietnam January–August 1963*, 337–38; Trueheart to Rusk, June 1, 1963, ibid., 339; Hammer, *Death in November*, 135, 138.

33. Transcript, Rufus Phillips Oral History Interview, 15, May 27, 1982, by Ted Gittinger, LBJL; Trueheart Oral History Interview, 1: 33–34, LBJL; Trueheart to Rusk, May 31, 1963, *FRUS*, 3: *Vietnam January–August 1963*, 338; "Tear Gas and Daggers," 40.

34. Trueheart to Rusk, June 1, 1963, *FRUS*, 3: *Vietnam January–August 1963*, 340–41, 340 n. 3, 341 n. 3; Hammer, *Death in November*, 135.

35. Trueheart to Rusk, June 1, 1963, *FRUS*, 3: *Vietnam January–August 1963*, 340–41; Saigon embassy to Rusk, June 1, 1963, ibid., 341 n. 4.

36. Trueheart to Rusk, June 1, 1963, ibid., 341.

37. Rusk to Saigon embassy, June 1, 1963, ibid., 342–43; Saigon embassy to Rusk, June 5, 1963, ibid., 343 n. 4.

38. Trueheart to Rusk, June 3, 1963, ibid., 343.

39. Ibid., 343–44.

40. Saigon embassy to Rusk, June 4, 1963, ibid., 346 n. 2; Trueheart to Rusk, June 4, 1963, ibid., 346–47; "Tear Gas and Daggers," 40; Newman, *JFK and Vietnam*, 333.

41. Saigon embassy to Rusk, June 3, 1963, *FRUS*, 3: *Vietnam January–August 1963*, 348 n. 2; Trueheart to Rusk, June 4, 1963, ibid., 349–50 n. 2; Rusk to Saigon embassy, June 3, 1963, ibid., 349; Helble to Rusk, June 3, 1963, ibid., 346 n. 3.

42. CIA Current Intelligence Memorandum, OCI no. 1561/63, June 3, 1963, NSF, Countries—Vietnam, box 197, JFKL; Helble to Rusk, no. 107, June 3, 1963, ibid.; Ho Chi Minh interview with Wilfred Burchett in *FRUS, 1961–1963*, vol. 4: *Vietnam August–December 1963* (Washington, D.C.: Government Printing Office, 1991), 85 n. 3.

43. NLF pamphlet, *Success in the International Field in 1962* (June 1963), 13–14, Indochina Archives: History of the Vietnam War, Unit 5: NLF, General Materials, External Relations, 1963 (University of California, Berkeley); Pribbenow, trans., *Victory in Vietnam*, 107, 121; Mao quoted in Zhai, *China and the Vietnam Wars*, 124; CIA Current Intelligence Memorandum, OCI no. 1561/63, June 3, 1963, NSF, Countries—Vietnam, box 197, JFKL.

44. Rusk to Saigon embassy, no. 1171, June 3, 1963, NSF, Countries—Vietnam, box 197, JFKL.

45. Trueheart to Rusk, June 4, 1963, *FRUS*, 3: *Vietnam January–August 1963*, 349–51; Hammer, *Death in November*, 136.

46. Trueheart to Rusk, June 4, 1963, *FRUS*, 3: *Vietnam January–August 1963*, 351; Trueheart to Rusk, June 4, 1963, ibid., 352–53; Saigon embassy to Rusk, June 6, 1963, ibid., 352 n. 3; Rusk to Saigon embassy, June 4 1963, ibid., 353 n. 4; Saigon embassy to Rusk, June 5, 1963, ibid.; Hammer, *Death in November*, 136; Hilsman, *To Move a Nation*, 473.

47. Hammer, *Death in November*, 137; Trueheart to Rusk, no. 1107, June 5, 1963, NSF, Countries—Vietnam, box 197, JFKL; Trueheart to Rusk, no. 1136, June 9, 1963, ibid.

48. Trueheart to Rusk, no. 1107, June 5, 1963, NSF, Countries—Vietnam, box 197, JFKL; Nolting Oral History Interview, 1: 15–16, LBJL.

49. Trueheart to Rusk, no. 1107, June 5, 1963, NSF, Countries—Vietnam, box 197, JFKL; Trueheart to Rusk, June 6, 1963, *FRUS*, 3: *Vietnam January–August 1963*, 359–60; Hammer, *Death in November*, 137; Nolting Oral History Interview, 1: 16, LBJL.

50. Hammer, *Death in November*, 137–38, 142.

51. Ibid., 142; Trueheart to Rusk, no. 1133, June 8, 1963, NSF, Countries—Vietnam, box 197, JFKL; Saigon embassy to Rusk, June 8, 1963, *FRUS*, 3: *Vietnam January–August 1963*, 362 n. 2; Trueheart to Rusk, June 8, 1963, ibid., 362–63; Trueheart to Rusk, June 8, 1963, ibid., 363 n. 3.

52. Madame Nhu quoted in Halberstam, *Making of a Quagmire*, 110; Rusk to Saigon embassy, June 8, 1963, *FRUS*, 3: *Vietnam January–August 1963*, 363; Hilsman to Saigon embassy, no. 1196, June 8, 1963, NSF, Countries—Vietnam, box 197, JFKL.

53. Trueheart to Rusk, no. 1136, June 9, 1963 (2 sections), NSF, Countries—Vietnam, box 197, JFKL; Rusk to Saigon embassy, June 3, 1963, *FRUS*, 3: *Vietnam January–August 1963*, 349.

54. Trueheart to Rusk, no. 1136, June 9, 1963 (2 sections), NSF, Countries—Vietnam, box 197, JFKL; Trueheart to Rusk, June 10, 1963, *FRUS*, 3: *Vietnam January–August 1963*, 371–72.

55. Forrestal Oral History Interview, 15–16, LBJL; Taylor Oral History Interview, 2: 14, 16, LBJL; Phillips Oral History Interview, LBJL; Hilsman Oral History Interview, 21, JFKL.

56. COMUSMACV to Joint Chiefs of Staff, June 12, 1963, *FRUS*, 3: *Vietnam January–August 1963*, 374 n. 2.

Chapter 12

1. Trueheart to Rusk, June 11, 1963, *FRUS*, 3: *Vietnam January–August 1963*, 375; Halberstam, *Making of a Quagmire*, 112–13; Trueheart to Rusk, no. 1146, June 11, 1963, NSF, Countries—Vietnam, box 197A, JFKL; "Monk Suicide by Fire in Anti-Diem Protest," *New York Times*, June 11, 1963, p. 6; "Fiery Protest," *Newsweek*, June 24, 1963; "The Battle of Time and the River," ibid., July 15, 1963, p. 37; "Trial by Fire," *Time*, June 21, 1963, p. 32; A. J. Langguth, *Our Vietnam: The War, 1954–1975* (New York: Simon and Schuster, 2000), 214–15; Hammer, *Death in November*, 144; Rust, *Kennedy in Vietnam*, 98.

2. Hammer, *Death in November*, 144.

3. Mecklin, *Mission in Torment*, 157; Frances Fitzgerald, *Fire in the Lake: The Vietnamese and the Americans in Vietnam* (New York: Random House, 1972), 176–79.

4. Halberstam, *Making of a Quagmire*, 113; Trueheart to Rusk, June 11, 1963, *FRUS*, 3: *Vietnam January–August 1963*, 375; "Monk Suicide by Fire in Anti-Diem Protest," 6.

5. Colby quoted in Rust, *Kennedy in Vietnam*, 98.

6. Saigon embassy to Rusk, June 11, 1963, *FRUS*, 3: *Vietnam January–August 1963*, 375 n. 2; Saigon embassy to Rusk, June 11, 1963, ibid., 377 n. 3.

7. Trueheart to Rusk, June 11, 1963, ibid., 375; Flowerree to Acting Deputy Chief of Mission Melvin L. Manfull, June 13, 1963, ibid., 375–76 n. 3.

8. JFK quoted in Rust, *Kennedy in Vietnam*, 102; Nolting Oral History Interview, 1: 13–15, LBJL; Harkins Oral History Interview, 1: 23, LBJL; Church quoted in "Vietnam: Crisis of Indecision," *Newsweek*, Sept. 23, 1963, p. 25; Trueheart interview, Washington, D.C., July 1989, cited in Anne Blair, *Lodge in Vietnam: A Patriot Abroad* (New Haven: Yale University Press, 1995), 28; Trueheart Oral History Interview, 32–33, LBJL; Hilsman in "Memorandum of Conversation, July 4, 1963," *USVR*, Book 12: 530. For other examples of self-immolation in Vietnam, see Hammer, *Death in November*, 145–46.

9. Trueheart to Rusk, June 11, 1963, *FRUS*, 3: *Vietnam January–August 1963*, 376 n. 2; Trueheart to Rusk, June 11, 1963, ibid., 376.

10. Rust, *Kennedy in Vietnam*, 98–99; Rusk to Saigon embassy, no. 1207, June 11, 1963, NSF, Countries—Vietnam, box 197, JFKL.

11. Memo for record of meeting in White House, June 14, 1963, *FRUS*, 3: *Vietnam January–August 1963*, 386 n. 5.

12. Trueheart to Rusk, June 12, 1963, ibid., 383; Winters, *Year of the Hare*, 52; Nolting Oral History Interview, 1: 15, LBJL. Nolting declared that Nguyen Van Thieu, South Vietnam's premier during the early 1970s, also considered Tri Quang a Communist. Ibid.

13. Trueheart to Rusk, June 12, 1963, *FRUS*, 3: *Vietnam January–August 1963*, 383–84.

14. Trueheart to Rusk, June 12, 1963, ibid., 385–86.

15. Trueheart to Rusk, June 13, 1963, ibid., 387–88; Trueheart to Rusk, June 13, 1963, ibid., 391 n. 3.

16. Trueheart to Rusk, June 13, 1963, ibid., 388–89.

17. Trueheart to Rusk, June 13, 1963, ibid., 389 n. 4; Trueheart to Rusk, June 14, 1963, ibid., 391; Trueheart to Rusk, June 14, 1963, ibid., 391 n. 3.

18. Frankel's article in *New York Times*, June 14, 1963, encl. in Rusk to Saigon embassy, no. 1222, June 14, 1963, NSF, Countries—Vietnam, box 197, JFKL; *New York Times*, June 17, 1963, cited in Gibbons, *U.S. Government and the Vietnam War*, 2: 144 n. 15; David Halberstam, "U.S. Avoids Part in Saigon Dispute," *New York Times*, June 11, 1963, p. 6.

19. Hilsman to Saigon embassy, no. 1219, June 14, 1963, NSF, Countries—Vietnam, box 197, JFKL; Hammer, *Death in November*, 21; Taylor, *Swords and Plowshares*, 248; Kattenberg, *Vietnam Trauma in American Foreign Policy*, 118.

20. Trueheart to Rusk, no. 1195, June 16, 1963, NSF, Countries—Vietnam, box 197, JFKL; Trueheart to Rusk, June 11, 1963, *FRUS*, 3: *Vietnam January–August 1963*, 378.

21. Ed. Note, *FRUS*, 3: *Vietnam January–August 1963*, 397–98.

22. Trueheart to Rusk, June 16, 1963, ibid., 396–97; Daily Staff Summary quoted ibid., 397 n.3.

23. Trueheart to Rusk, no. 1207, June 19, 1963, NSF, Countries—Vietnam, box 197, JFKL; Hammer, *Death in November*, 149.

24. Hilsman to Trueheart, no. 1247, June 19, 1963, NSF, Countries—Vietnam, box 197, JFKL.

25. Nolting Oral History Interview, 1: 16–17, LBJL.

26. Thomas Hughes, Department of State Bureau of Intelligence and Research, to Rusk, Research Memo RFE-55: "Implications of the Buddhist Crisis in Vietnam," June 21, 1963, NSF, Countries—Vietnam, box 197, JFKL.

27. Ibid.

28. Ibid.

29. Trueheart to Rusk, June 22, 1963, *FRUS*, 3: *Vietnam January–August 1963*, 409–10, 409–10 n. 3; Trueheart to Rusk, June 22, 1963, ibid., 411–12; Gravel, ed., *Pentagon Papers*, 2: 227; Hammer, *Death in November*, 152–53.

30. Blair, *Lodge in Vietnam*, 14; Henry Cabot Lodge, "Vietnam Memoir," chap. 1, pp. 4–5, March 20, 1978, P-373, reel 26: Part VIII, Papers of Henry Cabot Lodge II, Massachusetts Historical Society (MHS), Boston, Mass.

31. Transcript, Henry Cabot Lodge Oral History Interview, 18, by Charles Bartlett, Aug. 4, 1965, JFKL; Henry Cabot Lodge, *The Storm Has Many Eyes: A Personal Narrative* (New York: W. W. Norton, 1973), 212; Winters, *Year of the Hare*, 37; Reeves, *President Kennedy*, 526–27; McCone quoted in Kahin, *Intervention*, 151.

32. Nolting–Diem exchange in Hammer, *Death in November*, 163; Nolting, *From Trust to Tragedy*, 117.

33. Rusk to Saigon embassy, June 20, 1963, *FRUS*, 3: *Vietnam January–August 1963*, 414 n. 3; Trueheart to Rusk, June 22, 1963, ibid.; Trueheart to Rusk, June 25, 1963, ibid., 414; Rusk to Saigon embassy, June 26, 1963, ibid., 415; Ball, *Past Has Another Pattern*, 370; Nolting Oral History Interview, 30–32, JFKL.

Nolting learned of his removal over radio while on vacation. Nolting, *From Trust to Tragedy*, 111.

34. Hammer, *Death in November*, 78–79, 131, 154–57; CIA to Forrestal for Bundy, June 26, 1963, NSF, Countries—Vietnam, box 197, JFKL.

35. CIA Special Report, "The Buddhists in South Vietnam," 4–6, June 28, 1963, NSF, Countries—Vietnam, box 197, JFKL; CIA Information Report, June 28, 1963, *FRUS*, 3: *Vietnam January–August 1963*, 424.

36. CIA Information Report, June 28, 1963, *FRUS*, 3: *Vietnam January–August 1963*, 423–24; "Vietnam: Getting to Know the Nhus," *Newsweek*, Sept. 9, 1963, pp. 34, 36; Homer Bigart, "Rise of Vietnam's Religious Crisis Caught Many by Surprise," *New York Times*, Aug. 22, 1963, p. 3.

37. Trueheart to Rusk, June 28, 1963, *FRUS*, 3: *Vietnam January–August 1963*, 427–28; Trueheart to Rusk, June 29, 1963, ibid., 429–30.

38. Forrestal to Bundy, July 1, 1963, NSF, Countries—Vietnam, box 198, JFKL; Forrestal to JFK, July 3, 1963, *FRUS*, 3: *Vietnam January–August 1963*, 447–49.

39. Report by Krulak, JCS's Special Assistant for Counterinsurgency and Special Activities, undated, but early July 1963, *FRUS*, 3: *Vietnam January–August 1963*, 456, 460, 465.

40. Hilsman and Nolting to Trueheart, July 1, 1963, NSF, Countries—Vietnam, box 198, JFKL; Forrestal to Bundy, July 1, 1963, ibid.; Trueheart to Rusk, July 2, 3, 5, 1963, ibid.; Trueheart to Rusk, July 4, 1963, *FRUS*, 3: *Vietnam January–August 1963*, 449; Ball to Trueheart, July 2, 1963, ibid., 443–44.

41. Memo of conversation in White House, July 4, 1963, *FRUS*, 3: *Vietnam January–August 1963*, 452–53.

42. CIA Report, July 3, 1963, NSF, Countries—Vietnam, General, box 198, JFKL; Conein's background sketch in his testimony of June 20, 1975, p. 15, before the U.S. Senate Intelligence Committee Select Committee to Study Governmental Operations with Respect to Intelligence Activities—Record Group 46, Church Committee (SSCIA), box 47, 13-H-03, U.S. Senate, Record No. 157-10014-10094 (National Archives, College Park, Md.). Hereafter cited as Church Committee Hearings (NA). CIA quote in "Untold Story of the Road to War in Vietnam," *U.S. News and World Report*, Oct. 10, 1983, p. VN5, cited ibid., 147 n. 23.

43. Mecklin, *Mission in Torment*, 173; Langguth, *Our Vietnam*, 218–19; Halberstam quoted ibid., 219; Trueheart to Rusk, no. 210, July 7, 1963, NSF, Countries—Vietnam, General, box 198, JFKL; Hammer, *Death in November*, 157.

44. Browne, Halberstam, Kalischer, and Sheehan to JFK, July 7, 1963, *FRUS*, 3: *Vietnam January–August 1963*, 473.

45. Hammer, *Death in November*, 157.

46. "Battle of Time and the River," 37–38; Mecklin, *Mission in Torment*, 17.

47. CIA Information Report, July 8, 1963, *FRUS*, 3: *Vietnam January–August 1963*, 473–77; CIA Information Report, TDCS-3/552,822, July 8, 1963, NSF, Countries—Vietnam, box 198, JFKL; Tran Van Don, *Our Endless War: Inside Vietnam* (San Rafael, Calif.: Presidio Press, 1978), 84; Hammer, *Death in November*, 234, 248.

48. CIA Information Report, TDCS DB-3/655,523, July 13, 1963 (two reports of same day), NSF, Countries—Vietnam, box 198, JFKL; CIA Information Report, TDCS DB-3/655,517, July 12, 1963, ibid.; Gravel, ed., *Pentagon Papers*, 2: 228.

Hammer believes the coup rumors false and that Nhu intended to hunt out conspirators. *Death in November*, 287. Newman concurs. *JFK and Vietnam*, 338–39.

49. CIA Information Report, TDCS DB-3/655,523, July 13, 1963 (two reports of same day), NSF, Countries—Vietnam, box 198, JFKL; CIA Information Report, TDCS DB-3/655,524, July 13, 1963, ibid.; Rusk to Harriman, July 15, 1963, ibid.; Rice to Rusk, July 15, 1963, *FRUS*, 3: *Vietnam January–August 1963*, 488–89.

50. CIA Information Report, July 8, 1963, *FRUS*, 3: *Vietnam January–August 1963*, 477–78.

51. Forrestal to McGeorge Bundy, July 9, 1963, NSF, Countries—Vietnam, General, box 198, JFKL.

52. Special National Intelligence Estimate, SNIE 53-2-63: "The Situation in South Vietnam," July 10, 1963, *FRUS*, 3: *Vietnam January–August 1963*, 484–85.

53. Nolting to Rusk, July 16, 1963, ibid., 492; Nolting to Rusk, July 17, 1963, ibid., 494 n. 4.

54. Nolting to Rusk, July 17, 1963, (1), ibid., 494; Nolting to Rusk, July 17, 1963, (2), ibid., 494–95; Gravel, ed., *Pentagon Papers*, 2: 729; "The Plot Against Diem: 'Shameful and Disastrous'" (interview with Nolting), *U.S. News and World Report*, July 26, 1971, pp. 67–70; CIA Information Report, July 17, 1963, NSF, Countries—Vietnam, boxes 198–99, JFKL; Rust, *Kennedy in Vietnam*, 103–4.

55. Diem radio broadcast, July 18, 1963, *FRUS*, 3: *Vietnam January–August 1963*, ed. note, 514–15; Nolting to Rusk, July 19, 1963, ibid., 516; Nolting to Rusk, July 19, 1963, ibid., 517 n. 3; Gravel, ed., *Pentagon Papers*, 2: 227.

56. Rusk to Saigon embassy, July 19, 1963, *FRUS*, 3: *Vietnam January–August 1963*, 517–18; Nolting to Rusk, July 19, 1963, ibid., 517 n. 3; Rusk to Saigon embassy, July 23, 1963, ibid., 524; Hilsman to Nolting, July 23, 1963, NSF, Countries—Vietnam, General, box 198, JFKL; CIA Report, July 18, 1963, ibid.

57. Forrestal Oral History Interview, 13–15, LBJL.

58. Rusk to Saigon embassy, July 26, 1963, NSF, Countries—Vietnam, General, box 198, JFKL; Benjamin Read, executive secretary, to McGeorge Bundy, July 26, 1963, encl.: Manning's report on trip to Vietnam, 2–4, 6–9, 12–13, 28, ibid.

59. Nolting to Rusk, Aug. 1, 1963, *FRUS*, 3: *Vietnam January–August 1963*, 550 n. 2; Nolting to Rusk, July 31, Aug. 1, 1963, ibid.; memo of telephone conversation between Harriman and Hilsman, Aug. 1, 1963, ibid., 550; Rusk to Saigon embassy, Aug. 1, 1963, ibid., 550 n. 3.

60. Mme. Nhu quoted in Nolting to Rusk, Aug. 3, 1963, ibid., 553 n. 2; information on self-immolation in Nolting to Rusk, Aug. 5, 6, 1963, ibid., 553 n. 4; Rusk to Saigon embassy, Aug. 5, 1963, ibid., 553; Nolting to Rusk, no. 183, Aug. 6, 1963, NSF, Countries—Vietnam, boxes 198–99, JFKL.

61. Hilsman to acting sec. of state, Aug. 6, 1963, *FRUS*, 3: *Vietnam January–August 1963*, 554–55.

62. Gravel, ed., *Pentagon Papers*, 2: 183.

63. Nolting to Rusk, Aug. 7, 1963, *FRUS*, 3: *Vietnam January–August 1963*, 556–57; Ball to Saigon embassy, Aug. 8, 1963, ibid., 557–58; summaries of two press stories in Rusk to Saigon embassy, Aug. 8, ibid., 557 n. 3; Nolting to Rusk, Aug. 9, 1963, ibid., 559 n. 6; James Reston, *New York Times*, Aug. 21, 1963, pp. 1, 3; Langguth, *Our Vietnam*, 216; Herring, *America's Longest War*, 96.

64. Ball to Saigon embassy, Aug. 8, 1963, *FRUS*, 3: *Vietnam January–August 1963*, 558; Nolting to Rusk, Aug. 10, 1963, ibid., 560–62; reference to Chuong in Nolting to Rusk, Aug. 8, 1963, ibid., 561, n. 4; Hammer, *Death in November*, 10, 48–49, 150–51.

65. "Tiny Saigon Warrior: Mrs. Ngo Dinh Nhu," *New York Times*, Aug. 22, 1963, p. 3.

66. Langguth, *Our Vietnam*, 92; "Vietnam," 33–34.

67. "Vietnam," 34.

68. Ibid.; "Tiny Saigon Warrior," 3.

69. "Vietnam," 36; Kenneth Crawford, "Vietnam's Many-Sided War," *Newsweek*, Dec. 10, 1962, p. 38; "Tiny Saigon Warrior," 3; Bigart, "Rise of Vietnam's Religious Crisis Caught Many by Surprise," 3; "Battle of Time and the River," 37.

70. Nolting to Rusk, Aug. 12, 1963, *FRUS*, 3: *Vietnam January–August 1963*, 562–63.

71. Nolting to Rusk, Aug. 13, 1963, ibid., 564–65 n. 3; Rusk to Saigon embassy, Aug. 13, 1963, ibid., 564–65; Nolting to Rusk, Aug. 14, 1963, ibid., 565 n. 4; Nolting to Rusk, no. 226, Aug. 14, 1963, NSF, Countries—Vietnam, boxes 198–99, JFKL.

72. Hammer, *Death in November*, 163; Rust, *Kennedy in Vietnam*, 104; Diem quoted in *New York Herald Tribune*, Aug. 15, 1963, cited in *FRUS*, 3: *Vietnam January–August 1963*, 566 n. 3; President's Intelligence Checklist, Aug. 15, 1963, ibid., 566–67 n. 4.

73. Krulak to McNamara, Aug. 16, 1963, *FRUS*, 3: *Vietnam January–August 1963*, 584; article summarized ibid., 584 n. 2; JFK to McNamara and Rusk, Aug. 15, 1963, ibid., 589 n. 1; meeting between JFK and Lodge, Aug. 15, 1963, Oral History interview with Henry Cabot Lodge, Aug. 4, 1965, Oral History Program, JFKL; William J. Miller, *Henry Cabot Lodge, a Biography* (New York: Heineman, 1967), 337–38, both cited ibid., Ed. Note, 567; ministers' demands cited in Gibbons, *U.S. Government and the Vietnam War*, 2: 144.

74. Rust, *Kennedy in Vietnam*, 106.

75. CIA Information Report, TDCS-3/557,576, Aug. 27, 1963, NSF, Countries—Vietnam, boxes 198–99, JFKL; memo from Richard Helms, CIA Deputy Director, to Hilsman, Aug. 16, 1963, Attachment 2, *FRUS*, 3: *Vietnam January–August 1963*, 571–72.

76. Joint Chiefs of Staff to McNamara, Aug. 20, 1963, *FRUS*, 3: *Vietnam January–August 1963*, 591, 593–94. For optimistic appraisals, see Krulak to McNamara, encl.: "A Critical Analysis of the Article: Vietnamese Reds Gain Key Area," Aug. 19, 1963, ibid., 589 n. 4; Thomas Conlon of Vietnam Working Group to Hilsman, Aug. 20, 1963, ibid., 589–90; Gravel, ed., *Pentagon Papers*, 2: 168, 184; CINCPAC to Joint Chiefs of Staff, Aug. 17, 1963, NSF, Countries—Vietnam, boxes 198–99, JFKL. Nolting warned Rusk that the impression in Vietnam was that the United States had about 12,000 military personnel in the country. The actual numerical strength was 16,000 and by fall would peak at 16,700. With civilians, Americans would total 19,000. The correspondents, however, had been so preoccupied with the Buddhists that they had missed this growth. If the correct

figure leaked at the time of the announced withdrawal of 1000 men, the United States would "face [the] ridiculous prospect of saying, in effect, we [are] withdrawing 1,000 men [and] 'reducing' strength from 12,000 to 15,000." Nolting to Rusk, Aug. 8, 1963, ibid., General, box 198, JFKL.

77. Rusk to Lodge, no. 268, Aug. 20, 1963, NSF, Countries—Vietnam, box 198, JFKL.

Chapter 13

1. President's Intelligence Checklist, Aug. 21, 1963, *FRUS*, 3: *Vietnam January–August 1963*, ed. note, 598; Department of State Daily Staff Summary, Aug. 21, 1963, ibid.; memo from Director of Defense Intelligence Agency, Lt. Gen. Joseph Carroll of USAF, to McNamara, Aug. 21, 1963, ibid., 600; Gravel, ed., *Pentagon Papers*, 2: 203, 232; Hammer, *Death in November*, 167–68; "U.S. Denounces Vietnam for Drive on Buddhists; Charges Breach of Vow," *New York Times*, Aug. 22, 1963, p. 2; David Halberstam, "Anti-U.S. Feeling Rise in Vietnam as Unrest Grows," ibid., Aug. 24, 1963, p. 1; *New York Daily News* story in Trueheart to Rusk, No. 268G, Aug. 20, 1963, NSF, Countries—Vietnam, General, box 198, JFKL; Harkins to Rusk, Aug. 21, 1963, ibid.; "Crisis in South Vietnam Deepens as Diem's Forces Raid Pagodas; U.S. Sees Its Troops Endangered," *New York Times*, Aug. 21, 1963, p. 3.

2. *New York Times*, Aug. 22, 1963, pp. 1, 2; Department of State Daily Staff Summary, Aug. 21, 1963, *FRUS*, 3: *Vietnam January–August 1963*, 599; Carroll to McNamara, Aug. 21, 1963, ibid., 600; *New York Times* story by Halberstam in Trueheart to Rusk, no. 268F, Aug. 20, 1963, NSF, Countries—Vietnam, General, box 198, JFKL; *New York Daily News* story in Trueheart to Rusk, no. 268G, Aug. 20, 1963, ibid.; Trueheart to Rusk, Aug. 20, 1963, no. 268, ibid.; Sheehan's UPI story in Trueheart to Rusk, no. 268H, Aug. 20, 1963, ibid.; Trueheart to Rusk, no. 297, Aug. 21, 1963, ibid.; "Crisis in South Vietnam Deepens as Diem's Forces Raid Pagodas," 1; "U.S. Denounces Vietnam for Drive on Buddhists," *New York Times*, Aug. 22, 1963, p. 2; "Policemen Wrecked Interior of Saigon Pagoda," ibid., Aug. 22, 1963, p. 3.

3. Unsigned message to Rusk, Aug. 20, 1963, no. 268, NSF, Countries—Vietnam, General, box 198, JFKL; Sheehan's UPI story in Trueheart to Rusk, No. 268H, Aug. 20, 1963, ibid.; Trueheart to Rusk, Aug. 20, 1963, ibid.; Trueheart to Rusk, no. 283, Aug. 21, 1963, ibid.; "Policemen Wrecked Interior of Saigon Pagoda," 3; Reeves, *President Kennedy*, 557. The U.N. team concluded in late October 1963 that no one had died in the pagoda assaults. Hammer, *Death in November*, 168; Marguerite Higgins, *Our Vietnam Nightmare* (New York: Harper and Row, 1965), 180–81.

4. Higgins, *Our Vietnam Nightmare*, 181.

5. Department of State Daily Staff Summary, Aug. 21, 1963, *FRUS*, 3: *Vietnam January–August 1963*, 599; Department of State Daily Staff Summary, Aug. 23, 1963, ibid., 610; Mecklin, *Mission in Torment*, 183, 184; Harkins to Rusk, Aug. 21, 1963, NSF, Countries—Vietnam, General, box 198A, JFKL; Trueheart to Rusk, Aug. 20, 1963, ibid., box 198, JFKL; Ball to Trueheart, Aug. 21, 1963, ibid.

6. Trueheart to Rusk, no. 298, Aug. 21, 1963, NSF, Countries—Vietnam, General, box 198A, JFKL; "U.S. Denounces Vietnam for Drive on Buddhists," 2.

7. Trueheart to Rusk, Aug. 21, 1963, *FRUS*, 3: *Vietnam January–August 1963*, 595–96; Hammer, *Death in November*, 165. In a crowd of 3,000 demonstrators in Danang, a Vietnamese army captain and two soldiers in a jeep got entangled among the Buddhists and a dispute broke out. One of the soldiers fired three shots into the procession, wounding two of the demonstrators. They then turned on the soldiers, beating the captain, pummeling the soldier who fired the shots, and burning the jeep. "Crisis in South Vietnam Deepens as Diem's Forces Raid Pagodas," 1, 3.

8. Gravel, ed., *Pentagon Papers*, 2: 232–33; *New York Times* story by Halberstam in Trueheart to Rusk, no. 268F, Aug. 20, 1963, NSF, Countries—Vietnam, General, box 198, JFKL.

9. Trueheart to Rusk, Aug. 21, 1963, *FRUS*, 3: *Vietnam January–August 1963*, 596–97.

10. Ibid., 597; Ken Hughes, "JFK and the Fall of Diem," *The Boston Globe Magazine*, Oct. 24, 1999, pp. 10–24 (internet copy, p. 2).

11. Trueheart to Rusk, Aug. 21, 1963, *FRUS*, 3: *Vietnam January–August 1963*, 597; Mecklin, *Mission in Torment*, 182–83; Hammer, *Death in November*, 173; Rust, *Kennedy in Vietnam*, 121–22.

12. Rust, *Kennedy in Vietnam*, 122; "Nhu's Military Arm," *New York Times*, Aug. 24, 1963, p. 2.

13. "Deeper Dilemma in Vietnam," *New York Times*, Aug. 23, 1963, p. 24; "Diem Raids on Buddhists Shock U.S. Helpers in War on the Reds," ibid., Aug. 23, 1963, p. 2.

14. *New York Times*, Aug. 22, 1963, pp. 1, 2; "Two Versions of the Crisis in Vietnam: One Lays Plot to Nhu, Other to Army," ibid., Aug. 23, 1963, pp. 1, 2, 3.

15. President's Intelligence Checklist, Aug. 21, 1963, *FRUS*, 3: *Vietnam January–August 1963*, ed. note, 598; Thomas Hughes, Research Memorandum RFE-75, "Diem versus the Buddhists: The Issue Joined," Aug. 21, 1963, pp. 1, 4–5, NSF, Countries—Vietnam, General, box 198A, JFKL; Nolting Oral History Interview, 1: 17–19, LBJL; Trueheart Oral History Interview, 1: 42–44, LBJL; Mecklin, *Mission in Torment*, 181.

16. Carroll to McNamara, Aug. 21, 1963, cited in Gravel, ed., *Pentagon Papers*, 2: 233; Taylor to Rusk, Aug. 22, 1963: encl.: Harkins to Taylor, Aug. 22, 1963, *FRUS*, 3: *Vietnam January–August 1963*, 606–10; memo for record by Krulak, Aug. 21, 1963, ibid., 601–2; tape recording of White House meeting, Aug. 21, 1963, POF, Presidential Recordings Collection, Tape no. 106/A41 (cassette 3 of 3), JFKL. Colby became director of the CIA's Far East Division in Washington after leaving Saigon in 1962.

17. "Diem's U.S. Envoy Quits in Protest," *New York Times*, Aug. 23, 1963, pp. 1, 2; "Last 3 Vietnam Diplomats Quit Washington Embassy," ibid., Aug. 27, 1963, p. 1.

18. Memo by Office of Current Intelligence, CIA, Aug. 21, 1963, *FRUS*, 3: *Vietnam January–August 1963*, 602–3; Hilsman to Lodge, no. 299, Aug. 22, 1963, NSF, Countries—Vietnam, General, box 198A, JFKL; Reeves, *President Kennedy*, 560–61.

19. Ball to Harriman, Aug. 22, 1963, *FRUS*, 3: *Vietnam January–August 1963*, 604.

20. Lodge quote in Langguth, *Our Vietnam*, 220; mandarin quote in ibid.; Trueheart Oral History Interview, 1: 44–45, LBJL; Mecklin, *Mission in Torment*,

189–91; Blair, *Lodge in Vietnam*, 18; Karnow, *Vietnam*, 302; Hammer, *Death in November*, 170; Reeves, *President Kennedy*, 558, 560.

21. "Diem's U.S. Envoy Quits in Protest," 1; Halberstam, "Anti-U.S. Feelings Rise in Vietnam as Unrest Grows," ibid., Aug. 24, 1963, p. 2; Lodge's delayed submission of credentials explained in Department of State Daily Staff Summary, Aug. 23, 1963, *FRUS*, 3: *Vietnam January–August 1963*, 610; Lodge Oral History Interview, JFKL, cited ibid., 606 n. 3; Mecklin, *Mission In Torment*, 191.

22. Lodge, "Vietnam Memoir," chap. 1, pp. 4–7, 11–12, March 20, 1978, P-373, reel 26: Part VIII, Lodge Papers (MHS); Lodge Oral History Interview, 12, JFKL.

23. Lodge, "Vietnam Memoir," chap. 2, p. 1; Lodge to Rusk, no. 308, Aug. 23, 1963, NSF, Countries—Vietnam, boxes 198–99, JFKL; Hilsman, *To Move a Nation*, 483. The news correspondent was Joe Freed.

24. Lodge to Rusk, no. 308, Aug. 23, 1963, NSF, Countries—Vietnam, boxes 198–99, JFKL; Lodge to Rusk, no. 313, parts 1 and 2, Aug. 23, 1963, box 198A, ibid; Lodge to Rusk, no. 314, Aug. 23, 1963, ibid., boxes 198–99, ibid.

25. CIA Information Report, Aug. 23, 1963, ibid.; Reeves, *President Kennedy*, 569.

26. CIA Information Report, Aug. 24, 26, 1963, NSF, Countries—Vietnam, boxes 198–99, JFKL.

27. Don, *Our Endless War*, 91; CIA Information Report, Aug. 23, 1963, NSF, Countries—Vietnam, General, CIA Information Reports, box 198A, JFKL; CIA station in Saigon to CIA in Washington, Aug. 24, 1963, *FRUS*, 3: *Vietnam January–August 1963*, 614–15; Blair, *Lodge in Vietnam*, 41. Mecklin declared that Diem had taken a vow of chastity. *Mission in Torment*, 30. Independence Day in Vietnam is July 7.

28. CIA station in Saigon to CIA in Washington, Aug. 24, 1963, *FRUS*, 3: *Vietnam January–August 1963*, 616–17; Reeves, *President Kennedy*, 557–58.

29. CIA station in Saigon to CIA in Washington, Aug. 24, 1963, *FRUS*, 3: *Vietnam January–August 1963*, 618–19.

30. CIA Information Report, Aug. 24, 26, 1963, NSF, Countries—Vietnam, boxes 198–99, JFKL; Lodge to Rusk, Aug. 24, 1963, *FRUS*, 3: *Vietnam January–August 1963*, 613.

31. Lodge to Rusk, Aug. 24, 1963, *FRUS*, 3: *Vietnam January–August 1963*, 613–14.

32. Lodge to Rusk, Aug. 24, 1963, ibid., 611–12; Gibbons, *U.S. Government and the Vietnam War*, 2: 148.

33. Hilsman, *To Move a Nation*, 484–85; Lodge to Rusk, Aug. 24, 1963, *FRUS*, 3: *Vietnam January–August 1963*, 613.

34. Kattenburg to Hilsman, Aug. 24, 1963, *FRUS*, 3: *Vietnam January–August 1963*, 620 n. 3; Hammer, *Death in November*, 174; final quote in Rust, *Kennedy in Vietnam*, 111.

35. Lodge to Rusk, Aug. 24, 1963, *FRUS*, 3: *Vietnam January–August 1963*, 620–21; President's Intelligence Checklist (sent to Hyannis Port, Mass.), Aug. 24, 1963, ibid., ed. note, 626; Current Intelligence Memorandum, CIA, Aug. 26, 1963, ibid., ed. note, 626.

36. Acting sec. of state to Lodge, Aug. 25, 1963, *FRUS*, 3: *Vietnam January–August 1963*, 635; CIA station in Saigon to CIA in Washington, Aug. 25, 1963, ibid., 633–34; author's interview with Hilsman, Sept. 17, 2001; Hammer, *Death in November*, 177; Winters, *Year of the Hare*, 61.

37. Nolting Oral History Interview, 80–81 (May 6, 1970), JFKL; Trueheart Oral History Interview, 1: 53–54, LBJL; Nolting Oral History Interview, 115–16, May 7, 1970, by Joseph E. O'Connor, for JFKL Oral History Program.

38. Mieczyslaw Maneli, *War of the Vanquished* (New York: Harper and Row, 1971), 115, 117–18, 121, 125. A photograph had circulated among the diplomatic corps that suggested an immoral liaison between Maneli and Madame Nhu. Maneli denied both charges, although wittily remarking that "a love affair with as interesting and unusual a woman as Madame Nhu . . . could only adorn a man's biography." Ibid., 112–13. See also Langguth, *Our Vietnam*, 232, and Logevall, *Choosing War*, 6–12. Later exiled from Poland, Maneli came to the United States and taught political science at Queens College in New York. Hammer also emphasizes France's wish to reestablish its control over Vietnam. See *Death in November*, 222. Dinh told the press that the Diem government "had entered negotiations with the Communists . . . by contacting the Polish representative on the ICC." *Policy of the Military Revolutionary Council and the Provisional Government of the Republic of Vietnam* (Saigon: Ministry of Information, 1963), 32. Wason Pamphlet, Department of State Vietnam 373+. Echols Collection: Selections on the Vietnam War.

39. Maneli, *War of the Vanquished*, 121–22; Ho quoted in Hammer, *Death in November*, 221–22.

40. Maneli, *War of the Vanquished*, 127; Hammer, *Death in November*, 223; Lalouette quoted in ibid.

41. Maneli, *War of the Vanquished*, 127–28; Hammer, *Death in November*, 223–24; Winters, *Year of the Hare*, 43–44; Duiker, *Ho Chi Minh*, 534. Ho Chi Minh expressed the same peace terms in an interview with Wilfred Burchett that appeared in Moscow's *New Times* on May 29, 1963. See *FRUS*, 4: *Vietnam August–December 1963*, 85 n. 3.

42. Maneli, *War of the Vanquished*, 128–29, 131, 134.

43. Ibid., 135–37; Hammer, *Death in November*, 220–21.

44. Nhu's first quote in Hammer, *Death in November*, 221; Nhu's second quote in Maneli, *War of the Vanquished*, 138.

45. Remainder of conversation in Maneli, *War of the Vanquished*, 138–39.

46. Ibid., 136–37; Langguth, *Our Vietnam*, 232; Hammer, *Death in November*, 78.

47. David Halberstam, "U.S. Problem in Saigon," *New York Times*, Aug. 24, 1963, p. 2; Forrestal to JFK, Aug. 24, 1963, encl.: Ball to Lodge, Aug. 24, 1963, *FRUS*, 3: *Vietnam January–August 1963*, 625; Forrestal to JFK, Aug. 24, 1963, ibid., 627; Hilsman, *To Move a Nation*, 485, 485 n. 1; Newman, *JFK and Vietnam*, 346–51; Kaiser, *American Tragedy*, 231–34.

48. Forrestal to JFK, Aug. 24, 1963, encl.: Ball to Lodge, no. 243, Aug. 24, 1963, NSF, Countries—Vietnam, boxes 198–99, JFKL. A copy of Telegram 243 is in Ball to Lodge, no. 243, Aug. 24, 1963, National Security Adviser, Saigon Embassy Files Kept by Ambassador Graham Martin: Copies Made for the NSC, 1963–75 (1976), box 8, folder 1, Copies of Files Removed by Ambassador Martin, Henry Cabot Lodge, Including Diem Coup, 1963–65 (3 folders), Gerald R. Ford Library, Ann Arbor, Mich. (hereafter Martin Papers). According to Gilpatric, Mendenhall helped to draft Telegram 243. Gilpatric Oral History Interview, 1: 4–5, LBJL.

49. Forrestal to JFK, Aug. 24, 1963, encl.: Ball to Lodge, no. 243, Aug. 24, 1963, NSF Countries—Vietnam, boxes 198–99, JFKL; Ball to Lodge, no. 243, Aug. 24, 1963, Martin Papers, box 8, folder 1, Ford Lib.; Rusk, *Many Reasons Why*, 90–93.

50. This sequence of events derives from numerous sources: Gilpatric Oral History Interview, 1: 4–5, LBJL; Harriman Oral History Interview, 114, JFKL; Forrestal to JFK, Aug. 24, 1963, encl.: Ball to Lodge, no. 243, Aug. 24, 1963, NSF, Countries—Vietnam, boxes 198–99, JFKL; Transcript, George Ball Oral History Interview, 1: 4, July 8, 1971, by Paige E. Mulhollan, LBJL; Rust, *Kennedy in Vietnam*, 112, 114–16; Karnow, *Vietnam*, 303; Hilsman, *To Move a Nation*, 488; Winters, *Year of the Hare*, 57.

51. Gilpatric Oral History Interview, 30–31, JFKL; Nolting Oral History Interview (May 14, 1966), 23, JFKL.

52. Nolting Oral History Interview (May 7, 1970), 119, JFKL.

53. Transcript, William P. Bundy Oral History Interview, 7, May 26, 1969, by Paige E. Mulhollan, LBJL; Ball Oral History Interview, 1: 4–5, LBJL. Alexis Johnson opposed a coup involvement but termed the telegram the "green light" for Lodge to go ahead. Johnson, *Right Hand of Power*, 412.

54. Felt to Joint Chiefs of Staff, Aug. 25, 1963, *FRUS*, 3: *Vietnam January–August 1963*, 632.

55. Forrestal to JFK, Aug. 25, 1963, encl.: Lodge to Rusk and Hilsman, CAS (Controlled Action Source or CIA) station 292, Aug. 24, 1963, NSF, Countries—Vietnam, box 198A, JFKL; Ball to Lodge, Aug. 25, 1963, ibid.; Hilsman, "McNamara's War," 157.

56. William Colby, *Lost Victory: A Firsthand Account of America's Sixteen-Year Involvement in Vietnam* (Chicago: Contemporary Books, 1989), 138; Taylor, *Swords and Plowshares*, 292–94; Rust, *Kennedy in Vietnam*, 119; Hilsman, *To Move a Nation*, 487–88; memo for record by Krulak, Aug. 24, 1963, *FRUS*, 3: *Vietnam January–August 1963*, 630–31; Gilpatric Oral History Interview, 1: 5–6, LBJL; Hilsman, "McNamara's War," 157; Halberstam, *Best and the Brightest*, 263–64.

57. First JFK quote in Reeves, *President Kennedy*, 567; second JFK quote in Rust, *Kennedy in Vietnam*, 119.

58. Ball's interview of 1988 quoted in Winters, *Year of the Hare*, 57; Rust, *Kennedy in Vietnam*, 119–20; Ball, *Past Has Another Pattern*, 370, 372; Hilsman Oral History Interview, 31, 34–35, JFKL; Colby, *Lost Victory*, 138.

59. Hilsman Oral History Interview, 35, JFKL; Hilsman, "McNamara's War," 158; Schlesinger, *Thousand Days*, 825; Schlesinger, *Robert Kennedy and His Times*, 745–46.

60. Memo for record of meeting at White House, Aug. 26, 1963, *FRUS*, 3: *Vietnam January–August 1963*, 638–39, 639 n. 5; Hilsman memo of meeting, Aug. 26, 1963, Vietnam: White House Meetings, Hilsman Papers, box 4, JFKL. Those present included Rusk, McNamara, Taylor, Ball, Harriman, Gilpatric, CIA Deputy Director General Marshall Carter, Helms of the CIA, Hilsman, William Bundy, Forrestal, and Krulak.

61. Taylor quoted in Rust, *Kennedy in Vietnam*, 114; Memo for record of meeting at White House, Aug. 26, 1963, *FRUS*, 3: *Vietnam January–August 1963*, 639; Hilsman memo of meeting, ibid., 639 n. 7; Joint Chiefs of Staff to Felt, Aug. 27, 1963, ibid., 639 n. 7; Hilsman Oral History Interview, 34, JFKL.

62. Hilsman reference in testimony of Lucien Conein, June 20, 1975, p. 22, Church Committee Hearings (NA); memo for record of meeting at White House, Aug. 26, 1963, *FRUS*, 3: *Vietnam January–August 1963*, 640–41.

Chapter 14

1. VOA English Language Broadcast, 8 A.M., Aug. 26, 1963, Martin Papers, box 8, folder 1, Ford Library; VOA Broadcast, Saigon, Aug. 26, 1963, *FRUS*, 3: *Vietnam January–August 1963*, 636; Hammer, *Death in November*, 221.

2. Rusk to Lodge, no. 248, Aug. 26, 1963, Martin Papers, box 8, folder 1, Ford Library; Rusk to Saigon embassy, Aug. 26, 1963, *FRUS*, 3: *Vietnam January–August 1963*, 637 n. 5; memo for record of White House meeting, Aug. 26, 1963, ibid., 640; Saigon embassy via CIA channels to Department of State, CAS 0329, Aug. 26, 1963, ibid., 636–37; CIA report, Aug. 28, 1963, ibid., 637 n. 2. Karnow and Reeves blame Hilsman, but Hilsman's own defense, however shaky, seems closer to the truth. Both Karnow and Hilsman declared that Lodge had approved the broadcast, but with *no* speculation on aid cuts. See Reeves, *President Kennedy*, 566; Karnow, *Vietnam*, 304; Hilsman, *To Move a Nation*, 489–90.

3. Lodge to Harriman, Aug. 26, 1963, Martin Papers, box 8, folder 1, Ford Library; Trueheart Oral History Interview, 1: 46–47, LBJL; Mecklin, *Mission in Torment*, 194.

4. CIA report, Aug. 28, 1963, *FRUS*, 3: *Vietnam January–August 1963*, 637 n. 2.

5. CIA station in Saigon to CIA in Washington, Aug. 26, 1963, *FRUS*, 3: *Vietnam January–August 1963*, 642; Rust, *Kennedy in Vietnam*, 118–19; Hammer, *Death in November*, 127, 167.

6. CIA station in Saigon to CIA in Washington, Aug. 26, 1963, *FRUS*, 3: *Vietnam January–August 1963*, 642. The White House interpreted interim help to mean the "possibility of supplying military leaders in the field with logistic support directly without going through [the] Central Government." Rusk to Lodge, no. 249, Aug. 26, 1963, Martin Papers, box 8, folder 1, Ford Library.

7. CIA station in Saigon to CIA in Washington, Aug. 26, 1963, *FRUS*, 3: *Vietnam January–August 1963*, 643, 647.

8. CIA station in Saigon to CIA in Washington, Aug. 27, 1963, ibid., 653–54.

9. Saigon embassy to Rusk, Aug. 26, 1963, ibid., 650 n. 6; Lodge to Rusk, no. 335, Aug. 27, 1963, NSF, Countries—Vietnam, boxes 198–99, JFKL.

10. Memo for record by Lansdale, Aug. 27, 1963, NSF, Countries—Vietnam, boxes 198–99, JFKL; Forrestal to McGeorge Bundy, Aug. 28, 1963, *FRUS*, 3: *Vietnam January–August 1963*, 665 n. 1; Karnow, *Vietnam*, 307; Hammer, *Death in November*, 173, 194–95.

11. Memo for record of meeting at White House, Aug. 26, 1963, *FRUS*, 3: *Vietnam January–August 1963*, 641; Gilpatric Oral History Interview, 1: 6–7, LBJL.

12. Memo of conference with JFK, Aug. 27, 1963, folder on Meetings on Vietnam, Aug.–Nov. 1963 (Diem Coup), Papers of Bromley K. Smith, boxes 24, 26, 33, LBJL; memo of conference with JFK, Aug. 27, 1963, box 316, NSF, Countries—Vietnam, JFKL. Those present on August 27 included Rusk, Ball, McNamara, Gilpatric, Robert Kennedy, Taylor, General Carter, Murrow, Nolting, Krulak, Hilsman, Helms, Colby, McGeorge Bundy, and Forrestal. Smith was executive secretary of the National Security Council.

13. Memo of conference with JFK, Aug. 27, 1963, folder on Meetings on Vietnam, Aug.–Nov. 1963 (Diem Coup), Smith Papers, boxes 24, 26, 33, LBJL.

14. Ibid.; memo of conference with JFK in White House, Aug. 27, 1963, *FRUS*, 3: *Vietnam January–August 1963*, 660–61.

15. Memo of conference with JFK, Aug. 28, 1963, *FRUS*, 4: *Vietnam August–December 1963*, 1; Hilsman's memo of White House meeting, Aug. 28, 1963, ed. note, ibid., 7.

16. Memo of conference with JFK, Aug. 28, 1963, ibid., 1–3; Hilsman's memo of White House meeting, Aug. 28, 1963, ed. note, ibid., 7; Krulak's memo for record, Aug. 28, 1963, ibid.; memo of conference with JFK, Aug. 28, 1963, folder on Meetings on Vietnam, Aug.–Nov. 1963 (Diem Coup), Smith Papers, boxes 24, 26, 33, LBJL.

17. Memo of conference with JFK, Aug. 28, 1963, *FRUS*, 4: *Vietnam August–December 1963*, 4–5; Hilsman's notes on White House meeting, Aug. 28, 1963, ed. note, ibid., 8; memo of conference with JFK, Aug. 28, 1963, folder on Meetings on Vietnam, Aug.–Nov. 1963 (Diem Coup), Smith Papers, boxes 24, 26, 33, LBJL.

18. Memo of conference with JFK, Aug. 28, 1963, *FRUS*, 4: *Vietnam August–December 1963*, 5.

19. Ibid., 4–5; Hilsman's notes on White House meeting, Aug. 28, 1963, ed. note, ibid., 8; memo of conference with JFK, Aug. 28, 1963, folder on Meetings on Vietnam, Aug.–Nov. 1963 (Diem Coup), Smith Papers, boxes 24, 26, 33, LBJL; memo of conversation (by Hilsman), Aug. 28, 1963, Vietnam: White House Meetings, Aug. 8–Oct. 29, 1963, Hilsman Papers, box 4, JFKL.

20. Harkins to Taylor, Aug. 28, 1963, NSF, Countries—Vietnam, General, Defense Cables, box 198A, JFKL; memo of conference with JFK, Aug. 28, 1963, folder on Meetings on Vietnam, Aug.–Nov. 1963 (Diem Coup), Smith Papers, boxes 24, 26, 33, LBJL; Edward R. Murrow, director of USIA, to JFK, Aug. 28, 1963, *FRUS*, 3: *Vietnam January–August 1963*, 672.

21. Hilsman Oral History Interview, 34, JFKL.

22. Memo of telephone conversation between JFK and Hilsman, Aug. 29, 1963, *FRUS*, 4: *Vietnam August–December 1963*, 25–26, 25 n. 2.

23. Memo of conference with JFK, Aug. 28, 1963, ibid., 3; Logevall, *Choosing War*, 43.

24. Memo of conference with JFK, Aug. 28, 1963, *FRUS*, 4: *Vietnam August–December 1963*, 3–4; Hilsman's notes on White House meeting, Aug. 28, 1963, ed. note, ibid., 8–9; memo of conference with JFK, Aug. 28, 1963, folder on Meetings on Vietnam, Aug.–Nov. 1963 (Diem Coup), Smith Papers, boxes 24, 26, 33, LBJL.

25. CIA to White House, Aug. 28, 1963, NSF, Countries—Vietnam, boxes 198–99, JFKL.

26. Memo of conference with JFK, Aug. 28, 1963, *FRUS*, 4: *Vietnam August–December 1963*, 1991, 1–6; JFK to Lodge, Aug. 28, 1963, box 316, NSF, Countries—Vietnam, box 316, JFKL; Gilpatric Oral History Interview, 1: 7–8, LBJL; Gilpatric Oral History Interview, 31, JFKL; Rust, *Kennedy in Vietnam*, 122–23; Forrestal quoting JFK's August 28, 1963, comment, ibid., 123; McGeorge Bundy quoted in Walter Isaacson and Evan Thomas, *The Wise Men: Six Friends and the World They Made* (New York: Simon and Schuster, 1986), 618.

27. Harriman Oral History Interview, 105–6, 109, JFKL.

28. Rusk to Lodge, no. 268, Aug. 28, 1963, NSF, Countries—Vietnam, General, box 198A, JFKL.

29. Lodge to Rusk, Aug. 28, 1963, *FRUS*, 3: *Vietnam January–August 1963*, 668–71.

30. Lodge to Rusk, no. 371, Aug. 29, 1963, NSF, Countries—Vietnam, boxes 198–99, JFKL.

31. Ibid.

32. Ibid.

33. Ibid.

34. President's Intelligence Checklist, Aug. 28, 1963, *FRUS*, 4: *Vietnam August–December 1963*, 9; CIA Information Report, TDCS-3/557, p. 818, Aug. 28, 1963, NSF, Countries—Vietnam, boxes 198–99, JFKL.

35. CIA station in Saigon to CIA in Washington, Aug. 27, 1963, *FRUS*, 3: *Vietnam January–August 1963*, 654; Lodge to Rusk, Aug. 27, 1963, ibid., 650–1; Taylor to Harkins, Aug. 26, 1963, ibid., 648; CIA station in Saigon to CIA in Washington, Aug. 30, 1963, *FRUS*, 4: *Vietnam August–December 1963*, 40–41.

36. JFK to Lodge, Aug. 28, 1963, Martin Papers, box 8, folder 1, Ford Library; Lodge to JFK, Aug. 29, 1963, ibid.; Lodge to Rusk, Aug. 29, 1963, *FRUS*, 4: *Vietnam August–December 1963*, 21–22; Harkins to Taylor, Aug. 29, 1963, ibid., 23–25.

37. Memo of conference with JFK, Aug. 29, 1963, folder on Meetings on Vietnam (Diem Coup), Smith Papers, boxes 24, 26, 33, LBJL; memo of conference with JFK, Aug. 29, 1963 (noon), NSF, Countries—Vietnam, Meetings on Vietnam, box 316, JFKL.

38. Ibid., both references.

39. Ibid., both references.

40. Ibid., both references; memo of conference with JFK in White House, Aug. 29, 1963, *FRUS*, 4: *Vietnam August–December 1963*, 29–30; Lodge to Rusk, Aug. 30, 1963, ibid., 32 n. 3; Vice Adm. Herbert Riley, Director of the Joint Chiefs of Staff, to JFK, Aug. 30, 1963, ibid., 62.

41. Rusk to Lodge, no. 272, Aug. 29, 1963, NSF, Countries—Vietnam, boxes 198–99, JFKL; Taylor to Harkins, Aug. 29, 1963, Martin Papers, box 8, folder 1, Ford Library. Rusk's note to Lodge is also in the Martin Papers.

42. Rusk to Lodge, no. 272, Aug. 29, 1963, NSF, Countries—Vietnam, boxes 198–99, JFKL; Rusk to Lodge, no. 279, Aug. 29, 1963, ibid., or in Martin Papers, box 8, folder 2, Ford Library.

43. JFK to Lodge, Aug. 29, 1963 ("Personal for the Ambassador from the President"), Martin Papers, box 8, folder 2, Ford Library; Bundy to Gen. Chester Clifton, president's military aide, Aug. 30, 1963, encl.: JFK to Lodge, Aug. 29, 1963, NSF, Countries—Vietnam, boxes 198–99, JFKL; Lodge, "Vietnam Memoir," chap. 2, pp. 4–5.

44. Lodge to JFK, Aug. 30, 1963 ("For President Only, Pass White House Directly, No Other Distribution Whatever"), Martin Papers, box 8, folder 2, Ford Library; Bundy to Clifton, Aug. 30, 1963, encl.: Lodge to JFK, Aug. 30, 1963, NSF, Countries—Vietnam, boxes 198–99, JFKL.

45. Lodge, "Vietnam Memoir," chap. 2, p. 3; Lodge to Rusk, Aug. 30, 1963, *FRUS*, 4: *Vietnam August–December 1963*, 38–39; memo of conversation in Department of State, Aug. 30, 1963, ibid., 53–55; Bromley Smith's notes on meeting, Aug. 30, 1963, ibid., 53 n. 2, 54 n. 5; Taylor to JFK, Aug. 30, 1963, ibid., 43–48.

46. Memo of conference with JFK (not present), Aug. 30, 1963 (2:30 P.M.), NSF, Countries—Vietnam, Meetings on Vietnam, box 316, JFKL; meeting at

Department of State, Aug. 30, 1963, folder on Meetings on Vietnam (Diem Coup), Smith Papers, boxes 24, 26, 33, LBJL.

47. Memo of conversation in Department of State, Aug. 30, 1963, *FRUS*, 4: *Vietnam August–December 1963*, 53–56; Rusk to Lodge, no. 284, Aug. 30, 1963, NSF, Countries—Vietnam, boxes 198–99, JFKL.

48. Kai Bird, *The Color of Truth: McGeorge Bundy and William Bundy: Brothers in Arms: A Biography* (New York: Simon and Schuster, 1998), 256; Logevall, *Choosing War*, 14–15.

49. Lodge to Rusk, Aug. 30, 1963, *FRUS*, 4: *Vietnam August–December 1963*, 58; memo of conversation in Department of State, Aug. 30, 1963, ibid., 54–55; Karnow, *Vietnam*, 307.

50. Lodge to Rusk, Aug. 30, 1963, *FRUS*, 4: *Vietnam August–December 1963*, 59.

51. Conversation in Maneli, *War of the Vanquished*, 140–43; Langguth, *Our Vietnam*, 233.

52. CIA station in Saigon to CIA in Washington, Aug. 31, 1963, *FRUS*, 4: *Vietnam August–December 1963*, 64; Harkins to Taylor, Aug. 31, 1963, ibid., 65–66; meeting at Department of State, Aug. 31, 1963, NSF, Countries—Vietnam, Meetings on Vietnam, box 316, JFKL; meeting at Department of State, Aug. 31, 1963, folder on Meetings on Vietnam (Diem Coup), Smith Papers, boxes 24, 26, 33, LBJL; Harkins to Taylor, Aug. 31, 1963, Martin Papers, box 8, folder 2, Ford Library; Harkins's assurance to Khiem in Harkins interview quoted in Rust, *Kennedy in Vietnam*, 126.

53. Lodge to Rusk, no. 391, Aug. 31, 1963, NSF, Countries—Vietnam, boxes 198–99, JFKL; Gravel, ed., *Pentagon Papers*, 2: 240.

54. Memo of conversation in Department of State, Aug. 31, 1963, *FRUS*, 4: *Vietnam August–December 1963*, 69–74; Gravel, ed., *Pentagon Papers*, 2: 741–43; Kattenburg quoted in Gibbons, *U.S. Government and the Vietnam War*, 2: 155; meeting at Department of State, Aug. 31, 1963, folder on Meetings on Vietnam (Diem Coup), Smith Papers, boxes 24, 26, 33, LBJL; meeting at Department of State, Aug. 31, 1963, NSF, Countries—Vietnam, Meetings on Vietnam, box 316, JFKL; Reeves, *President Kennedy*, 577 n.

55. Rusk to Lodge, nos. 294 and 295, Aug. 31, 1963, NSF, Countries—Vietnam, boxes 198–99, JFKL; memo of conversation in Department of State, Aug. 31, 1963, *FRUS*, 4: *Vietnam August–December 1963*, 70, 73–74.

56. Lodge to Rusk, Sept. 2, 1963, *FRUS*, 4: *Vietnam August–December 1963*, 84–85.

57. CIA station in Saigon to CIA in Washington, Sept. 2, 1963, ibid., 89–90 (first report), 90–92 (second report); Kahin, *Intervention*, 153–55; Hammer, *Death in November*, 165; Karnow, *Vietnam*, 307. The fifteen generals were: Don, Big Minh, Little Minh, Khiem, Le Van Nghiem, Kim, Pham Xuan Chieu, Oai, Khanh, Nguyen Van La, Tran Ngoc Tam, Nguyen Giac Ngo, Van Thanh Cao, Mai Huu Xuan, and Huyn Van Cao.

58. Maneli, *War of the Vanquished*, 143, 145.

59. Ibid., 145.

60. Ibid., 145–46.

61. Ibid., 146, 149–50. Maneli later attributed these stories to at least three sources: Diem and Nhu, who sought to blackmail their U.S. ally; the Vietcong,

who was trying to divide the regime's followers; and the coup planners, who gained a ploy for seizing the government. Ibid., 148.

62. Ibid., 150–51. Years afterward, Maneli concluded that the French call for neutralizing Vietnam might have ended the war in 1963. Ibid., 151–52.

63. Memo of conversation in Department of State, Aug. 31, 1963, *FRUS*, 4: *Vietnam August–December 1963*, 71; Lodge to Rusk, Aug. 30, 1963, ibid., 32 n. 3; CIA station to CIA in Washington, Aug. 30, 1963, ibid., 42.

64. CIA station in Saigon to CIA in Washington, Sept. 2, 1963, *FRUS*, 4: *Vietnam August–December 1963*, 86–88.

65. Ibid., 92–93; "Vietnam," 33; Schlesinger, *Thousand Days*, 825; Mecklin, *Mission in Torment*, 197–98; Gravel, ed., *Pentagon Papers*, 2: 236.

66. Hilsman to Lodge, Aug. 31, 1963, *FRUS*, 4: *Vietnam August–December 1963*, 76; Reeves, *President Kennedy*, 577. Reeves makes this assertion about the White House directive, citing a memo for the record by John McKesson, deputy executive secretary at the state department, and dated September 24, 1963. The memo, located in the Harriman Papers in the Library of Congress, read that copies of the August 24 cable, "along with all similar cables between the period August 24–29, were recalled and destroyed by S/S [executive secretary of DS] on instructions from the White House. . . . It is also understood that similar instructions were given by the White House to CIA and Defense." Ibid., 746.

Chapter 15

1. Cronkite's interview of JFK, Sept. 2, 1963, NSF, Countries—Vietnam, boxes 198–99, JFKL; *Public Papers of the Presidents: Kennedy, 1963*, 650–53.

2. *New York Times* editorial, Sept. 6, 1963, quoted in Gibbons, *U.S. Government and the Vietnam War*, 2: 163.

3. Rusk to Saigon and other embassies, no. 306, Sept. 2, 1963, NSF, Countries—Vietnam, boxes 198–99, JFKL; Taylor to JFK, undated but c. Sept. 2, 1963, *FRUS*, 4: *Vietnam August–December 1963*, 98–99.

4. McGeorge Bundy to JFK, Sept. 2, 1963, *FRUS*, 4: *Vietnam August–December 1963*, 95–97.

5. Memo of conference with JFK in White House, Sept. 3, 1963, ibid., 102–3; memo of conference with JFK, Sept. 3, 1963, folder on Meetings on Vietnam, Aug.–Nov. 1963 (Diem Coup), Smith Papers, boxes 24, 26, 33, LBJL.

6. CIA Information Report, TDCS-3/656, p. 445, Sept. 5, 1963, NSF, Countries—Vietnam, boxes 198–99, JFKL. The three accused collaborators were Colonel Jose Banzor, Filipino military attaché; Lieutenant Colonel Peter Oxley, Australian military attaché; and Colonel H. L. Lee, British military attaché. Memo by Hilsman on luncheon meeting, Sept. 3, 1963, ibid.

7. CIA station in Saigon to CIA in Washington, Sept. 6, 1963, *FRUS*, 4: *Vietnam August–December 1963*, 125–27; Gravel, ed., *Pentagon Papers*, 2: 242; McNamara, *In Retrospect*, 51; Maneli, *War of the Vanquished*, 114–52; Rust, *Kennedy in Vietnam*, 138.

8. Lodge to Rusk, Sept. 4, 1963, *FRUS*, 4: *Vietnam August–December 1963*, 111 n. 3; Lodge to Rusk, Sept. 5, 1963, ibid., 110; "What to Do About Vietnam?" *Newsweek*, Sept. 16, 1963, p. 24; CIA Information Report, Sept. 20, 1963, NSF,

Countries—Vietnam, boxes 200–201, JFKL; Gravel, ed., *Pentagon Papers*, 2: 242; Hammer, *Death in November*, 204.

9. Hilsman to Lodge, Sept. 5, 1963, *FRUS*, 4: *Vietnam August–December 1963*, 113; Rusk to Saigon embassy, no. 341, Sept. 6, 1963, NSF, Countries—Vietnam, boxes 198–99, JFKL; Rusk to Saigon embassy, Sept. 7, 1963, *FRUS*, 4: *Vietnam August–December 1963*, 129 n. 5; Lodge to Hilsman, Sept. 6, 1963, ibid., 113 n. 2; "Vietnam: Crisis of Indecision," *Newsweek*, Sept. 23, 1963, p. 25.

10. Lodge to Rusk, Sept. 9, 1963, *FRUS*, 4: *Vietnam August–December 1963*, 136–37; memo for Forrestal, encl.: CIA, Monthly Situation Summaries from Saigon Station (Aug. 1963), Sept. 6, 1963, NSF, Countries—Vietnam, boxes 198–99, JFKL.

11. Ed. note, *FRUS*, 4: *Vietnam August–December 1963*, 121; memo of conference with JFK, Sept. 6, 1963, ibid., 117–18, 120–21; memo of conference with JFK, Sept. 6, 1963, folder on Meetings on Vietnam, Aug.–Nov. 1963 (Diem Coup), Smith Papers, boxes 24, 26, 33, LBJL; memo of conversation (by Hilsman), Sept. 6, 1963, Vietnam: White House Meetings, Aug. 8–Oct. 29, 1963, Hilsman Papers, box 4, JFKL; Gravel, ed., *Pentagon Papers*, 2: 214–15; Forrestal quoted in George Plimpton, ed., *American Journey: The Times of Robert Kennedy* (New York: Harcourt Brace Jovanovich, 1970), 207; Schlesinger, *Robert Kennedy and His Times*, 770; Hilsman, *To Move a Nation*, 501.

12. Rusk to Saigon embassy, Sept. 6, 1963, *FRUS*, 4: *Vietnam August–December 1963*, 130; memo of conference with JFK, Sept. 6, 1963, folder on Meetings on Vietnam, Aug.–Nov. 1963 (Diem Coup), Smith Papers, boxes 24, 26, 33, LBJL; Gravel, ed., *Pentagon Papers*, 2: 243; Gibbons, *U.S. Government and the Vietnam War*, 2: 170–71; Rust, *Kennedy in Vietnam*, 135–36.

13. Bell interviewed by Scali, Sept. 8, 1963, NSF, Countries—Vietnam, boxes 198–99, JFKL.

14. Lodge to Rusk, Sept. 7, 1963, *FRUS*, 4: *Vietnam August–December 1963*, 131.

15. Lodge to Rusk, Sept. 9, 1963, ibid., 141–43; Gibbons, *U.S. Government and the Vietnam War*, 2: 167–68.

16. Interview of JFK in White House by Chet Huntley and David Brinkley, Sept. 9, 1963, NSF, Countries—Vietnam, boxes 198–99, JFKL.

17. Lodge to Rusk, Sept. 9, 1963, *FRUS*, 4: *Vietnam August–December 1963*, 138; CIA station in Saigon to CIA in Washington, Sept. 10, 1963, ibid., 147–48.

18. Gravel, ed., *Pentagon Papers*, 2: 243; Mecklin, *Mission in Torment*, 206–7; Harkins Oral History Interview, 1: 30, LBJL; Rust, *Kennedy in Vietnam*, 135; Newman, *JFK and Vietnam*, 371.

19. Colby, *Lost Victory*, 142; Gilpatric Oral History Interview, 1: 33, JFKL; Lodge to Rusk, Sept. 9, 1963, *FRUS*, 4: *Vietnam August–December 1963*, 144–45; Krulak report, Sept. 10, 1963, ibid., 154, 156, 158; Gravel, ed., *Pentagon Papers*, 2: 243–44.

20. Memo of conversation in White House, Sept. 10, 1963, *FRUS*, 4: *Vietnam August–December 1963*, 161–63, 163 n. 5; Krulak's first quote in Rust, *Kennedy in Vietnam*, 135–36; Krulak's second quote in Gibbons, *U.S. Government and the Vietnam War*, 2: 171; Gravel, ed., *Pentagon Papers*, 2: 243–45.

21. Mendenhall to Hilsman, Sept. 17, 1963, Gravel, ed., *Pentagon Papers*, 2: 244–45.

22. Ibid., 245, 248–49.

23. Phillips Oral History Interview, 21–22, LBJL; memo of conversation in White House, Sept. 10, 1963, *FRUS*, 4: *Vietnam August–December 1963*, 161–63, 163 n. 5, 164; Rust, *Kennedy in Vietnam*, 136; Newman, *JFK and Vietnam*, 372–73; Kaiser, *American Tragedy*, 251–52.

24. Memo of conversation in White House, Sept. 10, 1963, *FRUS*, 4: *Vietnam August–December 1963*, 164–65; Phillips Oral History Interview, 20–22, LBJL; Harriman's outburst in Halberstam, *Best and the Brightest*, 279. Trueheart later asserted that Krulak's positive assessment had resulted from the advisers' hesitancy to criticize the program. They wanted to say what their superiors wanted to hear, and they also found it difficult to downgrade a program in which they were participants. Moreover, Krulak had spent most of his time in the north when the worst situation was in the delta. Trueheart Oral History Interview, 1: 48–50, LBJL. The military officer who had criticized the war effort received a new assignment, and Phillips's relations with MACV became "pretty chilly" as its officers tried for two days to prove that he had lied. Phillips Oral History Interview, 22, LBJL

25. Memo of conversation in White House, Sept. 10, 1963, *FRUS*, 4: *Vietnam August–December 1963*, 166.

26. Murrow to Bundy, encl.: memo by Mecklin for Murrow, Sept. 10, 1963, NSF, Countries—Vietnam, boxes 198–99, JFKL.

27. Nolting Oral History Interview, 1: 26–27, LBJL.

28. Memo of conversation in Department of State, Sept. 10, 1963, *FRUS*, 4: *Vietnam August–December 1963*, 170.

29. Meeting in White House Situation Room (without the president), Sept. 11, 1963, folder on Meetings on Vietnam, Aug.–Nov. 1963 (Diem Coup), Smith Papers, boxes 24, 26, 33, LBJL.

30. Memo for record of discussion at daily White House staff meeting, Sept. 11, 1963, *FRUS*, 4: *Vietnam August–December 1963*, 175; Madame Nhu quoted in ibid., 191 n. 4; memo of conference with JFK, Sept. 11, 1963, ibid., 191, 191 n. 4.

31. Memo of conference with JFK, Sept. 11, 1963, ibid.; memo of conversation in White House, Sept. 11, 1963, *FRUS*, 4: *Vietnam August–December 1963*, 185–87; last JFK quote in Rust, *Kennedy in Vietnam*, 137.

32. Lodge to Rusk, no. 478, Sept. 11, 1963, NSF, Countries—Vietnam, boxes 200–201, JFKL; Gibbons, *U.S. Government and the Vietnam War*, 2: 174; Rust, *Kennedy in Vietnam*, 137.

33. Research memo from Hughes to Rusk, Sept. 11, 1963, NSF, Countries—Vietnam, boxes 200–201, JFKL; memo to Bundy from Robert Neumann, Sept. 15, 1963, ibid.; Lodge to Rusk, Sept. 13, 1963, *FRUS*, 4: *Vietnam August–December 1963*, 203; memo of telephone conversation between Harriman and McCone, Sept. 13, 1963, ibid., 204; Saigon embassy to Rusk, Sept. 12, 1963, ibid., 204 n. 4.

34. Memo from Chester Cooper, chair of CIA's Working Group on Vietnam, to McCone, Sept. 19, 1963, NSF, Countries—Vietnam, boxes 200–201, JFKL; memo for McCone, Sept. 26, 1963, *FRUS*, 4: *Vietnam August–December 1963*, 295–96.

35. CIA memo from Ray Cline, deputy director of intelligence, for Bundy, Sept. 26, 1963, NSF, Countries—Vietnam, boxes 200–201, JFKL; Hughes to Rusk,

Sept. 15, 1963, ibid.; Nhu quoted in "Victory in Defeat?" *Newsweek*, Sept. 30, 1963, p. 38.

36. Gravel, ed., *Pentagon Papers*, 2: 252; NLF Central Committee Communiqué, Sept. 4, 1963, pp. 1–2, 4, Indochina Archives: History of the Vietnam War, Unit 5: NLF, Documentation (University of California, Berkeley); CIA memo from Cline for Bundy, Sept. 26, 1963, NSF, Countries—Vietnam, boxes 200–201, JFKL; Hughes to Rusk, Sept. 15, 1963, ibid.

37. Memo of conversation in Washington between Kattenburg and Madame Chuong, Sept. 17, 1963, *FRUS*, 4: *Vietnam August–December 1963*, 237–38.

38. Memo by McCone, Sept. 13, 1963, ibid., 206–7; Lodge to Rusk, Sept. 13, 1963, ibid., 205.

39. Langguth, *Our Vietnam*, 245.

40. Seymour M. Hersh, *The Dark Side of Camelot* (Boston: Little, Brown, 1997), 3, 427–28; Langguth, *Our Vietnam*, 690; author's interview with Langguth, March 22, 2002; author's interview with Ellsberg, March 27, 2002.

41. McNamara testimony, July 11, 1975, pp. 4, 7, 29, 61, Record No. 157-10014-10073, Agency File No. 10-H-05, box 3, Church Committee Hearings (NA).

42. The relative documents follow McNamara's testimony in the records of the Church Committee Hearings (NA). These include: Memo for record of meeting of Special Group (Augmented) on Operation Mongoose, Aug. 10, 1962 (among those in attendance: McNamara, Rusk, Taylor, McGeorge Bundy, Lemnitzer, Lansdale, and McCone); memo from Lansdale (the whited-out and the clean versions) to CIA, Department of State, and defense departments, and USIA, Aug. 13, 1962; Summary Record of NSC Standing Group Meeting, April 23, 1963; McCone's testimony, June 6, 1975, p. 15, Record No. 157-10011-10052, SSCIA; Goodwin's interview by Select Committee, May 27, 1975; David Belin, "Summary of Facts: Investigation of CIA Involvement in Plans to Assassinate Foreign Leaders," June 5, 1975, pp. 39–40, 45–50, 54–55, 69, Record No. 157-10005-10153, SSCIA. See also Thomas Powers, *The Man Who Kept the Secrets: Richard Helms and the CIA* (New York: Alfred A. Knopf, 1979), 129. The secretary at the meeting of the Special Group (Augmented) was Thomas Parrott.

43. Lodge to Rusk, Sept. 11, 1963, *FRUS*, 4: *Vietnam August–December 1963*, 171–73; Lodge to Rusk, Sept. 13, 1963, ibid., 203; Lodge to Rusk, Sept. 13, 1963, ibid., 205; memo by McCone, Sept. 13, 1963, ibid., 206–7.

44. Lodge to Rusk, Sept. 16, 1963, ibid., 215; memo of telephone conversation between Rusk and McCone, Sept. 17, 1963, ibid., 241; Lodge to Rusk, Sept. 24, 1963, ibid., 205 n. 4; Rusk to Lodge, no. 7623, Sept. 15, 1963, NSF, Countries—Vietnam, boxes 198–99, JFKL.

45. CIA station in Saigon to CIA in Washington, no. 0940, Sept. 17, 1963, NSF, Countries—Vietnam, boxes 200–201, JFKL; Hammer, *Death in November*, 176.

46. Gibbons, *U.S. Government and the Vietnam War*, 2: 177–81; White House to Lodge, Sept. 17, 1963, in Gravel, ed., *Pentagon Papers*, 2: 743–45.

47. JFK to Lodge, Sept. 17, 1963, *FRUS*, 4: *Vietnam August–December 1963*, 252–54; Lodge to JFK, Sept. 18, 1963, ibid., 255; JFK to McNamara, Sept. 21, 1963, ibid., 278; Gravel, ed., *Pentagon Papers*, 2: 247; JFK to Lodge, no. 431, Sept. 18, 1963, NSF, Countries—Vietnam, boxes 200–201, JFKL; JFK's draft memo to McNamara, Sept. 19, 1963, ibid.

48. Forrestal quoted in Bird, *Color of Truth*, 257.

49. Lodge to Rusk, no. 556, Sept. 20, 1963, NSF, Countries—Vietnam, boxes 200–201, JFKL; Young, *Vietnam Wars*, 47–48, 74; Kaiser, *American Tragedy*, 64; Rust, *Kennedy in Vietnam*, 122.

50. Lodge to Rusk, Sept. 19, 1963, *FRUS*, 4: *Vietnam August–December 1963*, 258–59; Lodge to JFK, Sept. 19, 1963, ibid., 262.

51. Harkins to Felt and Taylor, Sept. 20, 1963, NSF, Countries—Vietnam, boxes 200–201, JFKL; CIA station in Saigon to CIA in Washington, Sept. 20, 1963, ibid.; CIA Information Report, Sept. 26, 1963, ibid.

52. Report by McNamara, undated, but c. Sept. 27, 1963, *FRUS*, 4: *Vietnam August–December 1963*, 301–2.

53. Memo of conversation in Gia Long Palace among Diem, Thuan, Lodge, McNamara, Taylor, and Harkins, Sept. 29, 1963, ibid., 311, 313–14; extract from memo of conversation with Diem (author unidentified), Sept. 29, 1963, NSF, Countries—Vietnam, boxes 200–201, JFKL; tape recording of NSC meeting, Oct. 2, 1963, POF, Presidential Recordings Collection, Tape no. 144/A49 (cassette 2 of 3), JFKL.

54. Memo of conversation in Gia Long Palace among Diem, Thuan, Lodge, McNamara, Taylor, and Harkins, Sept. 29, 1963, *FRUS*, 4: *Vietnam August–December 1963*, 318–19, 318 n. 3; extract from memo of conversation with Diem (author unidentified), Sept. 29, 1963, NSF, Countries—Vietnam, boxes 200–201, JFKL.

55. Memo of conversation in Gia Long Palace among Diem, Thuan, Lodge, McNamara, Taylor, and Harkins, Sept. 29, 1963, *FRUS*, 4: *Vietnam August–December 1963*, 319; extract from memo of conversation with Diem (author unidentified), Sept. 29, 1963, NSF, Countries—Vietnam, boxes 200–201, JFKL.

56. Memo of conversation in Gia Long Palace among Diem, Thuan, Lodge, McNamara, Taylor, and Harkins, Sept. 29, 1963, *FRUS*, 4: *Vietnam August–December 1963*, 319–20.

57. Ibid., 321; extract from memo of conversation with Diem (author unidentified), Sept. 29, 1963, NSF, Countries—Vietnam, boxes 200–201, JFKL; Taylor quoted in Rust, *Kennedy in Vietnam*, 143.

58. Taylor, *Swords and Plowshares*, 297–98; Taylor to McNamara, Sept. 30, 1963, *FRUS*, 4: *Vietnam August–December 1963*, 327 n. 1; tape recording of NSC meeting, Oct. 8, 1963, POF, Presidential Recordings Collection, Tape no. 144/A50 (cassette 3 of 3), JFKL.

59. Lodge to Rusk, Sept. 30, 1963, *FRUS*, 4: *Vietnam August–December 1963*, 322–23.

60. Memo by McNamara of conversation in Saigon, Sept. 30, 1963, ibid., 323–24; memo by Undersec. of State for Political Affairs Special Asst. William Sullivan, Sept. 30, 1963, ibid., 325–26; memo for record by Taylor, Oct. 1, 1963, ibid., 327.

61. "McNamara Makes a Tour of Vietnam," *Newsweek*, Oct. 7, 1963, p. 45; "Win with Whom?" ibid., Oct. 14, 1963, p. 46; Forrestal, major, and Taylor quoted in Bird, *Color of Truth*, 257.

62. Bird, *Color of Truth*, 257–58; McNamara's report of interview with "Professor Smith" (pseudonym for Honey), Sept. 26, 1963, *FRUS*, 4: *Vietnam August–December 1963*, 293–95.

63. Quotes in Bird, *Color of Truth*, 258.

64. Gravel, ed., *Pentagon Papers*, 2: 169; memo for JFK from McNamara and Taylor, Oct. 2, 1963, NSF, Countries—Vietnam, boxes 200–201, JFKL.

65. Memo for JFK from McNamara and Taylor, Oct. 2, 1963, NSF, Countries—Vietnam, boxes 200–201, JFKL; memo from Taylor and McNamara to JFK, Oct. 2, 1963, *FRUS*, 4: *Vietnam August–December 1963*, 337–38; Gravel, ed., *Pentagon Papers*, 2: 169.

66. Memo from Taylor and McNamara to JFK, Oct. 2, 1963, *FRUS*, 4: *Vietnam August–December 1963*, 339.

Chapter 16

1. Author's interview with Galbraith, March 28, 2001; Galbraith's letter to author, April 18, 2001 (in author's possession). John M. Newman concurs that President Kennedy no longer regarded the war as winnable. See his essay, "The Kennedy–Johnson Transition," in Gardner and Gittinger, eds., *Vietnam*, 163.

2. McNamara, *In Retrospect*, x, 80; NSAM 263, Oct. 11, 1963. See also Newman, *JFK and Vietnam*, 402, 409; Kaiser, *American Tragedy*, 261–62; Logevall, *Choosing War*, 54–55. Logevall considers the 1,000-man withdrawal idea "a device" to exert pressure on Diem and *not* the first step in a major withdrawal plan. See ibid., 69.

3. Memo for JFK from McNamara and Taylor, Oct. 2, 1963, NSF Countries—Vietnam, boxes 200–201, JFKL; William P. Bundy Oral History Interview, 6, LBJL.

4. Memo from Taylor and McNamara to JFK, Oct. 2, 1963, *FRUS*, 4: *Vietnam August–December 1963*, 345–46; Gravel, ed., *Pentagon Papers*, 2: 753, 765; McNamara, *In Retrospect*, 79.

5. Summary record of NSC meeting, Oct. 2, 1963, *FRUS*, 4: *Vietnam August–December 1963*, 351; first Sullivan quote in second oral history interview with Sullivan, JFKL, quoted in Gibbons, *U.S. Government and the Vietnam War*, 2: 186; Taylor quote ibid.; Sullivan's quote on more troops needed in 1963 in Rust, *Kennedy in Vietnam*, 141; Harriman Oral History Interview, 110, JFKL; Newman, *JFK and Vietnam*, 403; Sullivan quote on honesty in Transcript, William H. Sullivan Oral History Interview, July 21, 1971, p. 6, by Paige E. Mulhollan, LBJL; Trueheart Oral History Interview, 1: 48–49, LBJL.

6. Harriman Oral History Interview, 110–11, JFKL.

7. Ibid., 111–12, 122–23, 126.

8. Tape recording of meeting in Oval Office, Oct. 2, 1963, POF, Presidential Recordings Collection, Tape no. 144/A49 (cassette 2 of 3), JFKL.

9. McNamara, *In Retrospect*, 80.

10. Tape recording of NSC meeting, Oct. 2, 1963, POF, Presidential Recordings Collection, Tape no. 144/A49 (cassette 2 of 3), JFKL.

11. Author's interview with McNamara, March 5, 2001; McNamara, *In Retrospect*, x, 80; Gilpatric Oral History Interview, 1: 8–9, LBJL; Gilpatric Oral History Interview, 4: 97–98, JFKL; Lodge to Rusk, no. 633, Oct. 5, 1963, NSF, Countries—Vietnam, General, State Cables, Sept. 22–Oct. 5, 1963, box 200, JFKL; Sullivan Oral History Interview, 6, LBJL.

12. Summary record of NSC meeting, Oct. 2, 1963, *FRUS*, 4: *Vietnam August–December 1963*, 351; memo for director of CIA by Chester L. Cooper, Oct. 2, 1963, NSF, Countries—Vietnam, boxes 200–201, JFKL; Gravel, ed., *Pentagon Papers*, 2: 163–64, 251; JFK quoted in O'Donnell and Powers, *"Johnny, We Hardly Knew Ye,"* 17.

13. NSC Action No. 2472 on McNamara–Taylor Report on Vietnam, Oct. 2, 1963, *FRUS*, 4: *Vietnam August–December 1963*, 353; White House Statement Following the Return of a Special Mission to South Viet-Nam, Oct. 2, 1963, *Public Papers of the Presidents: Kennedy, 1963*, 759–60; Rusk to Saigon embassy, Oct. 2, 1963, NSF, Countries—Vietnam, box 204, JFKL; Salinger news conference at White House, Oct. 2, 1963, ibid.; Chester L. Cooper, *The Lost Crusade: America in Vietnam* (New York: Dodd, Mead, 1970), 216; *New York Times* quoted ibid. The NSC staff member was Cooper.

14. Memo of Meeting in White House Situation Room, Oct. 3, 1963, *FRUS*, 4: *Vietnam August–December 1963*, 356; memo from Sullivan to Hilsman, Oct. 3, 1963, ibid., 358; meeting in White House Situation Room (without the president), Oct. 3, 1963, folder on Meetings on Vietnam, Aug.–Nov. 1963 (Diem Coup), Smith Papers, boxes 24, 26, 33, LBJL.

15. Taylor memo ("South Vietnam Actions") for Adm. David McDonald and Gens. Curtis LeMay, Earle Wheeler, and David Shoup, Oct. 4, 1963, JCS CM-935-63, Taylor Papers, box 1, National Defense University, Washington, D.C. I thank James Galbraith for calling this document to my attention.

16. Memo of meeting of Executive Committee, Oct. 4, 1963, *FRUS*, 4: *Vietnam August–December 1963*, 359; memo by Forrestal for files of conference with JFK, Oct. 5, 1963, ibid., 370; Gibbons, *U.S. Government and the Vietnam War*, 2: 189; memo for the file by Forrestal, "Presidential Conference on South Vietnam," Oct. 7, 1963, folder on Meetings on Vietnam, Aug.–Nov. 1963 (Diem Coup), Smith Papers, boxes 24, 26, 33, LBJL; tape recording of meeting in Cabinet Room, Oct. 5, 1963, POF, Presidential Recordings Collection, Tape no. 144/A50 (cassette 1 of 3), JFKL. I also acknowledge my gratitude to James Galbraith, who shared his unpublished paper, "Did John F. Kennedy Give the Order to Withdraw from Vietnam?"

17. Gravel, ed., *Pentagon Papers*, 2: 252–53.

18. Memo from Cleveland, Asst. Sec. of State for International Organization Affairs, to Hilsman, Oct. 2, 1963, *FRUS*, 4: *Vietnam August–December 1963*, 335–36; memo of conversation between Buu Hoi and Rusk at U.N. Mission in New York, Oct. 2, 1963, ibid., 347–48.

19. JFK's opposition to denying visa in memo of conversation in White House, Sept. 10, 1963, ibid., 167; Mme. Nhu quote on Kennedy in Lodge to Rusk, Oct. 19, 1963, ibid., 414; Ball to Saigon, no. 506, Oct. 1, 1963, NSF, Countries—Vietnam, boxes 200–201, JFKL; LBJ to Mme. Nhu, Sept. 20, 1963, ibid.; Mme. Nhu to LBJ, Sept. 30, 1963, ibid.; Gravel, ed., *Pentagon Papers*, 2: 217; tape recording of NSC meeting, Oct. 2, 1963, POF, Presidential Recordings Collection, Tape no. 144/A49 (cassette 2 of 3), JFKL.

20. Tape recording of NSC meeting, Oct. 2, 1963, POF, Presidential Recordings Collection, Tape no. 144/A50 (cassette 2 of 3), JFKL; Lodge to Rusk,

Oct. 5, 1963, no. 633, NSF, Countries—Vietnam, box 204, JFKL; Lodge to Rusk, Oct. 5, 1963, no. 637, ibid.; Lodge to Rusk, no. 639, Oct. 5, 1963, ibid.; Lodge to Rusk, Oct. 5, 1963, no. 641, ibid.

21. CIA station in Saigon to CIA in Washington, Oct. 3, 1963, *FRUS*, 4: *Vietnam August–December 1963*, 354.

22. Conein testimony, June 20, 1975, pp. 23, 38–39, Record No. 157-10014-10094, SSCIA, Church Committee Hearings (NA).

23. Karnow, *Vietnam*, 298–300; Lansdale, *In the Midst of Wars*, 162–63; Conein testimony, 14–15; Tom Wells, *Wild Man: The Life and Times of Daniel Ellsberg* (New York: St. Martin's Press, 2001), 229–30. Lowell Hukill was Lansdale's secretary.

24. CIA station in Saigon to CIA in Washington, Oct. 3, 1963, *FRUS*, 4: *Vietnam August–December 1963*, 355; Conein testimony, 15–18, 30–33.

25. CIA station in Saigon to CIA in Washington, Oct. 3, 1963, *FRUS*, 4: *Vietnam August–December 1963*, 354–55; Colby testimony, June 20, 1975, p. 11, Record No. 157-10014-10019, SSCIA, Church Committee Hearings (NA); Conein testimony, 24, 39.

26. CIA station in Saigon to CIA in Washington, Oct. 3, 1963, *FRUS*, 4: *Vietnam August–December 1963*, 354–55; CIA station in Saigon to CIA in Washington, Oct. 5, 1963, ibid., 365–67; Conein testimony, 25, 33–34; CIA station in Saigon to McCone, Oct. 5, 1963, Miscellaneous Records, Record No. 157-10014-10158, SSCIA, Church Committee Hearings (NA); Colby testimony, 56–57; Gravel, ed., *Pentagon Papers*, 2: 256–57; Gibbons, *U.S. Government and the Vietnam War*, 2: 190; Rust, *Kennedy in Vietnam*, 146–47. Trueheart was the observer.

27. Conein testimony, 34; CIA station in Saigon to McCone, No. 1447, Oct. 5, 1963, Miscellaneous Records, No. 157-10014-10158, SSCIA, ibid.

28. McCone testimony, June 6, 1975, pp. 4, 60 (McCone to CIA station in Saigon, Oct. 5, 1963, read into official record), 61, Record No. 157-10011-10052, SSCIA, ibid.; CIA station in Saigon to McCone, Oct. 6, 1963, Miscellaneous Records, Record No. 157-10014-10158, SSCIA, ibid.; CIA station in Saigon to McCone, Oct. 7, 1963, Church Committee Assassination Report: U.S. Cong., Senate, Select Committee to Study Governmental Operations with Respect to Intelligence Activities, *Alleged Assassination Plots Involving Foreign Leaders; Interim Report*, 94th Cong., 1st Sess., Senate Report No. 94-465 (Washington, D.C.: Government Printing Office, 1975), 221.

29. Colby testimony, 13, 58–59; for Smith's role, see ibid., 12. Lodge, Colby declared, considered Richardson "too closely identified" with Nhu. Ibid. Colby testified that McCone opposed CIA involvement in any assassination. Ibid., 14, 57. Conein testimony, 34–35.

30. McCone testimony, 62–63, 66.

31. Lodge to Rusk, Oct. 5, 1963, *FRUS*, 4: *Vietnam August–December 1963*, 367; McGeorge Bundy to Lodge, Oct. 5, 1963, ibid., 379.

32. Gravel, ed., *Pentagon Papers*, 2: 257.

33. Harkins quoted in Rust, *Kennedy in Vietnam*, 152; removal of Richardson explained in Hilsman, *To Move a Nation*, 515. It was probably Richardson's successor, David Smith, who later complained to McCone that Lodge was "running very much a vest pocket operation and not a country team or total American effort."

Richardson's recall was "the overture to the opera" and perhaps the prelude to replacing Harkins. CIA station in Saigon (Smith?) to CIA in Washington, Nov. 16, 1963, *FRUS*, 4: *Vietnam August–December 1963*, 602.

34. Rusk to Lodge, Oct. 5, 1963, *FRUS*, 4: *Vietnam August–December 1963*, 373–78; memo for files of conference with JFK, Oct. 5, 1963, ibid., 368.

35. Lodge to Rusk, no. 636, Oct. 5, 1963, NSF, Countries—Vietnam, boxes 200–201, JFKL; Joint Chiefs of Staff to CINCPAC, Oct. 5, 1963, ibid.; memo of White House Staff meeting, Oct. 7, 1963, *FRUS*, 4: *Vietnam August–December 1963*, 387.

36. McCone to Smith, acting CIA station chief, Oct. 6, 1963, *Alleged Assassination Plots*, 221; Rust, *Kennedy in Vietnam*, 151–52; Colby quoted ibid., 148.

37. Meeting of Oct. 8, 1963, POF, Presidential Recordings Collection, Tape no. 114/A50 (cassette 2 of 3), JFKL; Hughes, "JFK and the Fall of Diem," internet copy, 3.

38. CIA to Lodge, Oct. 9, 1963, *FRUS*, 4: *Vietnam August–December 1963*, 393.

39. Trueheart observed that Nhu's remarks in the *Expresso* did not fit the tone of those Diem was prepared to give in his "State of the Nation" address to the National Assembly on October 7. One of his passages in the draft expressed appreciation for U.S. aid and advisers. Lodge to Rusk, Oct. 5, 1963, no. 640, NSF, Countries—Vietnam, box 204, JFKL; Lodge to Rusk, No. 652, Oct. 7, 1963, ibid., boxes 200–201; Lodge to Rusk and McNamara, Oct. 7, 1963, *FRUS*, 4: *Vietnam August–December 1963*, 385–86. For Nhu's October 19 interview with the *Times of Vietnam*, see Forrestal to Bundy, Oct. 21, 1963, encl.: Nhu's interview in *Times of Vietnam*, Oct. 19, 1963, NSF, Countries—Vietnam, boxes 200–201, JFKL.

40. The other Americans were Trueheart, Manfull, and Special Assistants Frederick W. Flott and John M. Dunn. CIA station in Saigon to White House, Oct. 9, 1963, NSF, Countries—Vietnam, boxes 200–201, JFKL; Lodge to Rusk, no. 676, Oct. 10, 1963, ibid.; Lodge to Rusk and Harriman, Oct. 10, 1963, *FRUS*, 4: *Vietnam August–December 1963*, 394–95.

41. McCone–Harriman telephone conversation, Oct. 10, 1963, *FRUS*, 4: *Vietnam August–December 1963*, 395 n. 3; CIA Information Report, Oct. 14, 1963, ibid., 399.

42. NSAM 263, Oct. 11, 1963, ibid., 396; Kattenburg to Hilsman, Oct. 18, 1963, ibid., 408–9; Rusk to Lodge, No. 195, Oct. 19, 1963, NSF, Countries—Vietnam, General, State Cables, box 201, Oct. 15–28, 1963, JFKL; William C. Gibbons, "Lyndon Johnson and the Legacy of Vietnam," in Gardner and Gittinger, eds., *Vietnam*, 119–20, 138.

43. Col. Raymond Jones, army attaché in Vietnam, to Asst. Chief of Staff (Intelligence), Department of Army, Oct. 22, 1963, *FRUS*, 4: *Vietnam August–December 1963*, ibid., 419–20. Thieu later became president of South Vietnam.

44. CIA station in Saigon to CIA in Washington, Oct. 23, 1963, ibid., 423–24 n. 5; Anne L. Hollick, *U.S. Involvement in the Overthrow of Diem, 1963*, U.S. Congress, Senate, Committee on Foreign Relations, Staff Study No. 3, 92nd Cong., 2nd sess. (Washington, D.C.: Government Printing Office, 1972), 14, 22; Conein testimony, 36–37; Blair, *Lodge in Vietnam*, 65–66; Lodge, "Vietnam Memoir," 2, chap. 2: 10. General Don in his book highlights his October 22 conversation with

Harkins (which he says occurred at a British embassy party), and his October 23 meeting with Conein. See Don, *Our Endless War*, 98.

45. Lodge to Bundy, no. 1964, Oct. 25, 1963, NSF, Countries—Vietnam, boxes 200–201, JFKL.

46. See Hughes, "JFK and the Fall of Diem," internet copy, 6.

47. Ibid., 6–8; tape recording of White House meeting, Oct. 25, 1963, POF, Presidential Recordings Collection, Tape no. 117/A53 (cassette 3 of 3), JFKL.

48. Bundy to Lodge and Harkins, Oct. 25, 1963, ibid.; Harkins to Taylor, Oct. 30, 1963, ibid; checklist for NSC meeting, n.d. but c. late Oct. 1963, ibid.; CIA station in Saigon to CIA in Washington, Oct. 23, 1963, *FRUS*, 4: *Vietnam August–December 1963*, 427; Don, *Our Endless War*, 98.

49. Conein and John Richardson (After Action Report), "History of the Vietnamese Generals' Coup of 1/2 November 1963," Conein Exhibit no. 1, p. 15, after Conein testimony, June 20, 1975, Church Committee (NA). Conein and Richardson from the CIA compiled this report immediately after the coup. Charles Kirbow, Professional Staff Member of U.S. Senate, Select Committee to Study Governmental Operations, 12, ibid. See also ibid., 26–27. David Halberstam, "Coup in Saigon: A Detailed Account," *New York Times*, Nov. 6, 1963, pp. 1, 16; Stanley Karnow, "The Fall of the House of Ngo Dinh," *Saturday Evening Post*, Dec. 21–28, 1963, p. 76.

50. Halberstam, "Coup in Saigon," 16.

51. Ibid.

52. Dinh's press conference of Nov. 7, 1963, in Bo Thong-tin va Thanh-nien, *Policy of the Military Revolutionary Council and the Provisional Government*, 32; Conein testimony, 67; Karnow, "Fall of the House of Ngo Dinh," 77.

53. Karnow, "Fall of the House of Ngo Dinh," 77; Conein and Richardson, "History of the Vietnamese Generals' Coup," 13.

54. Karnow, "Fall of the House of Ngo Dinh," 77; Halberstam, "Coup in Saigon," 16; Hammer, *Death in November*, 286.

55. Halberstam, "Coup in Saigon," 16; Karnow, "Fall of the House of Ngo Dinh," 77; Hammer, *Death in November*, 280.

56. Gravel, ed., *Pentagon Papers*, 2: 256, 265; Halberstam, "Coup in Saigon," 16; Karnow, "Fall of the House of Ngo Dinh," 76–77; Gibbons, *U.S. Government and the Vietnam War*, 2: 189–90; Rust, *Kennedy in Vietnam*, 146.

57. Hollick, *U.S. Involvement in the Overthrow of Diem*, 14; Blair, *Lodge in Vietnam*, 65–66; Lodge, "Vietnam Memoir," 2, chap. 2: 10.

58. Lodge to Rusk, Oct. 28, 1963, *FRUS*, 4: *Vietnam August–December 1963*, 442–46.

59. Lodge to Rusk, Oct. 29, 1963, NSF, Countries—Vietnam, CIA Reports, Oct. 15–28, 1963 (misfiled), box 201, JFKL.

60. Ibid.; Hollick, *U.S. Involvement in the Overthrow of Diem*, 14; Blair, *Lodge in Vietnam*, 65–66; Lodge, "Vietnam Memoir," 2, chap. 2: 11.

61. Phillips Oral History Interview, 25–26, LBJL.

62. Ibid., 26–27. Diem expressed interest in having Lansdale back in Saigon. In July 1962, when Phillips had first arrived in Vietnam, Diem asked him to arrange for Lansdale's return. Phillips could not persuade Nolting on at least three occasions to do anything. Ibid.

63. Lodge to Rusk, Oct. 29, 1963, *FRUS*, 4: *Vietnam August–December 1963*, 450–51, 454–55.

64. Memo of conference with JFK, Oct. 29, 1963 (4:30 P.M.), NSF, Countries—Vietnam, Meetings on Vietnam, box 317, Oct. 29, 1963, JFKL; McGeorge Bundy to Lodge, Oct. 29, 1963, NSF, Countries—Vietnam, CIA Reports, Oct. 29–31, 1963, box 201, JFKL.

65. Memo of conference with JFK, Oct. 29, 1963 (4:20 P.M.), NSF, Countries—Vietnam, Meetings on Vietnam, box 317, Oct. 29, 1963, JFKL; White House meeting (4:20 P.M.), Oct. 29, 1963, *FRUS*, 4: *Vietnam August–December 1963*, 469–71; Hughes, "JFK and the Fall of Diem," internet copy, 8–9; tape recording of White House meeting, Oct. 29, 1963, POF, Presidential Recordings Collection, Tape no. 118/A54 (cassette 1 of 2), JFKL; Langguth, *Our Vietnam*, 249–50.

66. Memo of conference with JFK, Oct. 29, 1963 (6 P.M.), NSF, Countries—Vietnam, Meetings on Vietnam, box 317, Oct. 29, 1963, JFKL; White House meeting (6 P.M.), Oct. 29, 1963, *FRUS*, 4: *Vietnam August–December 1963*, 472–73; McGeorge Bundy to Lodge, Oct. 29, 1963, ibid., 473–75; memo of conference with JFK, Oct. 29, 1963, folder on Meetings on Vietnam, Aug.–Nov. 1963 (Diem Coup), Smith Papers, boxes 24, 26, 33, LBJL; Gravel, ed., *Pentagon Papers*, 2: 219.

67. To conceal the reason for boarding a military plane, Lodge had intended to explain that it was for his comfort and to save time. He also planned to reserve space on the aircraft for MACV emergency cases. Lodge to Rusk, Oct. 30, 1963 (several cables that day), NSF, Countries—Vietnam, CIA Reports, Oct. 29–31, 1963, box 201, JFKL; Lodge to Rusk, Oct. 30, 1963, *FRUS*, 4: *Vietnam August–December 1963*, 484–86. See also ibid., 487–88.

68. Gravel, ed., *Pentagon Papers*, 2: 262–63, 792–93; McGeorge Bundy to Lodge, Oct. 30, 1963, NSF, Countries—Vietnam, CIA Reports, Oct. 29–31, 1963, box 201, JFKL; tape recording of White House meeting, Oct. 30, 1963, POF, Presidential Recordings Collection, Tape no. 118/A54 (cassette 1 of 2), JFKL.

69. Lodge to Bundy, Oct. 30, 1963, *FRUS*, 4: *Vietnam August–December 1963*, 484–85.

70. Lodge to Rusk, no. 973, Nov. 8, 1963, NSF, Countries—Vietnam, boxes 202–3, JFKL; McGeorge Bundy to Lodge, Oct. 30, 1963, *FRUS*, 4: *Vietnam August–December 1963*, 500–501; Dinh's claim to secret negotiations between Nhu and Hanoi in Seth S. King, "Hanoi Problems Said to Increase," *New York Times*, Nov. 10, 1963, p. 4.

71. Gravel, ed., *Pentagon Papers*, 2: 260, 264; Bundy to Lodge, CAS 79109, Oct. 30, 1963, ibid., 783; Bundy to Lodge, Oct. 30, 1963, *FRUS*, 4: *Vietnam August–December 1963*, 502.

Chapter 17

1. Harkins to Taylor and Felt, Nov. 1, 1963, NSF, Countries—Vietnam, boxes 200–201, JFKL; Gravel, ed., *Pentagon Papers*, 2: 267; Karnow, "Fall of the House of Ngo Dinh," 77; Hammer, *Death in November*, 286. Minh and a coup committee of about twenty-two high ranking officers had chosen the daylight hours of this day for the coup because it was a holiday and they might keep casualties to a minimum since most people, including children, would be at home. Harkins to

Taylor, Nov. 4, 1963, *FRUS*, 4: *Vietnam August–December 1963*, 564; Harkins to Director of National Security Agency, Nov. 1, 1963, ibid., 505. Khanh later explained that they had planned the coup for October 31 but postponed it for one "nerve-wracking" day to take advantage of the presence of most of the generals in Saigon for a Strategic Hamlet conference scheduled by Nhu. Memo of conversation with Khanh and others, Nov. 24, 1963, NSF, Country File—Vietnam, CIA, vol. 1 (Nov.–Dec. 1963), LBJL.

2. "The Fall of the House of Ngo," *Newsweek*, Nov. 11, 1963, p. 27.

3. "Revolution in the Afternoon," *Time*, Nov. 8, 1963, p. 28; Karnow, "Fall of the House of Ngo Dinh," 77.

4. Karnow, "Fall of the House of Ngo Dinh," 77–78; Conein and Richardson, "History of the Vietnamese Generals' Coup," 11–12; Hammer, *Death in November*, 285–86.

5. Conein and Richardson, "History of the Vietnamese Generals' Coup," 12.

6. Ibid., 19; Halberstam, "Coup in Saigon," 16.

7. Rust, *Kennedy in Vietnam*, 166, 170; Conein and Richardson, "History of the Vietnamese Generals' Coup," 23; Saigon embassy to Rusk, no. 858, Nov. 1, 1963, NSF, Countries—Vietnam, boxes 200–201, JFKL; Saigon embassy to Rusk, no. 844, Nov. 1, 1963, ibid.; Saigon embassy to Rusk, no. 846, Nov. 1, 1963, ibid.; Gravel, ed., *Pentagon Papers*, 2: 221, 267.

8. Saigon embassy to Rusk, no. 858, Nov. 1, 1963, NSF, Countries—Vietnam, boxes 200–201, JFKL; Saigon embassy to Rusk, no. 844, Nov. 1, 1963, ibid.; Saigon embassy to Rusk, no. 846, Nov. 1, 1963, ibid.; Gravel, ed., *Pentagon Papers*, 2: 221, 267; Conein testimony, 63; Malcolm Browne, "Escape, Surrender and Death: How Diem and Brother Spent Their Final Hours," *New York Times*, Nov. 6, 1963, p. 17.

9. Rusk to Saigon embassy, no. 674, Nov. 1, 1963, NSF, Countries—Vietnam, boxes 200–201, JFKL; U.S. Department of State, Central Files, Office of the Historian, Vietnam Interviews (1984), *FRUS*, 4: *Vietnam August–December 1963*, 506 n. 3.; Hollick, *U.S. Involvement in the Overthrow of Diem*, 19–20; Conein testimony, 64, 68; Gravel, ed., *Pentagon Papers*, 2: 266, 268; Halberstam, "Coup in Saigon," 16; Karnow, "Fall of the House of Ngo Dinh," 78.

10. Rust, *Kennedy in Vietnam*, 163; Conein and Richardson, "History of the Vietnamese Generals' Coup," 8–9; Church Committee Assassination Report: U.S. Cong., Senate, Select Committee to Study Governmental Operations with Respect to Intelligence Activities, *Alleged Assassination Plots*, 222; Conein testimony, 49, 68–73. Senator Walter Mondale perceptively noted before the Church Committee in 1975 that the rebels used this money "to help carry out and pay the costs of the coup." Ibid., 73. Conein told the committee that he had on hand about $70,000 but took the lesser amount to the generals because that was all he could fit into the bag. He did not want to carry two briefcases. Ibid., 70, 77. Lodge had also alerted Washington to the need for monetary assistance to the generals for buying off "potential opposition." See Lodge to Rusk, Oct. 29, 1963, *FRUS*, 4: *Vietnam August–December 1963*, 454; Lodge to Rusk, Oct. 30, 1963, ibid., 487.

11. Conein testimony, 49, 69.

12. Minh and Conein exchange in Rust, *Kennedy in Vietnam*, 163–64.

13. Conein testimony, 75.

14. Saigon embassy to Rusk, no. 846, Nov. 1, 1963, NSF, Countries—Vietnam, boxes 200–201, JFKL; Saigon embassy to Rusk, no. 845, Nov. 1, 1963, ibid.; Lodge to Rusk, no. 842, Nov. 1, 1963, ibid.; Conein testimony, 49–50, 75; Conein and Richardson, "History of the Vietnamese Generals' Coup," 11; Oral History Interview with Frederick W. Flott, 1: 45–46, by Ted Gittinger, July 22, 1984, LBJL; Conein's report in CIA station in Saigon to Director of National Security Agency, Nov. 1, 1963, *FRUS*, 4: *Vietnam August–December 1963*, 506; Hollick, *U.S. Involvement in the Overthrow of Diem*, 22; Karnow, "Fall of the House of Ngo Dinh," 77; Halberstam, "Coup in Saigon," 16; Rust, *Kennedy in Vietnam*, 163; Hammer, *Death in November*, 284–85; Hughes, "JFK and the Fall of Diem," internet copy, 9–10; Gravel, ed., *Pentagon Papers*, 2: 267.

15. Nguyen Cao Ky, *Twenty Years and Twenty Days* (New York: Stein and Day, 1976), 40; Saigon embassy to Rusk, no. 857, Nov. 1, 1963, NSF, Countries—Vietnam, boxes 200–201, JFKL; Rust, *Kennedy in Vietnam*, 166–67; "Fall of the House of Ngo," 28.

16. Conein testimony, 50; CIA station in Saigon to Director of National Security Agency, Nov. 1, 1963, *FRUS*, 4: *Vietnam August–December 1963*, 511; CIA memo, "The Situation in South Vietnam," Nov. 1, 1963, NSF, Countries—Vietnam, General, Memos and Miscellaneous, Nov. 1–2, 1963, box 201, JFKL.

17. Halberstam, "Coup in Saigon," 16; Karnow, "Fall of the House of Ngo Dinh," 78.

18. Both quotes in Rust, *Kennedy in Vietnam*, 167.

19. Diem's first quote in Gravel, ed., *Pentagon Papers*, 2: 221, 268; Dinh quoted in Bo Thong-tin va Thanh-nien, *Policy of the Military Revolutionary Council and the Provisional Government*, 32; Diem's second quote ibid.; Rust, *Kennedy in Vietnam*, 168.

20. Lodge to Rusk, no. 867, Nov. 1, 1963, NSF, Countries—Vietnam, General, State Cables, Nov. 1–2, 1963, box 201, JFKL; Gravel, ed., *Pentagon Papers*, 2: 221, 268; "Fall of the House of Ngo," 28.

21. I have reconstructed this conversation from two sources: Lodge to Rusk, no. 860, Nov. 1, 1963, NSF, Countries—Vietnam, boxes 200–201, JFKL; Flott Oral History Interview, 42–45, LBJL.

22. CIA no. 61 no. 2, no. 77 no. 6, no. 88 no. 2, no. 113 no. 3, to Rusk, Nov. 1, 1963, NSF, Countries—Vietnam, boxes 200–201, JFKL; Gravel, ed., *Pentagon Papers*, 2: 221, 269.

23. CIA no. 61 no. 2, no. 77 no. 6, no. 88 no. 2, no. 113 no. 3, to Rusk, Nov. 1, 1963, NSF, Countries—Vietnam, boxes 200–201, JFKL; CINCPAC to RUHPA, 018996, Nov. 2, 1963, ibid.; JFKL; Harkins to Taylor and Felt, 1190, Nov. 2, 1963, ibid.; Lodge to Rusk, Nov. 1, 1963, *FRUS*, 4: *Vietnam August–December 1963*, 510; Conein and Richardson, "History of the Vietnamese Generals' Coup," 18; Gravel, ed., *Pentagon Papers*, 2: 221, 267–68; Conein quoted in Rust, *Kennedy in Vietnam*, 170.

24. Colby, *Lost Victory*, 155; Rust, *Kennedy in Vietnam*, 169.

25. Rust, *Kennedy in Vietnam*, 170; Conein and Richardson, "History of the Vietnamese Generals' Coup," 20; Browne, "Escape, Surrender and Death," 17; Tri Quang quote in Halberstam, "Coup in Saigon," 16.

26. CIA no. 61 no. 2, no. 77 no. 6, no. 88 no. 2, no. 113 no. 3, to Rusk, Nov. 1, 1963, NSF, Countries—Vietnam, boxes 200–201, JFKL; Harkins to Taylor and Felt, Nov. 1, 1963, ibid.; Harkins to Joint Chiefs of Staff, Nov. 1, 1963, ibid.; Harkins to White House, Nov. 1, 1963, ibid.; CIA to White House Situation Room, Nov. 1, 1963 (series of messages), ibid.; CIA station in Saigon to Director of National Security Agency, Nov. 1, 1963, *FRUS*, 4: *Vietnam August–December 1963*, 512; Hollick, *U.S. Involvement in the Overthrow of Diem*, 22–23; Trueheart Oral History Interview, 1: 55–56, LBJL; Harkins Oral History Interview, 1: 32, LBJL.

27. "Battle Went on under Full Moon," *New York Times*, Nov. 3, 1963, p. 24; Halberstam, "Coup in Saigon," 16; Browne, "Escape, Surrender and Death," 17.

28. "Fall of the House of Ngo," 28; Browne, "Escape, Surrender and Death," 17.

29. Harkins to Taylor, Nov. 2, 1963, *FRUS*, 4: *Vietnam August–December 1963*, 534; CIA to White House Situation Room, Nov. 1, 1963 (series of messages), NSF, Countries—Vietnam, boxes 200–201, JFKL; Hollick, *U.S. Involvement in the Overthrow of Diem*, 23–24; *Alleged Assassination Plots*, 223; Gravel, ed., *Pentagon Papers*, 2: 221, 269; Halberstam, "Coup in Saigon," 16; Karnow, "Fall of the House of Ngo Dinh," 78; Conein testimony, 52–53; Rust, *Kennedy in Vietnam*, 170; Langguth, *Our Vietnam*, 255.

30. "Battle Went on under Full Moon," 24; Langguth, *Our Vietnam*, 254.

31. Flott Oral History Interview, 47–48, LBJL; Conein testimony, 53; "Battle Went on under Full Moon," 24; "Fall of the House of Ngo," 28; "Revolution in the Afternoon," 30; Karnow, "Fall of the House of Ngo Dinh," 78; Rust, *Kennedy in Vietnam*, 172; Langguth, *Our Vietnam*, 254.

32. Conein testimony, 52, 54, 76–78; memo from Rhett Dawson to Fritz Schwarz and Curt Smothers, July 7, 1975, p. 10, SSCIA, Record No. 157-10014-10152, Miscellaneous Records, Church Committee Hearings (NA); Lodge to Department of State, Oct. 30, 1963, *FRUS*, 4: *Vietnam August–December 1963*, 487; Rust, *Kennedy in Vietnam*, 171–72; Hammer, *Death in November*, 294; Hollick, *U.S. Involvement in the Overthrow of Diem*, 23. That length of time was necessary, Smith explained, for the pilots to get their briefing and for the Saigon airport to open and the plane to arrive. The White House refused to consider either Taiwan or the Philippines as a refuge. Both were too close to Vietnam, and there were also political complications regarding Taiwan's problems with the Beijing government.

33. Minh quoted in Rust, *Kennedy in Vietnam*, 171; Senate commission quote in Hollick, *U.S. Involvement in the Overthrow of Diem*, 23 n. 80.

34. Conein testimony, 53, 55, 74; *Alleged Assassination Plots*, 223. See also Hughes, "JFK and the Fall of Diem," internet copy, 11.

35. *Alleged Assassination Plots*, 223; Conein testimony, 47, 52.

36. "Fall of the House of Ngo," 28–29; "Leader of Uprising," *New York Times*, Nov. 2, 1963, p. 2.

37. Conein testimony, 52, 62–63, 66; Conein and Richardson, "History of the Vietnamese Generals' Coup," 10.

38. See CIA to Department of State (several missives), Nov. 2, 1963, NSF, Countries—Vietnam, boxes 200–201, JFKL; Lodge to Rusk, no. 913, Nov. 4, 1963, ibid.; Harkins to Taylor, Nov. 5, 1963, *FRUS*, 4: *Vietnam August–December 1963*, 569; tape recording of meeting in Oval Office, Nov. 2, 1963, POF, Presidential Recordings Collection, Tape no. A55 (cassette 1 of 2), JFKL; Harkins Oral History

Interview, 1: 32–33, LBJL; Gravel, ed., *Pentagon Papers*, 2: 269; Halberstam, "Coup in Saigon," 16; Browne, "Escape, Surrender and Death," 17; Karnow, "Fall of the House of Ngo Dinh," 78; "Saigon 23126 Doesn't Answer," *Time*, Nov. 15, 1963, p. 42.

39. CIA station in Saigon to Director of National Security Agency, Nov. 1, 1963, *FRUS*, 4: *Vietnam August–December 1963*, 511; CIA to White House Situation Room, Nov. 1, 2, 1963 (series of messages), NSF, Countries—Vietnam, boxes 200–201, JFKL; CIA Memo, "The Situation in South Vietnam," Nov. 1, 1963, ibid.; Lodge to Rusk, No. 973, Nov. 8, 1963, ibid.; Lodge to Rusk, no. 883, Nov. 2, 1963, ibid.; Harkins to Taylor and Felt, Nov. 2, 1963, ibid.; Gravel, ed., *Pentagon Papers*, 2: 222; Bo Thong-tin va Thanh-nien, *Policy of the Military Revolutionary Council and the Provisional Government*, 5–7, 9–10; Gibbons, *U.S. Government and the Vietnam War*, 2: 202; "Young Tigers—And Cautious Optimism," *Newsweek*, Nov. 18, 1963, p. 41. The National Assembly had been elected on September 27, 1963.

40. CIA Memo, "The Situation in South Vietnam," Nov. 1, 1963, NSF, Countries—Vietnam, boxes 200–201, JFKL; "South Vietnamese Military Regime Lifts Curfew and Press Censorship," *New York Times*, Nov. 8, 1963, p. 8; Bo Thong-tin va Thanh-nien, *Policy of the Military Revolutionary Council and the Provisional Government*, 35. For Soviet and Chinese reaction, see "Izvestia Derides Revolt Leaders," *New York Times*, Nov. 3, 1963, pp. 1, 27, and "Peking [Beijing] Says Saigon Has New U.S. Puppet," ibid., Nov. 5, 1963, p. 12.

41. Duiker, *Ho Chi Minh*, 534; Duiker, "Hanoi's Response to American Policy" in Gardner and Gittinger, eds., *Vietnam*, 67; Macdonald, *Adventures in Chaos*, 247; CIA Report TDCS – 3/563,962, "Views of Vietnamese Communists in Phnom Penh Concerning the Military Coup of 1 November against the Ngo Dinh Diem Regime," Nov. 3, 1963, NSF, Countries—Vietnam, General, CIA Reports, Nov. 3–5, 1963, box 201, JFKL; Pribbenow, trans., *Victory in Vietnam*, 121–22; Harkins Oral History Interview, 1: 33, LBJL; Gravel, ed., *Pentagon Papers*, 2: 222–23, 273; Taylor Oral History Interview, 2: 24, LBJL; Vietnamese Communists and Tho quote in Colby, *Lost Victory*, 158. The NLF's demands came on November 17, 1963.

42. Harriman Oral History Interview, 117, JFKL; Hilsman Oral History Interview, 29–30, 33, JFKL; Taylor Oral History Interview, 2: 22, LBJL.

43. Lodge to Rusk, no. 973, Nov. 8, 1963, NSF, Countries—Vietnam, boxes 202–3, JFKL; Harkins Oral History Interview, 1: 31–32, LBJL; MacDonald, *Adventures in Chaos*, 247; Karnow, "Fall of the House of Ngo Dinh," 77.

44. Lodge to Rusk, no. 973, Nov. 8, 1963, NSF, Countries—Vietnam, boxes 202–3, JFKL; Blair, *Lodge in Vietnam*, 68.

45. Memo of conference with JFK, Nov. 1, 1963 (10 A.M.), NSF, Countries—Vietnam, Meetings on Vietnam, box 317, Nov. 1–2, 1963, JFKL; memo for record of discussion at Daily White House Staff Meeting, Nov. 1, 1963, *FRUS*, 4: *Vietnam August–December 1963*, 518; Rusk to Lodge, Nov. 1, 1963, ibid., 525; tape recording of White House meeting, Nov. 1, 1963, POF, Presidential Recordings Collection, Tape no. 118/A54 (cassette 2 of 2), JFKL.

46. Rusk to Lodge, Nov. 1, 1963, *FRUS*, 4: *Vietnam August–December 1963*, 521; Lodge to Rusk, Nov. 1, 1963, ibid., 521 n. 2.; Seth S. King, "Hanoi Problems Said to Increase," *New York Times*, Nov. 10, 1963, p. 4; Halberstam, ibid., Nov. 3, 1963, p. 24.

47. Unidentified source quoted in "Fall of the House of Ngo," 31; Mansfield quoted in Bo Thong-tin va Thanh-nien, *Policy of the Military Revolutionary Council and the Provisional Government*, 38; author's interview with Rusk, Aug. 16, 1989, Athens, Ga.; Rusk to author, Sept. 20, 1989 (letter in author's possession); memo of conference with JFK, Nov. 1, 1963, folder on Meetings on Vietnam, Aug.–Nov. 1963 (Diem Coup), Smith Papers, boxes 24, 26, 33, LBJL; Rusk quote on press in Hughes, "JFK and the Fall of Diem," internet copy, 10; Department of State quote in "Behind the Denials," *Time*, Nov. 8, 1963, p. 21. Richard Phillips was the press officer.

48. Mecklin, *Mission in Torment*, 169; Trueheart Oral History Interview, 1: 50–53, LBJL; Colby Oral History Interview, 8, LBJL.

49. "Revolution in the Afternoon," 28; U.S. official quoted in "Behind the Denials," 21–22; Frankel in *New York Times*, Nov. 2, 1963, pp. 1, 3; Smith, ibid., 1. Other Americans also expressed suspicions of U.S. involvement in the coup. See Robert Trumbull, "Diem under Attack as Authoritarian Ruler since He Took Power in Vietnam," ibid., 4; "Americans' Role Discussed," ibid., Nov. 7, 1963, p. 36.

50. Jack Langguth, "Mrs. Nhu Charges U.S. Incited Coup," *New York Times*, Nov. 2, 1963, pp. 1, 3; "Text of Statement by Mrs. Nhu on Vietnam Events," ibid., Nov. 3, 1963, p. 24; "Revolution in the Afternoon," 29. Madame Nhu's brother-in-law was Ngo Dinh Khoi.

51. Gravel, ed., *Pentagon Papers*, 2: 207; *Alleged Assassination Plots*, 256.

52. Memo of conference with JFK, Nov. 1, 1963 (10 A.M.), NSF, Countries—Vietnam, Meetings on Vietnam, box 317, Nov. 1–2, 1963, JFKL; tape recording of White House meeting, Nov. 1, 1963, POF, Presidential Recordings Collection, Tape no. 118/A54 (cassette 2 of 2), JFKL; "Eyes Only" from White House to Lodge, Nov. 1, 1963, NSF, Countries—Vietnam, boxes 200–201, JFKL.

53. Lodge to Rusk, Nov. 2, 1963, *FRUS*, 4: *Vietnam August–December 1963*, 526; Mrs. Lodge quoted in Blair, *Lodge in Vietnam*, 81; Lodge to Rusk, no. 890, Nov. 2, 1963, NSF, Countries—Vietnam, General, State Cables, Nov. 3–5, 1963, box 201, JFKL; Lodge to Rusk, no. 895, Nov. 3, 1963, ibid.; Lodge to Rusk, no. 898, Nov. 3, 1963, ibid.; Trueheart Oral History Interview, 1: 56, LBJL; Gravel, ed., *Pentagon Papers*, 2: 270; CIA Memo, "The Situation in South Vietnam," Nov. 2, 1963, NSF, Countries—Vietnam, Meetings on Vietnam, box 317, Nov. 1–2, 1963, JFKL. The CIA reported the total casualties among coup forces and loyalists as perhaps 100. Ibid.

54. Nolting Oral History Interview, 1: 20–21, LBJL.

55. Ibid., 21–22.

56. CIA to White House Situation Room, Nov. 2, 1963, NSF, Countries—Vietnam, boxes 200–201, JFKL; Lodge to Rusk, no. 876, Nov. 2, 1963, ibid.; Lodge to Rusk, no. 973, Nov. 8, 1963, ibid.; Conein testimony, 28, 39–40; observer quoted in "Young Tigers," 41; Bo Thong-tin va Thanh-nien, *Policy of the Military Revolutionary Council and the Provisional Government*, 33; Dinh quote in memo for the Record, Nov. 7, 1963, NSF, Country File, Vietnam, CIA, vol. 1 (Nov.–Dec. 1963), LBJL; "Americans' Role Discussed," 9.

57. Harkins to Taylor and Felt, Nov. 2, 1963, NSF, Country File, Vietnam, CIA, vol. 1 (Nov.–Dec. 1963), LBJL; Lodge to Rusk, no. 888, Nov. 2, 1963, ibid.;

CIA station in Saigon to Department of State, Nov. 2, 1963, *FRUS*, 4: *Vietnam August–December 1963*, 527 n. 2.

58. Taylor, *Swords and Plowshares*, 301; Colby, *Lost Victory*, 156; Schlesinger, *Thousand Days*, 830. Kenneth O'Donnell, the president's appointments secretary, asserted that the deaths had severely unsettled the chief executive, for he had "an agreement" with the coup makers not to hurt either Diem or Nhu. O'Donnell testimony, Sept. 15, 1975, pp. 79, 81–83 (quote on 81), SSCIA, Record No. 157-10002-10385, Church Committee Hearings (NA). Presidential tape, Nov. 4, 1963, quoted in Freedman, *Kennedy's Wars*, 395. See also Kaiser, *American Tragedy*, 276–77. Gravel, ed., *Pentagon Papers*, 2: 270.

59. Powers, *Man Who Kept the Secrets*, 165; Trueheart Oral History Interview, 1: 57, LBJL; Gravel, ed., *Pentagon Papers*, 2: 270.

60. Memo of conference with JFK, Nov. 2, 1963, folder on Meetings on Vietnam, Aug.–Nov. 1963 (Diem Coup), Smith Papers, boxes 24, 26, 33, LBJL; memo of conference with JFK, Nov. 2, 1963 (4:30 P.M.), NSF, Countries—Vietnam, Meetings on Vietnam, box 317, Nov. 1–2, 1963, JFKL; memo of conference with JFK, Nov. 2, 1963 (9:15 A.M.), ibid.; tape recording of meeting in Oval Office, Nov. 2, 1963, POF, Presidential Recordings Collection, Tape no. A55 (cassette 1 of 2), JFKL.

61. See Hughes, "JFK and the Fall of Diem," internet copy, 11–13.

62. Taylor Oral History Interview, 2: 22–23, LBJL; Nolting Oral History Interview, 24, 78, JFKL; Trueheart Oral History Interview, 1: 51, LBJL; Taylor, *Swords and Plowshares*, 302; Colby and Forbath, *Honorable Men*, 203; Lansdale Interview of Nov. 19, 1982, quoted in Gibbons, *U.S. Government and the Vietnam War*, 2: 203; Bundy quoted ibid., 205.

63. Conein testimony, 59.

64. Hammer, *Death in November*, 294, 297–98; Langguth, *Our Vietnam*, 256; Conein testimony, 59–60; Rust, *Kennedy in Vietnam*, 172; Don, *Our Endless War*, 112; Karnow, "Fall of the House of Ngo Dinh," 75, 78. Khiem had refused to join the mission, bitterly remarking that "Diem doesn't deserve two generals." Ibid., 78.

65. Conein testimony, 60–61; Nghia quoted in Karnow, "Fall of the House of Ngo Dinh," 78; Langguth, *Our Vietnam*, 256; Colby, *Lost Victory*, 154. Karnow actually quotes an "eyewitness," but Nghia was the only one (other than Nhung and the two victims) in the vehicle.

66. See CIA to Department of State (several missives), Nov. 2, 1963, NSF, Countries—Vietnam, boxes 200–201, JFKL; Lodge to Rusk, no. 913, Nov. 4, 1963, ibid.; Gravel, ed., *Pentagon Papers*, 2: 221–22, 269; Don, *Our Endless War*, 111; Blair, *Lodge in Vietnam*, 70; Hammer, *Death in November*, 292–93.

67. Don, *Our Endless War*, 111; Karnow, "Fall of the House of Ngo Dinh," 78; Langguth, *Our Vietnam*, 257; Hammer, *Death in November*, 298.

68. See Conein testimony, 55–58; *Alleged Assassination Plots*, 223; Hughes, "JFK and the Fall of Diem," internet copy, 11.

69. Halberstam to Rusk, no. 892, Nov. 2, 1963, NSF, Countries—Vietnam, boxes 200–201, JFKL; Sheehan to Rusk, no. 893, Nov. 2, 1963, ibid.; Lodge to Rusk, no. 913, Nov. 4, 1963, ibid.; news conference cited in *FRUS*, 4: *Vietnam August–December 1963*, 574 n. 5.

70. CIA to Department of State (several missives), Nov. 2, 1963, NSF, Countries—Vietnam, boxes 200–201, JFKL; CIA station in Saigon to Lt. Gen. Gordon Blake, Director of National Security Agency, Nov. 3, 1963, *FRUS*, 4: *Vietnam August–December 1963*, 545; "The Bodies," *Time*, Dec. 6, 1963, p. 42. That the generals had transported Diem and Nhu in an armored personnel carrier rather than a car, according to General Samuel Williams, provided a forecast of their fate. Williams Oral History Interview, 1: 47–48, LBJL. Authorities turned over the bodies of Diem and Nhu to former Minister of Defense Tran Trung Tung, whose wife was the niece of the two brothers. CIA Report TDCS DB – 3/657/ 724, "New Military Committee Formed," Nov. 4, 1963, NSF, Countries—Vietnam, General, CIA Reports, Nov. 3–5, 1963, box 201, JFKL. They were buried in a small military cemetery outside Saigon. "Relative Reports Burial," *New York Times*, Nov. 8, 1963, p. 8.

71. Rusk to Lodge, no. 704, Nov. 3, 1963, NSF, Countries—Vietnam, boxes 200–201, JFKL. Khanh told Lodge in late May of 1964 that when Diem was killed, he was carrying a briefcase containing one million dollars "in the largest denominations" of American currency. Big Minh kept the briefcase, along with forty kilograms of gold bars that he had taken earlier. Lodge advised Khanh to keep this news quiet, for it would undermine popular confidence in the generals. Lodge to Rusk, May 26, 1964, Martin Papers, box 8, folder 3, Ford Library.

72. Lodge to Rusk, Nov. 3, 1963 (2 parts: nos. 1386 and 1387), ibid.; Lodge to Rusk, no. 900, Nov. 3, 1963, NSF, Countries—Vietnam, General, State Cables, Nov. 3–5, 1963, box 201, JFKL; Gravel, ed., *Pentagon Papers*, 2: 222.

73. Higgins, *Our Vietnam Nightmare*, 224–25; Langguth, *Our Vietnam*, 257– 58; "A Sad Week for Mme. Nhu," *Newsweek*, Nov. 11, 1963, p. 30.

74. Langguth, *Our Vietnam*, 257–58; Hilsman to Robert Manning, Asst. Sec. of State for Public Affairs, Nov. 5, 1963, Hilsman Papers, Vietnam, Nov. 1963, JFKL; Flott Oral History Interview, 1: 51, 53–55, LBJL. Conein told the Church Committee that he "was instrumental in getting Ngo Dinh Nhu's children out of the country." Conein testimony, 66. Based on Conein's direct connections with the generals, it is probable that he again served as Lodge's liaison in securing their approval for evacuating the youths. Conein maintained contact with the military junta until November 7, the day that United States recognized the provisional regime in Saigon. Ibid., 61.

75. Jack Langguth, "Mrs. Nhu Says U.S. Will Bear Stigma," *New York Times*, Nov. 3, 1963, p. 1; "Sad Week for Mme. Nhu," 30; "Widow's Retreat," *Time*, Nov. 22, 1963, p. 27. That same day, Madame Nhu met with her father in the Beverly Wilshire Hotel, ending their estrangement. Jack Langguth, "Mrs. Nhu Off to Rome Tomorrow to Join Sons," *New York Times*, Nov. 5, 1963, p. 12.

76. Lodge to Rusk, no. 917, Nov. 4, 1963, NSF, Countries—Vietnam, boxes 200–201, JFKL; Helble to Department of State, Nov. 4, 1963, *FRUS*, 4: *Vietnam August–December 1963*, 563; Harkins to Taylor, Nov. 5, 1963, ibid., 570; Higgins, *Our Vietnam Nightmare*, 226; "Young Tigers," 42.

77. Helble quoted in Rust, *Kennedy in Vietnam*, 176; ibid., 176–77; Department of State to U.S. consulate in Hué, Nov. 2, 1963, *FRUS*, 4: *Vietnam August– December 1963*, 562–63 n. 2; "Military to Try Brother of Diem," *New York Times*, Nov. 6, 1963, p. 1.

78. Lodge quoted in Rust, *Kennedy and Vietnam*, 177. The *New York Times* likewise reported that U.S. officials had secured assurances that Can "would not be lynched and would receive due process of law." "Military to Try Brother of Diem," *New York Times*, Nov. 6, 1963, pp. 1, 17.

79. Lodge to Rusk, Nov. 30, 1963, *FRUS*, 4: *Vietnam August–December 1963*, 646; Conein and Richardson, "History of the Vietnamese Generals' Coup," 4, 10. Stories of torture included the police securing information by attaching electrodes from a portable radio generator to one young female student's breasts, and forcing captives to drink enormous amounts of soapy water that caused blood to seep from their inflamed intestines. Karnow, "Fall of the House of Ngo Dinh," 79; "Young Tigers," 41; Langguth, *Our Vietnam*, 258; Rust, *Kennedy in Vietnam*, 178. Diem's youngest brother, Ngo Dinh Luyen, resigned his post as ambassador in London, saying that he could not serve a government "the promoters of which have murdered my brother [Diem] and camouflaged it into suicide." He also resigned his posts as Minister in Austria, Belgium, and The Netherlands. *New York Times*, Nov. 3, 1963, p. 24.

80. Department of State Circular Telegram to all diplomatic posts, Nov. 2, 1963, *FRUS*, 4: *Vietnam August–December 1963*, 536; memo for record of White House Staff meeting, Nov. 4, 1963, ibid., 555–56.

81. Lodge to Rusk, no. 888, Nov. 2, 1963, NSF, Countries—Vietnam, boxes 200–201, JFKL; Conein testimony, 61, 65–66; Hollick, *U.S. Involvement in the Overthrow of Diem*, 24. Minh's assistant, Colonel Quan, claimed that Nghia shot the brothers point-blank with his submachine gun and that Nhung likewise shot them before using his knife. Don, *Our Endless War*, 112. But Quan was not there, and his story does not fit with the eyewitness account. Nhung became a liability. Sometime after the deaths, he confessed to the murders and attributed them to Minh. Nhung was thrown into prison, where he feared torture and execution and hanged himself with his shoelaces. Ibid., 112–13. "His life expectancy," according to Rufus Phillips, "was very low from that moment on." Phillips Oral History Interview, 28, LBJL. "So there goes your witness," remarked General Williams some years afterward. Williams Oral History Interview, 1: 48, LBJL.

82. Conein testimony, 61, 66; Colby, *Lost Victory*, 154; Don, *Our Endless War*, 112; Lodge to Rusk, no. 888, Nov. 2, 1963, NSF, Countries—Vietnam, boxes 200–201, JFKL; tape recording of meeting in Oval Office, Nov. 2, 1963, POF, Presidential Recordings Collection, Tape no. A55 (cassette 1 of 2), JFKL; Hammer, *Death in November*, 299. Nghia insisted that "the fate of President Diem was decided by the majority of the members of the Revolutionary Committee," but Conein denied that the generals ever discussed the matter. Nghia quoted in Rust, *Kennedy in Vietnam*, 173.

83. Conein testimony, 65; Hammer, *Death in November*, 299–300.

84. Harriman Oral History Interview, 117, JFKL; Phillips Oral History Interview, 27–28, LBJL.

85. Lodge to Rusk, no. 913, Nov. 4, 1963, NSF, Countries—Vietnam, boxes 200–201, JFKL; Lodge to Rusk, Nov. 5, 1963, *FRUS*, 4: *Vietnam August–December 1963*, Ed. Note, 567; Gravel, ed., *Pentagon Papers*, 2: 222, 272.

86. Nguyen Ngoc Huy quoted in Blair, *Lodge in Vietnam*, 79. Nguyen Ngoc Tho had been born in 1908 and served as minister of interior in Diem's first govern-

ment in 1954, ambassador to Japan in 1955, minister of national economy in 1956, and vice-president of South Vietnam from January 1957 to November 1, 1963. Bo Thong-tin va Thanh-nien, *Policy of the Military Revolutionary Council and the Provisional Government*, 18.

87. CIA Report, "The Situation in South Vietnam," Nov. 4, 1963, NSF, Countries—Vietnam, General, CIA Reports, Nov. 3–5, 1963, box 201, JFKL; Lodge to Rusk, no. 917, Nov. 4, 1963, NSF, Countries—Vietnam, boxes 200–201, JFKL; Gravel, ed., *Pentagon Papers*, 2: 222; Blair, *Lodge in Vietnam*, 77; Gibbons, *U.S. Government and the Vietnam War*, 2: 202; CIA Report, "The Situation in South Vietnam," Nov. 5, 1963, NSF, Countries—Vietnam, General, CIA Reports, Nov. 3–5, 1963, box 201, JFKL.

88. Rusk to Lodge, no. 729, Nov. 5, 1963, NSF, Countries—Vietnam, General, State Cables, Nov. 3–5, 1963, box 201, JFKL; CIA Report, "The Situation in South Vietnam," Nov. 4, 1963, NSF, Countries—Vietnam, General, CIA Reports, Nov. 3–5, 1963, box 201, JFKL; Bo Thong-tin va Thanh-nien, *Policy of the Military Revolutionary Council and the Provisional Government*, 10–13; "Vietnam Coup Leader Says He Feared Diem Was Losing War," *New York Times*, Nov. 5, 1963, p. 12; Lodge to Rusk, Nov. 4, 1963, *FRUS*, 4: *Vietnam August–December 1963*, 557–58; CIA Report TD CS – 3/564/022, South Vietnam Situation Report, Nov. 5, 1963, NSF, Countries—Vietnam, General, CIA Reports, Nov. 3–5, 1963, box 201, JFKL.

89. "Saigon Ban on Dancing Is Lifted with a Grin," *New York Times*, Nov. 8, 1963, p. 8; "Young Tigers," 41.

90. Hedrick Smith, "U.S. Recognizes Regime in Saigon; Talks on Aid Set," *New York Times*, Nov. 8, 1963, pp. 1, 9; "Britain Gives Recognition," ibid., Nov. 8, 1963, p. 9; Bo Thong-tin va Thanh-nien, *Policy of the Military Revolutionary Council and the Provisional Government*, 36; Gravel, ed., *Pentagon Papers*, 2: 222–23.

91. Lodge to Rusk, no. 917, Nov. 4, 1963, NSF, Countries—Vietnam, boxes 200–201, JFKL; Lodge to Rusk, no. 949, Nov. 6, 1963, ibid.

92. Lodge to Rusk, no. 949, Nov. 6, 1963, ibid.

93. JFK to Lodge, no. 746, Nov. 6, 1963, ibid. Kaiser argues that Diem and Nhu were "the two men most responsible" for the government's overthrow. Kaiser, *American Tragedy*, 275.

94. Forrestal to McGeorge Bundy, Nov. 7, 1963, NSF, Countries—Vietnam, boxes 200–201, JFKL; James Reston, "Why a Truce in Korea and Not in Vietnam?" *New York Times*, Nov. 6, 1963, p. 40; Mendenhall to Hilsman, Nov. 12, 1963, NSF, Countries—Vietnam, boxes 200–201, JFKL.

95. *New York Times* article, entitled "Saigon Coup Hurts Position of Harkins," cited in *FRUS*, 4: *Vietnam August–December 1963*, 593 n. 2; Forrestal to McGeorge Bundy, Nov. 13, 1963, NSF, Countries—Vietnam, boxes 202–3, JFKL.

96. "Pertinent Excerpts from Secretary Rusk's Press Conference November 8 on Viet Nam and Foreign Aid," Nov. 8, 1963, NSF, Countries—Vietnam, boxes 200–201, JFKL; Hollick, *U.S. Involvement in the Overthrow of Diem*, 25; Gravel, ed., *Pentagon Papers*, 2: 272.

97. Forrestal to McGeorge Bundy, Nov. 13, 1963, NSF, Countries—Vietnam, boxes 202–3, JFKL; Rusk to Lodge, Nov. 13, 1963, ibid.

98. CIA station in Saigon to CIA in Washington, Nov. 16, 1963, *FRUS*, 4: *Vietnam August–December 1963*, 602–3.

99. Jack Raymond, "High U.S. Officials Meet on Vietnam in Hawaii Nov. 20," *New York Times*, Nov. 13, 1963, pp. 1, 4; "The President's News Conference of November 14, 1963," *Public Papers of the Presidents: JFK, 1963*, 3: 846, 852; Jack Raymond, "G.I. Return Waits on Vietnam Talk," *New York Times*, Nov. 15, 1963, p. 13; "The Conference in Brief," ibid., Nov. 15, 1963, p. 18; "1,000 U.S. Troops to Leave Vietnam," ibid., Nov. 16, 1963, pp. 1, 6; "U.S. Aides Report Gain," ibid., Nov. 21, 1963, p. 8.

100. Honolulu Briefing Book, "The Transfer of US Military Functions to Vietnamese Forces," Southeast Asia, Department of State, Nov 15, 1963, NSF, Countries—Vietnam, box 204, JFKL; memo of discussion at special meeting on Vietnam in Honolulu, Nov. 20, 1963, *FRUS*, 4: *Vietnam August–December 1963*, 608–11; Gravel, ed., *Pentagon Papers*, 2: 170, 190.

101. Honolulu Briefing Book, Nov. 20, 1963, Parts I and II, NSF, Countries—Vietnam, Subjects, box 204, JFKL. According to one writer, the Honolulu meeting overflowed with optimism, so much so that the policymakers felt confident that all 16,500 soldiers could be home by 1965. "Optimism at Honolulu, Problems in Saigon," *Time*, Nov. 29, 1963, p. 40.

102. For the argument that President Kennedy intended to escalate the conflict, see Gibbons, "Lyndon Johnson and the Legacy of Vietnam," in Gardner and Gittinger, eds., *Vietnam*, 141–44. Bundy's memo to JFK, Nov. 21, 1963, in NSF, NSAM File, NSAM 273, South Vietnam, box 2, LBJL, quoted ibid., 141–43.

103. Forrestal quoted in Bird, *Color of Truth*, 260.

Conclusion

1. E. W. Kenworthy, "Johnson Affirms Aims in Vietnam," *New York Times*, Nov. 25, 1963, pp. 1, 5; Ball Oral History Interview, 1: 8, LBJL; Rusk to LBJ, early Dec. 1963, NSF, Country File–Vietnam, Memos and Misc., vol. 1 (Nov.–Dec. 1963), LBJL.

2. Situation Report prepared by Department of State for president, Nov. 23, 1963, *FRUS*, 4: *Vietnam August–December 1963*, 629–30; memo for record of meeting in Executive Office Building, Nov. 24, 1963, ibid., 635–37; Ted Gittinger, ed., *The Johnson Years: A Vietnam Roundtable* (Austin: LBJ Library, Lyndon B. Johnson School of Public Affairs, University of Texas, 1993), 14, cited in Gibbons, "Lyndon Johnson and the Legacy of Vietnam," in Gardner and Gittinger, eds., *Vietnam*, 119–20; NSC meeting, Aug. 31, 1963, Gravel, ed., *Pentagon Papers*, 2: 240–41; memo for record of NSC meeting, Aug. 31, 1963, ibid., 743; LBJ to JFK, May 23, 1961, p. 4, Vice-Presidential Security File, "Vice-Presidential Travel, Vice President's Visit to Southeast Asia, May 9–24, 1961," box 1, LBJL; Lyndon B. Johnson, *The Vantage Point: Perspectives of the Presidency, 1963–1969* (New York: Holt, Rinehart and Winston, 1971), 43–44; Tom Wicker, *JFK and LBJ* (Baltimore: Penguin, 1972), 205–6.

3. Hilsman Oral History Interview, 1: 8, 19–20, LBJL.

4. Ibid., 20, 35.

5. Langguth, *Our Vietnam*, 268–69.

6. Memo of conversation between Hilsman and Lodge in Washington, Nov. 24, 1963, *FRUS*, 4: *Vietnam August–December 1963*, 633–34. Lodge presented these

same ideas to Harriman as well. See memo of conversation between Harriman and Lodge in Washington, Nov. 24, 1963, ibid., 634, and Lodge to Harriman, Dec. 3, 1963, ibid., 657. Lodge told Harriman that North Vietnam would become "a Yugoslavia-like neutralist nation." Ibid. See also Blair, *Lodge in Vietnam*, 92–93. For Johnson and McGeorge Bundy's dismissal of the neutralization idea, see their telephone conversation of Feb. 6, 1964, in Michael R. Beschloss, ed., *Taking Charge: The Johnson White House Tapes, 1963–1964* (New York: Simon and Schuster, 1997), 226.

7. LBJ telephone conversation with Donald Cook, president of American Electric Power Company, Nov. 30, 1963, in Beschloss, ed., *Taking Charge*, 73–74; transcript of telephone conversation between LBJ and Fulbright, Dec. 2, 1963, in William C. Gibbons Papers, box 3, LBJL; LBJ's views on Lodge in Blair, *Lodge in Vietnam*, 97–98; memo of telephone conversation between Harriman and McGeorge Bundy, Dec. 4, 1963, *FRUS*, 4: *Vietnam August–December 1963*, 666. Lodge left Saigon on June 28, 1964.

8. Explanatory note in *FRUS*, 4: *Vietnam August–December 1963*, 637 n. 1; NSAM 273, Nov. 26, 1963, ibid., 638–40; Rusk to Lodge, Nov. 27, 1963, ibid., 640; Newman, *JFK and Vietnam*, 445–46.

9. Gravel, ed., *Pentagon Papers*, 2: 223, 3: 149–51; Gibbons, *U.S. Government and the Vietnam War*, 2: 210; 212, 214; Shultz, *Secret War against Hanoi*, 38–40.

10. Seymour Topping, "U.S. Seeks to Spur War," *New York Times*, Dec. 15, 1963, p. 24; Hilsman quoted in Rusk to Saigon embassy, Nov. 29, 1963, NSF, Country File–Vietnam, State Cables, vol. 1 (Nov.–Dec. 1963), LBJL; Harkins to RUEPDA/OASD/PA, Washington, D.C., Nov. 29, 1963, ibid., Defense Cables, vol. 1 (Nov.–Dec. 1963), LBJL; Gravel, ed., *Pentagon Papers*, 2: 171, 191; "End of the Glow," *Time*, Dec. 13, 1963, p. 32. Three planeloads filled with 220 servicemen, many of whom had experienced combat, departed Vietnam on December 3, the first contingent of 1,000 to be home by Christmas. A fourth jet had engine trouble, forcing the seventy-four soldiers on board to return to camp. Many of these were army men who vented their disappointment on the air force. Hedrick Smith, "220 G.I.'s Leave South Vietnam as Troop Reduction Gets Under Way," *New York Times*, Dec. 4, 1963, pp. 1, 11.

11. LBJ to Taylor, Dec. 2, 1963, *FRUS*, 4: *Vietnam August–December 1963*, 651; LBJ to McCone, Dec. 2, 1963, ibid., 651 n. 2; Ed. Note, ibid., 652; Joint Chiefs of Staff to Felt, Dec. 2, 1963, ibid., 653; Joint Chiefs of Staff to CINCPAC, undated but early Dec. 1963, NSF, Country File–Vietnam, Defense Cables, vol. 1 (Nov.–Dec. 1963), LBJL; Taylor to LBJ, Dec. 6, 1963, NSF, Country File–Vietnam, Memos and Misc., vol. 1 (Nov.–Dec. 1963), LBJL; Powers and LeMay quoted in Hilsman, *To Move a Nation*, 526–27.

12. Taylor to LBJ, Dec. 6, 1963, *FRUS*, 4: *Vietnam August–December 1963*, 679; Rusk to Lodge, Dec. 6, 1963, ibid., 685–87; memo of telephone conversation between Rusk and McNamara, Dec. 7, 1963, ibid., 690.

13. Serong quoted in Blair, *Lodge in Vietnam*, 91; Forrestal to Bundy, Dec. 11, 1963, quoted ibid.; Forrestal to LBJ, Dec. 11, 1963, *FRUS*, 4: *Vietnam August–December 1963*, 699–700; Gibbons, *U.S. Government and the Vietnam War*, 2: 211; Hilsman, *To Move a Nation*, 533–34.

14. Krulak's report on McNamara's visit of Dec. 19–20, 1963, Dec. 21, 1963, *FRUS*, 4: *Vietnam August–December 1963*, 722–27; memo for record by Sullivan, Dec. 21, 1963, ibid., 728–30; Pribbenow, trans., *Victory in Vietnam*, 80, 115, 124.

15. "'We Are Losing, Morale Is Bad . . . If They'd Give Us Good Planes . . .'" *Newsweek*, May 4, 1964, pp. 46–47, 49.

16. McNamara to LBJ, Dec. 21, 1963, *FRUS*, 4: *Vietnam August–December 1963*, 732–35; McCone to LBJ, Dec. 23, 1963, ibid., 735; memo of discussion between Taylor and LBJ, Dec. 23, 1963, ibid., ed. note, 739; Colby and Forbath, *Honorable Men*, 219–20; Gibbons, *U.S. Government and the Vietnam War*, 2: 213.

17. McNamara to LBJ, Dec. 21, 1963, *FRUS*, 4: *Vietnam August–December 1963*, 735.

18. LBJ quote in Karnow, *Vietnam*, 342; Langguth, *Our Vietnam*, 271. For Johnson's long-time enmity toward the military, see H. R. McMaster, *Dereliction of Duty: Lyndon Johnson, Robert McNamara, the Joint Chiefs of Staff, and the Lies That Led to Vietnam* (New York: HarperCollins, 1997), 52–53.

19. DIA/CIIC to Joint Chiefs of Staff, Dec. 11, 1963, NSF, Country File–Vietnam, Defense Cables, vol. 1 (Nov.–Dec. 1963), LBJL; "The Viet-Nam Workers' Party's 1963 Decision to Escalate the War in the South," Dec. 1963, Indochina Archives: History of the Vietnam War, Unit 5: NLF, General Materials, 1963 (University of California, Berkeley); Duiker, "Hanoi's Response to American Policy," in Gardner and Gittinger, eds., *Vietnam*, 67–68; Duiker, *Ho Chi Minh*, 534–35; Jian, *Mao's China and the Cold War*, 207–8; Zhai, *China and the Vietnam Wars*, 120, 125.

20. Gaiduk, *Soviet Union and the Vietnam War*, 6–10.

21. "Now It's a War against Americans in Vietnam," *Newsweek*, March 2, 1964, p. 35.

22. LBJ telephone conversation with McNamara, Feb. 20, 1964, in Beschloss, ed., *Taking Charge*, 249; "Is There a Way Out for U.S. in Vietnam?" *Newsweek*, Feb. 17, 1964, pp. 42–44.

23. Gravel, ed., *Pentagon Papers*, 2: 194–96; LBJ telephone conversation with McNamara, March 2, 1964, in Beschloss, ed., *Taking Charge*, 258.

24. "New Turn in a 15-Year War: The Real Story of Vietnam," *Newsweek*, March 23, 1964, pp. 51–52.

25. Gravel, ed., *Pentagon Papers*, 2: 197.

26. Jorden to Harriman, Dec. 27, 1963, *FRUS*, 4: *Vietnam August–December 1963*, 741–43; Sullivan to Harriman, Dec. 31, 1963, ibid., 749–52; Gravel, ed., *Pentagon Papers*, 2: 303; George C. Herring, *LBJ and Vietnam: A Different Kind of War* (Austin: University of Texas Press, 1994), 67; Currey, *Lansdale*, 291–92.

27. Transcript of Oral History Interview of Robert F. Kennedy, by John M. Martin, April 30, 1964, JFKL; Edwin O. Guthman and Jeffrey Shulman, eds., *Robert Kennedy in His Own Words: The Unpublished Recollections of the Kennedy Years* (New York: Bantam Books, 1988), 394–95; Sorensen, *Kennedy*, 660–61; William Bundy, unpublished manuscript under the title of "Vietnam Manuscript" (1969–72), chap. 10: "Retrospective: A Road Deepened and Another Not Taken," 8–11, William P. Bundy Papers, box 1, LBJL.

28. Gilpatric Oral History Interview, 1: 10, LBJL; author's interview with Galbraith, March 28, 2001; Galbraith to author, Oct. 16, 2001 (letter in author's possession); author's interview with McNamara, March 5, 2001; author's interview with Hilsman, Sept. 17, 2001. My view sharply contrasts with that of William C. Gibbons. See his essay, "Lyndon Johnson and the Legacy of Vietnam," in

Gardner and Gittinger, eds., *Vietnam*, 140. Much of my argument is in accord with that of Newman, *JFK and Vietnam*, Logevall, *Choosing War*, and Kaiser, *American Tragedy*.

29. For Kennedy's growth in office, see Robert A. Divine, "The Education of John F. Kennedy," in Frank J. Merli and Theodore A. Wilson, eds., *Makers of American Diplomacy: From Theodore Roosevelt to Henry Kissinger*, 2 vols. (New York: Charles Scribner's Sons, 1974), 2: 317–44.

30. Author's interview with Rusk, Aug. 16, 1989; author's interview with McNamara, March 5, 2001; author's interview with Hilsman, Sept. 17, 2001; Hilsman Oral History Interview, 35–36, JFKL; author's interview with Galbraith, March 28, 2001.

31. Rusk Oral History Interview, 4, 6, LBJL; Jorden Oral History Interview, 1: 5, LBJL; William Bundy Oral History Interview, 14–15, LBJL; Forrestal Oral History Interview, 16–17, 21–22, LBJL.

32. McNamara in congressional hearings on Tonkin Gulf crisis, August 1964, Gravel, ed., *Pentagon Papers*, 2: 200; quote ibid.; author's interview with McNamara, March 5, 2001. Although quoted earlier in this work, McNamara's words at the White House meeting on October 2, 1963, are worth quoting again: "We need a way to get out of Vietnam. This is a way of doing it. . . . I think, Mr. President, we must have a means of disengaging from this area." Tape recording of meeting in the Oval Office, Oct. 2, 1963, POF, Presidential Recordings Collection, Tape no. 144/A49 (cassette 2 of 3), JFKL.

33. Richard Winston, *Thomas Becket* (New York: Alfred A. Knopf, 1967), 346–47; W. L. Warren, *Henry II* (Berkeley: University of California Press, 1973), 508–9. There is disagreement over Henry II's actual words, but it is clear that he made known his dissatisfaction with his servants for permitting Becket to continue his provocative behavior.

34. Colby testimony, 29–34.

BIBLIOGRAPHY

Primary Sources

Unpublished Sources

John M. Echols Collection, Cornell University
    Selections on the Vietnam War (microform)
    Gerald R. Ford Library, Ann Arbor, Michigan
    Graham Martin Papers
        Saigon Embassy Files Kept by Ambassador Graham Martin
Indochina Archives, University of California, Berkeley
    National Liberation Front (microform)
        Documentation
        General Materials
        Military Operations
Lyndon B. Johnson Library, Austin, Texas
    William P. Bundy Papers
    William C. Gibbons Papers
    Lyndon B. Johnson Papers
        Vice-Presidential Security File
    Meeting Notes File
    National Security File
        Country File, Vietnam
        Files of McGeorge Bundy
        Head of State Correspondence
        Intelligence File
        International Meeting and Travel File
        Memos to the President
        Name File
        National Security Action Memorandums
        National Security Council Meetings
    Bromley K. Smith Papers
    Vietnam Country File
    Oral History Interviews
        George Ball
        Chester L. Bowles
        William P. Bundy
        William E. Colby
        Elbridge Durbrow

Frederick W. Flott
Michael V. Forrestal
Leslie H. Gelb
Roswell L. Gilpatric
Paul D. Harkins
W. Averell Harriman
Roger Hilsman
U. Alexis Johnson
William J. Jorden
Edward G. Lansdale
Lyman Lemnitzer
John A. McCone
Robert S. McNamara
Frederick E. Nolting
Rufus Phillips
Walt W. Rostow
Dean Rusk
William H. Sullivan
Maxwell D. Taylor
William Trueheart
Samuel T. Williams
John F. Kennedy Library, Boston, Massachusetts
Roger Hilsman Papers
John F. Kennedy Papers
National Security File
Countries—Laos
Countries—Vietnam
Meetings and Memoranda
President's Office File
Cabinet Meetings
Countries—Laos
Countries—Vietnam
Departments and Agencies
Presidential Recordings
Cabinet Room Meetings
National Security Council Meetings
Oval Office Meetings
Special Correspondence
Vietnam General
John Newman Papers
James Thomson Papers
Oral History Interviews
Chester L. Bowles
McGeorge Bundy
Roswell L. Gilpatric
W. Averell Harriman

Roger Hilsman
U. Alexis Johnson
Robert F. Kennedy
Edward G. Lansdale
Henry Cabot Lodge
John A. McCone
Robert S. McNamara
Mike Mansfield
Frederick E. Nolting
Kenneth P. O'Donnell
Walt W. Rostow
Dean Rusk
Maxwell D. Taylor
Massachusetts Historical Society, Boston
    Henry Cabot Lodge II Papers
       "Vietnam Memoir" (microform)
National Archives
    College Park, Maryland
        U.S. Senate Intelligence Committee Select Committee to Study Governmental Operations with Respect to Intelligence Activities—Record Group 46, Church Committee (SSCIA)
           William E. Colby Testimony
           Committee Memoranda, Diem Assassination
           Lucien Conein Testimony
           Lucien Conein and John Richardson, "History of the Vietnamese Generals' Coup of 1/2 November 1963" (After Action Report)
           John A. McCone Testimony
           Robert McNamara Testimony
           Miscellaneous Records
           Kenneth O'Donnell Testimony
           Operation Mongoose
           Recommendations for Key Positions in a Successor Regime
           Dean Rusk Testimony
           Maxwell D. Taylor Testimony
           Vietnam Cables, October 1963
    St. Louis, Missouri
        National Personnel Records Center
           Military Personnel Records
National Defense University, Washington, D.C.
    Maxwell D. Taylor Papers

Published Sources

Documentary Collections, Congressional Documents, and Periodicals

Beschloss, Michael R., ed. *Taking Charge: The Johnson White House Tapes, 1963–1964.* New York: Simon and Schuster, 1997.

Church Committee Assassination Report: U.S. Congress, Senate, Select Committee to Study Governmental Operations with Respect to Intelligence Activities. *Alleged Assassination Plots Involving Foreign Leaders; Interim Report.* 94th Cong., 1st Session, Senate Report No. 94–465. Washington, D.C.: Government Printing Office, 1975.

The Declassified Documents Quarterly Catalog and microfiche. Woodbridge, Conn.: Research Publications, 1977–.

Gibbons, William C. *The U.S. Government and the Vietnam War: Executive and Legislative Roles and Relationships.* 4 vols. Part II: *1961–1964.* Princeton, N.J.: Princeton University Press, 1986.

Guthman, Edwin O., and Shulman, Jeffrey, eds. *Robert Kennedy in His Own Words: The Unpublished Recollections of the Kennedy Years.* New York: Bantam Books, 1988.

Hollick, Anne L. *U.S. Involvement in the Overthrow of Diem, 1963.* U.S. Congress, Senate, Committee on Foreign Relations, Staff Study No. 3, 92nd Cong., 2nd Session. Washington, D.C.: Government Printing Office, 1972.

Kennedy, John F. "America's Stake in Vietnam." *Vital Speeches* 11 (Aug. 1, 1956): 617–19.

The Pentagon Papers: The Department of Defense History of United States Decisionmaking on Vietnam [Senator Mike Gravel Edition]. 4 vols. Boston, Mass.: Beacon Press, 1971.

Porter, Gareth, ed. *Vietnam: The Definitive Documentation of Human Decisions.* 2 vols. Stanfordville, N.Y.: Earl M. Coleman Enterprises, 1979.

Pribbenow, Merle L., trans., *Victory in Vietnam: The Official History of the People's Army of Vietnam, 1954–1975.* Lawrence: University Press of Kansas. 2002. Original Publication: Military History Institute of Vietnam, Ministry of Defense, *History of the People's Army of Vietnam, Volume II: The Maturation of the People's Army of Vietnam during the Resistance War against the Americans to Save the Nation (1954–1975).* Hanoi: People's Army Publishing House, 1988; rev. ed., Hanoi: People's Army Publishing House, 1994.

Sheehan, Neil, et al., eds. *The Pentagon Papers as Published by The New York Times.* New York: Quadrangle Books, 1971.

U.S. Department of Defense. *United States–Vietnam Relations, 1945–1967* [The Pentagon Papers]. 12 vols. Washington, D.C.: Government Printing Office, 1971.

U.S. Department of State. *Foreign Relations of the United States, 1958–1960,* vol. 1: *Vietnam.* Washington, D.C.: Government Printing Office, 1986.

———. *Foreign Relations of the United States, 1961–1963,* vol. 1: *Vietnam 1961.* Washington, D.C.: Government Printing Office, 1988.

———. *Foreign Relations of the United States, 1961–1963,* vol. 2: *Vietnam 1962.* Washington, D.C.: Government Printing Office, 1990.

———. *Foreign Relations of the United States, 1961–1963,* vol. 3: *Vietnam January–August 1963.* Washington, D.C.: Government Printing Office, 1991.

———. *Foreign Relations of the United States, 1961–1963,* vol. 4: *Vietnam August–December 1963.* Washington, D.C.: Government Printing Office, 1991.

———. *Foreign Relations of the United States, 1964–1968,* vol. 1: *Vietnam 1964.* Washington, D.C.: Government Printing Office, 1992.

U.S. National Archives and Records Administration. *Public Papers of the Presidents of the United States: John F. Kennedy, 1961–1963*. 3 vols. Washington, D.C.: Government Printing Office, 1962–64.

Memoirs and Personal Accounts

Ball, George W. *The Past Has Another Pattern: Memoirs*. New York: W. W. Norton, 1982.

Bowles, Chester L. *Promises to Keep*. New York: Harper and Row, 1971.

Colby, William. *Lost Victory: A Firsthand Account of America's Sixteen-Year Involvement in Vietnam*. Chicago: Contemporary Books, 1989.

Colby, William, and Peter Forbath. *Honorable Men: My Life in the CIA*. New York: Simon and Schuster, 1978.

Cooper, Chester L. *The Lost Crusade: America in Vietnam*. New York: Dodd, Mead, 1970.

Deitchman, Seymour J. *The Best-Laid Schemes: A Tale of Social Research and Bureaucracy*. Cambridge, Mass.: MIT Press, 1976.

Don, Tran Van. *Our Endless War: Inside Vietnam*. San Rafael, Calif.: Presidio Press, 1978.

Galbraith, John Kenneth. *Ambassador's Journal: A Personal Account of the Kennedy Years*. Boston: Houghton Mifflin, 1969.

Halberstam, David. *The Best and the Brightest*. New York: Random House, 1969.

———. *The Making of a Quagmire: America and Vietnam during the Kennedy Era*. New York: Alfred A. Knopf, 1964. Rev. ed., New York: Alfred A. Knopf, 1988.

Higgins, Marguerite. *Our Vietnam Nightmare*. New York: Harper and Row, 1965.

Hilsman, Roger. *To Move a Nation: The Politics of Foreign Policy in the Administration of John F. Kennedy*. New York: Dell, 1964.

Johnson, Lyndon B. *The Vantage Point: Perspectives of the Presidency, 1963–1969*. New York: Holt, Rinehart and Winston, 1971.

Johnson, U. Alexis. *The Right Hand of Power*. Englewood Cliffs, N.J.: Prentice-Hall, 1984.

Kattenburg, Paul M. *The Vietnam Trauma in American Foreign Policy, 1945–75*. New Brunswick, N.J.: Transaction Books, 1980.

Ky, Nguyen Cao. *Twenty Years and Twenty Days*. New York: Stein and Day, 1976.

Lansdale, Edward G. *In the Midst of Wars: An American's Mission to Southeast Asia*. New York: Harper and Row, 1972.

Lodge, Henry Cabot. *The Storm Has Many Eyes: A Personal Narrative*. New York: W. W. Norton, 1973.

McNamara, Robert S. *In Retrospect: The Tragedy and Lessons of Vietnam*. New York: Random House, 1995.

Maneli, Mieczyslaw. *War of the Vanquished*. New York: Harper and Row, 1971.

Mecklin, John. *Mission in Torment: An Intimate Account of the U.S. Role in Vietnam*. Garden City, N.Y.: Doubleday, 1965.

Nolting, Frederick. *From Trust to Tragedy: The Political Memoirs of Frederick Nolting, Kennedy's Ambassador to Diem's Vietnam*. New York: Praeger, 1988.

O'Donnell, Kenneth P., and David F. Powers. *"Johnny, We Hardly Knew Ye": Memories of John Fitzgerald Kennedy*. Boston: Little, Brown, 1970.

Reston, James. *Deadline*. New York: Random House, 1991.

Rostow, Walt W. *The Diffusion of Power: An Essay in Recent History*. New York: Macmillan, 1972.

_____. *The Stages of Economic Growth: A Non-Communist Manifesto*. Cambridge, Engl.: Cambridge University Press, 1960.

Rusk, Dean. *As I Saw It*. Ed. by Daniel S. Papp. New York: W. W. Norton, 1990.

Salinger, Pierre. *With Kennedy*. New York: Avon, 1967.

Schlesinger, Arthur M., Jr. *A Thousand Days: John F. Kennedy in the White House*. Boston: Houghton Mifflin, 1965.

Shaplen, Robert. *The Lost Revolution*. New York: Harper and Row, 1955, 1965.

Sheehan, Neil. *A Bright Shining Lie: John Paul Vann and America in Vietnam*. New York: Random House, 1988.

Sorensen, Theodore C. *Kennedy*. New York: Harper and Row, 1965.

Taylor, Maxwell D. *The Uncertain Trumpet*. New York: Harper and Brothers, 1960.

_____. *Swords and Plowshares: A Memoir*. New York: W. W. Norton, 1972.

Truong Nhu Tang. *A Viet Cong Memoir: An Inside Account of the Vietnam War and Its Aftermath*. San Diego: Harcourt Brace Jovanovich, 1985.

Newspapers and periodicals

New Republic
New York Times
Newsweek
Saturday Evening Post
Time
U.S. News and World Report
Washington Post

Author Interviews

Daniel Ellsberg. March 27, 2002
James Galbraith. February 21, 2001
John Kenneth Galbraith. March 28, 2001
Roger Hilsman. September 17, 2001
A. J. Langguth. March 22, 2002
Robert McNamara. March 5 and April 17, 2001
Walt W. Rostow. February 20, 2001
Dean Rusk. August 16, 1989

Secondary Sources

Books

Bird, Kai. *The Color of Truth: McGeorge Bundy and William Bundy: Brothers in Arms: A Biography*. New York: Simon and Schuster, 1998.

Blair, Anne E. *Lodge in Vietnam: A Patriot Abroad*. New Haven: Yale University Press, 1995.

Brigham, Robert K. *Guerrilla Diplomacy: The NLF's Foreign Relations and the Viet Nam War*. Ithaca, N.Y.: Cornell University Press, 1999.

Buttinger, Joseph. *Vietnam: A Dragon Embattled.* New York: Praeger, 1967.

Castle, Timothy N. *At War in the Shadow of Vietnam: U.S. Military Aid to the Royal Lao Government, 1955–1975.* New York: Columbia University Press, 1993.

Charlton, Michael, and Anthony Moncrieff. *Many Reasons Why: The American Involvement in Vietnam.* New York: Hill and Wang, 1978.

Conboy, Kenneth, and Dale Andradé. *Spies and Commandos: How America Lost the Secret War in North Vietnam.* Lawrence: University Press of Kansas, 2000.

Currey, Cecil B. *Edward Lansdale: The Unquiet American.* Boston: Houghton Mifflin, 1988.

Di Leo, David L. *George Ball, Vietnam, and the Rethinking of Containment.* Chapel Hill: University of North Carolina Press, 1991.

Duiker, William J. *The Communist Road to Power in Vietnam.* Boulder, Colo.: Westview Press, 1981.

_____. *Ho Chi Minh.* New York: Hyperion, 2000.

_____. *Sacred War: Nationalism and Revolution in a Divided Vietnam.* New York: McGraw-Hill, 1995.

Eliot, T. S. *Murder in the Cathedral.* New York: Harcourt, Brace, 1935.

Fairlie, Henry. *The Kennedy Promise: The Politics of Expectation.* Garden City, N.Y.: Doubleday, 1973.

Fitzgerald, Frances. *Fire in the Lake: The Vietnamese and the Americans in Vietnam.* New York: Random House, 1972.

FitzSimons, Louise. *The Kennedy Doctrine.* New York: Random House, 1972.

Freedman, Lawrence. *Kennedy's Wars: Berlin, Cuba, Laos, and Vietnam.* New York: Oxford University Press, 2000.

Futrell, Robert F. *The United States Air Force in Southeast Asia: The Advisory Years to 1965.* Washington, D.C.: Office of Air Force History, 1981.

Gaiduk, Ilya V. *The Soviet Union and the Vietnam War.* Chicago: Ivan R. Dee, 1996.

Gardner, Lloyd C., and Ted Gittinger, eds. *International Perspectives on Vietnam.* College Station: Texas A&M University Press, 2000.

_____. *Vietnam: The Early Decisions.* Austin: University of Texas Press, 1997.

Giglio, James N. *The Presidency of John F. Kennedy.* Lawrence: University Press of Kansas, 1991.

Gittinger, Ted., ed. *The Johnson Years: A Vietnam Roundtable.* Austin: LBJ Library, Lyndon B. Johnson School of Public Affairs, University of Texas, 1993.

Greene, Graham. *The Quiet American.* New York: Viking Press, 1956.

Hallin, Daniel C. *The "Uncensored War": The Media and Vietnam.* Berkeley: University of California Press, 1986.

Hammer, Ellen I. *A Death in November: America in Vietnam, 1963.* New York: E. P. Dutton, 1987.

Hammond, William M. *Reporting Vietnam: Media and Military at War.* Lawrence: University Press of Kansas, 1998.

Herring, George C. *America's Longest War: The United States and Vietnam, 1950–1975,* 4th ed. New York: McGraw-Hill, 2002.

_____. *LBJ and Vietnam: A Different Kind of War.* Austin: University of Texas Press, 1994.

Hersh, Seymour M. *The Dark Side of Camelot*. Boston: Little, Brown, 1997.

Isaacson, Walter, and Evan Thomas. *The Wise Men: Six Friends and the World They Made*. New York: Simon and Schuster, 1986.

Jian, Chen. *Mao's China and the Cold War*. Chapel Hill: University of North Carolina Press, 2001.

Joes, Anthony J. *The War for South Viet Nam, 1954–1975*. Westport, Conn.: Praeger, 2001.

Jones, Howard. *"A New Kind of War": America's Global Strategy and the Truman Doctrine in Greece*. New York: Oxford University Press, 1989.

Kahin, George McT. *Intervention: How America Became Involved in Vietnam*. New York: Alfred A. Knopf, 1986.

Kaiser, David. *American Tragedy: Kennedy, Johnson, and the Origins of the Vietnam War*. Cambridge, Mass.: Harvard University Press, 2000.

Karnow, Stanley. *Vietnam: A History*. New York: Viking, 1983. Rev. ed., New York: Penguin, 1997.

Kelly, Francis J. *U.S. Army Special Forces, 1961–1971*. Washington, D.C.: Department of the Army, 1973.

Krepinevich, Andrew F. *The Army and Vietnam*. Baltimore: Johns Hopkins University Press, 1986.

Langguth, A. J. *Our Vietnam: The War, 1954–1975*. New York: Simon and Schuster, 2000.

Lederer, William J., and Eugene Burdick. *The Ugly American*. New York: W. W. Norton, 1958.

Logevall, Fredrik. *Choosing War: The Lost Chance for Peace and the Escalation of War in Vietnam*. Berkeley: University of California Press, 1999.

Macdonald, Douglas J. *Adventures in Chaos: American Intervention for Reform in the Third World*. Cambridge, Mass.: Harvard University Press, 1992.

Mann, Robert. *A Grand Delusion: America's Descent into Vietnam*. New York: Basic Books, 2001.

McMaster, H. R. *Dereliction of Duty: Lyndon Johnson, Robert McNamara, the Joint Chiefs of Staff, and the Lies That Led to Vietnam*. New York: HarperCollins, 1997.

Merritt, Jane Hamilton. *Tragic Mountains: The Hmong, the Americans, and the Secret Wars for Laos, 1942–1992*. Bloomington: Indiana University Press, 1993.

Miller, William J. *Henry Cabot Lodge, a Biography*. New York: Heineman, 1967.

Newman, John M. *JFK and Vietnam: Deception, Intrigue, and the Struggle for Power*. New York: Warner Books, 1992.

Olson, Gregory A. *Mansfield and Vietnam: A Study in Rhetorical Adaptation*. East Lansing: Michigan State University Press, 1995.

Parmet, Herbert S. *JFK: The Presidency of John F. Kennedy*. New York: Dial Press, 1983.

Paterson, Thomas G., ed. *Kennedy's Quest for Victory: American Foreign Policy, 1961–1963*. New York: Oxford University Press, 1989.

Pike, Douglas. *PAVN: People's Army of Vietnam*. Novato, Calif.: Presidio Press, 1986.

———. *Viet Cong: The Organization and Techniques of the National Liberation Front of South Vietnam*. Cambridge, Mass.: MIT Press, 1966.

Plimpton, George, ed. *American Journey: The Times of Robert Kennedy*. New York: Harcourt Brace Jovanovich, 1970.

Powers, Thomas. *The Man Who Kept the Secrets: Richard Helms and the CIA*. New York: Alfred A. Knopf, 1979.

Prados, John. *The Blood Road: The Ho Chi Minh Trail and the Vietnam War*. New York: John Wiley and Sons, 1999.

Prochnau, William. *Once upon a Distant War: David Halberstam, Neil Sheehan, Peter Arnett—Young War Correspondents and Their Early Vietnam Battles*. New York: Random House, 1995.

Reeves, Richard. *President Kennedy: Profile of Power*. New York: Simon and Schuster, 1993.

Rust, William J. *Kennedy in Vietnam: American Vietnam Policy, 1960–1963*. New York: Charles Scribner's Sons, 1985.

Schlesinger, Arthur M., Jr. *Robert Kennedy and His Times*. 2 vols. Boston: Houghton Mifflin, 1978.

Schwab, Orrin. *Defending the Free World: John F. Kennedy, Lyndon Johnson, and the Vietnam War, 1961–1965*. Westport, Conn.: Praeger, 1998.

Shultz, Richard H., Jr. *The Secret War against Hanoi: Kennedy's and Johnson's Use of Spies, Saboteurs, and Covert Warriors in North Vietnam*. New York: HarperCollins, 1999.

Spector, Ronald H. *Advice and Support: The Early Years of the United States Army in Vietnam, 1941–1960*. Washington, D.C.: Center of Military History, 1983.

Tilford, Earl H., Jr. *Crosswinds: The Air Force's Setup in Vietnam*. College Station: Texas A&M University Press, 1993.

_____. *Search and Rescue Operations in Southeast Asia, 1961–1975*. Washington, D.C.: Office of Air Force History, 1980.

Toczek, David M. *The Battle of Ap Bac, Vietnam: They Did Everything but Learn from It*. Westport, Conn.: Greenwood Press, 2001.

Valentine, Douglas. *The Phoenix Program*. New York: William Morrow, 1990.

Walton, Richard J. *Cold War and Counterrevolution: The Foreign Policy of John F. Kennedy*. New York: Viking Press, 1972.

Warren, W. L. *Henry II*. Berkeley: University of California Press, 1973.

Wells, Tom. *Wild Man: The Life and Times of Daniel Ellsberg*. New York: St. Martin's Press, 2001.

Wicker, Tom. *JFK and LBJ*. Baltimore: Penguin, 1972.

Winston, Richard. *Thomas Becket*. New York: Alfred A. Knopf, 1967.

Winters, Francis X. *The Year of the Hare: America in Vietnam, January 25, 1963– February 15, 1964*. Athens: University of Georgia Press, 1997.

Wyden, Peter. *Bay of Pigs*. New York: Simon and Schuster, 1979.

Young, Marilyn B. *The Vietnam Wars, 1945–1990*. New York: HarperCollins, 1991.

Zhai, Qiang. *China and the Vietnam Wars, 1950–1975*. Chapel Hill: University of North Carolina Press, 2000.

Articles and Essays

Bassett, Lawrence J., and Stephen E. Pelz. "The Failed Search for Victory: Vietnam and the Politics of War." In *Kennedy's Quest for Victory: American Foreign*

Policy, 1961–1963, edited by Thomas G. Paterson, 223–52. New York: Oxford University Press, 1989.

Divine, Robert A. "The Education of John F. Kennedy." In *Makers of American Diplomacy: From Theodore Roosevelt to Henry Kissinger*, 2 vols., edited by Frank J. Merli and Theodore A. Wilson, 2:317–44. New York: Charles Scribner's Sons, 1974.

Duiker, William J. "Hanoi's Response to American Policy, 1961–1965: Crossed Signals?" In *Vietnam: The Early Decisions*, edited by Lloyd C. Gardner and Ted Gittinger, 58–82. Austin: University of Texas Press, 1997.

Gaiduk, Ilya V. *"Turnabout? The Soviet Policy Dilemma in the Vietnamese Conflict.* In *Vietnam: The Early Decisions*, edited by Lloyd C. Gardner and Ted Gittinger, 207–19. Austin: University of Texas Press, 1997.

Galbraith, James. "Did John F. Kennedy Give the Order to Withdraw from Vietnam?" Unpublished manuscript.

Gates, John M. "People's War in Vietnam." *Journal of Military History* 54 (July 1990): 325–44.

———. "Vietnam: The Debate Goes On." *Parameters: Journal of the U.S. Army War College* 14 (June 1984): 43–56.

Gibbons, William C. "Lyndon Johnson and the Legacy of Vietnam." In *Vietnam: The Early Decisions*, edited by Lloyd C. Gardner and Ted Gittinger, 119–57. Austin: University of Texas Press, 1997.

Hilsman, Roger. "McNamara's War—Against the Truth: A Review Essay." *Political Science Quarterly* 111 (Spring 1996): 151–63.

Honey, Patrick J. "Notes and Comment: North Vietnam's Workers' Party and South Vietnam's People's Revolutionary Party." *Pacific Affairs* 35 (Sept. 1962): 375–83.

Hughes, Ken. "JFK and the Fall of Diem." *The Boston Globe Magazine*, Oct. 24, 1999, pp. 10–24.

Jones, Howard. "Mistaken Prelude to Vietnam: The Truman Doctrine and 'A New Kind of War' in Greece." *Journal of Modern Greek Studies* 10 (May 1992): 121–43.

Jumper, Roy. "Mandarin Bureaucracy and Politics of South Vietnam." *Pacific Affairs* 30 (March 1957): 47–58.

Logevall, Fredrik. "Vietnam and the Question of What Might Have Been." In *Kennedy: The New Frontier Revisited*, edited by Mark J. White, 19–62. New York: New York University Press, 1998.

Newman, John M. "The Kennedy–Johnson Transition: The Case for Policy Reversal." In *Vietnam: The Early Decisions*, edited by Lloyd C. Gardner and Ted Gittinger, 158–76. Austin: University of Texas Press, 1997.

Paterson, Thomas G. "Bearing the Burden: A Critical Look at JFK's Foreign Policy." *Virginia Quarterly Review* 54 (Spring 1978): 193–212.

Pelz, Stephen. "John F. Kennedy's 1961 Vietnam War Decisions." *Journal of Strategic Studies* 4 (Dec. 1981): 356–85.

Shy, John, and Thomas W. Collier. "Revolutionary War." In *Makers of Modern Strategy: From Machiavelli to the Nuclear Age*, edited by Peter Paret, 815–62. Princeton, N.J.: Princeton University Press, 1986.

INDEX

advisers, 125, 126, 273, 275, 277, 314–21, 316–17, 421, 454–55. *See also specific individuals*

Agency for International Development, 153, 212

Agent Orange. *See* defoliants

agrovilles (fortified communities), 14, 24, 31, 35, 72, 99, 143, 147. *See also* strategic hamlet program

aid to South Vietnam. *See also* economic development: aid cuts, 344, 351, 362, 378–79, 390, 421, 423, 438, 439; press inquiries, 191; Special Forces, 359, 361, 375, 378, 390; U.S. provisions, 53, 74, 78, 189, 235; withdrawal plan, 246

air corps: bombing Independence Palace, 163; border issues, 148, 159; combat engagements, 144, 168; coup (1963), 412; disabling Vietcong airlifts, 130; Harriman on air strikes, 158; helicopters (*see main entry*); increasing, 220, 222, 239; initial deployment, 139; for Laos defense, 78; "Operation Farmgate," 89, 144, 152, 184; reconnaissance, 76; of South Vietnamese, 203–4; Taylor on, 76; 4400th Combat Crew Training Squadron (Jungle Jims), 89–90, 106, 158–59; training missions, 144; U.S. pilots, 152, 158, 159

Alsop, Joseph, 37, 363

ambassadors to Vietnam, 20–21. *See also* Durbrow, Elbridge; Lodge, Henry Cabot, Jr.; Nolting, Frederick

amnesty plan for deserters, 244

Anspacher, John, 137

Anthis, Roland, 203, 223

Ap Bac battle, 223–25, 226–27, 228, 231, 232

Army of the Republic of Vietnam (ARVN): Buddhist demonstrations and, 275, 307, 310; capacity of, 36; Chinese Nationalist forces compared to, 117; "Concept of Pacification Operations," 81; conventional warfare emphasis, 227; coup of 1963, 9, 282, 388; coup of 1960 (failed), 286; creating safe operational bases, 34; criticism of Nhus, 357; defoliant usage, 158; Diem and, 152, 165; discontent in, 33; document capture, 213; India's fears regarding, 75; Johnson's discussions with Diem, 62; Kennedy on, 108; in "kill area," 136; MAAG's interest in joining, 20; Nhu and, 257, 309; Parsons on, 26; performance of, 4, 73, 82, 98, 104, 117–18, 191, 194–95, 223–25, 354, 384; personnel numbers, 52, 80; in "Program of Action," 51; reconnaissance, 76; SEATO Plan 7 and, 162; Special Forces disguised as, 306, 307, 322; Taylor mission, 105, 118–20; Taylor's meeting with commander, 98–99; U.S. expectations of, 123, 124, 133; U.S. military presence and, 3, 83, 144, 159; Vietcong prisoners, 217; weakened state of, 25, 32, 91; withdrawal plan and, 349, 376

Arnett, Peter, 215, 228, 285, 290

arrests, 297, 301, 305, 347, 351, 358, 371, 400, 419

assassinations and attempts: attempt on Nolting, 75; Diem, 10, 12, 22, 69, 281, 286, 417, 425–31, 435–36, 439; generals' plans, 388–89, 391, 394; of Hoang Thuy Nam, 101–2; Independence Palace bombing, 163–64; KA on, 151, 305, 366, 375, 454–56; of Kennedy, 12, 443; of leaders and potential leaders, 75, 80; Nhu, 284, 286, 295–96, 388, 425–31, 435–36, 439; Nhu's plans for, 393–94; of U.S. officials, 65; Vietcong's reliance on, 18, 103, 141

Associated Press, 186, 187, 206

Bagley, Worth, 123
Baker, Russell, 178–79
Baldwin, Hanson, 226
Ball, George: Buddhist crisis, 281, 284;
    counterinsurgency program, 55, 178;
    coup plans, 304, 327, 328, 330–31;
    Geneva Accords violations, 168–69;
    Johnson administration, 443, 444; on
    seduction of Vietnam, 114; 'Telegram
    243,' 314, 315, 316, 319; on troop com-
    mitment, 120, 121, 125, 127
Bao Dai, 14, 252, 265
Bay of Pigs invasion, 7, 10, 47–48, 63, 67–
    68, 70–71, 81, 330, 339, 452
Becket, Thomas, 12, 454–55
Beijing. *See also* China: concern about
    Vietcong, 141; nuclear weapons consid-
    ered, 49; potential intervention from,
    120, 123–24
Bell, David, 43, 354
Berlin, Germany, 6, 7, 70, 72, 76, 77, 86,
    88, 122, 123, 124, 129–30, 136, 280
Big Minh. *See* Duong Van Minh ("Big
    Minh")
Bigart, Homer, 144, 145, 171, 294
bilateral treaty, 68–69, 83, 94, 182
Binh Hoa village, 148
Bissell, Richard, 34
Boggs, J. Caleb, 213–14
bombing. *See also* defoliants: Bathu bomb-
    ing incident, 148; citizenry's response
    to, 213; communication lines and
    roads, 235; Galbraith on, 132; of Inde-
    pendence Palace, 163; Johnson admin-
    istration, 447; napalm, 83, 158, 220,
    222, 223, 233; NLF on U.S. bombing,
    147; questionable effectiveness, 112;
    recommendations for, 110, 203–4, 223;
    South Vietnamese villages, 143; terror-
    ist campaigns, 450
Bonesteel, Charles, 55
border control issues: air strikes and, 159;
    Bathu incident cover-up, 148; Cambo-
    dia, 5, 43, 64, 76, 82, 86, 117, 159;
    China, 40; counterinsurgency plan, 35;
    Diem on, 147; expansion of patrols, 52;
    "flood control units" and, 107; joint
    study on, 64; Kennedy on, 108;
    Lansdale's assignment, 95; Laos, 82,
    86, 117, 136, 147, 149, 159; ranger
    force for, 124; Rostow on, 86
Bowles, Chester, 30, 46–47, 127–28, 172,
    242
British Advisory Mission, 154, 238
Browne, Malcolm, 144, 206, 215, 268–69,
    285
Buddhist uprising: bordello accusations,
    355, 372; demonstrations, 288–89;
    Diem and, 312–13, 372–73; formal
    agreements, 276, 289, 318; funeral for
    martyred bonze, 277; initial confronta-
    tions, 247–56, 258–67; martial law,

297–98, 307, 309; Operation Bravo,
    398; pagoda raids, 297–301, 302, 305,
    307, 322, 386, 414; political signifi-
    cance, 282; reparations, 341, 350; riot,
    276–77; self-immolations, 268–70, 291,
    294, 295, 296, 297, 317, 386; U.N. in-
    quiry, 385; U.S. response, 273–75,
    277–78; U.S. sanctuary, 299; Vietcong
    and, 334, 335; weaponry, 262, 263–64,
    297–98; withdrawal plans and, 8
Bui Dinh Dam, 223
Bui Van Luong, 264, 284, 300
Bundy, McGeorge: assassination of Diem
    and Nhu, 427; Buddhist crisis, 284;
    counterinsurgency program, 26; coup
    execution, 421, 434, 441; coup plans,
    331, 332, 338, 341, 392, 397, 402, 404;
    on culpability, 396; Diem regime is-
    sues, 349, 353, 361; Johnson adminis-
    tration, 444, 446; Kennedy on Jungle
    Jims, 89–90; Laos intervention, 45;
    McNamara-Taylor mission, 374, 375,
    380–81; Taylor's meeting with
    Kennedy, 39; U.S. involvement in war,
    14, 27, 40, 43, 56–57, 129, 197; with-
    drawal plans, 179, 442
Bundy, William, 26, 76, 88, 120, 123, 201–
    2, 317, 341, 369–70, 378, 428, 452
Burdick, Eugene, 19–20
Bureau of Intelligence and Research, 153
Burke, Arleigh, 44, 45, 46, 47
Burma, 98
Burris, Howard, 194
Buttinger, Joseph, 216
Buu Hoi, 385

Cambodia: border issues, 5, 43, 64, 76, 82,
    86, 117, 159; Buddhist uprising and,
    270–71; cooperative relationship with,
    34; Counterinsurgency Plan, 28;
    Decker on Southeast Asia intervention,
    46; Kennedy's concern regarding, 80;
    in "Program of Action," 50; sanctuary
    for Vietcong, 97; South Vietnam's rela-
    tions with, 35
"Campaign Plan" military strategy, 147
Can Lao party, 24, 35, 282, 370
Canada, 69
canine patrols, 76
Cao Dai religious sect, 24
Cao Xuan Vy, 308
Caravelle Manifesto, 336, 435
Carlson, Frank, 352
Carson, Rachel, 197
Castro, Fidel, 7, 330, 366–67
casualties: Ap Bac battle, 224–25; Buddhist
    uprising, 250, 251, 265, 297, 298; civil-
    ians, 148, 155–56, 419; coup (1963),
    419; Davis as first U.S. casualty, 142;
    Diem's desire to minimize, 227–28; In-
    dependence Palace bombing, 163; Plei
    Mrong battle, 225; press coverage, 161,

229; projections, 186; reports of, 159, 160, 194, 201; Strategic Hamlet Program, 349; of terrorist campaigns, 450; Vietcong, 174, 195, 229–30, 349
cease-fire, 38, 58, 128
Central Committee, 14–15, 16
Central Intelligence Agency (CIA): assassination of Diem and Nhu, 425, 430–31; assassination policies, 389; Bay of Pigs invasion, 38, 81; Buddhist uprising, 251, 255, 286; on Castro assassination, 366–67; Country Team in Saigon, 24; coup of 1963, 9, 282, 323–24, 326, 331, 333, 345, 402, 407, 411, 422, 426; covert actions, 74–75, 81; on Delta Plan, 154; on Diem, 289, 347; on duration of struggle, 221; in economic/military mission, 89; on generals, 356; generals' trust of, 346; on Harkins, 441; Johnson administration and, 453; Kennedy's distrust of, 38, 81; Lansdale and, 19, 368; on Minh's dissatisfaction, 290; Montagnards and, 217, 223; on Nhu, 245, 286–87, 290, 295–96, 304, 344; opposition to coup, 426; psywar, 233–34; recruitment of civilians, 52, 75; report on South Vietnam, 13; Special Group implementation, 153; sponsoring paramilitary activity in Laos, 71; on unification, 363; on Vietcong, 84, 230
Central Intelligence Organization, proposed by McGarr, 111
Central Military Party Committee of the Communist party, 263
Central Office for South Vietnam (COSVN), 18, 81–82
Chayes, Abram, 131
chemical warfare, 110–11. *See also* defoliants
Chen Yi, 165
Chiang Kai-shek, 80, 256
Child, Frank, 109
China: on 1963 coup, 419; concern about Vietcong, 141; domestic issues, 180; influence, 16, 362; Laos border with, 40; nuclear weapons considered, 49; potential intervention from, 87, 112, 115, 120, 121, 123–24, 129, 180; reaction to military presence, 122, 146–47; support for Communists, 34; threat of war with, 44, 46–47, 97, 449
Chinese Nationalist forces, 106, 110–11, 117
Chuong. *See* Tran Van Chuong
Church, Frank, 271, 352
Church Committee, 366, 367, 423
Churchill, Winston, 61
CIA. *See* Central Intelligence Agency (CIA)
CINCPAC (Commander-in-Chief, Pacific), 43, 45, 51, 89, 139, 140, 223, 296
civic services and programs: Diem on, 64, 157; emphasis on, 31–32, 34, 60, 90–

91, 108, 162; funding, 191; Hilsman on flood relief, 131; McGarr on, 91; in "Program of Action," 50; Saigon regime and, 65; Taylor mission on, 135, 153; Vietcong's effect on, 118
Civil Guard: Delta Plan, 154; Diem on, 62, 64, 69, 98; funding, 27; Kennedy on, 108; leadership of, 99; Nhu on, 393; performance of, 82, 189, 194–95, 223–25, 233; personnel, 52, 53; request for American instructors, 106; role in war, 190–91; targeted by Vietcong, 98; training and equipping, 24, 83, 124, 135
Civilian Irregular Defense Group program, 234, 244
civilians. *See also* Montagnards; peasantry: casualties, 32, 419; coup (1963), 412; press coverage, 161; recruitment of, 52, 75; student arrests, 301, 347, 351, 358, 400, 419; training and arming, 111, 204–5, 212
Cleveland, Harlan, 385
Colby, William: assassination of Diem and Nhu, 425, 428, 435; Buddhist crisis, 270; coup execution, 421, 422; coup plans, 303, 326, 327, 328, 389, 392, 402; coup responsibility, 455; Johnson administration, 449; McNamara-Taylor mission, 369–70; over CIA operations, 74–75; on Taylor's recommendations, 107; 'Telegram 243,' 318, 319; U.S. involvement in war, 55, 387
Cold War, 2, 40, 70, 71, 72, 128, 190, 280, 452, 456
combat troops: absent from "Program of Action," 53–55; buildup, 141, 204; calls for, 55, 56, 59, 63, 66, 76, 88, 93, 98, 129, 131, 157, 162; caution against, 68, 125, 126, 235, 444; Child on, 109; combat participation, 90, 144, 152; coup plans, 359, 362; Craig on, 110; as "flood control units," 104–5, 106–7; 4400th Combat Crew Training Squadron (Jungle Jims), 89–90, 106, 158–59; Geneva Accords and, 94; international reaction to, 122; Johnson administration, 447, 448; KA on, 60, 62–63, 112–13, 114, 118–32, 135, 164, 444; Legislature's interest in, 67; NSAM III on, 135; post-coup consideration of, 428; self-defense orders, 142, 152, 160; training mission, 89–90; U.S. Special Forces, 51, 52, 53–54, 143, 217
Commander-in-Chief, Pacific (CINCPAC), 43, 45, 51, 89, 139, 140, 223, 296
Commodity Import Program, 378, 390
communication systems, 35, 52
communism, 2, 5, 7, 14–15, 21, 40, 55, 67, 72, 115, 116. *See also* Vietcong

Comprehensive Plan for South Vietnam, 8,
    10, 234, 236, 238, 239, 244–45, 248,
    383, 442, 451
"Concept of Intervention in Vietnam" (A.
    Johnson), 88
Conein, Lucien: assassination of Diem and
    Nhu, 426, 427, 430, 435; Buddhist cri-
    sis, 284; coup execution, 410–11, 412,
    414, 416–17, 422, 424–25, 432; coup
    plans, 307–8, 324, 331, 336, 346, 386–
    87, 392, 400, 402; Don and, 400–401,
    410–11; generals and, 386–88, 389–90,
    395–97; on Ngo Dinh Can, 434
Congo, 2, 40
Congress on Vietnam involvement, 126,
    202, 203
Connally, John, 1
Constitution of United States, 160
conventional warfare emphasis, 227, 245
Cottrell, Sterling, 72, 89, 106–7, 110, 155–
    56, 159, 167, 173–74, 179–80, 183–84,
    194, 196
counterinsurgency plan: advisers on, 24,
    111, 112, 119, 135, 142, 157; agrovilles
    in, 72 (*see also* strategic hamlet pro-
    gram); Bureau of Intelligence and
    Research's suggestions for, 153; Delta
    Plan, 154–55; Diem's response to, 29,
    35, 56, 58, 62, 81, 155; effectiveness of,
    201; emphasized in "The Report the
    President Wanted Published," 64;
    flaws, 195; implementation, 27; Joint
    Action Program, 75; Jungle Jims, 89–
    90; Kennedy's emphasis on, 50, 60, 79,
    81, 90, 108, 145, 153, 157, 162, 235;
    Kiraly on, 70; lack of interest in, 49;
    MACV role in, 139; military measures
    balanced with, 157, 159; as official
    strategy, 143; personnel, 74, 80; priori-
    ties of, 51; "Program of Action" and,
    53; Special Group implementation,
    153; tactics, 28; task force, 34, 152;
    Thuan on, 155
Country Team in Saigon, 5, 24–25, 26, 50,
    190, 241, 315, 321, 363–64, 441
coup of 1963. *See also* coup threats and
    plans: assassination of Diem and Nhu,
    425–31, 435–36; counter-coup plans,
    401, 420; Dinh's boasts, 437–38; evacu-
    ation proposal, 413; initiation, 407,
    408; Kennedy administration's respon-
    sibilities, 12, 407, 454–56; Lodge as
    proponent of, 11–12; Ngo family, 431–
    32; palace siege, 414–15; popular ap-
    proval, 423; Provisional Government,
    419, 436, 437–38, 440–41; Seventh Di-
    vision, 409; surrender of Ngos, 416,
    417–18; U.S. involvement in, 9, 416–
    17, 420, 421–23, 424–25, 433, 438–39
coup of 1960 (failed), 13, 18, 20, 25, 26,
    36, 69, 281, 286, 399, 402, 412

coup threats and plans: Buddhist uprising
    and, 269, 279, 302–3; counter-coup
    plans, 401, 420; coup committee, 325;
    Dai Viet, 281–82; Diem's fear of, 22,
    29, 93, 97, 101, 134, 140–41, 281;
    Diem's unpopularity, 213; discussed as
    an option, 93, 193–94; Don's inten-
    tions, 152, 307; generals' plans, 286–88,
    296, 339–40, 375–76, 386, 388, 389–90,
    394–95, 401; Independence Palace
    bombing, 163; Jordan on possibility of,
    108–9; KA on, 62, 65, 104, 109, 133–
    34, 135; likelihood of, 291–92; Nhu's
    plans for, 286–87; NLF's intentions,
    18, 103; Nolting on possibility of, 104,
    132; potential sources of, 164–65, 286,
    306; rumors, 304; Seventh Division,
    399; 'Telegram 243,' 314–21; U.S. in-
    volvement in, 108–9, 133–34, 140–41,
    272, 275, 279–80, 288, 291–92, 296,
    304, 315, 317, 323–24, 331, 336–37,
    342, 347, 354, 364–65, 368–69, 379,
    391, 395, 397, 402–6, 416; White on,
    80, 88
covert actions, 52, 74, 81
Craig, William, 110
Cronkite, Walter, 348
crop destruction: areas defined, 189;
    citizenry's response, 213; defoliants,
    143, 197–98; Diem on, 106, 158; food
    supplies for Vietcong, 143, 144, 145;
    NLF on, 147; poison gas accusations,
    240–41; Trueheart on, 144; U.S. criti-
    cized for, 147, 221, 235
Cuba: Bay of Pigs invasion, 7, 10, 38, 47–
    48, 63, 67–68, 70–71, 81, 330, 339,
    452; emphasis on, 2, 6, 130; meeting
    regarding, 23; missile crisis, 201, 222,
    452
curfews, 154, 419

Dai Viet, 281–82, 285
Dang Duc Khoi, 136, 149, 207, 240
Dang Sy, 247, 249, 250, 251, 252
d'Asta, Salvatore, 311, 313
Davis, James, 142
deceptions and secrecy in war, 144, 146,
    148, 155–56, 159, 168–69, 203, 421–23,
    424–25
Decker, George, 45, 46, 186
'Decree Number 10,' 341
defoliants. *See also* crop destruction: alter-
    natives to chemical warfare, 110–11; in-
    troduction of, 76; Kennedy's
    restrictions on, 157–58; poison gas ac-
    cusations, 240–41; "Ranch Hand" op-
    erations, 135; supplied to South
    Vietnamese Air Force, 83; Trueheart's
    defense of, 144; U.S. criticized for, 221;
    use of, 143, 189, 197, 220, 233, 235
Deitchman, Seymour, 19
Delta Plan, 154–55, 167, 170–71

democracy, 115, 202, 216–17, 222, 371
Deng Xiaoping, 165
Department of Civil Action, 31
Department of Defense, 81, 127
Department of Rural Affairs, 31
Diem. *See* Ngo Dinh Diem
Dillon, Douglas, 328, 331, 340
Dinh. *See* Ton That Dinh
Do Cao Tri, 259, 401
Do Khac Mai, 276
Dodd, Thomas, 67
dog patrols, 76
Don (General). *See* Tran Van Don
Duc Nghiep, 335
Dulles, Allen, 14, 23
Dulles, John Foster, 38, 175
Duong Huu Nhgia, 429
Duong Nghoc Lam, 414, 429
Duong Van Minh ("Big Minh"): assassination of Diem and Nhu, 425, 427, 428, 431, 435, 436, 456; Buddhist crisis, 267, 308; coup execution, 408, 409, 411, 414, 416–17, 422; coup of 1960 (failed), 98–99; coup plans, 165, 192–94, 284, 286, 307, 317, 321, 324–25, 334, 336, 342, 346, 362, 369, 373, 386, 388, 391–92, 394, 397–98, 401, 406; criticism of government, 134–35; on Diem, 98–99, 290, 370; Diem's surveillance of, 140; Independence Palace bombing, 163; lack of authority, 152; leadership skills, 371; McGarr and, 137; military campaign plan, 140; military experience, 258; on Ngo Dinh Can, 434; Ngos' surrender, 417–18; as potential successor to Diem, 100; Provisional Government established, 437; Republican Youth demonstration, 308
duration estimates for conflict, 184, 189, 194, 213, 220, 230, 341, 391
Durbrow, Elbridge: alleged involvement in coup, 20, 26; Diem's distrust of, 35, 38; Diem's response to Counterinsurgency Plan, 35, 56, 58; Ladejinsky and, 33; Lansdale's assessment of, 20, 25–26; on Nhu, 326; on reforms, 29, 30, 37–38; replacement, 34, 326; Thuan's meeting with, 36

economic development: aid programs (*see* aid to South Vietnam); Diem's salary raises for villagers, 149; emphasis on, 31; financial resources of South Vietnam, 74; Ladejinsky on, 34; loans for, 36–37; Mansfield on, 115; "Program of Action," 50; Saigon regime and, 65; "Special Financial Group," 71; Taylor mission on, 135; Zhou Enlai on, 198–99
Eisenhower administration, 2, 7–8, 114, 121, 211, 456
Ellsberg, Daniel, 365

embassy. *See* U.S. embassy
equipment and nondisclosure policy, 159
evacuation plan for Americans, 320, 338, 402, 406
executions, 18, 24, 82, 103. *See also* assassinations and attempts
Expresso, 393

Fatherland Front, 14
Felt, Harry: coordination issues, 223; coup execution, 420; coup plans, 317, 329, 397; Hilsman-Forrestal mission, 231; Independence Palace bombing, 163; on infiltration from Laos, 94; military supplies approval, 106; on nature of war, 165; on patrolling north of 17th parallel, 148; progress reports, 162; 'Telegram 243,' 314, 320–21; U.S. involvement in war, 43, 92, 107, 197, 220, 228–29, 238, 239; Vietnam visits, 182
Findley, Paul, 68
First Lady. *See* Madame Nhu
First Observation Battalion, 52
Fishel, Wesley, 149–51, 202
Fitzgerald, Desmond, 41
flood relief task force, 104–5, 106, 107, 113, 120, 122, 131, 132
Flott, Frederick, 411, 413, 416, 432
Flowerree, Charles, 271
Forces for Liberation of the South, 102
Foreign Assistance Act (1961), 160
Foreign Liaison Assistance Group (FLAG), 131
Foreign Relations Committee, 214–16, 271
Foreign Service, 25
Forrestal, Michael V.: adviser, 445; assassination of Diem and Nhu, 425; Buddhist crisis, 255, 267, 271, 283, 284, 290; coup execution, 421, 439; coup plans, 288, 325, 333; Diem regime issues, 191, 349, 353, 364; Hilsman-Forrestal mission, 230, 232, 234; Johnson administration, 448; Kennedy's reflection on South Vietnam, 442; McNamara-Taylor mission, 369–70, 374, 379; Provisional Government, 440; 'Telegram 243,' 314–15, 316, 319, 321; U.S. involvement in war, 191, 194, 197, 198, 220, 222–23, 241, 362; withdrawal plans, 179, 242
4400th Combat Crew Training Squadron (Jungle Jims), 89–90, 106, 158–59
France, 51, 69, 78, 114, 122, 125, 129, 341, 362–63
Frankel, Max, 275, 422
Fulbright, J. William, 33, 159, 202, 446

Galbraith, John Kenneth: coup rumors, 134, 165; on Diem, 132, 135; flood relief task force, 132; ICC report, 183; inspecting Saigon, 132; on Laos, 40;

Galbraith, John Kenneth (*continued*)
LeMay and, 47; McNamara's pending appointment, 10; Rostow and, 133; U.S. involvement in war, 115–17, 118, 164, 169, 171–72, 175; withdrawal plans, 10, 132, 174, 221, 378, 453
Gaulle, Charles de, 78, 311, 341, 345–46, 351, 362
generals. *See also specific individuals*: alleged suicides of Diem and Nhu, 425, 426–27, 428, 429; assassination of Diem and Nhu, 435–36, 439; assassination plans, 388–89, 391; capabilities and willpower, 371; Conein and, 386, 395–97; coups, coup of 1960 (failed), coup threats and plans) (*see* coup of 1963); on Diem, 388; helicopters request, 333, 338; Lodge and, 440; Nhu and, 369; U.S. support of, 325–28, 332, 346, 356, 391, 397, 402–6, 420, 423
Geneva Accords of 1954: bilateral treaty and, 83; clandestine violations of, 144, 159; Diem on violations, 71; on division of Vietnam, 15, 17, 36, 85; Hanoi and, 85, 122; India on, 181; International Control Commission on, 167–68; Kennedy's desire to comply, 130; Morse on violation of, 160; on relocation of Vietminh forces, 21; Rostow on, 37, 43, 54; Task Force on, 51; Trueheart on, 144; U.S. forces in Vietnam, 2, 5, 51–52, 56, 69, 94, 104, 122, 139, 141, 159, 394
Gia Long Palace, 410
Gilpatric, Roswell: on aid cuts, 361; Harkins's MACV appointment, 139–40, 146; on LeMay, 47; memo to president, 42; on Mendenhall, 357; on Nolting, 325, 332; Presidential Task Force, 40–41; 'Telegram 243,' 316; U.S. involvement in war, 45, 54, 55, 63–64, 90; withdrawal plans, 381–82, 452
Goburdhun, Ramchundur, 311, 313
Good, Kenneth, 224
Goodwin, Richard, 367
Gore, Albert, 159
Great Britain. *See* United Kingdom
Greece, 55, 120, 129
Guevara, Ernesto (Che), 27
Gullion, Edmund, 4

Halberstam, David: Ap Bac battle, 228; assassination of Diem and Nhu, 430; Buddhist crisis, 259, 266, 282, 285, 295, 302; Buddhist monk self-immolation, 268–69; censorship accusations, 145; coup, 400, 416, 421; defoliants and crop destruction, 240; Diem regime issues, 360; McNamara-Taylor mission, 375; on neutralization, 440–41; on Nolting and Trueheart, 208; restric-

tions on, 209; 'Telegram 243,' 314, 320; U.S. involvement in war, 215; Vietnam assignment, 144
Hanoi: China and, 51; communist infiltration, 21; Geneva Accords and, 2–3, 85, 122; Jordan White Paper, 132; KA on, 77, 93, 97, 110, 119, 120, 130, 131, 164; Lao Dong party on, 102; Nam's assassination, 102; National Liberation Front (NLF), 14, 103; Nhu and, 10; objectives, 103, 118; origin of offensive, 85; potential intervention from, 123–24; potential offensive against, 46, 47, 49, 75, 76, 77–78, 79, 93, 126, 130, 131; reaction to military presence, 146–47; reluctance to act, 15; reunification efforts, 117; transition to armed struggle, 16; United Nations and, 83–84; Vietcong and, 93, 141
Hanoi Daily, 102
Harkins, Paul: Buddhist crisis, 257, 271, 275, 283, 304; changes to strategies, 149; coordination issues, 223; coup execution, 407, 415, 418, 420, 440, 441; coup plans, 303, 323, 327, 328, 329–30, 336, 337, 338, 339, 342–43, 346, 371, 387–88, 390, 395–96, 397, 403; coup's effect on war, 438; Diem regime issues, 152, 350, 356, 359; Harkins on napalm, 158; Hilsman-Forrestal mission, 231; Independence Palace bombing, 163; Johnson administration, 447; MACV appointment, 139, 146, 182, 194; McNamara-Taylor mission, 380; Ngo family, 432, 433; press, 145, 208; progress reports, 162; strategic hamlet program, 167, 190; 'Telegram 243,' 317; U.S. involvement in war, 148–49, 188–89, 191, 197, 203, 212, 214, 220, 226–27, 228–29, 233, 234–35, 240; withdrawal plans, 246
Harriman, W. Averell: as ambassador, 116; assassination of Diem and Nhu, 394, 427, 436; Buddhist crisis, 271, 284, 291; Cottrell on press restrictions, 156; coup execution, 420; coup plans, 288, 325, 328, 332, 333, 404; Diem regime issues, 310, 359; Laos issues, 58; McNamara appointment, 6; McNamara-Taylor mission, 379; on political remedies, 445; Task Force on Southeast Asia, 183–84; 'Telegram 243,' 314–15, 316, 319, 320, 321; U.S. involvement in war, 77, 127–28, 158, 171, 172, 173, 190, 196, 197, 198, 204, 210–11, 220, 239, 362–63; withdrawal plans, 179
Harvey, William, 366–67
Heavner, Theodore, 175–76, 216–18, 230
Heinz, Luther, 191
Helble, John, 205, 217, 247, 250, 262, 433–34

helicopters, 106, 113, 124, 139, 143, 204, 209, 236–37, 290, 333, 338, 393

Helms, Richard, 316, 367, 426

Hersh, Seymour, 365

Higgins, Marguerite, 178–79, 350, 431–32

Hilsman, Roger: assassination of Diem and Nhu, 426–27; Buddhist crisis, 257, 271–72, 275–76, 277, 284, 289–90, 291–92; coup execution, 420, 422; coup plans, 134, 288, 297, 303, 304, 325, 326, 327, 329–30, 331, 333, 338, 347, 383; Diem regime issues, 309, 310, 349, 350–51, 352, 357, 360, 361; Harkins's MACV appointment, 140; Hilsman-Forrestal mission, 230, 232, 234, 238; Johnson administration, 444–45, 447, 448, 449; on Kennedy and war, 443; on Kennedy's policies, 4, 10, 48; on Lansdale, 41; on "liberal press," 157; McNamara-Taylor mission, 379; on McNamara's inconsistency, 11; napalm preference, 158; Ngo family, 432; strategic hamlet program, 167, 178, 217–18; 'Telegram 243,' 314–15, 318, 319, 320, 321; U.S. involvement in war, 27, 131, 143, 148, 157, 171, 184, 197, 213, 222–23, 241, 362; withdrawal plans, 10, 243, 323, 453

Hilsman-Forrestal mission, 230, 232, 234, 238

Ho Chi Minh: caution exercised by, 15, 213; China and, 245; goals, 14, 18; on guerrilla warfare, 85; on hamlets, 212; leadership of, 192; on mandarins, 33; negotiations, 15, 263, 311; on neutrality, 58, 239; Nhu and, 312, 341, 374; People's Revolutionary party and, 141; on socialism, 17; support sought, 16; U.S. request for cease-fire, 116; on U.S. involvement in war, 187, 313

Ho Chi Minh Trail, 5, 16

Ho Tan Quyen, 411

Hoa Hao religious sect, 24

Hoang Thuy Nam, 101–2, 104

Hoang Van Hoan, 450

Honey, Patrick, 191–92, 375

House Foreign Affairs Committee, 257

Hué, 94, 247–48

Hughes, Emmet John, 12

Hughes, Richard, 231

Humphrey, Hubert, 202

Huntley-Brinkley Report interview, 355

Huynh Huu Hien, 401

Huynh Van Cao, 224, 228, 397, 399

Huynh Van Tam, 147

India, 75, 93, 116, 122, 181

indoctrination camps, 347

intelligence gathering, 35, 52, 83, 108, 111, 121, 134, 154

Inter-Ministerial Committee for Strategic Hamlets, 155

International Control Commission (ICC): commitment to end war, 345–46; defoliant usage hidden from, 158; on equipment, 181–83; on Geneva Accords violations, 167–68, 394; Geneva conference on Laos, 71; Harriman on, 128; on infiltration from Laos, 237; MAAG personnel increases, 57, 69; Nam assassination, 101–2; Nehru's intervention in Laos, 116; Nhu's negotiations, 311, 313–14, 374, 421; report on responsibility, 172; U.S. involvement in war, 122, 139; Vietcong activity, 103

Intersect Committee for the Protection of Buddhism, 291

Johnson, Alexis, 40, 44, 65, 72, 88, 113, 141, 197, 220, 315

Johnson, Lyndon: Communist expansion, 67; coup plans, 343, 444; Harkins's MACV appointment, 146; Kennedy assassination, 1; Lansdale's meeting with Kennedy, 23; Madame Nhu and, 290, 385; presidency, 11, 443–52; Taylor's meeting with Kennedy, 39; trip to Asia, 43, 60–65, 69, 74; U.S. involvement in war, 11, 65–66, 162, 443; Young on, 68

Johnson, Robert, 77, 79, 109, 112–13, 127

Joint Action Program, 71, 75

Joint Chiefs of Staff: assault recommendations, 234; border control issues, 86; CIA's authority transferred to, 81; on combat troop commitment, 49, 59, 63, 86, 121, 124; communication, 223; Comprehensive Plan for South Vietnam, 244; cover stories for war effort, 146; Harkins's MACV appointment, 140, 146; influence, 445; Johnson and, 11, 453; Kennedy on, 38, 452; on Lansdale's appointment to Task Force, 41; leadership, 41; MACV reporting to, 142; McNamara and, 10; on McNamara-Taylor mission, 390–91; on military reduction plan, 296; personnel increase recommendation, 78; in "Program of Action," 51; rules of engagement for helicopters, 236–37; on SEATO Plan 5, 86–88; Special Group implementation, 153; Taylor and, 75–76, 92

Joint General Staff headquarters, 401, 408, 410

Jones, Raymond, 373

Jordan, William, 83, 89, 108–9, 132, 138, 242, 451

Jordan mission, 102

Jungle Jims. *See* 4400th Combat Crew Training Squadron (Jungle Jims)

junk force of South Vietnam, 52, 53, 64, 184

Kalischer, Peter, 285
Karnow, Stanley, 61, 398
Kattenburg, Paul, 28, 309, 343, 364
Kennedy, John F.: assassination, 1, 443; assassination of Diem and Nhu, 425–28; Bay of Pigs invasion, 10, 38, 47–48, 63, 81, 452; Buddhist uprising, 271 (*see also main entry*); campaign for reelection, 1, 8, 12; caution exercised by, 78; civil action programs, 60; counterinsurgency emphasis, 48, 49, 50, 53–54, 79, 81, 90, 108, 145, 153, 157, 162, 235; coup execution, 403, 404, 405, 407, 439; coup possibilities, 135, 326–28, 339–40; deceptions of administration, 144, 146, 156–57; on defoliant usage, 157–58, 197–98, 233; Diem and, 48, 105, 108, 127; distrust of military, 10, 114; on failure, 322; foreign policy, 38; Galbraith and, 115–17, 118; Harkins's MACV appointment, 140; indecisiveness, 79; inner circle, 132; insurgency warfare interest, 19–20, 27–28; Khrushchev and summit talks, 70; Lansdale and, 42, 48; LeMay and, 47; Madame Nhu, 290; Mansfield and, 114–15, 118; at National Security Council meeting, 44; on neutralization, 267; on new Saigon regime, 423; on non-military factors, 185–86; reflection on South Vietnam, 442; response to Communist's May push, 57–58; response to *Time* article, 58; on Rostow, 77; Rusk on, 122; on South Vietnam's responsibility to win war, 28, 70, 115, 125–26, 136, 348, 376, 377–78, 452; Taylor and, 90, 114; Taylor mission, 107, 108, 114; 'Telegram 243,' 314–21; Thuan's meeting with, 74; U.S. involvement in war, 1–2, 50, 71, 74, 89–90, 125, 126–27, 131, 135–36, 143, 144, 146, 159, 232–33, 235; on weaponry, 129; on withdrawal, 219, 238, 257–58, 377–78, 440, 441, 442, 452–53
Kennedy, Robert F.: on Castro, 367; on contact with generals, 396; coup planning, 328–29, 389; Cuba crisis, 365; on culpability, 396; on false telegram, 327; Gore on optimism of, 159; influence, 445; on JFK's presidency, 452; on Laos intervention, 46, 47; Nhu analogy, 306, 424; Presidential Task Force, 41; president's reliance upon, 38; on Rusk's replacement, 11; Special Group implementation, 153; 'Telegram 243,' 319–20; U.S. involvement in war, 26; withdrawal plans, 384, 452
Kennedy administration. *See specific individuals*
Kent, J. R., 151
Khrushchev, Nikita, 7, 14, 16, 19, 40, 58, 65, 70, 72, 129, 450

kidnappings, 18, 24, 80, 103, 200
King, Benjamin, 89
Kiraly, Bela K., 70
Kleiman, Bob, 440
Kohler, Foy, 241
Komer, Robert, 38, 56–57, 76–77, 109–10
Korean War, 45, 53, 67, 75, 114, 115, 129, 147, 172, 180
Krock, Arthur, 40, 90–91, 229
Krulak, Victor "Brute," 167, 190, 283, 303, 316, 326, 353–54, 356–57, 359

Ladejinsky, Wolf, 32–34
Lalouette, Roger, 311–14, 341–42, 345–46, 352, 369
Lam Van Phat, 409
land mines, 142, 233
Langguth, A. J., 365–66
Lansdale, Edward: assassination of Diem and Nhu, 428; assignments, 23, 41–43, 89, 106, 119, 138; coup plans, 325, 364–67, 368; credentials and experience, 18–19, 359, 387; Diem and, 20, 22, 38, 56, 95–97, 106, 107, 138, 141, 346; Durbrow and, 25–26; Hillandale character, 20; Kennedy's meeting with, 455; Nhu and, 96, 101; report on South Vietnam, 13, 20–22; return to Vietnam, 452; Rostow's speech, 72; Taylor and, 94–95, 110, 111, 119; Thuan on, 108; U.S. involvement in war, 5, 31–32, 48, 53, 54, 110–11, 184–85; Vietcong, 22, 81, 141
Lao Dong party, 14, 15, 16, 18, 81–82, 83, 85, 102, 103, 141, 191–92, 449–50
Laos: airfields, 78; border issues, 82, 86, 117, 136, 147, 149, 159; cease-fire, 38, 116; China's border with, 40; CIA-sponsored paramilitary activity, 71; combined military force proposal, 77–78; communist threat in, 5; Counterinsurgency Plan, 28; Diem on, 210–11; emphasis on, 2, 7, 39, 43–46, 58, 80; Geneva conference on, 54, 57, 65, 67, 71, 116, 126, 144; India's fears regarding, 75; infiltration through, 82, 110, 111, 112, 149; KA on, 43–45, 46, 50, 77, 86, 128; neutralization, 117, 185–87, 196; Nhu on, 101; offensives in, 89; peasantry, 8; sanctuary for Vietcong, 97, 149; SEATO, 40; South Vietnam's ties with, 210; volatility, 190
Lausche, Frank, 352
Le Duan, 14–15, 16, 17, 102, 187, 213, 239–40, 449, 450
Le Duc Tho, 17, 450
Le Khac Quyen, 251
Le Quang Tung: aid cuts, 390; assassinated, 414, 429; assassination plans of, 393; Buddhist crisis, 297, 301, 302; coup execution, 408, 410, 411, 414; coup plans, 306, 310, 325, 331, 334,

388; Operation Bravo, 398, 399; Phillips on, 359

Le Van Kim: assassination of Diem and Nhu, 431; coup execution, 417, 419, 422; coup plans, 284, 308, 325, 334, 346–47, 394, 397–98, 401; on Diem, 134; on Nhu, 309, 310; Provisional Government established, 437

Le Van Nghiem, 134–35, 394

Le Van Ty, 208–9

Lederer, William, 19–20

Leger (priest), 430

LeMay, Curtis, 46–47, 89, 447

Lemnitzer, Lyman L.: Diem's meeting with, 58–59; at Kennedy's meeting with Lansdale, 23; president's disregard for advice, 39; U.S. involvement in war, 49, 58, 60, 92, 97–98, 111, 120, 130, 140, 142, 197; Vietnam visits, 182

L'Humanite, 241

Li Tianyou, 449

"A Limited Partnership," Taylor mission, 118–20

Lisagor, Peter, 350

Little Minh (Tran Van Minh), 307, 308

Liu Chang-sheng, 147

Liu Shaoqi, 245

Lodge, Henry Cabot, Jr.: ambassador assignment, 304–5, 313, 368, 386–87; assassination of Diem and Nhu, 426, 427, 429, 430, 431; Buddhist crisis, 280–81, 283, 284, 289, 291, 295, 297, 300, 302, 310; coup advocate, 11–12, 423–24; coup committee, 325; coup execution, 407, 412–14, 420, 424, 425, 440, 441–42; coup plans, 296, 322, 327, 328, 329, 330, 332, 334, 335, 336–37, 338, 339, 340, 342, 347, 364, 369, 370, 389, 390, 392–94, 395–96, 400–402, 404–6, 441; coup's effect on war, 438–39; Diem regime issues, 309, 349, 350, 351, 354–55, 356, 371–72, 400, 423; Johnson administration, 444, 445–46, 447–48, 451–52; on Madame Nhu, 361; McNamara-Taylor mission, 382; on Ngo Dinh Can, 434; Nhu and, 344–45, 349–50, 354; Provisional Government established, 437; 'Telegram 243,' 314–19; U.S. involvement in war, 362

Luce, Henry, 82

Luo Ruiqing, 240

Ma Tuyen, 418, 428

MAAG. *See* Military Assistance and Advisory Group (MAAG)

MacArthur, Douglas, 4, 44, 121, 452

MACV. *See* Military Assistance Command, Vietnam (MACV)

Madame Chiang Kai-shek, 372

Madame Nhu: assassination plots, 284, 286; background, 293–94; Buddhist uprising, 266, 267, 271, 278, 291, 292–93,

300, 385; as center of problems for Diem, 296; children and family after coup, 431–33; CIA coup article, 345, 350; coup execution, 407, 422–23, 431–32, 433; coup plans, 302; criticism of, 24, 150, 210, 282, 357; Diem and, 150, 294–95, 307; extended trip, 341, 344, 349, 351–52, 361, 384–85; husband (*see* Ngo Dinh Nhu); Independence Palace bombing, 163; influence, 9, 109; KA on, 279, 284, 290; Lodge appointment, 304, 305; morality emphasis, 99, 294; on opposition and dissension, 164; parents, Tran Van Chuong) (*see* Madame Tran Van Chuong); power struggles, 195–96, 303; press coverage of, 136, 145, 195–96, 207, 208, 305–6, 335; Robinson's interview, 136; "Social Purification Law," 150–51; statements by, 309, 315, 353, 371, 372, 400; on treatment of women, 245; U.S. visit, 384–86

Madame Tran Van Chuong, 305, 325, 364

Mai Huu Xuan, 429, 430, 435

Malaya compared to Vietnam, 97–98, 133

Maneli, Mieczyslaw, 311–14, 341–42, 345–46, 351, 369

Manila, communist infiltration, 21

manioc killer, 83

Manning, Robert, 290

Mansfield, Mike: on coup, 421; Diem and, 214–16, 243; Foreign Relations Committee, 213–14; Madame Nhu compared to, 294; on presidential policy in Southeast Asia, 202; Tran Van Chuong and, 192; U.S. involvement in war, 114–15, 118; withdrawal recommendations, 218–19, 221, 222, 230, 238, 243

Mao Zedong (Mao Tse-tung), 16, 27, 31, 80, 180, 192, 204, 256–57, 263, 449

Marcy, Carl, 203

martial law, 297, 302, 363, 419

Martin, Edwin, 158

Martin, Robert, 117

Mat Nguyen, 252

McCarthyism, 7, 128, 238

McCone, John: advising role, 445; assassination of Diem and Nhu, 426, 427; Buddhist crisis, 280; coup plans, 368, 388–89, 392, 395–96, 403; Cuba issues, 366, 367; Diem regime issues, 361, 385–86; Hilsman-Forrestal mission, 234; Johnson administration, 444; 'Telegram 243,' 316, 318, 319; U.S. involvement in war, 362–63

McGarr, Lionel: border issues, 43; "Campaign Plan" approved, 147; civil action programs, 91–92; Civil Guard, 98; command structure, 35; Diem on, 137; Harkins's appointment, 140; Minh and, 137; reaction to first casualty, 142; U.S. involvement in war, 20, 60, 62, 74, 93, 100, 104–5, 107, 111–12, 154, 162, 165

McNamara, Robert: advising role, 11, 14, 445; call for civic action, 162; Castro assassination, 366–68; coup execution, 441; coup plans, 303, 325, 326, 327, 330, 337, 340, 343, 373, 391–92, 396, 402, 403; defoliant usage, 158; Diem regime issues, 350, 359, 360; Geneva negotiations, 126; Greece intervention, 129; Harkins's MACV appointment, 139–40, 146; Hilsman-Forrestal mission, 234; Johnson administration, 444, 447, 448–49, 450–51; Lansdale and, 23, 42, 365–66, 368; Laos intervention, 44, 45–46; on MACV, 142; quantification emphasis, 6–7; secretary of state appointment, 452; speaking to press, 145; on Taylor's proposal, 113; 'Telegram 243,' 316, 318, 321; U.S. involvement in war, 13, 26, 37, 47, 49, 63, 88, 90, 120, 123–24, 125, 126, 130, 136, 162, 165, 170, 184–85, 189, 194, 197, 203, 204, 220, 238, 454; withdrawal plans, 10, 11, 246, 384, 440, 453
McNamara-Taylor mission, 369–76, 378–79, 380–81, 382, 383, 390–91
Mecklin, John, 162, 200, 207–8, 209, 211, 247, 268–69, 291, 356, 357, 359–60, 401, 422
Mekong Delta, 57–58, 75–76, 86–88, 104, 111–12, 147
"Memorandum of Understanding," 138
Mendenhall, Joseph, 193–94, 314–15, 325, 353–54, 356–58
Michigan State University, 150
Military Assistance and Advisory Group (MAAG): training missions, 91; "Campaign Plan" study, 147; Country Team in Saigon, 24; on defoliant usage, 158; Diem on, 64, 149; Geneva Accords on, 37; Harkins's command, 140; MACV and, 139, 143, 233; McGarr's call for more personnel, 60; objectives, 20, 110, 120, 162; personnel increases, 43, 45, 51–52, 57, 74, 108, 142, 183; on political solution, 59–60; propaganda against, 21; Self-Defense Corps, 52; self-defense of troops, 142
Military Assistance Command, Vietnam (MACV), 139, 143, 157, 182, 209, 231, 233, 291, 354, 364; reporting structure, 142
Military Assistance Program, 59, 212, 246
Military Revolutionary Council, 419
Minh. *See* Duong Van Minh ("Big Minh")
Ministers Vietnam Committee, 295
Mohr, Charley, 253–54
Monroe, Bill, 207
Montagnards, 188, 189, 190, 201, 217, 218, 223, 233, 237
Morse, Wayne, 159, 160, 202
"Movement of National Revolution," 282
Moyers, Bill, 445

Murder in the Cathedral (Eliot), 12
Murrow, Edward R., 197, 360, 366
Mutual Defense Assistance agreement, 160

napalm, 83, 158, 220, 222, 223, 233
National Assembly, 96, 265, 274, 335
National Campaign, 231, 234, 244, 246
National Conference on Foreign Affairs, 141
National Economic Council, 31, 149
National Emergency Council, 121
National Intelligence Estimate, 84
National Internal Security Council, 137
National Liberation Front (NLF): on 1963 coup, 419–20; on Diem, 18, 103, 165–66; goals of party, 18; Hanoi's promotion of, 14; intensification of, 81–82; Lao Dong's approval of, 18; legitimacy, 362; North Vietnam and, 192; origins, 18; on pagoda raids and U.S. aid policy, 363; People's Liberation Armed Forces (PLAF), 28; popular following of, 103; propaganda, 183, 187–88, 263; rally, 147; on Strategic Hamlet Program, 187–88; Vietcong support, 5
National People's Democratic Revolution, 17
National Plan, proposed by McGarr, 111
National Reunification Commission, 175
National Revolutionary Movement, 266
National Security Action Memorandum (NSAM), 81, 135–36, 442, 446
National Security Affairs, 153
National Security Council (NSC), 27, 43–44, 57, 129, 155, 353, 381, 382–83, 397, 402, 426, 440
naval power, 52, 53, 57, 64, 76, 148, 184
Nehru, Jawaharlal, 58, 115, 116, 122
New Frontier (Kennedy policies), 6
New York Times, 91, 139, 144, 208, 348, *See also* reporters
Newsweek, 163, 177–78, 195, 206, 262, 433, 438, 443, 448, 450, *See also reporters*
Ngo Dinh Can, 24, 205, 217, 253, 282, 293, 388, 432, 433–34
Ngo Dinh Diem. *See also* Ngo Dinh Nhu: assassination, 10, 12, 281, 425–31, 435–36, 439; Bathu bombing incident, 148; Buddhist uprising (*see main entry*); common view of, 16, 24, 48, 50, 83, 104, 150, 157, 205–6, 215, 279; condition of, 214; coup, coup of 1960 (failed), coup threats and plans (*see* coup of 1963); criticisms of, 9, 13, 98–99, 103, 145, 150, 283; dealing with opposition, 14, 15; distrust of U.S., 29, 61, 69; on economic development, 65, 66; First Lady (*see* Madame Nhu); Geneva Accords and, 71, 165–66; Independence Palace bombing, 163–64; Kennedy's partnership, 105, 127; Ladejinsky on, 32–34;

on Laos, 58–59, 210–11; martyr self-image, 286; Minh on, 134; Nhu and, 108, 134–35, 286–87, 296, 308–9, 314–15, 326, 334–35, 354–55; pacification and minimizing casualties, 227–28; philosophy, 29, 33, 48, 151, 253, 281, 288; press and, 145, 164, 171, 195–96, 207, 285; resistance to delegation, 29, 34, 61, 93, 99, 108–9, 113, 137, 140–41, 151; resistance to reforms, 30, 36, 40, 43, 56, 105, 108, 109–10, 151–52, 191, 243, 282–83, 318, 372–73; response to Counterinsurgency Plan, 35, 56, 58, 64, 155, 166; Thuan's influence on, 150; Tri Quang on, 249; U.S. advisers and, 26, 30–31, 35, 50–51, 56, 61–63, 64–65, 69, 74, 95–97, 98, 106, 107, 151–52, 214–16, 232, 280–81, 289, 403; U.S. military involvement, 48, 58–59, 62–63, 64, 66, 68–69, 74, 80, 83, 94, 96–97, 98, 105, 106–7, 108, 113, 114, 116–19, 121, 123, 130, 132, 135, 136, 137, 140, 141, 146, 152, 154, 158, 197, 243; U.S. support for, 2–3, 20, 22, 48, 65–66, 137–38, 173, 294, 298–99, 302–3, 323, 349, 400; Vietcong's attempts to undermine, 24, 36, 103
Ngo Dinh Luyen, 193
Ngo Dinh Nhu. *See also* Ngo Dinh Diem: army command and, 308; assassination, 284, 286, 388, 425–31, 435–36, 439; Buddhist pagoda raids, 307, 309, 314, 371, 414; Buddhist uprising, 247, 255, 256, 263, 265–66, 271, 291, 299, 300; call for removal, 282, 318, 364; CIA on, 290; Communist uprising (1946), 293; counter-coup plans, 401, 420; counterinsurgency effort, 243; coup, coup of 1960 (failed), coup threats and plans) (*see* coup of 1963); deluded thinking, 393–94; Diem and, 96, 108, 134–35, 286–87, 308–9, 314–15, 326, 334–35, 354–55; as Diem's biggest problem, 296, 310, 358; Don on, 303; drug use, 305, 363, 393; executive board considerations, 108; father-in-law, 242–43; generals and, 369; Hanoi talks, 310; Ho Chi Minh and, 312, 341, 374; influence, 9, 108, 150, 307–8; KA on, 96–97, 279, 284, 305–6, 344–45, 349–50, 354, 370–71, 420; on Laos neutralization, 101; Maneli and, 313–14; National Emergency Council proposal, 121; on need for revolution, 205; North Vietnam and, 10, 310–11, 312, 344, 351, 362, 369, 384, 406, 421; Operation Bravo, 398, 399–400, 410; on opposition and dissension, 164; popular dissatisfaction with, 24, 150, 210, 358, 376; as possible successor to Diem, 245, 295, 304; power struggles, 195–96, 303; press and, 207, 208, 209–10; R.

Kennedy analogy, 306, 424; refusal to leave Vietnam, 354; strategic hamlet program, 155, 167, 174, 176–77, 212, 214; 'Telegram 243,' 314–15; on Tho, 135; U.S. involvement in war, 69, 154, 211, 257; wife (*see* Madame Nhu)
Ngo Dinh Thuc, 193, 247, 253, 259, 282–83, 335, 344, 361, 432–33
Ngo Trong Hieu, 388
Nguyen Cao Ky, 412
Nguyen Chi Thanh, 17, 187
Nguyen Dinh Thuan: Buddhist uprising, 259, 263–64, 265, 272, 273, 274–75, 288, 300; counterinsurgency plan, 35, 71, 155; coup plans, 294, 317, 335, 356; cultivating U.S. support, 151; Diem and, 80, 108, 281, 283, 294, 308–9, 310; dislike of, 151; on duration of struggle, 220; on financial resources, 74; influence, 150; on intelligence gathering, 108; KA and, 74, 108, 137, 281, 371, 375; on Laos, 196, 210; on Madame Nhu's press campaign, 136; meeting with Rusk and Durbrow, 36; National Emergency Council proposal, 121; on Nhu, 310, 363; personnel, 80, 106; as possible successor to Diem, 100, 192–93; prime minister appointment, 350; surveillance of Minh, 140
Nguyen Huu Co, 398, 399, 409
Nguyen Huu Tho, 420
Nguyen Khanh: assassination of Diem and Nhu, 429, 436; coup execution, 414; coup plans, 320, 321, 324, 325, 334, 336, 401; on Nhu, 310, 314, 346; on reorganizing rangers, 188; on Tung, 301
Nguyen Khuong, 394, 395, 414
Nguyen Ngoc Huy, 437
Nguyen Ngoc Le, 287, 325, 417
Nguyen Ngoc Tho, 56
Nguyen Van Cao, 409
Nguyen Van Chang, 101
Nguyen Van Honshow, 101
Nguyen Van Nhung, 414, 416, 429, 435
Nguyen Van Quan, 429
Nguyen Van Thieu, 394, 414, 415, 435
Nguyen Van Vinh, 174–75
Nhu. *See* Ngo Dinh Nhu
Niebuhr, Reinhold, 283
Nitze, Paul, 23
Nixon, Richard M., 11, 452
Nolting, Frederick: ambassador post, 37, 116, 234; assassination attempt, 75; assassination of Diem and Nhu, 428; on bilateral treaty, 69; Buddhist crisis, 251, 254–55, 257, 263, 271, 273, 278, 280–81, 283, 291, 292, 294, 302; coup execution, 423–24; coup plans, 104, 132, 288, 296, 326–28, 329, 330, 337, 338, 341; Diem regime issues, 62, 121, 130, 136, 137–38, 140, 205, 206–8, 302, 310, 311, 332, 360; exclusion of, 325, 326;

Nolting, Frederick (*continued*)
    Independence Palace bombing, 163–64;
    Johnson's trip to Asia, 61; Lansdale on,
    56; on Laos neutralization, 196; on
    MACV, 142; Nam's assassination, 102;
    Nhu and, 108, 205; on objectives, 162;
    press relations, 145, 155–56, 161, 171,
    191, 196, 206–8, 241, 291; strategic
    hamlet program, 176; successors to
    Diem, 192; Taylor report, 130; 'Tele-
    gram 243,' 317; Thuan and, 74, 137;
    U.S. involvement in war, 51, 69, 94,
    104, 112, 127, 142, 144, 154, 159, 162,
    167, 168, 174, 181, 204, 210, 212–13,
    214–15, 220, 222, 227, 231–32, 237,
    240; withdrawal plans, 244
Norodom Sihanouk, 35, 174, 211, 254–55,
    271
North Atlantic Treaty Organization
    (NATO), 88
NSAM. *See* National Security Action
    Memorandum (NSAM)
nuclear weapons, 44, 49, 201

O'Donnell, Kenneth P., 219, 238
Office of Rural Development, 154
oil pipeline construction, 106
Operation Beef-Up, 138, 143
Operation Bravo, 398, 399–400, 410
Operation Farmgate, 89, 144, 152, 184,
    220, 222, 223, 231, 236, 239
Operation Mongoose, 365, 366, 368
Operation Plan 34A (OPLAN 34A), 26–
    27, 446
Operation Ranch Hand, 135
Operation Sunrise, 167, 171
Operation Switchback, 166, 449
Operations Mission. *See* U.S. Operations
    Mission (USOM)
Orlandi, Giovanni, 311, 313

palace, 163–64, 335–36, 410, 414–15, 416,
    418
"paper tiger" image of U.S., 67
paramilitary activities, 152
Parsons, Graham, 23–24, 26
Partial Test Ban Treaty, 295
Passavant, Sophie de, 342
Pathet Lao, 5, 44, 45, 46, 180
peasantry, 8, 14, 17, 35, 36, 177, 237, *See
    also* civilians; Montagnards
Pell, Claiborne, 213–15
Pentagon, 10, 38
Pentagon Papers: on 1963 coup, 423; on al-
    leged suicides of Diem and Nhu, 426;
    on breach of Geneva agreement, 52; on
    "Concept of Intervention in Vietnam,"
    88; on crisis meetings, 49; on Diem's
    reelection, 37; on Ho Tan Quyen as-
    sassination, 411; on Lansdale's appoint-
    ment, 41, 42; on minimal response, 63;

    on OPLAN 34A, 446; origins, 365; on
    Provisional Government, 440; on U.S.
    encouragement of coup, 69, 343; on
    withdrawal plans, 382, 451
People's Army of Vietnam (PAVN), 84–85,
    141, 230
People's Liberation Armed Forces (PLAF),
    28
People's Liberation Army of China, 240,
    449
People's Revolutionary Party, 141, 192
Pham Hung, 17
Pham Ngoc Thao, 286, 428
Pham Van Dong (North Vietnamese), 80,
    134–35, 181, 311, 312, 313, 351, 369
Pham Van Dong (South Vietnamese), 394
Pham Xuan Chieu, 325
Phan Van Tao, 207, 240
Philippines, 98, 120, 133
Phillips, Rufus, 155, 259, 267, 308–9, 346,
    347, 356, 358–59, 360, 362, 401, 422,
    436
Phoumi Nosavan, 211
Phuoc Thanh attack, 102
Pilcher, J. L., 202
Plei Mrong battle, 225
police, 289, 401, 407, 408
Policy Planning Council, 83
Politburo, 14, 16, 17, 18, 85, 239
Popular Force, 205
Powers, Thomas, 447
precedents in U.S. history, 78, 128–29
Presidential Task Force, 40–41, 42–43, 44–
    45, 50–53, 50–54, 51, 52, 54, 55, 63, 77
press coverage of Vietnam conflict. *See also*
    radio coverage: Ap Bac battle, 226, 227,
    228, 232; Buddhist uprising, 259, 262,
    266, 268–69, 275, 276, 298, 301–2, 335,
    386; casualties, 161, 229; CIA coup ar-
    ticle, 345, 350; controversies, 206–10;
    correspondents, 144–45, 290–91; coup
    (1963), 419; criticizing Kennedy ad-
    ministration, 145, 235–36, 241; defoli-
    ants and poison gas accusations, 197,
    241; Diem and, 30, 164, 195–96; em-
    bassy relations, 155, 161–62, 304; ex-
    pulsion of reporters, 171; on funding,
    191; Hilsman on "liberal press," 157;
    Ho Chi Minh, 263; information "black-
    outs" complaints, 155–57; Madame
    Nhu, 136, 292–93, 305–6, 335, 385;
    Ngo family, 206, 242; police alterca-
    tion, 284–85, 386; press restrictions,
    155–56; rules of engagement for heli-
    copters, 236–37; Strategic Hamlet Pro-
    gram, 177–78; Tho's succession of
    Diem, 417; on war efforts, 186, 187,
    290; withdrawal plans, 178–79, 256–57,
    296
prisons, 147
propaganda, 21, 24, 103, 118, 183, 187–88,
    282, 305

Provisional Government, 419, 436, 437–38, 440–41
psywar, 35, 53, 76, 81, 108, 233–34, 300
Pyle, Ernie, 145

Quang Duc, 268–69, 283, 284, 307–8
Quang Huong, 386

radar surveillance system, 52
radio coverage, 21, 102, 175, 192, 250, 277, 301, 322–23, 363, 398, 412, 419. *See also* press coverage of Vietnam conflict
Rangers, 189
Rayburn, Sam, 61
Red Cross, 240, 265
refugees, 32–33
"regroupees" (revolution leaders), 16–17
religion, 9, 150, 151, 252–53, 260, 270. *See also* Buddhist uprising
"The Report the President Wanted Published," 64
Republican Youth Organization, 282, 308, 322, 335, 370, 415–16
Reston, James, 40, 70, 144, 439, 440
rice crops. *See* crop destruction
Richardson, John, 310, 323, 336, 345, 346, 364, 371, 388, 390, 401, 420, 422
Riley, Herbert, 318
Robinson, James, 136, 145, 206–7, 208, 210
Roosevelt, Franklin D., 61
Rose, Jerry, 227
Rosson, William, 186
Rostow, Walt: on assassinations, 75; on Atlantic alliances, 40; on Beijing, 120; on border control, 86; on Chinese intervention, 129; on Communist insurgency, 72; coup plans, 62, 133–34, 135, 422; on Diem, 38, 62, 119, 140–41; on Geneva Accords, 37, 43, 54; on Hanoi's aggression, 180; KA, 13, 14, 33, 40, 77, 95, 127, 132, 133, 138; on National Security Council meeting, 44; on nuclear threats, 7–8; on role of South Vietnamese, 91; on U.N. observers, 101; U.S. involvement in war, 26, 31, 32, 37, 54–55, 72–73, 77, 78–79, 89, 94, 97, 110, 120, 126, 133, 136, 138, 172, 198; withdrawal plans, 11, 453
Rowan, Carl, 155–56
Rusk, Dean: assassination of Diem and Nhu, 426, 431; Bay of Pigs invasion, 38; Bowles on political solution, 127; Buddhist crisis, 263, 272–73, 280; coup execution, 421, 434, 440–41; coup plans, 287, 296, 327, 337, 338, 339, 340–41, 343, 344, 347, 364, 402, 403–4; Diem regime issues, 113, 130, 138, 353, 360–61; on Geneva negotiations, 126; on Greece intervention, 129; on Hanoi, 93, 130, 164; Hilsman on, 445; Johnson administration, 444, 447; KA, 6–7, 14, 23–24, 26, 51–52, 73, 136, 161, 368,

380, 382; on Laos, 44, 47; MAAG forces, 57, 69; MACV forces, 139–40, 142; negotiations opposed by, 128; on radio broadcast, 322–23; replacement of, 10–11, 452; Task Force, 27, 183; 'Telegram 243,' 315, 316, 317, 318, 321; Thuan's meeting with, 36; U.S. involvement in war, 7–8, 39, 49, 57, 73, 74, 78, 89, 107, 120, 122–23, 124, 126, 129, 164, 168, 171, 173, 198, 454; withdrawal plans, 179, 243, 453
Russell, Richard, 126

sabotage concerns, 18, 45
Saigon-Cholon Waterworks, 378, 390
Saigon Electric Power Project, 378, 390
Salinger, Pierre, 161, 382
sanctuaries, 28
Sarit Thanarat, 57
Saturday Evening Post, 64
Saund, D. S., 172
Scali, John, 354
Schlesinger, Arthur M., Jr., 19, 39, 49, 104, 125, 127, 207, 425, 434
Self-Defense Corps: Delta Plan, 154; Diem on, 64, 69, 98; funding requirements, 53; Heavner on, 217; Kennedy on, 108; leadership of, 99; Nhu on, 393; performance of, 189, 194–95, 233; request for American instructors, 106; role in war, 190–91; Strategic Hamlet Program and, 175–76; training and equipping, 83, 111, 124, 135
Senate Foreign Relations Committee, 67, 144, 159–61, 203, 352
Serong, F. P., 447–48
Seventh Division, 399, 409
Seventh Fleet, 94
Shank, Edwin, 448
Sheehan, Neil, 144, 209, 215, 226, 228, 229, 285, 360, 375, 430
Shoup, David, 45, 46
Sidey, Hugh, 350
Sihanouk. *See* Norodom Sihanouk
Smith, Benjamin, 213–14
Smith, David, 388–89, 416, 430
Smith, Hedrick, 422
Sochurek, Howard, 165
"Social Purification Law," 150–51
Sorensen, Theodore C., 37, 38, 39–40, 40, 43, 51, 54, 79, 367, 452
South Vietnam: according to Geneva Accords, 36, 85; commitment of U.S. to Southeast Asia, 64, 65–66, 76–77, 101, 124, 127, 178, 343, 355; defenses, 149; president (*see* Ngo Dinh Diem); responsibility to win war, 28, 70, 115, 125–26, 136, 348, 376, 377–78, 452; strategic significance, 34, 46; terrain, 21, 28, 116; U.S. political relationship with, 93, 110, 120, 127, 138, 142, 146

South Vietnamese Officer Corps, 189–90

Southeast Asia Treaty Organization (SEATO): anti-Communist policy, 6; bilateral treaty and, 83; border control issues, 86; counterguerrilla operations, 31; Diem on, 69; Felt on ground forces from, 94; on Hanoi offensive, 77; Johnson on, 67; Joint Chiefs on obligation of, 63; Laos handled through, 40; McNamara on, 130; 'Plan 5,' 86–88; 'Plan 7,' 162; in "Program of Action," 50, 51; Treaty of 1954, 161; U.S. involvement in war, 127

Souvanna Phouma (Laos Prime Minister), 231

Soviet Union, 16, 57–58, 75, 121, 128, 180, 201, 241, 362, 419, 449–50, 450

Special Assistant of Counterinsurgency and Special Activities (SACSA), 296

Special Financial Group, 71, 75

Special Forces of South Vietnam: aid cuts, 359, 361, 375, 390; arrests, 297, 301; coup, 346, 388, 399, 401, 410, 414; disguised as ARVN, 306, 307, 322; palace assignment, 335–36; press and, 206; training and equipping, 108, 189

Special National Intelligence Estimate, 288

Special Warfare School, Fort Bragg, 72

Spera, Al, 324, 422

Staley, Eugene, 71

Staley Group, 71, 74, 78, 81

State Department, 100, 106, 121, 138, 159–61, 444

Steeves, John, 46, 47

Stilwell, Richard, 387, 407, 422

strategic hamlet program: anniversary, 244; casualties, 349; defense of, 176, 190–91, 204–5; defoliant usage and, 158; Diem on, 283; emphasis on, 155, 200; food supplies for Vietcong, 256; Ho Chi Minh on, 263; implementation, 143, 166–67; issues with, 176–78, 212, 217–18, 295, 373, 380, 448; KA on, 144, 154–55, 190, 387, 401; Nhu's leadership of, 155, 167, 174, 214, 345, 370; NLF on, 187–88; objectives, 217, 234; press coverage, 208; Self-Defense Corps and, 175–76; skepticism, 230; success of, 194, 195, 199, 371

students, 301, 307, 308, 347, 351, 358, 393, 400, 419

Studies and Observation Group, 446

Sullivan, William, 39, 369–70, 379

Sully, François, 145, 171, 195–96, 206, 208, 210

Sun Tzu cited by Lansdale, 31

Sylvester, Arthur, 441

Symington, Stuart, 128

Syngman Rhee, 325

Szulc, Tad, 330

T-28 (Jungle Jim), 106

Taber, Robert, 32

Takashi Oka, 99

Task Force on Southeast Asia, 183–84

Taylor, Maxwell D.: ambassador position, 446; assassination of Diem and Nhu, 425, 428; Bay of Pigs analysis, 38–39; Buddhist crisis, 267, 276, 352; Colby on, 107; coup execution, 420, 422, 441; coup plans, 104, 303, 327, 329–30, 336, 339, 402, 403; on defoliant usage, 158; Diem regime issues, 96, 98, 105, 106, 110, 119, 360; Felt on role of military, 94; on Hanoi, 110; Harkins's MACV appointment, 139–40, 146; Hilsman-Forrestal mission, 234; Johnson administration, 447; Joint Chiefs' SEATO Plan 5, 88; Jordan on coup possibility, 109; Kennedy and, 75–76, 90, 107, 119, 380; on Kennedy's commitment to South Vietnam, 127; Lansdale and, 94–95, 110, 111, 119; McNamara-Taylor mission, 369–76, 378–79, 380–81, 382, 383, 390–91; mission assignment, 89, 93 (*see also* Taylor mission); press and, 95–96; recommendations to Saigon regime, 108; Special Group implementation, 153; strategic hamlet program, 195, 212; 'Telegram 243,' 316, 318–19, 320–21; U.S. involvement in war, 72, 77, 78–79, 92, 97, 98, 100, 104, 105, 107, 110, 111, 112–13, 114, 120, 124, 131, 197, 204; Vietnam visits, 104, 182; withdrawal plans, 391, 440

Taylor mission, 105, 108, 118–21, 124, 132, 135, 139

'Telegram 243,' 314–21, 322, 329, 356, 368, 391–92

terrain of South Vietnam, 21, 28, 116

terrorist campaigns, 14, 18, 36, 103, 149, 154, 195, 450

Thailand, 46, 76, 86

Thien Hoa, 265

Thien Khiet, 248, 265, 291, 295

Thien Minh, 264–65, 274

Third National Congress of Lao Dong party, 17

Third Party Congress, 102

Tho. *See* Tran Van Tho

Thompson, Robert G. K., 81, 154, 166–67, 173–74, 176, 184, 238, 243, 363, 380, 382, 424, 438

Thomson, James, Jr., 39

A Threat to Peace: North Vietnam's Efforts to Conquer South Vietnam (Jordan), 138

Thuan. *See* Nguyen Dinh Thuan

Time magazine, 58, 82, 422

Timmes, Charles, 441

Tinh Khiet, 264, 273–75

Ton That Dinh: assassination of Diem and Nhu, 429; coup execution, 409, 410, 412, 416, 421, 425; coup plans, 303, 306, 327, 331, 356, 388–89, 397–99; justifying coup, 406; on Nhu, 310; pa-

goda raids, 309; Phillips on, 359; power struggle, 301; Provisional Government established, 437–38
Tonkin Gulf incident, 447, 449, 454
torture, 18, 101, 147, 351, 394
Tran Chanh Thanh, 447
Tran Kim Tuyen, 136, 193, 286
Tran Le Xuan. *See* Madame Nhu
Tran Thien Khiem, 284, 307, 320, 321, 324, 331, 336, 342, 346, 369, 417, 424
Tran Tu Oai, 309, 317, 325, 430, 437
Tran Van Chuong, 30, 192, 242–43, 292, 293, 303–4, 335, 393, 398
Tran Van Don, 429, 431, 435, 436, assassination of Diem and Nhu; Buddhist crisis, 284, 300, 309, 310; concern about loyalty of, 395–96; Conein and, 386–88, 400–401, 410–11; coup execution, 411, 412, 416, 417, 420, 438; coup plans, 286, 303, 306–8, 317, 324, 325, 342, 364, 386, 389, 395, 397–98, 400–402; on Diem, 152, 424; on Ngo Dinh Can, 433, 434; notifying U.S. embassy, 407; Provisional Government established, 437; on student demonstrations, 307; tear gas issues, 264; U.S. support of coup, 439
Tran Van Huong, 435–36
Tran Van Minh ("Little Minh"), 307, 308
Tran Van Tho: Buddhist uprising, 264, 274, 282, 284; on citizens' dissatisfaction, 373–74; coup plans, 325, 334; on Diem, 99; on Madame Nhu's opinions, 294; on Michigan State University contract, 150; National Emergency Council proposal, 121; on neutralization, 173; Nhu on, 135; press coverage, 136; Provisional Government established, 437; as successor to Diem, 100, 135, 192–94, 258, 275–76, 279, 417, 419, 423; on U.S. withdrawal, 243
Tran Van Tu, 307–8
Tri Quang, 249–50, 251–52, 258–59, 260, 264, 265, 273, 286, 305–6, 353, 393, 405, 415
Trueheart, William: assassination of Diem and Nhu, 428; Buddhist crisis, 259, 263–64, 266–67, 271, 272, 273–75, 276, 279, 283–84, 285, 299, 300, 302; coup execution, 415, 422, 423; coup plans, 332, 388, 403; on defoliants and crop destruction, 144; Diem regime issues, 206, 281, 309, 310; on flood relief subterfuge, 107; on Geneva Accords violations, 144; Halberstam on, 208; on Independence Palace bombing, 163; on Lodge, 304; military emphasis, 142; press, 206; on radio broadcast, 323; strategic hamlet program, 177; U.S. involvement in war, 214–15
Truman, Harry S., 2, 330, 456

Truong Cong Cuu, 313
Tung. *See* Le Quang Tung
Turner, Nick, 228

The Ugly American (Burdick and Lederer), 19–20
An Uncertain Trumpet (Taylor), 38
Ung Van Khiem, 122
United Kingdom, 40, 50, 57, 69, 81, 122, 128, 129
United Nations, 40, 47, 83, 101, 105, 116, 362
United States v. Curtiss-Wright, 160
Unna, Warren, 179, 256
U.S. Agency for International Development, 354
U.S. citizens, terrorist campaigns against, 450
U.S. Department of State, 100, 106, 121, 138, 159–61, 444
U.S. embassy in Saigon, 22, 25, 58–59, 146–47, 153, 155–56, 161, 291, 393, 402, 407, 411, 415; ambassadors (*see* Durbrow, Elbridge; Lodge, Henry Cabot, Jr.; Nolting, Frederick)
U.S. Information Agency, 323
U.S. Information Service (USIS), 24, 355
U.S. News and World Report, 155–56
U.S. Operations Mission (USOM), 24, 154, 244, 267, 269, 299, 308
U.S. Special Forces, 51, 52, 53–54, 143, 217

Van Fleet, James, 121
Van Tieng Dung, 406
Vann, John Paul, 223–24, 227, 228
Vietcong: on 1963 coup, 419; activity escalation, 79–80, 81–82, 111, 447, 448; ARVN defense against, 73; battles, 82, 223–25; Beijing's concern regarding, 141; border issues, 43, 136; brutality, 101, 103; Buddhist uprising and, 250–51, 252, 254, 255, 260, 261, 263, 266, 278, 284, 288, 292, 300, 335; buildup, 111, 133, 141, 184, 203, 296, 349; casualties, 174, 195, 229–30, 349; civilian sympathizers, 32, 143; Diem administration and, 14, 24, 36, 106, 200; food supplies, 143, 144, 145, 177, 256; habits, 188; infiltration by, 36, 52, 73, 77, 82, 83, 116, 133, 147–48, 149; intelligence gathering, 83; interrogations, 102; KA on, 22, 24–25, 34, 73, 74, 93, 121; Lao Dong party and, 191–92; medical supplies, 187; Nam assassination, 101; national emergency declared, 96, 104; Nhu and, 310–11, 312, 344, 351, 362, 369, 384, 406, 421; objectives, 117; origins, 28; personnel estimates, 80, 84, 133, 223; progress of, 20, 21; recruiting efforts, 65, 118, 237, 373–74; sanctuaries, 5–6; tactics, 4;

Vietcong (*continued*)
   terrorism, 24, 36, 103, 195, 200; *Time* magazine on, 82; Vietminh in, 84; weaponry, 84, 98, 103, 195, 295; Zhang Yan on, 141
Vietminh Front, 18, 21, 36, 76, 84
Vietnam Democratic Party, 122
Vietnam Fatherland Front, 122
Vietnam Task Force, 167, 183
Vietnam Workers' Party, 263, 459
Vietnam Working Group, 183, 231, 233, 234, 364
Vietnamese Communists in Paris, 419
Vietnamese Workers' Party, 192
Vietti, Eleanor, 187
villages, 143, 177, *See also* agrovilles (fortified communities); strategic hamlet program
Vo Nguyen Giap, 14, 15, 36, 198, 204, 240
Vo Van Hai, 309, 310, 363
Vu Van Mau, 196, 299, 305

Wang Jiaxiang, 165, 192
The War of the Flea (Taber), 32
Warner, Denis, 401
Washington, George, 61
weaponry: Buddhist uprising, 261, 262, 263–64, 297–98; confiscated from Civil Guard, 98; coup (1963), 408, 409, 412; distribution, 204, 212; guerrilla warfare, 129; Kennedy on, 129; land mines, 142; nuclear weapons, 44, 49, 201; of Vietcong, 84, 98, 103, 195, 295; Zhou Enlai on, 198–99

Wheeler, Earle, 45, 233, 234, 236
White, Theodore H., 70, 80, 88
Williams, Samuel, 138, 145
withdrawal of troops from Vietnam: CINCPAC's plan for, 296; coup success and, 441; Diem on, 243; Galbraith on, 117; Johnson administration, 449, 450, 451, 453, 454; Kennedy's hesitation, 118, 348–49; Kennedy's plan for, 8, 10, 11, 221, 238, 245–46, 257–58, 377–78, 382–84, 391, 440, 441, 442, 452–53, 454, 456; Mansfield on, 115, 218–19; McNamara-Taylor report on, 375; Nixon administration, 452; *Pentagon Papers* on, 382; postponement, 12, 343–44; press coverage, 296
Women's Paramilitary Youth, 291
Women's Solidarity Movement, 245, 266, 282
Wood, Chalmers, 73, 207, 233, 245

Xuan Mai Training School, 17
Xuan Thuy, 311, 312

Yarborough, Ralph, 1
Ye Yianying, 141
York, Robert, 228
Young, Kenneth, 30–31, 68
Yugoslavia, 55

Zablocki, Clement, 202
Zhang Yan, 141
Zhou Enlai, 80, 165, 198–99